THE IMPERIAL HISTORY OF CHINA

RECORDS OF ASIAN HISTORY

Further volumes in preparation

THE IMPERIAL
HISTORY OF CHINA

Being a History of the Empire as compiled by the
Chinese Historians

BY

J. MACGOWAN

LONDON : CURZON PRESS
NEW YORK : BARNES & NOBLE BOOKS

First published 1897
Second edition 1906
New impression 1973

Published by

Curzon Press Ltd · London and Dublin

and

Harper & Row Publishers Inc · New York
Barnes & Noble Import Division

UK 7007 0027 7
US 06 494454 9

Printed in Great Britain
by Kingprint Ltd · Richmond · Surrey

PREFACE.

THE Imperial History of China is neither more nor less than the History of China, as it has been written, during successive ages, by the authorized historians of the Empire. This work, together with the writings of Confucius and Mencius, are the only truly authentic sources from which the story of this long-lived nation can be obtained.

During the past there have been many writers of note who have professed to give a history of their times, but their works have been so interlarded with manifestly fabulous stories and incredible statements that they could not possibly be accepted as genuine history.

It may seem strange to some of the readers of this History that the critical faculty has not been exercised more fully than it might have been in the preparation of the book. The fact is the author could only give what the Chinese historians supplied, and as historical criticism was a science that they had never studied, he did not dare to attempt what the ancient scholars of China had never dreamed of doing themselves. Besides, the materials for doing so do not now exist. China is a country that has taken scarcely any pains to preserve the books or monuments of the far-off past. The author consequently has simply been shut up to those documents that China has always considered to be authentic. In point of fact there are no others to be consulted, for any records outside of these are so few and so unreliable that to use them would land one in the region of fiction and romance.

That the authorized documents are on the whole to be relied upon, we have no reason whatever to doubt, especially when we consider the system that was adopted to protect the writers of them, when they had to record facts that might have been unpleasant to the Emperor and high officials of the time.

Ever since the Han dynasty (B. C. 206—A. D. 25) historians have been appointed by royal edicts to write the history of their times, and no one but themselves has ever been allowed to look upon what they have written. There have been times when a ruler has attempted to coerce them to reveal what they have said ab himself, but they have been willing to suffer death rather than betray the trust committed to them. The consequence has been that the writers have been able to write impartially, when they had to narrate some story to the discredit of the sovereign, or of some powerful statesman, or that reflected upon the honour of the nation.

As each document was written, it was deposited in an iron-bound chest, which remained locked up till that dynasty had ceased to rule. It was then opened by command of some sovereign of the next, when all the documents it contained were handed over to the regularly appointed royal historians, who edited them and formed them into a volume that contained the history of the dynasty that had just passed away. A sense of honour has seemed to rest upon this long line of writers, and a solemn sense of responsibility to posterity has made them feel bound to transmit the truth to it. That we have the actual story of China in their writings we are convinced. We must remember, moreover, however sceptical we may be about them, we have absolutely no means of proving their falsehood, for there are large portions of Chinese history that we cannot know anything about, excepting from this Standard History. Any history, therefore, of China that has ever been written, either by Chinese or by foreigners, that is of any historical value, must have been based upon it, and have obtained its facts from it.

The story of the present Manchu dynasty, being still concealed within the recesses of the historical chest, has not been available in the preparation of this History. The " Holy War," as well as other reliable sources, have been used in the writing of it.

In the production of this history, the following are the principal works that have been referred to :—The Shoo King, or Book of Historical Documents, by Dr. Legge ; The Chinese Repository ; Williams' Middle Kingdom and Dictionary ; Mayers' Chinese Readers' Manual ; China Review ; The Holy War ; Dr. Ross' the Manchus and the History of Corea ; Marco Polo's Writings ; Boulger's History of China, etc.

J. MACGOWAN.

Amoy, 1905.

TABLE OF CONTENTS.

THE

IMPERIAL HISTORY OF CHINA.

CHAPTER I.

THE MYTHICAL PERIOD.

THE beginning of Chinese history is buried in the profoundest mystery and obscurity. Where the forefathers of the present race originally came from, and how they reached China, are matters simply of speculation.

It is believed by many scholars that they first started from the neighbourhood of the Caspian Sea, and travelling eastwards they in due time reached the waters of the Yellow River. It has been asserted by later writers that the original home of the Chinese was on the great Euphrates plain, and that commencing their emigration they travelled in a north-east direction till they struck the waters of the Yellow River. They then travelled along its northern banks, and following its course till they reached the present Shansi, they determined to make a permanent settlement upon its fruitful plains. As the people grew in numbers and in strength they diverged in all directions, east, west, north and south, extending their rule and consolidating their power. In doing this they were sometimes engaged in fierce conflicts with the earlier emigrants of other races that had preceded them, and at others they found themselves fighting side by side with them, when as allies they helped them in some crisis of their history.

From the very beginning, as far as we can gather from the few and imperfect glimpses that we have of them in the early periods of their history, they were a sturdy race, and destined to become a conquering people. They were not simply a nomadic horde of shepherds that depended upon their flocks and herds for subsistence. It is true that as late as Shun his governors of districts are called "Pastors," and still further on Mencius, when speaking of them, terms them "Pastors of Men." In the later histories of China, however, there are comparatively few allusions to their ancestors having been a pastoral people.

As soon as they settled down they began to cultivate the soil. They not only planted the various kinds of grain for the sustenance of their families, but flax also, which was to be woven into garments for their use. They had some knowledge of the silkworm, and planted mulberry trees, on the leaves of which they might feed the worms. With the commercial instinct that is strong in the Chinaman of to-day they began a system of barter, and established fairs, where the farmers might gather from their farms and hamlets for the exchange of their commodities.

The first figure that appears on the horizon of Chinese history is P'an-ku. There is absolutely nothing known as to how this mythical personage originated, and yet he lives to-day in the popular mind as the man that first gave the heavens and the earth the shape they have ever since retained.

In the pictures we have of him he is represented as a huge figure, with axe in one hand and a chisel in the other, striking at the dome above, which is made of stone, to fashion it in the form that the firmament has to-day.* Next after him came the three great rulers, impersonations of a trinity of powers, viz., the celestial, terrestrial, and human sovereigns, who are said to have each reigned for eighteen thousand years, or even longer according to the particular author who is writing on the subject. These long lived potentates simply embody an idea so commonly expressed by the Chinese that Heaven, earth and man are the three great forces of nature, and in this crystalizing of them in the persons of these three great rulers that governed the world for so many ages, they merely mean that during that time the great forces that contain within them the essence of all things had ample time for their development.

After the long reign of these three celebrated monarchs Yu-chau (Nest-having) appears. In this fabulous personage we have another idea embodied, and he represents the advance that men were making in civilization. In his reign men began to build houses, for up to his time they had lived in forests, under the branches of the spreading trees, but these had been an imperfect protection against the inclemency of the weather, and consequently sickness had prevailed and men had gone mad through the sufferings they had been compelled to endure. Others who had taken refuge in caves and holes in the hill sides had suffered from cramps and rheumatism and various kinds of fevers. From 'the appearance of Yu-chau men began to fashion in a primitive way the houses that have since grown into the mansions and palaces that abound throughout the land.

Sui-jin (Producer of fire and wood) next appears upon the scene, another mythical personage, that still further embodies the idea of progress that the world was gradually making. Hitherto men had not learned the use of fire in the cooking of their food. They had simply devoured it raw, and had taken the flesh of the animals they had killed in the chase, and satisfied their hunger with it, as it was cut from the bleeding bodies of the beasts or birds they had slaughtered. The same had been the case with the productions of nature.

---

* The compilers of legendary history have made P'an-ku to be the first developed figure that appeared out of chaos. The great historian Sze Ma-ts'ien makes no mention of him, and it is not till we come to the writers of the Sung dynasty that we find him seriously discussed or made the hero of the Chinese cosmogony.

These had been plucked as they grew spontaneously, and had been eaten without any preparations to make them more wholesome or palatable.

It was not simply in the matter of the use of fire, however, that Sui-jin proved a benefactor to his fellowmen. Before his time the people had not learned the art of writing. There was no method therefore by which a record of events could be kept, and so the greatest confusion arose in public life. In order to meet this difficulty Sui-jin invented a plan, which has travelled down many centuries, and into lands where the highest civilization obtains, of tying knots, not on their handkerchiefs, for they had none, but on strings. A large knot called to mind an important matter, and a small one a more trivial affair. We assume incidentally from this that the people had learned the manufacture of twine at least, if not of the larger kinds of rope. During his time fairs and markets were established, and men were formally appointed as preachers of religion amongst the people.

With the passing away of Sui-jin, and the reign ot Yung-ch'eng Service accomplished), of whom we have no record more than his name, the purely mythological character of the early history may be said to have disappeared, and from this time what may be termed the legendary period begins.

CHAPTER II.

THE LEGENDARY PERIOD.

B. C. 2852—B. C. 2355.

THE next person that appears on the scene is the celebrated Fuh-hi, the first of the five great Rulers that occupy so prominent a position in the early history of China. He is an exceedingly shadowy and misty personage, and the pictures we have of him have been limned mainly by the imagination and the romance of succeeding ages. With regard to the date at which he commenced his reign various opinions have been given. One author puts it down at B.C. 3322, another at B.C. 2953, but the year B. C. 2852 is the one that is most generally received as being more approximately correct than any other.

Nothing is known of his father or mother. In order to increase his reputation it is stated that he was an incarnation of some powerful spirit, and therefore supernaturally conceived. The historian tells us that he was born at Ch'eng-ki, near the modern Singan, but that he subsequently established his rule in Ch'en near the present K'ai-fung-fu in Honan.

The great object of his life seemed to have been the carrying out of plans for the benefit of those over whom he was called to rule. He instituted the laws of marriage, for before his time the greatest laxity existed in regard to the relationship of the two sexes, such as one would expect to find in a very primitive and uncivilized state of society. He taught men how to fish with nets and to rear domestic animals. He also invented the lute and the lyre, that the people might be charmed with music, and thus be enabled to bear more cheerfully the burdens of life. Having found it difficult to distinguish his people one from another he invented the system of family names and divided the people into clans, and gave them surnames, which they were to retain, and by which they might be registered for purposes of taxation.

His original genius was shown in his devising a method of writing, which was to supersede the more clumsy plan of knotted cords hitherto used for the record of events. He invented the six classes of written characters. These were first, characters resembling objects ; second, characters having borrowed meanings, such as *ling*, which means an ensign of authority, but is used in the sense of to rule ; third, characters pointing out objects ; fourth, characters formed by combining ideas, such as the word for sincerity, which is made by uniting together the two words for man and to speak ; fifth, characters that inverted the significations; and sixth, characters that united sound to the object.

From these primitive beginnings have grown the six classes of written characters that have developed into the finished forms that they have at the present time. It is declared that he was assisted in his great efforts for the development of his people by the sudden appearance of a dragon-horse from the Yellow River as he was one day standing by its brink. On its back was a scroll inscribed with mystic diagrams, which were ultimately developed by him into the eight diagrams, which have played so momentous a part in the early systems of divination and in those of philosophy in almost every century since then. In commemoration of the appearance of the monster he gave the title of "dragon" to his officials.

Fuh-hi is revered to-day as one of the great benefactors of the Chinese race and as the real founder of it too, for it is his capital that is looked upon as the cradle of this people, from whence have sprung the multitudes of the black-haired race that to-day hold rule over this vast Empire of China. After a reign of one hundred and fifteen years he bequeathed his power to Shen-nung.*

When Shen-nung grew up to manhood he determined to make farming a science. He examined the various kinds of soils and gave directions to the farmers what should be cultivated in each. He taught them how to make ploughs, so that they could turn up the soil, and instructed them in the best methods of husbandry. Immediate results began to be seen in the improved condition of the people, and succeeding generations have been so grateful to him for his methods, which have been handed down through successive ages, that his image is now worshipped by every heathen farmer under the title of "The Prince of Cereals." Shen-nung also went very deeply into the study of herbs, in order to find remedies for the diseases of his people. He is said to have been very successful in his investigations. As an example of this it is declared that in one day he discovered seventy poisonous plants and as many that were antidotes to them. He is looked up to as the father of medicine, for he was able by practical experiments to demonstrate the value of an immense number of herbs. Tradition tells us that he had a glass covering to his stomach, in consequence of which he could watch the process of digestion of each herb and mark its influence on the system. A pharmacopeia which is in use at the present time is said to have been written by him, and it describes the properties of a large number of herbs, their uses, etc. In every druggist's shop there is an image of him, and he is looked

---

* Shen-nung. (B. C. 2737–2697). This man was the son of Nang-teng, the daughter of the chief of a district called Yu-kiau, and wife to the ruler of Sian-tien. The Chinese not satisfied with his being born in the way that ordinary mortals are, have invented the fable that he was of supernatural origin. It is told how that before his mother was married she was walking along the road one day, when having placed her foot upon a step she felt a strange sensation all over her. After a time a son was born, but she determined to reject him, so she had him placed in a lonely spot on a mountain, where she expected he would die. The wild beasts, however, gathered round him, and he was nurtured and protected by them. When his mother saw this she had him brought home and cared for him herself.

upon as the presiding deity of a business that he loved so much and that he had the honour of starting.

Shen-nung was succeeded by eight men of no fame or note whatever, and history has determined that they shall not be allowed to break the sequence between him and his famous successor Hwang-ti. There is consequently difficulty here in settling the dates satisfactorily. These eight are spoken of as rulers, and yet no years are reckoned to them, though the last of them—Yu-wang—must have been a real character, for it was the rebellion against him that led to a change of dynasty and to the placing of Hwang-ti on the throne. Yu-wang had bec⸍me utterly corrupt and worthless, and his life was such a vicious one that he lost the respect not only of his own people, but also of the feudal chiefs that paid him fealty. One of these, Ch'ih-yew, a man of power and very ambitious, raised the standard of rebellion against him, and tried to dethrone him. In this he was successful, when Hien-yuan raised an army and marched against him. The two armies met in Cho-luh in the modern province of Chih-li, and Ch'ih-yew would have been over-come, but by his enchantments he hid his men in a mist and escaped. Hien-yuan was, however, a match for him, for he constructed a wooden figure, which he fixed on his own chariot, whose hand invariably pointed to the south, no matter in what direction he drove. Guided by this he followed Ch'ih-yew into the very midst of the fog in which he had enveloped himself and captured and slew him.*

With the overthrow of Ch'ih-yew the feudal chiefs elected Hien-yuan to the supreme power (B. C. 2697–2597), which he consented to assume, and he took the title of Hwang-ti, the Yellow Emperor, from the colour of the earth, by virtue of which he believed he had come to his present eminence. In order to account for his great deeds he is said to have wrought, history gravely tells us that he was the offspring of a miraculous conception. His mother's name was Fu-pau, and he was born near the river Ki, which became the surname of his family. In addition to his title of Hien-yuan, given to him because he was the inventor of wheeled vehicles, he was also called Yew-hiung, from a territory that he inherited.†

---

*Another account represents Ch'ih-yew as having been one of Hwang-ti's ministers, against whom he rose in rebellion. On the day of the battle at Cho-luh he invoked the spirits of the wind and of the rain to come to his assistance, and a mighty tempest arose, but Hwang-ti sent the daughter of Heaven to quell it, and Ch'ih-yew was caught and slain. Ch'ih-yew is looked upon with horror by the earliest writers on historical subjects as the man that broke in upon the peace and innocence that for a certain period prevailed in primitive society and became the first great rebel. In the Historical Classic it says of him : "According to the teachings of ancient times Ch'ih-yew was the first to produce disorder, which spread amongst the common people, till all became murderers and robbers, owl-like in their conduct, traitors and villains, snatching and filching, dissemblers and oppressors. See Shu-king. Vol. III, page 590 ; also Mayers' Chinese Reader's Manual, page 36

† Yew-hiung is supposed to be the present Hsin-ch'ing in Honan.

Hwang-ti had the good fortune not only of being a man of great power and intelligence, but also of having ministers of considerable genius to aid him in the reforms that he wished to introduce into his administration. Under his direction Yung-ch'eng composed a calendar and made astronomical instruments that greatly assisted men in the study of the heavens. Musical instruments made of bamboo, called Ta-hia, were made for him by Ling-lun, and Yung-yuan by his command made twelve bells to denote the different seasons of the year. New methods of reckoning were devised, and weights and measures regulated, so that the people should have some standard to go by in their commercial transactions. Experiments were also made in dyeing, efforts being made to imitate the various colours of nature, and bows and arrows to be used in warfare were first constructed during this reign.

One of the most important and permanent of all the inventions of this celebrated Emperor was that of the Sexagenary Cycle which has been used ever since his day in the reckoning of time. His system was perfected in the sixty-first year of his reign, B. C. 2637, and consists of sixty combinations of two words each. The whole will therefore cover a period of sixty years. After the entire series has been used the reckoning is resumed from the first in it till the whole is again exhausted.*

Hwang-ti was fortunate in having a queen that forwarded as far as was in her power the plans of her husband for the prosperity of his people. Her name was Lui-tsu, and she was the daughter of the feudal chief of Si-ling. Having watched the operations of the silk-worms she determined to utilize their labours for the good of mankind, and she accordingly had the silk unwound from the cocoons and woven into cloth. Succeeding ages have been grateful to her wherever the silk-worms are reared for purposes of trade ; there they have an image of Lui-tsu, and her protecting influence is implored for an industry that was first instituted by her.

Hwang-ti was no dreamer, but exceedingly practical in all his thoughts for the welfare of his people. He taught them for example how to make utensils of wood, pottery, and metal, and he commanded Kung-ku to build boats and make carts. In order to prevent the disputes and serious quarrels that would necessarily arise, where the boundaries of the land were not well defined, he appointed officers,

---

* From the year B. C. 2637, A. D. 1863, there have been exactly seventy-five cycles. This method is followed by the Japanese, Coreans, and the people of Lew-chew. It may be remarked here in regard to the cycle that writers are by no means of one mind that Hwang-ti was the originator of it. Dr. Legge indeed does not believe that there ever was such a man as he, and that if he ever did exist he lived somewhere else than in China. The fact that Ta-nan, the man who is said to have compiled the cycle under the direction of Hwang-ti, is not heard of for more than two thousand years after the time in which he is said to have lived is a very suspicious circumstance. There is another fact worthy of observation, viz., that up to the era of the Former Han Dynasty the cycle simply chronicled days, and not years. It is used in this way by fortune-tellers at the present time. See Dr. Legge's Shoo-king, Vol. III, Part I, page 82.

whose business it was to arrange with the owners of property throughout the country the exact limits of their lands, thus placing on a secure basis the property which each claimed as his own, and preventing the encroachment of the more powerful on the lands of the poor. Besides being practical he was highly religious, and recognizing the fact that no people can be virtuous or prosperous without some settled faith and worship he appointed public places where the worship of God and the myriad spirits in nature might be reverenced, and where the people might be instructed in religion.*

After a reign of one hundred years he died, and was buried in Shensi, when he was succeeded by his son Kin-t'ien, whose dynastic title was Shau-hau (B. C. 2597). With regard to this ruler history has almost absolutely nothing to say. It is recorded that when he ascended the throne phœnixes appeared in large numbers.†

As these birds are believed to be particularly auspicious we may gather that this reign was a prosperous one, though the only thing that history has to tell us of what happened during it was that the various orders of both civil and military mandarins were distinguished from each other by distinctive dresses that he devised, and that the colours of them were taken from the plumage of birds that had attracted his attention. After a reign of eighty-four years he died in Ch'u-feu in the present province of Shantung, whither he had removed his capital from Ch'ih-chow in Kiang-nan.

Shau-hau was succeeded by Chwan-hu (B. C. 2513-2435), whose dynastic title was Kau-yang. Why none of the four sons of his predecessor were selected to succeed his father history does not tell. It was the theory in those early days that the throne was not necessarily hereditary, but was given to the man who had shown by a virtuous life and by special ability that he was the one that Heaven had raised up to govern the people. Neither do the ancient records tell in all cases who it was, Emperor, or chiefs, or people, that decided the question as to who was the fittest person to succeed to the imperial power. Although he became Emperor when he was only twenty years old he was not ignorant of the art of governing, for he had assisted Shau-hau from the age of ten, so that his mind must have been an exceptionally clever one, and he himself more precocious than the most of the young men of his time. He had another recommendation in his favour, viz., that he was the grandson of

---

* Legends and fables innumerable abound regarding this famous sovereign. One of these is that a certain kind of grass grew in his palace yard that immediately became agitated when any glib-tongued person entered, and that they pointed their leaves at him. Another is that Ts'ang-hieh by a careful study of the foot-marks of birds elaborated the art of forming written characters. There is a good deal of uncertainty about this man. One legend makes him to have been not a minister of Hwang-ti, but an Emperor that succeeded Fuh-hi, and that he got his idea of devising a system of written records from the tracings on the back of a supernatural tortoise that appeared to him from the River Loh. This one thing is certain, the Chinese scholars of to-day believe in him, for when they meet in their literary halls to worship Confucius the statue of Ts'ai.g-hieh is also reverenced.

† The four supernatural creatures which the Chinese look upon as omens of good are the K'i-lin, the fung or phœnix, the tortoise, and the dragon.

Hwang-ti, and therefore he had royal blood in his veins. He fixed his capital in Puh, in Shantung, where he lived and died.

We know exceedingly little of his life. He made corrections in the calendar, in order if possible to obviate the errors in regard to times and seasons which were constantly occurring in consequence of the defective astronomical knowledge of those times. He also had bells cast, and he appointed officers, whose special duties were to examine into the mineral resources of the country, and report to him upon them. He was very musical, and he composed a piece entitled "The Response to the Clouds," and he took measures to see that the harmonies of the music that was used in the solemn service of God by himself and chief officers should be as perfect as possible. He appointed the four sons of Shau-hau as well as the son of Shen-nung and his own grandson to preside over the five elements or primordial essences, viz., water, fire, wood, metal and earth, and to-day the spirits of these men are worshipped as the presiding deities of these elements. After a reign of seventy-eight years he died, and was succeeded by Hau-sin (B. C. 2435-2365), whose dynastic title was Ti-kuh.

This Emperor was the grandson of Yuan-hiau, a son of Hwang-ti. According to the annals of the Bamboo Books he was distinguished at his birth by being born with double rows of teeth. He ascended the throne when he was thirty years old, and established his capital in Honan-fu. As a ruler he was noted for his justice and for the profound interest he took in the concerns of his people. He knew what was going on in the furthest extremity of his dominions, and he sympathized with the sorrows and sufferings of those on whom misfortune had fallen. There was such a mingling of love and majesty in him that men were drawn to him, and yet they had the most profound reverence for him. Ti-kuh had attained the unenviable reputation in history of being the first ruler of whom it is recorded that he had more than one wife.*

Besides his queen he had three concubines, and it is stated that on the occasion of his espousing each of them a religious service to God was performed, in which His blessing was implored. It must be acknowledged that Ti-kuh was exceedingly fortunate in at least three of his marriages. His queen bore him a son of the name of K'i, who was distinguished for his virtue and ability. He became minister of agriculture under Shun, and his descendants founded the great dynasty of Chow. One of his concubines was the mother of Sieh, who was minister of instruction under the same famous Emperor as his brother, and one of whose duties as defined in the Historical Classic was to see to the carrying out of the five orders of relationship, viz., parent and child, sovereign and subject, hus-

---

* There is a legend, indeed, that Hwang-ti had at least four, and that one of these was Mu-mu, who was noted for her ugliness and for the wisdom with which she ruled the imperial household. History says nothing about her, and if Hwang-ti was really a fabulous personage the story falls to the ground.

band and wife, brother and brother, and friend with friend. His descendants were the founders of the Shang dynasty. Another bore the famous Emperor and sage Yau, whilst the last had the misfortune to bear the ill-fated Chi, who was named successor to his father, but having fallen into habits of intemperance and dissipation was set aside, and Yau was made the heir-apparent instead. History gives no reason why the latter was selected in preference to either K'i or Sieh. He may have shown pre-eminent abilities that led his father to believe he was the most suitable one to follow him on the throne. After nine years' trial of Chi he was compelled to depose him and substitute his younger brother in his place.

CHAPTER III.

THE LEGENDARY PERIOD (Continued).

Yau—B. C. 2356-2255.

Shun—B. C. 2255-2205.

THESE two names are the most conspicuous in Chinese history. They are the ideal Emperors, by whom every sovereign has been measured since they lived. The Chinese have endowed them with almost every conceivable virtue and given them credit for such high administrative abilities that they stand worthy of being the first prominent figures in such a grand and stirring history as this Chinese Empire has had. That they were chiefs of the Chinese people in very early times seems on the whole probable, though we are surrounded by so much that is misty and nebulous in regard to these two worthies, that the statements we have in regard to them have necessarily to be received with the greatest possible caution. The fame they have got and the halo that surrounds them are entirely due to Confucius and his distinguished disciple Mencius, who adopted them as the great heroes of China, and who in the true spirit of hero worship endowed them with every perfection and made them to be fit models for every ruler that should succeed them.*

Yau was the son of Ti-kuh by one of his concubines. Historians prefer to believe that he was miraculously conceived by a red dragon as being more consistent with the heroic character he afterwards became. Whilst his brother Chi was on the throne he was ruler of the principality of T'au, whence he removed his residence to T'ang, in consequence of which he was known by the title of Prince T'ang of T'au.† When, however, "both men and Heaven determined to discard" the unworthy Chi, and he was driven from his throne, Yau at age of sixteen became the ruler of the Chinese people.

The latter proved to be a man of sagely virtues, as was seen by the remarkable results of his government. "He was able to make the clever and virtuous distinguished, and thence proceeded to the love of the nine classes of his kindred (viz., four on the father's side, three on the mother's and two on the wife's), who all became harmonious. He regulated and refined his people, who all became

---

* That this is so can be proved by the very few references that are made to them in the very earliest books. In the Historical Classic, in the books of Hia, Yau is mentioned only once, and Shun not at all. In the books of Shang they are named but once, whilst in the book of Chow we have simply but two references to them. Again the Books of Odes and the Yih-king are absolutely silent with regard to them. This state of things could hardly have been possible had this men been as distinguished during their life-time as tradition has made them to be.

† T'au is the present Ta-yuen in the prefecture of Ping-yang in Shan-si.

bright and intelligent. He united in perfect harmony the myriad states (*i.e.*, the feudal tribes beyond the royal domain), and the black-haired people (the Chinese people) were transformed, and the result was concord." *

His fame spread in every direction, and when he made his visitations round his kingdom young and old flocked about him to see the wonderful man that ruled over them, and to invoke bless-ings on his head for the happiness he had been the means of bring-ing down upon them. On one of these occasions, when he came to the district of Hoa-yin, the people crowded around him and prayed that Heaven might give him the three great blessings of wealth, sons and long life. He declared that he did not desire any of these. "Wealth," he said, "brought many troubles, children many anxieties, and old age much sorrow and contempt." "Not so," they replied, "sons are the gift of Heaven, and it finds a place for each on earth, where he can fulfil his duties, therefore you need not have any anxiety about them. Old age never brings insult on anyone, excepting where virtue has been lost. At the close of life the aged man ascends on a cloud to the place where God lives. How then can it be said that mature age brings contempt? With regard to wealth it is true it brings many responsibilities, but you can divide it with others, who will share with you the burdens that it has brought you and help you in the management of the country." †

The most abundant prosperity was the result of Yau's wise and benevolent government. Even nature seemed to be touched by his virtuous rule, for the rain fell once in every twelve days, and the wind blew in such gentle breezes that men's bodies were refreshed and the crops were encouraged in their growth, so that they came forth in such abundance that want was a thing unknown. Men, too, dwelt in perfect safety, for every one was honest. No door was shut at night for fear of thieves, for none existed, and if a man passed some article of value that some one had accidentally dropped, he would find it still there on his return, for no one coveted it.

The next important thing that is mentioned in the Historical Classic is the measures that he took to secure a correct calendar for the guidance of the farmers in their cultivation of the land. "Thereupon Yau commanded Hi and Ho, the astronomers royal, in reverent accordance with their observation of the heavens, to calculate and make a map of the sun, moon and stars and zodiacal spaces," and so deliver respectfully the seasons to the people. ‡

---

* See Legge's Shoo-king, vol. 1, page 17

† The three blessings invoked by the men of Hoa-yin are still coveted by the people of to-day, and amongst the scrolls pasted over the doors at the new year's time one often sees these, on which is inscribed the prayer that the three-fold hap-piness may descend upon the family within.

‡ See Canon of Yau, Legge's translation, p. 19.

After he had reigned sixty-one years a mighty inundation of the Yellow River took place, so vast that the waters were said to have enveloped the mountains and covered the tops of the hills, and seemed as though their object was to rise to the very heavens.* One of Yau's ministers, by the name of Kwun † was, after some hesitation, appointed to the task of devising measures for the relief of the flooded country, but after nine years of unsuccessful efforts he was degraded as incompetent, and after a time imprisoned, either for this or other offences.‡

After Yau had reigned seventy years, feeling the cares of government too much for him, he addressed the president of the nobles of the empire and the one whose duty it was to stand between him and his feudal chiefs, and told him that he desired to resign his throne to him. The man meekly replied that he had not the virtue for so high and responsible a position, and that he "should only disgrace the imperial seat." Yau then asked him to "point out some one among the illustrious, or set forth one from among the poor and mean," that could worthily succeed him. The officers of the court upon this unanimously recommended to him a man of the name of Shun, whose reputation for filial piety had spread far and wide and had reached even the ears of the Emperor himself. In order to test him he gave him his two daughters—Ngo-hwang and Nu-ying—in marriage,§ believing that if he could stand such a severe strain as this he would demonstrate his ability for becoming the ruler of his people. After three years of trial, during which Shun gave the utmost satisfaction to Yau and showed his knowledge of men by introducing the famous Yu to the notice of the Emperor as a competent man to control the ravages of the Yellow River, he was formally installed as colleague with him in the government of the country. The ceremonies connected with this important act were of the most solemn character possible. Standing out in the open air Yau told the story of his choice to Heaven and appealed to it to ratify what he had done. They next repaired to the ancestral temple of the Emperor, and there in the presence of the spirits of the dead he narrated all that he had done to secure a suitable man to succeed him on the throne, and thus preserve the heritage that once was theirs, and which they had entrusted to him.¶

---

* See Canon of Yau.

† This man was the father of the famous Yu and Baron of Ts'ung, a district that now corresponds with Hu, in the department of Si-ngan in Shan-si, and that lies south of the river King.

‡ What finally became of him is uncertain. Some say that he was imprisoned for life, others again affirm that he was put to death.

§ This story seems to us somewhat apocryphal, and ought to be relegated to the region of legend. One thing seems certain that polygamy must have been practised at this very early age of Chinese history.

¶ From this ceremony we see at what a very early age ancestral worship was practised by the Chinese, and thus we can understand how it is that it is more deeply rooted in the minds and faith of this people than any other religious system that has a purely human origin.

That he was perfectly sincere in his action is manifest from the fact that he had passed by his own son Chu, who was lacking in moral character, and had selected a stranger to succeed him as the ruler of the Chinese.

The only important event that took place during the remainder of Yau's life was the division of the country into twelve grand divisions and the appointing the spirit of the highest mountain in each to be the tutelary god of all the region within its boundaries. The country had prospered under his rule, and under the wise administration of K'i, who had been made minister of agriculture, the farmers enjoyed the highest prosperity. Yau died in the year B. C. 2258 in Yang, in the present province of Honan, and was in due time succeeded by his virtuous colleague Shun.

Shun (B. C. 2255-2205.)

The accounts that we have of this distinguished man's early days are very conflicting and not altogether satisfactory. Some hold that his ancestors had been lords of Yu, but they had lost their inheritance, and the family had been reduced to the condition of common people. Mencius says, he was born in Chu-fung ; the Historical Records in K'i-chow, the Shansi of to-day, and the writers of the Sung dynasty make his birthplace to have been T'si-nan in Shantung. According to Sz-ma-ts'ien he was of royal origin, for he was a descendant of the Emperor Chwan-hu.

His father was named Ku-seu, and was blind. After the death of Shun's mother he married another wife, who had a son of the name of Siang. This stepmother hated Shun, and so managed to infuse her own wicked feeling into the hearts both of her husband and son, that they made several attempts to deprive him of his life. On one occasion they sent him into a loft of a granary, and taking away the ladder by which he had ascended they set the building on fire. Shun narrowly escaped with his life. On another his father ordered him to open a well. Shun, who was suspicious of some deep-laid scheme to injure him, opened a side way by which he could escape. It was well he did so, for after he had got down a considerable depth the hole was suddenly filled up, and he would inevitably have perished had he not been able to ascend to the upper world by the road he had previously dug. Some of the more veritable historians prefer to believe that he was saved by a dragon that had especially taken him under its protection. In spite of all the hatred of his family to him Shun acted with the most profound filial reverence to his father and his unnatural stepmother, so that he became the model for filial piety to the whole region in which he lived. His influence over his fellow-men seemed to have been remarkable. If he went to fish in the Lui lake the fishermen abandoned their boat for him to use as he liked. When he went for a time to the banks of the Yellow River to make pottery the workmen employed there were so influenced by his upright conduct that they would pass nothing from their hands but what was of the best material and the most perfect workmanship. He could not, indeed, reside anywhere without attracting people by the magic of his person, who were content to abandon their homes to settle down beside him, in order to be benefitted by his example.

His fame spread everywhere, and at last reached the ears of Yau, and when he was thirty years of age he was introduced to his notice as a suitable person to succeed him in the government. After the lapse of three years, being satisfied with him in every respect, Yau appointed him to be his colleague in the management of the kingdom, and for twenty-eight years he acted with him in that high and honourable capacity.

On the death of Yau, Shun with the modesty that was characteristic of him, for three years refused to ascend the throne He wished to give an opportunity to Chu, the disinherited son of his celebrated colleague, to become the successor of his father. It is presumed, moreover, that his heart was so filled with sorrow for the loss of Yau that he felt it would be unbecoming in him to take part in public business before the three years of mourning had elapsed.* Mr. Chu, however unworthy he may have been in other respects, seemed to have had the common sense to refuse an honour that he knew he could not worthily sustain. He accordingly kept himself retired in Fang-ling and left the throne open to Shun. That the will of the people and of the feudal chiefs was in favour of the latter is manifest from the distinct evidence of Mencius, " Shun ruled with Yau for twenty-eight years. This was more than man could have done ; it was from Heaven. After the death of Yau, when the three years' mourning was ended, Shun got out of the way of Yau's son, and went to the south of south river. The nobles, however, when they went to the audience repaired not to Yau's son, but to Shun. Those that had disputed cases went not to Yau's son, but to Shun. Those that sang ballads did not do so in honour of Yau's son, but of Shun. Therefore I said that it was Heaven made him rule." †

Shun reigned independently fifty, or rather fifty-three years, since the period of interregnum must be counted to him. The whole time that he governed, whether as colleague or as sole ruler, was a most busy as well as a prosperous period for his kingdom. It is said that he engaged in astronomical studies, and by instruments observed the " Seven Regulators," i.e., the sun, moon and five planets. He also took special care that the service of religion should be so regulated that it should be carried out with the utmost order and ceremony. Not only did he worship God, but also the spirits

---

* The example set by Shun has been followed in official life ever since, and though his royal successors have not imitated his example in refusing the throne on the death of their predecessors etiquette demands that a similar period should be spent in mourning for those that have passed away.

† See Mencius in loc.

of the hills and rivers, and a host of other miscellaneous deities, thus proving that the very highest type of men that the Chinese have to present us at this period of their history had taken the first steps that were finally to lead to universal idolatry in the future.

In order to terrify the evil that still existed in spite of the benign influences of this great sage, he had pictorial representations made of the five kinds of statutory punishments. As he wished, however, to temper mercy with judgment he allowed banishment to take the place of the more severe of these, and he ordered that the whip should be used in the magistrates' courts, and the cane for the school boys throughout his dominions.* Branding and the cutting off the nose and feet were abolished by the Emperor Wen of the Han Dynasty, B. C. 178-156. Castration was done away with by the first Emperor of the Sui Dynasty, A. D. 589-600. If one may judge by these terribly severe punishments these high-minded sages could be exceedingly cruel when they liked, and could calmly pass enact ments which their less famous successors deemed it necessary in the interests of humanity to abolish.† The extent of country over which Shun ruled cannot of course be known with any preciseness. Taking the account that is given of his visitation of the Empire, we should conclude that on the west his territories extended to the eastern part of Shensi ; on the north to nearly a half of Shansi ; on the east that they occupied the western half of Shantung, and on the south embraced only the northern part of Honan.‡

After he had ruled alone thirty-three years Shun feeling himself incompetent for the many arduous duties that devolved upon him as ruler of a prosperous people appointed Baron Yu to be his colleague and successor to his throne, thus debarring his own son, Shang-chun, who had not turned out as satisfactory as his father had desired, from the succession.§ With the assistance of Yu he continued to rule the "black-haired people" with vigour and success. Ministers of Agriculture, and Crime, and Works, and even of Music were appointed. Whatever was considered to be for the interest of the people, either practically or ethically, was attended to by Shun.

He died at the good old age of one hundred and ten, whilst he was making a visitation through the country, and was buried in Ts'ang-wu, on the Kiu-i hills in Kiang-nan.

---

* The five great punishments were : (1) Branding on the forehead, (2) Cutting off the nose, (3) Cutting off the feet, (4) Castration, and (5) death in various forms.

† See Legge's Canon of Shun.

‡ In making his visitation Shun first travelled east to T'ai-tsung, now called T'ai-shan in Shantung. From this place he proceeded to probably Mount Hwang in Honan ; though being so far south other mountains have been suggested that lay further north of it. He then travelled west to Mount Hwa in Shensi, and thence north to Mount Hang in Shansi. His object in visiting these mountains was for the purpose of worshipping Heaven from their summits. Having made the round of these mountains he returned to the capital, which was in P'ing-yang, and there offered to his refined ancestor (probably Hwang-ti) a bullock in the ancestral temple. See Legge's Canon of Shun, page 35.

§ The chiefs of the Empire were divided into five great classes, the heads of which were known by the titles of Duke, Marquis, Earl, Viscount and Baron.

Yau and Shun are the two greatest men in Chinese history. Although the names of other rulers are mentioned with honour they do not hold the distinguished place in the nation's past that they do. Their characters, if we are to believe the records that we possess of them, must have been very excellent, and they seem to have been just the kind of men with whom a mighty Empire like China should begin its national life. They contrast favourably with the founders of almost any other great nation, for it was for what the men were in themselves, and not for the performance of any heroic deeds, that the historians of China have placed them on the high pedestal on which they stand to-day. No doubt there is a great deal that has been said about them that will not bear investigation, still the conception that a king can be a renowned one only in as far as he is a good and virtuous man, is a great one for a nation to have, and gives it a high ideal of what a sovereign ought to be.

CHAPTER IV.

THE LEGENDARY PERIOD (CONTINUED).

The Hia* Dynasty—B. C. 2205-1766.
The Great Yu—B. C. 2205-2197.

THE name of Yu is a very famous one in Chinese history. He was the son of Baron Kwun, who was employed by Yau for nine years in endeavouring to control the great inundation of the Yellow River, but without success. In the seventy-fifth year of that ruler he was introduced to his notice by his colleague Shun as a fit person to accomplish the task that his father had failed to accomplish.

This overflow of the Yellow River forms one of the great epochs in Chinese history. It not only made the fortunes of Yu, but it enabled him to found a dynasty that lasted over four hundred years, and it has been a prominent feature in the ancient history of China, to which writers in all subsequent ages have often referred. According to the Historical Classic it must have been an unusually severe one. Yau is represented as saying to the President of his nobles : "How destructive are the waters of the inundation. They envelop the mountains and rise higher than the hills, and they threaten the very heavens, so that the people complain."

Mencius, who of course got his information from this Classic, and giving what he considered to be a legitimate interpretation of the above famous passage, says : "In the days of Yau, when China had not been reduced to order, the mighty waters did not flow in their regular streams, and so there was an inundation in the country. Vegetation was rank, and birds and beasts abounded. The various kinds of grains could not be grown, and birds and beasts encroached upon man. The Middle Kingdom was marked with the tracks of the feet of birds and animals."

To control this inundation and restore the flooded lands to their owners was the work assigned to Yu (B. C. 2286). Although he had abundant helpers in his great task it was his mind that conceived the plan by which he was to divert the waters back again to their channels, and it was his untiring energy that for eight long years kept him incessantly at his work till he could report to Yau that the commission he had entrusted to him had been fulfilled.

Four days after his marriage he began his labours, and so absorbed was he in them that though he thrice passed his own door, and on one occasion heard the wailing of his own child, he never entered till the completion of his task. He tracked the great rivers

---

* The dynastic title of Hia was taken from a small territory in Honan, which had been given to Yu for his signal service in controlling the great flood.

to their sources, and burned the woods upon the mountain sides, and built up embankments, and made cuttings through the hills, and deepened the channels until the waters were drained off into the eastern sea, and the inhabitants could again return to the lands from which they had been driven.   There is a legend that states that Yu got his idea of how he was to manage the flood by looking at the lines on a turtle's back.   Following the inspiration that these gave him he divided the country into nine provinces and proceeded by degrees to drain off the waters from them.   Having accomplished this he then more accurately defined the boundaries of his provinces, their productions and the amount of revenue they had to pay to the government.   There is no doubt but that there has been a great deal of exaggeration in the accounts that have been given of the labours of Yu in connection with the inundation of the Yellow River.   That some merit, however, is due to him is unquestionably true, though it is difficult to say how much.   Any one that would dare to cope with such an one as has occurred in recent years would deserve the greatest credit, and therefore much more so in the ancient times in which Yu lived, when the people were more rude and the appliances for battling with such a disaster fewer than they are to-day.

We lose sight of Yu till the 14th year of Shun, who then ordered him to consult with him about affairs of state, and nineteen years after insists that Yu should act as his vicegerent.   After various attempts to evade this honour the latter finally consents, and is associated with Shun in the government of the people.   Two years after he proceeds on a punitive expedition against some of the aborigines, who had refused to submit to the government, and for thirty days he strove in vain to gain the victory over them.   He saw that there was something morally wrong, for if his virtue had been more complete he must have got the advantage of them.   He accordingly returned to the capital and began to make serious reforms in his own life, with the result that in seventy days the Miautze, influenced by his change of character, came voluntarily and made their submission.

When Shun died, Yu who did not wish to dispossess his son I-kiun of the succession, endeavoured to withdraw into private life, but the nobles and the people were determined to have him as their ruler, and so after the three years of mourning were over he was established on the throne, and I-kiun made no efforts to dispute his right to it.   He removed his capital to Ping-yang in Shensi and made the royal colours black.   In his first year he made a tour as far as T'u-shan, the native place of his wife, and there met the assembled nobles of the various states of the Empire and addressed them on matters concerning the welfare of the nation.

Yu was a ruler that desired to stand in the closest relationship to his people, and to be easy of access to them at all times.   For this purpose at the entrance to his palace he caused to be hung a drum, a gong, a triangular musical instrument, and a rattle.   If any one desired to discourse with him upon any of the virtues that adorn a monarch, he had but to strike the drum, and he was at once admitted. If any one, again, thought there was room for a reforma- tion in his life, he had simply to strike the gong, and the doors were flung open and he was ushered into his presence. If rebellion or famine existed anywhere of which he was unaware a tap on the triangular instrument, and the man who was possessed of the news was at once led to where Yu was, and if any magistrate had decided a case unjustly or unwisely one shake of the rattle gave him instant admission into the presence of his sovereign, to whom he could state his grievance.*

An important thing happened shortly after Yu ascended the throne, and that was the discovery of spirits by I-ti by distillation of various kinds of grain. Specimens were brought to him, which he tasted, and though agreeable to the palate, he professed himself much distressed at the discovery. "The days will come," he said, "when some of my successors through drinking this will cause infinite sorrow to the nation." These were prophetic words, and destined to be fulfilled by the last ruler of the dynasty he was now founding. He then expelled I-ti from the country as a man dangerous to the state.

In the second year of his reign his chief minister Han-yan died, and Yih was appointed in his place with the idea of succeeding him on the throne when he died. Two years after he caused to be made nine golden tripods on which he had engraven the maps of his nine provinces, one on each, which he solemnly placed in the royal ancestral temple, as a permanent record of the great work he had achieved in delivering China from the great flood.

In his fifth year in one of his tours, he passed a criminal in chains. He immediately descended from his chariot, and weeping asked him how it was that he was in this condition. The by-standers said, "Great Yu, don't pity this fellow, or weep for him, for he is a bad man and deserves no sympathy." "I weep," replied Yu, "because of the state of things in my kingdom. When Yau and Shun were rulers, their people were of one mind with them, and so were good. Now because of my deficiency in virtue, every man follows the bent of his own will, and so evil prevails."

Up to Yu's time trade had been carried on by barter, but now gold and silver were minted and used as a currency. He showed his benevolence by issuing an order that if any family through poverty had been compelled to sell a son, if they applied to him he

---

* The rattle is still in existence, but is now only used by peddlers. The drum, however, is still used, though in a modified way, much in the same way as it was in the days of Yu. In front of every Mandarin's Yamên there is one hung and any one who fails to get justice by the ordinary channels, can strike this, when he is at once admitted into the presence of the official, to whom he can personally appeal for redress. This method, however, is not always efficacious in securing justice, for the magistrates of to-day have fallen far below the ideal ones of those early days.

would supply them with money sufficient to redeem him. In his eighth year he made a tour of visitation and reached Hwuy-k'i in Cheh-kiang, where he met his nobles. One of these, Fang-fung, he put to death, because he had shown disrespect to him in not arriving at the meeting in proper time. Before the assembly had finished its discussions the aged ruler fell ill and died at the advanced age of one hundred, and was succeeded by his son.

K'i—B. C. 2197-2188.

According to the intentions of Yu, Yih should have been the man that should have succeeded him on the throne. He was no doubt influenced to this decision by the belief that he had in his ability. He had helped him in devising measures for controlling the great inundation of the Yellow River, and had been appointed by Shun to superintend the works for cutting down the trees and grass that had run wild during the flood, and for destroying the birds and beasts that had become so numerous during that time that they had become a danger to man. He had a most kindly feeling towards him, and infinite faith in the probity of his character. There was a profounder reason, however, than all this for his action. The throne hitherto had not been hereditary, but had been given to the most suitable man without any family partiality. Yu knew that posterity would stigmatize his conduct, as being wanting in that unselfish concern for the state that had marked both Yau and Shun, and he would suffer in the estimation of it. The nation, however, resented this plan, and though it is probable that they allowed Yih to govern during the three years of mourning for Yu, the Princes of the feudal states, and the people at large, decided that K'i was the proper man to succeed his father.*

He fixed his capital in the present prefectural city of Honan. The only event of any importance that is recorded of him is his battle with Hu at a place named Kan, in Shensi. This man was a powerful and ambitious noble, and no doubt he thought that he had as good a right to reign as K'i. Hitherto the succession had been to the fittest, and Yu's son, therefore, had the right to become Emperor, only as he excelled other men in his virtues. He did not believe that he was a better man than himself, and consequently he was determined to try issues with him, and see who it was that Heaven intended should reign, he or K'i.

Just before the engagement K'i called together the officers of the six divisions of which his army was composed and addressed them. He tells them in language, which it is difficult now fully to understand, that Hu was a rebel that Heaven had determined to

---

* It may be stated here that a ruler's reign counted to the end of the year in which he died. For example, if he died in January his successor's years did not begin to count till the beginning of the following year. There is at least one notable exception to this, which will be noted at the place where it occurs in this history. K'i's reign therefore is reckoned from the next year to that in which his father died.

destroy, and that they were the instruments it had selected to carry out its purpose.   He then exhorts the men on the right, as well as those on the left, to show themselves courageous in the conflict that was imminent, and he urged upon those that fought in chariots to listen well to the orders of their officers, so that there might be no confusion in the coming battle.* Rewards were promised to those that distinguished themselves, whilst the death of themselves as well as of their families would be the portion of those who showed themselves cowardly before the enemy.† What was the issue of this battle is left in doubt.   Sz Ma-ts'ien, the historian, declares that K'i obtained a decisive victory, and that Hu was slain, but as he lived fully two thousand years after the event his evidence must not be considered decisive.   K'i died after a brief reign, and was succeeded by his son.

T'ai K'ang—B. C. 2188-2159.

This ruler was the eldest son of K'i, but he was in no sense fitted to be a successor to his father.   He was indolent and vicious, and therefore unwilling to govern the country with the same regard to justice as had distinguished his predecessors.   The consequence was that the hearts of his people became alienated from him.   This, however, did not seem to give him any concern, for he continued his dissipations and spent his time in the most frivolous amusements, whilst the affairs of the kingdom were allowed to take care of themselves.

In the nineteenth year of his reign he went on a hunting expedition across the river Loh,‡ and for a hundred days no news came to his people of his whereabouts.

I, the Prince of K'iung, taking advantage of the discontent of the people, and looking upon this as a good opportunity for seizing the crown for himself, raised an army and prevented his return to his capital.   For ten long years he was thus compelled to live in exile, and finally died in it.   During this time I usurped the power, though T'ai K'ang still nominally remained Emperor.   After a troubled reign of twenty-nine years, the latter died, and was followed by his brother.

---

* From this it would appear that in those very early days, just as amongst the ancient Gauls and Britons chariots were used in war. The war chariot was armed with three men. The left one was a bowman, the right was armed with a javelin or spear, whilst the third drove the horses.

† It seems from the Historical Classic that it was the custom when going into battle for the Emperors to carry with them the tablets which they believed enshrined the spirits of their ancestors, as well as others that contained the spirits of the land. They supposed that by so doing they were carrying with them all the unseen influences that gathered round these beings, which would be put forth for their benefit in the coming struggle. It is noticeable in these threats of extending punishment to the families of the delinquents, K'i was departing from the practice of the amiable Shun, of whom it was declared, "That his punishments did not reach to men's heirs, whilst his rewards extended to future ages." The history of China shows that its people have preferred to follow the example of the former, rather than that of their great sage and ruler.

‡ This river is a tributary of the Yellow River, rising in the S. E. of Honan and flowing into it to the west of K'ai-fung-fu.

Chung K'ang—B. C. 2159-2146.

This Emperor was appointed to his position by I, who seems to have had power enough to control the succession. His object appears to have been to retain for himself the real authority in the state, whilst allowing Chung K'ang to have the semblance of rule in the Empire. He found, however, that he was not going to be such a puppet in his hands as he had planned him to be, for shortly after his elevation he proceeded to appoint the Marquis Yin to be the chief amongst all the feudal nobles and at the same time his Prime Minister. The position of the latter was thus a very exalted one. He was not only always near the Emperor, and gave him advice in all political matters, but he had also the power, for example, if any of the feudal princes rebelled of leading the royal troops to punish them.

I was completely outmanœuvred by this action of Chung K'ang, for in any attempt to claim the sovereignty he would have to contend not only with the royalists but also with the Marquis, as well as the other feudal princes, who were not yet ready to upset the dynasty in favour of himself.

In the beginning of this reign the Marquis Yin was sent on a punitive expedition against Hi and Ho, Ministers of the Board of Astronomy. In the time of Yau these officials had each an independent feudal state of his own, but in this dynasty the two were merged into one. They had miserably neglected their duties, and had given themselves to pleasure and dissipation. The consequences were that the calendar got out of order, and the business of the country became deranged. They had been so absorbed in their drunken excesses that the observation of the heavens had been omitted, and so when in the autumn an eclipse of the sun took place all the great officers of state were taken by surprise.*

It was the duty of the Astronomical Board some days before an eclipse to formally notify the Emperor, so that preparations might be made and orders given to the Board of Music to be ready to beat their drums and shoot arrows against the moon, so as to deliver the sun from the impending danger. The sin of Hi and Ho was considered so serious that it could only be met by an army being led against them and their territory being devastated. The laws up to this time had been very explicit with regard to the punishment that was due for such

---

*The mention of this eclipse brings up a very important question, and could its date be satisfactorily settled it would help the student of Chinese history very materially in his researches in this remote and ancient period of the world's history. Dr. Legge in his valuable notes concerning it says: "The astronomers of the T'ang dynasty determined that the eclipse took place in the fifth year of Chung K'ang . . . . . Father Gaubil brought out the result, in harmony with the conclusions of the T'ang scholars, that it occurred on 11th Oct. (old style) of the year B. C. 2155, and that it was visible at Gan-yih at 6h. 49m. in the morning . . . . Rev. Mr. Chalmers confirmed Gaubil's conclusion so far as regarded the year, month and day, but considers that it must have occurred during the night and before the rising of the sun." The Bamboo Annals declare that the eclipse took place in the 5th year of the Emperor. Comp. Journal N. C. B. R. A. S., Vol. XXIV.

a crime. "When the astronomers give notice of the eclipse too soon let them be put to death without any forgiveness, and when after the time let the same happen to them."*

According to Sz Ma-ts'ien, the expedition was successful, and the dominion of Hi and Ho was added to the royal domain, though the Historical Classic is silent on the subject. Chung K'ang died after a reign of thirteen years, and was succeeded by his son.

Siang—B. C. 2146-2118.

With the accession of this ruler to the throne calamities of severer character than had ever yet fallen upon the dynasty now came upon it. Yin, the faithful vassal and wise minister, was dead, and I seeing that there was no one that could successfully resist him seized upon the supreme power, and Siang was compelled to flee to Chin-kwan, where the members of his own clan resided in the greatest numbers. I ruled for eight years, but as he was a famous archer, and delighted in the exhibition of his skill with the bow, he neglected the interests of his people and spent the most of his time in hunting. All his able and loyal ministers he dismissed, and employed only worthless and scheming men to carry on the business of the State. One of these was Tsuh, of the principality of Han, who pretended great friendship for I, but who all the time was secretly undermining his influence amongst the people.

On one occasion I had gone hunting, when an uprising was organized by Tsuh. The palace was filled with his soldiers, and an ambush laid near the road by which the usurper was to return. Unsuspicious of evil he was seized and hacked to pieces, whilst Tsuh ordered that his body should be boiled in a cauldron. The latter seized upon his throne and married his widow, by whom he had two sons—Kiau and Hi—though it is supposed by some that they were really the sons of I. When the former reached the age of twenty he was ordered to go and murder Siang, which he did in the city of Shang-k'iu, which was the chief town in the State of Shang.†

The Interregnum—B. C. 2118-2079.

After the murder of Siang, his queen, Min, fled to Jing in Shantung, where her father was chief, and not long after her arrival gave birth to a son, whom she named Shaw K'ang. The usurpation of Tsuh was a long one. He was a worthless dissipated man, and in the end the nation became weary of his rule. The people rose in rebellion, and having put Tsuh to death set Shau K'ang on the throne of his fathers, an action which was ratified by the approval of all the feudal nobles.

---

* "See Punitive Expedition of Yin."
† This was an ancient State, now in Kwei-teh to the E. of Honan.

Shau K'ang—B. C. 2079-2057.

The story of the early days of this ruler is quite a romantic one. Born at the home of his grandfather in Jing, when he became old enough he was put in charge of his flocks and herds. Compelled to flee from this place in consequence of the hostility of Tsuh, who sought his life, he fled to the Chief of Yu, who appointed him his chief cook. Here he so won the good will of his master that he gave him his two daughters in marriage and the city of Lun to rule over. This was the commencement of the good fortune that finally led to his becoming Emperor.*

When he became firmly seated on the throne the good effect of his wise reign was seen in the gradual disappearance of disorder throughout the Empire. Even the wild tribes on the borders felt its civilizing influence, and some of them submitted to him. In the 11th year of his reign an overflow of the Yellow River took place, and the Prince of Shang was ordered to take measures to control it. We see from this that the State of Shang was beginning to take a prominent place in relation to the other principalities, and that from this time it comes more and more conspicuously into view, until at length it is strong enough to overthrow the Hia dynasty and become the ruling power in the Empire.

Two years after, Wu Yu, one of Shau K'ang's sons, established himself in Yueh, in the north-east of the present Cheh-kiang province, and there founded a feudal State of his own. Shau K'ang died after a reign of twenty-two years, and was succeeded by his son.

Ch'u—B. C. 2057-2040.

History has scarcely anything to relate of this man. The Bamboo Annals state that he made Yuen, in Honan, his capital, that he went on a punitive expedition to Shan-show, where he caught a fox with nine tails, and that he died after a reign of seventeen years, and the throne was occupied by his son, *Hwai* (B. C. 2040-2014,) who reigned twenty-six years, and then was succeeded by his son *Mang* (B. C. 2014-1996), who ruled eighteen years, and then left the throne to his son, *Sieh* (B. C. 1996-1980). Of this man's reign of sixteen years, except what little we get from the Bamboo Annals, we know nothing. It is stated in them that the Prince of Yin was murdered by that of Yu-yih who, however, was put to death by the combined forces of Yin and Ho.

Pu Kiang (B. C. 1980-1921). After a lengthy reign of fifty-nine years he was followed by his younger brother, to whom he resigned his throne.

Kiung (B. C. 1921-1900). After twenty-one years he left the throne to his son.

---

* See Bamboo Annals in loc.

Kin (B. C. 1900-1879). According to the Bamboo Annals this man removed his capital from Honan to Shen-si, and adapted the national music to the requirements of the people of the West. He died after an uneventful reign of twenty-one years.

K'ung Kia (B. C. 1879-1848). This man was a son of the former Emperor Pu Kiang. He was dissolute and profligate, and gradually lost the sympathies of his people. In the 27th year of his reign the Prince of Shang had a son born to him of the name of Li, who subsequently became the founder of the Shang dynasty.

Kau (B. C. 1848-1837). After eleven years' reign he was followed by his son.

Fa (B. C. 1837-1818). The nineteen years of this ruler's reign were uneventful, excepting for two events mentioned in the Bamboo Annals, viz., that various tribes of aborigines came and made submission to him, and that when he died the great mountain T'ai, in Shantung, shook to its very base, an omen that predicted that unusual calamities were about to come upon the dynasty. His son, who succeeded him, was the notorious Kwei or Kieh as he is more popularly known.

Kwei or Kieh—B. C. 1818-1766.

This sovereign is one of the most infamous in Chinese history. He is said to have been a man of immense physical strength, and could manipulate bars of iron and twist them into any shape it pleased him. Unfortunately his main aim in life seemed to be to use this for selfish purposes rather than for the benefit of his people. In the year B. C. 1785 he proceeded to attack the Chief of Shih, who averted the threatened danger by the present of his daughter Mei-hi to Kieh. She was remarkable for her beauty, and so gained the heart of the emperor that he became an absolute slave to her. She was a woman, however, without a redeeming virtue ; her whole purpose in life seeming to be the desire to do evil.

Kieh, in order to gratify her, built her a palace of the most costly materials and laid out gardens that contained everything that would please the eye. A passionate love for the beautiful, however, was not the distinguishing feature of her mind, and she was not satisfied unless grosser pleasures were mingled in the fairy scenes that the emperor had created for her. In these gardens a vast host of at least three thousand dissolute people were assembled to participate in the orgies that she had instituted. The trees were hung with all kinds of dried meats, and a pond in the midst of the gardens was filled with spirits, on which boats were rowed. At the sound of drums every one jumped into this and drank and sported, whilst Kieh and his concubine looked on, watching with glee how many got drunk and how others were drowned in the fiery waters.

This state of things went on for four years, when T'ang, the Prince of Shang, who was distressed at the immorality of the imperial court, introduced to the Emperor I-yin, a man of distinguished ability, who proceeded to expound to him the principles on which Yau and Shun founded their government, and urged upon him to follow their brilliant example. Kieh refused to be guided by his advice, and dismissed him from his court. Five times in all did he approach the monarch in the hopes of saving him, and as many times was he driven from the capital. Years again went by, and matters instead of improving grew worse. In the 51st year of his reign Kieh built an underground palace, and for thirty days he and his dissolute companions disappeared from sight to carry on their scenes of wickedness unobserved by the world. The high officials now began to desert to T'ang. The astronomer royal, Chung-ku, finding all his remonstrances in vain, transferred his allegiance to him and implored him to intervene and save the country from a monster that was unfit to govern.

Nature, too, at this time seems to have joined in the universal condemnation of Kieh by acting in a very extraordinary and unusual manner. Two suns were seen in the sky struggling with each other ; the planets by night wandered about out of their courses ; a portion of the great T'ai mountain fell down with a tremendous crash, and the rivers I and Lo became dry.

At this crisis of the Empire's history T'ang felt himself called upon by Heaven to be the minister of its vengeance. He accordingly summoned his men to take the field and march with him to overthrow Kieh. When his army had assembled he addressed them in a speech that is still extant. It is brief and to the point, and is the utterance of a man that knows his own mind. It seems that there were many amongst his own subjects that doubted the propriety of their Chief engaging in such a hazardous enterprise as a conflict with the forces of the Empire. He, therefore, explains to them the reason why he is not afraid to undertake it. "It is not I," he said, "who am but a little child, who dare take in hand what may be termed to be a rebellious undertaking. The crimes of Hia are many, and Heaven has ordered his destruction. Some of you say," he continued, "our Prince does not pity us, but takes us away from our farms, simply to punish the ruler of Hia. I indeed have heard such words from many of you. But the King of Hia has sinned, and I dare not refrain from punishing him." To clinch his argument he closes with the significant words, "Those of you who do not obey these orders of mine shall be put to death with your children, and no forgiveness shall be extended to you, whilst those that help me shall be rewarded."

The battle was fought at Ming-t'iau, and resulted in the overthrow and flight of Kieh, who halted not till he reached Nan-ch'au, in Ngan-hwui, where he was imprisoned till his death three years afterwards. This defeat put the crown upon T'ang's head, and though his conscience afterwards pricked him for his conduct in this matter succeeding ages have justified him, and his name is recorded amongst those that are considered to have been the benefactors of China.

CHAPTER V.

THE LEGENDARY PERIOD (Continued).

The Shang Dynasty, B. C. 1766-1122.   Also called the Yin Dynasty.

T'ang—B. C. 1766-1753.

T'ANG, the founder of the new dynasty, was of distinguished ancestry, being descended from the famous Hwang Ti through Sieh, the son of the Emperor Ti Kuh, who was Minister of Instruction to Yau, and who for his services had the principality of Shang bestowed upon him. In giving a name to the dynasty he was now founding he took that of his ancestral fief as the most fitting one with which to transmit it to posterity.

On his ascending the throne at Po,* T'ang issued an address to his people, which has fortunately been preserved in the Historical Classic. It is brief but pithy, and shows him to have been a very thoughtful man, and one with a lofty ideal of what a king ought to be. He shows that all men, even those of the lowest orders, have been endowed by God with a sense of what is right, and that it is the business of the sovereign to direct this into the path in which, if obeyed, it would continually lead them. He next proves that the calamities that had come upon the exiled king were sent directly by Heaven for his crimes, and he expresses his own fears, lest he should offend the powers of Heaven and Earth and thus excite their anger against himself, and he winds up by an earnest exhortation to his nobles and people to continue in the path of right. "With regard to all the States that now come under my control," he says, "do not walk in unrighteous ways, and let there be no high-handed viciousness. Let every one observe the laws, and so he shall have the blessing of Heaven. If there is any good in any of you I shall not dare not to acknowledge it, and any evil in myself I shall not presume to forgive myself. When any of you do wrong the guilt shall be on me, and when I transgress the sin shall be my own." These are noble words, and well worthy the founder of a dynasty.

T'ang was fortunate, like his predecessors, in having a prime minister of rare ability and excellence named I-yin,† to assist him in the government of the nation.

---

* Po was in the modern Shang-k'iu in the East of Honan. Shang was in the present Kwei-teh Fu, also in the E. of the same province.

† Mencius says of him that he was a farmer in Shan, who had gained a reputation for wisdom and virtue. T'ang sent him presents of silk and invited him to enter his service, but he refused. Three times he sent messengers to him, and the last time he relented, because finally he had the ambition of making T'ang like Yau and Shun. Confucius speaks in the highest terms of him, and says in his Analects that T'ang, having become Emperor, chose him from all the men in his kingdom, and the result was "that those that had failed to fulfill their social duties disappeared from the State."

Having ascended the throne T'ang in order to show that the former dynasty had finally passed away changed the royal colours from black to white, made the twelfth month of the Hia the first of his reign, and ordered that all sacrificial animals should be white. He then made a visitation round the eastern part of his dominions, rewarding the nobles that had done anything meritorious and punishing those that had misbehaved themselves. He also made provision for the royal descendants of the last dynasty by assigning them lands, where they could live in comfort.

In the second year of his reign a drought began to be experienced, which lasted for seven years, and resulted in a terrible famine that caused much suffering amongst his people. During this time the rain almost entirely ceased to fall, and sorrow and distress prevailed throughout the country. Many of the poorest were reduced to such straits that they were compelled to sell their children in order to keep starvation from the home. Money was coined and freely distributed amongst such, but where grain was so scarce even this availed not to relieve the distress. The suffering at length became so extreme that it became the universal conviction that some human victim would have to be sacrificed before Heaven would be appeased. T'ang with a noble generosity expressed himself willing to surrender his life in order that the nation might be saved, and after having fasted he cut off his hair, and then seated in a simple carriage drawn by white horses and clad in white rushes, as though he were the sacrifice all ready to be offered up, he proceeded to a mulberry grove. There he confessed his sins and offered himself a victim to God. The response to this was a copious rain that fell for hundreds of miles over the parched country, and that brought joy and hope to the people. Deeply impressed by the delivery that God had wrought for his kingdom T'ang composed an ode of thanksgiving, which he called "The Great Salvation."

Shortly after this joyous event the Emperor decided that the spirit of Chu, the grandson of Shen Nung, that had acted as tutelary god of the land during the Hia dynasty, should be degraded from its office and be replaced by that of K'i, the son of Ti Kuh, as a more competent one to occupy such a responsible position. The former had shown its want of power by allowing the severe drought to desolate the land for so long a period. In this proceeding we see that T'ang, in spite of his belief in God as the Supreme Ruler, was still a believer in the inferior spirits that popular superstition had made the protectors of the land and the mountains and the products of the earth.

The records of this reign are exceedingly meagre and disappointing. From the few fragments that we have respecting T'ang we feel ourselves instinctively drawn towards him. There is something so manly and robust about him, and moreover he is so unselfish that when we contrast him with the rulers of the later ages of China we are struck with the fact that the governme ᵗ was carried on by him on entirely different principles from those that actuated them. He seems to have subordinated every passion and feeling, and even his own life, to the good of his people. His overthrow of the Hia dynasty was in no sense a usurpation. The feudal chiefs recognized him as the one man that could save the empire, and the consent of the people after Kieh was defeated ratified their action. He undertook the conflict with the emperor with great reluctance, and only at last because he was convinced that it was the will of Heaven that he should do so.

The question did indeed come up in after days, whether T'ang acted rightly in taking up arms against his sovereign. The common sentiment of the Chinese, who do not believe in the divine right of kings to rule as they like, has upheld his action, and he is to-day looked up to as a model ruler, whose example every occupant of the dragon throne may imitate with advantage.

He died at the good old age of one hundred, and was succeeded by his grandson.

T'ai Kia*—B. C. 1753-1720.

This sovereign was of a weak and vacillating nature and wanting in that strong character that distinguished his famous grandfather. The consequence was that the stronger-minded companions at the court with whom he associated began to lead him astray. Fortunately for him and the Empire I-yin was by his side, who was too patriotic to allow the young man to endanger his own crown and the public peace. He remonstrated with him in writing, and reminded him how the chief concern of T'ang had been to obey the laws of Heaven, and how it had blessed and honoured him in return. He warns him to take heed to the terrible disasters that had fallen on the Hia dynasty, and urges him to play the part of king well, so that he may not bring disgrace upon the name of his great ancestor.

T'ai Kia refused to listen to the words of his faithful minister, who, however, once more personally remonstrated with him and implored him to begin a life of greater self-restraint and to strive after virtue, so that he might have the satisfaction of feeling that the serious trust that had been committed to him by T'ang had been faithfully and loyally carried out. Still no impression was made upon him, and he continued in his old courses. I-yin, however, was just as strong as T'ai Kia was weak, and evidently being backed up by the powerful nobles at court he determined to take strong measures with him and save him and his dynasty in spite of himself. He accordingly had rooms fitted up for him in a palace that had been built for him in T'ung, in Shan-si, where T'ang had been buried, and thither he

---

* According to Mencius and the Bamboo Annals there were two kings that came between T'ang and T'ai Kia, viz., Wei Ping and Chung Jin, sons of the former. All attempts to explain the discrepancy are unsatisfactory, and it is better therefore to follow the standard history of China, which makes T'ai Kia to be the immediate successor of T'ang.

forcibly removed him and kept him in very easy confinement during the whole period of mourning. In this place he was dissociated from the pleasures of the capital and the dissipated companions that were leading him astray.

In the comparative solitude of this place he had leisure to think over his evil courses and to reflect upon the advice which I-yin had given him. The better nature of the young Emperor prevailed, and by the end of three years he was a thoroughly repentant man. * Dressed in imperial cap and robes he was escorted back to his capital by I-yin with great pomp and ceremony, where he resumed the position that he had been deprived of for a time.

That his repentance was sincere is evident. His confession, as recorded in the Historical Classic, is a very touching one. He says to I-yin, "I, a little child, did not comprehend the full force of virtue, and thus I made myself unworthy. My passions caused me to subvert all good rules and my over-indulgence to transgress the laws of courtesy. The end would have been speedy ruin to myself. Sorrows sent by Heaven may be avoided, but those that one brings upon oneself can never be escaped." He then goes on to beg I-yin still to counsel him and be a mentor and a guardian to him, so that he may not transgress again as he had done before. His altered life bore out his profession of repentance. He began to cultivate virtue, and paid special attention to the good government of his people. He was kind to the widow and the fatherless. His nobles gave him their loving homage and allegiance, and after a reign of thirty-three years he died in his capital, Po, and was succeeded by his son Wuh Ting.† With the death of T'ai Kia we come to an almost absolute blank in the history of the nation for fully three hundred years. What is left of the documents of the Historical Classic says nothing of the events that took place during the reigns of fourteen Emperors that followed T'ai Kia. From the standard histories we get the names of these men and a few of the more remarkable of the events that happened in the lives of the more conspicuous of them. But after all, to an English reader, even those that have been chronicled, will frequently appear very trivial and hardly worth the serious study of the student of history.

Yuh Ting—B. C. 1720-1691.

The great event of this reign, and one that overshadows every other, was the death of I-yin, who acted as prime minister to the time of his death. His decease was followed, it is said, by a great mist that enveloped the kingdom for three days. The Emperor decided

---

* The Bamboo Annals differ entirely from the Historical Classic in regard to T'ai Kia's repentance. They say that he escaped from T'ung and put I-yin to death, but for this statement we have no evidence.

† He was really only a little over two years away. In counting time the Chinese reckon a part of a year as a whole year. A child, for example, is born in the last month of the year and on the last day of it, and still he is considered to be a year old.

that he should have a royal funeral. He visited the body whilst it lay in state, and wept as though he had lost his father, and he ordered that a bullock should be sacrificed at his tomb.* The whole nation mourned for him, for they felt they had lost the one man that could keep the nation together and make it to be respected by all classes.

The great commentator Chu Hi says of him, "T'ang proclaimed I-yin to be a sage. Now as far as I have examined his life I have found him a man of virtue and of marvellous ability, and when on several occasions he used his power, neither the people nor the nobles thought of opposing him. Although he approached Kieh five times with his remonstrances, that king, though so vicious, dare not lay hands on him, and though he returned four times to T'ang with his mission unfulfilled he never doubted his ability. He only became more firmly convinced than ever that Kieh could not be cured of his vices. He was a man of such great ability that he helped T'ang, the successful, to the Empire. The whole nation was at rest when this was accomplished. When T'ai Kia would not repent he drove him to T'ung, and the whole of the officers of state never for a moment doubted his loyalty. The whole nation too had implicit faith in him. The consequence was that T'ai Kia became reformed, and was one of the good kings of the Shang dynasty. There was none in the whole nation that could have used the power that he had, and yet not have usurped the regal authority for himself. I-yin was a man the most famous of all men in history that have known how to use power rightly."

Wuh Ting died after a reign of twenty-nine years, and was succeeded by his brother T'ai Keng.

T'ai Keng—B. C. 1691-1666.

After a reign of twenty-five years this ruler was followed by his son, *Siau Kia* (B. C. 1666-1649), who was in turn succeeded by *Yung Ki* (B. C. 1649-1637).

During this ruler's reign government became so weak that the nobles refused to appear once in every five years at court, as was the custom, to pay their acknowledgments to the Emperor as over-lord. The consequence was that the royal authority extended very little beyond his own domains. After a rule of seventeen years he was succeeded by his brother T'ai Mow.

T'ai Mow—B. C. 1637-1562.

Not long after this Emperor came to the throne there was an exceedingly bad omen that boded ill to the nation. A mulberry sapling and a stalk of grain appeared in the palace yard, growing from the same stem, which in the course of a few hours became so large that a man could not clasp them with both his arms. This

---

* According to Chinese law a bullock is offered only to the following, viz., the Emperor, the spirits of the mountains, streams and land, to the spirits of the dead in the royal ancestral temples, and to Confucius.

phenomenon could only mean that some great calamity was about to come on the Empire. The king was exceedingly afraid, and consulted his Prime Minister I-chih, the son of I-yin, as to what ought to be done under the circumstances. He replied, "Calamities cannot prevail against virtue. There must be some defect in your government. I pray you, from this time, be earnest in the cultivation of righteousness."

T'ai Mow listened respectfully to this advice and began to follow the noble example of former kings. So great was the influence of this in the sight of Heaven that in three days the abnormal growth withered away and disappeared. From this time he paid great attention to his morals and made special efforts to impress on his people the duty and privilege of caring for the old. He made enquiries as to who were sick or in trouble, and he helped them and comforted those that were mourning for the dead. His fame spread so widely in the course of three years that no fewer than seventy-six countries sent ambassadors to congratulate him upon the greatness of his kingdom and the wisdom of his rule.

During his reign carriages were made that afterwards became famous. Confucius more than a thousand years later refers to them as the style that the nation ought to adopt. The country revived under him, and the power of the state became recognized by all the feudal chiefs. After a prosperous reign of seventy-five years he left the throne to his son Chung Ting.

Chung Ting—B. C. 1562-1549.

This ruler removed the capital from Po, in consequence of an inundation of the Yellow River, to Ao. His reign was disturbed by internal disorders and incursions of the barbarians of the south. Having no heir to succeed him there were troubles in the capital after his death, but finally his brother Wai Jin was made Emperor.

Wai Jin—B. C. 1549-1534.

Great confusion existed in the country during the reign of this man, and many of the nobles refused to acknowledge him. His brother Ho Tan-kia succeeded him.

Ho Tan-kia—B. C. 1534-1525.

This Emperor's reign was a feeble one, and the Shang dynasty showed signs of decay. He moved the capital from Ao to Siang in the present prefecture of Chang-teh in Honan. His son Tsu Yih got the throne after him.

Tsu Yih—B. C. 1525-1506.

The overflow of the Wei River necessitated the removal of the capital from Siang to Kêng in Shansi, but after nine years he had again to move to Hing-t'ai in Chihli. He had a vigorous Prime

Minister of the name of Wu Hien, who caused the authority of the
Emperor to be respected by the nobles and by the people. His son
Tsu Sin took his place.

Tsu Sin—B. C. 1506-1490.

This man was followed by his brother *Wu Kia* (B. C. 1490-
1465), and he, after a reign of great confusion, by his son *Tsu Ting*
(B. C. 1465-1433) who, after a long but unhappy reign of thirty-two
years, died and left the throne to *Nan Kung* (B. C. 1433-1408), a
son of Yu Kia. He again was succeeded by *Yang Kia* B. C. 1408-
1401), under whose rule the fortunes of Shang grew more and more
desperate, and undoubtedly, had there been any strong ambitious
man amongst the nobles, he could easily have wrested the sceptre
from the hands of this weak monarch. Yang Kia was followed by
his brother P'an Kung.

P'an Kung—B. C. 1401-1373.

The most remarkable event of this reign was the removal of the
capital from King-t'ai in Chihli to Yin, a town N. of the Yellow
River in Honan. His reason for this was because his kingdom was
not prospering, and righteousness was declining throughout the
nation. He therefore wished to return to the region where the great
kings of former days had had their seat of government, in the hope
that their spirits, lingering about the place, might influence his
people, and so bring back the prosperity of other days. Honan,
moreover, was more central than their present situation, and all
parts of the country could be more easily reached from it.

The people of the capital were at first unwilling to consent to
this removal. They did not like to endure the sacrifices demanded
by it. Their lands and property would have to be abandoned, and
for this they were not prepared. The Emperor, knowing this,
wrote out his reasons for the step he was advocating, and they have
been handed down to us in the Historical Classic. Finally, after
much grumbling, the people consented to his wish, and the capital
was moved to Yin, or the Western Po, as it was also called, and
henceforth the name of the dynasty was changed from Shang to Yin.

From this time P'an Kung followed the methods of T'ang
in his government of the people, and in consequence there was a
marked improvement in every department of life. After a successful reign of twenty-eight years he was succeeded by his brother
Siau Sin (B. C. 1373-1352), and after twenty-one years he again
was followed by his brother *Siau Yih* (B. C. 1352-1324), who
occupied the throne for twenty-eight years. It is recorded that
in the 26th year of this sovereign's reign Tan Fu, a descendant of
K'i, the son of the Emperor Ti Kuh, the chief of Pin, removed his
people from that place to K'i and took the title of Chow.* His

---

* Pin was a small principality in the south of Shensi, whilst K'i was in the S.
W. of the same province, near the river Wei.

descendant was the founder of the famous Chow dynasty that ruled so long over China. Siau Yih, after an uneventful reign, was succeeded by his famous son Wu Ting.

Wu Ting—B. C. 1324-1265.

If any man could have restored the declining fortunes of the Shang dynasty it would certainly have been this ruler, but even he, with all his virtues, found the task too great for him. All that he could do was for a time to arrest its downfall. It is recorded that during the three years of mourning for his father he never spoke. Whether he kept absolute silence all that time, or whether he simply abstained from interference in the government of the country, is matter of conjecture. "He never left his palace or uttered a sound," one historian says, but handed over the management of public affairs to his Prime Minister. Even after the full time of mourning was over the silence continued to be unbroken, to the great distress of his officials, who represented to him that the government of the country was impossible, so long as he abstained from taking a share in it.

Still unwilling to speak he explained in writing the reasons for his conduct. He said that he was conscious that his virtues were so far inferior to those of the great models of former days that he had deemed it the highest wisdom to keep silence. He showed, however, that his three years of total inaction had not been without its benefits. Whilst he was pondering over the state of his kingdom, and thinking how he should live a noble life, he said he dreamt that God had presented to him a man that should assist him in the government of his Empire.

This person seems to have appeared in a most vivid form to him in his dream, for he could distinctly recollect his appearance when he awoke. He not only minutely described it to his ministers, but he also drew a picture of him, and ordered that search should be made for him throughout his kingdom. This resulted in the discovery of a man of the name of Hu-yueh, who corresponded in the minutest detail to the picture drawn by the royal hand. He turned out to be a man who lived in Fu-yen in Kiai-chow, in Shansi. He was exceedingly poor, and when discovered was engaged in repairing the public roads that had been injured by the overflow of a mountain stream.* He was at once taken to court, and the Emperor recognized him as the man of his dream.

Upon conversing with him he found him to be a person of profound ability, and as the conversation went on he was delighted to find that he had the most exalted ideas of goodness and morality.

---

* Mencius says that he came from amidst the building frames to the high office he subsequently held. Many houses in China, especially those of the poorer classes, are built of earth and lime pounded hard within a wooden frame of about a foot in width and four feet in length. When plastered outside with good mortar these walls are quite as lasting as those built of bricks.

Never had he met a man that was so worthy the appellation of sage, and impressed, not only with his character, but also with the fact that he was given him by a direct revelation from God to be his assistant, he at once appointed him to be his Prime Minister.

The Emperor became so anxious to be instructed by Yueh that he gave him orders never to be far away from him. "Morning and evening" he said, "bring your instructions that my virtue may be helped by them. Let me be a weapon, and you shall be the grindstone on which I may be sharpened. Imagine me crossing a river; you shall be the boat in which I shall pass over. Fancy me as a year when no rain has fallen; you shall be the abundant showers that shall come down upon me. Imagine yourself medicine, which will only cure in proportion as it distresses the patient. Think of me barefoot and unless I look down to the ground my feet will be wounded." Yueh was only too delighted to obey the royal commands. He found in him a pupil after his own heart, and it was a pure labour of love to instruct a man so eager for knowledge as Wu Ting was. The affairs of state now fell entirely into his hands, and he managed matters so well that its decline was arrested. The fame of Wu Ting's virtues spread beyond the confines of his kingdom, and six nations sent ambassadors with their interpreters to visit his court and pay their respects to him.

In the 6th year of his reign, whilst he was offering a sacrifice in the royal ancestral temple to the spirit of his ancestor T'ang, a pheasant flew in, and alighting upon the ear of one of the golden tripods of Yu, began to crow. This was considered a very bad omen, and one of his ministers advised the Emperor that if he would avoid sorrow he must make haste to correct something in his conduct that was deficient in some respect. He then proceeded to show him that his offerings to the spirit of his father had been excessive, whilst he had comparatively neglected those of his ancestors. He at once felt the force of this advice, and in order that he should not easily forget the warning that Heaven had sent him he had pheasant's feathers stuck in several parts of his dress, to be a constant reminder of the errors into which he had fallen.

During the year B. C. 1292 Wu Ting was engaged in a fierce conflict with the people that inhabited the demon land, which lasted for three years. These are supposed to be the wild tribes that then dwelt in the countries beyond the northern boundaries of the Empire, and which were destined to play so important a part in the coming history of China, and which eventually, about twenty-five centuries after they were conquered by Wu Ting, were to become the masters of this country and give rulers to sit on the dragon throne that should govern the black-haired race. After a reign of fifty-nine years this famous Emperor died, and the title given him in the ancestral temple was Kau-tsung, or "The High and Venerable."

We get the impression that Wu Ting was a man of unusual ability and with an exceedingly sensitive conscience. He had a high conception of his duty as a sovereign, and was prepared to put himself in the background and be taught by others so long as the interests of the nation were conserved. He was a strong king too, for peace was maintained not only within the Empire, but also without, and a new lease of life would have been given to the dynasty if there had been men of the same calibre to succeed him.

Tsu Kung (B. C. 1265-1258). This was a son of the above, and after an uneventful reign of seven years he died, and was succeeded by his brother *Tsu Kia* (B. C. 1258-1225) who, it is stated, was a wicked licentious man, whose reckless conduct tended further to the weakening of the hold of this dynasty upon the affections of the people. The statement contained in the Bamboo Annals differs entirely from this. It says that when he was a young man he lived away from court and amongst the common people. The result was that when he became Emperor he knew how to sympathize with his subjects. Towards the end of his reign, however, his punishments became so excessive that their hearts were alienated from him. He was followed by his son *Lin Sin* (B. C. 1225-1219', who governed six years, when his brother *Kung Ting* (B. C. 1219-1198) became Emperor, who was again succeeded by his son Wu Yih.

Wu Yih—B. C. 1198-1194.

In the same year that he ascended the throne he moved the capital from Western Po to the north of the river Ho. This man has the reputation of having made the first idols in China. He did this to show his utter disbelief in any religion. Heaven and the spirits of the mountains and streams that were reverenced by the people were looked upon as mythical by him. To show his contempt for them he had figures made in wood and clay, which he said represented them. He then made some of his people fight with them, who of course came off victorious, and they were then assured by Wu Yih that they were stronger than the gods they worshipped, and therefore that it would be folly for them any more to trust in them. In his 4th year, whilst out hunting between the rivers Ho and Wei he was struck with lightning and was killed immediately. This has been considered by historians a just punishment by Heaven for his attempt to hold it up to contempt in the eyes of his people. His son *T'ai Ting* (B. C. 1194-1191), whose reign of three years was unmarked by any event worthy of record, was succeeded by his son Ti Yih.

Ti Yih—B. C. 1191-1154.

This ruler had a son by one of his concubines named K'i, a man of great ability, and who subsequently became the founder of a dynasty in Corea. His mother was afterwards raised to the position of Empress and had another son, Chow Sin, who, because he was born whilst his mother was queen, became the legal heir to the throne, to the sorrow of China and the downfall of his house.

In the meanwhile the chiefs of Chow had been growing in power and influence.* Ch'ang, the present chief, was a man of great benevolence, and won the hearts of the people by his sympathy and consideration for them. He is now known in history by the title "Chief of the West," an honour conferred upon him by Ti Yih. In the year B. C. 1167 he was ordered to punish a fierce tribe of barbarians that were ravaging the northern boundaries of his Empire. Although he gained no great victory he was able to prevent them from crossing the borders into China and to force back the stream of invasion that threatened the nation with calamity.

Ti Yih died after a reign of thirty-seven years. Before his death he wished to appoint his eldest son K'i, the Viscount of Wei, his successor, but his ministers opposed this on the ground that he had no legal claims to the throne. Chow Sin accordingly became the next Emperor after his father's decease.

Chow Sin—B. C. 1154-1122.

This man is one of the most infamous in all Chinese history. He was extravagant, a drunkard and a most abandoned character, and yet he was a man of great ability. Physically he was so powerful that he was not afraid to meet the fiercest of wild animals. History informs us that he was the first to use ivory chop-sticks. This was considered such an extravagance that his uncle remonstrated with him, and predicted that his over-indulgence would cost him his Empire.

In the year B. C. 1146 the royal forces made an expedition against the small state of Su, and the only significant thing recorded in connection with this campaign was the obtaining of T'a-ki, a most beautiful woman, as a prize of war. She was presented to the Emperor, who at once became infatuated with her. T'a-ki was a most infamous character, and in the story of the events in which she took a leading part there is not a single redeeming act, nor a single feature about her that showed that the womanly instinct existed in her at all. She was not only very licentious, but she was also excessively cruel. The king ordered his Minister of Music to have the most licentious songs composed and the most indecent dances arranged for her. He also built her the famous "Stag Tower," which it took seven years to erect, and was more than a mile square, and was surrounded by a splendid park, which was stocked with the rarest animals.

Another palace was built at Sha-k'iu, also on a most magnificent scale, where the most abominable orgies were carried on night and day. In imitation of the last king of the Hia dynasty a pond

---

*In the time of T'ai Ting, Ki, the son of Tan Fu, the Duke of Chow, had distinguished himself in a compaign against the barbarian tribes on the north. In B. C. 1184 Ki died, and was succeeded by his son Ch'ang.

was made and filled with spirits. The trees around were hung with all kinds of viands, and drinking and debauchery were carried on without any regard to public opinion. The people by and by became dissatisfied with the heavy taxes levied to meet all these expenses. When T'a-ki heard this she urged the Emperor to make the penalties more severe than they were, and rule his subjects with greater rigour.

She herself devised two new modes of punishment that have helped to make her name execrated. One of these was called the "Heater." This was a piece of metal, which was made almost red hot, and which the poor unfortunates were compelled to take up in their hands. The other, which was called the "Roaster," consisted of a copper pillar well greased, which was laid over a pit full of burning charcoal. The condemned had to walk over this, and when his feet slipped he fell into the fire and was roasted alive. T'a-ki, who watched the carrying out of these terrible punishments, was delighted with the agonies of the sufferers.

Another instance of her cruelty is recorded. Walking in the garden every morning and evening she noticed that when the men were wading across a stream near by the young men seemed to feel the cold more than the old ; a discussion arose between her and Chow Sin as to the cause of this. T'a-ki said it was because the young men had more marrow in their legs than the old. The king denied this, and in order to settle the matter he had a number of both old and young seized and their legs broken, in order that they might see which of them was right. Ch'ang, for expressing his distress at these cruelties, was denounced by Hu, the Earl of Ts'ung, and cast into prison at Yew-li. It is said that he occupied himself whilst there in studying the famous diagrams of Fuh-hi and in composing a large part of the classic called the Book of Changes.*

After about seven years' imprisonment his son, by the payment of a very large sum of money, got his release, and it is said that Ch'ang, who was now once more in favour, by a present of part of his territories, got the punishment of roasting abolished. He died in the year B. C. 1134, and was succeeded by his son Fa.†

---

* Ch'ang, or as he is better known by his posthumous title of Wen Wang, is said to have invented a system of divination. He used a hollow turtle, into which a certain number of cash were placed. These were shaken and allowed to fall on to the eight diagrams which were arranged in a circle. Each of these had significations of their own, and it was observed where the cash fell, and which of these they touched. The answer was considered favourable or otherwise from the position of the cash on the drawing.

† One of the most fragrant names in the long history of the past is that of Ch'ang. He was a statesman and a patriot. His system of government was the admiration of all the surrounding states. It is said that two princes had a dispute about the boundaries of their territories, and they determined to let Ch'ang arbitrate in the matter. They proceeded to his capital to beg his interference, but they were astonished after they had entered his state to find how the farmers yielded to each other. Travellers on the road did the same. They also observed that it was the law that no old man should carry a burden. When they reached the palace they noticed how the officials were full of courtesy to each other, and gave precedence to each other. They were so impressed by this that they at once returned home without having seen Ch'ang, and settled their dispute amicably by themselves.

The Emperor and his wicked consort still went on in their evil ways. Whatever minister dared to remonstrate with either of them had either to be prepared for death or to fly to escape their vengeance. His uncle Pi-kan ventured to counsel Chow Sin, but he soon showed him that his near relationship to him was no protection whatever. Indignant at his reproofs he said to him, "I have heard that the heart of a sage has seven apertures ; let us see if it be so." With this he made Pi-kan to be put to death, had his heart cut out, and glutted his eyes with the sight of it.*

In the thirty-first year of Chow Sin's reign, his enormities having excited the indignation of his whole Empire, Fa thought the time had arrived for him to take action. He accordingly raised an army with the professed object of insisting upon a reform in the life and conduct of the Emperor and his consort. No sooner had he led his forces across the Yellow River than, without any previous agreement, eight hundred princes and petty chiefs flocked to his camp, who all urged an immediate advance on the capital. This, however, Fa refused to do. "Heaven has not yet cast him off, and therefore we may not yet punish him. When we know that it has done so then let us work its will and destroy him. As long as Heaven stands by him we are still his officers, but when he has been abandoned by it we are then free to act as we please, for he will then be but an ordinary mortal without any divine authority." Instead, therefore, of advancing against Chow Sin they marched against the chief of Li,† who had distinguished himself by his bad government, and whose punishment, therefore, would be a warning to the Emperor of what would be attempted against him if he did not reform.

The expedition against Li was successful, and Fa ‡ led back his troops to his own state and waited to see if there would be any reformation in Chow Sin's conduct. As might have been expected there was none ; rather, indeed, did it become more arbitrary and oppressive. Not only had Pi-kan been barbarously murdered, but the Viscount of Wei was imprisoned, and escaped death only by feigning madness.

Fa felt convinced that Heaven had now deserted Chow Sin, and that the time had arrived for him to execute its decrees. Once more his army was collected and led to Muh,§ where the royal forces advanced to meet him. The disparity between the two armies seems to have been very considerable, but it is impossible with the imperfect data at our command to say either what this was or how large either of them was.‖ Fa, on the morning of the battle,¶ with

---

* See Dr. Legge's Shoo King, page 279.

† Li was a district in the S. E. of Shansi, on the upper waters of the river Chang.

‡ The more popular and best known name of this man is his posthumous one of Wu Wang.

§ This celebrated battlefield was in the north of Honan in the present country of K'i.

‖ The historian Sz Ma-ts'ien puts down the royal army at 700,000 men, but Dr. Legge thinks that number a great exaggeration. See his Shoo King, p. 315.

¶ It took place on the 3rd day of the Chinese 2nd moon, B.C. 1122.

an axe in his left hand and a white flag in his right, addressed the assembled hosts, and after detailing the crimes of Chow Sin urged them to quit themselves like men and to imitate the courage and ferocity of panthers and tigers.

In such a battle as was fought that day there could be no doubt about the issues. Fa and his men were fighting for their lives, for they knew that but scant mercy would be extended them were they defeated. At the first shock of the two armies it was seen to which side victory would be given. The royalist troops not only gave way, but the front ranks actually turned their spears against those behind and drove them into them as though they had been their enemies. The slaughter that ensued was terrible, and blood flowed so freely that the wooden pestles of the mortars which the soldiers carried with them in which to prepare their rice actually were floated by it.*

Chow Sin, seeing that all was lost, fled with all speed to the "Stag Tower," and arraying himself in his most gorgeous apparel set fire to the building and was burned to death. His body was discovered amongst the ruins, and the general of the troops that captured the place cut off the head with his own hand, and had it elevated on a long pole. Next day the victorious army entered the capital, where it was received with shouts of delight by the populace. T'a-ki shared in the downfall of the unhappy Chow Sin. After the victory of Muh she was seized and executed, to the delight of nearly every one that knew her.†

The conduct of Fa after his victory was quite in keeping with his general character. He proceeded to free the unhappy men that were languishing in prison, and he raised a splendid monument over the spot where Pi-kan had been buried. In order to relieve the necessities of the people he ordered that all the treasures that had been accumulated in the Stag Tower, and all the immense stores of grain that had been laid up in the public granary in Chihli, should be distributed amongst the necessitous. He also showed his magnanimity by appointing territories where the descendants of the former great Emperors might reside, and where they might have the means of offering the proper sacrifices to the spirits of their ancestors. He also proceeded to pass such laws as would tend to the peace and prosperity of a people that for many years had groaned under the burdens imposed by the two tyrants that were happily no more.

---

* There are two points in this story that need elucidation. First, how is it that with the universal discontent against Chow Sin he was able to muster an army so much larger than Fa's, which was in arms to rescue the people from their oppressor: and second, how was there so much bloodshed, when there was so little real oppsition to Fa's men that at the very first assault the royalists flee without serious fighting. History does not help us in our difficulty

† There is a legend to the effect that her beauty was so great that no one had the courage to execute her. At length an aged councillor of Fa covered his face, so that he could not look upon her, and dealt the fatal blow that deprived her of life. The popular belief throughout China to-day is that she was a human incarnation of a wolf demon.

CHAPTER VI.

THE SEMI-HISTORICAL AND HISTORICAL PERIOD.

The Chow Dynasty—B. C. 1122-255.
Wu Wang—B. C. 1122-1115.

WU WANG, the founder of this dynasty, was descended from K'i, the Minister of Instruction under Shun and the son of the Emperor Ti Kuh. The family home had been in Pin in the present province of Shensi ; but, harassed and annoyed by the continual incursions of the barbarians, in B. C. 1326, Tan-fu, the chief at that time, migrated to K'i and changed the name of his principality to Chow.

The first act of the new sovereign, after he ascended the throne, was to order that the 12th month of Shang should become the 1st of his reign. He also changed the royal colour from white to brown and disbanded his soldiers and sent his cavalry horses to Mount Hoa, in Shensi, and dispersed the oxen that had been used in the campaign amongst the farmers to help them in the cultivation of the soil. He also rewarded those that had distinguished themselves in his service by grants of territory and titles of honour,* and he founded the five orders of nobility, viz., Duke, Marquis, Earl, Viscount and Baron, and ordained that each should have a certain amount of territory connected with it to enable it to maintain its dignity.†

Whilst he lavished honours on the living he did not forget the dead. His grandfather and great-grandfather had high sounding titles given them, whilst his father Ch'ang was called Prince Wen, a title by which he is universally known throughout China to-day. Being of a highly religious nature Wu Wang offered a solemn sacrifice to his great ancestors in the ancestral temple of Chow, and a burnt offering to Heaven, and worshipped the spirits of the mountains and rivers and informed them all that he had brought his campaign to a successful issue.

As he was very anxious to govern his people well and wisely he enquired of his ministers what should be the principles on which his government should be founded. His Prime Minister Lu-shang informed him that if he would only read a treatise entitled Tan Shu he would get the precise information that he needed in it. In that the rule was laid down that righteousness should be superior to passion, that there should be untiring perseverance in any plan that

---

* Wu, like William the Conqueror, established a feudal system in China by the erection of eighteen large states and seventy-two smaller ones, which he bestowed upon the statesmen and warriors that had helped him to the throne. This was a generous act, but one fatal to the interests of his kingdom.

† To each of the first two were assigned a hundred square *li* (a *li* equals a third of a mile), to the third seventy, and to each of the last two fifty *li*.

was undertaken, and that in order to have rectitude of conduct there must be a reverent spirit. Wu Wang was so impressed with the value of these sentiments that he had them inscribed on his walking stick, shoes, girdle, wash bason, tables, windows, doors, etc., so that he might have them constantly before him, and thus never be tempted to forget them.

Wu Wang also consulted the Viscount of Wei as to the best methods of governing his people.* His reply was the "Great Plan" that is recorded in the Historical Classic, which is a mixture of common sense, abstruse doctrines and superstition, for one of the essential ideas contained in it is that divination by the eight diagrams and the turtle should be a prominent feature in any plan that might be devised for the government of a nation.† For the

---

* The Historical Classic says that this was done in the 13th year of his reign, whilst really it was in his 1st. The solution of this difficulty is easy. Wu Wang counted his thirteen years of rule over Chow as forming part of his reign over China.

† Fuh-hi is said to have been the one that had first to do with the diagrams. A dragon horse one day appeared to him from the Yellow River with a scroll upon its back, on which were inscribed mysterious symbols. From these were developed the system that is believed in by the scholars and the thinkers of China to-day. Briefly stated it is a combination of triple lines, viz :—

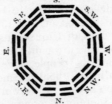

The 1st unmixed male principle=Heaven ; 2nd=vapour, lakes, etc. ; 3rd=fire and light ; 4th=thunder ; 5th=wind ; 6th=water ; 7th=mountains ; 8th=unmixed female principle.

In explanation of the above it may be stated that a straight line ——— represents the young or male principle, and a broken line —— the Yin or female principle. An advance upon this are the double lines, such as ===== =sun, heat, mental disposition, etc.; ===== =the moon, cold, passions, etc. ; ===== =stars, daylight, the outward form, etc.; === =the planets, night, the bodily frame, usurping rulers, etc. A still further development results in the triple forms explained above.

As indicating the unseen revolutions of nature these diagrams are sometimes arranged as follows :—

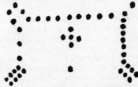

By duplicating the original triple forms of course a larger number of combinations may be obtained, and from them the believer in them may obtain the most remarkable results in metaphysics, philosophy, astrology, etc.

The tortoise is indelibly associated with Yu. The lines on its back are indicated thus :—

The head has nine marks and the tail one. The two and four were on the shoulders, and the six and eight by the feet. Three were on the left and seven on the right side, whilst five were in the centre. It can easily be imagined how these, in combination with the figures of the eight diagrams

advice thus given him the Emperor bestowed upon him the government of Corea. As it was outside the limits of the Empire the viscount, who had vowed that he would never become the officer of a new dynasty, was thus enabled to remain faithful to the Shang, and still be on friendly terms with Wu Wang.

In order to meet the expenses of the government it was enacted that the whole country should be divided into allotments of one thousand mow each, to be occupied by ten families that should each have one hundred mow, and that they should pay a tenth of their produce of their land to the state.* In the central part of the Empire where cities were more numerous it was more difficult to carry out the allotment system, so the people there were required to pay a tenth of their incomes for the support of government.

Wu Wang established schools of various grades throughout the country and built houses for old infirm people, where they might end their days in comfort at the expense of the country. He now composed an ode entitled "The Great Wu," in which he recounted the victories he had gained, and he gave orders that it should be sung by the officials and people throughout his dominions, in order that the memory of his great achievements might not be forgotten. This proves him to have been a foreseeing prince, for there is no better way of keeping alive the recollection of heroic deeds than by the words of some stirring song set to music that has caught the popular ear.

The fame of Wu Wang spread beyond the nine provinces of the Empire, and in the second year of his reign the wild tribes from the district Leu in the west sent him a present of some blood hounds. One of his ministers remonstrated with him for accepting them, as to do so was to endanger his own virtue and to place himself too much on a level with the barbarians. We have here a significant hint of the low estimation in which foreigners were held in those very early days of Chinese history, and we need not, therefore, be astonished at the arrogant tone of superiority in which the rulers of China and its people have always spoken when either addressing or talking about them. The theory of this country is that there is no nation in the world that can be compared with China, and that, therefore, foreign powers must always be treated as inferiors. It was this inborn belief and consequent

---

that could be multiplied to almost any extent, in the hands of mystic thinkers, could be manipulated to mean almost anything in heaven or on earth. See Dr. Legge's Shoo King, p. 321, and Mayer's Chinese Reader's Manual, p. 333.

* For this statement we have the authority of Mencius, who also declares that in the Hia dynasty each family had fifty mow, a tenth of the produce of which was paid to the state. Under the Yin the allotment consisted of nine equal squares, each containing seventy mow, and occupied by eight families, the centre square being left vacant and cultivated by the occupiers of the rest for the benefit of the government. The Chinese character that represented this system was 井. If enclosed by outside lines it would be 田, thus showing at a glance the shape of the allotment. A mow has varied in different ages and in different localities, but there are about six of them to an English acre.

incessant insults to the English that caused the first war with China. The conviction is the same to-day, though the authorities are afraid to express it. It is a very significant fact that when the audience question was granted, and the ministers of foreign powers were presented to the Emperor, the ceremony was performed in a building where the bearers of tribute from states in subjection to China are received. In the eyes of the nation these ambassadors, by consenting to meet there, acknowledged themselves to be vassals of China.

Wu Wang had a serious illness, and the Duke of Chow, anxious lest his brother's death should endanger the new-born dynasty, determined to appeal to the spirits of his father, grandfather and great-grandfather to spare him. He accordingly built three altars in an open place facing the south, and there he made supplication to their spirits. He prayed them to take his life, but spare Wu's, on the ground that he could serve them better in the other world than his brother, and because the Empire having been bestowed upon him by Heaven, it would not be right to remove him from his high position too soon. The prayer which had been written out was then enclosed in a metal bound box, in which it may be presumed important state documents were kept, and he awaited the result with confidence.

The very next day Wu recovered and lived for five years, when he died at the age of ninety-three, and was succeeded by his son Sung, but who is known in history by the title of Chung.

Chung—B. C. 1115-1078.

The meaning of this Emperor's name is Completer, or Perfecter, because he was enabled to finish the work of his father in the establishment of the dynasty on a firm basis, which Wu had not been able to do in consequence of the shortness of his reign. As he was only thirteen years of age when he came to the throne his uncle, the Duke of Chow, was appointed regent, a man of large abilities, a profound statesman and a most conscientious and upright prince. His wisdom is shown in the able manner in which he tried to instruct Chung in goodness and in the proper management of his kingdom.

Although he was his uncle he did not dare to take those liberties with him that he would have been entitled to do in private life. His nephew was his sovereign, and the majesty of his person demanded that the utmost reverence should be paid him. How was he to correct what was wrong in the young king and yet not transgress the rigid etiquette of the court. He hit upon a very happy and successful expedient. He had a son, who in time would succeed him in the government of Chow. He used therefore to lecture him in the presence of Chung upon what would be expected from him when he became a duke. He also instructed him in the five human relationships, viz., the duties of parents and children to each other, of Emperor and ministers, of superiors and inferiors, of friends and friends and of elder and younger brothers, and whenever the Emperor did any wrong he had his own son whipped as though he had been the guilty party.

Chung had not been long on the throne, when a very serious rebellion took place in the eastern part of the empire, which might have proved most dangerous to the dynasty had not a man like the Duke of Chow been in control of the executive. This disturbance arose from the clemency that Wu had shown his enemies after the battle of Muh. Among other acts of generosity he preserved the life of Chow Sin's son, Wu-kung, and actually made him Prince of Sung, where he and his followers might live in comfort, and where he could offer the yearly sacrifices to the spirits of the former kings of the Shang dynasty. In order to guard against treason he appointed three of his brothers to be residents at his court to watch his movements. The eldest of these, Kwan-shuh, was very angry when Wu Wang died that he had not been appointed regent instead of his younger brother. Disappointed and reckless he plotted with Wu Kung and his other brothers to upset the government, and as a preliminary step to this he began to circulate reports throughout the Empire that the Duke of Chow was not loyal to the Emperor. These got to the ears of Chung and produced an estrangement in his mind towards his uncle.

The duke, feeling that the very existence of the dynasty depended upon immediate action, at once proceeded against the traitors, and though it took him two years to crush the rebellion he did so most effectually. Wu-kung and Kwan-shuh were executed, another brother was confined in a frontier prison, and the third was deprived of his rank and allowed to go. The members and followers of the Shang dynasty were transplanted to another part of the country, and the Viscount K'i, the elder brother of Chow Sin, was made the chief of the clan, and thus peace once more reigned throughout the country.

In the autumn of B. C. 1112, and whilst the campaign was still being carried on, a great storm of wind and thunder visited the country near the capital. Trees were torn up by the roots, and the grain, which was very abundant that year, was levelled with the ground. The king and his officers were in great distress at this, and did not know what it foreboded. They dressed themselves, therefore, in their robes of state and went with great ceremony to consult the important documents that were in the copper-bound chest, to see if they would not give them some hint as to the cause of the present calamity. The first that met Chung's eye was the one containing his uncle's petition to be allowed to die in the place of Wu. He was startled, and asked the chief historian whether this document was genuine, and why he had never been informed of its existence before. He was told that the duke had forbidden all mention of it. The Emperor's heart was then wrung with sorrow that he had ever entertained suspicions of him. "There is no need," he said hastily, "to further examine the documents in the chest. It is quite manifest that the design of Heaven in sending the storm was to vindicate the loyalty of the Duke of Chow. It is only in harmony with the laws of courtesy that belong to my Empire that I should go and meet him a new man." He then proceeded to the borders of the imperial domain to welcome the duke back from his successful campaign. On this, it is said, Heaven sent a strong wind, that raised the fallen crops, so that the harvest after all was a most abundant one.*

When Chung was seventeen the Duke of Chow resigned his office as regent and handed over the government to him. Two years after there appeared ambassadors from the south of Cochin China, the king of which was named Yueh Ch'ang. On their journey to the court they had been compelled to use no fewer than three different sets of interpreters. They were received with great distinction, for never before had representatives from so distant a country appeared at the Chinese capital. Amongst the presents that they brought was a white pheasant, a thing unknown in China.

When they were questioned as to the reason why they had undertaken so long a journey they replied that the old men of their country had remarked that for three years in succession their country had not had tempestuous winds or storms of rain, neither had the sea been lashed into great waves. They were convinced that all this was caused by some sage ruler that occupied the throne of China. They, therefore, felt bound to send ambassadors to visit this wonderful personage, whose virtue was able to procure such blessings for people situated at such a distance from him.

When the time came for them to return it was discovered that they had forgotten the way. The Duke of Chow, however, was prepared for this emergency, for among the presents that Chung gave them were five chariots which were to carry them home. By the orders of the duke a certain kind of instrument was fixed in each that always pointed to the south, no matter what direction the drivers took. By means of this they reached the sea coast without difficulty, where taking ship they arrived at their own country after a year's voyage. †

---

* There is a division of opinion in regard to the time when the Duke of Chow proceeded against the rebels. The Bamboo Books and some commentators hold that when he found Chung suspicious of him he retired to the east for two years, and when his innocence was manifested he then proceeded with the royal troops to punish them. We prefer the version we have given in the text.

† The statement here made in reference to the south-pointing chariots is evidently mythical as far as the duke is concerned, for we find in the life of Hwang-ti that he is said to have used just the same kind of vehicles in his contest with the rebel Ch'i-yew. The Chinese refer the discovery of the mariner's compass to the duke, but this is simply a legend, as there is no historical evidence that it was his invention.

In the year B. C. 1108 Chung gave orders that a new city, to be called the Eastern Capital, should be built at Loh in Honan. Wu had planned to do this same thing, but his reign was too short to allow him to carry out his intentions. Now, however, his son for filial and state reasons determined to commence the building of the city. The present capital in Shensi was not central enough for the convenient carrying on of the government. Loh would be more in the heart of the Empire, and when the Emperor made his royal visitations the chiefs of the feudal states could better assemble here than in the Western capital. He at the same time decided to move the nine tripods of Yu to it, so as to give it a prestige that an entirely new city would otherwise lack.

After the city had been walled in, the government of it was handed over to the Duke of Chow, whilst at the same time the family of the late Yin dynasty was removed to its vicinity, in order that they might be near him, so that any attempt at rebellion could be easily crushed at its very beginning. Unfortunately for the country the duke lived only four years after his appointment. Before his death he requested that he might be buried in it, but his nephew overruled his request, and had him interred in the old dukedom of Pi in Shensi near his father Wen. This he did to do him honour, and that the same sacrifices might be offered to his spirit as were presented to the royal dead.

In the 12th year of his reign Chung made a royal visitation to different parts of his Empire. He was particular in seeing whether the unreclaimed parts of the country were being opened for cultivation, whether the aged were being cared for and men of ability honoured, and whether persons of good character were being put into office to the exclusion of the bad. Where these things were being attended to the chiefs were rewarded, and where not they were punished. In the following year a coinage of cash was ordered. Hitherto gold only had been minted, but now it was determined that there should be a currency of copper coins. It was decided that they should be round, with a square hole in the centre. Chung also at the same time ordered that when cotton cloth was woven each piece should be of a regulation size, viz., two feet two inches in width and forty feet in length. This was also to be used as a currency, and being of one determined size its exact value could be more easily fixed. In order to have a place where to store the new coins he ordered that nine large treasuries should be built in the capital.

After a prosperous and happy reign of thirty-seven years the Emperor died. The day before his death he called together his six principal ministers and commended his son Ch'au to their loyal care and affection. This is the first record we have in Chinese history of a sovereign doing this. He was no doubt moved to this action by a desire to make the throne as secure as possible to his son. During his own life rebellion would probably have wrecked his dynasty had it not been for the ability shown by the Duke of Chow. He knew that those same revolutionary elements still existed, and he therefore wished to secure the allegiance of the chief men in the state, so that when he was gone his son might have them to depend upon.

K'ang—B. C. 1078-1052.

This prince was a weak pleasure-loving man, whose reign was distinguished by nothing special. On his ascending the throne the chiefs of the Empire gathered loyally around him and acknowledged him as sovereign. Those from the west were headed by Shih, the Duke of Shau, and those from the east by the Duke of Peih.* They appeared with their teams of light bay horses, and holding up their sceptres, and presenting their presents, and they declared they were there to pay him fealty and bring him the productions of their various states. They then bowed down reverently before the king who, according to the etiquette of the Chow dynasty, returned their obeisance.

The Grand Guardian, the Duke of Shau, who was also the Emperor's grand uncle, then addressed K'ang and prayed him to be careful by his wise government to secure the firm establishment of his kingdom, that by the special appointment of heaven had passed from others to his own family. The king replied in a very graceful and modest way and begged the princes to be as loyal to him as they had been to his predecessors, so that his anxieties might be removed and his Empire saved from shame and disorder. After an uneventful reign of twenty-six years he died, and left the throne to his son Hia, whose dynastic title was Chau.

Shortly before his death the Duke of Shau, who had been entrusted with the government of the west, also died. Like Wu and the Duke of Chow he had been a remarkable man, and showed, like them, exceptional powers of administration. He was a profoundly just man, and so he gained the affections of his people, who were enthusiastically devoted to him. He was particularly anxious that every one that was oppressed should be righted. The disposition of the mandarins of those early days seems to have been very much what it is to-day, and justice was dispensed with a liberal hand only to those who could afford to pay for this privilege. In order to rectify this state of things men were given access to him at all times, and as his residence was far distant from some of the districts over which he ruled he made frequent visitations, when disputed cases were heard by him. It was his custom to go round not only to the important centres, but also to small villages, and there, mingling with the common people, he listened to their complaints. As there was often no house large enough to contain himself

---

* The territory of Peih was in the present district of Ch'ang-ngan, in the prefecture of Si-ngan, whilst that of Shau was in the imperial domain, in the prefecture of Kiang, in Shansi.

and suite he would try the appeal cases under the largest tree near the village. One of these, a crab tree, became famous, because under it he frequently dispensed justice, so that when he died no one was allowed to touch it, and it stood there till old age laid its hand upon it, and it finally passed away like one of the patriarchs of the village. Long after he was gone his memory was kept alive by the songs that the people sung of him, in which his virtues and his goodness were recounted.

Chau—B. C. 1052-1001.

With the commencement of this reign there began to be a decline in the prosperity of the country. Historians tell us that for a period of more than forty years the Empire had enjoyed the most profound tranquillity, so that all punishments were dispensed with, and there was no disposition on the part of the people to evade the laws of the land. This of course is an extreme statement, and simply means that peace and plenty had existed within the Empire in consequence of the wise rule of such men as the Dukes of Chow, Shau and Peih. The reign of Chau was uneventful, and was marked by only one prominent event, that took place B. C. 1038, and that was the murder of Yin, the Duke of Lu, by his brother Wei, who thus has the unenviable notoriety of being the first regicide mentioned in Chinese history.* So weak was the central government that nothing was done to avenge this wrong or punish the murderer.

In the last year of his reign Chau made a visitation to the south of his Empire, and came to what are now the provinces of Hunan and Hupeh. The people of this region had a reputation, which attaches to them to-day, of being exceedingly turbulent and unruly. During his travels the Emperor was drowned with a number of his chief officers in the River Han. There is some mystery as to how this happened. It is said to have been the fault of the people that lived near the river, who showed their contempt for Chau by rowing him and his suite over in a boat, whose planks had been simply glued together. When it got to the middle of the stream the glue gave way, and the whole party were precipitated into the river and drowned. This explanation is manifestly an unsatisfactory one. One thing is certain, the king was drowned, and no punishment of any kind was ever meted out to those connected with his death. He was succeeded by his son Man, who, however, is known in history by his title of Muh.

Muh—B. C. 1001-946.

This sovereign had sat upon the throne for seventeen years without anything very important having happened. The chief of the state of Su, who was distinguished for 'is goodness and

---

* The State of Lu, whose ruler was murdered, is frequently mentioned by Confucius and Mencius. It was first given to Tan, the Duke of Chow, in B. C. 1122, but his eldest son Peh-kin first made his capital at Kieh-fu about B.C. 1115, and was called Duke Lu.

benevolence, because some one had given him a red bow and arrow,
thought about this time that heaven had intended him to become
Emperor.   He therefore rose in rebellion, and thirty-six other
states were preparing to join him.   Muh, who was absent from his
capital on a visitation, hastened back with all speed to collect his
forces and march against the rebel.   He was specially helped in
his return by his charioteer Tsan-fu, who had accompanied the
Emperor with a very fine breed of horses that were famous for their
speed and their powers of endurance.

The rebel chief finding the royal army on its march against him,
out of pity for his people, fled without meeting it, and the rebellion
died a natural death.   For his services on this occasion Tsau-fu was
made chief in the place of the one that had disappeared.   In the
year B. C. 966 the wild tribes of Turfan showed signs of discontent
with the Chinese rule, and Muh organized an expedition against
them.   His ministers endeavoured to dissuade him from this, and
tried to prove to him that the best way of restraining these unruly
people was by living such a life of virtue that they would, without
any exhibition of force, submit to him, as had been the case in the
history of former Emperors.   Muh refused to listen to this advice,
and led a large army against the unruly tribes, but the campaign
was a failure, and all that he could show as the results of his
expedition were four white deer and as many white wolves.

In the fiftieth year of his reign Muh passed his famous decrees
in reference to the redemption of punishments by the payment of a
money fine.   He was not acting absolutely without precedent, for
we find by a reference to the Canon of Shun that that distinguished
sage referred to crimes that might be redeemed by a money payment.
What these were we have no means of knowing now.   Muh's
enactments were more definite, and referred specifically to the five
great punishments, viz., cutting off the nose, excising the ears,
castration, branding and death.   After warning the judges to be
very careful in their trial of criminal cases, so as to be sure that they
have grasped the facts concerning them, he lays down the law that
where the evidence is doubtful the punishment of branding may be
commuted for one hundred copper hwan,* cutting off the nose for
two hundred, cutting off the feet for five hundred, castration for the
same, and the punishment of death for one thousand.   There were
a thousand different kinds of crimes that belonged to each of the two
first classes, five hundred to the third, three hundred to the fourth,
and two hundred to the last.   In all there were three thousand
crimes of the most serious character that could be avoided simply
by the payment of a fine that had been settled by the state.

It may easily be imagined what a blow this must have been to
the majesty and power of the law, for in spite of the statement that
these decrees affected only doubtful cases the way was now opened

* The ancient weight of a hw n was 6⅔ taels or ounces, equivalent to 8⅓
English oz.   In later times a hundred hwan weighed only 48 taels.

under unscrupulous judges for the release of the most desperate criminals, if they had only the means of paying for their crimes. From the time of this weak monarch down to the present day the system of redemption of punishments has had a place in the penal codes of nearly every subsequent dynasty. Muh died after a reign of fifty-five years, in his 104th year, and was succeeded by his son, whose dynastic title was Kung.

Kung—B. C. 946-934. After a reign of twelve years he was followed by his son I.

I—B. C. 934-909. This ruler in the first year of his reign removed the capital for a time to Hwai-li. According to the Bamboo Annals barbarian tribes made frequent incursions into China, as there was no strong hand at the head of the government to restrain them. After ruling for twenty-five years he was succeeded by his brother Pei-fang, whose dynastic title, however, was Hiau, "The Filial."

Hiau—B. C. 909-894.

The one significant event of this reign was the appearance of a man whose descendants were destined to overthrow the Chow dynasty and themselves to become the rulers of China. This was Fei-tze, who could trace his ancestry up to Yih, an official of the great Shun. He had become famous for his skill in rearing horses, and so he was taken into the service of the Emperor to superintend the royal studs near the K'ien and Wei rivers in Shensi. He was finally invested with a small territory, ten miles square, in Kansuh, whose chief town was named Ts'in. Hiau appointed him the head of his clan to offer the sacrifices to the spirits of his ancestors, and from this time the family begins to take a prominent position in the Empire. His selection was attended, it is said, with the most unlucky omens, for there was a great fall of hail in Shensi, so that the oxen and horses died in great numbers, owing to the extreme cold, and the Han River was frozen over. Hiau died after a reign of fifteen years, and was succeeded by his nephew, the son of his predecessor, who is known by the name of I.*

I—B. C. 894-878.

This Emperor was raised to his high position by the action of the feudal chiefs, and consequently he never after seemed to be able to take that independent course that a sovereign ought to adopt if he is to rule with any success an Empire composed of so many different and powerful elements. Instead, therefore, of upholding the dignity of the kingly power he appeared to be afraid of the men that had elevated him, for when they came into his presence he would descend from his throne and advance to meet them, instead of

---

* Though this name seems identical with that of his father it is not so in reality, for the two Chinese characters are essentially different in form and meaning.

waiting until they had paid obeisance to him. The contempt with which some of them treated him was seen in the case of the chief of Tsu, who extended his possessions and invested his sons with the conquests he had made, without any reference to the will of I.

In the third year of his reign, the Turfans having become unruly, the Emperor led an army against them, and returned with a thousand horses, which he had captured from them. The people of Hunan and Hupeh now began to make encroachments upon the neghbouring states, and when these latter appealed to I for assistance he was compelled from want of sufficient force at his command to refuse it. After an inglorious reign of sixteen years he was followed by his son, who was named Li, "The Stern One."

Li—B. C. 878-827.

This man was exceedingly cruel and remorseless in his treatment of those that opposed him. The Chief of Tsu, who had acted so arbitrarily in the previous reign, deterred by the stern and passionate character of Li, at once made his submission to him. In his 11th year the wild tribes in the neighbourhood of the Hwai were in a state of rebellion, and Li led his troops against them, but as history does not record what the result was it may be inferred that the campaign was not a very successful one.*

In the 30th year of his rule Ying-i was made president of all the nobles. This man was grasping and avaricious, and a most active helper of the king in all his plans of cruelty and misrule. The Emperor was remonstrated with, but without effect. The people who had been grievously oppressed for so many years now began to express their indignation in the strongest terms. The Duke of Shau, too, ventured to advise him to correct his conduct and to rule his people with more justice. Li was exceedingly indignant that any one should dare to take such liberties with the royal person, and so he employed a wizard, who pretended to be able by his magic powers to point out any one, no matter how remote in the kingdom, who had been speaking evil of the king's majesty. Li believed in this impostor, and the consequence was that many people were put to death. A universal terror reigned, and no one dared to express his opinion to his neighbour, and when men walked the streets they could only greet each other with their eyes, for they were afraid, lest their simplest actions might be misinterpreted by spies, and they should be put to death. The Emperor sneeringly said to the Duke of Shau, "I have stopped the profane talk of my people and given them a lesson in good manners." "You have only dammed up their words in their hearts," he replied, "and that is a dangerous thing for even a king to do. When the waters of a river are obstructed they will by and by carry everything before them. The wise way is

---

* The Hwai drains Honan and Nganhui and reaches the Yang-tze through the Grand Canal.

to open channels by which the waters may run free. Let the people have the widest freedom of speech, and listen to what they say and correct the things in which you are wrong.'' The Emperor refused to listen to this wise advice, and instead of reforming became more cruel than ever in his treatment of his subjects.

At length, in the year B. C. 841, his people rose in rebellion, and to save his life he fled to Chi in Shansi. The populace, hearing that his son Tsing had taken refuge with the Duke of Shau, surrounded his house and demanded his surrender. This minister was remarkable for his loyalty, so seeing that there was no possibility of keeping the mob out, he determined upon a most heroic sacrifice, in order to save the life of the young prince. Taking his own son, who was about the same age as Tsing, he delivered him to the crowd, who, believing that he was the heir apparent, instantly murdered him. Li remained in banishment till B. C. 826, the Dukes of Chow and Shau acting as regents till then. His son, who is known as Suan, succeeded him.

Suan—B. C. 827-781.

This prince had evidently learnt a lesson from the misfortunes of his father, for when he came to the throne he took good care to put himself under the guidance of those great men that had loyally governed the Empire during the expatriation of his father, and had delivered it intact to himself. The great majority of the feudal chiefs returned to their allegiance to the imperial family.

For a long time his kingdom was disturbed by the incursions of the barbarians, who, however, were met boldly by the royal troops. After a time the energy and activity of Suan seemed to have deserted him, and he became indifferent to the affairs of his kingdom. When the spring came round, and, according to custom, he should have gone out dressed as husbandman to guide the plough with his own hand in the field set apart for this royal husbandry, he refused to do so.* His ministers remonstrated with him, but in vain. At length a device used by his queen, who seems to have been a remarkable woman, saved her husband from the evils into which he was falling. One morning she divested herself of her rich dress and her ornaments. She took her gold pins out of her hair and her earrings out of her ears. She then repaired to the imperial prison, which was in the palace, and desired to be shut up within it, as she declared she was no longer worthy of being queen, since she had been the means of leading the king into indolent habits that prevented him from ruling his Empire

---

* It has been the custom from the earliest times for the Emperor to go out in early spring and plough with his own hand. This is done for two reasons, viz., to acknowledge that the welfare of the Empire depends upon its agriculture, and also to be an example to the farmers. The queen accompanies him with a basket in her hand, and her dress tucked up like a country maiden, and plucks some mulberry leaves, which she puts into it. This is in consequence of the tradition that one of the queens in early history was the means of the introduction of the rearing of silk worms and the manufacture of silk.

properly. Suan was greatly moved by this devotion of his queen, and from this time he gave up his whole soul to the management of public affairs.

In the year B. C. 788 he suffered a severe defeat in the battle of "The Thousand Acres" at the hands of a western tribe of barbarians, named K'iang, that lived to the west of Szchwan and Kansuh. His mind never recovered from this disaster, and he became morose and moody, and capriciously put some of his ministers to death. He died after a long reign of forty-six years, and was succeeded by his son.

Yiu—B. C. 781-770.

This ruler was a thoroughly bad and unprincipled man. According to the Chinese, nature seemed to have combined her forces to·show her abhorrence of him, for it is said that in his second year the waters of the rivers King, Wei and Lo became dry, and their beds were agitated as if by an earthquake.* In the following year he met with the woman that was to prove his ruin. This was the famous beauty named Pau-sze, to whom he became completely enslaved. Under her influence he put away his queen, who was a daughter of the chief of Shin, and made her his consort, whilst at the same time he disinherited his son I-k'iu in favour of that of Pau-sze. Nature again, the Chinese declare, signified her abhorrence of this wicked conduct of Yiu by the famous eclipse of the sun, which took place August 29th, B. C. 775. This was an important event for historians, because in consequence of it and other subsequent ones they have been able to fix the date of many events with chronological accuracy that they could not have otherwise done.†

The influence of Pau-sze was altogether a mischievous one, and like the famous beauties that were the cause of the overthrow of the Hia and Shang dynasties she seemed to delight in inciting the Emperor to the wildest acts of folly. One of these has become historical, and forms a scene which Chinese artists have delighted to depict. Yiu could never extract a smile from Pau-sze, though he tried every art and blandishment to cause her to do so. At last he hit upon an expedient that was successful. There was in existence

---

* The first of these takes its rise in Kansuh and joins the second in Shen-si, whilst the third has its source in Honan and flows into the Yang-tze.

† From this time we emerge from semi-historical region into that of more authentic history, for we cannot conceive it possible that the Chinese should have been able to fix with certainty an imaginary eclipse and to have given the date on which it occurred unless it really had happened. This eclipse is mentioned in the Book of Odes, and a translation of one of the verses referring to it is here given.

"The lightnings flash and blaze, the thunders roll :
All is unrest, and nature's out of joint :
The hundred streams pour forth their fountains high :
The highest mountain peaks come thund'ring down :
The banks subside, transformed to valleys deep,
Whilst valleys rise, and mount to lofty hills.
Alas ! alack a day ! for this man (Yiu);
What stays his fears that he should not reform "?

in his time, as there is to-day, a system of beacons, which were lighted in times of extreme danger, and the feudal vassals were bound when they saw these signals to hurry with all speed to the capital to the assistance of the Emperor.

Yiu caused these to be lighted, and the nobles and chiefs of the various states hastily collected all the forces they could immediately command and hastened by forced marches to the capital, when, to their extreme annoyance, they found they had been summoned simply to make an infamous woman smile. The king's purpose, however, was accomplished, for the cold face of Pau-sze was wreathed in smiles as she saw the princes marching at the head of their troops, as they supposed, to the relief of the metropolis.

After a time Yiu wrote to the chief of Shin and demanded from him his son I-k'iu, who had hitherto been in his charge, but his order was disobeyed, because it was known that the father intended to have his son put to death, in order that he might not by and by struggle for the crown with the son of Pau-sze. The Emperor was exceedingly indignant at this, and raised an army to compel him. The prince of Shin seeing that a crisis had now come to the Empire, and that he alone could not dare to meet the imperial forces, called in the aid of a tribe of the barbarians called "The Dog Jungs." Yiu, conscious of the extreme danger in which he was placed, now lighted the beacons in real earnest, but no one responded to the call. The barbarians captured and plundered the capital and carried off Pau-sze, who became the property of their chief. In the assault Yiu was slain, and after the nobles succeeded in expelling the Jungs I-k'iu became Emperor, who is known by the name of P'ing, "The Pacificator."

Before the death of Yiu the feudal chiefs, many of whom had begun to look with contempt upon the authority of their suzerain, indignant at his wickedness, refused to acknowledge his orders. Each man began to act as an independent lord in his own state, and to make war and to enter into treaties with each other, quite ignoring the existence of the Emperor. From the death of this ruler the states in reality threw off their allegiance to the sovereign and acted without any reference to him, except when it suited them to do so.

CHAPTER VII.

THE CHOW DYNASTY (CONTINUED).

P'ing—B. C. 770-719.

THE Jung barbarians who had so successfully assisted the chief of Shin in his contest with Yiu, now refused to leave the country, as they found it more pleasant than their own native wilds in which they were wont to roam. The aid of the powerful states of Tsin, Ts'in, Wei and Ching* was invoked, and after a brief but terrible contest they were expelled, and P'ing was sent for and placed upon the throne. Almost the very first measure that he carried out was the transference of the capital from Shensi to Loh-yang in Honan, the city that was built by the Duke of Chow. The main reason that influenced him to take this rash step was no doubt his dread of the numerous tribes of barbarians that occupied the regions to the west. It was a fatal one, however, for the dynasty, for it may be said with truth that from this time the power of the crown was transferred to the nobles of the vassal states. Another unwise act of the Emperor helped to make this a fact. Out of gratitude to the chief of Ts'in for sending soldiers to guard him on his way to his new capital he not only raised him to the rank of noble, but he also gave him sufficient territory to sustain his new position, the chief town in which was the old capital which he had just abandoned.† This not only gave him great prestige, but also a commanding position in the Empire, for he now occupied a place of great danger, where he would have to face the invading hosts of the barbarians that would try to wrest his territory from him. The very duties that he would be called upon to perform would inevitably develop his ambition, for the martial ardour of his people could not but be stimulated by their constant collision with tribes whose very existence depended upon their successful forays upon their richer neighbours, the Chinese.

Fifteen years went by, during which the power of Ts'in had been slowly but surely growing, and then the independent spirit of its chief was seen in his building an altar to God, and sacrificing to Him. As this was entirely an imperial prerogative such an act could only be considered as a usurpation of the royal function. The authority, however, of the Emperor had by this time sunk to so low an ebb that he dared not resent it. Four years after, the

---

* Shin was a small state in the south of Honan, on the head-quarters of the river Han ; Tsin, a powerful state in the southern half of Shansi, and N. W. of Honan, on the Yellow River ; Ts'in, a state that arose with Fei-tze, B. C. 897, and which gradually extended over the whole of Shensi and Kansuh, and Ching was an important state (B. C. 774-500), occupying about half of the present province of Honan.

† Namely, Hanking.

power of the Ts'ins was greatly increased by a great victory that they gained over the Western barbarians, and the recovery of all the lands which had been wrested from China, which were incorporated with those of the conquerors.

The year B. C. 748 was distinguished by wars between several of the states, but which the Emperor felt himself too weak to forbid. Matters went on growing worse and worse and the states getting more independent till B. C. 722, when the Duke of Lu also built an altar to God, thus virtually casting off his allegiance to P'ing.* The Emperor on this occasion sent one of his ministers to protest against this, but he was arrested by the Duke and forbidden to return home. P'ing died after reigning fifty-one years. He was so poor that he had not left enough to bury him in a royal manner, and when an application was made to the Duke of Lu for assistance a rude refusal was returned to this request, so low had the descendant of the great Wu fallen. He was succeeded by his grandson.

Hwan—B. C. 719-696. The one important event that took place during this reign was an eclipse of the sun, B. C. February 14th, 719.† After an inglorious and uneventful reign of twenty-three years he died, and was succeeded by his son, who is known as Chwang.

Chwang—B. C. 696-681. The late Emperor had originally designed that the younger brother of Chwang should succeed him, but he was overruled by his great ministers, who represented to him that this would be illegal. Three years after his ascending the throne the Duke of Chow combined his forces with those of the younger brother and made an attempt to dethrone him. This rebellion, however, was unsuccessful, and the Duke was executed. The story of this reign is mainly concerned with the quarrels of the two powerful states of Lu and Ts'i.‡ The ruler of the latter was the celebrated Duke Hwan, who played a most important part in China during the greater part of the seventh century. His success was mainly due to his prime minister Kwan-chung, who for many years guided his counsels and developed the commerce of the state till it took a leading place in the Empire. After a reign of fifteen years Chwang died, and was succeeded by his son Hi.

Hi—B. C. 681-676.

The only event worth recording in this reign was the appointment of Duke Hwan of Ts'i to be the chief of the five states that then practically engrossed the whole power of China. It is said that at the conference that was held to decide this question

---

* The Duke that set himself in opposition to P'ing was Hwui. It may be interesting to note here that Confucius' "Spring and Autumn" commences with his reign and ends two years before his own death, B. C. 481.

† Some Chinese scholars, Rev. Dr. Chalmers being amongst them, consider that Chinese authentic history dates from this year.

‡ The state of Ts'i lasted from B. C. 1122-265, and comprised a large part of Northern Shantung and Southern Chihli.

Tso-mui, a general of Lu, drawing out his sword from its scabbard, declared in an angry voice that the Duke was always making war upon his state and encroaching upon its lands. "If you return the territory you have wrested from us, he said, we will acknowledge you." The Duke agreed to this, but after he had been formally recognized and returned home he determined not only not to abide by his promise, but also to kill Tso-mui for the insult he had offered him. Kwan-chung, however, remonstrated with him, and showed him that if he broke faith with the chiefs in this matter they would certainly distrust him in the future, and in time he would lose all the power he had gained. Fortunately the Duke listened to this advice, and the result was that when the chiefs saw this powerful ruler restoring the lands he had taken from Lu they all felt such confidence in his integrity that they never dreamed of disputing his supremacy. He died, and was followed by his son Hwui.

Hwui—B. C. 676-651.

The accession of this prince was attended with some disorder, because some of the influential Chinese wished his brother to be Emperor. The plan, however, did not succeed, and the brother was compelled to flee, and three years after he was slain by the chief of Ting. Things went on pretty smoothly till B. C. 668, when troubles arose in the state of Lu in consequence of a disputed succession. In reading the history of these times one is deeply impressed with the vast mischief that arose from the system of polygamy. An Emperor or a feudal prince would have a favourite concubine, and under the pressure of her influence he would be induced to appoint her son to succeed him, though he knew that this was illegal and utterly opposed to the instincts of the Chinese. Then would arise murder and sedition and disorder, and after all the real heir would obtain his rights, who would cruelly avenge himself upon those who had endeavoured to deprive him of them.

In the year B. C. 660 the Western barbarians invaded and took possession of Hing that lay in the S. W. of Chihli, near Shansi, and would have remained permanently there had they not been defeated and driven across the borders by Hwan, the Duke of Ts'i.

Meanwhile the state of Tsin had been rapidly increasing in power and importance till its standing army consisted of fifty thousand men. It now began to look around for opportunities of conquest. It had not long to do so, for the three principalities of Hing, Kang and Wei, being small and powerless, lay before it a ready prey. They were accordingly attacked and conquered, and their territories were annexed to those of Tsin. Two years after it cast longing eyes on Kwo and Yu, but as these had combined for purposes of protection their conquest was not so easy. The prime minister of Tsin, who was a crafty and astute politician, hit upon a plan that resulted in success. The chief of Yu, being very fond of jewelry and fine horses, he promised him magnificent presents of both if he would detach himself from Kwo. In spite of the warning of his officials he agreed to this. The troops of Tsin were then allowed a passage through his territory to attack Kwo, which, being left alone in the struggle, easily succumbed. A nemesis, however, was soon to fall on the faithless Yu. On their return the soldiers of Tsin occupied the country, killed its chief and recovered all the presents that had been made, and then absorbed both it and Kwo.

In the year B. C. 655 eight large states combined to attack a small state that was a dependency of Ch'u.* The Duke of this latter sent an ambassador to the Duke of Ts'i, the head of the confederacy, to complain of this, and to ask how it was that he allowed armed men to forcibly enter territories that were under his control. Duke Hwan, advised by Hwan-chung, replied by asking him how it was that he had hitherto failed in paying his annual tribute of grass to the Emperor.† The Duke acknowledged that he had failed in his duty in this respect, but promised to be more faithful in the future. Upon this the confederate army withdrew from the attack, and peace was restored.

In the year B. C. 654 the state of Tsin was greatly disturbed by the plots of one of the "fatal beauties" of Chinese history, named Li-ki. She was one of the concubines of Duke Hien, who had been captured by him in an expedition that he had made against the Jung barbarians, and she was determined that her son should be the successor to the dukedom, to the exclusion of the rightful heir. To secure this she entered into a most infamous plot against him and his brothers. One day, whilst the Duke was out hunting, she told the eldest son that in her dreams the previous evening the spirit of his mother had appeared to her. This of course necessitated a sacrifice to it. The son at once prepared the customary articles of food, and when the service was over brought them to Li-ki to be kept to allow of his father partaking of them. Li-ki put some deadly poison in the food, which so discoloured it that when the Duke saw it he became suspicious. Throwing some to a dog, that shortly after died in great agonies, he came to the conclusion that his son wished to destroy his life. The latter, feeling that circumstances were too strong for him, committed suicide, whilst his two younger brothers, whom Li-ki got the Duke to believe were accomplices in the plot, fled for their lives. Soon after the Duke died, and Hi-ts'i, the son of Li-ki, succeeded to the dukedom, but he was murdered almost immediately by the minister

---

* The powerful state of Ch'u existed from B. C. 740-330. It occupied parts of Hu-kwang, Honan and part of Kiang-su. Its capital was K'ing-chow.

† Every district of the Empire from the time of great Yu had been required to send to the Emperor a tribute of some of the articles specially produced in it. The grass here spoken of is a particular kind that is used in ancestral worship. When the wine was poured out to the spirits of the dead this grass received it in pots that were placed before the ancestral tablets, and through it, it was said to be conveyed to the waiting spirits. In Foh-kien leeks are used instead of grass.

Li-k'eh. Two other brothers followed, and finally, after nineteen years of wandering and adventure, Wen, the son that had been compelled to escape from his father's home, obtained his rights (B. C. 635), and was the means of raising the state of Tsin to the highest pre-eminence amongst the others.

The Emperor died after a reign of twenty-five years, and was succeeded by his son Siang.

Siang—B. C. 651-618.

In the fourth year of this Emperor his younger brother endeavoured to dethrone him by calling in the aid of the Western barbarians. Siang called upon the Duke of Ts'i to come to his assistance, who sent an army under Kwan-chung, who defeated the enemy. Very grateful for this deliverance he wished to treat him as one of the nobles of the Empire, but Kwan-chung, with the wisdom and modesty that distinguished him through life, refused to have this honour thrust upon him, and wished to be looked upon simply as an official of his powerful master. Three years after, when he lay dying, Duke Hwan suggested, one after the other, three persons as proper ones to succeed him as prime minister. Against each of them he warned the Duke, who, however, disregarded his advice, and made all three his cabinet ministers, which was the cause, in time, of serious loss to the country. In two years more the Duke died, and at once there was a fierce contest between his five sons for the dukedom. His body was left uncoffined, whilst the savage contest went on even in the very courtyard of the palace, and sixty-seven days were allowed to pass before the hideous, putrifying corpse was consigned to the grave.

In the year B. C. 638 the Duke of Sung* invited six of the chiefs of powerful principalities to a meeting, when he proposed that he should be made the president of the confederacy. The Duke of Ch'u resented this, and publicly insulted him before the rest. Smarting under this, in the following year he raised a large army and advanced to the attack of Ting, a small state under the protection of Ch'u. The Duke of Ch'u, who was a warlike and ambitious prince, needed no stronger challenge than this to bring him into the field. The two armies approached each other and were posted on the opposite banks of the river Fung. As the troops of Ch'u were in the act of crossing, the general of the Sungs advised that they should be attacked whilst they were in the water, but his advice was disregarded. He again strongly urged that the Sung soldiers should rush upon them whilst they were forming in battle array after they had come out of the stream, but once more his voice was unheeded, and the result was that the troops of Sung suffered a most serious defeat.

---

* Sung was an important state that lasted B. C. 1113-285, and occupied the lower part of the valley of the Hwai.

In the year B. C. 635 Wen, the long lost heir to the dukedom of Tsin, appeared upon the scene, and with the help of some soldiers that he had raised in Kiu got possession of his rights. In his long wanderings he had been reduced to the greatest straits, and so had five of his most devoted followers that clung to him through all his misfortunes. It is said that on one occasion, when crossing a desert country, they were reduced almost to starvation, and one of his friends saved his life by cutting off the flesh of the calf of his leg and cooking it for him. With his restoration to power he liberally rewarded his faithful followers, but strange to relate he entirely forgot the one that had rendered him such a signal service. This man, however, seemed to have been made of the sterling material out of which heroes are formed and made no complaint. His mother, however, bitterly complained of the neglect, and so they both agreed to retire to a range of mountains, where the world could be entirely forgotten. After his disappearance the Duke's memory was one day suddenly refreshed by a parable in verse that was written over the entrance to his palace. Displeased with himself for the wrong he had done his friend he caused a search to be made for him throughout the hills, but all in vain. At length he ordered the forests to be set on fire, in the hope that his friend might be driven out by the heat, but unfortunately he and his mother were burnt to death. When the news was brought to Wen he cried with sorrow. He built a splendid temple, where his spirit could be sacrificed to, and he gave all the land in the neighbourhood of where he died to provide the funds for the offerings. The people far and near sympathized with the Duke in the loss he had suffered, and refrained from food for one entire day. This story is handed down to the present time, and the day before that on which the feast of tombs commences ought by rights to be observed as a day of fasting in memory of this ancient hero, whose name was Kiai Chitui. (Mayer's Manual 253.)

After Siang had governed for sixteen years, through the treachery of his brother he was compelled to meet an invasion of the barbarians. Not feeling strong enough to do this alone he invoked the aid of Wen, who at once responded to the call, and the foe was ignominiously defeated, and the Emperor, who had taken refuge in the state of Tsin, was again restored to his capital. As a reward for this Wen prayed Siang to allow him a royal funeral when he died.[*] This he refused to grant, as it was not fit that a subject should have such an imperial privilege, but instead he bestowed upon him four districts with their

---

[*] In those early days when a king died a vast excavation was made in the ground, and rooms were built and furnished as though for a royal residence. Then a certain number of men and women, to the number sometimes of sixteen, were enclosed with the corpse, and with food to sustain life for a certain time. The whole was then built in, and by and by these wretched people died. It was believed that their spirits would be ready to act as attendants to that of the deceased sovereign, so that he could be served in the same manner as when he was alive.

cities. One of these towns refused to be transferred to the jurisdiction of Wen, so he raised an army and proceeded against it.

When he reached it he found the walls strongly fortified, whilst at the same time he discovered that by some gross blunder his own army was provisioned for only four days. When the place was summoned the people inside indignantly refused to surrender. Upon this Wen promised that if he did not capture it in four days he would retire from it. Four days passed by but still the city was untaken. News then came from spies that the provisions of the city were nearly exhausted, and Wen was urged by his officers to hold on for a day or two more. Wen replied that he had made the promise, and he must carry it out. His army was commencing its march home, when the people, touched by his sense of honour, voluntarily opened their gates and admitted his soldiers.

In the year B. C. 632 five states united to attack Sung, the Duke of which applied to Tsin for aid. This was granted, and the confederate army was compelled to retire without having accomplished its purpose. Wen was now appointed president of the nobles, for he had shown by his recent action that he was qualified to occupy a position that was only granted to the most powerful of the states. Five years after, this famous man died, and was succeeded by his son. Shortly after, the Duke of Ts'in, who had always aimed at being the chief amongst the vassal states, attacked Tsin, but he was defeated. Three years afterwards, however, he again crossed the Yellow River, and burning his boats that had carried his soldiers across he determined to conquer or perish. A great battle was fought, and the Tsin soldiers, lacking the genius and generalship of Wen, were defeated, and the conqueror assumed the honourable position that he had so long coveted.

In the thirty-third year of his reign Siang died, and was succeeded by his son K'ing. He was so poor that an application was made to the Duke of Lu for the expenses of his burial. These were granted, and officials were sent from that state to see that the funeral ceremonies were performed with the dignity becoming an Emperor.

K'ing—B. C. 618-612.

In the fifth year of this ruler's reign the chief of Tsu* was minded to move his capital to another city within his dominions. Before doing so he determined to ascertain by divination whether it was proper for him to do so or not. The reply was that it would be profitable for his people, but disastrous for himself. "Well then," he replied, "I shall move, for whatever is for the benefit of my people is for mine too. The ruler has been appointed for the good of his people, and it must be his object to consider their welfare." "But," said one of his ministers, "if you allow your capital to remain where

---

* Tsu was in the south of the present province of Shantung, and existed B. C. 700-469.

it is your life will be prolonged." "My life," he replied, " is in
the hands of Heaven, and it can dispose of me as it likes. I am
satisfied so long as my subjects are prosperous." He then made the
transfer, and in the course of a few months he was dead.

After reigning six years K'ing died, and was succeeded by his
son K'wang.

K'wang—B. C. 612-606.

This ruler had hardly ascended the throne when the Duke of
Ts'i attacked Ts'au, a dependency of Lu in the S. W. of Shantung.
Three years after the Duke of Lu died, but his son was murdered by
a relative, who usurped the dukedom.*

In the year B. C. 605 the Duke of Tsin, who was a most arbitrary
and lavish ruler, began to make his people disgusted with him, because
of the extravagant and cruel manner in which he ruled them. He
increased the taxes to build himself magnificent palaces. Because on
one occasion his cook did not prepare the royal dish of bear's paws
properly he had him slain, and in order to conceal the murder he
had the body carried out by the female slaves and hastily buried in
a hole dug by them. A virtuous minister of the name of Chau-tun
ventured to remonstrate with him for his cruelty, but the Duke was so
angry that he employed a man of the name of Tsu-ni to assassinate
him. About two o'clock in the morning† this man stealthily
approached that part of the palace where the Duke met his ministers
for the transaction of public business, and there sat Chau-tun in his
official robes waiting for the rest. He was so moved by this display
of virtue on the part of this venerable statesman that, conscience
stricken, he dashed his head against a tree and killed himself. The
Duke next arranged that a company of soldiers should lie in wait and
murder Chau-tun as he returned from a banquet to which he
proposed to invite him, but again his life was saved by a friend,
who warned him of his danger. He now fled the country, but
before long he was recalled by his brother, who had killed the cruel
tyrant in his own peach garden.

After a reign of six years K'wang died, and was succeeded by
his brother Ting.

Ting—B. C. 606-585.

In the first year of this Emperor's rule the Duke of Ch'u who,
however, had taken the higher title of Prince, led an army against
the aborigines that lived in the West of Honan. In order to impress
Ting with his power he marched it close by the capital where he
could see it. The Duke ostentatiously asked one of the Emperor's

---

* It may be noted here that many of these chiefs assumed the title of Duke
without having any right to it. Lu for example was only a marquisate. With the
weakness of the monarchy every state was aiming at a power that it did not
rightfully possess.

† This is the time at which the Emperor meets his ministers to discuss the
affairs of the nation at the present day. The custom is certainly a most ancient one.

officers if the nine tripods of Yu were heavy. This individual, who saw that he had the idea of grasping the supreme power for himself, replied that their weight depended upon the virtue of the man who would endeavour to lift them. "If it was slight," he said, "they were heavy and immovable, but if it was great then they were as light as a feather." "These tripods," he continued, "were given by the direct interference of Heaven to the Hia, Shang and Chow dynasties, and none could possess them except by its will."

In the year B. C. 596 the Duke of Ch'u marched an army against Chang* and defeated the forces of Tsin that had come to its rescue. Three years after the Duke of Lu raised the taxes from one to two-tenths, much to the sorrow and discontent of his people. Again, in B. C. 588, Wei fought with Ts'i, but was defeated, upon which Lu, Tsin and Ts'au came to its aid, and Ts'i was compelled to sue for peace. Ting died after a reign of twenty-one years, and was followed by his son Kien.

Kien—B. C. 585-571.—Nothing of importance occurred in this reign, excepting quarrels between Tsin and Ch'u, in which the latter suffered a severe defeat, which so increased the pride of the ruler of the former that he became arrogant and dissolute, and was finally killed by one of his officials. His son Ling succeeded him.

Ling—B. C. 571-544.

In the first year of this reign the states of Tsin, Ts'i, Sung, Lu, Wei, Ts'au and Tsu combined to build a wall along the border of the state of Chang, so as to prevent the encroachments of the latter. Formerly it had been in alliance with Tsin, but thinking that Ch'u was more powerful, and could aid it in its attempts to enlarge its territories, it suddenly deserted Tsin and paid homage to Ch'u.

In the year B. C. 568 a barbarian tribe of Jungs sent a present of tiger and leopard skins to the Duke of Tsin, who was at first doubtful whether he ought to receive them, or lead an army into their territory and annex it to his own. His prime minister dissuaded him from the latter, and showed him what advantages would accrue to his state from being on friendly terms with the Jungs. "These," he said, "do not cultivate the soil, but they have many things that our people can buy from them, and thus our commerce might be improved. Our farmers, too, could go into their territory and till their lands, which they do not care to cultivate for themselves; again, too, when other states see that we have such powerful allies they will all fear us." The Duke, impressed by these arguments, concluded a treaty of peace with the barbarians.

In the year B. C. 563 twelve states combined to punish Chang, and so thoroughly was it subdued that it broke off its connection with Ch'u and returned to its alliance with Tsin. The Duke of this

---

* Chang, an important feudal state in Honan, B. C. 774-500.

latter state now thought it time to give his people a rest and to pay special attention to their welfare. Instead of hoarding up the public money he lent it out to the needy and the struggling. A strict economy, too, was observed in the palace in regard to dress and the general expenses of the court, so that in the course of a year there was a remarkable improvement in the condition of the state. The effect of this was seen in the strong attitude it took in reference to the other powerful principalities. Three times did Ch'u attack it, but every time it was repulsed.

In the year B. C. 551, in the tenth month and the twenty-first day of it, was born in the state of Lu, in the present department of Yenchow in Shantung, the famous sage and philosopher Confucius, a man who was destined to exercise a mighty influence over the Chinese during the succeeding ages of their history.*

In the twenty-seventh year of his reign Ling died, and his brother King succeeded him.

King—B. C. 544-519. After an uneventful reign of twenty-five years this Emperor died, and the throne was occupied by his son King, the "Reverential."

King—B. C. 519-475.

In the year B. C. 505 the chief of the small state of Ts'ai went to pay court to the Duke of Ch'u.† One of the leading ministers in the palace refused to let him see him unless he gave him a handsome bribe. This he refused to do, upon which he treated him with the greatest rudeness. Indignant at this he at once left the state, and repairing to the Duke of Wu he implored him to avenge his wrongs. This prayer was granted, and the men of Ch'u suffered a most severe defeat, and its Duke was compelled to fly, and his capital was held for a whole year by the troops of Wu. It was only by the devotion of one of his ministers that he finally got possession of his dominions

---

* Many fabulous stories are told about the birth of this great man. We know very little about him till he was nineteen, when he married, and next year a son of the name of Li was born to him. He was a profound student at this time, and attracted a number of young men around him, who listened to his teachings. His power lay not in any original doctrines of his own, but rather in the able manner in which he drew pictures of the famous men that had figured in Chinese history and who had helped by their virtuous lives and wise enactments to build up the Chinese Empire. He lived for a time in Loh-yang, where he studied the records of antiquity, but he afterwards returned to his own state, where he was made a magistrate in the town of Chung-tu. Here the most marvellous results followed, for by the application of his own maxims the people became virtuous and orderly in their lives. Duke Ting, hearing the reports about him, made him Minister of Works and afterwards Minister of Justice, and his fame spread because of the able manner in which he fulfilled the duties of each. In the year B. C. 481 he commenced his original work, the "Spring and Autumn," which is one of the standard works studied by every scholar to-day in China. He died B. C. 478, mourned and lamented by his followers and all who had at heart the welfare of China. His merits were not fully recognized, however, till fully three centuries after his death, but succeeding ages have made up for the neglect that was shown him by his contemporaries. Kau-tsu, of the Han dynasty, gave the first impetus to the recognition of the great sage.

† Ts'ai was situated on the river Hwai. This river drains the provinces of Honan and Ngan-hwui and flows into the Hung-tsih lake.

once more.   This man repaired to the Duke of Ts'in and implored him to come to the help of his master.   At first he utterly refused to have anything to do with the matter, but Pau-sz was not to be denied, and it is said that for seven days and nights he refused all food and spent the time in weeping and lamentation.   At length the Duke, moved by his extreme devotion, marched to Ch'u, and having driven out the invaders, restored the fugitive Duke to his home.

In the following year was born in the state of Lu, Ts'ang-ts'an, a distinguished disciple of Confucius, and one that continued his teaching after his death.   In the year B. C. 500 Confucius was made a magistrate in his own state, and the most remarkable results soon followed from his new methods of government.   He made laws in reference to both the living and the dead.   He arranged that the aged should be cared for, and that they should be supplied with good food, so as to make them strong and robust.   He decreed that employment should be found suitable for the capacities and strength of all, so that those who were weak should not be burdened with tasks that they could not perform well.   He also passed a law that men and women in walking on the public roads should take different sides of it, so that there should be no promiscuous mingling of the sexes, to the detriment of public morals, and he gave orders that valuables that might have been dropped by the way should not be picked up by the passers-by, but be left to be found by the owner, who would come in search of them.   He was very severe against bad work, and he would not allow it to be exposed in the market for sale, and in order to restrain the lavish expenditure incurred at funerals he decreed that the wood of the inner shell of the coffin should be only four inches in thickness, and that of the outer one, five.   After one year's experience of these measures there was such a marked improvement in his district that all the surrounding counties began to imitate the example of Confucius and to adopt his laws.

In the following year he was made Minister of Justice.   About this time Lu and Ts'i were going to enter into a treaty of friendship, and Confucius was asked by the Duke to accompany him to meet the Duke of Ts'i and help him in drawing up the treaty.   Confucius consented, but warmly recommended that a strong force of soldiers should accompany them to the place of meeting.   This was agreed to, and when the other parties arrived they were found to have come with a very considerable body of troops.   A collision would inevitably have taken place had not the Duke of Ts'i been much influenced by the language and bearing of Confucius, for he not only signed the treaty, but also agreed to restore all the territory he had taken from Lu.

In the year B. C. 497 Confucius having received reliable information that three men, high in office, were going to rebel, issued an order that no mandarin should be allowed to have coats of mail in his house, and also that the walls of the cities where these men had a following should be reduced in height.   It is needless to say that these measures were so effectual that the threatened rebellion never broke out. In the next year Confucius was made Prime Minister, and at once a wonderful reformation of manners took place throughout the state. The men became honest and the women virtuous, and all classes of tradesmen refrained from the special tricks that belonged to their trades. The consequence of this was that Lu became highly prosperous and powerful, so that its old rival Ts'i became alarmed; lest this should endanger its existence. Its Duke therefore conceived a plan by which he would stop this happy state of things. He carefully selected eighty of the most beautiful women that could be found, and together with one hundred and twenty of the finest horses in his stud he sent them a present to the Duke of Lu.

This ruler unwisely accepted this dangerous gift, and of course Confucius retired from court. He waited in his home for three days to see whether the Duke would send for him and intimate his willingness to be guided by his teachings, but no message came, so he made preparations for leaving Lu. He was now in his fifty-seventh year, and travelled about from state to state, attended by some of his most faithful disciples, who were willing to resign all the ties of life to listen to his teachings.

After wandering about for twelve years, being received with great honour in some places and with scant courtesy in others, he returned to Lu. During the remaining five years of his life he accomplished a large amount of literary work. He wrote a preface to the Historical Classic and selected from the ancient poems, of which there were upwards of three thousand, the three hundred and eleven that now constitute the Book of Odes. He also devoted much time to the study of the Yih Classic, commonly known as the Book of Changes. He had a great admiration for this book, and he has declared in his Analects that if his life were to be prolonged to any extent he would willingly spend fifty years of it in the study of it, in order that he might attain to the one desire of his life, viz., to be able to live without serious error.

It is said that he had as many as three thousand disciples, of whom seventy-two were distinguished for their abilities. In the early part of the year B. C. 480 he was informed that a strange monster called the Ki-lin, or Chinese unicorn, had been caught, during a hunting expedition of the Duke. This he looked upon as an evil omen and as presaging his own death, and was accordingly much depressed. Two years after he died, and was buried in a cemetery that remains to the present day, being perhaps the most unique and remarkable one in the whole world.*

The Emperor King died after a long reign of forty-four years, and was succeeded by his son.

---

* Williamson's Journeys in North China. Vol. I., p. 224. I have slightly swerved from the strictly chronological order of events in order to give the story of Confucius in a more connected form.

Yuan—B. C. 475-468.

This short reign was distinguished, as many of the former ones were, simply by the contests that went on between the more powerful of the vassal states. In the year B. C. 472 the state of Yueh conquered Wu and incorporated it with itself. Twenty-three years ago the troops of Wu had invaded Yueh and carried off its Duke, who had been kept a prisoner for three years. The memory of his sufferings so rankled in his heart that he vowed a most terrible revenge. In order to carry this out he knew it was essential that the material resources of his dominions should be improved, and also that he must so win the hearts of his people that they would be prepared to make any sacrifice for him when the hour for the supreme struggle should arise.

To gain these objects both he and his wife entered upon a course of the most rigid self-denial. Kau-tsien endured all kinds of hardness and discarded every luxury, and himself cultivated his land like any common farmer, whilst his wife wove cloth for the use of her household. Scholars and eminent men were treated with the greatest honour, and strangers received the politest attentions from both. They gave alms to the poor and attended the funerals of the people and wept with sorrow over the dead. For twenty long years this went on, and still the passion for revenge never slumbered. By this time the feeling of devotion to their prince was so great that Kau-tsien knew they were ready for the greatest sacrifices for him. He accordingly assembled his forces and attacked Wu and gained a most decisive victory. Its Duke was obliged to flee and leave his dominions in the hands of his conquerors. He sent ambassadors to Kau-tsien, praying for mercy, and reminding him how he had released him when he formerly had him in his power and restored him to his state. Do the same to me now, he pled. The Duke might have listened to his appeal, but his Prime Minister Fan-li, who had aided him in all his plans, and who had been the means of his success, strongly advised him not to do so. "When Heaven," he said, "gave the Duke of Wu the grand opportunity of gaining power he did not take advantage of it, and so he is a fugitive to-day. Should you fail to accept the fortune it has now given you, you too may be driven from your state, and then all the twenty years of hardships that you and your wife have borne will have been endured in vain." This cold-blooded sophistry made a deep impression on Kau-tsien, and the Duke of Wu, finding his entreaty for mercy unheeded, committed suicide.* Kau-tsien, as a matter of policy, now paid his annual tribute to Yuan, who at once sanctioned the seizure of Wu and appointed him the president of the nobles of the Empire. After a brief reign the Emperor died, and was succeeded by his son.

---

* His family are said to have fled to Japan, whither one of their ancestors, Tai-pi, had gone in the twelfth century B. C. and became the founder of the present Japanese dynasty.

Ching Ting—B. C. 468-440.

This reign was marked by great disorders amongst the states, the rulers of which acted without any regard to the royal authority, and carried on war with each other as though the Empire consisted of so many distinct kingdoms and had no connection with the dynasty that claimed their allegiance.

He had hardly ascended the throne before the three powerful families that had been on the point of rebellion in Lu during the time of Confucius, began to gather together their adherents to contest for supremacy in the state. The Duke of Lu, in his extremity applied to the now powerful state of Yueh, but before relief could come to him he was driven from his capital, and his son was put in his place, though without any real power, for the most influential of the rebel chiefs held that within his grasp. Eleven years after, Tsin was rent by internal dissensions. Six high officials refused to acknowledge their Duke, and held their districts in their own right. Shortly after four of them combined and seized the districts of the other two. The Duke of Ts'i was appealed to for help, but before it could arrive the unhappy Duke was obliged to take refuge at the court of Ts'i. The result was that the state of Tsin was now divided into five, viz., Tsin, Wei, Chau, Han and Chih.

In the year B. C. 443 the Jung barbarians were signally defeated by the Duke of Ts'in, and from this time they dissappear from sight and are no more mentioned by this name in Chinese history. The Emperor died, and was succeeded by his son K'au (B. C. 440-425), who was again followed by his son.

Wei Lieh—B. C. 425-401.

The strife between the states became more severe, and the authority of the supreme government proportionately diminished during the reign of this monarch. In his twenty-third year the nine tripods of the great Yu began to utter sounds, which men looked upon as exceedingly ominous and portending coming disasters to the kingdom. In the principality of Tsin the four chiefs that had rebelled and now ruled independently were recognized by Wei Lieh and titles of nobility given them, an act that was exceedingly unjust and impolitic. Before long three of these joined their forces, and conquering the other, divided his territories amongst themselves. Wei Lieh was succeeded by his son.

Ngan—B. C. 401-375.

The only things that are mentioned during this sovereign's reign are the overflow of the Yellow River and the murder of the Duke of Ts'i by one of his ministers. The murderer at once took possession of the Dukedom, and instead of being punished was confirmed in his usurpation by the Emperor, who gave him a patent of nobility. After a weak and inglorious reign Ngan was succeeded by his son.

Lieh—B. C. 375-368.

In the first year of this Emperor the three great Houses that had divided part of the state of Tsin between them now absorbed the remainder of the country into their different governments, so that from this date the old state of Tsin disappears. Lieh seems to have been a man of uncommon firmness and decision of character, and had he lived in the earlier years of the dynasty he might have been celebrated as one of the famous kings of history. It is said that on one occasion he called one of his great officers, who had been accused of malversation, to his presence. "I have been greatly troubled," he said, "by complaints that have been made to me of you. No one in the palace has a good word for you, and I am assured that you are an exceedingly incompetent man. I have, however, thoroughly examined your case, and I find that these evil reports arise entirely from the integrity of your character, and because you would not condescend to propitiate your enemies by bribes. I am glad to have such an honest man in my service, and I shall now advance you in rank as a reward for your fidelity." To another he said, "I hear nothing but good about you. Every one is loud in your praises, which ring in my ears the livelong day. I have examined your history, and I find that you have been a most dishonest public servant, and that all these eulogiums are the result of the large sums you have given dishonest men to proclaim your so-called virtues. I mean, therefore, to punish you so severely that no one will ever dare to imitate your example so long as I am Emperor." He then ordered that he should be boiled in a huge cauldron that he had specially prepared for the occasion.

About the year B. C. 371 was born Mencius, the famous moralist and philosopher, who stands second only to Confucius in the estimation of the Chinese, and who became the distinguished expounder of the great sage's teachings. He was born either in Lu or Tseu, for the precise place of his birth is not positively known.* Lieh, after a brief reign, was succeeded by his son.

Hien—B. C. 368-320.

In the year B. C. 362 the Duke of Ts'in gained a great victory over the combined forces of the three chiefs that had absorbed Tsin, upon which Hien sent him a present of some royal apparel which he authorized him to wear. This was an exceedingly unwise thing to do, especially when it is considered that the power of Ts'in had been gradually overshadowing that of the other great states, and that its Duke was making no effort to conceal the ambitious view that he had of overthrowing the old dynasty and of establishing his own in its place. Two years after this man died, and was succeeded by his son Han. At this time six great states and ten or twelve

---

* See Dr. Legge's Chinese Classics. Vol. II. prolegomena.

smaller ones combined to resist his encroachments, and they agreed to treat him as a barbarian ruler and to hold no correspondence with him whatever. Hau saw that his only chance of maintaining his power was by obtaining the assistance of gifted men, who would by the display of extraordinary talents raise his state to such pre-eminence that all others would tremble before him. He accordingly sent abroad notices that he was prepared to employ men of ability, no matter to what state they belonged, and that he would confer honours upon them and lands to enable them to sustain their position. This invitation reached the ears of a young man, who was then in the employ of one of the high officials of the state of Wei, who at once hastened to Ts'in and presented himself before the Duke. This was the famous Wei-yang, who from this time became the most important factor in this important state.

In his youth he had given himself to the study of law, and more especially to the criminal department of it. He proposed to the Duke to make a complete change in many of the most important laws of the country. This, of course, was vigorously opposed by Hau's council, on the ground that it would be highly dangerous to abandon what had come down to them from their ancestors. Wei-yang laughed at this, and declared that it was only the ignorant and stupid that were held in bondage by anything that had come down from the past, and that the truly wise man was one who was prepared to accept of any thought or suggestion that would be serviceable to his fellow-men. "The sage could change," he said, "but the fool never." The Duke was so impressed with his arguments that he gave him permission to carry out his reforms. The chief of these were : (1) the ten house system ; * (2) in every family where there were two grown up sons one of these should go out and form a new household, or else double taxes should be levied ; (3) the rich should not be required to do personal service on the public works, but be permitted to compound by a money payment to the state. The poor, however, and especially the indolent, were required to attend with their wives. They would be thus cured of their laziness, and at the same time earn money that would go to the support of their families; (4) every man that travelled through the state must have a passport, and any inn-keeper that lodged strangers without such would be liable to a severe penalty.

The people at first were very unwilling to obey these laws, and even the son of the Duke showed his disapproval by breaking them whenever he had an opportunity. Wei-yang did not dare to punish

---

* This was a small division of a ward in a city, and consisted of ten dwelling houses. Each of these was responsible to the government for the conduct of the rest. This system holds good to-day, except in the villages, which often consist of one clan ; there every family in it has to answer for the misdeeds of any of their number, should he escape, and be beyond the reach of the law.

him, so he seized his two tutors and branded them on the face with Chinese words that held them up to public contempt for not having properly taught their young pupil. The people were so struck with this severity that they everywhere submitted to the new laws. After they had been in force ten years the whole character of the state was changed, for thieves disappeared from it, the indolent became industrious, and a spirit of widespread loyalty was engendered.

Twelve years after (B. C. 349) the institution of these reforms Wei-yang made still further important changes. Instead of the old territorial divisions he divided the country into thirty districts or counties. He also abolished the law relating to the apportioning of land to be cultivated by ten families, instituted by Wu, and he allowed each farmer to till whatever lands were most suitable, whilst those on the outskirts of the state could reclaim the waste country, the only condition being that they should pay taxes for lands actually under cultivation.

In the year B. C. 340 Wei-yang advised that war should be waged against the state of Wei. An army was accordingly marched against it, and the troops of Wei, headed by the son of its Duke, advanced to meet it. Wei-yang, who used to be intimate with him when he lived in his father's court, invited him to a conference to see whether they could not settle their differences without fighting. The invitation was accepted, but no sooner had he arrived in the Ts'in camp than he was arrested, and at the same time an immediate attack was ordered by Wei-yang on the army of Wei. Unprepared for treachery it was signally defeated and pursued to the very capital of the state, which was occupied by the victorious troops. The result was that a very considerable slice of the Wei territory was added to that of Ts'in.

Three years after the Duke of Ts'in died, and was succeeded by his son. The two tutors who had been branded on the face, and who all these years had never forgiven the author of their disgrace, now meditated a most terrible revenge. They persuaded the Prince that Wei-yang was meditating rebellion, and that he was preparing silently but surely to seize the power of Ts'in for himself. Prejudiced as he was against him he listened only too readily to the charges that were brought against him, and he issued orders for his arrest. Wei-yang, who had received secret information of the designs of his enemies, fled during the night, but when he reached the frontiers he could not pass the guards there, because he had no passport. Next day the soldiers of the Duke arrived in pursuit and arrested him and carried him back to the capital. Not all the years of service to the state could save him, and he was put to a most horrible death. His head and arms and legs were each tied to chariots in which were spirited horses. At a given signal the drivers started their animal in different directions, and Wei-yang, the builder up of the fortunes of Ts'in, was torn to pieces, whilst

every member of his family was put to death.   Five years after this
tragedy six states combined and entered into a solemn treaty to
defend each other against the growing power of Ts'in.   This
confederacy, however, was broken up by the skill and diplomacy
of the Duke's statesmen.

In the year B. C. 340 the Duke of Ts'in took the higher name
of king, and Hien was unable to take any action to prevent him
assuming a title that threatened his dynasty.   Four years after the
latter died, and was followed by his son.

Shin Tsing—B. C. 320-314.

The only facts recorded during this brief reign were the
combination of the states of Ch'u, Chau, Wei, Han and Yen against
Ts'in and their ignominious defeat ; and a great victory gained by
the latter power over the barbarians that lived near the river Min
in the present province of Sz-chwan and the appropriation of their
territory.   The next ruler was the unfortunate Nan.

Nan—B. C. 314-255.

The first year of this Emperor was marked by the invasion of
Yen* by the Duke of Ts'i.   The reason for this was because the
ruler of the former state had been persuaded by a clever minister of
his that he would gain imperishable fame if he were to imitate Yau
and Shun, by resigning his power to him.   This he did, and he
actually allowed him to be Duke whilst he acted as his prime
minister.   This was considered to be a very disgraceful thing,
which ought to be severely punished.   The Duke of Ts'i consequently led an army against the usurper, and being successful in
his campaign chopped both the Duke and his cunning minister into
a thousand pieces.

Ts'in looked on this success with no friendly eye, and military
operations were commenced.   In order to secure the neutrality of
the Duke of Ch'u he was promised that he should be given territory
to the extent of two hundred miles if he stood aside whilst the
contest was going on.   Contrary to the urgent advice of his
ministers he agreed to this proposition, and Ts'i was conquered.
When the promised reward was claimed, Chan-gi, the minister who
had conducted the negotiations, declared that he had only agreed to
give him two miles.   Enraged at this breach of faith the Duke of
Ch'u determined to attack Ts'in.   His ministers endeavoured to
dissuade him from this by showing him the great risk he ran, but
he was impervious.to all their arguments, and led an army against
that powerful state.   In the first battle that was fought he was
defeated, and in a second he suffered still more severely, because

---

* This state was founded in B. C. 1122 and lasted till B. C. 265.   It extended N.
and E. to the desert and the Songari river.   Its capital, Yen-king, was not far from
Peking.

Han and Wei joined their forces against him. He could finally secure peace only by the sacrifice of a considerable portion of his territory, which was annexed to Ts'in.

From this time there were interminable wars between the states. Sometimes one would be victorious, and then again it would be crushed and absorbed by a more powerful adversary. It is remarkable what a large number of able men appeared during these later years of the Chow dynasty, whose names are as household words to the scholars of to-day. Their history is generally a sad one. By their abilities they would retrieve the fortunes of the state they served, and victory would crown their plans, and the state once more hold its head proudly amongst the rest. Some evil-minded person, jealous of their success, would then whisper some envenomed words into the ear of the Duke, and at once the distinguished statesman would be consigned to the most miserable death. It seemed as though all generosity and all public faith had disappeared from the country in these interminable strifes for pre-eminence.

Amidst all the fluctuations of war Ts'in was gradually gaining the first place amongst the other states. In the year B. C. 280 the Duke of Ch'u threatened to invade the royal domain and seize it for himself. The Emperor, however, sent an ambassador to him and begged him to refrain from his purpose. ''Supposing you were to gain possession of my small territory,'' he said, ''what advantage would it be to you, who have so much larger a one of your own? You would only have the evil reputation of having been a rebel and of having murdered your sovereign.'' The Duke, influenced by these representations, now abandoned his ambitious purpose and remained loyal to Nan.

During the next few years the history mainly centres in Ts'in, which, victorious in its contests with the other states, was growing larger and larger at the expense of the conquered. Things at last came to such a serious pass that the Emperor organized a league of the nobles against it, a proceeding that so enraged its Duke that he at once led his armies into Chow, and, defeating the royal troops, he captured Nan. The Emperor was compelled to submit to the greatest indignities. He had to surrender all his lands and his soldiers to the conqueror, and himself to kneel in his presence, and knocking his head upon the ground confess his wrong and entreat forgiveness. He was then set at liberty, but he soon after died of grief and mortification. The only part of the royal domain that was not seized was the small feudal territory of Kung, which the Emperor had bestowed upon a branch of the imperial family, and which the usurper thought it prudent, for the present at least, to refrain from appropriating. From this time the Chow dynasty may be said to have ceased to exist, though historians have been accustomed to consider its actual extinction to have taken place six years later when the Duke of Kung was dispossessed of his small domain and the Chow family disappeared from the scene. This mode of reckoning is not a correct one, for the Duke was never invested with the supreme power, nor did he ever exercise imperial functions.

The Chow dynasty is in some respects the most remarkable one among the many that have ruled over China, and it has exercised a more powerful influence over the thought and manners of succeeding ages than any other. It has had the honour of producing the three great thinkers that have moulded the opinions and determined the philosophy of the scholars of the land, viz., Lau-tze, Confucius and Mencius. The first of these, born about B. C. 604, became the founder of the Tauist philosophy, and through that, though in a most perverted form, of the Tauism of to-day. The second is the author of a system of morals that is taught and studied throughout the eighteen provinces of China. He is looked upon as a god, and no human being has ever received such profound and enduring homage from such a vast number of people as he. The writings of the last are placed nearly on a level with those of the great sage, and studied with almost the same veneration as his.

Besides these great names a large number of statesmen and generals who distinguished themselves by their ability, and who played a conspicuous part in the history of the times, were produced in this dynasty. Their names and their deeds are known to learned and unlearned, for in the plays that are acted upon the streets these men figure upon the stage, and the virtues of the good are applauded, and the traitorous schemes of the men that thought only of their own aggrandisement are greeted with scorn and contempt. The extraordinary length of this dynasty is remarkable, when it is considered that with the exception of a few of its rulers they were all men of very moderate abilities. The fact is, its existence was prolonged, simply because there were so many powerful states within the Empire, all jealous of each other and ready to combine against any one that presumed to aim at a power that was beyond their own reach.

CHAPTER VIII.

THE TS'IN DYNASTY (B. C. 255-206).

Chau Siang—B. C. 255-250.

WITH the death of the Emperor Nan begins the Ts'in dynasty, though thirty years have to elapse before it is recognized by the whole of the nation. The only reason why the king of Ts'in did not assume the imperial title was because he did not feel himself strong enough to do so yet. Though his power was greater than that of any other ruler of the most powerful of the feudal states he did not dare to face the combination of them, which he was sure would be made were he to proclaim himself Emperor. Before Chau Siang could do this he must subdue his rivals, and if needs be absorb their territories within his own, and then he could step into the place that had been for so long occupied by the rulers of Chow.

Chau Siang had already ruled for fifty-two years over the state of Ts'in, so that he was an old man when he defeated Nan. The chief states that now existed as obstacles in his way to supreme power were Ch'u, Yen, Wei, Chau, Han, Ts'i and Kung, the last of which was ruled over by the last representative of the Chow family.

In his second year the state of Han submitted to Ts'in and agreed to pay tribute and acknowledge its superiority. Chau Siang began to assume the duties of the Imperial office by offering a solemn sacrifice to God. As only the Emperor is entitled to do this it soon became manifest to the rulers of the other states what his ambition was. Three years after this he died, when he was succeeded by his son *Hiau Wun*, who, however, died after a reign of only three days. He in turn was followed by his son.

Chwan Siang—B. C. 249-246.

This prince occupies a very important position in the history of his time. Whilst he was living as a hostage in Chau he became acquainted with a travelling merchant of remarkable ability, who was drawn towards the prince as a man through whom his own fortunes might be made. This was the famous Lu Pu-wei, who played so important a part in the history of this dynasty. By a liberal use of the fortune he possessed he managed to get the young prince free, and finding that his own wife, who was an exceedingly beautiful woman, was pregnant, he managed to inspire him with such a love for her that he requested her from him as his wife. With apparent great reluctance he granted this request, and so in course of time he had the pleasure of finding his own offspring the acknowledged heir to the throne. When he became king of Ts'in he made Lu Pu-wei his prime minister, and for the next ten years he was the ruling force in the state, and so consolidated its power that he gradually prepared it for the ruling position it was ere long to take.

In the second year of Chwan Siang the Duke of Kung endeavoured to get the great states to combine to resist the growing power of Ts'in, when an army was sent by Chwan Siang, and the last remnant of the Chow family disappeared from history, and his principality was attached to that of Ts'in. In the following year his soldiers were led against Wei, when they captured two of its cities, but fearing utter destruction it leagued with four other states, whose soldiers combined overcame those of Ts'in, who were compelled to retreat. A few months after Chwan Siang died, and was succeeded by the famous Chung, who subsequently took the exalted title of Shih Hwang-ti,* by which he is best known in history.

Chung, or Shih Hwang-ti—B. C. 246-221.

This man came into power when he was thirteen years old, and he may be considered really to be the founder of the Ts'in dynasty. He is one of the most remarkable men that has ever figured in Chinese history. Fortunately for him, in the second year of his reign the two powerful states of Chau and Wei, that had often been rivals of Ts'in, instead of uniting their forces against the growing power quarrelled and fought with each other. In his fourth year there was a great plague of locusts that devastated the state of Ts'in. Everything green was eaten up by them, and famine stalked throughout the land. In this emergency Chung sent notices far and wide that every one that brought any kind of cereals to a certain amount for the use of the state would be given official employment. Historians remark that this is the first instance in history where government honours were obtained by purchase. Four years after there was a combination of five states to overthrow Ts'in, but it failed. The confederacy was broken up, and the power of Chung was consequently only the more firmly established.

In the year B. C. 237 severe domestic troubles marred the happiness of the youthful ruler. He discovered that his mother had been guilty of the gravest immoralities, that Lu Pu-wei was giving out that he was his father, and that the latter had actually been guilty of facilitating the excesses of the Queen Dowager. His mother he banished to a strong fortress in Shensi, whilst Lu Pu-wei was dismissed from his office of prime minister and sent home to his estate, with a warning that he was on his good behaviour, and that any indiscretion would be visited with the severest punishment.

---

* Hwang means sovereign, and Ti divine ruler. The three great rulers Fuh-hi, Shen-nung and Hwang-ti used this title of Hwang. Chung would therefore combine in himself the highest names that had ever been used before him.

Though so prudent in ordinary life Lu Pu-wei had not the wisdom to follow out this advice, and before long Chung found that he was actually going to become the prime minister of the Duke of Ch'u, the most dangerous rival that he now had in the Empire. To accept that office was a public manifesto that he was going to throw all the talent and ability he had shown in the government of his own state for the last ten years into the hands of a prince whose sole aim and ambition was the overthrow of Ts'in. Chung was not a man to stand by and see this done with impunity. He accordingly sent messengers to him, upbraiding him for his wickedness and requiring him, in order to avoid extreme measures that he was prepared to adopt regarding him, to put an end to his life. Knowing that he could not get beyond the reach of the king's vengeance he poisoned himself, and thus passed from this stage of history, a man whose force and vigour of mind had impressed themselves upon the government and given it the stability it then possessed. Influenced no doubt by these home troubles Chung passed an edict ordering that all foreigners should leave his state. This would have been undoubtedly carried into effect, but for the representations of his prime minister the famous Li-sze.* He showed what a loss it would be to the state to deprive it of the valuable services of men of ability who, attracted by his renown, were flocking to it in order to be employed by him. He also pointed out that it had ever been the object of the great men of other days to secure men of advanced thought and largeness of mind, and that their renown had been enhanced by the employment of such, though many of them had not been natives of the kingdoms in which they had been so honoured. "You get your precious things from abroad," he said, "and your country is benefitted, and trade is increased, and the prosperity of the state is advanced. Why should you not exclude them too, if you have made up your mind that everything foreign should be expelled from your state?" Chung saw the force of his reasoning and repealed the law which would have deprived him of the services of Li-sze, and might thus have prevented him from carrying out those great plans of reform with which his name is indelibly associated.

The next great event during this reign was the destruction of the state of Yen and its absorption into that of Ts'in. The circumstances that led to this are very romantic. Tan, the heir of the dukedom, for some cause or other had been living in Ts'in as a

* Li-sze, who is so intimately associated with Chung in some of the most momentous acts of his reign, was a native of the state of Ch'u, the greatest rival of Ts'in. In early life he entered the service of the conquering chiefs of Ts'in, and for upwards of twenty years he was the counsellor, and finally the prime minister of Chung. He was a scholar, and is said to be the inventor of a special kind of writing called by the Chinese the seal character. His name is hateful to every Chinese scholar, and has been ever since he lived, because it was by his advice that the king issued a decree for the destruction of all the classical books that had been handed down from antiquity.

hostage. There he had been treated most cruelly by Chung, so that when he returned to his home his heart was burning with a desire to revenge his wrongs. He was determined that Chung should die, for nothing short of his death would satisfy him. In order to accomplish his purpose he consulted with a man named King-k'o as to the means by which it could be carried out. The latter volunteered to do the bloody deed, but the question was, How was he to penetrate through the guards that surrounded the king, so that he could get near his person?

At that time there was living in Yen a fugitive from Ts'in, for whose head Chung had offered a thousand pieces of gold and high official employment. King-k'o proposed that this man should be executed, and that he should take his head to Chung and seize the opportunity of murdering him. The prince, who by this time had become Duke, revolted from this proposal, not only because he was under his protection, but also because he had been kind to him when he was living in Ts'in. King-k'o said, "If you have any scruples about the matter I shall settle it with Fan-yu himself."

He accordingly visited him and told him that a plan was being matured to kill Chung, and that he was the man that had been appointed to assassinate him. He soon found that he had a willing listener, for he had suffered terribly, and he was prepared to assist in any scheme that would bring sorrow upon his enemy. King-k'o then showed him that his great difficulty was in devising some way by which he could approach the tyrant. "There is only one way," he continued, "that I can see out of the difficulty." "And what is that?" eagerly asked Fan-yu. "By taking your head," he replied, "for you know that he has offered a large reward to the man that brings it to him." "Most willingly will I give my life," he said, "to rid the world of a man who has not only sought my destruction, but has also murdered my wife and family and driven me a hopeless fugitive from my home."

He accordingly committed suicide, and King-k'o, with his head and a map of Yen, showing its boundaries and productions, proceeded to the court of Chung, under the pretence of bringing Fan-yu's head, and also of pointing out to him how easily he could conquer Yen and add it to his dominions. He was received with the greatest honour by the king, but whilst King-k'o was showing him the map, and waiting for a propitious moment in which to stab him, Chung saw the gleam of his knife, and starting up in the greatest alarm began to struggle with the would-be assassin, who was soon overcome and slain. He was so enraged at this attempt on his life that he determined to avenge himself by invading Yen. This he did, and soon this state was added to his own.

In the year B. C. 232 the Duke of Han, in terror of Chung, who gave signs that he was going to invade his dominions, very wisely surrendered them to him, and as a reward was made a high official under him. Four years after preparations were made for an assault on Chau. This was a most serious undertaking, for many attempts had been made to conquer it, but they had all been foiled by the consummate generalship of a famous commander named Li-muh, who had led the armies of Chau. For a considerable time he had held the post of warden of the northern frontier, and in many a successful engagement he had routed the wild forces of the Hiung-nu and prevented them from entering the state. He once more proved his ability as a general by several times repulsing the armies of Ts'in. Chung now saw that as long as he had to face Li-muh he could not hope for success. He accordingly bribed one of the officials at the court of Chau, who insidiously represented to the Duke that his successes had turned his head, and that he was actually making preparations to rebel. Orders were at once sent for his recall, and another commander appeared in his camp to take command, but the sturdy general refused to accept his dismissal, upon which he was put to death. With this tragedy the history of Chau as an independent state ceased, for its soldiers seemed to be deprived of all their courage with the loss of their leader, and were so thoroughly defeated by those of Ts'in that they dared no longer meet them in the field, and so Chau passed under the control of the conqueror.

In the twenty-first year of his reign Chung determined upon one of the most serious enterprises that he had yet undertaken, and that was the conquest of Ch'u. Applying to his general, Li-sin, he asked him how many men he would require for the purpose. Two hundred thousand, he replied. He then asked the famous veteran Wang-tsien how many troops he would need were he to entrust the campaign to him. He promptly replied, six hundred thousand. "Oh!" answered Chung, "you are getting old, and with age your courage is vanishing. Why should you demand so many men when Li-sin is ready to march with a third of the number that you deem requisite." "Yes," replied the wary old man, "it is true I am getting old, and I feel myself incapable of enduring the hardships of a severe campaign, such as must be borne in the invasion of so powerful a state as Ch'u. Your majesty has shown extreme wisdom in appointing a younger and more able man to the command of your forces, and of course with his conspicuous ability he will bring more honour to you than I could." The exquisite sarcasm of these words, and yet the profound submission that they showed to the will of the strong-minded king, can only be appreciated by those who have lived long amongst the Chinese and observed the ability with which a man can conceal his thoughts under the most ceremonious and refined language. If Chung had been a profound student of human nature he ought to have taken alarm at the polite and self-depreciatory language of the old captain, but he had been too long accustomed to success, and so he took his words in their literal sense.

Li-sin's army met with a terrible defeat. It was chased by the men of Ch'u for three days and nights, until it was utterly demoralized and dispersed. Chung, in his great anxiety and distress, came personally and prayed Wang-tsien to take command of his troops. "I am too old," he said, with that child-like smile with which a Chinaman can wreathe his face when he wants to affect profound humility, "and besides I have lost my courage, and dare not face such an enemy as Ch'u." "Oh! yes, you can," replied the king, "and you are not a bit too old. Come," he said, "grant my request, for my kingdom is in disorder, and this great defeat of my men must be avenged by a crowning victory over Ch'u." At last Wang-tsien consented, "but I must have six hundred thousand men he said. I would not march with a man less."

The king assured him that he should have all the soldiers he required. The magic of Wang-tsien's name soon brought back the soldiers to their colours, and men flocked into his camp, so that in a short time he had the number he had demanded. When the army marched Chung was so anxious about the results that he attended it in person for a considerable distance. On the march, whenever they passed by a fruitful district where the lands were in high state of cultivation, he would ask these as presents from the king. He, laughing, would instantly grant his request. When they came in sight of some magnificent building again he would ask the king to give it to him. Chung said to him, "You need not fear about your reward. Only defeat the enemy, and you will never have need to reproach me for my want of generosity." "But I would rather, if it pleases your majesty, have the gifts now than wait for them by and by. Your manner of bestowing rewards is different from that of the dynasties that have preceded yours. You reward men with high office which ceases with their death. They bestowed titles and fiefs that they transmitted to their children. My office dies with me, and so I ask you for these lands and houses that I may bestow them on my children in case I am killed in the war on which I am entering." The king smiled when he heard this statement, and promised to give him whatever he asked. Even after Chung had left him to return to the capital he was constantly sending messengers after him to request this land and that house, and praying for letters royal from himself securing the gift beyond any doubt. When some of his officers remonstrated with him and told him that this continual begging from the king would incense him and turn his heart away from him the crafty old general said, "My action will have the very reverse effect of what you dread. This continual demand of gifts from Chung is a premeditated scheme of mine in order to save my reputation and perhaps even my life. You observe," he continued, "that I am put in command of a very large army with vast and unlimited powers. This is sure to raise up enemies, who would like to ruin me. If I succeed, these men will whisper doubts into the ear of my sovereign and insinuate that I am plotting treason and meditating rebellion. When the king, however, sees the estates that he has given me in various parts of his dominions he will feel that in them he has a guarantee of my loyalty. By rebellion I should risk them all, and by treason I could not gain more."

When Wang-tsien entered the territories of Ch'u the whole country was moved by one common desire to save it from this vast army that had come to conquer it. The fame of Wang-tsien was known, and mighty exertions were made to bring sufficient forces into the field to meet him. Voluntee· from every part of the country flocked to swell the army in this great crisis of the state's history. Wang-tsien was determined, however, not to risk his reputation by a rash engagement with the enemy. He knew the valour of the men of Ch'u and how desperately they would fight now, when it was not simply that their honour was at stake, but their very existence as a separate power. He accordingly entrenched his army in a strongly fortified camp, and there he acted as though his soldiers had not come for the serious purpose of war, but for a huge and prolonged picnic. In the rivers and lakes near by he practised his soldiers in the art of swimming. Dinner parties, and singing songs, and mirth and jollity were the order of the day amongst his troops. The enemy by and by began to look with contempt upon this immense force of Wang-tsien, and thought that he had lost his senses. They became careless in their own military discipline and less watchful for any movement that might be made by the invading force. At last the fatal opportunity for which Wang-tsien had been looking with eager eyes, during all the months of his apparent indifference, came. Silently, but with deadly purpose, his army was put in motion, and an attack made on the ill-prepared soldiers of Ch'u, who suffered a tremendous defeat. Their prince was taken prisoner, their general slain and the whole army scattered, never to be assembled again in defence of home and hearth. The state itself was at once attached to Ts'in, and thus became part of the already extensive dominions of Chung.

Whilst Wang-tsien had been engaged in the conquest of Ch'u the state of Wei had been attacked and overcome, and its independent rule put an end to, and four years later Ts'i was also treated in the same manner, so that Chung remained supreme throughout China with none to dispute his assumption of imperial power. He now thought fit (B. C. 221) to assume titles that no previous sovereign had ever ventured to take. Instead of the modest appellation which the kings before him had been accustomed to use when they were speaking of themselves, he took the high-sounding ones of "We," "Us." The term Wang, signifying king, was now given up, and Hwang-ti was used instead. He vindicated his action by declaring that his virtues were equal to the three great Hwang, or sovereigns of ancient history, and his achievements not a whit behind those of the five Ti, or rulers, that figured in remote times, and that therefore he had a right to the combined honourable titles of those distinguished potentates.

In accordance with the custom of all founders of dynasties he ordered that the tenth month should be the first in the new *régime*, and that it should be the commencement of the new dynasty, and that black should be the imperial colour. He also divided the whole country into thirty-six governments or provinces, and set over each three great officers, that corresponded very much with those that are in existence to-day.* One of his ministers now suggested to him that he should appoint his sons and members of the royal family to the command of some of these provinces with the title of Prince. He peremptorily rejected this advice as most injurious to the country and even to the continuance of his own dynasty, and declared that the feudal system that had been so disastrous to the Chow dynasty should never, with his consent, be again established in China.

Although Shih Hwang-ti was a man of great intellect and force of character he was exceedingly superstitious and in constant dread of death. In consequence of this he became the tool of any charlatan that pretended to have a knowledge of the future, or that professed that he could find for him the elixir of life. On one occasion he applied to a magician to know how long he had yet to live. Imitating the method of the Delphic oracle he gave him an answer that could be read in two ways. He said that his kingdom would be endangered by some one of the name of Hu. Now Hu was one of the characters that applied to the Hiung-nu, and it was also one in the name of his second son, who afterwards succeeded him, and really wrecked the dynasty. The Emperor, however, took it to apply to the former, and at once raised an immense army, invaded the territory of those powerful barbarians and conquered them. Immediately after this he began the great work that has immortalized his name, viz., the building of the Great Wall, in order to act as a barrier against them should they or any other tribes think of invading his kingdom.

In the year B. C. 212 a great council was held in Hien-yang to discuss the affairs of the kingdom. It was advocated by some that the old methods of government under the previous dynasty should be adopted and the same division into states. This idea was strenuously opposed by Li-sze, who showed how the nobles, under that system, had fought with each other to the detriment of the common weal, and how the scholars had been a source of mischief to the nation, because they had been accustomed to offer their services to the highest bidder without any reference either to their own particular states or to the Empire at large. To stop this latter

---

* The three great officials of each province to-day are the Governor-General, or Viceroy, the General and the Provincial Treasurer.

evil he advised that all the classical literature should be burned, and that only those on medicine, divination, agriculture, etc., should be preserved, and that all students should give their minds to the study of law, which they were to learn from the recognized officials of the Empire. The Emperor was highly pleased with this idea, and at once promulgated an edict to this effect, which was carried out with the utmost stringency. It was enacted that all classical books should be handed over to the nearest magistrate to be burned ; that if two scholars were found talking together about the classic they were to be put to death ; and that if they were heard expressing their belief that the ancient books and customs were superior to those of to-day they and their families were all to be executed. In the following year, finding that the scholars had not obeyed his order, Shih Hwang-ti ordered that four hundred and sixty of the most conspicuous of them should be decapitated as a warning to the rest.

In the same year in which the Council was held, the Emperor having consulted a magician to find some medicine that would prevent him from dying, was told that he was pursued by malignant spirits that wished to kill him, and that he must arrange to spend his nights in different rooms, and that no one but himself should know what particular one he was going to occupy. His wives even must not be informed, as otherwise the spirits might get information and so kill him during the darkness of the night. Terrified beyond measure at this news he built the splendid palace of A-fang Kung, a building of such enormous extent that every one of his numerous wives could have an establishment of her own. Seven hundred thousand criminals and prisoners were employed in the erection of it. The great central hall could seat ten thousand persons, and the money lavished upon it was enormous. After it was completed the Emperor thought he could evade the spirits by selecting a room every evening that none but he himself knew he was going to pass the night in.

His eldest son Fu-su gently remonstrated with his father for spending so much money on this palace, who, to punish him for his audacity, sent him to join Mung-t'ien, the General who was then superintending the building of the Great Wall.

After a reign of thirty-seven years this great sovereign died whilst on a tour through his kingdom at Sha-k'iu in modern Chihli. As death was a terror to him none dare speak of it to him, and of course he would never refer to the subject. He left no message and gave no commands about the succession. He died in the company of a few of his high officials. Two of these were now to play an important part in the present crisis, viz., Li-sze and the eunuch Chau-kau, the tutor of the second son of the deceased Emperor. Both of these men dreaded the accession of Fu-su, for it meant the disgrace of them both. They accordingly concealed the death of Shih Hwang-ti and sent an order signed with his name that he and

Mung-t'ien should commit suicide. The latter suspected a plot, and told the prince that he had three hundred thousand men under his command building the wall that would follow him to the death, and he advised him, before he put himself to death, to appeal to his father for an investigation into his conduct. Fu-su did not dare to take this step, as his father was so cruel and relentless that he dreaded lest some horrible punishment might be inflicted upon him for his disobedience, so he quietly put an end to his life. This left the throne open for Hu-hai, who had thus infamously plotted for the destruction of his brother, but who was not destined to enjoy his usurpation for any considerable time. With the death of Shih Hwang-ti the power of the Ts'in dynasty may be said to have vanished. It had been upheld simply by his statesmanship and ability, and when his strong hand was removed disaffection was sure to break out into rebellion that would soon sweep away the structure that had been upreared by his genius. His destruction of the classical books, and his severe treatment of the scholars of his time, have given him an evil reputation that no lapse of time has been able to remove, and to-day there is no sovereign in the history of the past whose name is so execrated and abhorred as his.

Urh Shih Hwang-ti—B. C. 209-206.

This man, who ascended the throne through the murder of his brother, was weak and cruel, and about the worst one to hold the reins of power at this particular time that could have been possibly selected. Fu-su, on the other hand, was a man of power and greatly beloved by the people, and his rule would have been accepted by the great majority of the nation. By the advice of Chau-kau, who had a complete ascendency over the young Emperor, twenty-four members of the royal family, and Mung-t'ien, the one general that could have saved the dynasty, were ordered to commit suicide, which they did by drinking poison.. Urh Shih Hwang-ti was so wrapped up in his own folly that he was not aware of the actual condition of his kingdom and that men everywhere were ripe for rebellion. The very honours that he determined to pay his father were the means of hastening the sorrows which it was fated should fall upon his house. A huge palace was built underground, where the body of the late Emperor was laid. This was adorned with every luxury that art could suggest and enriched with immense treasures of gold, and silver, and jewels. When all was completed several hundreds of the most beautiful of the concubines of the late sovereign, with their attendants, were entombed in it with the royal corpse.

Lest thieves should be tempted by the treasures it contained to break open this huge tomb, cunningly devised machines were placed all round, immediately inside it, that would shoot the most deadly arrows upon any that would dare to desecrate it.

The building of this mausoleum was a great tax upon the people, and led finally to the rebellion that overthrew the throne. The men employed on it, as in the case of the magnificent palace that his father had built, were criminals of every degree that the Emperor ordered should be sent from every part of the kingdom to work on it. On one occasion a petty officer of the name of Ch'en-sing was conducting a party of prisoners to the work, when some of them managed to escape. The punishment for this, under the stern criminal laws of Ts'in, was death. He thought that as he must die anyway he might as well perish in a nobler cause than this, so he released the remainder of the prisoners, who gladly joined in the project of rebellion, and in a very short time several thousand men had joined his standard, and cities were captured, and his power grew to so formidable an extent that a large army had to march against him. Though he was defeated, the royal cause was not much benefitted, for the standard of rebellion had been raised by other men, the most prominent amongst whom were Liu-pang, Hiang-liang and Hiang-yu. In the meantime affairs were going on badly at the palace. The ambitious eunuch Chau-kau, who had the absolute confidence of the Emperor, persuaded him that Li-sze was plotting against him and was aiming at founding a new dynasty. He was at once seized, and without any trial ordered to suffer the most cruel death. He was cut in two from the waist, and died in the most terrible agonies. Not content with this the Emperor commanded that all the relations connected with his father, mother and wife should be exterminated, thus at once blotting out three families. Chau-kau, under mortal terror, lest his own misdeeds should be found out and be as ruthlessly punished by the Emperor, conceived that his only mode of safety consisted in destroying this cruel monster, and so he had him assassinated by men whom he had hired for the purpose. His son Tze-ying immediately was proclaimed Emperor. He was of an amiable and loving disposition and very different from the sanguinary rulers that had preceded him, but he came too late to avert the doom that was coming with sure and certain footsteps upon his family, and that in less than two months after the assassination of his father was to destroy the dynasty and put the capital into the hands of a new power. His first act was to cause Chau-kau, as well as all his relatives, to be put to death. This was an act of stern justice, for never had a more wicked or cruel man incited his sovereign to more diabolical acts than he had done.

Whilst this tragedy was being enacted the two lieutenants of Hiang-yu, who had proclaimed himself ruler of Ch'u, and I, a member of the ducal family that ruled in that state before it was conquered by Shih Hwang-ti to be Emperor, were marching on the capital, and Hiang-yu had promised that the title of prince should be bestowed upon the first that captured it. Liu-pang had the good fortune to be the man, and Tze-ying surrendered to him the imperial seal of state, when he was dismissed to his home without any injury. Liu-pang's position was a very critical one. He had only ten thousand men, whilst Hiang-yu was coming on as fast as he could travel with six hundred thousand. He doubtless would be jealous of his success, and, being a bloodthirsty man, would be inclined to get rid of so troublesome a rival. Liu-pang was fortunate at this time in having a most wise and faithful adherent of the name of Siau-ho to counsel him. He warned him that the greatest care was needed, lest he should excite the hatred of Hiang-yu. "You have to act, moreover, so as to gain a reputation with the people that shall secure you the throne in the future. You must not plunder them and you must leave untouched the magnificent palace of A-fang Kung. By doing this you will gain a name for moderation that will exalt you greatly in the estimation of the people." Liu-pang acted on this advice, and before Hiang-yu arrived he retired to the west, and there ruled over a territory in the present province of Sz-chwan.

Hiang-yu no sooner reached the capital than he showed his savage character by murdering the unfortunate Tze-ying, whom Liu-pang had spared. He also broke open the grave of Shih Hwang-ti and plundered it, and rifled the palace of A-fang Kung, and burnt it. After three months had been spent in thus enriching himself and his soldiers he retired to Shantung, where he ruled as king. To become Emperor, however, was the main ambition of his life, and so after two years he murdered I, and would have assumed the imperial title, but Liu-pang entered into the lists against him, and after two years' conflict, during which fortune inclined sometimes to one and then again to the other, Hiang-yu was so thoroughly defeated that he committed suicide, and Liu-pang, who was now known as the Prince of Han, became the founder of the famous Han dynasty.

In this premature fall of the Ts'ins we have an illustration of the instability of anything that has been founded on injustice or wrong. The reign of the Ts'ins was distinguished by its cruelty. Its criminal code is amongst the most severe of all those that have ever been put into practice in the long history of China. Shih Hwang-ti was a man of marvellous power and energy of character. He was a true statesman, and with the instincts of a man of genius he was quick to appreciate the enlightened views of the able minister that assisted him in the government of the kingdom. He was the real founder of the Chinese Empire, for he found it a disjointed mass of warring states, and he left it one and undivided as it is to-day. He was, however, full of superstition, and towards the close of his life terribly under the influence of charlatans, who pretended that they could secure to him immortality. He was, moreover, savage and fierce in his resentments, and thought but little of the human life in others that he was so much afraid to part with in his own. He was wanting, too, in manliness, and would scheme to blacken the name or destroy the life of the statesmen of other states that stood in the way of his ambition. Unlike T'ang, the founder of the Shang dynasty, whose picture we ponder over with pleasure, he was stern and inhuman, and though he stands out pre-eminently above the many sovereigns that preceded him, we part with him gladly, and feel that the fall of the Ts'ins was a righteous judgment from Heaven.

CHAPTER IX.

THE HAN DYNASTY (B. C. 206—A. D. 25).

Kau Ti or Kau Tsu—B. C. 206-194.

LIU-PANG, whose dynastic title was Kau Ti, claimed the throne from B. C. 206, though he did not ascend it till the year in which his fierce competitor Hiang-yu disappeared from the scene in B. C. 202. He would never have attained to the dignity of being the founder of a dynasty had he not been assisted by men of extraordinary abilities, both as statesmen and generals. His famous prime minister Siau-ho was a man of remarkable talents, and besides him he had the services of three men who in Chinese history are known by the name of the Three Heroes, viz., Han-sin, Chang-liang and Ch'en-p'ing, to whose energy and self-sacrifice it was mainly due that he finally acquired the kingdom.*

He gave his dynasty the title of Han, from the important river of that name that flows into the Yang-tze, and near which he was born, and by the advice of Chang-liang he removed his capital which he had first established in Loh-yang to Ch'ang-ngan in Shensi. He took brown as the imperial colour, and he ordered that the first month of the first year of his reign should date from the third month of the late dynasty. Kau Ti was a broad-minded, generous man, and though his temper was quick and furious he had the generosity, when it subsided, to confess his wrong to the persons to whom he had been unjust. Determined that his dynasty should be a permanent one, and that he would avoid the severities and cruelties that had turned all hearts from the Ts'ins, he remodelled the laws of etiquette for his officials, so as to make them less oppressive and exacting. He also ordered Siau-ho to draw up a new code of laws for the better government of the country, and he caused Han-sin to write a treatise on military tactics, which

---

* Siau-ho is renowned for the care he took, when the capital of the Ts'ins was captured, in rescuing from destruction the official archives, which were of incalculable value in after times. It is said that he gained nothing pecuniarily by the capture of the city and of the famous palace of A-fang Kung. Han-sin was of noble family, the grandson of the last Duke of Han, whose territory was conquered by Shih Hwang-ti, and in consequence of which he was left penniless and starving. He joined himself to Liu-pang, and his splendid generalship soon swept away every enemy that dared to face him. In the last great defeat of Hiang-yu, whom he had completely surrounded, his victory over him was achieved by a stratagem. This latter was noted for his strength and courage. Though placed in such a critical position he was not in the least terrified, for confident in his strength he had no fear of any number that might be brought against him. Han-sin caused his soldiers during the evening to play the music of Ch'u, the state from which Hiang-yu came. The latter listened with alarm, for he thought that the men of Ch'u had rebelled against him, and were now in the camp of the enemy. He became so depressed at this thought that he committed suicide. Han-sin was made Prince of Ch'u, but having subsequently been found harbouring treasonable designs he was executed by the Empress Lu.

should be the text-book in the education of men who were being trained for the army.

In the year B. C. 199 the Hiung-nu, finding that feebler hands held the reins of government than those of the great man that had subdued them, determined to win back the lands that had been wrested from them. An immense army of between three and four hundred thousand men, under the command of Mau-tun, marched against the Chinese, and they soon not only recovered what they had lost, but also gained a considerable area of new territory. They had penetrated as far as Shensi before Kau Ti could advance to meet them. As Han-sin was mistrusted, the Emperor commanded in person. Mau-tun on this occasion proved himself to be the better general of the two, as he skilfully managed to lead Kau Ti into a trap, where he was surrounded by overwhelmingly large forces, that to save himself from destruction compelled him to take refuge in the city of P'ing. There he was surrounded for seven days with a three-fold cordon of his savage foes. No provisions could reach him, and no succours could penetrate the three rings of these sturdy and courageous barbarians. It was under these distressing circumstances, when there was nothing left but surrender, that Ch'en-p'ing delivered the king from his danger by a stratagem. He had the picture of an exceedingly beautiful woman drawn and sent by a sure hand to the wife of Mau-tun, with the message that Kau Ti was going to win the favour of her husband by sending him a present of one of the famous beauties of China. Mad with jealousy, and fearful that her arrival would alienate her husband's heart from her, she persuaded him to break up the siege and return to his home.

Delighted with the success of the trick that had relieved him from his danger Kau Ti returned to his capital, when to his astonishment he found that Siau-ho had built him a magnificent palace. Kau Ti was exceedingly indignant with him, and asked him if this was a time to be lavish in expenditure when the enemy was at the gates and when the revenue was utterly exhausted. The great minister, who had wished to bind him to the capital in Shensi, where he could defend the Empire better from the inroads of the Hiung-nu, and who had taken this plan to keep him from removing from it to Loh-yang, said, "The Emperor is the greatest man in the kingdom, and unless he has a palace to live in suitable to his dignity he will not get the respect and reverence of his people." This reply satisfied the Emperor, and from this time he abandoned the idea of removing his capital to Honan.

In the year B. C. 197 the Hiung-nu again made an irruption into the kingdom, and Kau Ti was preparing an army to go and meet them, when one of his ministers dissuaded him from doing so and advised him to send an embassy to Mau-tun, proposing that their differences should be healed by a royal marriage. The savage chief was delighted with the idea, and as the Emperor had no daughter of his own he palmed off upon him one of the beauties of his harem as his own child. The marriage took place, and Mau-tun returned to his own home with his bride and with splendid presents that had been given him by Kau Ti.

Next year he was compelled to lead a force against one of his officers that had rebelled. Whilst he was away subduing him Han-sin was denounced for being in correspondence with the rebel. The Empress Lu, who had been left in charge with Siau-ho, at once seized him and had him executed and all his relatives utterly exterminated. After Kau Ti's return from his successful campaign the Lady Ts'i made a desperate effort to have her son appointed successor to the throne. Both from love of her and because of the ability of her son he was willing to consent to this, but the whole of his ministers were opposed to it as being illegal, and therefore injurious to the interests of the state. He was compelled to submit, but knowing what terrible vengeance would be exacted from the Lady Ts'i and her son after he was gone, he requested one of his faithful ministers to promise that he would shield them to the utmost of his power after they had lost his protection.

Two years after, he had again to march against another rebel, and though he was victor in the battle that was fought he came away with a wound that was destined to be fatal to him. On his way home he called at his native place, P'ei, and summoning his old friends to a banquet he seems to have become once more one of the people. Taking a lute he improvised a song, in which he declared that he would never forget his birth-place, and that even after his death his spirit would hold it in remembrance. He decreed on the spot that it should be for ever exempt from taxation. When he reached his palace he was very ill, but he refused all medicine. "Heaven," he said, "has made me Emperor, and my life is in its hands, and I will trust in none else."

He died a comparatively young man, being only fifty-two years old, and was succeeded by his son.

Hwei Ti—B.C. 194-187.

The prince was only fourteen years old when he came to the throne. He was a gentle, kind-hearted youth, and abhorred anything like cruelty. He was fortunate in having the famous statesman Ts'au-ts'an as his prime minister. The ruling force in the state, however, was his mother Lu, who no sooner saw that her husband was dead than she seized the Lady Ts'i and had her chopped into a thousand pieces, and in spite of the entreaties of Hwei Ti despatched her son with poison. The youthful sovereign was so terrified by the sight of the lady's remains that had been cast on a dunghill that he became impaired in mind, so that from this time the government remained in the hands of his cruel mother.

In the year B.C. 191 Mau-tun was again restive, and sent to the Chinese court a demand for another royal princess. The Queen Dowager was highly incensed at his presumption, and would have treated him in her own forcible manner, but by the advice of her council she sent him a courteous reply refusing his request, but soothing him by a magnificent present of horses and chariots. Hwei Ti's reign was not distinguished by anything remarkable, and after ruling nominally for seven years he was succeeded by his ambitious mother.

Lu Shih—B. C. 187-179.

As Hwei Ti had no son of his own his mother previous to his death surreptitiously brought in a child, whom she got her daughter-in-law to acknowledge as her own, whilst in order to prevent disclosure she had the real mother put to death. On the decease of Hwei Ti she forcibly occupied the position of regent, and as she was a strong and masterful woman, and held the threads of power in her own hands, the great officers of state were compelled to yield to her. From the moment that her authority was acknowledged she began to take measures for the elevation of her own relatives and for the founding of a new dynasty to supplant the present one. For this purpose she made some of her nearest of kin princes, in utter violation of the law that exists to the present day, that none can be elevated to this rank, excepting those of the same clan as the Emperor.

The prime minister opposed her action as illegal, and she then appealed to Ch'en-p'ing, who replied that she had the right to do so if she liked. This astute statesman, who had helped the dynasty on six critical occasions, determined to prevaricate, in order to save the Hans when the time for action should arrive. He saw that if he were to oppose the Empress now he should be dismissed from office, whilst if he temporized he would be promoted to still further honours. Events turned out precisely as he had forecast, for the prime minister was dismissed, whilst he was appointed to his vacant office.

In her second year of power, finding that the youth whom she had given out to be her grandson was not so pliable as she wished, she had him murdered and another puppet put in his place. During this same year the copper cash, which during the times of the Ts'ins had been half an ounce in weight, were reduced to only a tenth of an ounce, and a little later on to only a twentieth, to the great convenience of the people, who had found the heavy coins a serious hindrance in their commercial transactions.

The queen's reign was a peaceable and a prosperous one, for though cruel she was a woman of great ability. In her eighth year, according to custom, she went to bathe in the river, when she was attacked by a huge monster, which, though it struck its teeth into her side left no mark, thus showing, according to the popular belief, that it was a supernatural animal that had sought her life. She returned to the palace in great distress of mind and seriously ill. She at once summoned her diviners, who pronounced the monster that had bitten her to be the spirit of the Lady Ts'i, whom she had so barbarously murdered.

From this time she gave up all hope of life, and yet even now she showed the strong determination of her character by calling the chiefs of her family to the capital and commanding them to seize upon the supreme power after her death. More astute brains, however, were at work than hers. Ch'en-p'ing and the commander of the troops, the famous Chow-p'o, were all ready prepared for the crisis when it should occur. No sooner was the regent's death announced than there was a stir amongst her kinsmen, but Chow-p'o, summoning his soldiers, commanded that those that were for the Lus should bare their right shoulders, whilst those that were for the Hans should do the same with the left. The men enthusiastic-ally bared their left arms, when he fell upon the Lus, dispersed their following and put the traitorous princes to death. The great officers by a unanimous vote elevated a son of the late Emperor, by one of his concubines, to the throne, who is known in history by the name of Wun Ti.

Wun Ti—B. C. 179-156.

This Emperor is famous in history for his generous, humane feelings, for his stern economy, and for the unceasing care that he took of his people's interests. In his first year, distressed with the severity of some of the laws that had been enacted by the Ts'ins, he made it his business to have them modified, so that they should no longer bear oppressively on the innocent. He decreed that a wrong-doer should suffer for his own crimes, but that his family should be exempt from punishment. He also enacted that old men over eighty should be provided by the state with meat, rice and a certain amount of spirits, and for those over ninety sufficient silk for a dress should be added.* He also repealed the law of the Ts'ins that any man that criticized the Emperor should be put to death, and he invited the people, whenever they had any grievances, to come and complain of them, even though in doing so they should have to express an adverse opinion of himself. He next passed an act in reference to the coinage, and decreed that each cash should be one-tenth of an ounce in weight, and that the liberty that the people had hitherto possessed of coining for themselves should cease, and the government have the sole right of issuing the currency. Two royal mints were established, one in Chehkiang and the other in Sz-chwan.

---

* The edict to this effect runs as follows : " It is now the spring time, and all the vegetable world is opening out in a thousand different forms, and nature is everywhere rejoicing. Now I, who have been Emperor for nearly a year, how shall I act so as to make my people's lives to be full of happiness? How shall I plan so as to bring gladness to the old man whose wife is dead, or to the old widow whose husband has long since left her, or to the little ones who have been bereft of their parents, or to those who have no children to brighten their lives whilst they are treading upon the very borders of death, etc., etc.; and then follows the regulations with regard to how such should be treated.

This reign was very much disturbed by the frequent incursions of the Hiung-nu. A great council was convened to concert measures to prevent these, and it was decided, after much discussion, that a tribe of Jungs that had submitted to the arms of China should be transferred to the northern frontiers, and that in addition large colonies of Chinese, who should be provided with lands, houses and implements, should be invited to settle down and assist in bringing a barrier against the inroads of their barbarian neighbours. This plan was carried out, but, of course, at first with only a partial success.

The great humanity of Wun Ti led to a modification of the five great punishments, which were : branding on the face, excision of the nose, chopping off the feet, castration and beheading. The last of these was left unaltered, but the other four were abolished, and flogging was enacted in their place. The immediate cause of this change was the filial and heroic conduct of a young lady of the name of T'i-ying, who has thus become famous in the annals of her country. Her father, Ch'un-yu, was an officer of high rank, and had charge of the public granaries of Ts'i. He made himself distinguished for his wondrous knowledge of medicine, and because he refused to attend certain influential persons he was denounced to the Emperor as a defaulter and condemned to the punishment of mutilation.

Ch'un-yu, who was entirely guiltless of the offence for which he had been condemned, bemoaned his fate bitterly and lamented that he had no son who might at this time have helped him to avert his terrible doom. T'i-ying was so moved by the anguish of her father that she started for Ch'ang-ngan, and sending in her memorial to the Emperor had the good fortune to be led into his presence. With great modesty and power she laid the case of her father before him. She not only proved that he was innocent, but she also showed the injustice of the punishment that was going to be meted out to him. "If a man is worthy of death," she said, "let him die, that is just, but to mutilate him defeats the ends of justice, because you leave no place for repentance. No amount of sorrow for his offence will ever bring back the limbs that have been once cut off. You thus make a man desperate, as by this one act of punishment you shut off all hope for the future." She then appealed in a most pathetic way to the Emperor to be allowed to suffer for her father. "Let me be sold as a public bond-servant, and let my father go free," she cried entreatingly to Wun Ti. The Emperor, who was a tender-hearted monarch, was so touched by her devotion that he not only reversed the sentence against her father, but also abolished the four punishments as narrated above.

In the year B. C. 163 Wun Ti sent commands throughout the Empire that search should be made for any of the classical books that might have escaped the destruction that had been ordered by Shih Hwang-ti. Large numbers that had been secreted were thus brought to light, and scholars once more began their study of them, which has gone on uninterrupted till the present day.   Three years after this one of the most terrible invasions of the Hiung-nu that had happened for many years took place.   A widespread slaughter of the Chinese was the result, and beacon fires turned night into day over a large extent of the north of China.   Wun Ti raised six large armies to meet the overwhelming forces of the barbarians, and the command of the whole was given to Chow Ya-fu, a distinguished general, and one noted for the strictness of his discipline.   When the Emperor visited his camp on the frontier before it marched against the invaders, wishing to enter without any formality, he was stopped by the lieutenant in charge, who declared that none could pass the gate without the order of Chow. "But I am the Emperor," he said, "and need no such authority to be able to visit my own soldiers."   "In the camp, the only one we obey," he replied respectfully, "is our general.   His word, not the Emperor's, is our law," and Wun Ti had actually to wait until the commander came himself and admitted him.   The Hiung-nu were defeated and driven back, and peace was restored to the Empire.

After a reign of twenty-three years Wun Ti died, to the great regret of his people, by whom he was sincerely beloved.   His last request was in harmony with what he had practised all his life. "Let the public mourning for me," he said, "extend over three days only, and not three years ; let no expense be gone into in erecting a monument over my tomb, but let me be buried on the hill side like any of my officials, and let my corpse be buried in the simplest clothing and lay my head on an earthenware pillow."   He was only forty-eight years old when he died, and he was succeeded by his son.

King Ti—B. C. 156-140.

This Emperor seemed determined upon following in the footsteps of his father, for he reduced the number of strokes in the flogging that had been enacted in the previous reign.   He also regulated the size of the bamboo rod with which the punishment was to be inflicted, for he had heard that many deaths had been caused by the unscrupulous use of a power that vindictive hands had used unmercifully.   It was to be five feet in length, an inch thick at the handle and a half an inch at the end, and it was to be planed smooth so as not to be used with cruelty.

In his second year there was a serious rebellion of seven princes of the blood, headed by the Prince of P'ei, who declared that the only object they had in rising was to defend themselves from the machinations of Ch'au-ts'o, one of King Ti's privy counsellors, who they said had intrigued against them, and they promised to disband their forces if he were executed.   The real offence of this faithful minister was that he had strongly advised the Emperor to abolish the feudal dependencies that he saw were becoming a danger to the state. Wun Ti had failed to see the peril such brought upon the Empire, and had allowed matters to take their own course, and now they had come to a crisis in the life of his son. King Ti weakly conceded the demands of the rebels, and ordered Ch'au-ts'o to be beheaded. He found, however, that this concession only increased their demands, and finally Chow Ya-fu had to be launched against them with a powerful army, when they were defeated and scattered.

The Hiung-nu were again troublesome during this reign, but the Emperor secured peace with them by giving his daughter in marriage to their chief. After a reign of sixteen years he was succeeded by his son.

Wu Ti—B. C. 140-86.

This prince was only seventeen when he ascended the throne, but he showed himself thoroughly in earnest to rule his subjects to the best of his ability. He surrounded himself with able scholars and experienced statesmen. Chief amongst these were Tung Chung-shu, Sz-ma Siang-ju* and Ki-jen, noted for his policy of governing by letting things alone. The influence of these three men caused the rapid spread of Confucianism, which would have become supreme in the state had it not been that the Queen Dowager threw all her power on the side of Taoism, in which she had a most profound belief. This latter system had greatly degenerated since the days of Lau-tze, its founder. Instead of being a profound system of philosophy it had deteriorated into one of magic and pretended control over the supernatural.

Through her influence some of Wu Ti's advisers were put to death, and others had to retire from public life, whilst she surrounded him with magicians, who declared that they could assist him to govern the kingdom with more wisdom than could all the scholars of the country. Her sudden death interrupted the influence of these men for a time, and the disgraced Confucianists were recalled to court, but Taoism had evidently a fascination for the superstitious Wu Ti, and he has the reputation of being the first ruler through whose influence and support this degraded system got the footing in the Empire that it has never lost till to-day.

In the year B. C. 133 Wu Ti came under the teaching of Li Shau-kun, a famous professor of the magic arts, and his life from this was greatly influenced by the doctrines of Taoism. This man professed to be an adept in the mysteries of alchemy and to know where the elixir of life could be obtained. He assured the Emperor that he knew the secret of the transmutation of metals into gold and silver, which he had learned from the chief of his

---

* The first of these was a scholar and statesman, who vigorously opposed the charlatans that deceived the Emperor, whilst the second was a scholar and poet, who rose to distinction under Wu Ti.

sect, who, he said, had lived a thousand years. Wu Ti implicitly believed every word that he said, and sent him on a mission to obtain the elixir, but he died on the journey. The credulity of this sovereign's mind may be learned from the fact that he believed that his favourite had been called away to become a god, and therefore could not procure for him the precious liquid that was to secure him immortality.

The Hiung-nu had been a source of trouble to the Empire ever since Wu Ti had come to the throne. A great Council was therefore called to devise some plan for averting this incessant danger to the country. It was proposed that the Chinese, instead of waiting for their incursions, should become the aggressors, and marching into their territories crush their power once and for all. It was also decided that a stratagem should be employed to circumvent their savage enemies. They were to be invited into a certain territory where gold was said to abound, and they were to be informed that the whole was to be theirs, so that they would be so enriched they need never dream of making any more forays into China. Should they accept this invitation immense forces were to lie in wait for them and destroy them as they marched to the golden land.

The Hiung-nu only too readily listened to the words of the Emperor's envoys, and between three and four hundred thousand of them started for their new homes. On the way, however, they found out that an ambuscade was prepared for them, upon which they instantly returned to their own country. From this time no more royal marriages bound the Empire to the barbarians, but the conquest of each was the aim of both. Fortunately for China she possessed at this time generals of great ability, who were able to stem the torrent of barbarian invasion and to teach their men and the settlers on the northern frontiers such lessons in the art of war that they never shrunk from facing their fierce antagonists. The chief amongst these were Li-kwang, Wei-ts'ing and Ho K'u-ping.* On many occasions they met the assembled forces of the barbarians, and inflicted severe losses upon them. In B. C. 121 Wei-ts'ing and Ho K'u-ping invaded their territories, and advancing far into them slaughtered immense numbers of them. It was on this occasion that they penetrated into Turkestan and brought away the golden image that was worshipped by one of their chiefs named Hiu-chu.

---

* Li-kwang was victorious in more than seventy battles. In a great battle in B C. 119, in which he was second in command, a great disaster happened to the division under his orders, and when called upon to give account of his conduct he committed suicide rather than submit to the indignity of a trial. Wei-ts'ing gained distinction by constant success in battle. In B. C. 121 he led an army into Turkestan, and when he returned from the conquest of the Hiung-nu he brought with him a golden image used in worship by them. Historians are inclined to believe that this was an image of Buddha, and that Buddhism may have been introduced thus early into China, and that the "golden man" of this age may have inspired the dream of Ming Ti that caused him to send messengers to the west that led to the formal introduction of Buddhism into China during his reign.

As a reward for this successful expedition the Emperor rewarded the latter with a district containing five thousand families. So discouraged were the Hiung-nu with their losses, and so discontented were they with the conduct of some of their chiefs that their Khan summoned the latter to his presence to give an account of themselves, when two of the most influential fled to the camp of their enemy and gave in their submission to Wu Ti.

In the twenty-first year of his reign there was great difficulty in raising enough revenue to meet the expenses of the state. The wars with the Hiung-nu had been so frequent and so expensive that the country was drained of its resources. The Emperor had a considerable supply of raw silver and tin in his own private treasury. He had also a very large number of white deer in the royal park. It was decided to utilize these for the benefit of the country. They were killed, and their skins, cut into pieces of a foot square, were beautifully embroidered. Every official that came to pay his respects to the Emperor was required to purchase one of these at a fancy price. By this means considerable sums were procured for the public service. An amalgam was made of the silver and tin, and three different kinds of coin were made from them. The largest was round, with the figure of a dragon on it, and worth about ten shillings. The next in size was square, with a horse stamped on it, and was valued at about eighteenpence, and the third was oblong, with the figure of a turtle on it, and was worth about a shilling.*

During this same year Wu Ti determined to make an expedition against the barbarians, and to carry it out on such a scale that success would be absolutely certain. Two armies, each of fifty thousand foot, and the same number of cavalry, were despatched against them. The campaign on the whole was most successful, and proved to the Hiung-nu that their deserts were no barriers to the soldiers of the Empire, but that they could be reached in any part of their country whenever the Chinese armies wished. Over seventy thousand of them were slain, but the losses of the Chinese were serious, because the division of Li-kwang and that of another were almost annihilated in a sand storm.

All this time Wu Ti was under the absolute dominion of the Taoist magicians. By the advice of one he built a high tower, in order that he might have freer intercourse with the heavenly spirits who desired to bestow upon him immortality. After waiting and worshipping for more than a year he became suspicious. To quiet his doubts he was told that if he killed a certain cow he would find a revelation from the gods to him. When it was opened Chinese writing was discovered, which the impostor had previously caused

---

* These values are altogether approximate. It is impossible, with the changes in currency, and with our imperfect knowledge of the precise value of the coins of those early days, to say absolutely what they are equivalent to in English money now.

her to swallow, but the Emperor recognizing the magician's hand caused him to be instantly put to death. This discovery made not the slightest difference in his belief in magic.

In this twenty-third year the Emperor, driven to desperation for money, imposed a property tax on his subjects, being the first the Chinese had ever been asked to pay. Everyone was required, by royal edict, to send in an estimate of all the goods of any kind that he possessed, and he was compelled to pay five per cent. of their value to the crown. The wealthy man, with his large substance, and the fisherman, with his small boat with which he supplied the wants of his family, and the carter, who looked to his cart for the means of subsistence, all were taxed alike to the same amount. It was also enacted that those that refused to send in an account of their property, or who gave a false one, should have the whole confiscated to the state, and that informers should have the half for themselves.

This law was exceedingly unpopular, and largely disregarded. It was soon seen, however, that Wu Ti was not a man to be trifled with. Most stringent orders were given to carry it into effect, and the result was that vast numbers were reduced to absolute poverty. Informers and officials, whose consciences were dead to truth, availed themselves of the provisions of the new law to enrich themselves. The result was that many of the wealthy were stripped of all they had through false accusation made against them, and of the middle and lower classes vast numbers were reduced to poverty. Widespread discontent was the consequence. The poorer classes refused to work, for they declared that all their earnings were seized by the mandarins When this was reported to the Emperor he issued an edict commanding that all that were found unwilling to follow their several occupations should be compelled to work for the state, in whatever way the officials of a district should decide. With a less vigorous ruler than Wu Ti there would have been rebellion throughout the country.

Through all the political concerns of his life his mad passion for immortality led Wu Ti to be the dupe of the vilest men in the kingdom. One man deceived him to such an extent that he made him a high official and gave him his own daughter in marriage. This raised up an army of charlatans throughout the country, everyone of whom declared that he had discovered the infallible remedy. The capital was filled with Taoist temples that resounded day and night with the incantations of men that represented themselves as being in a perpetual conflict with the powers of darkness on behalf of his majesty.*

---

* The Chinese term for "Your Majesty," which means "a thousand years," came into use at this time. Walking amongst hills one day, with his heart full of the one thought that continually oppressed him, one of his attendants told Wu Ti that he heard mysterious sounds echoing and re-echoing amongst the mountains, and that he could distinctly make them out to be "a thousand years," "a thousand years." This was an intimation from the gods, he said, that his life was to be prolonged for that length of time. The Emperor was delighted, and from this time this phrase became a part of the court language.

During all this time the war with the Hiung-nu was carried on with varying success, though on the whole it was decidedly in favour of the Chinese. In his 36th year Li Kwang-li was despatched with a large army, who penetrated as far as the confines of Persia and took the city of Ur-shih. On his return he was ennobled with the title of Viscount of Ur-shih, and his sister was taken into the royal seraglio. Five years later (B. C. 99) Li-ling, a grandson of the famous Li-kwang, led immense forces against the Hiung-nu, but advancing with a force of five thousand men ahead of the main body he was surrounded by them, and he escaped with only four hundred men. Knowing that death awaited him, if he returned to China, he took service with barbarians. The Emperor was so enraged at this that he doomed to destruction his entire family, and because Sz-ma-ts'ien, the great historian of China, attempted to defend him, he was most barbarously mutilated and cast into prison.*

In the 46th year of his reign, Fuh-ling, who succeeded him on the throne, was born. He was the son of the Lady Chau, one of his concubines. Li, the rightful heir, had completely vanished from sight in consequence of a court intrigue against him. One of the ministers having a feud with him represented to his father that he was using magical arts for the destruction of his life, and that evidences of this could be found in the young man's own room.† When officers were sent to search it a great many wooden figures of Wu Ti, which had been placed there by the accuser, were found in it. The superstitious mind of the Emperor was terribly affected by this discovery, and he ordered the immediate arrest of his son, though he was fondly attached to him, but he and his partisans resisted, and for five days the capital was filled with the clamour of the two hostile sides. Finally the prince escaped, and was never heard of again. All the soldiers that had aided him were put to death, and even the queen, who had sided with her son, was ordered to commit suicide.

He discovered before his death the foul wrong that had been done his son and a fearful revenge he had upon the man who had deceived him. He and all his relatives were exterminated. He built a temple to the memory of the lost heir, over the front of which were inscribed the words, "I am thinking of my son." He also erected a high tower, on the top of which was engraved the sentence, "I am looking for his return." Towards the close of his life he confessed his folly in listening to the Taoists, and he ordered the destruction of their temples and the cessation of all their

---

* Sz-ma-ts'ien wrote the "Historical Records," which give a comprehensive view of Chinese history from the time of the mythical Emperor Hwang-ti down to B. C. 104.

† The magical arts referrred to are practised even to the present day in China. When a person wishes to destroy another one's life he has a wooden figure resembling him made. It is then pierced with sharp instruments, and all kinds of imprecations having been uttered against it, it is buried in the ground. It is believed that certain death will be the result of this.

religious services throughout the empire. His cruel disposition was seen in his order for the execution of Lady Chau a short time before he died. When asked by his ministers what wrong she had done he replied, "She has done no wrong, but her son is only seven years old, and when I die she would become regent. I fear the intrigues of a woman in the palace during the minority and the dangers she might bring to my dynasty, so I have had her executed." Just before his death he left the regency in the hands of Ho-kwang, the king maker of the Han dynasty, Kin Jiu-ti and two others, and after a short interval this very able, superstitious and sanguinary monarch passed away. His son succeeded him, whose dynastic title was

Chau Ti—B. C. 86-73.

This ruler was a very wise and intelligent person and singularly humane in his treatment of his people. An elder son by one of Wu Ti's concubines, and who had been made Prince of Yen, thought that by the law of succession he should have succeeded his father, and began to make preparations to assert his rights. Ho-kwang was, however, on the alert, and the incipient rebellion was nipped in the bud and his followers severely punished, though the prince, through the forbearance of Chau Ti, was forgiven and allowed to hold his estates in Yen as before.

In the second year of his reign he made a tour round his dominions, and perceiving the poverty of the people, and that many of them were without money, and could not till their lands, he remitted the land tax in the places where the distress was extreme. Three years after a pretender to the throne, in the person of a Shensi man, who said that he was Li, the lost son of Wu Ti, appeared one day at the palace gates and declared that he was the rightful Emperor. He was apprehended and cut in two through the waist, and those that had had the temerity to accompany him vanished.

The year B. C. 80 was a disastrous one for the farmers and for the country generally. The crops through a large area of the empire failed, and Chau Ti, anxious to know how to remedy this state of things, appealed to his ministers for advice, who recommended that more attention should be paid to the good government of the people. The Emperor thought that this was very good, but he decided to ask his subjects what opinions they had in a matter that so nearly affected them. When they were consulted they said they wished the taxes on salt, iron, spirits and property to be abolished. Chau Ti was inclined to grant their request, but his ministers, having declared that they could not carry on the government without them, a compromise was made, and the last two only were remitted. During this year the famous Subu returned from a nineteen years' captivity amongst the Hiung-nu. Having been sent on a mission to their Khan he and his followers were detained as prisoners, and his life was offered to him on the condition that he should renounce his allegiance to the house of Han. This he refused to do, when he was immured for many days in an underground dungeon and left to perish. He sustained life, however, by imbibing the moisture that was in his clothes at the time of his arrest, and the Tartars finding after some time that he was not dead sent him to tend the flocks of their chief. After long years of servitude he was restored to freedom and allowed to return to his home. History praises his loyalty to his country, and his name to-day is held in high honour by all classes of the Chinese.

The Prince of Yen having once more raised the standard of rebellion he was seized and executed. Chau Ti died after a reign of thirteen years, greatly regretted by his people, who had a sincere affection for him. As he died without issue Ho-kwang had to settle who should succeed him. After considerable thought an uncle of the late Emperor was placed upon the throne, but he showed such incapacity, that after three months he was set aside as incompetent. During this brief reign of power he spent his time in hunting and in the pursuit of such pleasures as proved that his mind was essentially low and debased. With the consent of the Queen Dowager a grandson of the missing Li was proclaimed Emperor in the place of the one that had been so summarily dismissed.

Suan Ti—B. C. 73-48.

The story of the early days of this Emperor is a most romantic one. After his grandfather Li had fled from the vengeance of Wu Ti not only were the adherents of the former condemned to death, but also his wife and infant son. Being thrown into prison previous to execution the governor of the jail, being moved to pity for the child, gave it to one of the jailers, who adopted it as his own. He was then reared in his own family, and when he grew up he gave him his daughter in marriage. When Ho-kwang was in search of an Emperor the history of the young man was related to him, and having found that the story was a genuine one he raised him to the throne with the unanimous consent of all the members of the Privy Council. His life having been spent amongst the people he knew them better than any ordinary ruler that had ever sat upon the dragon throne. His sympathy was manifested for them by his appointing a special minister, whose business it should be to keep the government informed of their wants and sorrows.

In the third year of Suan Ti's reign a terrible tragedy happened in his family. With a noble fidelity to his plebeian wife he had insisted, when he was raised to the throne, that she should be recognized as his queen. Ho-kwang's wife was exceedingly disappointed at this, for she had planned that her own daughter should occupy that distinguished position. Matters came to a crisis when the queen came to be confined, for the doctor who was attending her was bribed to poison both mother and child, which she did. Being apprehended she was about to be put to the torture, when Ho-kwang, to save the reputation of his family, ordered her release, and reported to the Emperor that the death of his wife and child cou d be accounted for on natural grounds. In the following year Ho-kwang's daughter was made queen, whilst he himself died, and was buried with royal honours.

In the year B. C. 66 the Emperor's eldest son, who was born when he was one of the people, was formally appointed successor to the throne, to the unbounded anger of Ho-hien, his mother-in-law, who wished the succession to run in the line of her own family. She planned the murder of the heir, but his father, who was suspicious, guarded him so carefully that all her designs were frustrated. The Emperor from this time, with the help of his adopted father, gradually dismissed the relatives of the queen, who filled all the important posts in the palace and replaced them by others not under her influence. Taking alarm at this Ho-hien plotted to murder Suan Ti, when she and her son were arrested, and not only were they both executed, but the queen also was divorced, as being unworthy of the lofty position she and her mother had plotted to obtain.

In the following year a great famine extended over the region of Hai-po in the north-east of China, and as a consequence brigandage existed on a very large scale. The famous Kung-sui was appointed to the command of this district, with orders to put down the disorders. Before starting to assume the duties of his office he was asked by the Emperor how he intended to deal with the brigands. He replied that his intention was to turn them into peaceable citizens, "for you know," he said, "the people are poor and the mandarins are bad, and therefore they are to be pitied." When he arrived in his district he gave out that every man that was found with a hoe on his shoulder would be treated as an honest man, whilst everyone with a gun would be proceeded against as an enemy. "Every man that is poor let him come to me, and I will examine his case," he said, "and wherever a farmer has no seed I will assist him." Ere long his people became the most peaceable and happy in the Empire.

Chau Ti, seduced by the promises of some Taoists that they would find the elixir of-life for him, was nearly becoming their dupe as Wu Ti had been, but being warned by his ministers he refused to have anything more to do with them. In the 18th year of his reign a Tartar chief of considerable importance, named Hau-han, made his submission to the Emperor and became tributary. Chau Ti was so overjoyed at this that he built a tower to commemorate this event, which he called "The Unicorn Tower." Eleven statues of the great men that had been prominent in raising the fortunes of the house of Han were placed in it, amongst which were those of

Subu, Ping-kieh and Ho-kwang, though the name of the last was not inscribed on his, because of the treason in his family. After a reign of twenty-five years Chau Ti died, and was succeeded by his son.

Yuan Ti—B. C. 48-32.

This prince was twenty-seven years old when he came to the throne, and with his appearance in history come the first shadows of the coming disasters that were finally to destroy the dynasty. Yuan Ti married a lady, who is best known as the aunt of Wang Mang, a man that played a prominent part in the history of the next three reigns. On his first becoming Emperor he gave every promise of being a wise and statesmanlike ruler. He asked his Prime Minister Kung how he should best rule his people. His reply was, that "Economy, light taxes, and above all profound love for his people, were essential elements in the good government of a nation." The Emperor was so impressed with the truth of this statement that he at once issued an edict to cut down all unnecessary expenses in the royal household, particularly specifying that the number of horses in the stables should be reduced, and that the funds thus saved should be expended in assisting the poor. Unfortunately these bright promises were soon overclouded, as Yuan Ti, instead of being guided in his counsels by the wisest of his ministers, put himself almost absolutely under the control of a eunuch of the palace, who by his ability and shrewdness managed to gain complete mastery over the royal mind. Instead of leading him into good he seduced him into the most immoral habits, that soon made him entirely oblivious of the people's welfare.

In the year B. C. 41 there was a rising of the barbarians that were settled in Shensi, and an army of sixty thousand men was sent against them. The insurrection was put down with terrible severity. Thousands of heads were decapitated and forwarded to the capital for the inspection of the Emperor, and those who survived were so terrified that they fled the kingdom in terror, and the vacated district was ere long occupied by Chinese settlers. The year B. C. 35 was distinguished by a great victory over Chih-chih, a noted chief of the Hiung-nu, who had refused to submit when Hau-han gave in his adhesion to China. The commander of the forces that were guarding the frontiers conceived the idea, whilst there was no suspicion of war, of marching suddenly upon him and surprising him. His second in command refused to consent to this, until they got the permission of the Emperor. Chin-tang was opposed to delay, as he knew the plan would be frustrated by the eunuch Shih-hien, through jealousy of the renown he would obtain if he were successful. He accordingly made several forced marches and managed to surround the capital of Chih-chih with forty thousand men, which he captured and burnt, and sent the head of the chief to Yuan Ti. The latter was prepared to lavish signal honours upon the general for his distinguished services, but the eunuch opposed this. "He deserved punishment," he said, "because he had dared to undertake so perilous an expedition without the permission of the Emperor." Completely under the control of this miserable man Yuan Ti's mind was uncertain how he should act. The whole of his ministers now interposed to save Chin-tang. "He had no doubt been wrong," they said, "in thus acting upon his own responsibility, but his merits far transcended his guilt, and therefore he ought to be rewarded." The result was that he was created a Viscount. Hau-han was now summoned to court, and formally recognized as ruler, both of the territory that used to be his own and also of that over which Chih-chih lately ruled, with the title of king. In order to bind him to the Chinese the famous beauty Chau-kun was given him in marriage, who was elevated to the position of queen when she reached her new home.*

After a reign of sixteen years Yuan Ti died, and was succeeded by has son.

Ch'eng Ti—B. C. 32-6.

The first important act of this monarch was to banish the eunuch who had exerted such a baleful influence over his father to a distant part of the empire. He never reached his destination, however, for through the severity of the journey he died on the way. His next was to ennoble seven of his uncles with the rank of princes and to bestow upon them sufficient territory to enable them to maintain their new rank.

He soon began to show the essentially low and dissipated turn of mind with which he was naturally endowed. He was very fond of going out at nights in disguise and in engaging in the lowest amusements and in associating with men of the vilest character. On one of these midnight adventures he fell in with Chau Fei-yen, with whom he was so bewitched that he took her into his seraglio, and in time, after divorcing his queen, made her his consort.†

---

* This lady is the heroine of a romance that has been translated into English under the title of "The Sorrows of Han." The story of her life in that differs materially from that given in history. In it, it is told how the Khan of the Hiung-nu, hearing of her peerless beauty, invaded China with overwhelming forces and consented to retire only on the condition that Chau-kun should be given him. As she was a member of the Emperor's harem this the latter agreed to, and weeping and sorrowful she was handed over to the savage chief, who carried her away with him. When they reached the banks of the Amoor, however, she managed to escape the vigilance of her guards, and plunging into its waters she was drowned. The historical account is of course the genuine one. See Mayers' Chinese Reader's Manual, page 14.

† Chau Fei-yen was a famous beauty and the daughter of a man of low position in society. She, as well as her sister Ho-tuh, had been trained as dancers, and she was so lithe and graceful that she got the appellation of Fei-yen, or the flying swallow. In time they found their way to the capital, where they became courtesans till their fortunes were changed by meeting with Ch'eng Ti.

In the 18th of this reign Wang Mang comes prominently on to the stage of history. He is represented as a man whose whole aim in life was the gaining of power. His ambition was unbounded, and in obedience to that he made everything he did subservient to this one great purpose. He strove, however, to make men believe that he was animated by the noblest aims. He was diligent in his pursuit of knowledge, he was careful in his expenditure, and he was most subservient to his uncle, who was prime minister. Fortunately for him the sons of the latter were all wild and dissipated, and when their father lay dying it was Wang Mang who waited on him and soothed him in his last hours. This so touched his heart that he strongly recommended him to the Emperor, who at once gave him a high official position. Being a man of great ability his promotion was rapid. All this time he was diligently making friends amongst the great, and with a lavish hand he was giving away his money to those that wished to borrow from him, until he became the most popular man in the palace.

In the year B. C. 7 one of Ch'eng Ti's ministers made an attempt to get the divorced queen into the harem as a concubine. Wang Mang informed the Emperor of what was going on, and he was so pleased with his fidelity that he made him commander-in-chief of all the royal forces and imprisoned the minister. He had now risen to great honour, but still his ambition was unsatisfied. He consequently carried on his dissimulation in order to win golden opinions from those in power. He associated with scholars and put them in important government positions. He divided his salary amongst them, whilst he himself lived in the most modest style, and always wore dresses made of cotton cloth. The one thing real about him was his devotion to his mother, and this, together with his modesty and simplicity, gained him the praises of all classes of people.

Ch'eng Ti died after a reign of twenty-six years. His death was mysterious. The evening previous to it he was in robust health, and had been superintending the making of new seals for some patents of nobility that he was going to issue. Next morning when his attendants entered his room he was found speechless, and shortly after he died. Suspicions were aroused in regard to Ho-tuh, the queen's sister, who had been appointed lady-in-waiting, but though she was examined there was no proof that she was implicated in his death ; still she committed suicide immediately after her examination. As Ch'eng Ti had no son he was succeeded by his nephew.

Ngai Ti—B. C. 6–A. D. 1.

This prince had hardly come to the throne, when Wang Mang resigned all his appointments and retired into private life, though his ambitious designs were never for a moment laid aside. His successor as commander-in-chief was Tung-hien, whose name is associated with the introduction of laws that were intended to effect a radical change in regard to the tenure of land. Observing that the rich and the noble were gradually absorbing the lands of the country, and that vast numbers of people were in great poverty, and could never hope to possess farms of their own, he got the Emperor to pass a law that no one in the empire should possess more than thirty ch'ing of land.* The only classes exempt from the operation of this law were the princes of the blood, dukes and viscounts, to whom the Emperor had made special grants of territories for distinguished services. It was also enacted that no man should possess more than thirty male or female slaves. These laws were not to come into force for three years. After that time any one that possessed more land or slaves than the enactments allowed was to be punished by having the excess confiscated to the state. Great was the consternation amongst the high officials about the court, and especially amongst the royal princes, who possessed large tracts of lands in different parts of the country. They managed to have the promulgation of the edict stopped for several years, so that the nation at large should know nothing of this special legislation. After a brief reign of six years, during which nothing special happened, Ngai Ti died at the early age of twenty-five, and as he had no son to succeed him Hu-how, the Empress-Dowager, who was an ambitious woman, and wished to reign herself, selected a youth of only nine years of age, a great-grandson of Yuan Ti, whom she made Emperor.

P'ing Ti—A. D. 1-6.

Hu-how immediately installed herself as regent and invited Wang Mang to act with her in the government of the country. This position exactly suited the ambitious views of this able and unscrupulous Chinaman. From this time he began gradually to drop the mask he had been wearing so long, and to take measures for the accomplishment of a purpose that had never slumbered, and that was destined to carry him through bloodshed and murder to the highest power in the state.

His first prominent act was to destroy Tung-hien, the able minister who had proposed the new land law, and to seize upon all his money, which history says amounted to an enormous sum. Gradually the whole administration of the government fell into his hands, as the ministers, who were all his own creatures, petitioned the regent not to appear at the council, as Wang Mang was fully competent to relieve her of the burden of governing. After this farce was enacted Wang Mang dismissed or killed all the men of character and integrity in the palace, till he was surrounded only by a set of sycophants, who were ready to carry out every measure that he proposed. In order to deceive the people and make them believe

---

* A ch'ing was equal to about 15.13 square acres.

that his government was the admiration of far-distant nations he bribed men to come with the present of a rare animal, who pretended that they had travelled thousands of miles, when in reality they were a tribe that bordered on China.

In the year A. D. 3 Wang Mang married his daughter to P'ing Ti, and fearful of the influence of his relatives upon him he banished his mother and uncles from the palace. Men now began to talk openly of his intended usurpation of the throne and to condemn him for the crime he meditated. His own son was indignant with him for preventing the young Emperor from seeing his mother, and began to take steps to have this wrong righted, when the father hearing of his intentions cast him into prison, where in anger he poisoned himself. Wang Mang, who had tasted blood, now put the uncles to death, and spared the mother only, because he deemed her too insignificant to be a danger in his path.

When P'ing Ti reached the age of fourteen he began to show signs of resentment against Wang Mang for his treatment of his mother that alarmed him, and he accordingly determined to get rid of him. On New Year's day, when in keeping with the usual custom, the high officials appeared before the Emperor with pepper wine to wish him a happy New Year and long life, he also came with his cup and presented it to P'ing Ti. Being afraid of treason he would not drink it, but Wang Mang forced the liquid down his throat. He was at once seized with sickness, and news spread throughout the palace that the Emperor was dangerously ill. His murderer pretended to be extremely affected about this, and filled the palace with his cries. Imitating the Duke of Chow he appeared in the chief temple in the city, and there before the five great gods he read a paper, in which he entreated them to spare the life of P'ing Ti, and if they demanded a sacrifice let them take his. The document was then dropped into a casket, which was kept in the building for the reception of such, in order that posterity might be deceived in regard to the murder of the king. He forgot that the national historian was, as if with the hand of fate, recording his misdeeds, which should be read by the peoples of China for countless generations.* As P'ing Ti had none to succeed him, a descendant of Suan Ti, a child two years old, was selected by the Queen Dowager, and Wang Mang was named regent. The baby Emperor is known in history by the title of

---

* The historians that record the story of the nation's life belong to the academy, and are solemnly entrusted with a duty that in all the ages of the past they have executed with the utmost fidelity. No one is allowed to see what they write, and so they feel free to record events as they actually occur, without fear of those whose crimes they may describe. There have been times in the past when Emperors or usurpers have demanded to see what they have written about them, but they have refused to comply with such requests, and have even been content to suffer death rather than betray the trust the nation has reposed in them. The records of each dynasty are put away in archives, to which none has access, excepting these historians. When the dynasty passes away it is the business of the next to collect these and make a history of the period during which it exercised power over China.

Ju Tz Ying—A.D. 6-9.

The usurpation of Wang Mang was now apparent to every one, and the princes belonging to the house of Han began to organize measures to resist this.   They were, however, entirely unsuccessful, because the whole power of the army was at the usurper's command, and because he could say to the nation that he was simply regent, and that in opposing the princes he was fighting against men that were in rebellion against their sovereign.   At last, after three years of this farce, he deposed the Emperor and gave him the title of duke, but he put the poor little boy into such strict confinement that he grew up without being taught even how to speak.   He now styled himself the "New Emperor," thus intimating that the old dynasty had passed away and a new one had been inaugurated.   Historians, however, have refused to acknowledge that there was any change of dynasty at this time, and Wang Mang has been known as

Wang Mang, the Usurper—A.D. 9-23.

In order to support his usurpation Wang Mang pretended that he had received a revelation from Kau Ti, the founder of the Han dynasty, giving his sanction to it.   He declared that he had found two caskets in his ancestral temple that had come there mysteriously one night, and which he desired to be opened in the presence of his ministers.   One of them contained a document which declared that Kau Ti specially wished Wang Mang to occupy the throne at this crisis.   The other also had a writing, but it purported to come from the god of heaven and earth, and commanded that all men should accept him as a legitimate monarch and the founder of a new dynasty.   The high officials, with true Chinese complaisance, now formally acknowledged him as Emperor, though they were astute enough to know that the whole thing was a fraud. Wang Mang, apparently overcome by the force of the revelation that he had concocted, gracefully yielded to the wishes of the nobles, and according to royal precedent ordered that the twelfth month of the Hans should be the first in his new dynasty.

Shortly after this event he issued an edict ordering that the laws that had been enacted in a previous reign with regard to the tenure of land and the possession of slaves should now come into operation. Much of his time, however, was taken up in endeavouring to put down the rebellions that, headed by some of the Han princes, sprung up throughout the country.   In order to aim a blow at these leaders of revolt he passed a law that no person of the name of Liu (the royal surname) could hold any official position in the country, and that everyone with that name, from the moment of the passing of the act, should be stripped of every title that he then possessed. This of course robbed every royal prince or noble in the country of the power of using the forces of the state in raising an insurrection. Matters, however, had gone too far for peace to be restored by the passing of an act. Wang Mang had no hold on the affection of the country. He had used his power in a harsh and ungenerous manner, and he had excited the hostility of large classes of people by the unscrupulous way in which he had gradually usurped the functions of the state.

In order to guard against any possible incursion of the Hiung-nu he sent twelve armies under separate generals to different quarters of the frontiers with orders to remain there and be ready for emergencies. These measures had the very opposite effect from what was intended. "We owe submission to the Hans," the barbarians said, "but we now feel free from the obligations under which we were bound, for we utterly refuse to acknowledge any allegiance to Wang Mang, and we shall march on China whenever it is convenient to do so." The history of the subsequent years of his usurpation is that of numerous rebellions that broke out in various parts of the country. The suppression of one had no moral effect in discouraging others. The country had no king, and ambitious spirits everywhere felt that the time had come when they could have a chance for the throne just as much as Wang Mang had had. The most serious of all the risings took place in Shantung, headed by a man named Fan-chung, and lasted for several years, to the great detriment of the country and the grief and sorrow of the people. They pretended to be in rebellion against Wang Mang, but plunder and an easy life were the chief motives that led them to become insurgents. They grew in time to such vast proportions that they could number their men by hundreds of thousands and could defy with impunity the royal forces that were sent against them. In order to show their determination and ferocity their leader ordered their eyebrows to be dyed red. This distinguished them from their foes, and was an omen of the kind of warfare they intended to wage. They declared by this sign that they would not only slay their enemies without mercy, but they would also be ready to shed the last drop of their own blood in defence of the cause for which they had risen in arms. Army after army was sent against them, but they were defeated with great slaughter, and the cause of Wang Mang began gradually to decline.

It was not simply with the "Eyebrows," however, that he had to contend. Rebellion was in the air. His own treason had caused demons of ambition and war to start up in the hearts of men as ambitious as himself, who were determined to fight to the bitter end for the power he now possessed. In the fourteenth year of his usurpation two men, named Liu-huan and Liu-siu, appeared at the head of a formidable gathering, and as they were both of the royal house of Han they soon had an army of a hundred thousand foot and the same number of cavalry at their command. A. a council that was held it was decided that one of the two cousins should be elected to be their chief, and finally, should they be successful, Emperor. Liu-siu was a man of the highest reputation with the army. He was of noble physique, and straightforward in character, so that he had a reputation for honesty and manliness with every one. Liu-huan, on the other hand, was indolent and easy going, and was in his present position simply because he was of the royal blood and had a right to the throne that Wang Mang had not. The leaders unanimously chose Liu-huan, because they dreaded to put a man of such force of character and popularity as Liu-siu over them, and because some of them hoped that his very weakness would present them an opportunity of carrying out their own ambitious plans. The new Emperor is known in history by the name of

Hwai Yang Wang—A. D. 23-25.

Wang Mang, terrified at the progress of events, sent an army of over four hundred thousand men against the new Emperor, but after some slight successes it was defeated, and the enemy marched upon the capital. Everywhere the people submitted to them, and there was no opposition to their entry into it. No sooner had they gained possession of the city than the citizens and soldiers fraternized with them, and rejoicings everywhere showed how detestable the rule of the usurper had been.

Wang Mang, with the cowardice that had always characterized him, fled for refuge to a tower in the city, where he concealed himself. His palace had been set on fire, and he had seen his own daughter throw herself into the flames rather than be captured by the soldiers. Whilst the city was in confusion this wretched man was hidden in the tower, under the firm conviction that his virtues would after all enable him to triumph. He was under the delusion that his miserable life was under the special protection of heaven. In proof of this historians preserve one sentence that he uttered in this crisis of his life : "Heaven produced the virtue that is in me," he said ; "the house of Han, what can it do to me?"*

Wang Mang soon found to his sorrow that heaven would not interfere on his behalf, for ere long the tower was filled with soldiers and citizens, who seized him, and, after beheading him, cut him into a thousand pieces. His head was hung in the market place, and soon in contempt it was tossed about in the streets by the people over whom he had tyrannized.

Hwai Yang Wang proved himself incompetent for the position to which he had been elected. Whilst his cousin was away battling with armies and winning victories he gave himself up to all kinds

---

* This was a quotation with a slight change from Confucius, who said, Heaven produced the virtue that is in me. Hwan-t'ui, what can he do to me? This expression was used by the great sage when he was on his way from the principality of Sung to that of Ts'in. Whilst performing some ceremonies under a tree he was attacked by Hwan-t'ui, who wished to kill him. His disciples were terrified, but Confucius was calm, under the conviction that he was sent of heaven, and that therefore no mortal hand could injure him.

of dissipation and amusement. The affairs of state were left entirely
to the mercy of the mercenary officials that surrounded him.
These quarrelled amongst themselves as to who should hold the
highest offices. Justice and right were obtained by bribery, and
the people were taxed and crushed by their rulers in the mad race
for wealth. In the meanwhile those about the Emperor whispered
in his ears that Liu-siu was becoming famous, and that he would
before long overshadow him, and they counselled him to order his
return to the capital, where he would be under his own immediate
supervison. When the command reached him in Honan his
generals dissuaded him from obeying it, on the ground that he
would certainly be murdered at the instigation of men that wished
to get rid of him. They declared that neither they nor the army
would ever consent to acknowledge Hwai Yang, who was utterly
useless as a ruler at this crisis when the kingdom was rent with
rebellion and when the " Eyebrows " required a general that could
crush them. Yielding to their entreaties, because he knew that his
own life was in danger, he at last consented to be made Emperor,
and he is known in history under the title of Kwang Wu Ti, or the
Glorious Martial Emperor.

CHAPTER X.

THE LATER HAN DYNASTY.

Also styled Eastern Han, from its Capital being at Lohyang.
A. D. 25-221.

Kwang Wu Ti—A. D. 25-58.

THE difficulty as to what Kwang Wu Ti should do in regard to his cousin, who now divided the empire with him, was settled by the "Red Eyebrows." They marched all their forces from the east and besieged Hwai Yang Wang in his capital at Ch'ang-ngan, and after a very feeble resistance captured it. With the ruthless ferocity of robbers they not only murdered a great many of its citizens, but Hwai Yang Wang himself, who had surrendered to the rebel chief. Kwang Wu, who was of a noble, generous disposition, hearing of the advance of the rebels on the old capital, had sent an army of twenty thousand men under the famous general Teng-yu* to the succour of the city, and had given express orders that none should injure his cousin unless he wished to excite his displeasure and punishment. When Teng-yu arrived the city had been already captured, and as the forces of the rebels were far in excess of his own all that he could do was to entrench his army and wait for a favourable moment to strike. That he was not wanting in bravery is evidenced by the fact that shortly after, when he did engage the enemy, his men fought so bravely and stubbornly that out of all his host only twenty-four ever reached their homes. In the 2nd year of Kwang Wu Ti the capital of the re-established dynasty was set up in Lohyang. The "Red Eyebrows" were still in possession of Ch'ang-ngan, as well as the region which they had desolated with their plundering and marauding. The Emperor thought it was now high time to measure his forces with an enemy that was a national danger. In order to give them the semblance of right in their rebellion they had raised a young man to the throne by the name of Liu, the family name of the royal family, and they asserted that they were acting under his authority. But this was a farce that deceived no one.† Kwang Wu sent another of his great generals, P'ing-i, who managed to completely crush out the rebellion by his military tactics.

---

* This man was one of the twenty-eight commanders who assisted in establishing the dynasty, and whose portraits had the honour of being placed in the "Cloud Tower" which was built by Ming-ti in A. D. 60 in his southern palace.

† The young man who was suddenly elevated by the rebels to this high position was only fifteen years old, and was taken from the very lowest ranks of life. He was a cowherd of the name of Liu-pun. His clothes were in rags, his hair dishevelled, and he was barefooted when he was first elected. When the chiefs came round him and paid him obeisance as their sovereign he was so startled that he burst into tears.

Before his great engagement which he had determined to have with them he dressed several thousands of his soldiers in the same kind of clothing as the rebels and painted their eyebrows red. He then placed them in ambush, whilst he sent a strong division a long way round to the rear of the enemy. The battle began in the morning and lasted the whole of the day, with varying success, until the ambushed contingent appeared upon the field. The "Eyebrows" thought it was a party of their own men that had come up to their rescue, and were welcoming them with raptures of joy, when all at once they were fiercely assaulted by them. The insurgents were at once routed, and fled in the greatest consternation, but before long they were met by the force that had been sent to intercept them, and being thus placed between two fires they threw down their arms and submitted. The only conditions they could secure were that their lives should be spared. The rebel Emperor and his chiefs were made petty mandarins, whilst the great force that had so recently threatened the very safety of the state gradually dissolved and melted into society.

For the next few years the Emperor's forces were engaged throughout the country in attacking the leaders of insurrection that had risen in arms against Wang Mang, and who still competed with Kwang Wu for the possession of the throne. They were one after the other defeated, until at last Kwang Wu found the house of Han once more firmly established in the kingdom.

Although so successful as a warrior Kwang Wu was a man of so kindly a nature and of such large sympathies that the arts of peace had a greater attraction for him than those of war. He spent the most of his time in study and in converse with literary men. He refused to talk even about war. On one occasion when his son asked him to tell him how armies were marshalled in the field and how they were marched he replied to him : "When the Duke Ling, of Wei, asked Confucius very much the same questions that you have enquired of me, he answered, 'I have heard about the vessels that are used in sacrifices, but I have not studied military questions;' so I say to you, my son, don't desire to know about armies and warfare, but rather spend your strength in mastering the principles of good government, so that in time you may be able to rule your people well."

His kindly disposition was also shown in the manner in which he treated a number of his followers who had distinguished themselves by their valour when they were fighting in his cause. A considerable number of these were at his court. Calling them together he spoke to them of his gratitude to them for the illustrious services they had rendered him, and begged them to allow him to give them a little advice. "You will be expecting, of course," he said, "that I should reward your services by giving you official posts under the government. This I could easily do, but there is danger in this to yourselves. Many men who have been distinguished in the field have lost their good name when they became mandarins, through the temptations connected with their office, and have died dishonoured. Now what I advise is that you should all retire to your homes. I will give you presents of money and lands that will enrich you, and there amongst your relatives and the people in the midst of whom you were reared you may enjoy yourselves.'' It is needless to say that they accepted his offer with the greatest avidity, and thus he not only rewarded these distinguished soldiers in a way that would bring honour to them amongst their friends, but he also removed them from the temptations of the capital and from the seductions of evil men to use their military knowledge against the state.

Amongst the most notable of his wars was the one which he was compelled to wage against the modern Tonquin, in order to prevent it from casting off its allegiance to China. A female chieftain, of the name of Ching-tseh, had headed a rising of her countrymen, in order to shake off the Chinese supremacy. Kwang Wu, kind and generous though he was, could not afford to lose prestige by allowing so important a tributary as this to defy its suzerain. He accordingly sent one of the most famous generals of the age, Ma-yuan, to suppress the rebellion. This intrepid commander embarked part of his army in junks on the Canton river and sent it by sea, whilst he led the remainder overland. He was completely successful in all his operations. The heroic Ching-tseh, together with her sister Ching-urh, were seized and beheaded, for there was not enough chivalry in those days to make men look with admiration upon the noble efforts of these two women to free their country, or to cause them to spare lives. To commemorate his successful campaign Ma-yuan erected a pillar of bronze on the boundary of the country that future generations might not forget the victory he had won. *

In the year A.D. 48 Ma-yuan again at his own request was sent in conjunction with another commander with forty thousand men to suppress a rising of some native tribes in Wuling, in the present province of Hunan. Disagreeing with his second in command in regard to the route they should take after they entered the hostile territory Ma-yuan led his army into a district where it suffered terribly from disease, and more than half his men died.

---

* Four years after (A.D. 45) this veteran general, finding that the Hiung-nu were again invading the northern frontiers, asked permission to lead the armies of the Emperor against them. Out of pity for his old age the latter gently expressed his doubts about his being able to do so at his time of life. The old hero declared that he could wear his armour and mount his horse with the youngest. Upon Kwang Wu's expressing a wish to see him do so he had his orderly bring his weapons, and mounting his horse rode in front of him. He was so delighted with this exhibition of his strength that he cried out, '' How strong and stalwart is this old man !'' When he was leaving the palace to join the army the great officers came to the gate of the city to see him off, when, just as he was departing, he said, '' A man ought to die in the field fighting with his enemies, and be brought home wrapped in a horse skin, rather than die in his bed surrounded by his weeping wife and children.''

He had his wish in not dying at home, for he too succumbed to the prevailing epidemic, and his body was carried home in the way he had desired. Immediately upon his death being made known, his enemies at court brought the most serious charges against him, viz., that in his Touquin compaign he had secretly brought back immense quantities of pearl and ivory, which really belonged to the state, but which he had appropriated to his own use. His widow, indignant at the charges which she knew were unfounded, hastily buried the corpse of her husband in a private way and demanded an investigation of these and the restoration of her husband's good name, after which, she said, a proper funeral should be given him. A commission was appointed for this purpose, when it turned out that all the precious things he had brought with him was a chariot load of the seeds of the water lily, which were considered a specific against infectious diseases. The old general, whilst so lavish of his life in the presence of the enemy, had yet with a natural instinct been desirous of preserving it against disease, and so he had taken the trouble of bringing across the empire these seeds that gave an occasion for the calumnies of his enemies. The charges made were proved to be false, and so his reputation stood still higher than it did before. Kwang Wu died in the thirty-third year of his reign and in the sixty-third of his life, and was succeeded by his son.

Ming Ti—A.D. 58-76.

This prince was thirty years of age when he ascended the throne. He found the empire at peace, in consequence of his father's vigor and the ability of the great captains that with true military instincts he had gathered around him. In this third year he married Ma-how, the daughter of Ma-yuan, who is celebrated in history for her intelligence and virtue and for the simple way in which she dressed and conducted herself generally.*

In his third year he built the famous "Cloud Tower," in which were placed the portraits of the twenty-eight great generals that had been the means of re-establishing the Han dynasty. Ma-yuan had not the honour of a place in it from a false feeling of etiquette. The Emperor was afraid that the people would say that he had such an honour done to his memory, simply because his daughter was queen, and so the great commander was excluded from the company of those amongst whom by right he would have taken the first place. This Emperor has the unenviable reputation of having introduced Buddhism and consequently idolatry into China. Hearing that there was a very powerful and influential spirit in the west named Fo (Buddha) he sent ambassadors to make investigations into its

---

* She was childless, but the Emperor was so fond of her that he did not find fault with her for this, and he got her to adopt her cousin's son, who was a member of the Seraglio, named Kia. She bestowed extreme love upon this child, and so treated him as her own that he did not know till he had become Emperor, and she was dead, that she was not his own mother.

nature and powers, with orders to learn what its teachings were and to bring back all books that taught the doctrines that were inculcated amongst its disciples. He did this in the eighth year of his reign (A. D. 65).

In due time his messengers reached India, where they came in contact with Buddhism. They collected a number of its books, and, what was still more important, they persuaded some of its priests to return with them to China, in order to instruct the Emperor and his court in the mysteries of the new faith. History records that Buddhism was received by the learned with a great deal of scepticism, as the priests brought forward the most unreliable statements as evidence of its truth. There were five main doctrines that it inculcated:—first, the forbidding of the destruction of animal life; second, metempsychosis; third, rewards and punishments for good and evil conduct; fourth, meditation and absorption in thought; and fifth, abstinence and self-denial through which men might become gods. The Emperor at once accepted the new faith as part of his own religion, and temples were built in the capital, and the people imitating the court, others were ere long erected in other parts of the country.

During this year the criminal law was revised, and it was decided that capital crimes might be commuted by a money payment, or by the criminals being sent to the frontiers to be enrolled in the army that was stationed there to repel the Hiung-nu. Less serious offences were remitted by a money fine at a fixed rate for certain breaches of law. This showed that the government was distressed for want of funds to carry on the business of the country, as this remission of crime by a pecuniary payment was a favorite resource with the rulers of ancient times when the finances were low. The remainder of this reign was spent in comparative peace. There were indeed one or two risings against the throne, but they were soon put down. One was headed by the Emperor's younger brother, whom he had treated with the greatest kindness. The court officials were urgent in their demands that he should be put to death, but Ming Ti was unwilling to do this, so he was banished, but on his way to the place appointed he committed suicide. After a reign of eighteen years he died, and was succeeded by his son.

Chang Ti—A. D. 76-89.

This prince ascended the throne under the most favourable circumstances. The country was at peace, and the Hiung-nu were quiet within their own territories. He had besides the advantage of the wisdom and virtue of his mother Ma-chi to help him in his plans for the good government of his people. As he was only eighteen years of age it may well be imagined what valuable service she could render him at this time. Unfortunately, his barbarian foes, despising the young Emperor, and thinking that the time was opportune for another invasion of China, gathered their hordes, and once more marched on the northern frontiers. Fortunately, at this time the Chinese were supplied with generals of the highest order, who were quite competent to meet the invading forces. Tau-hien and Pan-ch'au in A. D. 80, and again in A. D. 88, defeated them with great slaughter. In the first engagement the latter had the command of the troops, but in the second they had joint control.* After a quiet and uneventful reign of thirteen years Chang Ti died at the age of thirty-one and was succeeded by

Ho Ti—A. D. 89-106.

As the young Emperor was only ten years of age, his mother, the Empress-Dowager Tau, was appointed regent.† During the first year of his reign an incident occurred that led to great wars and important successes that raised the fame of China as a military power higher than ever it had been before. On the accession of Ho Ti the princes and viceroys, as in duty bound, came to pay their respects and renew their oaths of allegiance to the new sovereign. His cousin Tau-hien, who had once acted as chamberlain in the palace, but had subsequently been raised to the position of commander-in-chief, also attended. Being jealous of one of the nobles that presented himself he caused him to be murdered. According to law he ought to have paid the penalty of his crime with his life, but he begged so hard for mercy, and that he should be allowed to redeem his wrong by fighting with the Hiung-nu, the hereditary enemies of China, that his aunt, the regent, granted his petition and set him free.

The high officials were exceedingly opposed to any warlike measure being adopted against the barbarians, but the Queen-Dowager refused to listen to their arguments, and Tau-hien was appointed to take command of a large army, with Pan-ch'au as his lieutenant, to proceed at once against the Hiung-nu. He led his forces into Central Asia, and there achieved a splendid victory over the enemy near Yen-jan, in memory of which he ordered an account of the battle to be engraven on the rocks near by.

On his return to China he was loaded with honours, but his haughty demeanour excited the suspicion of his cousin, whom he was too much inclined to treat as an equal. Not long after he joined in a conspiracy with the Tau princes to dethrone Ho Ti, but their plans becoming known, the latter consulted with the chief of his eunuchs, and on a certain day the gates of the city were suddenly closed, and a body of troops having been led to the palace, Tau-hien and all the members of the Tau clan were massacred.

---

* Pan-ch'an had previously distinguished himself in Turkestan, in the state of Shen-shen and in Khoten, in his wars with the Hiung-nu. Some time after the victory in A. D. 88 he led his men as far as the region of the Caspian. He died in the year A. D. 102.

† There are four persons mentioned with this name of Tau in history. (1) The Queen of Wun Ti. B. C. 179; (2) The Queen of Chang Ti, A.D. 79; (3) The Queen of Hwan Ti, A. D. 165; (4) The Queen of Kau Tsu, A. D. 618.

For this service the eunuch was made a high mandarin, and was called to the councils of the Emperor in the government of the empire. This was a most dangerous innovation on previous custom. No eunuch up to this time had ever had such an honour conferred upon him, but well would it have been for posterity had the eunuchs been sternly relegated to their own special duties within the palace. It would have saved the empire from many a sorrow and have prevented the pages of history from being blotted with the accounts of their intrigues and seditions, which led to the murder of kings and the overthrow of dynasties.

In the year A. D. 96 a great drought was experienced in the northern part of the empire, and the people were reduced to such extremities that vast numbers of them perished of starvation. The Emperor did everything in his power to relieve them, and he remitted all taxes due to the government for this year. Six years after he divorced his queen and married a granddaughter of the famous general Teng-yu, mentioned in the previous pages. About this same time Pan-ch'au, feeling himself worn out with old age and the toils of many a severe campaign, asked permission to be allowed to retire from active service. Unwilling to lose the advice and influence of such a distinguished man Ho Ti at first refused to do so, but finally, through the intercession of Pan-ch'au, the desired leave was granted.*

The Emperor Ho Ti had been very unfortunate in his sons, for they were all weakly, and several of them had died. Two remained, but they were so frail and delicate that in order to give them a chance for life they were put out to nurse, in order to preserve them, if possible, from the fate of their brothers. When the Emperor died, which he did after a reign of seventeen years, the elder of the two was rejected, because of his state of health, and the younger, who was only a little over three months old, was proclaimed successor to the throne. He is known in history by the title of

Shang Ti—A. D. 106-107. He died in eight months, and was succeeded by

Ngan Ti—A.D. 107-126.

This ruler was a nephew of Ho Ti, and was twelve years old when he came to the throne. The widow of Ho Ti, who was appointed regent on his death, was again asked to fulfil the same

---

* Pan-ch'au is a famous literary character, whose name is well known among the scholars of every age. Her brother Pan-hu was historiographer under Ming Ti, who appointed him to this office for the pr pose of compiling the history of the Western Han Dynasty from the documents that had been accumulating during its existence in the historical archives. He was engaged in the composition of a work on history and philosophy, but before he could complete it he was involved in the conspiracy of Tau-hien, and being cast into prison he died there. The Emperor Ho Ti subsequently commissioned his gifted sister with the duty of finishing it. She also wrote a work entitled " Lessons for Women," which had a great reputation amongst scholars. When her husband died she was admitted into the palace in the capacity of Lady-in-waiting to the Empress. See Mayer's Chinese Reader's Manual, page 166.

duty for the present Emperor. She was a woman well qualified for this responsible position. In her second year of power the country was afflicted with a great drought. She was greatly distressed at this, and supposed it must have been caused by some misgovernment of hers, by which there had been a failure of justice. She accordingly examined into all the cases where men had been condemned to death, but who had not yet been executed. The result was that she found a considerable number that had been adjudged to die unjustly. These she caused to be set at liberty, and it is said that copious rains at once fell throughout the country, and the drought was at an end.

It is pleasant to think that amidst the general corruption of those in high places there were men of honour in the service of the state who felt the responsibility of their exalted position and were determined to act so as to gain the approval of the best of mankind. One of these was Yang-chun, who, though he became a great mandarin, still continued to be poor, to the great discontent of his own family. When they urged him to consider them and to plan more for the enriching of them he said he had done so ; for the greatest wealth he could give them he believed to be the inheritance of a spotless character. One night a man for whom he had done some favour came secretly to him and urged upon his acceptance a considerable sum of money, saying that no one need know anything about the transaction. He utterly refused to receive it, and said, "You are quite mistaken when you say that no one would ever know that you gave it me. Heaven would know, the earth would know, and you and I would know. I beg you, therefore, to take back your gift, for I dare not receive it."

In the year A. D. 110 a formidable outbreak of brigandage occurred in Honan, caused almost entirely through the poverty of the people, bad harvests, and the misrule of the local authorities. Yu-hu, an official of great merit and distinction, was appointed with full powers to put it down, which he did within a year. It was by an ingenious device that he succeeded in his object so soon. When he arrived in the district over which he had authority he issued a notice that he was going to organize a military force that should consist of three classes of men, to whom immunity for all past offences was promised. The first was to consist of those who had committed robbery and murder, and to these a considerable monthly salary was to be paid ; the second, of those that had been merely robbers, and they were to be paid less ; and the third, of men that had joined the brigands because they were lazy and liked an easy life. These were to receive a still smaller salary. Before long between two and three hundred men were enrolled in this new kind of regiment. Yu-hu had them paraded before him, when he addressed them and told them that their past was now all forgiven, but he expected them to atone for the wrongs they had done society by discovering to him their old comrades who had not answered to his call.   This they did, and the result was the utter extinction of the robber fraternity.

In his seventh year Ngan Ti issued an edict ordering all the officials in the empire to report to him the names and histories of men in common life who had distinguished themselves for virtue and filial piety, so that he might reward them by making them government officials.   Next year his son Po was appointed successor to the throne, and about the same time he made one of the eunuchs member of the Privy Council.   He also elevated his foster mother, who had nursed him as a baby, and of whom he was inordinately fond, together with her daughter Peh-ying, to be officials ; the first instance in history of such an anomaly.   The result was most disastrous.   From this time corruption prevailed throughout the court, and justice was perverted and honest men driven from it by the shameless system of bribery that these two women openly carried on under the protection of the Emperor.

Ngan Ti died after a reign of nineteeen years, whilst making a visitation through a portion of his kingdom.   His queen, who was afraid that Po would avenge his mother, whom she had caused to be murdered,* immediately appointed one of the descendants of Chang Ti to be Emperor.   As he was but a child she established herself as regent, and she made her brother Yen-hien commander-in-chief.   This man at once ordered the execution of the eunuch who had been so powerful during Ngan Ti's reign, and banished Wang-sheng and her daughter Peh-ying to a distant part of the empire.   The infant that had been made Emperor, but whom history declines to recognize, died after six months, when the great officials insisted upon the rightful heir to the crown being acknowledged.   The Queen-Dowager, finding her power gone, wisely yielded to the force of circumstances, and giving her consent, Po succeeded to the throne of his father.   His historical name is

Shun Ti—A. D. 126-145.

The first official act of this young sovereign, who was only thirteen, was to order the execution of Yen-hien and the imprisonment of the Queen-Dowager, who from this time drops out of history.   In his seventh year a very important law was passed that no persons henceforward could hold any government employment unless they had been brought forward by the magistrates of their districts as men noted for their filial piety and for their purity of character.   They must also be at least forty years old.   Nine years went by without anything of importance happening in the state, when (A. D. 141) a serious outbreak of brigandage took place in the region in which the capital was situated.   Alarmed by this the Emperor appointed Li-ku, an able and upright mandarin, to endeavour to suppress it and to enquire into the causes that produced it.   An

---

* The queen had no children of her own ; so she adopted Po, the son of one of the ladies of the harem, whom, to avoid friction, she caused to be put to death.

investigation brought to light that the officials, by their injustice and rapacity, were entirely responsible for the disturbances. He degraded forty of these, and would have punished more, but he was stopped in his good work by some of the accused bribing Liang-ki, who influenced Shun-ti to remove Li-ku to another district.*

The young Emperor had the determination to rule his country with justice, but the influence of his queen Liang, and her corrupt and ambitious brother, frustrated every effort that he made to do so. In the year A. D. 142 eight great mandarins were ordered to proceed throughout the country and examine into the conduct of the rulers. The bad were to be reported that they might be punished, and the good that they might be rewarded. One of these was observed to be in the capital after his colleagues had started on their journey. The Emperor summoned him to his presence and asked him the reason of this. His reply was significant, "Why should I go through the country looking for foxes when the big tiger is in the palace?" He then proceeded to an indictment of Liang-ki and brought forward fifteen serious charges, for any one of which he was worthy of condign punishment. The Emperor had not the courage to stand by this faithful officer against a man of such power, and so nothing was done to curb the wrong doing of Liang-ki, who soon found an opportunity of revenging himself on his accuser by having him transferred to a distant part of the empire, from which he was never allowed to return. Shun-ti died, and was succeeded by his son.

Ch'ung Ti—A. D. 145-146.

This child, who was only two years old when he came to the throne, died in a year, and was followed by

Chih Ti—A. D. 146-147.

This ruler was a descendant of Chang-ti in the sixth generation, and was only eight years old when the perilous honour was thrust upon him. The Queen-Dowager Liang, who had acted as regent since her husband's death, was still continued in office, who, with her brother, now absorbed in themselves all the power of the state. The regent had the merit of appointing one loyal man, Li-ku, to assist her in the government. One important measure proposed by him that became law was that all students, after they had mastered the Confucian classics, should repair to the capital to spend three years in the study of law and of the methods of governing a state. After that time they were to pass an examination, and the fittest were to be selected and made magistrates. In one year thirty thousand assembled in Lohyang in obedience to this decree.

The young prince, though of so tender years, was a keen discerner of character, and instinctively could mark out the good

---

* Liang-ki was a brother of the queen, and a famous actor in the tragedies that were soon to be enacted in the House of Han.

and bad officials that thronged his court. Liang-ki was his special aversion, and he could not bear the sight of him. One day when the latter was entering the palace he said to one near him, "There goes a man of perverse temper." This fatal speech cost him his life. It was repeated to Liang-ki, who sent him some poisoned cakes, of which he ate and died. Another descendant of Chang-ti, a youth of fifteen years, was now approved of by the murderer, and he became Emperor. He is known by the name of

Hwan Ti—A.D. 147-168.

Although the regency was continued in the hands of the Queen-Dowager the real power was exercised by her brother. He was invested with a grant of territory that contained thirty thousand families, together with all the revenues that came from it. About the same time his younger sister was married to the Emperor, so that the family of the Liang seemed firmly established in the highest honours.

Hwan-ti took the government into his own hands when he was nineteen, and he made Liang-ki his prime minister. The arrogance of the latter was only the more increased by these facilities for power that seemed naturally to come to him, and the consequence was he became more insolent in his conduct and did things that no other in his position would have ventured to have done. On one occasion he had the audacity to appear at an audience with his sword on. This was a capital offence, and some of the mandarins cried out that punishment should be meted out to him, but the Emperor, in consideration of his having placed him on the throne, and because of his relationship to him, spared his life, and only punished him by fining him a year's salary.

In the year A.D. 158 one of the censors petitioned the throne, stating that the miseries of the empire were extending in consequence of the misrule of Liang-ki and his excessive exactions. Next day, when he should have appeared before the privy council to explain his charges, it was found that he was dead, having been murdered by the premier's authority. In the following year the Queen-Dowager died. Together with Liang-ki she had exercised rule for twenty years, during which time the latter had used it so arbitrarily that he had excited universal hatred. His last act of cruelty was the cause of his overthrow and death. For some reason or other he had determined on the death of the father of one of Hwan-ti's most beloved concubines. The men that were coming to murder him had reached the door of his house, when he managed to escape to the palace and appeal to the Emperor for protection. This he at once granted him, and ordered a thousand of the household troops to march to Liang-ki's and put him to death. Before the latter was aware of it his house was surrounded, and knowing full well that the hour of reckoning had come, and that no mercy would be shown him, he and his wife put an end to their lives by drinking a deadly poison. All the members of both sides of his house were ruthlessly slain, and all his treasures of money, for which he had bartered his honour and his reputation, were seized and confiscated to the state. It is said that these amounted to three hundred millions of taels. *

In consequence of this vast amount being added to the treasury the whole of the taxes throughout the country were remitted for one year. In the 19th year of his reign Hwan-ti commissioned a eunuch to build a temple in Lung Hu Shan, in the present province of Kiangsi, in honour of Lau-tze, the founder of Tauism. He also appointed a man of the clan of Chang to be the high priest of the sect, with the title of "Heaven's Teacher." This office is still in existence, and the reputed successors of this man exercise his functions with the same title and in the same manner as he did seventeen centuries ago. †

This same year the Emperor put away his queen and married the daughter of Tau-bu, who became prime minister, being at the same time ennobled with the title of viscount. After a reign of twenty-one years he died, and having no children of his own a descendant of Chang-ti was selected to succeed him.

Ling Ti—A.D. 168-190.

As this prince was only twelve years old the Queen-Dowager was appointed regent, whilst her father still continued in his office of prime minister. The latter was loyal and sound-hearted, and wished to govern the kingdom with justice, but he was thwarted in all his efforts by the eunuchs, who through the folly of preceding monarchs had attained to the highest power and offices in the state. Not only had they been given titles that carried with them control over considerable districts of country, but they had also been permitted to adopt children who could succeed to their honour and estates. Tau-bu, in conjunction with another, schemed their destruction. A letter was sent by him to the regent detailing a plan by which they might all be murdered. Unfortunately this fell into the hands of the chief eunuch, who, seeing the peril that hung over him and all his fraternity in the palace, determined to save himself by the destruction of Tau-bu. He instantly sought Ling Ti and persuaded him that the latter was plotting his dethronement and murder. Terrified by the fearful picture that this wretched man drew of the horrors that were in store for him he signed a decree ordering the instant execution of Tau-bu and his colleague, and more than a thousand of their friends and adher-

---

* "The standard tael weighs 579.84 grs. or about 1½ oz. It is worth from $1.38 to $1.47, according to its purity, and is usually reckoned at six shillings and eightpence." With the reduction in the price of silver the present value of the tael has considerably diminished. See Williams' Dictionary, page 526.

† This patriarch of the Tauist body was named Chang Tau-ling, and his residence was called "The Palace of the Supreme Azure." The idol which was placed in the new temple was styled Li Peh-yung, a name by which Lau-tze was known.

ents were slain, whilst the regent was banished to a distant part of the empire. In the seventh year of Ling Ti's reign a serious rebellion broke out in the present province of Chehkiang, but it was suppressed by an army under General Sun-kien. Next year the famous scholar Ts'ai-yung was engaged in superintending the cutting on stone tablets of the authorized text of the Five Classics.* The characters were written so beautifully that thousands of scholars came from far and near to take impressions of them, and crowds of wealthy people came in their chariots to ·witness this exhibition of this distinguished scholar's learning.

In the year A. D. 177 a formidable tribe called the Sienpi made an irruption into China, but they were defeated by the skill and bravery of Chau-pau. It is said that on their march they seized his mother, and when the two armies came in front of each other they dragged the old lady and placed her where her son could see her, and threatened that unless he submitted to them they would murder her before his very eyes. A terrible conflict ensued in Chau-pau's breast as to whether he should betray his country or abandon his mother to a terrible death. Loyalty to his Emperor prevailed and the barbarians carried out their fierce purpose in the sight of the horrified Chinese soldiers ; but a fearful retribution fell upon them. Infuriated by the spectacle the soldiers sprung upon the enemy, when a terrible slaughter ensued. Thousands were slain upon the field, and those that could escape fled terror-stricken across the borders into their own territories. Not long after Chau-pau died of grief. "If I had betrayed my country," he said, "I should have been disloyal. I have been the cause, however, of my mother's death, and so I have been unfilial." This thought made his life so wretched that he pined away, and ere long joined his mother in the spirit land.

The following year is a famous one in the annals of China, for in it the system of examination for degrees, similar to that which exists at the present day, was first put into practice. Hitherto the recognized plan had been to promote to the magistracy and other government offices those that were distinguished for their filial piety, or their purity of character. From this time it was no longer a question of morals but of education. The candidates were to be examined in the Confucian classics, in the writing of poetry, in letter writing and in penmanship.

In the 11th year of his reign Ling Ti raised his concubine, the Lady Ho, to the rank of queen, and she and another member of the harem had each a son, of whom we shall hear more by and by. Through her influence her brother Ho-tsin was made prime minister, a very exalted position for him, for he came from a very low rank in society, and before long he was made commander-in-chief of all the royal forces. The year A. D. 184 may be said to

---

* These were the Book of Changes, the Historical Classic, the Book of Poetry, the Record of Rites and the Spring and Autumn.

have ushered in the series of calamities that brought about the downfall of the Han dynasty. Chang-kioh, a native of North-eastern China, who pretended to have a knowledge of the occult arts, raised a rebellion, and in a very short time gained possession of all the northern provinces. His followers were known as the "Yellow Turbans." An army was sent against them under Ho-tsin, and his two famous lieutenants—Tung-cho and Ts'au-ts'au.* The rebels, after several months' most sanguinary warfare, were subdued, and peace was once more restored to the country, but it was only the lull that preceded the hurricane.

Ling Ti died after a reign of twenty-two years, and his son succeeded him ; his widow being appointed regent. One of the ministers now advised Ho-tsin to put an end to the tyranny of the eunuchs by the massacre of the entire body of them. He gladly listened to this advice, but his sister refused to give her consent, because of the cruelty of the plan. Upon this a scheme was devised for bringing the army under Tung-cho to the capital and of using it to destroy these wretched men. Ts'au-ts'au opposed this, on the ground of the great danger of doing so in the present weak condition of the executive ; but his counsels were unheeded, and Tung-cho was ordered to march with all his forces to Lohyang. This command was obeyed with the greatest pleasure, for this commander was ambitious, and he saw in the present disturbed condition of things an opportunity for advancing his own interests, and perhaps finally for becoming Emperor.

The arrival of this army at the capital now drove the eunuchs to extreme measures, for they had found out by this time that their destruction was determined upon. They were decided that they would not tamely submit to this, and as they believed the death of Ho-tsin would mean their deliverance from their peril they devised a plan by which he was to be got out of the way. Issuing an order as if from the regent to present himself at the palace, Ho-tsin, too confident of success and unsuspecting treachery, obeyed the order, but he had no sooner got within its walls than he fell beneath the knives of the infuriated eunuchs. Their triumph, however, was but short-lived. One of his generals, suspecting foul play, set fire to the palace, when the eunuchs, to the number of two thousand, streamed out with the young Emperor and his brother, and fled towards one of the gates of the city. The troops led by Yuan-shan set upon them with the greatest fury, and with the exception of a few, who managed to escape, they were all slain.† The young princes escaped to the hills, but they were brought back to the palace next day, where the regent was discovered hidden away in an inner room. At this crisis Tung-cho stepped out from the comparative

---

* The three famous traitors of the Han dynasty were—War̄g-mang, Tung-cho and Ts'au-ts'au.

† Yuan-shan was a commander under Tung-cho, but he deserted his standard when he found him harbouring traitorous designs. He joined Ts'au-ts'au and became the leader of the party that opposed Tung-cho's pretensions.

obscurity in which he had hitherto lived and took the direction of the state into his own hands. Observing that the young Emperor was the stronger-minded of the two brothers he deposed him and proclaimed the other as sovereign of China. He then put the regent to death and assumed that office himself. The boy prince that was now made ruler is known by the title of

Hien Ti—A. D. 190-221.

The throne to which this youth now succeeded was one full of peril to one much stronger in intellect than he. A man of indomitable will and stern in purpose might have weathered the storms that were gathering thick and dark around the house of Han, but for Hien-ti there was no hope. His mind was weak and imbecile, and utterly incapable of coping with the daring spirits that were already stretching forth their hands to grasp the sceptre that was falling from his feeble hands.

Tung-cho soon showed what kind of a man he was by murdering the deposed Emperor, and by acts of cruelty such as aroused a bitter hatred against him in the breasts of all classes of people. Yuan-shan became the leader of a powerful party that were determined to resist the usurpation of this upstart, but Tung-cho unfortunately had the advantage of legality on his side, for he could declare that all he did was sanctioned by the young Emperor, for whom he was acting. The confederates finding it dangerous to remain in the capital fled with their followers to different parts of the country, and there unfurled the flag of rebellion. Liu-piau, a scion of the house of Han, subdued a considerable territory to the south of the Yang-tze and ruled there till his death. Ts'au-ts'au fled to Shantung and gathered large bodies of men around him, with which ere long he raised himself to almost regal power. Sun-kien, who ruled in Wu, the modern Kiangsu and Chehkiang, also opposed Tung-cho, but he was killed in battle, leaving four sons, two of whom became distinguished in the coming struggles. Liu-chiong became supreme in Sz-chwan, till finally he was dispossessed by Liu-pei, whose romantic story, and those of the heroes that fought with him, have supplied the writers of romance with marvellous tales and hair-breadth escapes such as have thrilled the hearts of countless readers ever since.

Tung-cho, alarmed by the near proximity of some of the able men that were in arms against him, determined to remove his capital from Lohyang to the old one in Shensi. The former at this time was said to contain several millions of people, and the vast palaces that had been built and gradually added to in the course of time, to occupy an area of nearly forty miles in circumference. The most loyal and patriotic of the high officials opposed this, but an unanswerable reply to their protests was an order for their execution.

Having made up his mind to the removal Tung-cho had it carried out in the savage barbaric manner that suited the cruel character of his mind. First of all, the great palaces that contained the records of the doings and tragedies of the past centuries were set on fire and burnt to the ground. The houses of the people were then entered and plundered of their most valuable property by bands of robbers that collected amidst all this disorder and misrule. Even the very tombs of the mighty dead were opened and stripped of the treasures they contained. After the struggling, sorrowful crowds had quitted their homes for their long and dreary journey, the city was fired and destroyed. It appeared as though a mighty inroad of barbarians had been made upon the capital, and after plundering it the destroyers were hurrying off with their spoil to their native deserts. It seemed altogether inconceivable that such terrible miseries and disasters could have been brought upon the country by any of its own people. To the sorrows of the crowds that struggled along the weary roads they were attacked by the forces of Ts'au-ts'au, which, however, were signally defeated by the commander of Tung-cho's army that accompanied them on the journey to defend them from such assaults.

The deserted capital was taken possession of by Yuan-shan, who endeavoured to restore some order to the wilderness of desolation that now covered the scene, where only a short time before busy crowds and happy homes had existed. He endeavoured to repair the palace, but this he found an impossible task ; yet he did manage to restore somewhat the graves of the Emperors that had been rifled and left open to the winds and storms of heaven. He was fortunate in one thing, viz., the discovery of the great seal that had been lost at the time of the massacre of the eunuchs. It was discovered down a well on the person of one of the royal ladies who in her flight had cast herself into it.

An endeavour was now made by Yuan-shan to give a semblance of legality to his rebellion by appointing one of the princes of the Han family to the throne, but as he wisely declined the dangerous honour all pretence of fighting for the dynasty was given up, and he and the other competitors in the field boldly proclaimed that their aim was the advancement of their own interests.

In the year A. D. 192 the career of Tung-cho came to a sudden end. His cruelty had not only alienated every heart from him, but had also filled all that had anything to do with him with terror for their own lives. A savage and morbid desire to shed blood had seized upon him, and no one knew the moment when an altered look or some negligence in etiquette would not consign him to the executioner's axe. He even designed to murder his trusty and faithful lieutenant, Lu-pu, through whose devotion his elevation to his present position had been alone possible. Wang-yun, a loyal officer in the court, having discovered this, so worked upon his feelings by showing him the extreme danger in which he stood, that finally he consented to murder the usurper. To help him to this decision he informed him that the Emperor had already issued an edict commanding his death, and that therefore he would be acting strictly within the law were he to carry out the intentions of his sovereign.   A day was at once arranged when the deed should be done.   On the morning appointed, whilst Tung-cho was getting into his carriage within the palace gates, a number of soldiers, who lay in ambush, rushed upon him and attacked him.   As he was a large, powerful man, he managed to defend himself for a time. Whilst struggling for his life he kept calling for Lu-pu to come to his rescue.   This officer, who was not far off, seeing the doubtful issue of the conflict, rushed out, and with sword in hand stabbed him to the heart, saying, "By command of the Emperor I slay a robber."   His head was next cut off and his body thrown outside of one of the gates of the city, where it lay for days, the derision and scorn of every passer-by.   Every member of his father's, mother's and wife's families that could be got hold of were ruthlessly slain, in accordance with the savage customs of the times.

His death, instead of bringing peace to the empire, caused only more dire confusion.   Four generals, having heard of Tung-cho's death, returned home without leave, with the forces that were under their command.   They appealed to Wang-yun for forgiveness for this breach of military discipline, the punishment for which they knew was death.   Being rudely repulsed, they determined to rebel, and having induced the commander of the troops in the city to open the gates for them, they marched in with their soldiers and surrounded the palace.   This, of course, soon capitulated, when Wang-yun, now terrified beyond measure, not only promised them forgiveness, but also high official employment, an offer that was sternly rejected, and he was seized and slain.

At this crisis, when the capital was in the utmost disorder, Ts'au-ts'au appeared on the scene.   It was time he did, for the four generals were quarrelling amongst themselves as to which should be the greatest.   One held possession of the palace, and another the person of the Emperor, who managed, however, to escape from his guards, and returned to Lohyang in Honan.   When he arrived there it was with the greatest difficulty that he could find a place for himself and retinue to live in.   It is said that even his great ministers had to take shovel in hand and help to clear away the rubbish and ruins that had once been magnificent palaces, the wonder and admiration of the empire.

Ts'au-ts'au at the head of three hundred thousand men appeared before Hien-ti and offered him protection against his enemies. The feeble monarch could not do otherwise than accept the aid that this man with such a force behind him rudely thrust upon him. He was immediately invested with such large powers that in a short time he became the real ruler of China, and Hien-ti but a simple puppet in his hands, whose only function was to legalize his acts by special edicts in his favour

From this time Liu-pei begins to take a prominent position in the struggle which ended in China being rent into three kingdoms.* At first he fought under the banner of Yuan-shan, when the latter served under Tung-cho. Finding that treason was in the camp he and his leader deserted to Ts'au-ts'au, but being equally disappointed in him he withdrew his men and became an independent leader, with the professed intention of seizing the crown if he could.

In the 11th year of Hien-ti's reign the oppression of Ts'au-ts'au became so intolerable that an effort was made by one of the ladies of the harem, with the assistance of friends outside the palace, to obtain deliverance from a burden that was crushing them all. The unhappy monarch had so little character of his own that he had to rely on the superior energies of the ladies of his household. Unfortunately Ts'au-ts'au got information of the correspondence that was being carried on, and he inflicted a terrible vengeance upon the poor woman who had so heroically determined to free her lord. She was seized by this cruel usurper, and though the Emperor went down on his knees to him, and prayed him to spare her life, she was murdered in the most ruthless and savage manner, and all her kindred, both on her father's and mother's side, were butchered. There is hardly anything that strikes the student of Chinese history so vividly as the barbarous way in which human life was dealt with by those in authority in early days. Not only were men hurled from power and they and their relatives sacrificed without mercy, but this was done with a refinement of cruelty that shocks one. It would be horrible to describe these murders here, so revolting are they. As one reads them in the Chinese records one gets an insight into the possibilities of cruelty that lie hidden behind the placid eyes and easy going exterior of this people, which to one who does not know them would seem to indicate a child-like nature and gentleness of character that would make them abhor inhumanity of any kind whatsoever.

Two other figures now appear to take their share in the tragic events that were hastening the fall of the house of Han. These were Sun-k'wan and Sze-ma-i. The latter of these was invited by Ts'au-ts'au to take office under him, but fearful of his imperious temper he declined to do so. He was not to be put off, however, for he knew that he was a man of great ability, and would be serviceable to him at this time in consolidating his power ; so he threatened him with death if he continued to refuse. To save his

---

* Liu-pei was a distant relative of the imperial family. Fortune had not been kind to him, for we find that in his early life he gained his living by making straw sandals. These are worn chiefly by sedan chair bearers and by the poorest class of travellers, who cannot afford shoes, but who need some protection for the feet when travelling along the bad roads of China. They cost only a fraction over a half-penny a pair. He got some notoriety by commanding a body of volunteers that marched to fight the "Yellow Turbans" in A. D. 185. In consequence of his association with his two sworn brothers—Chang-fei and Kwan-yu—he became a man of note, and finally a competitor for the throne.

life, therefore, he was compelled to accede to his demand, and he gradually rose to the highest offices in the government of Wei.

The year A. D. 208 was a memorable one for Ts'au-ts'au in more ways than one. One of his great competitors, Liu-piau, who had established himself in Kingchow, the modern Hunan, died, and his son, having tendered his submission, Ts'au-ts'au led his army to take possession of it. Liu-pei, who was living in this territory, knew nothing of this surrender till the enemy's troops were upon him. He was so taken by surprise that he had to abandon his wives and his only son Atau, who, however, was rescued by the bravery of Chau-yun, who burst through the enemy's lines and carried off the infant in his bosom. Liu-pei fled from this disastrous battle of Ch'ang-pan Bridge into Chehkiang, where he was beyond the power of his conqueror. Ts'au-ts'au, flushed with victory, and believing that the time was favorable to crush Sun-k'wan, who had established himself along the southern bank of the Yang-tze, led his army of eighty-three thousand men to the edge of the river, where he had ordered a flotilla of boats to await his coming to carry him and his men over.

Whilst these events were transpiring, Liu-pei joined his forces with those of Sun-k'wan, whilst his famous general and strategist, Chu Ko-liang, accompanied him. This man was a host in himself, and, together with Chow-pu, also a distinguished leader, he inflicted a crushing defeat on Ts'au-ts'au at the great battle of Red Ridge. The fleet of boats was burnt and his soldiers slaughtered in vast numbers, and it was with great difficulty that he escaped being annihilated. After this defeat Sun-k'wan took possession of King-chow, which, however, he bestowed upon Liu-pei, and shortly after he gave him his sister in marriage. The latter, after ruling in this district for three years, was invited by Liu-tsang, the chief of Sz-chwan, to join his forces with his and resist Ts'au-ts'au, who was threatening to take his territory from him. Delighted with the larger prospect that was thus suddenly opened up before him he at once set out for the west, leaving Chu Ko-liang and Kwang-yu in charge during his absence. He was met on the frontiers of Sz-chwan by a large detachment of troops sent by Liu-tsang to escort him to the capital, where he was received with the greatest demonstrations of joy.

Ts'au-ts'au, having learnt of his departure, thought it was a good opportunity to attack Sun-k'wan, but the latter, by the advice of his general, Lu-mung, threw up a line of embankment at the mouth of the river Ju-su, near Luchow, so that when Ts'au-ts'au arrived with seventy thousand men to attack him he found the place too strong to capture, and he had to return without accomplishing anything.

In the year A. D. 214 Liu-pei, by the urgent advice of his generals, determined to seize Sz-chwan for himself. He accordingly besieged Liu-tsang in his capital, and having carried it by assault his benefactor was banished to a remote district, where he would have time to ponder over his past, and Liu-pei was installed in his place. From this point the history of the Three Kingdoms may be said to date. It was in this same year that Ts'au-ts'au showed the ambitious designs that he cherished in reference to the throne. The Empress Fuh, having more spirit than her imbecile husband, entered into correspondence with her father, entreating him to find means to free her husband from the tyranny of this mayor of the palace. This having come to the knowledge of the latter he sent a company of soldiers into the palace to arrest her. The unfortunate lady hid herself in a closet, but she was discovered and dragged out in the very presence of Hien-ti. The unhappy woman, knowing that a terrible doom awaited her, appealed to her husband to save her. Instead of being moved by the cries and tears of his devoted consort he burst out weeping, and declared that he could scarcely save himself, much less her. She was then led away to be put to death by the most refined tortures that human ingenuity could devise. At the same time her two sons were compelled to drink poison, so that they should not be in the way of the ambitious schemes of this cold-blooded monster. Nothing will show better the craven spirit of Hien-ti than the fact that two years after this triple murder he consented to take the daughter of Ts'au-ts'au to be his queen in the place of the one that had perished so miserably at the hands of her father.

In the year A. D. 217 Ts'au-ts'au again led an expedition against Kingchow. He was defeated by Kwang-yu, but on the latter's return he met the forces of Sun-kw'an, who was determined to retake this territory for himself. This hero, and victor in many battles, nothing loath, advanced to meet the new foe, but he was overthrown and slain, and so the long disputed territory came under the control of Sun-kw'an once more.*

In the 31st year of his reign Hien-ti resigned his throne, and was made Duke of Shan-yung. About the same time Ts'au-ts'au died, and was succeeded in all his offices by his son Ts'au-p'ei, who, after pretending for ten months that he was administering the government in the name of Hien-ti, forcibly seized the crown, when the latter, handing him over the great seal, retired into private life, where in the same year he was put to death by the orders of the usurper ; and so, amidst weakness and sorrow and murder, ended the career of the house of Liu, that in this famous Han dynasty played so important a part in Chinese history.

---

* Kwan-yu is a famous hero with the Chinese. He was a mighty warrior, but his chief merit lies in the fidelity with which he clung to Liu-pei, whilst he could have bettered his position had he but listened to the overtures of Ts'au-ts'au, who was prepared to bestow honours upon him if he would but come over to his side. He is styled "the loyal and true," and his image is worshipped as the god of war in countless temples throughout the empire to-day. He was deified in A. D. 1594 by the Ming Emperor, Shen-tsung, and the present dynasty has adopted him as their patron god.

CHAPTER XI.

THE EPOCH OF THE THREE KINGDOMS.
(A. D. 221-265.)

The Sz-chwan Han Dynasty.

Chau Lieh Ti—A. D. 221-223.

WE have now arrived at one of the most exciting periods of the whole of Chinese history, namely that of the Three Kingdoms. It is full of romance and heroism and hard fighting and great generalship such as have never been exhibited since then. It is to the Chinese what King Arthur and his knights of the round table are to the English, or as the most prosperous days of chivalry when gallant heroes met to decide by some feat of arms some great question, or in some fierce and deadly conflict to fight in defence of right and honour.

To the public story-tellers and to the play-actors this period is a perfect mine of incident and adventure that never fails to arrest the attention, and to keep an audience spellbound as the thrilling stories of this eventful period are described. Who had not read "The Three Kingdoms?" a book infinitely more marvellous and entertaining than those contained in the most exciting romances in the English language. Every scholar has studied it, and even the unlettered who have been denied by fortune the privilege of dipping into its pleasures can yet relate the marvellous adventures and hair-breadth escapes and the unlooked for stratagems by which their favourite heroes on some occasion escaped destruction from the foe.*

In writing the history of this period we have in reality to do with the story of Three Kingdoms. The first and largest, named the Wei, embraced the central and northern provinces with its capital at Lohyang. The second, named the Wu, controlled the provinces south of the Yang-tze, with its chief city at Nanking; and the third, called the Sz-chwan Han, ruled over the large province of Sz-chwan, having its seat of government at Ch'ungtu.

As the ruler of this last was a distant relative of the imperial house of Han historians have always treated him as the legitimate heir to the throne left vacant by the resignation of Hien-ti, and

---

* "The Three Kingdoms," which gives a most vivid description of the struggles of this time, was written by Ch'un-shau. The main facts of his story agrees with the standard history of the time, but he has gone into descriptions of men and things that do not appear in it. As he was alive at the time when the great events which he describes took place we may suppose that many of them that he records must be true, whilst the fabulous and the incredible must be put down to the effects of a vivid imagination. As Ch'un-shau has endeavoured to prove that Ts'au-ts'au was no usurper but had a right to the succession, he is not considered by the scholars of China to have done his duty as an historian.

they have refused to recognize the others, whom they look upon as mere soldiers of fortune, who were usurpers and not worthy to be reckoned amongst the sovereigns of China.*

When the news reached Liu-pei that Hien-ti had handed over the great seal to Ts'au-p'ei, and that he was shortly after murdered by him, his court and the people of his capital went into mourning for him.   He then assumed the functions of royalty and declared himself to be the rightful heir to the throne of China.   Chu Ko-liang, or, as he is more popularly known, K'ung-meng, was made prime minister ; his wife, Sun-k'uan's sister, was publicly installed as queen, and his son Atau, whose mother, surrounded by Ts'au-ts'au's troops, threw herself into a well, was made heir to the throne.†

It was at this time that Liu-pei remembered his friend Kwan-yu, who had been slain by Sun-k'uan's general, Lu-meng.   In the sworn friendship that he had made with him and Chang-fei it had been agreed between them that they should live and die together. As he had not been able to die fighting by his side he determined to take a terrible revenge upon the author of his death, and he accordingly gathered an immense army of over seven hundred thousand men and prepared to invade the dominions of Sun-k'uan and inflict a signal vengeance upon him for his friend's death. Chu Ko-liang in vain remonstrated with him upon his folly.   He showed him that his affairs were not in such a settled condition as to permit him to engage in war with a distant enemy, and besides it was his duty as a sovereign to consider his empire first and his private friendship second.   Liu-pei was, however, in such a condition of mind as to be impervious to all arguments, and Chang-fei being of the same opinion, the preparations were hurried on for the campaign.   So impetuous was the latter, who had the superintendence of these, and so overbearing in his treatment of his men, that they rose against him and murdered him.   Liu-pei, nothing discouraged by this, still determined on carrying out his purpose.

---

* In the present history we have decided to follow the example of these great authorities and to make the minor Han the legitimate successor to the previous dynasty.   It is not an altogether satisfactory plan, because it ruled over such a very small portion of the empire, and was inferior in many ways to the Wei kingdom, that ultimately emerged the superior power in the contest of the three for universal dominion.

† Chu Ko-liang is one of the greatest heroes in the whole range of Chinese history, and there is hardly a man in the empire at the present day who does not know his name and get excited at the mention of his wonderful genius as a general. He was certainly the founder of Liu-pei's fortunes, for without him he would have been a wandering soldier of fortune without any of the success that ultimately attended him.   When he first met with him he was leading the life of a recluse, and for some time resisted all the entreaties of Liu-pei to abandon the reed hut in which he lived and enter upon the world of action in which he was to gain such fame.   He not only served Liu-pei with the greatest fidelity, but he also led the armies of his son, and died in one of his campaigns against the house of Wei.   It is a singular fact that he had two other brothers, each of which served one of the usurping dynasties.   In this way the three sons of one family were the important actors in each of the Three Kingdoms into which the empire was now divided.

Sun-k'uan, having heard of his determination to attack him, sent ambassadors to him and urged that instead of quarrelling with each other they should unite in a treaty of friendship, in order the better to withstand the power of the house of Wei, which was no insignificant opponent in the present position of affairs. Finding that he could make no impression upon him he began to arm, whilst at the same time he sent an ambassador to Ts'au-p'ei and tendered his submission to him and offered to hold his territory as his vassal. The latter accepted his offer with joy, although his ministers endeavoured to dissuade him from doing so, on the ground that Sun-k'uan was not in earnest, but was simply moved by fear of Liu-pei. Ts'au-p'ei refused to listen to their advice, and created Sun-k'uan Duke of Wei, with the command of the large district he already occupied. In the second year of Liu-pei, his vast preparations having been all completed, he set his army in motion for the great enterprise on which he had set his heart. Chu Ko-liang, knowing that the Emperor had not military skill enough to lead such an immense host, was confident that disaster only would attend it, and so made his preparations to minimize it as much as possible. He accordingly built his famous "eight line of battle plan" and awaited the result with intense anxiety.*

Liu-pei led his immense army to the frontiers of Sun-k'uan's territory, where he was met by Luh-sun, the general of the latter, with a greatly inferior army. What was lacking in numbers, however, was made up in strategic ability. After some months fencing with each other a grand battle took place at Hian-ting, when Liu-pei was defeated with great slaughter and compelled to fly for his life, and he never stopped till he had gained the city of Ying-ngan.

Luh-sun, not content with the numbers he had slain and captured on the field of battle, followed hard in pursuit of the beaten foe, until he came up with the famous structure that Chu Ko-liang had erected right across what he knew would be the line of pursuit. Arriving in front of this strange looking city he halted his army, and advancing to one of the gates he saw the inscription over it, "This is the eight line of battle plan. Let any one who thinks himself clever enter in and see what it is like."

---

* This eight line of battle plan was modelled on the eight diagrams invented by the famous Fuh-hi. Historians are exceedingly divided in their opinions as to what was the exact description of this celebrated structure that ultimately foiled Sun-k'uan's general after he had defeated Liu-pei. The general idea is that in outward appearance it resembled a huge stone city with eight gates. Inside strange sounds were revelling amongst the solitary deserted streets, and the rumbling of thunder and the rushing of mountain streams could be distinguished among them. Whoever trusted himself within its mazes wandered about in a hopeless way, and happy was the man who ultimately succeeded in getting out from what seemed to be enchanted ground.

The principle of this wonderful city was adopted in the formation of the army when it was going to battle, and granted that the commander had sufficient ability and the troops courage enough to carry it out steadily, any army that attacked it in this condition must infallibly be defeated. This famous military disposition of an army is well known in the present day, and is said to be sometimes employed by Chinese commanders.

Luh-sun, who no doubt thought this a direct challenge to him, and who modestly believed that his abilities were great enough to permit him to enter a building of this kind, boldly advanced through the gate, but in a few moments he found himself so bewildered in the mazes of this marvellous city that the more he attempted to disentangle himself from them the more involved he became. When he found it hopeless to win his way out he began to mourn and lament his unhappy fate, but just then his father-in-law, who had been captured by Chu Ko-liang, and who had given him the clue to the city, appeared and led him safely to the outside.* He was so terrified with his late experience, and so fearful of being led into some other well-planned contrivance for his destruction by Chu Ko-liang, that he stayed his pursuit of Liu-pei at this spot and returned to his own territory. In the meanwhile Ts'au-p'ei, having heard of this great victory, and fearing the effect on Sun-k'uan's mind, sent to him and demanded that his son should be given him as a hostage, as a proof of his good faith in the submission he had made to him. Sun-k'uan refused to do this, when Ts'au-p'ei sent an army against him, but it had to return without having accomplished anything. Liu-pei, who had never recovered from the effect of the great defeat that he had suffered at the hands of Luh-sun, and who never again returned to the capital, but remained in the city of Yung-ngan, became seriously ill the following year. He then sent for Chu Ko-liang and his son Atau to come to him. When they arrived he summoned them both to his bedside and said to his prime minister, "Your abilities are far superior to those of Ts'au-p'ei, and in the coming conflict you need not fear defeat at his hands. I entrust my son to you. He is still young. If you find him to be a good man and worthy of your support, then I pray you to defend him with every power you possess and help him to be a good king. If he is not, then take the reins of power into your own hands and reign in your own right."

Touched to the heart by these pathetic words Chu Ko-liang knelt by his bedside, and with tears declared that as long as life remained to him he should be loyal to his son, and no traitorous thought should ever enter his heart. Liu-pei, turning to his son, who was deeply affected by this scene, said to him, "Be a good man and you will be a good ruler. Never for a moment dream that to do evil is a matter of no consequence, and do not give way to small wrongs. A small wrong is still an evil, and can be called by no other name. Do good, even in slight matters, for even though insignificant they still belong to the class of right. I have unfortunately no good qualities that I can ask you to imitate. Chu Ko-liang has both ability and character. Imitate him and be a loyal, affectionate son to him, and your reign will be long and my house will be established on the throne of China."

---

* This story of the eight line of battle plan is not found in the regular history of China. It appears in "The Three Kingdoms."

He was sixty-two years old when he died, and he reigned only three years, which had been troublous ones for him and full of sorrow. His son's dynastic title was How Chu.

How Chu—A. D. 223-265.

This prince, who was only seventeen when he succeeded his father, implicitly followed his dying commands, for he at once handed over the whole management of the state to Chu Ko-liang, who loyally repaid his confidence in him by the most unswerving devotion. His first advice to him was to make peace at once with his uncle Sun-k'uan, especially because of the common danger to which they were both exposed from the formidable foe they had in the house of Wei. This he hastened to do, when Ts'au-p'ei, hearing of this treaty of amity between his two enemies, immediately marched a large army to the banks of the Yang-tze with the intention of crossing over and making his vengeance felt on Sun-k'uan.

There seemed a fatality, however, in this great river to the house of Ts'au. Armies had been repeatedly brought up to its edge, but they had never yet been able to get across, and so it happened once more. Luh-sun had made such efficient preparations to meet the coming danger that Ts'au-p'ei's soldiers found themselves baffled in every attempt to get into Sun-k'uan's territory. Just then it fortunately happened for the latter that a terrible storm of wind arose that distressed the soldiers very much. Coming from an interior province and unaccustomed to big waves, they were not only terrified at the sight of them, but, becoming seasick, they were perfectly helpless in the management of their boats. They consequently had to return to Lohyang without accomplishing anything.

Chu Ko-liang, having made peace with Sun-k'uan, now felt prepared to march his armies against the house of Ts'au, the destroyer of the Hans and the usurper of the domains that should by right belong to How Chu. There was only one thing that prevented his immediately carrying out his purpose, and that was his fear lest the Burmese in his rear should take advantage of his absence in the east to march their forces into Sz-chwan and ravage and destroy the country. He determined, therefore, to invade Burmah, and, having conquered it, to carry out his great project of destroying the dynasty of Wei.

The news of the preparations for the invasion of Burmah having reached the king of that country, he determined to anticipate the enemy by invading his territories. He accordingly led an immense army into Sz-chwan, which Chu Ko-liang had no hesitation in meeting.

At first his men found great difficulty in contending with the Burmese, for they were clad in coverings made of rattan. The swords of the soldiers could not pierce this armour, and the Burmese fought so courageously that the Chinese general was compelled to call forth all the resources of his inventive mind to prevent his being beaten by them. At last he devised a plan by which he succeeded in defeating them. He ordered his soldiers to bring with them lighted torches, which they applied to the bodies of the enemies, and at once the irresistible armour gave way.

Seven distinct engagements were fought, in each of which the Burmese were defeated, and each time their king was captured. Chu Ko-liang, who wished to touch his heart by his generosity, set him free after each battle, hoping in this way to convert him from a foe into a friend, so that he could carry on his great enterprise against the house of Wei without any fear of molestation from an enemy in his rear. Chu Ko-liang had during these successive engagements penetrated far into Burmah, and the king seeing the hopelessness of continuing the contest with such a general, and moved too by the magnanimity with which he had been treated, sent and signified his willingness to confess that he was conquered and to make a treaty with the house of Han. As the acquisition of territory was not the object of Chu Ko-liang, an arrangement was easily come to, and in a short time he was leading back his victorious army to Ch'ung-tu.

In the following year Ts'au-p'ei died, and was succeeded by his son Ts'au-jui, who took the imperial title of Ming Ti (A. D. 227-240).

For more than a year Chu Ko-liang was busily engaged in perfecting his arrangements for the great conflict which he was now determined to wage with the usurping house of Wei. As he would have to advance far from his base, from whence all his supplies would have to be drawn, and as the roads were of the worst possible description, he had to think and plan, not merely that his army should be in a fit state to meet the enemy, but also to provide against the thousand and one accidents that might happen, and which might wreck his enterprise more thoroughly than the swords of his foe. At length, every preparation having been made he advanced into Shensi, which for some time was to be the battle ground between the rival forces. Having sent one of his generals, Ma-su, ahead with a large detachment, he himself brought up the rear with the main body of his army.

Sze-ma-i, the enemy's commander-in-chief, had also sent on one of his generals with fifty thousand men, who, encountering Ma-su, so thoroughly defeated him, that his whole force was almost entirely annihilated.*

---

* Sze-ma-i is one of the most famous men, next to Chu Ko-liang, that appears in the conflicts during the time of the Three Kingdoms. He was no unworthy rival of his great adversary. He had not his brilliant genius, but that he was a commander of no mean ability is shown by the fact that the author of the "Three Kingdoms" declared that he managed his armies not like a mere man, but as though he had been inspired by the gods. His policy was a Fabian one and it was by persisting in it, in spite of all the discontent that frequently arose in his camp, that he was able to prevent Chu Ko-liang from accomplishing the great purpose that seemed to dominate his life.

The panic reached even Chu Ko-liang's army, which soon became a disorganized mass, heedless of the orders of their general, who was compelled to fly to the strong city of Hanchung, which he entered with only three followers.

And now we have one of the most famous incidents that has been recorded in the whole of the conflict during these stirring times, and one that has taken such hold upon the popular imagination that to-day it is known amongst every class of society, from the highest to the lowest. The great general was in the most imminent peril, for he had not long entered the city before the force of Sze-ma-i appeared before it, and escape from it was now rendered impossible. It was then that he had recourse to a stratagem that has made his name famous. He ordered the four gates of the city to be thrown open, whilst he himself took his position on a tower over one of them and began to play upon his guitar. As the enemy drew near they caught the strains of music, but not a soldier appeared upon the walls, neither could an opposing force be seen within the gates, which were ostentatiously thrown wide open. The commander-in-chief was seen approaching to examine this strange sight, but still Chu Ko-liang, with his face wreathed in smiles, sang his joyous songs to the accompaniment of his instrument. "He seems too happy, does that man," said Sze-ma-i, "for our comfort, and he evidently has some deep-laid scheme in his brain by which he means to bring disaster upon us all." As they stood spellbound, still the notes of the guitar sounded in the air, and its strains fell upon the ears of the thunderstruck soldiers that gazed in wonder upon the lately vanquished general.

Chu Ko-liang had long had the reputation of being more dangerous after he had been beaten than even when he was in the field at the head of his army, and so Sze-ma-i, fearful of some terrible disaster coming upon him, ordered the instant retreat of his army. As the serried ranks of his enemy were seen marching with quick step away from the city the joyous strains of music fell upon their ears and made them hurry away all the faster, for it seemed to them as though they contained a scornful challenge to them to come back and fight it out with their unseen foe. As soon as the last lines of the retreating enemy were seen vanishing in the distance, Chu Ko-liang, who was transported with joy at his marvellous escape, fled with his three friends in the opposite direction to that which the terrified Sze-ma-i had taken. Having ordered that his unfortunate general Ma-su should be put to death for the disgrace he had brought on the country he sent a report to How-chu of his defeat, and requested that he himself should be punished by being degraded three steps for his folly in entrusting so important a command to so incompetent a general. His request was granted, and instead of being prime minister he was made general of the left, though he was still kept in command of the army.

During this same year Ts'au-jui had set an army against Sun-k'uan, and Chu Ko-liang, hearing of this, detached a part of his force, to the number of thirty or forty thousand men, and went to the assistance of the latter ; but he could not do anything effective, as he had to retreat through failure of provisions. The general of Wei, thinking he had an easy prey in an enemy that was retreating, followed with all his forces, but Chu Ko-liang placed an ambuscade so skilfully that his army was defeated and he himself killed. The next year Chu Ko-liang was restored to his honours in consequence of victories he had gained in Shensi and for the capture of two important cities that had belonged to Ts'au-jui. In this same year Sun-k'uan took to himself the title of Emperor, with the royal appellation of

Ta Ti—A. D. 222-229.

The following year Sze-ma-i endeavoured to capture Han-chung, but failed before the forces of Chu Ko-liang. This city was strategically a most important one, as the man that held it controlled in a great measure the whole of Sz-chwan. Vigorous efforts were therefore made at various times by Sze-ma-i to capture it, but hitherto all his generalship had only ended in defeat.

In the year A. D. 211 Chu Ko-liang again led an army into Shensi, where he was once more met by his old antagonist Sze-ma-i. The latter, as usual, feeling that he was no match for him in the open field resorted to his Fabian tactics. On the other hand, Chu Ko-liang was eager for an engagement, knowing that delay was fatal to him, for after a time, when his provisions should all be exhausted, he would simply have to retreat. The one great sorrow of his life in these campaigns had been the impossi-bility of keeping his army in the field, because of the immense difficulty that he always had in bringing supplies over the bad roads of Sz-chwan to such a great distance as where the war was usually carried on. He accordingly used every means in his power to get Sze-ma-i out of his entrenchments. His men came out daily and taunted the enemy with cowardice and with all the epithets that they knew would excite the anger of the more daring amongst them. These tactics after a time prevailed. The commanders and officers of Sze-ma-i were so galled with these that they reproached their general with being afraid of his opponent. " You fear him," they said, "as though he were a tiger. All the world is laughing at us, because we stay behind our earthworks and dare not advance to meet the enemy that we have come here to fight." This bold language to their general shows the excited feeling there was in the camp, and how the taunts of the foe had entered into the hearts of Sze-ma-i's men. Goaded at last by the reproaches of his soldiers, and fearing that the moral effect of these daily insults of the enemy would be disastrous to his army, he at length reluctantly led it out to battle. The result was as he had expected. He suffered a great defeat, and he was saved from being utterly destroyed only by the fact that Chu Ko-liang's commissariat having by this time become completely exhausted, instead of pursuing the enemy he was compelled to hurry back as fast as he could into Sz-chwan. Sze-ma-i seeing this, sent a large division in pursuit, but Chu Ko-liang, with his usual genius, laid in wait for it, and signally defeated it, the general in command being slain in the fierce onslaught that was made upon it by Chu Ko-liang's men. Two years after this, this great general, who had spent his time in incessant preparations for another campaign, was again in the field in Shensi, and once more the army of Sze-ma-i was in front of him, and, as usual, behind their entrenchments.

For the last three years the mind of Chu Ko-liang had been greatly exercised as to the best means by which to get his supplies carried from his base along the bad and dangerous roads of Sz-chwan into Shensi, beyond which he had never been able to penetrate. His genius had always been foiled and the fruits of victory snatched from him by his inability to command abundance of provisions for his soldiers. It must be remembered that he was not simply a great general; he was also a man of a mechanical turn of mind. It is said that he invented a kind of an alarm clock that he used to put under his pillow that would wake him at any particular hour of the morning that he wished to rise. He set his mind to think, and the result was he designed a number of self-acting machines that when wound up would proceed along the roads by themselves, subject only to the guidance and control of those that had the charge of them. The name given to them in the history of "The Three Kingdoms" is "the fleet of wooden oxen and horses." What these were no one at the present day knows, though Chinese writers have discussed them, and men have taken the measurements that have been given in the history and striven to construct similar machines. It would seem that the spring was wound up by the tongue, for as the name implies they were made in the form of oxen and horses.* Once more Chu Ko-liang was anxious for the fight, whilst Sze-ma-i was just as concerned to defeat his great enemy by the slow process of delay. The former's men came out every day and taunted the foe with the most insulting epithets, and sneered at them in language in which the Chinese are perfect masters, but nothing could induce the latter to accept the challenges that were daily hurled at him. At last this astute general sent him a covering for the head, such as widows wear when they attend the funeral of their late husbands, and which they also keep on their heads in the home as a sign of sorrow and bereavement. Sze-ma-i was exceedingly enraged when the messenger brought this, but he restrained himself in the presence of his suite, and merely sent back a sarcastic message to Chu Ko-liang, praying him not to wear himself out by such hard

---

* Some have imagined that we have in them the first wheel-barrows that were ever in China. See "Three Kingdoms" in loc.

work, for he had reliable information that he was shortening his life by want of rest and food. The receipt of this female article of attire roused the wrath of the more fiery spirits in the army to perfect fury, and they insisted that the foul insult upon their general and themselves should be washed over by a battle, in which they would soon show Chu Ko-liang what kind of material they were made of. The commander-in-chief, finding that he would soon lose all control over his men, agreed to write to Ts'au-jui and ask him what should be done under the circumstances. This pacified his officers, and they promised to abide by his decision. Sze-ma-i took care to write a private letter, urging upon him the policy of his forbidding him to fight, as he would soon have a bloodless victory through the death of Chu Ko-liang, who he had heard was at that time dangerously ill. This was only too true. Not long after, this great commander breathed his last, to the sorrow and consternation of his whole army. Before his death he gathered his captains about him and told them not to be afraid of Sze-ma-i. He instructed them to make a figure representing himself, and ordered them to place it in such a manner amongst the soldiers that it would be seen by the enemy, and thus make them believe that he was really alive, and still in command of his men. After Chu Ko-liang was dead, and the rumour had gone abroad, Sze-ma-i was still afraid to take decided action. He did not know whether this report was not got up by him in order to draw him out of his strongly entrenched camp. Even when the enemy began to retreat towards Sz-chwan he followed him with the greatest circumspection, afraid lest some ingenious stratagem should involve his army in disaster. At length, catching a sight of his great enemy, as he thought, he was so terrified that he hastily retreated with all his forces in the direction of Honan. For several years after this the contest was given up by both sides, and each of the Three Kingdoms busied itself more especially about the concerns of its own government.

About this time T'au-jui, having no son of his own, appointed one that had been adopted to succeed him on the throne. He also became more extravagant, and built four or five palaces, and also laid out an immense garden called "The Garden of the Fragrant Forest," in which were trees and plants and flowers of the rarest description, and all kinds of wild animals that had been brought from distant parts of the country to make the collection as complete as possible. In the 16th year of Kow Chu, Ts'au-jui, otherwise Meng Ti, became very ill, and fearing that his end was near, he called his great general Sze-ma-i to his bedside, and taking him by his hand, he said, "I have been in great trouble and distress of mind, as I was afraid I should die before you could arrive. Now that I have seen your face and can speak to you my last commands I shall die in peace." He then solemnly delivered over to his care his son Fang and prayed him to be loyal to him and to see that no intrigues of the great mandarins should threaten either his life or his peaceable succession to the throne. Sze-ma-i and a relative of the sick man named Ts'au-sung, who held high office in the palace, and who was present at this interview, both promised that they would loyally stand by his son, and that they would defend his rights with their lives. Soon after, Ts'au-jui died, and Fang, under the name of Fei Ti (A. D. 240-254), became his successor in the government of the kingdom of Wei, under the guardianship of Sze-ma-i and Ts'au-sung.

Eight years passed away after this closing scene in the life of Ts'au-jui, and during them great changes had taken place in the condition of affairs in at least two of the Three Kingdoms. Kow Chu, after the death of his great mentor Chu Ko-liang, began to degenerate and to show that his character was an essentially feeble one and inclined to that course of dissipation that had marked the end of every previous dynasty. Learning nothing by the sad experience of the past in his own house of Han he made a worthless eunuch of the palace his prime minister and placed the whole government in his hands, whilst he gave himself up to the wildest indulgence. Sze-ma-i and Ts'au-sung had by this time forgotten the solemn promises they had made to Ts'au-jui, and both entertained the most ambitious views for themselves and their families. Ts'au-sung, being of the royal blood, had more facilities for carrying out his designs, and at last he became so overbearing that Sze-ma-i retired from court, and for two years waited with his friends for the favourable moment when he could crush his enemies and seize the supreme power for himself. At last the opportunity for which he had waited so patiently came. At the feast of tombs Ts'au-fang, Ts'au-sung and his four brothers set out to visit the ancestral graves of the family and to perform the annual ceremonies before them. Hwan-hwan, the political adviser of Ts'au-sung, endeavoured to dissuade him from accompanying the royal party by showing the extreme danger to which he was subjecting the dynasty of Wei by leaving no one in the palace to guard against the intrigues of Sze-ma-i and his three sons. He refused to listen to this politic advice, and the party proceeded on their way to the tombs. They had not gone long before Sze-ma-i with his party took possession of the palace, and wishing to secure Hwan-hwan, who was a man of exceptional ability, and murder him, he sent him a message as if from the Queen-Dowager, saying that his presence was requested by her. Hwan-hwan was too wise a man to fall into this transparent snare, and instead of obeying he fled with all haste to Ts'au-sung and the royal party and informed them that the capital was in the hands of Sze-ma-i and his friends. Sze-ma-i was greatly concerned about the escape of Hwan-hwan, as he was a man of great ability and quite competent to advise Ts'au-sung in such a manner as to give him a vast amount of trouble in the dangerous step he had taken. One of his sons comforted him with the thought that he need not distress himself about the matter, as Ts'au-sung had not the mind to grasp a great idea, and that therefore Hwan-hwan would find himself utterly disregarded in any measures that he proposed to him in the present emergency. This prophecy turned out to be exactly true. Hwan-hwan's advice was that the whole of the royal family should stay where they were, and summoning the troops of Wei from all parts of the state, they would soon find themselves at the head of a force that would more than match that which the usurper could assemble. Because his family and his property were in the capital Ts'au-sung refused to listen to this advice, and preferred to run any risk rather than endanger them. Hwan-hwan spent a whole night with him discussing the matter with him, and showed him not only the risk he ran in returning to the place that was held by a man that was now fighting for his life, but also the certainty of success if he followed his counsels. When Hwan-hwan found that his advice was rejected he burst into tears, because he saw the sad fate that was in store for himself and the members of his family in consequence of the obstinacy of a man who had not the brain to perceive the danger he was incurring by his folly. Next morning the whole party returned to Lohyang, and Sze-ma-i could hardly believe his eyes when he saw how the very men that he was anxious to destroy were calmly walking into the very jaws of destruction. Ts'au-sung and his four brothers were at once seized and executed, and so was Hwan-hwan and every member of his family on whom they could lay their hands. Ts'au-fang alone was spared, because the time had not yet arrived for his destruction, and Sze-ma-i was made his prime minister with unlimited powers in the government of the country. In the 26th year of How Chu an attempt was made to overthrow Sze-ma-i by two high officials, who were indignant at the oppressive way in which he ruled, and because they saw that Ts'au-fang was too weak to be able to resist his tyranny. They resolved to elevate another member of the Ts'au family to the throne, of greater age and experience, who would draw around him a large number of the influential men who were dissatisfied with Sze-ma-i and his doings. Before the plans were fully matured they were divulged to Sze-ma-i, who came upon the conspirators with an army, and, seizing those most deeply implicated in insurrection, caused more than a thousand of them to be executed. In the same year Sze-ma-i died, and was succeeded in all his offices by his son Sze-ma-sze ; only in addition to all he was given the post of commander-in-chief of the army. In the 29th year of How Chu, Sun-k'uan, of the kingdom of Wu, died, and was succeeded by his son Liang, and as there appeared signs that the troops of Wei would again invade the kingdom, the embankment that had been built by Lu-meng at the mouth of the river Ju-su was repaired, and the army put into a state of readiness for an attack. The consequence was that when they did appear they were easily repulsed by Chu Ko-liang's general. The result, however, was fatal to himself, for he became so overbearing and haughty because of his success that he incurred the hatred of his own men and also of some of the high officials, who whispered into the ear of Liang that he meditated rebellion. This was enough to seal his doom. He was invited to a feast given in his honour by Liang, where he was murdered, and, as was customary in those barbarous days, his father's, mother's and wife's families were exterminated.

Ts'au-fang, of Wei, had fallen into evil hands when he came under the control of Sze-ma-sze. The latter was a most cruel and relentless tyrant. He first put to death a high official with whom the king was seen to talk too often, because he felt convinced they were plotting his destruction. Then he had the queen and her father executed for the same reason, and finally in the same year he deposed the young king (A.D. 254) and put a nephew of Ts'au-jui, a lad fifteen years old, named Ts'au-mau, in his place, whose dynastic title was Shau Ti. This same year How Chu's general, Ch'iang-i, met the forces of Ts'au-mau in Shensi, but the commander of these, adopting the tactics of Sze-ma-i with Chu Ko-liang, kept behind his entrenchments till Ch'iang-i's provisions were all exhausted, and he had to retreat without accomplishing his purpose. The oppression of Sze-ma-sze became so unbearable to Ts'au-mau that he entered into a plot with three of his ministers to murder him. The difficulty was in carrying it out, for all the officials in the palace were friends of the usurper. At last it was determined that on a certain day they should gather their adherents before notice could be given to any one of their intentions, and that they should at once proceed to the house of Sze-ma-sze and capture and put him to death. This plan would have succeeded, but two out of the three conspirators went and divulged it to the usurper. When the party arrived they found his general with his soldiers ready to receive them, and in the melée Ts'au-mau was killed by his order. Sze-ma-sze soon after arrived at the palace, and having ordered the execution of the mandarin that was faithful to Ts'au-mau he found his power more firmly fixed than ever. As he was not yet prepared to seize the imperial power, he put Ts'au-hwan, a descendant of Ts'au-ts'au, in the place of the murdered prince, who took the title of Yuan Ti (A. D. 260). In the thirty-eighth year of his reign How Chu gave still further evidence of the weakness of his character morally by the abandoned life that he openly led. Instead of being guided in the government of the country by wise and faithful counsellors, he put himself entirely into the hands of a eunuch and a Tauist priest, who pretended to be able to control the supernatural and to have a knowledge of coming events. The only general of any note that he had was Ch'iang-i, but he was so disgusted with the way things were managed in the capital that he withdrew with his soldiers to guard the frontiers against the irruption of the barbarians. The time, however, had now arrived when all the abilities of Ch'iang-i would be required to protect the last

s cion of the house of Han in his limited sovereignty. Sze-ma-chau,*
b eing exceedingly annoyed at the persistency with which How Chu
c ontinued to send armies into Shensi to endeavour to overthrow his
dynasty, determined to put forth all his energies, and not only for
ever stop this perpetual annoyance and expense, but also crush out
the last remains of the Han dynasty and add its territories to his
own. There was a division amongst his advisers on this point,
and the majority were against such a hazardous undertaking; but
one of them, more courageous than the rest, raised his voice loudly
for the expedition, which he declared was sure to succeed. He felt
certain of this for two reasons : because the great Chu Ko-liang
was dead, and How Chu had no general of his ability to meet
their troops in the field ; more important still, however, was the
fact that How Chu was leading a dissolute life, and therefore
heaven would withdraw its support from such a man, who would
in consequence inevitably fall. This advice so harmonized with
the wishes of Sze-ma-chau that the campaign was there and then
decided upon. An immense force was collected, and before Ch'iang-i
could organize his troops more than three hundred thousand men
were marching on Sz-chwan. Ch'iang-i hastened with what men
he could hastily collect towards the enemy, and at the same time
he sent messengers as fast as fleet horses could carry them to the
capital, and urged upon How Chu if he would save his kingdom
to send on soldiers as fast as he could, to enable him to meet the
large army that had already nearly reached the borders of Sz-chwan.
How Chu, terribly alarmed, consulted the eunuch and the Tauist
priest, who were the real governors of the state, as to what should
be done in this important crisis. The latter, after consulting the
spirits, declared that there was no danger from the enemy, as they
would soon retire broken and defeated to their own territory, and
that he need not therefore have any concern about the future.
How Chu, who was completely under the control of this man, was
so satisfied with his reply that nothing whatever was done to relieve
Ch'iang-i, neither did he think it necessary to inform any of his
ministers of the danger that was hanging over the state. Ch'iang-i
boldly advanced into Shensi to meet the enemy, but he was soon
defeated by the overpowering numbers he had to contend with,
and he retreated across the border into Sz-chwan and occupied the
strong town of Chien-ko. Here Chung-hwei, the commander of
Sze-ma-chau's army, followed and invested the place. He could,
however, make no impression upon it, and as the time went by and
provisions became scarce he began to think of retreating. His
second in command, Ting-ai, strongly dissuaded him from this,
as he showed him that certain and complete success was almost
within their grasp. Having obtained a large flying column from
him he set out on the hazardous but brilliant idea of surprising the

---

* Sze-ma-sze after four years exercise of power died, and was succeeded by his
brother, Sze-ma-chau.

capital, which he had learnt was entirely undefended. Diving off into the mountains and avoiding the main roads by which intelligence of his movements could be carried to How Chu, he gradually worked his way towards Ch'ung-tu. This road was of the most perilous and romantic character. Ting-ai and his men had to travel over most dangerous paths, from which men of ordinary nerve would have shrunk. They had to ascend high mountains and crawl along the edges of precipices, and cross great gullies, and climb down the face of the rocks by the aid of the creepers that covered them. But nothing could shake their courage, for they knew that the enterprise would be crowned with a success that would bring them honours and rewards. For more than two hundred miles this heroic band pursued its way, till like a thunderbolt it burst upon the devoted capital and demanded its instant surrender. As no preparation had been made for such a calamity the greatest consternation prevailed amongst all classes of the people. The eunuch Wang-ho, who had been the cause of this terrible disaster, advised How Chu to submit, and get the best terms he could from the enemy. The crown prince opposed this cowardly way of settling things, and urged that the city should be defended and messengers sent post-haste to summon soldiers from all parts of the state to meet the foe that had dared to appear before their gates.

How Chu, of a naturally feeble character, and weakened in mind by his excesses, was not prepared for the bold advice of his son, and declared his intention of doing as Wang-ho advised. Finding that remonstrances were of no avail, the son went away to the ancestral temple of Liu-pei, and there wept out the story of the disasters that had come upon his children in the hearing, as he believed, of his spirit. After this he went home, and having slain his wife and children he committed suicide, determined that none of them should be subjected to the indignities and sufferings that he knew awaited them at the hands of the victorious enemy. When this tragedy was over, How Chu, with his chief officials, proceeded to where Ting-ai was encamped, outside the city, with their hands tied behind their backs and with their coffins accompanying them, where they made an unconditional surrender of themselves and the capital. How Chu's life and those of his ministers were spared, but after his entry into the city Ting-ai ordered the execution of the eunuch Wang-ho. This wretched man, through whose ambition and folly the Emperor had lost his throne and his kingdom, escaped the due punishment of his offences by bribing heavily the officials who had influence with Ting-ai. As he was immensely rich he could do this to some purpose, and he was allowed to escape the death he so well merited.

Ting-ai, dazzled with the ease with which he had overthrown a dynasty that the most skilful commanders had so repeatedly failed to do, began from this time to entertain the idea that this was a grand opportunity for his founding a dynasty of his own, and for his taking possession of a throne that lay temptingly before him. He accordingly memorialized Sze-ma-chau to be allowed to remain in Sz-chwan two or three years, in order not only to rest his soldiers after their exhausting campaign, but also to thoroughly conquer the country, so that all disaffection might be crushed out of it.

Sze-ma-chau, catching at once the intention of his successful general, immediately sent orders for his being superseded in his command and for his instant return to the capital, which order he refused to obey. In the meantime treason was spreading further than in the camp of Ting-ai. The commander-in-chief who had been detained before the entry of Chien-ko, but which had been handed over to him in consequence of a command of How Chu after he had surrendered, began to believe that he was the fittest man to grasp the sceptre that had just fallen from the feeble hands of the late king. To carry out his purposes with more certainty of success he felt he must have Ch'iang-i to co-operate with him. He accordingly entered into a secret correspondence with him, promising him a high position in the government if he would throw in his fortunes with him and help him to become Emperor. Ch'iang-i, who was thoroughly loyal to his king, saw in this proposition a plan by which he might still save the dynasty. He therefore pretended to go heart and soul into the conspiracy, and that it might not fail, he said it was essential that Ting-ai should be removed from the country, as he was too able a man and too well beloved by his soldiers to have him to contend with in the carrying out of their dangerous projects. Chung-hwei readily agreed to this, and as the most successful way of getting rid of a formidable rival he memorialized Sze-ma-chau and declared that Ting-ai was meditating rebellion, and the sooner, therefore, that he was recalled the better it would be for the state of Wei. Upon the receipt of this at Lohyang orders were sent to Wei-hwan, who had superseded Ting-ai, to have him sent home under arrest, and if he resisted to have him at once slain. This order was immediately carried out, and Ting-ai was sent home under arrest, whilst far greater traitors than he were left behind to carry out their treasonable schemes. Ch'iang-i now proposed to Chung-hwei, in furtherance of his own secret design, to get rid of the most prominent of his enemies, that all the chief officers in his army should be slain, as they were not likely to be all willing to go in for the treason they were plotting. This scheme, unfortunately for him, came to the ears of these men, when they rose in insurrection and murdered both the commanders, and the camp for several days was in the greatest possible disorder. Wei-hwan, who was also in the plot, hearing of the tragedy that had taken place in the camp, and fearful that Ting-ai, when he got to the capital, would make disclosures that might implicate him, at once sent express messengers that overtook him on the road and murdered him. With the death of these men the conspiracy ended, and Sz-chwan was added to the already large dominions of Wei. How Chu was carried to Lohyang and kindly treated by Sze-ma-chau, who saw in him a dissolute, weak-minded rival, who cared much more for the enjoyments of life than for the power of a throne, and in contempt for him he made him "Duke of Pleasure."

With the fall of How Chu the Han dynasty disappears from history, excepting in so far as the influence of the laws that were passed and the men that lived in those stirring times have affected the national life ever since. After these successes Sze-ma-chau thought it was time to take more decided steps to show what was the purpose and aim of his life. He assumed the title of king and made his wife queen, and his son was recognized as the heir apparent. He only refrained from actually becoming Emperor, because the risings in Sz-chwan were not entirely suppressed, and he felt, before he did this, he must leave no trouble abroad that might endanger the position he had taken. There was one year therefore in which Yuan Ti was still allowed to have the nominal sway over the country. During this the king of Wu, King-ti, died, and was succeeded by his cousin, whose title is Mo-ti (A. D. 265). Next year Sze-ma-chau died, and was succeeded by his son Sze-ma-yen. Yuan Ti, knowing that the farce of his ruling was now at an end, resigned his perilous position and retired into private life, thus giving way for the founder of the new dynasty.

CHAPTER XII.

THE WESTERN TSIN DYNASTY (A. D. 265-317).

Wu Ti—A. D. 265-290.

WHEN Wu Ti seized the imperial power he was thirty years of age, and he gave the name of Tsin, the ducal title that had been bestowed upon his father by Mo Ti, to his new dynasty. He seems to have been an easy-tempered man, and not of that ferocious description that would have caused him to initiate his rule by the wholesale slaughter of all the members of the late dynasty. His first acts indeed showed that he had a sincere desire to rule his people well and to consider what was for the welfare of the state. He introduced a system of economy into the palace and amongst the mandarins, which he hoped would influence the people generally. The rulers of Wei had been noted for their lavish expenditure, and the example thus set had been imitated by the wealthy classes, and they again by those below them, so that the people were in danger of being impoverished by the extravagance that characterized every grade of society. He set an example of moderation in his own person. When he went to the ancestral temple of his fathers to offer the usual bullock to their spirits he ordered that it should not be led by a silken rope as usual, but by a hempen one. This was but one of the many reforms which he introduced for the good of the people. His son Chung was appointed heir to the throne, much to the disgust of the great mandarins, for he was half an idiot, and altogether incapable of ruling at a time when mind and energy were required to guide and strengthen the new dynasty.

In his fifth year Wu Ti made plans for the overthrow of the Wu dynasty, so that China should no longer be a country divided into several kingdoms, but should be one, as it was before the troubles and rebellions that resulted in the division of the empire into three kingdoms. To assist him in this enterprise he employed the famous statesman and commander Yanghu. This man was of noble ancestry, of great military skill, and noted for his virtues, both in public and private life. Wu Ti made him governor of that part of Kingchow that was under the rule of the Emperor. This was to be the base from which the movements were to be made that would finally end in the extermination of the house of Wu. No better man in the whole empire could have been found for this purpose than he. Without meeting of hostile armies, or the clash and sound of battle, the victory was gained by the gentle life and by the conspicuous virtues that made him loved both by friend and foe. When he reached his government his first care was for the welfare of his soldiers. He found that only ten days' provisions remained in the commissariat, and that he was expected, like other great commanders, to make the land of the enemy support his men.

This he utterly refused to do, not only because it was contrary to his own instincts of justice, but also because it would defeat the very end he had in view, and that was to subdue the people of Wu, not with the sword, but with his righteous way of administering his government. He wanted to let them see that in submitting to the Emperor they were exchanging an oppressive rule under which they now groaned for a just one under the Tsins. He therefore turned the great majority of his men into farmers. A plot of land was given to each, and with the natural instinct that a Chinaman has for cultivating the soil not many months had passed by before the camp was filled with abundance of food that made them quite independent of friend or foe.

In the eighth year of Wu Ti's reign an event took place that was destined to work evil consequences to the new dynasty. The heir Chung married a wife from the family of Ku. She was a clever woman and greatly beloved by her half-witted husband, but she was cruel and wicked, and just the kind of person that would wreck the fortunes of any person or thing over which she had any control. We shall meet with her by and by, when she begins to take a prominent place in the counsels of the state. This same year was marked by an irruption of the "White-horsed Barbarians" into Sz-chwan. The commander-in-chief sent his second in command with an army against them, but for some reason, which history fails to give, he killed his chief, and then with those of his soldiers that would follow him, joined the barbarians. As this was an act that could not be overlooked, another army larger than the first was sent the long dreary journey into Sz-chwan, and after vast toil and hardships, it met the daring intruders and sent them swiftly back across the river of the golden sands into their own country.

During this same year Wu Ti made serious preparations for an invasion of the Wu territory. The soldiers of Yanghu were called away from their fields and their agriculture to the banks of the Yang-tze to prepare boats in which they might cross the river, which during so many campaigns had always proved a most successful barrier to the hosts that had endeavoured to invade the land beyond. The versatility of the Chinese is shown in this remarkable undertaking. The great majority of these men had never seen a boat in their life, and yet when the order came to them to leave their fields and march to the great river's brink they complied, with the conviction that they could accomplish anything that men of their own rank had done before them. When the ruler of Wu saw the vast preparations that were being made for an invasion of his dominions he began to take such measures as would thwart the designs of his enemies. He had iron stakes driven into the river at regular intervals along the shore for a great distance along it, and he had also chains fastened from point to point in the islands which studded the river, so that no boats might pass. The river was thus so strongly fortified that the attempt to cross it was given up for the present as impracticable. Meanwhile Yanghu, with his noble policy of doing right, and his generous treatment of his people, was doing more for the subjugation of the kingdom of Wu than all the armies of Tsin and all the ships that were being built to carry the armed hosts across the unwilling river could accomplish. He made it a principle that everything his soldiers got from the people should be paid for. If a wild animal, wounded in the territory of Wu, was pursued and hunted down by himself or his retinue in the chase, it was sent back again across the boundary. The result of all this ended in extreme friendliness between Yanghu and Luh-k'ang, the commander of the Wu forces. Compliments were continually being exchanged between them. The latter made a present of wine to Yanghu, and when his officers warned him against drinking it, as it might be poisoned, with the generous and unsuspicious feelings of a large-hearted man, he at once tasted it to show that he believed in the honesty of the man that sent it. When, too, Luh-k'ang was ill, Yanghu sent him some medicine which he believed was good for the complaint from which he was suffering. This generous rivalry as to who should outdo the other in kindness is an exceedingly beautiful sight, especially in an age when men were wont in war and rival politics to consider the lives of their opponents as of no value whatsoever. In the 10th year of Wu Ti, Luh-k'ang died, and left his five sons in command of the army that was opposed to that of the Tsins. This year another famous captain in Chinese history, Chow-ch'u, was appointed to the command of the army in Sz-chwan, whose duty it was to guard that beautiful region from the incursions of the Burmese and other barbarians, and also to overcome any of the adherents of the late dynasty who might be inclined to rise in rebellion against the present one.*

This year, too, the queen died, and in the following one the Emperor married her younger sister. Her father agreed to this,

---

* Chow-ch'u in early life was a man of very indifferent morals. He was of very powerful physique and a rough, fierce fellow that caused alarm and terror to the neighbourhood in which he lived. One day he was walking along the road, when he came upon an old man sitting by the side of it with sad and mournful countenance. Standing before him, in a rough and boisterous voice he said to him, "Why are you so miserable looking? The times are good, and no disaster is happening to the people; why should you be so full of sorrow as you appear to be?" The old man said, "I have three causes for sorrow which are quite enough to make me as wretched as I seem to be." "What are these?" he asked; "perhaps I may be able to remove them." "The first is the tiger with the white forehead on the hills over yonder that descends into our plain and devours people," he replied. "The second is the dragon by the 'Long Bridge' that devours people that cross over, and the third is yourself." "Oh!" replied Chow-ch'u, struck to the quick that he should be considered one of the public enemies of society. "I'll undertake to remove them all, so that you need not sorrow over them any more." Shortly after he slew both the tiger and the dragon, and then, associating only with good men, he became so reformed that every one instinctively turned to his great strength as a protection against violence and injustice.

but her uncle was violently opposed to the marriage, and in a memorial to the Emperor he showed him the danger of putting such honour upon any one family, as it might prove perilous to the state from the great influence it would give it.   He also showed him what calamities it might bring upon the members of it at his death, when the enemies that his favour towards it had created would revenge their grievances by the murder of every member of it, as was the common custom of the day.   The Emperor, who was deeply in love with the lady, would not listen to any of these remonstrances, but consented to give him a document that would secure him from violence in the future by declaring that he had used all his influence in endeavouring to prevent the marriage.   Future events will show that this did not save him from the fate that he knew would be likely to fall upon him.

In the thirteenth year of his reign Wu Ti made Yanghu a viscount and appointed him commander-in-chief of the armies that were being gathered for the overthrow of the kingdom of Wu ; but the next year he returned to his home and died, to the great regret of the people of Wu.   When the news reached them every one was oppressed with sorrow, as though some dear friend had died.   All business was stayed for a time, and the people were affected even to tears.   They erected a stone tablet on a hill that he was fond of walking on, and it was called the "Tablet of the Falling Tears," for as the crowds came to look at it out of respect to his memory the tears fell fast from every eye for the loss of a man who was a public benefactor to the whole region.

In the meantime things were going on badly in the state of Wu, in consequence of the licentious and wicked conduct of its ruler, Sunhau, who neglected his duties and gave himself up to the most dissipated and abandoned of pleasures.

His cruel disposition was shown in the reckless way in which he murdered the officials about his palace.   He would invite a certain number at a time to a banquet which he had prepared for them.   He would there insist upon their drinking freely of the liquors which were purposely placed in profusion on the tables. None might refuse to drink without incurring the anger of Sunhau, though they were aware of the terrible consequences to themselves should they drink.   After the liquor began to take effect, the actions and words, and even the very looks, were carefully taken down and recorded by eunuchs in an ante-room, who were stationed there by the ruler's orders, and next day a fearful reckoning was made with those who, when under the influence of the strong drink, had been guilty of any indiscretion or any breach of court etiquette.   The man that had become drowsy and had dared to sleep in the royal presence had his eyes torn out.   The one whose face was flushed and red had the skin flayed from off his cheeks, and those who had spoken disrespectfully had their teeth broken to pieces.

Such terrible cruelties alienated the hearts of all men from him, and they were only too ready for the change of masters and submission to the Tsin Emperor. The general of the Tsin army in Kingchow, Towyin, memorialized Wu Ti to come and take possession of the country, for he would not find any to oppose his march into it. The latter willingly complied with this request, and immediately sent a force of over two hundred thousand men with which to occupy the country.

The five sons of Luh-k'ang, who had command of the troops, at once submitted, but thus at one stroke this important district was added to the possessions of Tsin. The imperial army was then marched to the bank of the Yang-tze, when Towyin floated down immense rafts of wood, which were covered with combustibles which, being set on fire, were allowed to drift on to the iron chain barriers, which melted under the great heat. The army then crossed the river, for this time the foe made no attempt to thwart the enterprise, and marching to Nanking they invested the city.

Sun-hau, seeing no hope of delivery, acted the part of How Chu when his capital was besieged, and with his hands tied behind his back, and with his coffin accompanying him, he marched out of the gates and delivered himself up to the enemy. Express messengers were at once despatched to inform Wu Ti of the success, who is said to have wept when he heard the joyful tidings, and to have exclaimed, "Ah! this victory belongs not to my soldiers, but to Yanghu, and now he is gone and cannot share in the success that his goodness and justice have obtained for me."

The life of Sun-hau was spared, and Wu Ti, in gratitude to Heaven for what he believed was its decision that he should rule over this whole empire, made him the "Duke Resignation to the Will of Heaven." He also took the five thousand women that composed Sun-hau's harem into his own, which now consisted of the modest number of ten thousand.

Wu Ti, now finding himself the recognized sovereign of the whole empire, and peace prevailing throughout its borders, gave himself up to luxurious indulgence, to the neglect of the best interests of the state. The court soon became too hot for the old and loyal ministers, who were gradually replaced by the relatives of the queen, of whom the Emperor was greatly enamoured. One day Wu Ti asked one of the imperial censors, with which one of the Emperors of the Han dynasty he would compare him. He promptly replied that the only ones that he could think of were Hwan Ti and Ling Ti. "But why should you couple my name with theirs," he asked in astonishment, "since they caused the overthrow of that dynasty." The censor replied, "You are worse than either of those two. When Hwan Ti, for example, sold the government offices the money obtained was put into the public treasury, but now it goes to your own private account."

"There is one thing," said the easy-going, good-tempered monarch, in which I am superior to him. "I have a faithful and loyal minister to tell me of my faults, which he did not have, and for this I am thankful." Two years after his defeat and submission Sun-hau died, and with him disappears the kingdom that had played such a stirring part in the great contests of the Three Kingdoms.

For four years the empire was engaged in a deadly struggle with the Sienpi, who came in great force into Shensi, and wished to take possession of that part of the country. It was only after severe fighting and a large number of lives had been lost that they were finally subdued and the barbarians were driven back. The next year after the victory had been gained over them, and in the twenty-fifth year of his reign, Wu Ti died, when his idiotic son Chung succeeded him on the throne. His dynastic title is

Hwei Ti—A. D. 290-307.

No sooner did this prince ascend the throne than his vigorous and wicked queen at once took the reins of power into her own hands.

It is true that for a time she dissembled and allowed the wife of the late Emperor to remain in the palace with the honour and a certain amount of power that a queen-dowager always has in China, and that her father held the great and important position of generalissimo of the forces. She was, however, only biding her time when she would in a most tragic way remove every one of the house of Yang out of the way, so that she could reign with undisputed sway. Her husband, imbecile as he was, was in mortal dread of his spouse, and consequently carried out her orders most implicitly. In this way he gave a legal sanction and authority to all her acts, the most of which he would have shrunk from acknowledging had he been sane enough to have known the meaning of them. His son Luh, by a concubine, a clever, intelligent lad, and one deeply beloved by his late grandfather, was appointed heir to the crown, as he had no children by his own queen.

Not many months had passed by before the queen had put her terrible purpose of murder into such a shape that she could carry it out. She plotted with some of the court officials, and they agreed to make the accusation to the Emperor that Yangtsun was conspiring to rebel and seize the throne, and that his daughter, the queen-dowager, was concerned in the plot. At the same time she brought soldiers into the capital, and quietly, before he was aware of it, had surrounded the house of the commander-in-chief with four hundred troops. She also got her poor weak husband to sign a decree that he should be put to death for treason. The queen-dowager realized the extreme danger to which she and every one of her name were exposed, and yet she was so surrounded by the friends of the queen that she could take no active measures to save her father. Driven

to despair, she wrote a short note, and tying it to the end of an
arrow shot it at random from her window. In this she promised
great rewards and high honours to any one that would rescue him
from his peril. The queen, who soon got to know of what had
been done, at once circulated the report that the family of the
queen-dowager was meditating rebellion, and declared that any one
that moved in her behalf would be implicated in her wrong. In
consequence of this no one durst lift a finger in aid of the doomed
family, for not only were people afraid of her vengeance, but they
also shrunk from complicity with a crime which the Chinese have
always looked upon with the utmost abhorrence, namely, treason
to the state. Yangtsun's house was set on fire by the soldiery, and
when he attempted to escape and fled into the stables he was cut in
pieces by the soldiers. Three of his brothers were killed at the
same time, one of them being the uncle who protested against
his niece marrying Wu Ti, and who had been given a document
insuring his safety should any danger come to him through the
alliance in the future. When the officers came to seize him
he produced the safeguard that Wu Ti had given him ; but the
queen was not a person to mind the existence of any number
of such documents, and he was murdered whilst protesting
against the injustice that was being done him. The queen-
dowager was sent to the city of Kinyang, where she was left
without any food or attendants, and in eight days she died of
starvation.

In the fourth year of the Emperor the Sienpi again made an
irruption into China and penetrated as far as Honan, but after
capturing some important places they were defeated and had to retire.
Two years after, the country was once more distressed by a tribe
of nomad shepherds that lived to the west of Sz-chwan and Kansuh,
called the Ch'iang barbarians. The Emperor sent Hia-heu, his
commander-in-chief, against them, with Chow-ch'u as his second,
to meet them in the field. When the chief heard that the latter
was to be opposed to them he is said to have remarked to his
officers, "We shall never be able to contend with a man of such
abilities and sterling character as he ; our only chance of success is
by meeting the enemy when another commands." As the Ch'iang
had not penetrated further than Shensi it took the imperial troops
some time to march from the capital to where they were. The
commander-in-chief, who was jealous of the fame of Chow-ch'u,
determined during the present campaign that it should suffer an
eclipse. He accordingly sent him forward with five thousand men
to attack the barbarians, who, with their chief, were stationed
near Singan-fu with seventy thousand. Chow-ch'u was too
brave a soldier to refuse the perilous honour that was assigned to
him. He only requested the commander to hasten to his aid as
speedily as possible, as otherwise he and his men must inevitably
perish.

They fought the livelong day, till their arrows were all spent and their bow-strings broken. Many an agonizing glance did they cast back in the direction of their comrades, but not a single soldier came to their relief.

After performing prodigies of valour and killing large numbers of the foe, Chow-ch'u and nearly all his men were slain.

Next day the main body came up and engaged the Sienpi, but it was defeated with great slaughter and utterly demoralized and dispersed. The barbarians were now free to work their will on the lands and people of Shensi, and most terrible were the sorrows that these ruthless invaders brought upon the inhabitants. For a whole year they were left in undisturbed possession of the region, and it was not till a new army under Mungkwan reached the scene that retribution came upon them, and they were driven ignominiously across the borders into their own territories. The queen, who more and more absorbed the power of the state, and of whom the weak Emperor had a growing apprehension, showed the utter wickedness of her heart by the immoralities of which she was guilty. Her expenditure, too, was on a most lavish scale, and to meet it she had recourse to the most shameless and open sale of government offices.

She seemed to have no regard for public opinion, either as to her own private life or to her methods in the government of the country. She removed every one from her path that seemed in any way likely to be a hindrance to her, and even Luh, the sharp, intelligent son of her imbecile husband was poisoned by her orders, lest when he came of age he might revenge upon her the injuries that he and his mother had received from her.

At length, in the year A. D. 300, Sze-ma-lun, seeing that she was determined upon the destruction of all the family of Sze-ma-i and of placing her own in possession of the royal power, took measures to forestall her, and hastily gathering a body of men devoted to him he entered the capital unexpectedly, and seizing the person of Hwei Ti he placed him in a secure part of the palace. He then ordered his men to convey the queen to the same place where the queen-dowager had been starved to death. She was left there without any attendants and without any food, and by a just Nemesis she suffered the same fate as her unhappy victim.

He next proceeded to exterminate as many of the queen's family as he could lay his hands upon, and thus in this tragic way the house of Ku disappears from the prominent place it had just occupied in history. After this Sze-ma-lun made himself prime minister of Hwei Ti and assumed the direction of affairs with Sun-siu as his political adviser.

By the advice of the latter he put to death the great mandarins who had made any opposition to his late action, and he took a terrible revenge upon all his enemies. The millionaire of his time, too, suffered death, simply because Sun-siu had been denied a beautiful concubine of his, which he had refused to give up to him.*

Sze-ma-lun, from the time he stepped into power, formed the design of making himself Emperor, but nature had not given him the mental capacities for such a distinguished position. He was a coarse and illiterate man, and his only excuse for being in the exalted rank he now occupied was entirely owing to his being a relative of the reigning Emperor. He showed his incapacity for comprehending the responsibility of governing a great empire like China by elevating all his friends, no matter how unsuited, to offices under government. The lowest menials about the palace who had accompanied him in his raid on the capital were elevated to be high officers, and even his cook was enabled to bid adieu to his kitchen forever and become a magistrate and exercise judicial functions over the people.

Several of the brothers of Hwei Ti, seeing the treasonable designs that Sze-ma-lun entertained, and judging that any one of them had a better right to the throne than he, combined their forces, and meeting him in battle they overthrew and slew him.

One of them was made commander-in-chief, and the rest were all elevated to responsible positions, where their powers were very large, and poor Hwei Ti, who was unconscious of all the plots and counter-plots by which his power had been threatened, again went through the farce of being recognized as the supreme authority in the state.

The real ruler was not he, but one of his brothers, Prince Ts'i. This man was prodigal and dissipated, and employed men to be the rulers of the people who were bad and wicked like himself. People became discontented with his rule, for Hwei Ti, as usual, was a mere puppet in the hands of the intriguers that thronged his palace.

Before the year was out prince Ts'i was murdered by another brother, who at once stepped into the offices he had held and pretended to administer the government in the name of the Emperor. Two other brothers—Yung and Ying—being dissatisfied at this state of things, and deeming that they were the proper persons to have the guardianship of the Emperor, rose in rebellion. The new minister, Prince Ngai, accompanied by Hwei Ti, led an army against Ying, but whilst they were fighting, Yung advanced upon the capital with his forces and took possession of it. He showed the kind of spirit by which he was animated by murdering ten thousand of the citizens. The Emperor now returned to face the

---

* Shih-ch'ung, the wealthiest subject that we meet with in history, and who had the reputation of being the Crœsus of China, was a man of unbounded hospitality, but was also, in accordance with the habits of the wealthy men of this land, dissipated and immoral in his habits. No doubt Sun-siu had his eye more on his wealth than upon the concubine, and therefore he determined to take this opportunity of acquiring it for himself. When he was about to be executed, Shih-ch'ung cried out, "Alas! my wealth on which I prided myself has been the cause of my ruin." "Why then," said a by-stander, "did you not scatter it abroad sooner?" A question underlying which there is a profound philosophy, but which wealthy men are never able to understand or appreciate.

danger that was threatening his existence, but his army was defeated, and he had to retreat. Finally Ying joined his brother in the capital, and having killed Prince Ngai, Hwei Ti was permitted to return to his palace and take undisturbed possession of it, whilst the two brothers divided between them the power of the state.

This state of things was soon interrupted by a rebellion in the south, which was destined to have a serious effect on the fortunes of the Tsin dynasty. Liuyen, who ruled a large district to the south of the Yang-tze, declared that he was the rightful successor to the throne of the Hans, and that therefore he was going to lay claim to it and oust Hwei Ti, who, after all, was but a mere usurper. The person who now professed to have a legitimate claim upon the throne was a Hiungnu, and a hostage that had come to the court of Wu Ti in the course of that Emperor's reign. His family name was the same as that of the house of Han. This is not astonishing, for in former days marriages had been contracted between the families of the sovereigns of China and those of the Hiungnu. Besides, in addition to this, the name of the reigning house had sometimes been given as a matter of compliment or honour to members of the great families of the barbarians, whom it was advisable at the time to please with such a distinguished favour. Liu-yen had been put in authority over the five clans of the Hiungnu that had submitted to the Chinese government, and who had been distributed throughout various parts of the empire. Considering the present moment favorable for carrying out his own ambitious designs, he proclaimed himself a descendant of the Han dynasty, and therefore entitled to the throne.

In the year A. D. 307 another formidable insurrection broke out in Shantung, which was headed by Yueh, the Prince of the Eastern Sea. This man appeared at the head of over two hundred thousand men, and overcoming all opposition he killed all the mandarins that opposed him, and taking possession of the Emperor again removed the capital to Lohyang He appointed himself prime minister and ruled the country in his name. Next year the unfortunate Hwei Ti died suddenly after eating some cakes which were supposed to have been poisoned by Yueh, and thus, after a troubled reign of seventeen years, during which many a tragedy had been enacted in his name, he passed away, leaving his country in a state of disorder and unrest. He was succeeded by his brother Sze-ma-chi, who is known by his dynastic title of

Hwai Ti—A. D. 307-313.

This prince was of the mature age of forty-two when he ascended the throne. He was a man of great intelligence and profoundly versed in the arts of government, and he began his reign with the sincere desire of ruling his people well. The Prince of the Eastern Sea was obliged to retire from court for a time, but it was only to more fully mature his schemes for overthrowing the Tsins.

In the meantime troubles were gathering thick and fast in other parts of the empire. In the 2nd year of Hwai Ti, Liuyen proclaimed himself King of Han, and shortly after, the Prince of the Eastern Sea again entered the capital and murdered nearly a score of high officials in the palace, on the ground that they were traitors to the country, but really, because they were loyal men and true, who would have opposed his usurpation.

Hwai Ti was perfectly helpless to prevent this, and he had to submit to the greatest indignities from the man that wished to oust him from the throne. In the 4th year of his reign Liuyen died, and was succeeded by his brother Liuch'ang. Next year the Prince of the Eastern Sea was made commander-in-chief of all the troops, the highest post he could hold under the Emperor, and which he looked upon as the final one he had to take before he stepped on to the throne. Fortunately Hwai Ti was relieved from any anxiety with regard to him by his death, which happened shortly after, as he was on his way to oppose the troops of Liuch'ang, who had begun the conquest of Kingchow. The command of the troops now fell to Wangyen, who, however, was defeated by the Hiungnu and pursued and captured by his savage enemies. He was immediately slain, and the coffin that contained the remains of the Prince of the Eastern Sea was opened and the body burnt. The imperial troops were so utterly routed that they were of no use to stem the tide of the victorious Hiungnu, who speedily marched on to Lohyang. Here three of their armies converged, and no fewer than twelve engagements were fought between them with the soldiers of Tsin that had been hastily summoned to the aid of the Emperor, but who were invariably defeated.

Things were now reduced to such a desperate pass that Hwai Ti, who saw that his life was in danger, fled with his suite to Ch'angngan in Shensi, but he was captured on the road and sent to Liuch'ang, who had fixed his capital in Peking. Here he was deposed from his kingly office and made Duke of P'ing-yang, whilst Liu-yau, the general who had seized him, was put in charge of Lohyang. After two years had passed by, the Tsin general, who had made Ch'angngan his headquarters, seeing that the Emperor was not likely to be restored to his throne, and feeling the need of some responsible head at the present critical state of affairs, placed Yeh, a brother of Hwai Ti, on the throne and sent orders throughout the length and breadth of the empire for all the loyal soldiers to come to the aid of the country and drive out its savage oppressors. The new Emperor is known by the name of

Min Ti—A. D. 313-317.

After Hwai Ti had been held a prisoner by Liuch'ang for two years the latter began to tire of his presence and to wish that by some decent pretence he could get rid of him. He accordingly began to treat him with the greatest indignity. He made him dress as a slave and attend at the dinners that he gave his great officers and pour liquors that they drank into their glasses. He was so ill-used that he and the officials that had followed him into captivity often wept over the hard lot that had befallen them. This only roused the anger of Liuch'ang, who treated them with still further unkindness. At length one of his officers, through malice, informed him that his prisoners were meditating flight, when, glad of an excuse, he ordered the execution of them all. When the news of Hwai Ti's death reached Wangtsun, who was Governor of Chihli, he thought that this was a fitting time for him to come forward and amidst the present disorder seize upon the supreme power. Whilst he was meditating upon this and maturing his plans, Liu-yau, who saw through his design and perceived the danger that would arise to Liuch'ang were another army in the field to oppose him, sent messengers to him and assured him that he was ready to submit to him and raise him to the throne, and that if he consented he would march his soldiers to his aid and fight for him.

Wangtsun only too readily fell into the snare of his wily opponent and granted permission for the troops to march into his camp, although he was opposed by his generals, who assured him that the only purpose of Liu-yau was to murder him. He very soon found out that he had been deceived, for no sooner had Liu-yau's army reached his than it made a sudden onslaught on it, when it was routed and he was killed. The whole of Chihli was thus added to the dominions of Liuch'ang.

In the 3rd year of Min Ti, Wangchi, the Governor of Kwang-chow, raised a rebellion and determined to found a dynasty of his own in the south of China. The famous statesman and General T'au-k'an was sent against him, and crushed the insurrection, and was himself appointed governor of the district. *

---

* T'au-k'an was specially noted for the talents he displayed in governing. When a young man he was extremely poor, but his mother was one of those clever women that seem to have the power of extracting good fortune out of the most desperate circumstances. Her great ambition in life was to forward the interests of her beloved son, and everything was made to bend to this one idea, and suffering and misery were endured by her willingly, in order that she might bring happiness and renown to him. She also put herself out to entertain scholars and distinguished men, for she wished her son to keep company with such, as she believed they would be the people amongst whom his coming years would be spent.

T'au-k'an was a man that never lost a moment. He was most indefatigable in everything that he undertook, and he dreaded lest through indolence he should degenerate in his character to that of the rest of the mandarins who entered office simply as a matter of livelihood. After he became Governor of Kwangchow he made it a practice of carrying from his study door every morning, when he went out to engage in his public duties, a hundred bricks, and when he returned in the evening to take them back within the house. When some of his officers, who were surprised at this, asked him why he, the governor of a province, should engage in such menial employment, T'au-k'an instantly replied that he wished to inure himself to hardness, so that he should never grow effeminate and thus be inclined to neglect his public duties. He was severe in his discipline. Those of the officers of higher rank who gambled or got drunk he punished by having their cards or their drinking cups thrown into the river. The common soldiers who indulged in these vices were beaten.

In the 4th, that is, the last year of Min Ti's reign, Ch'angngan was captured by Liu-yau, as well as all the cities that lay on the way to it. He also made prisoners of two generals whom he had defeated, named Lu and Liang. He was so much struck with their bravery that he offered to spare the lives of both if they would but take service with him. They resolutely refused the tempting offer and said that their lives and services had been devoted to the house of Tsin, and as the fortune of war prevented them from serving it the only wish they had now was to die.

Struck with admiration at their loyalty he ordered a sword to be handed to them, when they instantly put an end to their lives. The wife of the former was an exceedingly beautiful woman. Liu-yau offered to make her his wife if she would consent, but she declined, and said that a true woman could be the wife of only one man. She was allowed to follow her husband's example.

After the capture of Ch'angngan Min Ti was sent to Liuch'ang in Peking, where he was made in derision the Viscount of "The Peaceful Heart." Thus the fortunes of war had delivered the two last kings of the Western Tsin into the power of a man who was a barbarian. It was a strange turn in the wheel of fortune that made a member of the despised race of the Hiungnu the arbiter of the fate of the sovereigns of so great a country as China.

CHAPTER XIII.

THE EASTERN TSIN DYNASTY (A. D. 317-420).

Yuan Ti—A. D. 317-323.

AFTER the capital had been entered and Min Ti carried away to the court of Liuch'ang the empire was again practically left without a ruler, for no one expected that the captive would ever be restored to his home again; indeed it was almost certain that he would be got rid of in the same distressing manner as Hwai Ti had been. One of the descendants of Sze-ma-i, by the female line, was at this time a prince, in the territory of which Nanking was the chief city. Reading in his own favour a prophecy that the "House of Horse," which was the family name of Sze-ma-i, would be overthrown by a man of the name of Ox, which was his own, he determined, as far as he was able, to accomplish the prediction by seizing the throne now made vacant by the disappearance of Min Ti. It seems that whilst Sze-ma-i was alive a stone was brought to him one day that had been dug up out of the ground. On it were cut the figures of seven horses and one ox. This was interpreted to mean that seven members of his family would hold power in the state and then it would be overturned by some one of the name of Ox. So thoroughly did Sze-ma-i believe in the silent prophecy of this stone that he would never endure any one of this name to hold office under the government, and because one of his captains had it he caused him to be put to death. The time and the circumstances certainly favoured the ambition of the prince, and he was urged by his officers and friends to take advantage of them and proclaim himself Emperor of China. He refused at first, as he said that Min Ti, the real ruler, was still alive, and might any day return to dispute with him the possession of the throne.

He still, however, so far followed their advice that he built an ancestral temple after the manner of the founders of dynasties, and he had an altar built to Heaven and Earth, such as only the ruler of a state was allowed to offer sacrifice upon. The prince had not long to wait for the throne to become vacant. Liuch'ang made Min Ti's life as miserable as he had done that of his predecessor. When he went out hunting he forced him to assist in dragging his chariot. He caused him to wear the dress of the barbarians, and he gave him the servile office of cup-bearer to himself and his captains at their feasts. Having incurred the anger of Liuch'ang by their sorrowful countenances he and all his faithful followers were cruelly murdered. When the news reached Nanking there was great outward mourning and lamentation, but none the less the prince announced himself the legitimate successor of the house of Tsin and proclaimed himself Emperor of China. His son Shau was made the heir to the throne, and was immediately put under the charge of a famous teacher, Yuliang, to be trained for the important position that he was destined to occupy by and by. This man seemed well qualified for his high office, for when his father expressed a wish that his son should be trained in a knowledge of the laws and customs of his country Yuliang dissented, on the ground that such a study would teach him to become cruel to the people, as the example of many of the Emperors before his time would only tend to make him haughty and overbearing, and would cause him to fancy that the duty of a king was not to rule well and wisely the people of his empire, but to gratify his own ambition. He further advised that he should be allowed to read with him books that were intended to develop the moral character and give him a high sense of the duties of life. Yuen Ti admired the goodness and wisdom of Yuliang and gave him permission to train the young prince in his own way.

A few months after the murder of Min Ti a terrible disaster happened to Liuch'ang. His palace caught fire, and twenty-one of his sons, with other members of his family, perished in the flames, and only one son was left. He was so overwhelmed with this awful calamity that he died of grief, and his surviving son Ts'an succeeded him. Within a very short time, however, he was murdered by the commander-in-chief, who had fallen in love with a beautiful concubine of his, and who not only aspired to have her, but also to seize upon the power that Liuch'ang had so lately held.

When Liu-yau, the relative of Liuch'ang, got intelligence of this he at once hastened by forced marches from Ch'angngan with all his troops to meet the usurper and murderer. At the same time Shihleh, one of the generals in Lohyang, was hastening with fifty thousand men with the same object, and arriving first he killed the recreant general, and thus put a sudden stop to his ambitious projects. After his arrival on the scene Liu-yau proclaimed himself Emperor and appointed Shihleh his commander-in-chief.

Liu-yau removed his capital from Peking to Ch'angngan and called his dynasty by the name of Chau. Not long after some of his officers, who hated Shihleh, insinuated to him that he was going to rebel. Angry at this he put to death some messengers that the latter had sent him, upon which the accused, indignant at the unjust suspicions that had been entertained about him, and finding his life in danger, broke out into rebellion and declared that he was going to found a new dynasty, to which he gave the name of the Later Chau.

In the 4th year of his reign the Emperor was seriously troubled by the signs of coming disorder that promised to interfere with the stability of his government. There were two brothers—Wangtun and Wangtau. The latter of these was a loyal, trustworthy officer, and had charge over the palace and many of the affairs connected with it. The former was proud and inclined to rebellion, and held the influential post of Governor of Kingchow. Yuan Ti not only hated but also feared him, because he was greatly beloved by his soldiers, who were prepared, without looking closely into the reason or rights of things, to follow him wherever he might wish to lead them. The loyal officials in the palace were exceedingly anxious that some plan should be adopted by which his power might be restrained, and suggested that an officer with full powers should be sent to Kingchow to watch his proceedings and report them to the Emperor. Wangtun agreed to this plan, and the uncle of Yuan Ti was sent on this special mission. When he arrived, Wangtun, wishing to know the kind of metal of which he was made, invited him to dinner, and whilst they were sitting chatting, and he supposed he was off his guard, he asked him how it was that he, who was such a celebrated scholar, dared to undertake the command of an army, about which he was in perfect ignorance. "It is quite true," he replied, "that my experience is small, and I may be like a leaden knife that cannot make very severe cuts, but even that can make one at least." When the meal was over Wangtun told his officers that the man that had come to watch them was of no ability whatsoever, and that they need not concern themselves any further about him. Next year Wangtun gathered his chief men about him and told them he was going to rebel, for it was evident that Yuan Ti meant his destruction, and that he might as well die with arms in his hands as by the axe of the common executioner. They endeavoured to dissuade him from this, but he would not listen to them, as his mind was fully made up.

His first step in the programme was to memorialize the Emperor and demand that two of his officials, named Liu and Tiau, should be degraded and punished, as he declared that he knew for certain they were both engaged in a treasonable conspiracy against the throne. Yuan Ti was exceedingly enraged at this boldness of Wangtun, and immediately issued an imperial edict declaring that any one that killed him would be ennobled and made a viscount, and at the same time he proceeded to raise an army to fight against him. Wangtun took the initiative by attacking the city in which his uncle, the imperial commissioner, was living, and after capturing it he put him to death. Liu and Tiau now advised the Emperor as a matter of safety, and in accordance with the usage on such occasions, to put to death all the relatives of Wangtun that were about the palace. This he declined to do, as he was unwilling that his brother Wangtau, who had been most loyal, should be sacrificed for a crime with which he had had nothing to do. The latter, however, was prepared for such a measure, and in order to show his acquiescence in it, should the Emperor determine upon it, and to prove that he had no complicity with the treason of his brother, he collected all the members of the Wang family and stood within the palace gates waiting for the command of Yuan Ti that should consign them to the executioner's hands.

As they waited mournfully and in silence the prime minister, Chow-i, passed in to wait on the Emperor. Wangtau and he had been bosom friends, and he now besought him to intercede with Yuan Ti and save their wives and little ones from a fate that was coming upon them for crimes that they all abhorred. This Chow-i was a man rugged and stern in his demeanour, but one of those noble characters that we find even in the most depraved periods of Chinese history. He was loyal to his country and true to his friends, but he unfortunately was wanting in those external graces that would have helped men to understand and appreciate him better, and so he was apt to be thought hard and severe when in reality his heart was full of sympathy and kindness. On this occasion, at least, he was terribly misunderstood. Instead of replying to Wangtau's entreaties he passed by him as though he had never seen him. The reason of this was that there were spies about who would have reported to Yuan Ti any expression of kindness to Wangtau at that time, as a sign that he was in league with him for treasonable purposes, and instead of serving his friend he would only have hastened his ruin as well as his own. Wangtau was greatly distressed at the apparent desertion of his friend in this his time of extreme peril, and his heart was filled with anger against him. No sooner had he entered the palace, however, than he at once drew up a memorial to the Emperor, in which he pled for his friend's life, and showed that he was a loyal officer and one that could be ill-spared in this crisis when rebellion was abroad. Yuan Ti at once granted his request, not only because it harmonized with his own feelings, but also because he recognized in Wangtau a man of rare ability and nobility of character. Next day the Emperor restored him to his official position, but he did not know till too late that Chow-i had nobly done his part to bring this about. Unfortunately for himself Chow-i did not think it necessary to explain to his friend his apparent coldness. He had done his duty and he had saved his life, and he thought there was no need for any further reference to the matter.

When Wangtau entered the presence of Yuan Ti he knelt before him, and with sighs and tears complained of his unhappy lot in being connected with such a brother as Wangtun. The Emperor made him get up and assured him that he had the utmost confidence in him, and that he was going to show that he had by appointing him to the command of a large army that he was going to despatch against Wangtun. The latter in the meantime had been advancing with his forces towards the capital and had carried everything before him. He had given out a proclamation that he had sent broadcast throughout the country that he was not in arms against his sovereign, but against the disloyal officials—Liu and Tiau—who had got the ear of Yuan Ti, and who were determined on his destruction. Wangtun had entrenched himself in the strong city of Wuchang, and on five different occasions he had had engagements with the royal troops, and each time had been victorious.

After these Wangtun slowly advanced upon Nanking, when the Emperor gave Liu and Tiau some troops, and advised them to fly, as he could no longer protect them. Chow-i, together with Wangtau and the eldest brother Wangpin, went to the camp of their brother to try and make the best terms they could with him. When Chow-i came into his presence he demanded in stern tones what right he had to come with an armed force against his sovereign, and what were the demands that he had to make, in order to restore peace to the empire. His manner was that of a man who was conscious of integrity and indignant with wrong, but it would have been better for him had he worded his protest in more gentle language, for a conqueror with the sword of victory in his hand is not apt to brook reproof even from the most virtuous with complacency. Wangtun was highly offended with the manner in which he was addressed, and his anger was not abated by the suggestion of some of his officers, who whispered to him, "This man will one day not spare you, should you be unwise enough to let him go whilst you have him in your power." Disliking, however, to adopt severe measures with a man that he recognized to be of sterling honesty he turned to his brother and asked him what he thought should be done in this case.

Wangtau, smarting under the sense of ill-treatment that he thought he had received from Chow-i, told his brother how he had deserted him in the hour of extreme danger. Wangtun no sooner heard this story than he ordered him out for instant execution, which was accordingly carried out in the barbarous manner of those ancient times.

When the Emperor heard of the death of his loyal and devoted minister he sent Wangpin to the rebel camp to see if he could make terms with his brother. The first business of the latter, when he arrived there, was to weep and wail for Chow-i, and the next was to upbraid his brother for his murder. This so enraged him that he was about to issue orders for his execution, when Wangtau intervened and pleaded on his behalf. Drawing Wangpin aside he advised him to kneel to his brother and ask his forgiveness. "I have a pain in my leg," he replied, "and I cannot kneel, and besides it would be unbecoming for me to bend the knee to my younger brother."* Wangtau reminded him that it was a much less serious thing to have a pain in the leg than one in the neck, which he was in great danger of having if he did not humble himself. History does not record whether he went through the humiliation of bowing to his brother. We do know that he escaped with his life, and was afterwards employed in the service of the state.

---

* In China the elder brother takes precedence of the younger, and it is not considered proper that he should pay any such token of respect to him. The younger may kneel to the elder, as he is his superior.

The interference of the brothers seemed to have been successful in preventing Wangtun from going to the extreme to which his ambition urged him, for after having received a present from Yuan Ti of cattle and spirits for his army he retired from the neighbourhood of the capital to Kingchow. Wangtau, both because he was a loyal minister, and also as a reward for the meritorious services he had rendered, was appointed prime minister in the place of the murdered Chow-i. He had scarcely entered upon the duties of his office when he discovered from the documents he found in the archives the noble service that his dead friend had rendered for him when his life was in danger. When he thought of his ingratitude he wept bitter tears of sorrow, but they could not bring back the man whose death had been really caused by himself.

A few months after the withdrawal of Wangtun, Yuan Ti died. He had been so annoyed and distressed by the rebellion and the indignities he had suffered in connection with it that his health was seriously affected, and he passed away after a brief reign of only six years. He was succeeded by his son Siau, who is known in history by the name of

Ming Ti—A. D. 323-326.

After the death of Yuan Ti, Wangtun again determined that he would carry out the ambitious schemes that had been thwarted before by the influence of his brothers. He accordingly sent a memorial to Ming Ti praying that an appointment might be given him nearer the capital. The Emperor was afraid to grant this request, and yet he dared not refuse it, lest he should expedite the rebellion on which he knew he was intent. He therefore temporized, but this had only the effect of quickening Wangtun's purpose. In spite of the entreaties of his two brothers that he should remain loyal he began his preparations for his march on the capital.

To show what he really meant he appointed his son commander-in-chief, an act which usurped the royal function. Just as the expedition was on the point of starting Wangtun became seriously ill, and it seemed as though it must be given up, for there was no one that could take his place as a leader of the army. His officers, however, entreated him, in spite of his sickness, to begin the campaign. "Everything is ready," they said, "and the men are filled with enthusiasm. The armaments and the provisions are all provided, and we shall never be again in such a good condition as we are now, and therefore, we strongly advise you to order us to march." Wangtun, ill as he was, agreed to this, more especially as he wished to surprise Ming Ti, who, he supposed, was in entire ignorance of his plans. He was mistaken in this, however, for there were loyal men in the camp, who constantly sent information to him of the plan of campaign, so that he had time to collect his forces, and even take the field before Wangtun.

Four different armies were despatched against the latter, and a royal edict was published, showing the reasons why such a formidable force was in arms against the rebel, and declaring that all that submitted at once to the royal clemency would be pardoned, but that if they delayed till hostilities commenced they would be treated with the greatest severity. Wangtun now saw that the die was cast, and that any hesitation would be fatal to his cause. He, therefore, got his army in readiness to march out and meet the imperial troops. Before taking the final step he called a diviner named Chia to tell him what the future had in store for him. The latter was a man devoted to the Tsin dynasty, and so in order to dissuade him from his treason he declared that his expedition would turn out fatally both to him and his family. Wangtun, who was somewhat suspicious of the man, then asked him, how long he had to live. "Your life will be long spared if you do not rebel, but it will be a short one if you do," he promptly replied. Wangtun, now convinced that the man was not true, grimly asked him, "And how long do you think you have to live?" Chia immediately replied, "I die to-day." "You are right for once," said Wangtun sternly, "and I'll make it certain that your prediction comes out right." He then summoned an officer and ordered the execution of the unhappy man.

Unable to lead his army himself he sent it under the command of Chau, but in the battle that ensued the latter was defeated. This so annoyed Wangtun that he expired shortly after the news was brought him. His son Ying, knowing that the troops would disband the moment they knew he was dead, concealed the fact, and wrapping the body in mats buried it under the floor of one of the rooms of the house. The secret was kept most faithfully for some time, for even the general in command was kept in ignorance of it, so that when Ming Ti after his victory invited him to surrender, with the promise that he would be rewarded with high official honours, he refused to do so.

A second engagement took place, when the rebels were once more defeated and the army broke up in confusion and fled in every direction. Ying made all haste to reach Kingchow, but he was drowned by the boatman that was carrying him across the Yang-tze. Wangtun's body was dug up and decapitated, and his head was hung up in a conspicuous place, a warning and a lesson to all such as were meditating treason against their country. The famous T'au-k'an was now made Governor of Kingchow, and soon by the wisdom of his government he restored it to peace and prosperity. Ming Ti died after a brief reign of three years. On his deathbed he handed over the care of his son, who was only five years old, to the care of Yu-liang, his brother-in-law, Wangtau and Pien-k'un, three men in whom he had implicit faith, and who, he trusted, would see that in due time he should come into the inheritance of his father. The child's mother, Queen Yu, was appointed regent at the same time.

Ch'ung Ti—A.D. 326-343.

With the death of Ming Ti, Wangtau determined to withdraw from all political life. The rebellion of his brother had imperilled his very existence. Indeed, if he had not had such an indulgent sovereign to deal with he and his whole clan would inevitably have perished. When, therefore, he was summoned to court as one of the guardians of the young prince he declined, on the ground of illness. Being seen shortly after escorting a friend, who was starting to take up his government in a distant part of the empire, Pien-k'un memorialized the regent that he should be stripped of all his offices for disrespect to the throne. Nothing, however, was done to him, for the regent knew his fidelity and how loyally he had stood by her husband when his crown was in danger.

Gradually all power became vested in the hands of Yuliang, who was a thoroughly incompetent man, and, as is usually the case with such, exceedingly obstinate. The way in which he ruled the people gave great offence, and a rebellion in the palace seemed to be imminent. He behaved also with the greatest cruelty to any one that his small mind had reason to suspect. One of the princes of the blood was supposed by him to be meditating treason, when without any investigation he ordered him to be beheaded. A few days after the young Emperor, who had been greatly attached to him, asked Yuliang where the old gentleman with the white hair was. "Some one said he was going to rebel," he said, "and so I had him executed." The boy began to weep and to express his great sorrow, and then turning suddenly to him he asked him, "If some one said that you were going to do the same thing would your head be cut off?" Yuliang turned pale with fear, for he did not know but that in the turn of the wheel of fortune the words that had been so innocently uttered might not be those that would seal his doom, when the power of life and death had passed to other hands. In the 2nd year of Ch'ung Ti's reign Yuliang became suspicious of a commander in the imperial service, and he determined to crush him. He, therefore, recalled him to the capital. Both Wangtau and Pien-k'un tried to dissuade him from doing so. They showed him that Sutsun knew of his dislike of him and that a return to the capital would mean his destruction, and that therefore he would also, in self-defence, excite his men to rebellion as the only method of saving his life.

Yuliang refused to listen to their advice, and the result was precisely what they had predicted. When the order came to Sutsun to give up his command he appealed to his troops, by whom he was greatly beloved. He told them that his life was aimed at, because he had been only too faithful to his sovereign and successful in the field. His men declared that they were all prepared to stand by him and to risk their lives in his defence, and that the only course in the present disordered state of the country was to set up his own standard and found a dynasty of his own.

Sutsun taking advantage of the enthusiasm of his men, and hoping to surprise the capital before adequate preparations had been made to meet him, crossed the river some distance above Nanking and marched for it. During the night his men unfortunately got entangled amongst marshes they had to pass, and losing their way and becoming disordered, they could not accomplish the surprise they had planned, but instead they had to face an army that was commanded by Pien-k'un, and that lay across their path to the city. They were not deterred, however, by this, and advancing boldly against the royal troops a battle ensued, in which the latter were defeated and the commander and his two sons slain. Sutsun entered Nanking with his victorious soldiers and made himself master of the place.

In the meanwhile Wangtau, hearing of this disaster, led the young prince, dressed in his royal robes, and with the crown upon his head, and seated him on his throne. Ere long some of Sutsun's soldiers, flushed with success, came rushing into the palace, when Wangtau called out in stern tones that they must stand back, as the Emperor's person was sacred, and the common people must not dare to look upon him. With the dread instinct of loyalty that is deep in the heart of every Chinaman they instantly withdrew, and waited the coming of their general to see what orders he had to give them, and whether he would not seize the throne that their valour had put within his grasp. After a time Sutsun arrived, and being hardly yet prepared for the great act of making himself Emperor, declared that he appointed himself prime minister. This he did, he said, in the interests of Ch'ung Ti, who was too young to govern himself, and who unfortunately was surrounded by evil advisers, who did not know how to appreciate those of his servants who were loyal and devoted to him.

Yuliang in the meanwhile was collecting all the forces he could summon from every possible direction to deliver the Emperor from Sutsun. He sent a pressing message to T'au-k'an, the Governor of Kingchow, to come to him with all the men at his command and help him to overthrow the rebel. T'au-k'an, who felt slighted, because he had not been appointed one of the guardians of the young prince, replied that the duties of his province prevented him from complying with his request, and that he could only send him a captain with a few hundred men to help him in his emergency. One of the high officials upon this wrote him and showed him the folly he was committing in not obeying the order of Yuliang, who was really his superior officer, and who held his position by virtue of the commands of the dying Ming Ti. "You must remember," he said, "that in refusing to come with every man you can collect in your district you are doing an act that will be the cause of your own destruction. Sutsun is a bad man, and as soon as he gets possession of the throne he will have no regard for all your services to the state, but will give your government of Kingchow to some one of his followers as a reward for helping him in his rebellion. Your wisest policy, therefore, is to lay aside your jealousies and come with every soldier you have got and help to overthrow the enemy of your country."

T'au-k'an saw the force of this appeal, and without any further delay he donned his armour and quickly gathering his army together he led it with all speed towards Nanking. As this was not a strongly-fortified city Sutsun was afraid he could not hold out against so distinguished a commander, so he withdrew to Wuchang, taking with him the young Emperor.

In the meanwhile the forces of the empire were gradually assembling to the aid of Yuliang, and soon two large bodies of men joined him to assist him in the destruction of Sutsun. One of these was commanded by a man named Yu, who, if he were at all like his mother, must have been a man of most heroic stamp. When he was starting from his home she said to him, "Be loyal, and if your country demands your life then willingly render it up for her sake, for from this time you belong to the Emperor to serve the state at his bidding." She had already sold all her property to procure funds for enlisting men to accompany him, and every available man set forth with him to join the army.

As the forces gathered round Wuchang Sutsun began to dread lest the issue should be fatal to himself, but trusting to the strong defences of the city he determined to hold out to the very last and die fighting rather than surrender. For many months the imperialists could make no impression on the town, so strongly fortified was it and so bravely did the rebels repel every attack. At last the provisions of the army under Yuliang began to fail and the prospect of a retreat became imminent. He appealed to T'au-k'an, whose camp was abundantly provided, for assistance, but he refused, under the plea that he had only sufficient for his own men. He was still sore under a sense of his wrongs, and even at this time meditated withdrawing to Kingchow and leaving Yuliang to deal alone with Sutsun. One of the officers seeing what was in his mind said to him, "Be careful what you do at this crisis of your country. We are like men that are riding tigers. It is dangerous to be where we are, but it is still more perilous to get down, as we might be eaten up by the animals we bestride. If you leave us now then many others will follow your example, and should disaster come upon the royal arms the sin will lie with you."

T'au-k'an was so much impressed with these words that he determined to consult his captains as to the best mode of procedure under the present circumstances. They were unanimous in their opinion that there should be no desertion of the royal cause, and that a supply of their provisions should be given to Yuliang's army. One of them, a man named Maupau, offered, if a strong detachment were given him, to make a raid upon Kuyang, the city where Sutsun's commissariat was stored, and destroy it and the provisions that were laid up in it for the use of his army. His request was granted, and he had the good fortune to carry out his plans to the very letter.

Sutsun was terribly distressed when the news of this disaster reached him, for his power of resistance had depended upon his supplies regularly reaching him. In self-defence he was now compelled to assume the offensive, and leading out his troops he attacked the besiegers. In the battle that ensued he was routed, and during the retreat he was killed by an officer of T'au-k'an. Although their chief was dead the rebels had no intention of surrendering, for they knew that no mercy would be extended to them. They accordingly made Suyih, a brother of their late leader, their chief, and bidding defiance to the armies outside they prepared to be buried under the ruins of the town rather than deliver themselves up to certain destruction. The serious nature of this rebellion is shown by the fact that notwithstanding the death of Sutsun, and the large preparations that had been made by the whole power of the state, it was more than a year after this that the city was taken and the captive Emperor restored to freedom.

In the year A. D. 329 a great battle was fought between Liu-yau and Shih-leh, in which the former was defeated and slain and his army entirely dispersed. Next year Shih-leh became still more powerful, through the murder of Liu-yau's son, who had succeeded his father, and by the adhesion to himself of all the soldiers that had lately been under the banner of the former.

In the year A. D. 330 Shih-leh proclaimed himself Emperor, but he died only three years after, and was succeeded by his son Fung, who enjoyed his honours but one year, when he was assassinated by his commander-in-chief, Shih-hu, who at once stepped into his vacant place. Whilst these events were transpiring in the East, Liying, who had assumed the dignity and state of an independent prince in Sz-chwan, died, and was succeeded by his son Chi. In the year A. D. 335 Shih-hu removed his capital from Peking to Lohyang. He was a most reverent worshipper of idols and a firm believer in Buddhism. He issued an edict permitting Chinese to become priests. Up to this date the priestly office had been filled by foreigners, but from this time (A. D. 336) it was open to the citizens of China.

In the 17th year of his reign Ch'ung Ti became seriously unwell. Both his sons were young and ill-qualified to meet the dangers and care that would come upon them after his decease. One of his ministers advised him to nominate his brother as his successor. The Emperor remembering his own sorrows during his minority gladly consented, and so Yo was appointed heir and his sons made princes. After commending them to the care of his most loyal ministers he died, and was succeeded by

K'ang Ti—A. D. 343-345.

The only important event of this reign was the issuing of a royal edict, declaring Shih-hu a rebel against the Emperor. An army was immediately after sent against him, but it was defeated, and its general was so chagrined at his disgrace that he committed suicide. Hwan-wan, a man who is now going to play a prominent part in the history of his country, was appointed to succeed him. After a brief rule of two years K'ang Ti was followed by his son, but as he was only three years old his mother, the Queen-Dowager Ch'u, was made regent during his minority.

Muh Ti—A. D. 345-362.

At the commencement of this prince's reign Hwan-wan was made Governor of Kingchow, and Yin-hau became a prominent official in the palace through the recommendation of Ch'u-p'eu, the uncle of the young Emperor. Hwan-wan, having taken charge of his new government, determined to lead a small army into Sz-chwan and recover that province for the Tsins. Chi, having been murdered by his general, Li-shih, the latter, who styled himself Prince of Han, occupied Ch'ung-tu as his capital. Some of Hwan-wan's officers endeavoured to dissuade him from attempting such a daring undertaking by magnifying the dangers and difficulties of such an enterprise. He was not the man, however, to be daunted by any number of real impediments, and he certainly was not going to have his plans thwarted by imaginary ones. He quieted the fears of the more timorous by reminding them how the thing had been done before, when the last feeble scion of the Han dynasty was taken by surprise and captured by a flying squadron, and he promised them that he would not be less successful on this occasion. The bolder spirits were of course delighted with the project, and were full of enthusiasm at the idea of the adventures they were likely to meet with and the substantial honours that would come to them after their enterprise was over.

Hwan-wan at once memorialized the throne for permission to undertake the recovery of Sz-chwan, and fearing delay or a refusal he had no sooner sent off his despatch than he at once put his troops in motion and commenced his famous march to the west. When the news arrived at court there was great consternation. Every one was troubled, lest disaster come upon the arms of Hwan-wan, and so the enemies of the dynasty be encouraged to attack it. One of the ministers, who knew the great general well, re-assured them by asserting that he was certain of success. He had never known him, he said, make a move of any kind without laying his plans so well that failure was impossible. Even in his games of chess he had never moved a piece that he had not taken the one he was attacking. His only concern in the matter, he declared, was that he had taken the liberty of engaging in a momentous business without first getting the permission of his sovereign, and his fear, lest he should turn out disloyal if his campaign were successful.

After a sixteen months' terrible march by unfrequented paths and over mountain passes, during which they were often delayed by want of provisions, this adventurous band appeared before the city of Ch'ung-tu. Li-shih, who was entirely unprepared, led out what men he had on the spot to meet this unexpected foe, but he suffered a severe defeat, and the town was taken by assault. Li-shih now appeared before Hwan-wan with his hands tied behind him and with his coffin following him, ready to receive his body in case he should find no mercy from his conqueror. He was forwarded to Nanking, where he was reduced from his royal rank, and the lower title of viscount was bestowed upon him. Hwan-wan, after leaving a garrison in Ch'ung-tu, returned to his province, when he was created a duke for the services he had rendered the state. His fame from this time was very great, and soldiers flocked to his banner, and men talked of his exploits and the wonderful march he had made to the far off province in the west.

The palace, however, was greatly disturbed by his increased reputation, and feared lest he should become a power that would overshadow the very throne itself. Yin-hau, who was considered to be a very astute statesman, was appointed by the court to watch his movements and to be ready with counter-plans of his own to thwart any that the great general might be supposed to be making in a treasonable direction. The consequence was that a deadly feud soon arose between these men. This was a subject of regret to the patriotic men at court, as it promised trouble to the country. One of these, Wang Hi-chi, remonstrated with Yin-hau upon the impolicy of two such prominent men as he and Hwan-wan disagreeing, as their feuds were not about private matters, but such as concerned the well-being of the empire.* His advice, however, was not accepted, and the quarrel grew more intense and bitter.

In the year A.D. 349 Shih-hu, the King of Yen, whose capital was in Lohyang, died, and was succeeded by his son, who, however, was murdered, together with his mother, by his uncle Tsun. One of his relatives advised him, now that he had grasped the kingly power for himself that he should destroy Fu-fung, a general of commanding influence in the army and in the country. Acting on this advice the latter was ordered to report himself to Tsun, who, however, disregarded the command, as he knew that his death was determined upon. On the contrary, he sent messengers to Muh Ti, offering to surrender to him and become one of his servants. The Emperor signified that he was pleased to accept his submission, but shortly after, finding himself

---

* Wang was a politician and a scholar, but he was specially noted for his beautiful penmanship. He is said to be the inventor of the Chinese square character, called Kiai-shu, which is used in the printing of books, scrolls, etc.

at the head of a hundred and twenty thousand men in Chihli, he determined to found a dynasty of his own instead of being the subject of another.   Next year Tsun was killed by a man named Kan, who in his turn was murdered by Shih-min.   This man had formerly been adopted into the family of the Shihs, but he now resumed his own name of Jan and showed his gratitude to the clan that had helped him by murdering every member of it, with the exception of Shih-chi, who happened to be beyond his reach. He changed the title of the dynasty from Chau to Wei.   Tu-fung the same year (A. D. 351) was killed by one of his officers, and his son Kien became king, and called his dynasty the Ts'in, and made his capital at Singanfu in Shensi.   The reign of Shih-min lasted barely two years, for the northern barbarians, the Sien-pi, invaded his dominions, and having murdered him they took possession of Lohyang and set up a dynasty of their own, which they named the Yen.

In the year A. D. 355 Hwan-wan raised an army of one hundred thousand men and marched into Shensi to attack Kien, the ruler of the new dynasty of Ts'in.   The latter sent his son with fifty thousand men to meet him, when a great battle was fought at a place called the "Blue Field," where Hwan-wan obtained a decided victory.   He pursued the beaten army almost to the capital, and all the officials by the way submitted to him. Whilst his army was encamped one evening during their pursuit a man entered the camp in a ragged dress and with the air of a strolling beggar.   Although he got into the presence of the commander he seemed only anxious to show his contempt for his ability by doing the most discourteous things in his presence. This man was the famous Wang-mung, who afterwards played such an important part in the history of the Ts'ins.   Hwan-wan, who was a quick discerner of character, saw in this ragged, dirty looking fellow a man of great ability, and he determined to secure him as one of his followers.   He accordingly offered him a position in his army, which was accepted.   He held this, however, for only a brief period, as Hwan-wan shortly after suffered a most disastrous defeat in a battle that he had with another army of the Ts'ins. So severe was the contest, indeed, that the general, who was none other than the brother of the King Kien, died from over-exertion, and was succeeded in his command by his son Fu-kien.

In the year A. D. 356 Kien died, and was succeeded by his son Sheng, who, however, was such a bad, dissipated man that he became the terror of his subjects, and recklessly murdered his ministers without any reason for doing so.   In his drunken fits some of them were sure to be sent to the block.   At length, terrified lest they should all perish, his cousin Fu-kien was sent for, and by the advice of Wang-mung, who now appears for the first time in the history of the Ts'ins, Sheng was murdered in one of his drunken fits, and Fu-kien was crowned king, to the great delight of every one in the capital, and indeed of the people throughout the whole of his kingdom.

Wang-mung was made prime minister, for his genius was so manifest that Fu-kien advanced him to this important post, which is usually given to men of more mature years and to such as have performed some meritorious service for the state. One of the great mandarins, who had won his titles by heroic service during the last few years of desperate fighting, rebelled against the idea of an upstart like him getting such a distinguished post near the very person of the king. One day he said to Wang-mung, "You are eating the harvest without having done anything to secure it." "That is quite true," he replied, "and not only will I eat the food you have produced, but I shall also make you cook it for me." The indignant warrior was enraged at this reply, and angrily said, "I shall not be content to live if I do not have your head off and see it fixed over one of the city gates as a warning to upstarts." Wang-mung, feeling that matters were becoming serious, complained to Fu-kien of the language that had been used to him, who to satisfy his minister, who was of more value to him than all the others in his service, ordered the immediate execution of the man who had threatened him. From this time the profoundest respect was paid to Wang-mung and full play was given to his talents in the government of the country.

In the 16th year of Muh Ti, the chief of the Sien-pi, whose capital was in Honan, died, and was succeeded by his son Wei. The Emperor was planning to attack him, but he was dissuaded from doing so by Hwan-wan, who declared that he would do so at considerable peril so long as the famous general Muh Yang-k'o was alive, for there was no living commander that was a match for him. This same year a man who was to have a powerful influence over the destiny of the Ts'ins now came into prominence, viz., Sieh-ngan, a protegé of Hwan-wan.

After a reign of seventeen years Muh Ti died, and as he had no one to succeed him, P'ei, one of the sons of the former Emperor, Ch'ung Ti, was raised to the throne. He was twenty-one years of age, and his dynastic title was Ngai Ti, which means the Sad and Sorrowful Emperor, because of the early death of his father and his own short reign of only four years.

Ngai Ti—A. D. 362-366.

The only events worthy of being recorded during this reign were the wise government of the Ts'ins and the growing ambition of Hwan-wan, who began to make no secret of his intentions of usurping the throne. Fu-kien, the Ts'in king, made a law with regard to the appointment of men to official posts that tended to secure the best men of the country for them. The qualifications required were that they should have been good and filial sons; that they should be thoroughly educated; that they should be men that could not be bribed, and finally that they should be well versed in the laws of the state. All candidates were to be introduced by prefects and district magistrates, who were to be responsible for the men they brought forward.* Ngai Ti was succeeded by his brother Yih, who was twenty-two years old. His dynastic title is

Ti Yih—A.D. 366-371.

In the year A.D. 368 the valiant commander of the Yens, Muh Yang-k'o, was about to die. His king came in great distress to visit him. During their conversation the dying general was asked who he thought was the best man to succeed him. He promptly replied, that the one man in his dominions that could well maintain the honour of the state was Muh Yang-shui, and he urged upon the king to secure his services at once. Very earnest was the old man that the king should attend to his last request, for he knew that after he was gone the ruler of the Ts'ins would endeavour to add the territories of Yen to his own. Unfortunately his hearer neglected to act upon the advice of his far seeing general, whose predictions were verified two years after his death.

In the year A.D. 370 Hwan-wan raised a large army and advanced into the dominions of Yen with the purpose of subjugating them, and as there was no general of ability to meet him there seemed every prospect that his purpose would be accomplished. In this extremity the King of Yen sent to Fu-kien and requested military aid, promising if he gave it to repay him by giving him part of the western portion of Honan. The latter replied by sending him twenty thousand men. Hwan-wan suffered a great defeat from the combined armies and fled to Kiangnan. He was exceedingly chagrined at the disaster that had happened to him, and laid the whole blame upon one of his generals, Wantsin. In his memorial to the throne giving an account of the battle he requested that this officer should be deprived of his rank and be dismissed the army. This was accordingly done, more from fear of Hwan-wan than from anything else, for it was evident to every one that there was no one to blame excepting Hwan-wan himself.

This same year Muh Yang-shui got into trouble through the jealousy of another member of the clan, and with his four sons he fled to the court of Fu-kien, who received him with the most marked attention. When he arrived at the palace the king went to the door of the audience hall to meet him, and taking him by the hand led him to a seat. He then expressed the great pleasure he had in receiving him, and assured him of his pro-

---

* A district magistrate is the chief magistrate of a country. A prefect is the principal one over a prefecture, which includes several counties.

tection. He was greatly taken with the man, because of his superior. ability, and besides he had hopes that he would help him in case of an invasion of the territories of Yen, which he always kept before his mind as a possibility in the future. Wang-mung, who was a better discerner of character than his master, strongly advised him either to get rid of him or to put him to death. "He is a danger to our country as long as he is in it," he said. "He is like the dragon on the tiger, which was never known to submit to man. When the dragon comes then the flying clouds rush before him, and when the tiger appears he is preceded by the storm of wind." *

If you give him any power you will not be able to control him by and by. Wang-mung spoke his prophetic words to ears that were unwilling to listen. "I have received him as a friend," the king said, "and I have promised him my protection, and I cannot break my word to him." Instead of injuring him he gave him a command in one of his armies.

This same year Fu-kien made a demand upon the state of Yen for the territory that had been promised him for sending an army to assist in repelling the attack of Hwan-wan. Instead of honorably complying a distinct refusal was made, on the ground that no such promise had ever been given. "They had indeed been assisted by his troops," they said, "but it had been simply the friendly act of one prince towards another, for which they were deeply grateful to him. Should he ever be in a condition to require the like service he would find in the soldiers of Yen willing allies to help him to repel any invader that might dare to attack his dominions." Fu-kien was exceedingly irritated at this breach of faith, and immediately despatched Wang-mung with thirty thousand men to demand by their swords what had been refused to his ambassadors. Before starting the general asked of the king that one of the sons of Muh Yang-shui should be made a captain of the advanced corps that was to precede the main army, ostensibly to show the way, as he was well acquainted with the roads of his own country, but really for the purpose of carrying out a plot that Wang-mung was maturing for the destruction of the whole family. When the army reached Lohyang, Wang-mung secretly instructed one of the followers of Muh Yang-shui to go to his son and represent that he had been sent by his father and to tell him that he was afraid of Wang-mung, who sought his life, and that he was going to escape back again to Yen, and advised him as soon as he got word from his messenger that he was at once to fly into the lines of the Yen soldiers. The son readily fell into the snare, and that night he passed over to his countrymen, who, however, distrusted him and thought it was a deep laid plot of the father to betray them. He was at once sent under a strong guard to a distant part of the state. When Wang-mung

---

* "The dragon follows the clouds and the tiger the storm." Book of Changes.

heard of the success of his plot he at once memorialized Fu-kien and told him of the treachery of Muh Yang-shui's son and advised that the father, who was evidently a traitor, should be seized and put to death. When the latter heard of the extraordinary conduct of his son, despairing of life he at once made his escape, but he was soon captured and brought into the presence of Fu-kien. The king gently upbraided him for his want of confidence in him. "I told you when I received you at my court that I would protect you. You should have had more faith in me. I don't blame you for what your son has done, and I shall most certainly not punish you for his treachery, with which I believe you had nothing to do. I am sincerely sorry for your son," he continued, "because the kingdom of Yen is undoubtedly going to be destroyed. As for you, you need have no fear. I shall protect you and care for you as I have promised." Wang-mung attacked and captured Lohyang, when the King Wei removed his capital to Yeh. From there he managed to despatch three hundred thousand men to meet Wang-mung, who had advanced to take the city of Hu-kwan. Before the battle that now was fought (A.D. 371) Wang-mung made a speech to his soldiers. Standing in the midst of his army that had been gathered round him he reminded them that they had received innumerable favours from their king. "Soldiers and commanders and officers," he continued, "have also been well treated by the state. We have come into Honan to meet this great horde of thieves and banditti. Let us be ready this day to lay down our lives for our king. Let none dream of retreat, but may the word 'advance' be the one that shall ring through every heart. In this way we shall gain great honour and pay back the favours we have received from our sovereign."

The battle began in the early morning and lasted till the evening shades began to fall. Prodigies of valour were performed by both men and officers. One of these, named Ting-kiang, killed several hundred with his own hand. The men of Yen suffered a great defeat. Fifty thousand of them were either taken or slain, and in the pursuit as many more were similarly disposed of. One hundred thousand fled to Yeh, where the king was, but it was soon surrounded by the victorious foe, when Wei, finding himself unsafe in his new capital, fled from it into Chihli. The troops of Wang-mung, however, pursued and captured him. When he was brought before Fu-kien he was sternly rebuked for the resistance he had made, and he was asked how it was that he had not given himself up, when the battle had gone so decidedly against him. Wei replied, "When the fox dies he always does so with his head towards his hole. I was but following its example, for I was hastening to the home of my fathers, where I might have died in peace."* A most pathetic reply was this, and one that

* It must be remembered that Wei's countrymen were Sien-pi and not Chinese, and that the home of his ancestors lay beyond the frontiers of China

excited the pity of the generous-hearted Fu-kien.   His life was spared, and forty thousand of his people, who at his command submitted to the conqueror, were removed to Ch'ang-ngan and its neighbourhood.   The Yen dynasty was now destroyed and its territory absorbed in that of Ts'in.

This same year Hwan-wan planned with his military adviser Ch'i, a man of great ability, the best methods for usurping the throne.   All the plans were laid down, even to the murdering of the Emperor, when his heart failed him at the critical moment. All that he dared accomplish for the time was the setting aside of Ti Yih, who was made Prince of the Eastern Sea, and the placing of Yih, the prime minister, on the throne in his stead. The dynastic title of the latter is Kien Wen Ti.

CHAPTER XIV.

THE EASTERN TSIN DYNASTY (Continued).

Kien Wen Ti—A. D. 371-373.

KIEN WEN was fifty years old when he was placed upon the throne, and he reigned but two years. His age and weakness were the chief reasons why Hwan-wan selected him instead of a younger and more vigorous person. He knew that he had not long to live, and he counted upon his gratitude that when he came to die he would name him as his successor. The chief powers at the court besides Hwan-wan were Ch'i and Sieh-ngan. The latter, though a protegé of the former, was a thoroughly loyal man, and could not endure the treasonable conduct of his patron. In order to give him a hint as to how obnoxious his conduct was to the patriotic men of the kingdom he one day fell upon his knees before him as he entered the audience hall. Hwan-wan rebuked him and said, "I am not the Emperor, why should you kneel to me?" Sieh-ngan replied, "I saw the Emperor do this to you, and I thought it my duty to follow the example of His Majesty."

In the 2nd year of his reign Kien Wen became very ill, and he sent an order to Hwan-wan, who was away from the capital in Ku-shih, that he should at once return home. This he refused to do, because he hoped he would be named successor by Kien Wen, and he wanted the nation to believe that the idea of becoming Emperor did not originate with him, but was entirely the suggestion of the late ruler. Finding that he did not appear Kien Wen named his own son Ch'ang-ki, a youth of ten years old, his heir, and Hwan-wan regent during the minority. He also left a will, in which the following words were addressed to the latter: "Help my son to the utmost of your power and be a loyal minister to him. Should, however, you find that he has neither the ability nor the character to be a worthy ruler degrade him from his office and become Emperor yourself." Wang Tan-chi, a loyal minister who was standing by whilst this document was being read, seized it and tore it in pieces, saying, "It must never be known that such commands as these were left by his Majesty. Hwan-wan is only too anxious to become Emperor, and these words would only encourage him in his traitorous designs."

Kien Wen, shortly after this famous scene was enacted, died, and his son, whose dynastic title is Hiau Wu Ti, became Emperor.

Hiau Wu Ti—A. D. 373-397.

As soon as Hwan-wan heard of the Emperor's death and that he had not been named successor by him he was grievously disappointed, but he attributed the failure of his plans to the counter-plots of Wang Tan-chi and Lieh-ngan. He now determined to visit the capital and see whether the time was not ripe for the carrying out of his treasonable designs. When it was known that he was on his way to Nanking Wang Tan-chi and Lieh-ngan were sent with a large retinue to meet him on the way and escort him with due honour to the presence of the Emperor. Both these ministers felt that the crisis of the Tsin dynasty had now come, and a great deal depended on them whether it should have a longer lease of life or whether it should end in tragedy and bloodshed. When Hwan-wan came in sight he was attended by a retinue of soldiers that amounted almost to an army. All the mandarins of the region lined the road as though an Emperor was passing by. Wang Tan-chi was so terrified when he appeared in his presence that the perspiration poured from his back, and the tablet that he held before him was unconsciously to himself turned upside down.*

Sieh-ngan, on the other hand, was completely self possessed and talked with Hwan-wan as though he had been his equal. Seeing the very large escort of soldiers that followed him he said to him, "What a large number of men you have attending you to the capital. When the nobles are loyal and virtuous," he continued, "they need no retinue, for their virtues are their most efficient guard." Hwan-wan, upon hearing these words, immediately ordered his men to be marched away, and they entered the capital with only the royal guard and a few of the most intimate of his officers.

He had come thus far with the intention of discovering some great errors in the government, but under the able management of Sieh-ngan everything had been so wisely administered that no fault of any kind could be found. After he had been in the capital a month he fell seriously ill, and after a short time died. Previous to his death he handed over all his authority to his brother Hwan-ch'ang, a loyal and devoted officer, because his own son was a person of no talents or ability of any kind. The widow of the former Emperor, K'ang Ti, became regent in his place.

During the present year, A. D. 373, the king of the Ts'ins sent an army into Sz-chwan and captured the important city of Han-chung, and after a time Ch'ungtu, the former capital of the last of the Hans. The latter city was given up by its commandant, in order to deliver his wife and mother, who had been made prisoners in their flight from the city on the approach of the Ts'in army. Fukien offered to take him in into his service and give him a high command in his army, but he resolutely refused to accept this generous offer.

---

* When high officials had an audience of the Emperor or some great minister they held in their hands a tablet nearly three feet long and a few inches in breadth. It was made of ivory, gem, wood, or even bamboo, and the person who held it kept his eyes steadily fixed on it. This tablet was in use down to the time of the Ming dynasty. It is not used now, but a string of beads thrown round the neck takes its place.

"I only surrendered," he said, "to save my mother and family, and all that I want now is simply to be allowed to live." It shows how utterly weak the Tsin empire had become, that no attempt was made to prevent the conquest of the large province of Sz-chwan, and no soldiers were sent to the rescue of the loyal men that were hopelessly fighting the battles of the empire there. In the year A. D. 376 the great statesman and warrior of the Tsins lay a-dying. Fu-kien in great distress came to see the man who had not merely been a friend of his, but who had also been the cause of the great prosperity of his kingdom. When he entered his presence, after some words of sympathy and sorrow, he asked him if he had any dying commands to give him that might be of service to him after he was gone. Knowing what was in the mind of his royal master he said, "I would strongly urge you to give up your intention of attacking the empire of Tsin. You should rather make a treaty of peace with it. What I am most concerned about is the large numbers of Sienpi and western barbarians that you have about your capital, and I should strongly advise that you get rid of their leaders,—Muh Yang-shui and Yau-ch'ang,—as soon as you can, otherwise they will bring sorrow upon you and the kingdom." Shortly after he died. Fu-kien was deeply moved by the great loss he had sustained, and said to his son, "Heaven does not mean that we should obtain possession of the whole empire, and therefore it has called him away."

Unfortunately for himself and his dynasty he failed to take the advice of Wang-mung, and he acted in the very opposite way to that in which he had been warned, for he spared the traitors that the latter would have had destroyed and attacked the Tsin empire, with which he would have had him make peace.

When Hiau Wu Ti was fifteen years old he married and took the government of the country into his own hands. It now became a matter of great concern to find an able commander to lead the armies in the war, which it was seen would soon have to be waged with the ambitious Tsins. Sieh-ngan introduced his own nephew Sieh-huan, a man of great military genius, and who he felt convinced would bring the country safe through any crisis which the invasion of a hostile army might bring upon it. The Emperor was so convinced of the sterling qualities of Sieh-ngan that he at once accepted him and gave him the command of the great province of Kiangnan, though if he had been introduced by another man he might have hesitated in giving him such an important position. Subsequent events showed that Sieh-huan was just the man that was suited for this perilous time of the nation's history. His management of his district was judicious in the extreme. He was specially famous for his discernment of character and his choice of the best men for the offices they were to hold. He had the misfortune, however, to lose his military adviser Ch'i, a man of consummate military ability, and who for years had acted in the same capacity to Hwan-wan.*

Fu-kien in the year A. D. 383 met with his nobles and great officers in his Hall of Audience to discuss the question of the subjugation of the Tsins. He addressed them and said, "My kingdom is now at peace in all its quarters, and no enemy exists throughout it to distract it. Tsin possesses but a corner of the whole of China. My soldiers are numerous, for I have nine hundred and seventy thousand ready to take the field ; my opinion is that we should at once proceed to march on their capital and add its dominions to ours. What do you all think ? "

Immediately uprose Kwan-yih, a loyal man and true, and said, "It is true that the Tsins just now are weak, and their territories as compared with ours are small. They have done no wrong, however, that we should attack them, and to justify ourselves we must have some good reason to give the world for our invasion. The Emperor and his nobles are most harmonious with each other, and the nation possesses as prime minister a man who is famous for his wisdom and statesmanship. I would, therefore, beg the king to give up his idea of war for the present." Another got up and said "that he concurred in all that Kwan-yih had said, and besides there was a danger in this idea of invasion that seemed very formidable to him, and that was, they would have to cross the Yang-tze with all its difficulties and perils."

Fuk-kien scorned this last suggestion as unworthy of a man possessed of such unlimited resources as he had, and waived it gently away with the remark that if each one of his cavalry only threw his riding whip into it they would be able to cross over dry shod.

A general discussion then arose. Some sided with the king and others disagreed with him. Fu-kien, seeing that there was no likelihood of an agreement of opinion, at last said, "We are now like a builder who is going to erect a house by the roadside. He asks of each passer-by how the house shall face. Each one has his own particular theory in the matter, and the builder stands with mind distracted as to whose counsel he shall take. Finally he settles it by adopting his own, and after that the building of the house goes on speedily. Now in this matter, when there is such a diversity of opinions, I shall take my own, and I therefore determine that Tsin shall be invaded and conquered ! " The members of this great meeting then dispersed, and Fu-kien sought the counsel of Prince Fuyung, a relative of his, and asked him what he thought of his decision. The prince replied that he was exceedingly grieved at it for three reasons : "First, it is not the will of Heaven ;

---

* It had been the custom from the earliest times for the commanders and generals to have a military adviser always with them to give advice on important occasions. It exists to the present day, and the same class of men is still employed in the Chinese armies.

second, we have no quarrel with the Tsins; and third, you have
had so many wars lately that your people are becoming dissatisfied,
and hate the very idea of fighting. Did you not mark that all the
loyal men in the assembly to-day were against the invasion, and the
loudest in its favour were the disloyal and the men who would gain
the most by any disaster that might happen to you?" Fu-kien's
countenance fell, and he said bitterly, "If you are against me then
whom shall I trust in at all?"

The prince on hearing these words wept, and still urged him
to give up his designs. "Have you so soon forgotten the warnings
of Wang-mung, and do you still ignore the fact that your capital is
filled with Sienpi and Western barbarians from Tangut, who are
traitors at heart, and who are only waiting for an opportunity to rise
and hurl you from the throne?"

In A. D. 384 Fuyung was sent forward with two hundred and
fifty thousand men, whilst Fu-kien followed with six hundred
thousand more. When the news of this immense armament having
started to invade the domains of Tsin reached the capital, there was
the greatest consternation amongst every class of the community.
Sieh-ngan was the only one that never lost his composure, or showed
any alarm at the idea of such immense armies marching for the
destruction of the Tsins. His younger brother was made commander
of the advanced force that went out to meet the foe, whilst his
nephew commanded the main army. No more than eighty
thousand men could, however, be collected to meet the enormous
forces of Fu-kien. Sieh-huan came with great anxiety to his uncle
and asked him if he had any plans that he wished him to carry out
in order to meet the enemy successfully.

Sieh-ngan, who knew that he was a man of consummate ability,
replied, "No, I shall allow you to make your own dispositions and
carry them out as you please; but," he continued, "don't let us be
too anxious about matters. Let us go and have an outing on the
hills." They spent the day together, the greater part of which was
occupied in playing chess, a game of which he was passionately
fond, and it was quite late when they returned.

Hwan-ch'ang, the brother of the late Hwan-wan, was so
distressed with the tidings of the march of the huge host that was
on its way to capture Nanking that he led three thousand of his best
men from the district over which he ruled to the capital to assist in
the coming struggle. When Sieh-ngan met him he gently chided
him for his anxiety and ordered him to send his men back again.
"The capital is quite safe," he continued. "Let your men guard
well your own province and see that no disorder arises there from
the plots of any disloyal men who might wish to take advantage of
the present crisis to cause trouble to the state."

Hwan-ch'ang almost cried with vexation at the ease and
unconcern that Sieh-ngan manifested in this most critical hour of
the empire's history. "The prime minister," he said bitterly to

his friends, "knows nothing of military matters. He spends his time in picnicing on the hills and in playing chess, and he makes me send back the detachment of my men that I brought to defend the capital. He does not realize how powerful the enemy is and how weak we are. The Tsin dynasty is about to be destroyed, and the sooner we put on the dress of the barbarians and submit to them the better for us all." In the meanwhile Fu-yung had reached the banks of the Yang-tze and had taken the city of Sheu-yang, and Fu-kien, anxious to be in the front, hurriedly advanced with eight thousand men and joined him. The latter immediately sent a messenger across to Sieh-huan and commanded him to surrender. He promised him good terms if he would, and promotion and honor, but if he refused, then the direst calamities were threatened him. The officer that brought the message was originally a Tsin man, who in the many wars of Fu-kien had taken service with him. His heart, however, now turned to his own people in the hour of this distress, and he urged Sieh-huan that instead of submitting he should at once attack the enemy. "If you wait till the two armies have joined you will have no chance of success whatsoever, but there is no reason why you should not beat the one before you, and in so doing you might strike terror into the one that is coming up, so that it might hesitate to advance to confront a victorious enemy."

Whilst they were discussing these matters the Tsin army was marching down to the bank of the Yang-tze. Fu-kien and his commander-in-chief standing on the walls of the captured town could see them. Their martial bearing and the steady way in which they advanced struck Fu-yung forcibly, and turning to the king he said, "This is no mean enemy that we are about to face, and we shall have to use all our skill and bravery to defeat him."

Fu-kien had been equally impressed with the appearance of the heroic army as it moved down the hill to engage the immense forces that were threatening the capital. As its columns marched down they became magnified in appearance, for he could not well distinguish between the men and the trees in the distance, and it seemed as though the whole hill was covered with the moving host.

Sieh-huan returned for answer by the captain that had ordered him to surrender that he had no intentions of betraying the trust that his sovereign had committed to him, and that his only anxiety was to face the enemy in the field that had dared to pollute the territory of the Tsins with their presence. He then requested Fu-yung to withdraw his army a space that he might have room to fight in. "Your men," he said, "are so close to the river that I have nowhere to land my army. Give me room to dispose of my force, and I'll cross at once, and then we shall be able to decide by a pitched battle who shall be master of the country."

Fu-yung, who was no match for him in military skill, very unwisely granted his request and gave orders for his army to withdraw a mile or two into the country to a place called Fei-shui. Whilst this operation was being performed Sieh-huan's army was being rapidly passed over the river, and as the various detachments landed they were formed into ranks, and took their position to be ready for the coming battle.   After a time Sieh-huan, observing that there was considerable disorder amongst the enemy whilst they were falling back, ordered an instant attack.   Fu-yung, now greatly alarmed, endeavoured to recall his men to meet the advancing foe, but before the orders could be fully carried out the soldiers of Tsin were upon them and were carrying death and destruction amongst them.   A panic seized the front ranks that speedily spread throughout those in the rear, and ere long filled them with the utmost terror.   There was no longer any thought of resistance. The great aim of every man now was how to save himself. Fu-yung, whilst bravely leading on the few men that he could collect, fell from his horse that stumbled, and was immediately slain by the Tsin soldiers.   The cry flew through the panic-stricken army that their commander was slain.   This intensified the fears of the already terrified soldiers, and arms were cast aside, and it became one great race for dear life.   Men, forgetting the ties that bound them to each other, trod each other to death till the plain and the hills over which they flew were covered with the slain. So utterly demoralized were they that the screaming of the wind and the cry of the crows overhead were taken as the voices of the pursuing foe, and again they started off afresh, though the enemy was far in the rear of them.

Fu-kien, wounded and in great sorrow of mind, reached the camp of Muh Yang-shui with only a thousand men.   This general had remained behind, and so far none of his men had aided in any way to retrieve the disaster of that fatal day, and now it was too late to attempt to bring back victory to the scattered and demoralized army.   The son of Muh Yang-shui advised his father to kill Fu-kien and regain their lost inheritance, of which he had robbed them.   This, to his honour be it said, he indignantly refused to do. "He relieved me and you when we were fugitives," he said, "and protected us contrary to the advice of Wang-mung, who would have had us murdered.   He is in sorrow now, and it would be the basest ingratitude to turn against him, when his fortunes have sunk so low.   Should he ever try to crush us, or should he be destroyed by his many enemies that are sure to rise against him, then I shall feel no hesitation in gathering my countrymen around me and again endeavouring to establish the house of Yen in its old inheritance."

Muh-yang petitioned Fu-kien to be allowed to go with a force to the north of Honan and rule it for him.   The latter, who was no statesman, or at least had no suspicion of his fellow-men, granted his request.   Muh-yang had represented that the people of that region, hearing of his great defeat at Fei-shui, were about to rise in rebellion, and Fu-kien, believing that he was actuated by feelings of loyalty, gave him a force with which to suppress any rising that might be threatened. When his ministers heard of this they were astonished at his folly, and one of them begged him to withdraw the permission he had so rashly given.

Kwan-yih said, "This man is exceedingly clever and powerful, and the Sienpi, who look to him as their leader, are numerous and warlike. He came to us like a fierce eagle, and we have since then been keeping him in a cage. He has heard the blowing of the wind, and he wants to try his wings and fly up to the heavens. Instead of opening the cage door and letting him out you ought to make it stronger and keep him more closely confined." Fu-kien said that he had given his word, and he could not break it, and besides, he continued, to whomsoever Heaven has decreed to give the kingdom that man shall have it, and not all the wisdom or might of this world can prevent it. "I can guarantee," said Kwan-yih, "that if you once let him go you will never see him again."

When Muh-yang reached the district in the north of Honan, which he said was going to rise in rebellion, Fu-kien's son, P'ei, who was governor of the whole province, gave him the region of Yeh to command. From this time his whole thought was how to bring back the good fortunes of his house and make himself King of Yen. Not long after he had taken charge of this district the barbarians that occupied the territory to the north of Shensi gave symptoms of uneasiness, and rumours flew abroad that their chief, Tipin, was going to march on Lohyang. Fu-kien at once ordered his son to supply Muh-yang with troops and to command him to advance and meet the invaders. The advisers of the prince urged him to disobey the impolitic orders of his father. "He is meditating rebellion," they said, "and to supply him with men and arms is like giving wings to a tiger with which he may fly away."

P'ei, not daring to take such a responsibility upon himself, compromised matters by giving him the weakest and feeblest men he had under him and by sending a high official with them to watch his movements, who was to deprive him of his command the moment he saw anything suspicious in his actions. Instead of mending matters this actually brought about the crisis that everyone, excepting Fu-kien, saw was inevitable. Muh-yang, seeing himself suspected, and that he would never have such a good opportunity as the present again, killed Fu-fei, the commissioner, and then wrote a letter to Fu-kien, in which he told him that he no longer owned his authority, but that he was going to fight for his own hand. He was driven to take this course, he said, as his life was in danger from the officer that his son had sent to watch his movements. Instead of attacking the enemy he actually joined his forces with those of Tipin, and together they were prepared to march to the conquest of the entire province of Honan.

The year A. D. 385 saw rebellion rife throughout the dominions of the unhappy Fu-kien. His kingdom, which had been established by the power of the sword, began to fall to pieces the moment it seemed to be dropping from his hand. He now realized, when too late, that it would have been better for him and his kingdom had he followed the advice of his loyal ministers instead of obeying the whims and fancies of his own mind. Muh Yang-fung, another of the Sienpi leaders, hearing of the rebellion of Muh Yang-shui, collected a large force of his countrymen, and marching south took the important city of Singan-fu, which was not far from Fu-kien's capital. An army of fifty thousand men was sent against them under the command of Jui and his subordinate Yau-ch'ang. As the Tsin forces drew near the Sienpi exhibited signs of fear and began to retreat. Yau-ch'ang was exceedingly earnest in his advice to Jui not to attack them. "Don't you see," he said, "that they simply now want to get home. Let them go in peace. We can accomplish all we want by simply sitting still. If you interfere with them they will be compelled, in order to save themselves from destruction, to fight to the bitter end, and you may suffer a great defeat. When you touch a rat's tail he will turn about and bite you." This sound advice was rejected by his chief; indeed it seemed at this time as though any particular policy that would have been for the benefit of the kingdom was invariably rejected and the opposite counsels put into practice. A battle took place, in which the Tsin troops were worsted, and the Sienpi, instead of retreating, now took up a permanent position in the country. Yau-ch'ang, who was annoyed that his advice had not been taken, memorialized Fu-kien on the subject and showed how it was through the incompetency of Jui that disaster had come to their arms.

Fu-kien, with his usual short-sightedness, instead of listening calmly to his complaints and having them investigated, actually put his messengers that brought the document to death. Yau-ch'ang, fearing for his own life, fled to the Western barbarians, where he soon found himself at the head of an imposing force of these hardy warriors and advanced to attack the tottering throne of the Tsins. About this time Sieh-ngan, at the request of Fu-kien, sent an army under his redoubtable captain Liu Lau-chi to his assistance in Honan, and not only delivered Yeh, but also provisioned it, so that it might stand a siege from the gathering forces of the Sienpi. The next year saw important changes in the relative positions of those who were now engaged in a death struggle for mastery. Muh Yang-fung, who had been murdered by one of his officers, was supplanted by his brother Muh Yang-ch'ang, who set up his throne in Ch'angngan, from which he had been expelled by Fu-kien, and called his dynasty the "Western Yen." Muh Yang-shui, who had been driven from Honan by Sieh-ngan's lieutenant Liu Lau-chi, established himself in Chih-li with the title of "Later Yen." Fu-kien, who was now a fugitive, was repesented by his son P'ei, who had his capital in Lohyang, the sole remaining district to which the lately powerful house of the Tsins was confined. Thus there was, in addition to the Tsin empire, three other rival dynasties that were contending for supremacy in the centre and west of China.

Next year saw another change in the many shifting scenes that characterized the history of this period. Muh Yang-ch'ang was murdered, and was succeeded by his nephew, who in turn was killed and supplanted by Muh Yang-yung, who removed his capital to Lungan-fu in Shansi, when Yau-ch'ang, who had murdered Fu-kien, occupied Ch'angngan, and calling himself Emperor, gave his dynasty the name of the "Later Tsin."

Muh Yang-yung, leading an army into Honan, defeated P'ei and obtained his capital, and pursuing after him as he retreated, killed him, and thus obtained his territory. Upon hearing of his death his brother Futing, considering himself to be the real successor to the Tsins, took the title of King and made his capital in Nan-ngan, in the prefecture of K'iangch'ang, in Shansi. This same year there appeared on the scene a man who was to play a prominent part in the history of China, and whose descendants were for the next two centuries or so destined to take a leading position in the events of those times. His name was Topa, who, assuming the title of king, called his dynasty by the name of Wei.* He placed his capital in Tai-t'ung, in Shansi.† The year A.D. 389 was marked by the death of Sieh-ngan, the victor in the great battle of Fei-shui, and also by the perpetual conflicts between Yau-ch'ang, the slayer of Fu-kien and his son Futing. In these the former was always unsuccessful, mainly, it was believed, because the spirit of the murdered man fought against him, determined to have its revenge upon him for his destruction. Yau-ch'ang, hoping to propitiate this spirit, had a wooden image carved of Fu-kien. He then offered sacrifices to it and implored it to give him the victory in his next battle. Futing, hearing of this, was highly enraged, and sent a message to him to ask

---

* This Topa was a Sienpi. It seemed that a forefather of this man had done important service to the Tsin dynasty during the reign of Hwai Ti (A. D. 311) in meeting an inroad of the Hiungnu, in which he had driven them back with great slaughter. For this, Hwai Ti had given him the title of the Duke of Tai, in Shensi. In the third year of Min Ti (A.D. 316) he was advanced to the further honour of being called Prince of Tai. Subsequently, in the disorders that arose in China, family dissensions occurred, and murders took place, when Fu-kien came with his soldiers and took possession of Tai. Topa, who was a child at the time, but who was next in succession, became the feudal ruler when he had attained to manhood, under the Tsins. Seeing that Fu-kien was dead, and the Tsin dynasty almost disappearing, Topa thought that in the struggle for supreme power he had as good a chance as any one else, and so he took the name of King and changed his title from Tai to Wai, A.D. 386.

† At this time, besides a very large number of petty chiefs that aimed at independence, there were six principal powers in China, viz., the Tsins in Nanking; Muh Yang-yung in Lungan, in Shansi; Yau-ch'ang in Ch'angngan; Futing in Nan-ngan; Topa in Tai-t'ung, in Shensi, and Muh Yang-shui in Chihli.

him how he, the murderer of his king, could expect to be given success over the son of the very man he had slain. He sent also contemptuous messages to him to show the utter scorn he felt for his character.

Failing again in the next engagement, Yau-ch'ang in a fury cut off the head of the image and sent it to his son. Upon this Futing, to revenge the insult, led out his troops to attack him, but the former, whilst the battle was going on, sent a body of troops by a roundabout way that entered the capital of Futing and captured it. The wife and family were seized and brought before Yau-ch'ang. This lady was a remarkably beautiful and powerful woman, and Yau-ch'ang offered to make her his wife, but she indignantly refused, saying, "You have killed your sovereign, and now you want to take away his son's wife. Be sure that Heaven will not long endure such a man as you!"

The ferocity of his disposition was seen in his ordering her to be instantly put to death. Meanwhile Hiau Wu Ti, by his infamous and profligate life, was gradually insuring the destruction of his dynasty. He never attended to the government himself, but gave over all power to the disreputable associates with whom he spent a great deal of his time. Many of these were Buddhist priests and nuns, for he was a devout believer in the Buddhist faith. In order to get supplies for his lavish expenditure the public offices was sold with the most unblushing effrontery. Loyal men shook their heads and said, "The house is good, but it is now only waiting for others to live in."

In the year A.D. 394 Yau-ch'ang died, and was succeeded by his son Yau-hing, who no sooner attained to power than he invaded the territory of the now reduced Tsins and took possession of the country for himself, and nearly about the same time Muh Yang-shui marched an army of Sienpi and wiped out the rival branch in Shensi, named the Western Yen.

Two years after this a comet appeared in the heavens, to the great consternation of every one, for it is one of the most deeply-rooted beliefs of the Chinese heart that this physical phenomenon is the invariable harbinger of war or revolution. There is no doubt but that the immorality of the court coincided with the coming of the comet, and was the efficient cause of the confusion and civil wars that were continually being carried on by the rival aspirants for power in different parts of the country.

Hiau Wu Ti, after having reigned twenty-four years, came to a miserable end in the thirty-fifth year of his age. One of the fairest and best beloved in the harem was Lady Chang, who was at this time about thirty years of age. One day, when he was half drunk, he said to her half in joke and half in earnest, "You are getting old, and before long I shall have to dismiss you for a younger person." He did not know that whilst he was holding this jocular tone with her the wildest feelings of hatred and jealousy were already raging through her heart. She who had been supreme so long could not bear the thought of being cast aside to be neglected or ill-treated, and so she determined that her close of power should at the same time be the end of the Emperor's life. That night, whilst he was hopelessly drunk, she and her maidens smothered him to death, and history gives no account of what terrible punishment fell on her and them for this murder. His son Tuh-chung succeeded him. His dynastic title is

Ngan Ti—A. D. 397-419.

This prince was only seventeen years old when he succeeded his unhappy father. No more ill-qualified person could have come to the throne at this troublous time of China's history than he, for he was an absolute idiot. He could not talk properly, and he could take no rational part in anything that was going on. He had to be dressed and fed by other hands, for heat and cold, and hunger and satiety, were all alike to him. He was left entirely to the charge of his younger brother Tuhwun who, with loving affection, kept him company and guided the life which he had not the wisdom to direct himself. As might have been expected the greatest irregularities prevailed in the palace. The great men and loyal, such as Sieh-ngan, had died, and worthless men, such as often appear at the end of a dynasty, were scrambling for power around the poor demented monarch. Tautze, who acted as prime minister, was worthless in every way, for he had not even the ability that would have justified, in some measure, his being in such an exalted position. He introduced into high offices in the palace men who were even worse than himself, and who helped to hasten on the downfall of the dynasty that was now tottering to its ruin.

During the year A.D. 397 momentous events were taking place in the western part of China. Topa, the founder of the new dynasty of Wei, which by and by was to attain to such power in the northern part of China, was gradually making himself felt and extending his authority over new districts. The first to come under his dominion was the fast decaying dynasty of Yen. Quarrels and murders amongst themselves had made the leaders of it a ready prey for this strong-minded man. Having set his soldiers in motion against them, vast numbers of the Sienpi, with their king, fled across the Yellow River, hoping to form a new settlement in the districts south of it. Topa then obtained that part of the present province of Chihli that had been formerly held by these redoubtable barbarians.

Topa soon gave evidence that he was no mere military adventurer that never dreamt of any conquest excepting that gained by his sword. He evidently had a vision of an empire founded upon a more durable basis than it, for he was exceedingly anxious that his people should have the blessings not only of a well-established government, but also of refinement and learning. In order to this in the year A. D. 400 he appointed throughout his dominions three hundred and sixty advisory judges, as well as a board of eight great officials, to be a court of appeal, who had power to revise their decisions. He also established imperial colleges, where he soon had three thousand graduates studying the Five Classics. He one day asked one of his scholars, "What do you consider the best thing in all the world for increasing men's wisdom?" He at once replied, "Books." "How many are there of such," he again asked, "and how are these to be obtained?" "There are many such," the scholar replied, "as every age has had its own special productions. As to obtaining them that is a very simple matter. You have merely to give an order that a collection of them should be made and formed into a library, and the thing is at once accomplished." Topa, delighted at the easy process by which the books he longed for could be obtained, at once gave an order to all the chief officials in his dominions that they should, without delay, send to the capital specimens of all the books that existed in the districts under their jurisdiction.

In the year A. D. 400 Muh Yang-tuh, who had fled across the Yellow River, now made an inroad into the present province of Shantung, and having carried all before him made his capital in Yinchow.

This same year the prime minister's son Yuan-hien was made governor of the district of Yang-chow. He was a proud and tyrannical man, and so ill-treated the people under his charge that he was most thoroughly hated by them. The utmost discontent prevailed amongst them, and it required but a leader of position and ability, and the long-suffering Chinese would have risen in rebellion against him. His cruelty did indeed result in the rising of one man with a considerable following, who soon spread terror along the northern seaboard of China. This was the famous pirate San-wen. This man first advanced on the city of Hwui-che, in the Cheh-kiang province. The governor of this place was an infatuated Taoist, and believed in incantations and spiritual powers, whom he believed he could summon to his aid to repel any force that might attack him. In this case, instead of repairing the walls of his town and manning them with hardy soldiers to meet the coming foe, he went through a series of Taoist services, by which he believed that the invisible soldiers of heaven were summoned by an irresistible power that they dare not disobey to aid in the overthrow of Sun-wen, when the towns-people anxiously asked how he expected to defeat the latter with his bands of robbers. He replied, "Oh! it is all right. I have stationed hosts of heavenly soldiers all around the walls, and Sun-wen will soon find himself engaged with a force which will destroy him and his followers." Sun-wen was of a character that was not easily frightened, so regardless of all the hosts of the unseen world that were said to be arrayed against him, he soon captured the city and killed the governor.

The government that was terrified at the rapid progress that Sun-wen was making in conquering the country sent Liu Lauchi, a valiant commander, and one who greatly distinguished himself in the great battle of Fei-shui, to destroy him. On his way to meet him he fell in with a man of the same clan as himself, Liu-yu, whom he at once enlisted in his service and gave him the command of sixty or seventy men.*

He at once proved that he was a man of most distinguished courage, and that he had within him the makings of a hero. His commander sent him forward to reconnoitre the position of Sun-wen, who, with several thousand men, was encamped not far off. Liu-yu, not being skilled in the nice way of approaching an enemy, found himself unexpectedly in the presence of Sun-wen's entire force. Disdaining to fly before even such terrible odds he soon found himself in the greatest possible peril. Every one of his men was killed, and he himself barely escaped with his life.

For the next four years the history is mainly concerned with the story of Liu-yu's fighting with Sun-wen, whom he invariably discomfited whenever he could bring him to close quarters on shore. The difficulty in entirely subduing him arose from the fact that whenever the latter was conquered in any battle he immediately took to his ships that were lying off some appointed place on the coast and sailed away to the islands where his fleet used to have their head-quarters.

In consequence of his repeated successes Liu-yu was rewarded with honours by the state, and he rapidly rose to a high position under the government.

In the year A. D. 403 Hwan-yuan, the son of the late famous Hwan-wan, who was governor of Kingchow, rebelled, and a large army was sent against him to crush him. The commander was Yuan-hien, whilst the advanced forces were under Liu Lau-chi. Hwan-yuan, believing that a bold front was the surest way to obtain success, did not wait for the coming of the imperial army, but marched his men in the direction of Nanking.

Yuan-hien, who was utterly unfit for so important a command, but who had obtained it merely through the influence of his father, Tautze, the prime minister, became terrified when he heard of his approach, and timidly kept his army from crossing the Yang-tze to meet him.

---

* This man who was soon to be the founder of the Sung dynasty, belonged to the town of Suchow, in the north-west of the present province of Kiangsu. He was originally of low birth, but he was exceedingly ambitious and a man of great physical powers and commanding presence. His life had been a dissatisfied one, and most of it was spent in gambling. What time he gave to honest work was employed in making straw sandals. This occupation shows at once the straits into which he had fallen, for only the very poorest, and those who have absolutely no capital, would engage in a business that is so very unremunerative as this.

In the meanwhile Liu Lau-chi, who had crossed the river with his flying squadron, seeing himself deserted by his commander, and believing perhaps in the final success of Hwan-yuan, marched his men into his camp and signified his submission to him.

The combined forces now together crossed the Yang-tze and attacked Yuan-hien, whose army was routed and scattered to the winds. They then entered the capital, when Hwan-yuan, having put to death the prime minister and his incompetent son, took the whole power of the state into his own hands and ruled the country in the name of the imbecile Emperor Ngan Ti.

This year saw the final defeat and death of Sun-wen. Although Liu-yu had been the cause of many of his disasters, and had unquestionably prevented him from succeeding in his rebellion, he had not the honour of ultimately delivering the empire from this terrible scourge. It was to Sinking, the governor of Linhai, that the opportunity was given of rescuing the people of the districts that he had oppressed for years from this noted pirate. Being defeated in a great battle in which he fought with his usual bravery, but where the fortune of the day was decidedly against him, Sun-wen, seeing no way of escape, and dreading the fearful tortures to which we would be put were he captured, put an end to his life by jumping into the sea, where he was drowned.

Next year Hwan-yuan determined to do away with the farce of pretending to be simply a minister of the Emperor, and he deposed him, and giving him the title of prince, sent him off into retirement into Kiangsu, whilst he himself took the title of which he had deprived him. As he was about to ascend the throne for the first time the floor in front of it gave way, and he fell heavily to the ground. Some of the officials around shook their heads and muttered that heaven was not going to give the empire to him, as was manifest by this unlucky omen. Hwan-yuan, greatly disconcerted, rose hastily, when his fears were all dissipated by the more sycophantic of his ministers, who declared that his virtues were so great that the very ground gave way under him. This view of the case appeared very natural to him when it was told him in the hearing of his court, and the rest of the courtiers, who only the moment before had had such gloomy feelings about the incident, with ready wit joined in applauding the sentiment, so that the whole affair passed off happily and pleasantly. Shortly after this famous scene Liu-yu appeared at court to pay his obeisance to the new Emperor.

Not only was Hwan-yuan greatly struck with the appearance of the man and his noble bearing, but his wife also. She said to her husband, "Look at him, he has the walk of a dragon and the imperious step of a tiger. Look around on all your ministers. There is not another that has anything like his noble gait. He has the air more of a mandarin, and I should advise you to kill him now you have got him in your power, else the day will come when you will rue it that you did not do so!'' Hwan-yuan agreed with his wife in her estimate of the man, but he refused to take the severe measures that she proposed. ''We are all busy now,'' he replied, ''in pacifying the empire, and such a man as he is invaluable at such a time as this. I need his services, but the moment I can dispense with them I'll make short work with him.'' It would have been well for him had he acted on his wife's advise. It might have saved his own life and those of his kindred, and he might have been able to transmit the empire to his children.

Liu-yu must have got some inkling of what was in the mind of Hwan-yuan, for on his way home he gathered around him a few able men and declared that he was rising in defence of Ngan Ti, who had been illegally deposed by a usurper, and he called upon all loyal men and true to come to his aid. When Hwan-yuan heard of this he was paralyzed with terror, and when some of his officials attempted to comfort him by showing him the miserable character of the rising, he replied that it was enough to look at the men that were acting with him to see that the affair was an exceedingly serious one, and needed all their wisdom and resources to cope with successfully. This was quite true, for Liu-yu was no common man unknown to fame. His years of struggle with Sun-wen had made his name familiar to the people, and now when he was standing forth as the deliverer of his sovereign his influence in the minds of all loyal men was immensely magnified.

A large army was sent against him, but it was routed and pursued to the very capital, which Liu-yu entered with the flying soldiers. Hwan-yuan fled, but every one in the city that bore his name and had not escaped with him was ruthlessly murdered. Hwan-yuan now bent his course to the place where Ngan Ti was kept in confinement, and bringing him forth carried him off to Kingchow, his own province, so that he should not fall into the hands of Liu-yu, and thus give his rebellion a semblance of legality. Another army of Kingchow men was soon in the field, but once more Liu-yu was victorious, and Hwan-yuan, as he was in full retreat, was killed by one of the officials who was still loyal to the house of Tsin. Ngan Ti, too, was taken and conducted with all due ceremony and placed in the palace. He was nominally he Emperor, but he had only changed masters, for Liu-vu now ruled instead of Hwan-yuan.

In the year A. D. 404 Topa, who was gradually consolidating his power and showing by his legislation that he was a statesman as well as a warrior, made a law in regard to the distinctive dresses that his mandarins, both civil and military, should appear in when in full dress. He decided that the insignia with which the breast and back should be adorned should bear the figures of dragons and birds.* Another unfortunate undertaking was shortly after this begun in the now-diminished kingdom of the Tsins. Yau-hing, its ruler, was a most devout believer in Buddhism, and spent a large part of his time in the study and practice of that faith. He had men direct from India to be the public teachers of it. One of these, of the name of Lo-shih, was held in high reputation. Mandarins and scholars were compelled to assemble by order of the king to listen to his expositions of the doctrines of his church, and the man himself was treated with the reverence that was paid the idols. Monasteries and pagodas soon sprung up throughout the Tsin dominions, and so largely were the people influenced by the example of their ruler that nine out of every ten families of the common people were Buddhists. Yau-hing, anxious to be able to study the more profound doctrines of Buddhism, had Lo-shih translate a considerable number of Buddhist classics into Chinese. This was done to the great annoyance and vexation of the Confucianists, who saw this foreign religion perpetuated by these new books whilst their own were neglected.

In the year A. D. 406 a new actor in the struggles that were rending China appeared upon the scene. This was a Hiungnu, of the name of Holien Pohpoh. This person had formerly made his submission to Yau-hing, and served him faithfully. Seeing his opportunity in the universal restlessness that prevailed throughout the country he rebelled, and gathering his followers together he built a small town and highly fortified it on the northern boundary of the Tsin dominions. Here he bided his time, and watching the course of events prepared to take advantage of any opportunity that might occur to advance his own interests.

In the meantime Liu-yu had been gaining distinction and honour in his conflict with the various independent kings. He first of all invaded the present province of Shantung and obliterated the dynasty of the Later Yen, and in the year A. D. 416, the same in which he was made Duke of Sung, hearing of the death of the king of the Tsins in Shensi, he sent an army to take possession of the territories that had been held by Yau-hing.

---

* When a mandarin to-day appears in his official robes the breast and back of the outside dress are decorated with the insignia peculiar to his rank. These in the case of civilians are all birds. The first rank has a Manchurian crane ; the second, a golden pheasant ; the third, a peacock ; the fourth, a wild goose ; the fifth, a silver pheasant ; the sixth, a lesser egret ; the seventh, a mandarin duck ; the eighth, a quail ; the ninth, a long-tailed jay ; and the tenth, an oriole. The insignia of military men are all animals, as more consonant with their profession of arms. The first is the unicorn of Chinese fable ; the second, the lion of India ; the third, a leopard ; the fourth, a tiger ; the fifth, a black bear ; the sixth and seventh, a tiger cat, though the sixth has also the mottled bear ; the eighth, a seal ; and the ninth, a rhinoceros. The oriole is worn by the lowest grades of underlings. The wives of officials wear the same embroidery as their husbands. The ranks in both services have been further distinguished in the present dynasty by different coloured knobs on their caps. The first two wear red coral ; the third, clear blue ; the fourth, lapis lazuli ; the fifth, quartz crystal ; the sixth, opaque white stone ; and the last three, gilded yellow. See Williams' Dictionary, p. 698.

The general who commanded the advanced forces was a very brave and resolute man of the name of Wang-chin. Just before he started he swore to Liu-yu that he would never return alive to his home again unless he succeeded in the attempt he was going to make, for he was determined to conquer or to die. This brave officer was able to keep his word. Everywhere the most decided successes were given to his arms, and at the beginning of the next year, when Liu-yu came up with his force, Ch'ang-ngan was captured, and Fung, the king of the Tsins, seized and sent a prisoner to Nanking.

After these decided victories had been gained the army began to demand that they should be led home. The object of the campaign had been accomplished, the men said, and now it was but right that they should be allowed to return to their families, who would be all the time anxious about their welfare.

Liu-yu determined to accede to their request, and leaving a strong garrison in Ch'ang-ngan under the command of Wang-chin and a colleague of equal rank, he returned to Nanking.

There he was received with the greatest joy, both by the court and the people. Honours were heaped upon him, and he was made a prince of the empire, and territory to the extent of thirty-two chows were bestowed upon him.*

Soon after his departure for the east most important events began to take place in the region that had lately been conquered, by which the fruits of the recent campaign were snatched from the conquerors. Holien Pohpoh, mentioned above, who had been watching the progress of events, and had been gathering his forces together for years, now saw that the time had come for him to make a move. Immediately after the march of Liu-yu's army for Nanking he called his officers together and explained to them his plans. "Liu-yu," he said, "the great general that I have always feared, has gone, never to return as commander of an army again. He has now higher projects in view, for he means before long to seize the throne of the Tsins. We have therefore nothing to fear from him, for as an Emperor he will have to entrust his armies to be led by his lieutenants. There is not one of these that we need fear to face. Let us then move on to the conquest of the country formerly held by the Tsins and let us seize Ch'angngan to be our capital, and let us call our new dynasty the Hia, after the ancient one that ruled China in the days of the great Yu." The plan of their chief was eagerly adopted by his men, and before many days had elapsed twenty thousand of the Hiungnu were on their march to Ch'angngan. When they arrived before the city Wang-chin was anxious to lead out his men and fight with them, but his colleague Tientze, who hated him because of the fame he had obtained and of the high estimation in which he was held by Liu-yu, opposed

---

* A chow in ancient times comprised two thousand five hundred families. At present it means a district, the next in rank above a prefecture.

this. Wang-chin, indignant at the cowardice displayed by Tientze, said to him indignantly, "This place has been put in our hands by Liu-yu to be kept for our Emperor. Shall we then basely allow the enemy to approach and not make some effort to drive them away?" "Let us march out," he continued, "and we shall soon make these barbarians fly back to their native wilds, and if we cannot conquer we can at least die fighting like men." Tientze, finding that he must either fight or be disgraced, determined to get rid of Wang-chin. He therefore whispered to the leading officers that his colleague was going to rebel and set up an independent rule of his own. These deadly suspicions were believed in by the men, and taking advantage of this Tientze placed a body of soldiers in ambush and slew the valiant commander. He did not long survive the commission of this crime, however, for in the same year he was executed by a son of Liu-yu for this detestable murder that he had committed. Ch'angngan was captured by Holien Pohpoh, and though it was recovered by the next general that was sent in the place of Wang-chin, a few months after, it was again captured by the Hiungnu and made the capital of their new dynasty of Hia.

Holien Pohpoh had been a true prophet. From the time that Liu-yu reached Nanking he had planned to get rid of Ngan Ti. He had employed messengers to kill him, but his brother Tuh-wen, who never left his side, saved him from them. On one occasion, however, being sick, he had to consign the care of him to others, when the assassins, finding him one day alone and unguarded, strangled him. Liu-yu, who was hardly yet prepared for the great act of usurpation, made Tuh-wen Emperor in his place. His dynastic title was

Kung Ti—419-420.

After this prince had been on the throne a little under two years Liu-yu sent him a message, saying that he wished him to issue an edict announcing that he was going to resign his throne in favour of himself. Tuh-wen, bowing to the inevitable, did as he was requested. In the document that he put forth he recounted how the dynasty of the Tsins had been prolonged by the heroism of Liu-yu when it was threatened by the usurper Hwan-yuan, and that now he was but performing an act of justice in handing it over to one who had acted such a noble part, and who since then had enlarged the empire by his successes in the campaigns that he had carried on. The resignation was made in a building that had been specially erected outside the south gate of the city of Nanking, and thus the dynasty of the Tsins passed away after having ruled for one hundred and fifty-five years and having given fifteen Emperors, who, with more or less ability, occupied the throne during the troublous times when China was divided out amongst so many independent rulers. We see this dynasty disappear without any regret, for it seems to have done but little good for the people over whom it ruled.

CHAPTER XV.

EPOCH OF DIVISION BETWEEN NORTH AND SOUTH.

THE SUNG DYNASTY (A. D. 420-479).

Wu Ti—A. D. 420-423.

THIS Emperor is also known by the name of Kau-tsu. He was sixty-four years old when he came to the throne, and he reigned only three years. Although the historical Emperor of China, it must not be supposed that he, by any means, ruled over the whole of it. Six other kingdoms existed in different parts of it outside of the territory over which he himself reigned.* He had four sons, the first of whom was made heir to the throne, the second minister of education, and the third governor of Kingchow.

In the second year of his reign he sent a poisoned cup by the hands of one of his ministers, named Chang-wei, to the late Emperor Kung Ti. The former, who was a loyal subject of the house of Tsin. was terribly distressed with the commission that had been given him. He thought within himself, "If I take this poisoned liquor to Kung Ti, I shall be asking my sovereign to put himself to death, a thing that I cannot do. If I don't do so I shall certainly be put to death by Wu Ti. Better that I should die at once," said the brave man, and he accordingly drank off the cup that was intended for Kung Ti.

When Wu Ti heard of the failure of his plans he sent another dose of poison by the hands of another, who was less scrupulous than Chang-wei, and who soon presented himself before the unhappy prince. Kung Ti refused to have an end put to his life in this way, so the messenger of Wu Ti had him smothered to death. Next day, when the news was brought to Wu Ti, he met with his mandarins in the palace, and pretending that the death was a natural one, they all wept together as though their hearts were broken with grief for the loss of the unhappy captive. Three days after a royal funeral was given him, when lamentations and mourning were again manifested, according to the universal Chinese custom, around his tomb.

In the third year of his reign Wu Ti became dangerously ill, and it was manifest that his life was drawing to a close. Feeling anxious about his son, who was only seventeen years old, he called him to his bedside and urged him to put himself into the hands of

---

* The names of these were the Wei, ruled over by a grandson of Topa; the Hia, whose chief was a Hiungnu of the name of Hilien Pohpoh; the Northern Liang, ruled by Mongsun; the Western Liang, whose king was named Lisun; the Later Yen, ruled over by Fangpo, and the Western Ts'in, whose chief was Yau-ch'ang.

T'an Tau-ts'i, Su Sien-chi, Puliang and Sieh-hwui. "These are all distinguished men," he said, "and of marked ability. The only man that I have any doubts about is the last. His ambition is far reaching, and unless he is watched there is danger that he will rebel when a good opportunity presents itself to him." Whatever talent Wu Ti may have had as a warrior he certainly was extremely deficient in his power of reading men. Three of those that he recommended his son to look to for advice were about the worst he could have selected for so important a position. Calling them to his side after his son had left the room he commended him to their care and besought them to be loyal to him after his death. Shortly after this interview he ordered an edict to be issued, in which he laid down the law that never in the history of his house should any queen-dowager ever be allowed to exercise the functions of regent in the case of minors, but commanded that the prime minister of the day should invariably fulfill this duty. He shortly after died, and was succeeded by his son, whose dynastic title was

Shau Ti—A. D. 423-424.

About the beginning of this reign a northern tribe of barbarians, named the Jujan, invaded the dominions of Wei and began to harass the inhabitants that lived near the frontiers. In order to protect these the king of Wei, Topatau, built a wall nearly six hundred miles in length, from P'ing-lien to Yen-ngan, in Shensi, and manned the towers that he had built on it at various points with soldiers. This had the effect of stopping their ravages for a time and of giving some rest to the people that had hitherto been troubled by their inroads.

The people of Wei at this time were great believers in both Buddhism and Taoism, but one of the king's ministers, named Ch'ui, ridiculed both. He said the idols were things that barbarians only worshipped, and as for the jugglery of the Taoists it was simply the acting of men who were able to cheat the people by sleight of hand. He soon got into such disfavour that the king, though very fond of him and a great believer in his integrity and ability, was compelled to dismiss him from court. Not long after, coming in contact with a celebrated Taoist of the name of K'ow Kien-chi, he was converted from his unbelief and became an ardent believer in the mysteries of Taoism. He at once presented a petition to the king, in which he showed that of all certainties in this world Taoism was the most real, for it was founded on writings that had been left by the founder of it, and therefore was superior to the revelations that had been made to Fuh-hi by the celebrated Dragon Horse, or by the "Divine Tortoise" that had suddenly appeared to Yu when he was engaged in the gigantic work of draining off the waters that deluged China in his days. The king was so delighted with this conversion that he at once sent a present to K'ow Kienchi of precious stones and silks and satins as a token of his gratitude to him for restoring to him such an invaluable servant as Ch'ui, who was at once recalled to court and placed in his old position of honour and trust. A Taoist temple was also built to commemorate the happy event.

In the second year of Shau Ti his reign came to a disastrous end.

Su Chin-chi, who had a mortal hatred to his brother Yi-chin, the minister of education, brought false charges against him to the Emperor, when he was degraded from his high rank and reduced to the position of one of the people. A few months after Shau Ti himself was deposed by Su Chin-chi, Pu-liang and Sieh-hwui and made prince of Ying-yang, a district in Hunan, and only one short month after he was murdered by their order as well as his unfortunate brother Yichin. A younger brother, named Yiliang, was then raised to the throne, whose dynastic title was

Wen Ti—A. D. 424-454.

This prince was seventeen years old when he came to the throne, and though he abhorred the men that had put him on the throne he had to wait his time before he could execute his vengeance upon them, for they were too powerful for him to dare to attack at once. When he was twenty, by the advice of Tau-ts'i, who was his prime minister, and the only one of the four men that had been recommended by Wu Ti that had remained faithful to the trust committed to them, he determined to have them punished. When the edict went forth that they were to present themselves at the capital to give an answer to the question how it was they had dared to murder their sovereign, Puliang fled, but wass oon captured and ignominiously executed, and Su Chin-chi, who felt himself to be the most guilty of the three, and therefore who had the least hope of forgiveness, committed suicide. Sieh-hwui, who was governor of Kingchow, was the most difficult of all to deal with, for he was not only an exceedingly able man, but he had all the resources of his province to enable him to resist any measures that might be taken against him. Conscious of the treasonable part he had taken in causing the deposition and death of Shau Ti he determined to forestall any action on the part of Wen Ti by rebelling himself and by leading his forces against Nanking before preparations could be made to meet him. He accordingly sent a memorial to the Emperor, in which he complained of the wrong done to Puliang and Su Chin-chi, whom he declared to have been loyal subjects of the empire, and he stated that he was leading an army to the capital in order to deliver the Emperor from the evil counsellors by whom he was surrounded.

If he thought to take Wen Ti at a disadvantage he was grossly mistaken, for Tau-ts'i, a man just as clever as he was had got everything in readiness to meet just such an emergency as this. Before he could reach Nanking an army was on its way to meet him, and a battle was fought, in which his soldiers were defeated and he himself slain.

In the year A. D. 427 a son was born to Wen Ti. Immediately after its birth the queen sent in haste to her husband to tell him that the child that was born was so ugly and of so frightful a visage that she feared if it lived it would cause either some disaster in the family or the destruction of the dynasty. She therefore recommended that it should at once be put to death. Wen Ti rushed to the queen's apartments, and the child was just about to be strangled when he got there. The king, who was of a kindly nature, at once ordered it to be saved, and accordingly it was reared, to be in after days the murderer of its father. During the same year Topatau led an army against the Hia dynasty, and after a campaign of over a year he took the important city of T'ungman and conquered the district of Panchow in Shansi. After this was accomplished he marched his victorious army against the Western Tsins, when he captured their king Ch'ang, and when the people put his brother Ting in his place, Topatau, who had followed after the army that had rallied round him, was defeated, and the capital Ch'ang-ngan again fell into the hands of the Tsins. In the year A. D. 431 Wen Ti made great preparations to win back to the empire the province of Honan. He got an army together of fifty thousand men and put over it Tau Yenchi. He then sent ambassadors to the prince of Wei, who informed him that Honan belonged to the sovereign of China, that it had been taken by force from him, and that an immediate restoration of it was demanded. "Let your territories extend north of the Yellow River and ours to the south of it," they said, "and peace may then be maintained between us." "Your Emperor," Topatau replied, "claims Honan to be his, but in this he is mistaken. Ever since I was born, and before my hair was dry, I ever heard that it belonged to us. He is coming with his soldiers to take possession of it, and I shall quietly let him enter it, for I shall not fight with him. I shall recall my soldiers and my officers, but tell him that when the winter arrives, and the river is frozen over, I shall then come and demand it back again from him."* Topatau was as good as his word, for the whole of the places occupied by his men were evacuated on the approach of the Sung soldiers, who were highly delighted at their easy victory.

The only man that was anxious and foreboded disaster in the future was Wang Chung-tuh, a prominent military leader. "The northern barbarians," he said, "have no feelings of compassion and no generosity. To-day they do not fight, but in the meantime they

---

* The reason of this apparently tame submission of this warlike king was because his men were afraid of having to cross the river in boats. The northern men easily get seasick, and they have a great dislike to anything connected with the sea. There is a proverb that says, "The southern men sail in boats, whilst the northern men ride on horses."

are getting ready, and by and by they will come in all their strength and·drive us out of the country.'' This year Fangpo died, and was succeeded by his brother Fung, who killed his son, and thus became the next in succession. When the winter came round Topatau, true to his word, sent his general Ngan-ch'ieh to reconquer Honan. The Sung general, seeing the rapidity with which the Wei men marched, and the ease with which they captured two important cities, became filled with fear and retreated before them. Wen Ti then sent Tau-ts'i to the rescue, when the state of things assumed a different appearance. After he had arrived and taken charge of the army he advanced boldly in the direction of the enemy. More than thirty different engagements took place, in nearly all of which he was victorious. The Wei men in despair of success thought of the expediency of destroying the convoys of provisions that were coming for Tau-ts'i's army. This they managed to do, when he was reduced to such distress for food for his men that he found that he would have to retreat. This was a most perilous undertaking in the face of such an enemy and with his own men starving. Some of his soldiers, having deserted to the enemy, told the Wei army of Tau-ts'i's intention to retreat. They consequently made all arrangements to fall upon him whilst he was doing so, and the army was got ready so as to be able to move as soon as any motion was observed in that of the foe. The news somehow or other spread amongst the Sung men that they were to be fallen upon and annihilated by the soldiers of Wei the moment they began their retreat home, and there was to be seen the marvellous effect that a panic has upon the bravest and most disciplined men. Hitherto the Sung army had never feared to face the one that lay encamped before them, for victory had almost invariably attended them whenever they came to close quarters with it, and yet now they were so paralyzed with fear that every man in his anxiety to save his own life threw discipline and comradeship to the winds, and it seemed impossible to keep the men together. In a day or two more this valiant army that had gained such fame for its prowess would be dissolved and scattered over the roads of Honan in a wild and mad flight towards their homes.

In order to avert this terrible calamity Tau-ts'i had to resort to a stratagem. During one whole night he kept his soldiers carrying sand in baskets and laying it up in heaps by the road side. As each man went by officers who had been appointed to the task called out in as loud a tone as possible the number of loads that each had carried. The sound of these men's voices, and the bustle and tread of those who were carrying the sand, could be heard in the enemy's camp. Speculation was rife there as to what this all should mean. Some of the more daring drew near in the darkness to spy out what was going on. They could hear the incessant tramp of feet and the regular voices of the officers calling out numbers, that increased steadily on from one to hundreds. They were perplexed, and could only wait till morning light to see what mysterious cause had set in motion the whole army of Tau-ts'i. Just before dawn the general ordered the large heaps of sand that had been piled up by the road side to be covered with a thin covering of rice to make them appear as if they were heaps of that article, that had arrived for the use of his army. When the sun broke out and the Wei men who were gathered in crowds to catch a first glimpse of the opposite camp saw, as they thought, the vast heaps of rice they were struck with amazement. This did not look like destitution in the army. The story of the deserters was evidently a ruse of Tau-ts'i to lead them into attacking his camp, to be annihilated by some deep laid plot of this ingenuous commander. So enraged were they at the thought of being thus deceived that they at once led all the deserters to execution. After two days' interval Tau-ts'i quietly led his army away, and finally it reached the Sung territories in safety, but all the previous conquests were lost and Honan reverted to the rule of Wei.

The year A. D. 435 saw the further advance of Wei in power by the submission of the Later Yen to it. The ruler of the latter, in order to obtain easy terms from Topatau, made him a present of a very beautiful daughter that he had for his seraglio. This so pleased Topatau that he refrained for the present from absorbing the Yen districts with his own, and he still continued to allow his father-in-law a semi-independent rule over them.

Two years after this the great general and statesman Tau-ts'i came to a melancholy end. Since his return from his Honan campaign he had been held in high honour, not only because of his successes in it, but also because he was the only general that could keep the Wei from invading the territories of Sung. The fear of him and of his army that guarded the borders of the empire restrained the fierce soldiers of Wei from endeavouring to overthrow the dynasty. Wen Ti had lavished honours upon him, and prosperity attended him in every direction. He had eleven sons, all men of ability. He went about always surrounded by valiant men, heroes that had seen many a bloody fight and who at the word of their chief were ready to follow him against whatever enemy he might choose to lead them. Seeing the popularity of the man and the power he could command, the court began to have fears lest he might be entertaining ambitious views of overthrowing the dynasty. Unfortunately about this time Wen Ti fell dangerously ill, and there seemed no hope of his recovery. Yi-k'ung, his younger brother, sitting by his bedside, said, "If anything should happen to you there is no power that will be able to restrain Tau-ts'i from attempting to become Emperor. Better now, whilst you are alive, that you should put him out of the way than leave him to be a source of danger to your family." Wen Ti listened to his brother's advice, and Tau-ts'i was invited to the capital. After a month's waiting, during which Wen Ti did not improve in health, it was decided that the fatal act should be carried out. Tau-ts'i was told that he might return to his government, but that before doing so a royal banquet would be given him as a parting sign of the goodwill of the Emperor for him. On the morrow, when he entered the palace he was seized by men lying in wait and dragged away with the greatest indignity. The moment he was arrested he knew that his fate was fixed. Indignant at the wrong that was being done him he became convulsed with passions, and he inveighed against the ingratitude that was shown to a man that deserved so well of his country. Taking off his hat and throwing it down on to the ground he said, "You are casting down your great wall," meaning of course that they were destroying the only safeguard that they had against the inroads of the soldiers of Wei. In spite of his struggles and protestations he was ruthlessly murdered, and two of his officers that attended him shared his fate. When the news reached the capital of Wei everybody was delighted. The officers in the army clapped their hands in the exuberance of their joy, and they declared that they no longer feared the armies of Sung, as there was no one to lead them to victory as Tau-ts'i had always done. Shortly after this Topatau absorbed the territories of the Later Yen, and its king Fung fled to Corea.

In the year A. D. 439 Wen Ti gave great attention to learning, and established four royal colleges, in which the Confucian literature in all its branches was studied. The head of one of these was a distinguished scholar of the name of Lei. who had been repeatedly invited by Wen Ti to appear at court, but who had hitherto invariably refused. No honours could tempt him, and so devoted was he to study that he refused even to attend the examinations where degrees were to be obtained. When he heard from the Emperor that he was going to make him president of a college, where all his time would be spent in acquiring knowledge, he left the seclusion in which he had so long buried himself and appeared at the capital.

Wen Ti, who was fond of literature, often attended at the college to learn from the distinguished president. He used to drop in like a friend, for he insisted that Lei should not be troubled with any court ceremony in their intercourse as students of the same books. The description that is given of Wen Ti at this time is a very attractive one. He is said to have been full of benevolence, straightforward, frugal and very diligent. He never neglected any matters that pertained to the welfare of his kingdom. He was very forbearing, but he frowned upon anything like license or wickedness. He was very thoughtful about his people, and refused to take any tax from them, excepting the land tax. In consequence of all this the empire was prosperous, and contentment prevailed throughout it. The example of the Emperor led men to study, and as a result of this the manners and customs of the people gradually improved. About this time Topatau, after having extinguished the Northern

Liang dynasty, was also giving great attention to education and established national colleges like those of Wen Ti. He this year made the learned scholar Ts'ui-ho the royal historian.

It is pleasant to find in the historical records of China, which concern themselves mostly about wars and conquests and court intrigues, occasional glimpses of men who endeavoured to do their duty to their country in a humble way without any regard to the pleasure or anger of their rulers. One such is Kau-pih, the master of the horse to Topatau. On one occasion the king was going out with his suite on a grand hunting expedition, and he ordered Kau-pih to provide the very best horses he had on which to mount them all. When the time arrived and the horses appeared, they were the sorriest and most miserable looking set of animals that could be got together. The king was exceedingly indignant at this, and retired in a passion, saying that he would have Kau-pih executed for the insult that had been offered him that day. Some of the other officials who were slightly implicated in the affair began to express their concern lest some calamity should fall on them too. Kau-pih said, "This is a matter for which I am alone responsible, and I am willing to bear the whole brunt of the king's anger in my own person." "Is this a time," he continued, "for us to refrain from exhorting his majesty to have a special care for his kingdom now that the northern tribes of the Jujan are becoming every day more powerful, and when, too, the Emperor of the Sungs is seeking a quarrel with us to embroil us in a war? I have kept back therefore the best horses to have them in readiness to mount our soldiers to meet the enemy when he dares to come and attack us." Topatau, who had been listening to this speech of Kau-pih, was most delighted with it, and said, "I have at least one treasure in my kingdom," and, coming forth, he praised his integrity and loyalty before all the rest of his ministers and made him a present of a handsome suit of clothes.

In the year A. D. 446 Yi-k'ung, the younger brother of Wen Ti, and the one that had been the cause of the death of Tau-ts'i, was degraded from all his offices and reduced to the rank of a common person. Five years previously he had acted with such arrogance in the palace that Wen Ti was compelled to have him removed, and so he gave him the governorship of the province of Kiangsi. Whilst there he met a charlatan who pretended to be able to read and interpret the enigmatical sentences in a book on astronomy, and which were supposed to contain prophecies of coming events. One of these sentences said, an Emperor would come out of Kiangsi, and that a sovereign of the Sungs would be murdered by one of his own relatives. Yi-k'ung was easily persuaded that this referred to himself, and he raised the standard of rebellion. All his followers were seized and executed. His own life was spared, but he was stripped of all his titles and made incapable of ever holding office again. Next year (A. D. 447) Wen Ti determined to inflict severe punishment on Cochin China, which was then one of the tributaries of the empire. The reason for this was that the people on the coast of China had been terribly troubled and harassed by the pirate junks that came from that country and plundered their cities and villages. An army was equipped and sent under the command of Hochi, with Tsung-ch'ueh second in command. When the army reached the country the soldiers were terribly frightened at the sight of the elephants that the Cochinese had brought with them into battle, and they refused to meet such frightful looking creatures. They had never seen such in their own far-off homes, and they believed that they must be something unearthly. The heavy, solemn tread of these huge beasts, and their noses stretched far away into the air before them, inspired only feelings of the utmost terror, and they refused to advance to meet them.

There seemed to be a possibility of great disaster to the royal army, and consequently the disgrace of the house of Sung, when the inventive genius of Tsung-ch'ueh, the hero of the campaign, saved it from this terrible disgrace and brought instead victory and renown to its standards. He thought with himself that amongst the barbarians of the West there was a fierce kind of lion, which was the natural antagonist of these elephants, and before which they were accustomed to fly in the utmost terror. "If I could only get some of these animals now to help us fight them," he said, "we should be certain of victory. It is impossible, however, to obtain them now, and so we must do the next best thing in our power." He accordingly had images made of these ferocious beasts, which he placed in the van of the army. No sooner did the elephants behold their implacable foes than they turned tail and fled in the greatest consternation. Nothing could hold them back, and they crashed through the ranks of their friends, bringing consternation and death wherever they trod. Tsung-ch'ueh, seeing the happy consequences of his ruse, advanced rapidly upon the Cochinese whilst they were in disorder, and completely routed them. The king of the country fled, and the capital was taken. A vast amount of booty and treasure was seized by the soldiers, and gems and precious stones, such as had never been seen before, fell into their hands. Tsung-ch'ueh, who was known for his integrity, took nothing for himself, and when he reached his home it was noted that he not only returned empty handed, but his clothes were torn and ragged with the wear and tear of the campaign and the long wearisome journey to and from Cochin China.

This same year Ts'ui-ho, who was an inveterate hater of idolatry, memorialized Topatau and begged him to do away with the idols and Buddhism out of his kingdom. "They are all false," he said, "and moreover they are an injury to the people of your dominions, and ought therefore to be expelled from it." Topatau, anxious to see for himself what the exact state of the case was, entered a monastery one day unexpectedly. He found the priests all drinking whiskey, and looking around he saw swords hanging about in all directions. He was exceedingly enraged at these two things, and at once commanded the magistrate of the district to execute all the priests of this establishment for being guilty of offences that they were bound by their vows to avoid. He also ordered that an examination should be made into all such buildings throughout his kingdom. The results were not at all satisfactory. Many of them contained stills, where the whiskey was distilled on the premises, and in some of the larger ones secret cellars were found below, where persons of immoral character were lodged and maintained. Topatau determined to sweep out these abominations from his country, so he issued an edict, which ran somewhat as follows : " The unprincipled and ignorant minded Emperor to the Later Hans, Ming Ti, had a firm faith in what was corrupt and false. In consequence of his action neither the principles of Heaven could be carried out, nor the government of the country, nor the teaching of the people. All rules of ceremony and propriety were overturned. Now I have been appointed by Heaven to establish the right and to sweep away what is false. I am determined to destroy every trace of Buddhism from my kingdom. I therefore order every prefect and county magistrate in my dominions to destroy every idol and temple within his jurisdiction and to put to death all the Buddhist priests they can find."

This edict was kept back for a few days through the influence of the heir apparent Hwang, who was a believer in Buddhism, and information was secretly conveyed to the priests, a large number of whom escaped before the royal proclamation was issued. Many, however, did not get the news in time, and a considerable number were seized and executed. All the idols were burnt, as well as the Buddhist classics that the mandarins could lay their hands on, and every temple, small and great, was soon a mass of ruins.

In the year A. D. 451 two enemies of Ts'ui-ho, the royal historian and the prime instigator of the destruction of Buddhism, wishing to ruin him, advised him in order to show to the world his fidelity as an historian that he should have the record of what he had written so far cut in tablets of stone, which might be set up in some prominent place, where the people could see them. Ts'ui-ho did not show his usual acuteness or sharpness of intellect on this occasion, for he fell into the snare. Either he was becoming too confident of his own power or he had become vain, because he conceived himself to be possessed of an integrity that cared neither for the praise nor censure of kings, and so he consented to do an entirely unprecedented and illegal act. The rule had hitherto been that no eye but that of the historian should look upon the story of the dynasty, but that it should be hidden away in the royal archives, where not even the Emperor himself could reach them, and that when a new dynasty sat upon the throne then and only then the secrets of the past should be revealed to the world. As soon as the tablets were put up where everyone could read them the indignation of the country was aroused against Ts'ui-ho. The misdeeds of the men who had founded their dynasty were cut in letters of stone. The meanness, the treachery, the cruel murders and the intrigues of the palace were all put down as if with an iron finger alongside with what had been glorious and exalted in the history of their past. Ts'ui-ho had indeed been a faithful historian, but peoples and potentates do not like to have their vices paraded before the world, and so a terrible punishment fell upon the unfortunate man and his family. Not only was he put to a miserable death, but every member of his father's, mother's and wife's family was exterminated with relentless barbarity. This same year Wen Ti determined again to take the field against Topatau and endeavour to recover the long-coveted province of Honan. The most of his ministers were opposed to the idea, but others were favourable to it, so an army was sent under command of Wang-yuan, which marched into Honan. Topatau, who was a warlike prince, immediately took up the challenge and himself led in person an immense force, which rumour magnified into more than a hundred thousand men. In the battle that took place Wang-yuan was defeated and lost forty thousand men in killed and wounded. After this success Topatau's army marched into Shantung. On their way they passed by the tomb of the great Confucius, when the king offered a sacrifice of an ox before it. From this place the course of the army was to the south, and its track was marked by atrocities of the most savage kind. These wild soldiers of the north spared neither man, woman nor child. They seemed to take a delight in spearing the little ones and holding them high in the air and gloating over their agonies and contortions. These monsters, however, soon began to find that a nemesis was pursuing them. The people fled in terror before them, carrying or destroying what provisions they had, so that none should fall into their hands. Soon famine came into their camp. They then turned their steps, after they had been repulsed from the city of Hu-i, in the north-eastern part of Nganhwui, in the direction of Nanking, subsisting only on what provisions had been left by the people when they fled from their homes.

As soon as they arrived on the banks of the Yang-tsze they began to build boats to cross over it. The greatest fear and consternation filled the hearts of the people of the capital. Wen Ti was greatly distressed that his own wilfulness had been the means of bringing such misery upon his people. As he stood on the walls of the city of Shih-t'eu and looked across the Yang-tsze and saw the tents of the savage troops on the other side he confessed aloud that he was wrong in not listening to the advice of those that warned him not to attempt to recover Honan, and then with his spirit full of sadness he exclaimed, "If Tau-ts'i were only here the enemy would never have dared to have invaded my country!" In the following year, A. D. 462, the army of Wei, that was now utterly destitute of provisions, was compelled to retreat to its own country. They had devastated six provinces and had left them a wilderness. So extreme was the desolation that it is said that when the swallows came to them in the spring they could not find a house standing, and so they were compelled to build their nests in the trees.

The next year Topatau was murdered by one of his officers. This tragedy was the result of a miserable quarrel between two men, one of whom accused the other to the king of malpractices in which the heir apparent was implicated. Topatau, with his usual impetuosity, ordered the accused to be put to death. The prince, who was deeply attached to him, was so affected by this that he sickened and died. His father, who was passionately fond of him, mourned for him and refused to be comforted. The cause of all this, Chung-ngai, was so terrified lest Topatau in his anger should cause him to be executed that he entered into a conspiracy with a number of others and murdered him. The fatal deed was concealed by the conspirators for several days, during which they were planning whom they should raise to the throne. They dare not place the true heir on it, lest he should avenge the murder of his grandfather and the death of his father, so they elevated a prince of the blood named the Prince of Nan-ngan to the dangerous position, but a few months after he in his turn was murdered by Chung-ngai. This double murder aroused the indignation of the chief men of the kingdom, and gathering their forces together they seized the regicide and put him to death, and all the members of his father's, mother's and wife's family, and placed the legitimate heir, Chun, whose dynastic title was Wen-ch'ung Ti, on the throne. Almost the first act of this man was to re-establish Buddhism in his kingdom and to give permission to the bonzes again to practise their religion throughout the country.

The year A. D. 454 saw a similar tragedy enacted in the palace of the Sungs. Wen Ti was unfortunate in his two eldest sons, Shau and Chun. They were wild and dissipated, and the reproofs of their father only caused them to hate him with a most unnatural hatred. They became so unruly that Wen Ti determined to disinherit the eldest and put to death the second. Having unfortunately heard of this decision through one of the ladies of the harem, they determined they would be avenged on their father. Shau, in company with about sixty wild and dissolute companions, entered the palace one morning just before daybreak. Wen Ti, who had spent the night with one of his trusted ministers planning for the succession, was taken completely by surprise when the band of murderers burst in upon them. For some time he defended himself with a small table which he held in front of him, but his fingers having been cut off the table dropped, and he was speedily despatched by the swords of the conspirators. Shau, who was naturally of a blood-thirsty disposition, caused all the loyal ministers of his father to be put to death, but a nemesis was hastening with impatient strides to execute vengeance on the parricide. Wen Ti's third son Tsun, who was governor in Kiangsi, hearing of the terrible doings in the capital, gathered every soldier he could command, .and by forced marches soon reached Nanking. He entered without any opposition, for none lifted a hand in favour of the miserable Shau. His crime was such a detestable one that men felt that neither heaven nor earth could endure him, and therefore it was perilous to be associated with him. Tsun, at the head of his troops, entered the palace, and seizing Shau and Chun, had them at once executed. He himself now became Emperor with the title of Hiau Wu Ti, which means the Martial Filial Emperor.

Hiau Wu Ti—A. D. 454-465.

This prince was only twenty-four years old when he came to the throne. Nothing of importance happened in the empire or in the kingdom of Wei for several years. In the year A. D. 460 another son of the late Wen Ti, of the name of Tan, conspired with an official named Yen-chun against his brother Hiau Wu Ti and aimed at becoming Emperor instead of him. The conspiracy, however, was nipped in the bud. Tan was killed, and Yen-chun had his legs broken to pieces till he died of anguish. His wife and her daughters were banished to Cochin China, and the sons on their way there were drowned in the first river they came to. After this nothing important happened in the empire during the remaining years of Hiau Wu Ti's reign. He was a man given more to his own enjoyment than was meet for the ruler of a great people. He used to spend a large part of his time in hunting, to the neglect of public business. The time unfortunately produced no famous minister who could have stimulated him by his lofty ideas to a nobler conception of his duties as a sovereign. There was nothing dignified, moreover, in his manner of treating his high officials. Instead of the rigorous etiquette, which is deemed one of the most important essentials of an eastern court, there was an unbecoming frivolity, which undermined that respect and fear for the throne which ought to exist in the minds of the people for it. In speaking to the nobles of the court, instead of addressing them by their proper titles, he would give them some nickname from some peculiarity in their person or their manner, and he delighted to see a black man, that was in the palace, chase about these great stately mandarins with a stick, whilst he would sit by convulsed with laughter at the comical sight. He died in the eleventh year of his reign, and his son Yeh succeeded him. It was noticed that when the imperial seal was carried in to him he showed no emotion and expressed no sorrow at the death of his father. The officials who had taken it to him were so shocked at his want of feeling that they could not refrain from crying out aloud when they joined the other ministers, "The dynasty will not be long before it perishes." The Emperor is known in history by the name of Fei Ti, or the Discarded.

Fei Ti—A. D. 465.

This year, A. D. 465, Topa Fung became king of Wei, under the title of Hien Wen Ti. Fei Ti was a man of low and brutal passions, and seemed to delight in the commission of murder, not simply as a safeguard to his throne, but because he took pleasure in cruelty. Although he was only sixteen years of age he had the passions of a more mature man. His first act was to imprison three of his uncles, because he had a suspicion that they were meditating rebellion. He again remembered that his father and grandfather were each of them the third son in the family, and superstition made him believe that the luck ran in the line of the third sons. He therefore determined to destroy the next youngest brother but one to himself and so prevent the throne becoming his by some turn in the wheel of fortune. This man, whose name was Chu, was governor of Chinkiang in Kiangsi. He sent a high official with a dose of poison to him with orders that he should drink it. The messenger, who disliked his commission, managed to delay by the way, so that some of Chu's friends brought him timely information of the fate that was intended for him. He at once called together his principal men and advisers and asked them what should be done under the circumstances. His brother could find no offence in him, but simply because of a superstitious idea that had come into his head he was going to take away his life. After a good deal of discussion it was at last decided that the standard of rebellion should be raised. In ten days they had five thousand men in arms. Proclamations were sent broadcast over the country, explaining that the rising was simply in defence of right, and because Fei Ti was a ruler that had no regard for justice, and therefore he was rejected both by Heaven and by men.

In the meantime one of his uncles, named Hwo, who was in prison, was planning, with the aid of some of the eunuchs of the palace, to overthrow his nephew, and was simply wanting an opportunity to murder him and seize upon the supreme power. Fei Ti himself soon supplied the occasion. He had taken one way of amusing himself which showed the shameless and debased character of his mind. He had got together a large number of the ladies of his harem, and compelling them to strip off all their clothes, made them run round his royal gardens catching each other. One of the ladies, more modest, or at least more courageous than the rest, resisted the will of this savage and refused to join in the immodest sports. Fei Ti, who had no tenderness or gallantry in his nature, slew her with his own hand on the spot. That same night the murdered woman appeared to him in his dreams and reproached him for his wickedness and warned him that he would not be spared long enough to eat the fruits of the next harvest. Fei Ti, who was a coward at heart, awoke in the greatest terror, and sending for a Taoist priest asked if he had any way of warding off the danger to his life that the spirit of the woman he had slain predicted. The priest explained that the spirit of his late concubine was in the garden close to the place where she was killed by him, but that he undertook by his magic and his control over the supernatural powers to drive it away, when he would be saved from the fate she had threatened him with, and peace and happiness would return to his mind.* In order to this the Emperor had to attend with a special number of his harem, all supplied with bows and arrows. They were then directed to shoot over the spot where the unhappy woman had fallen, for, he said, some of their arrows would certainly hit the unappeased spirit and slay it, and Fei Ti would then be delivered from its vengeance. Whilst they engaged in this childish occupation serious events were taking place in the palace. Hwo with his confederates deemed the time had now arrived when the rising they proposed should take place. The Emperor was unguarded and the night was dark, so that the approach of the conspirators could not be perceived. They accordingly assembled, and creeping along unobserved they came into the garden before Fei Ti knew of their approach. He was at once despatched, not very far from the place where his victim had fallen, and thus her prophecy was fulfilled, and no doubt, as the Chinese believed, by her special agency.

An edict was issued next day, saying that the death of the Emperor had been ordered by the queen-dowager because of the reckless murders he had committed. Hwo was the eleventh son of Wen Ti, and was twenty-seven years old when he seized the throne. He is known by the title of Ming Ti, the "Intelligent."

Ming Ti.—A. D. 465-473.

This year Chu, the brother of the late Fei Ti, who had risen in rebellion in Kiangsi, also took the title of Emperor, and large numbers flocked to him. Ming Ti consulted with his ministers as to what should be done to meet this danger. One of these, Ts'ai-hing, counselled the Emperor to issue an edict declaring that the relatives of those who were in rebellion should not suffer the usual penalties, but be held guiltless of the treason of their friends. As there were large numbers with Chu whose wives and families were resident in the capital, this had an excellent effect upon them, for finding, contrary to expectation, that their families were in no danger, many of them deserted and secretly returned to their homes, fearful lest Ming Ti might change his mind by their continuance in

---

* The Chinese believed, and do so at the present day, that when a man loses his life in any way, whether by murder or by accident, the spirit of the person wanders about till it gets relief in some way or other. When a person, for example, is drowned, the spirit dwells in the water till some unwary bather comes to the same place to swim, when the spirit endeavours to paralyze the new comer. If it can succeed in this and cause his death, the lately unhappy spirit is at once released from the fate that bound it to the vicinity of its accident, and it is then free to wander wide afield in the spirit land.

rebellion and order their destruction.   A few months after an engagement took place between Chu and the royal army, when the former was defeated and slain.   If Ming Ti at this point had only shown the wisdom that his name implies that he was possessed of, the rebellion would have been completely crushed, and the empire would have been at peace.   Two of the governors of provinces that had been connected with Chu sent a memorial to him, confessing their fault and saying that they wished to surrender and become his faithful subjects.   Their names were Sieh-ngan and Siang-tin. Ming Ti, instead of pleasantly accepting their submission, determined to show them that whilst he forgave them it was not because he had not the power to bring them to their knees.   He accordingly ordered an army of fifty thousand men to march into their districts and take them over from them.   Ts'ai-hing endeavoured to dissuade the Emperor from this unwise course.   "These men," he said, "are quite sincere in the submission they are tendering you.   If you send such an army as that they will fancy that you mean their destruction, and fear will drive them into desperate courses.   One man is enough, and fifty thousand far too many."   The Emperor was obstinate, and insisted upon having his own way.   The army accordingly marched, and the results were exactly what his prescient minister had predicted.   Sieh-ngan got all the men together he could collect, and making his submission to the king of Wei, claimed his help in this emergency.   The latter was only too glad for an excuse to march into the Sung territory, and in the battle that followed Ming Ti's army was overthrown with the loss of over ten thousand men.   What was worse than even the defeat was the fact that four departments to the north of the river Hwai and the country to the west of it from this time came under the dominion of the kingdom of Wei.   When the news of the defeat reached Ming Ti he called Ts'ai-hing to his side, and showing him the despatch, deplored that he had not taken his advice, and thus have saved himself from a great disaster.

In the year A. D. 468 a prominent character came to the front. His name was Siau-tau, a descendant of Siau-ho, who played such a prominent part at the close of the Ts'in and the beginning of the Han dynasties.   Physically he was a remarkable man, and everyone predicted that he would one day become Emperor.   He was an exceedingly handsome and well made man.   His body was covered with scales like those on a dragon, and he had a mark on each shoulder that represented the sun and the moon.   Everyone read in these two the destiny that was to cause him to fill a throne.   Two years after, Ming Ti, who had made him a military commander, heard of the way in which he was being talked of as a man whom Heaven seemed to have destined for a throne.   He determined that he would do his best to defeat its purpose, so he sent orders to him to return to the capital, where he would soon have put it out of his power to do anything more in this world.   Siau-tau, who saw through his design, decided to refuse to obey this order. To do so, however, meant rebellion ; but that he was far from intending to engage in. By the advice of one of his captains he adopted a stratagem, by which he was delivered from his dilemma. He and a considerable number of his friends gathered on the frontiers of Wei as if for the purpose of creating trouble there. The commander of the troops guarding those districts, seeing a number of the Sung soldiers, and not understanding why they should be there if not with a hostile intention, became alarmed. A treaty of peace had been made between the two powers some two years ago, and this collecting of soldiers on the borders must mean that the Sung Emperor was intending to make an invasion of their dominions. He accordingly sent a corresponding number of Wei troops to watch their movements. This was all that Siau-tau wanted. He immediately memorialized the Emperor to be allowed to remain at his post, as he had seen large numbers of Wei soldiers on the frontiers of the Sung territory, looking as though they were meditating an incursion into his dominions. The necessary permission was given, and the imminent peril to which he had been exposed for the time being was avoided.

Next year Ming Ti killed four of his brothers, lest they should interfere with the prospects of his adopted son, when he wished to succeed him. Again Siau-tau was summoned to the capital, and upon his friends warning him of the danger he ran in obeying the command, he replied, "This time I am safe. Ming Ti has murdered his brothers, and he wishes me to help him in keeping the throne for his son." "Troubles," he continued, "are coming upon the empire, and the time for me to act has arrived."

The king of Wei, Topa Fung, was a great believer in both the Buddhist and Taoist religions, and as he wished to give all his time to the practice of these two faiths he resigned his throne in favour of his son, who was only five years old. His ministers protested against this, but all that they could gain from him was the promise that in all important matters of state he would give his advice, but that in the ordinary routine of business he would leave everything to be decided by his son and his ministers.

Ming Ti was a profound believer in Buddhism, and showed his devotion by building a magnificent temple to Buddha, upon which he lavished so much money that his subjects were distressed by the heavy taxes he levied to carry on the work.

When it was finished, Ming Ti one day in the presence of his ministers said, "Now my merit and my virtues are exceeding great, and the only reward that would be commensurate to them would be that I should in the future become a god myself." One of them replied, "If Your Majesty considers the amount of suffering that this building has caused to your people you will see that instead of merit and virtue your sin is higher than that pagoda that you have erected by the side of it. If those wooden, foolish idols were indeed endowed with life they would weep their eyes out with tears, for in order to provide the money to build the temple in which they are enshrined, men have even had to sell their wives and their children and to endure all the horrors of extreme poverty.''

Ming Ti died in the 8th year of his reign, and was succeeded by his son Tze, who took the title of Ts'ang Wu-wang, and also Chu Li. He reigned four years, but nothing of importance happened during the time that historians deemed worthy of note. He was killed by Siau-tau, and the prince of Ngan-ch'ung, the third son of the late Ming Ti, was raised to the throne. His dynastic title was Shun Ti.

Shun Ti—A. D. 477-479.

No sooner did this prince ascend the throne than an insurrection took place in Kingchow. The governor of it declared that he was going to demand the life of Siau-tau for the murder of the late Emperor. Two of the high officials in the palace, who sympathized with the movement, were in readiness to act when the time came, but their design becoming known to Siau-tau, they were ruthlessly put to death, and he, marching an army into Kingchow, defeated the governor, who fled, but died in his flight. The victor now took upon himself the airs of a sovereign and acted as though he were already in possession of the throne. When he appeared before Shun Ti he wore his sword and dispensed with some articles of court dress that only one with the views he entertained would dare to have done. In the autumn of A. D. 479 Shun Ti was made to resign, though he utterly refused to carry the imperial seal to Siau-tau, and, bowing before him, pay him obeisance as his successor. An official was therefore sent to demand it from him. When he unceremoniously appeared in his presence, Shun Ti asked him, whilst he wept, ''if he was come to take away his life.'' ''No,'' he replied, ''I have no order to kill you,'' and then trying to soothe him he said, ''Why should you weep? Your ancestors got the throne in the same way that you are being deprived of it now. Your family has had a turn in governing an empire, and now be content to let another have a share in the good fortune that you have had.'' ''Better then,'' replied the unhappy monarch, ''that a man should not be the descendant of an Emperor, but that he should be the son of a common man.'' The messenger left with the Great Seal, and Siau-tau became Emperor, whilst Shun Ti was made prince of Juyin, in Kiangnan, to which place he was sent under a strong escort of soldiers.

CHAPTER XVI.

EPOCH OF DIVISION BETWEEN NORTH AND SOUTH.

THE TS'I DYNASTY (A. D. 479-502).

Kau Ti—A. D. 479-483.

KAU TI was fifty years old when he dispossessed Shun Ti of the throne, and he reigned but four years. He is represented as being very clever and an accomplished scholar, and one that studied the interests of the people by a strict economy in his own life and in his court. He was a large-hearted man, and in the fulness of his desire to see the nation prosper he promised that if he lived but ten years he would make gold and silver as common as earth, so that the poorest should never be in want. Unfortunately, he did not live long enough to carry out this prophecy, for he died after only too brief a reign, to the great regret of his subjects.

The royal historian of the time had absolutely nothing of importance to record regarding the founder of this dynasty, who seemed deficient in some of the more heroic qualities.* He was succeeded by his son, who was forty-three years of age, and who reigned eleven years.

Wu Ti—A. D. 483-494.

In the first year of this Emperor's reign, the king of Wei, To-Pa Hung, who had succeeded to the throne when his father Fung was murdered by his wife, passed a law in imitation of his Chinese neighbours, that no person should be allowed to marry another of the same family name. This law had already been in existence amongst the Chinese from the time of the Duke of Chow, at the commencement of the Chow dynasty, and is in operation to-day throughout the empire. Great progress was made during this reign by the Buddhist church. Tze-liang, the eldest son of Wu Ti, was a devoted adherent of it, and was in the habit of collecting the most famous bonzes he could hear of in the empire and getting them to expound their doctrines in the hearing of himself and a large company of the élite who were attracted by his example.

---

* In the unauthorized history of the time, "The Former Five Dynasties," many details are given of his life and doings, but they are entirely unreliable. The author of that work has undoubtedly played with his imagination, but the precise place where romance comes in, and where facts are stated, it is impossible to tell. It has been thought better to adhere to the standard history, for here we are on firmer ground. The same may be said about some of the Emperors of the preceding dynasties : volumes have been written which contain marvellous stories about their lives, which make very pleasant reading, and decidedly enliven a page, but the historian looks askance at all such, for they belong more to the region of romance than to the sober domain of history.

One of the subjects that was specially dwelt upon was that of Rewards and Punishments. As Confucianism is profoundly atheistic in its tendencies, giving no thought to anything beyond the present life, and not even discussing the question of the future, men in all ages have been glad of a system that professed to deal with it, even in the imperfect way that Buddhism has done, and therefore it can be easily understood how rapidly it took hold of the popular imagination, and even claimed the attention of many scholars, both among the Sienpi of the Wei dynasty and the more civilized peoples of Chinese origin.*

This year, A. D. 435, a law was passed by Wu Ti that no prince of the blood should have more than forty attendants. He had seen the evil effects of men with large numbers of retainers, and how easily a man might be led into rebellion when he had so many willing followers all ready to help him in his treason. His relatives were highly displeased with this, but they had to submit, and it was no doubt for the welfare of the empire, as well as the security of the newly-founded dynasty that they should. Three years after this Topa Hung, the ruler of Wei, whose dynastic title is Hiau Wen Ti, and who was a remarkably intelligent and enlightened man, became greatly concerned because there were so many robbers throughout his kingdom. The wars in which the Wei and the Sung had been engaged had left disastrous consequences, in rendering many of the

---

* That Buddhism had its opponents, notwithstanding the favour shown it by the heir apparent, is manifest from the discussion that took place between him and one of his intimate friends, who was a scholar. Tze-liang, in his enthusiasm for Buddhism, began to descant upon its merits, and showed how true it was, especially in its doctrine of the transmigration of souls. " You see many confirmatory proofs of the truth of this tenet," he said to his friend Hwan-sin. " Men who in a previous life were good and virtuous and filial, in this are rewarded by being placed in positions of honour and ease in society whilst those who were immoral and profligate are now reaping the reward of their evil deeds in being made beggars and outcasts and the very scum of human life to-day." Hwan-sin, however, was not going to be convinced so easily as the prince imagined, so he replied, " I have no faith whatsoever in your idols or in Buddhism, and I entirely demur to the idea that men's relative positions in society have anything to do with the absurd fiction that they are the result of deeds done in a previous state of existence. Men are like the flowers of a tree, which grow naturally. A great wind comes, and they fall—some here, some there, some on the stony rock and some in the pleasant garden. So it is with man. Some are kings, some are beggars, some in poverty, some in silks, but all the result of mere natural law. As for the soul, it never existed before. It is a growth of the body. You see," he continued, " the sharpness of a knife blade. That is one of the accidents of the blade. If there were no knife there would be no sharpness, and if there were no body there would be no soul." Tze-liang, whose mental powers do not seem to have been of the highest quality, was completely flabergasted at such profound logic, for history significantly remarks that he was silent. He does not seem to have wished to meet such a sledge hammer reasoner again, so he sent a messenger to Hwan-sin to tell him that if he were not such an old character he would have made him a mandarin, as he plainly showed that he had ability enough to occupy such a position. This was a delicate hint to his opponent that he should swallow his principles and come over to his side, for he was convinced that a man with such transcendant power of reasoning would have been a powerful advocate for Buddhism. Hwan-sin, however, was made of sterner stuff than he imagined, for he returned answer that he did not want to be a mandarin, and that he still held on to his belief that there was nothing in idolatry that a sensible man could accept.

common people homeless. Having no means of livelihood, many of them had been compelled to take to the roads, and so they became unsafe for honest travellers. Hung consulted with one of his most intelligent officers as to how the difficulty should be met. The latter replied that the one panacea for extirpating robbers out of his country was good and righteous government. He then referred to the example of Sung-kun, who, through his wise and liberal rule, caused even the wild beasts to desert the country over which they had wildly roamed. *

Hung, feeling the force of this statement, began at once to examine his life and to see where corrections could be made. He also opened schools throughout the country and encouraged education. In the year A. D. 494, having become dissatisfied with his present capital, P'ing, in Shansi, he determined to move it further south to Lohyang, in Honan. He was of a more refined nature than his countrymen, and he could not stand the severe winters and cold weather of the north. He knew that he should experience a violent opposition from the more conservative of his ministers, so he determined to effect by a ruse what he felt convinced he could never accomplish by argument. All at once he gave out, in an audience that he had with his nobles, that he was going to make war on the Ts'i dynasty. The astonishment of most of them was unbounded, for there was no ostensible reason for such an unwise proceeding. One of them, and he the most powerful, was very violent in his opposition, and in order to be able to carry out his scheme Hung had to take him into his confidence and let him know that it was not war he meant, but the removal of the capital. The king then ordered that an immense army should be raised, and that the various chiefs should bring their contingents into the field.

The Ts'i Emperor, hearing of this vast preparation that was being made to invade his territories, began to arm too, and soldiers from all parts of his dominions began their march towards the capital to defend it when the Wei army should have arrived to attack it. Now it happened fortunately for Hung that when his army got near Lohyang it began to rain in torrents. The soldiers were wet through, the roads were bad, and the difficulty of locomotion depressed everyone. The officers who had originally been opposed to the invasion, represented to the king the folly of continuing to carry out a purpose that nearly everyone in the army opposed. "Better that we should return home," they said, "than persevere in an enterprise that must turn out disastrously with the present temper of the men."

---

* Sung-kun was an officer who lived in the first century of our era, and held at first a position under the famous commander Ma-yuan. He was subsequently made governor of Kiukiang, in the province of Nganhwui. When he took up his government he found the people terribly oppressed by the officials who had been sent to destroy the tigers that infested the country. He at once put a stop to their exactions, and his rule was so beneficent that the animals of their own accord deserted the country and left the people.

Hung, who was secretly delighted with the turn that things had taken, tried to show the scorn that would be showered upon them, should they give up their plans without striking a blow. "The kingdom," he said, "has been put to great expense, and vast trouble has been taken in getting together and providing for such a large body of men. I see your difficulties," he continued, "and I sympathize with you all. What I propose, then, is that we shall take possession of Lohyang, that is close by, and make it our capital; we shall then be nearer the enemy should we desire by and by to conquer him, and we shall be in a more central position from which we can govern and care for the lands under our rule." This proposition was carried by acclamation. Anything, they said, rather than persevere with this disastrous expedition. Hung at once sent several of his ministers back again to P'ing to rule in it until he could arrange for the removal of the government offices and the public archives to his new capital. In this same year tragic events were taking place in the Ts'i capital. Wu Ti had died, and Siau-lun, a nephew of Siau-tau, had determined that the succession should now run through his family. The late Emperor had only two grandsons that could succeed him, namely, Ch'iau-yeh and Liang. The first of these was made Emperor, with the historical name of Yu-lin Wang, but the Siau family were soon in rebellion, and this unfortunate prince was murdered by Siau-lun, who at once took the title of Prince. A few months after he also killed the other brother, who had been allowed to succeed to the throne with the title of Hai-ling Wang. Siau-lun is known in history by the title of

Ming Ti—A. D. 494-499.

This murderer of his relatives was thirty-five years of age when he became Emperor, and he reigned five years. At the same time, the king of Wei, whose proclivities were altogether Chinese, issued an edict commanding his people to adopt the dress of their neighbours and abandon their own. He also raised an army and marched into the Ts'i dominions. In order to justify this conduct he issued proclamations throughout the country, saying that he was moved to this action because of the abominable conduct of Ming Ti, who had violated the first principles of Heaven by murdering the two last Emperors. Although he led his army himself he was defeated by the Ts'i troops, and had to return to Lohyang without having accomplished anything. Soon after his arrival, he commanded that the native language of his people should be given up and the Chinese used instead. He also ordered that it should be taught in all the schools, and that the classical books of China should be collected and formed into a great library, so that scholars could read the history of the empire and be indoctrinated into the teachings of its sages and great men, and thus have their minds enlightened by them. Lohyang was now formally recognized as the capital of their kingdom, as the king and all the members of the royal family removed to the palace that had been built to receive them (A. D. 496). In the next year Topa Hung took another step that greatly displeased the able men of his kingdom. Discovering, as he thought, that his family was descended from the great Hwang Ti of Chinese history, he changed the name of his dynasty from Wei to Yuan. He also sought out all the best families in his kingdom and made them mandarins, with the power of transmitting their office to their sons, making, in fact, official position hereditary instead of the result of competitive examinations, or a reward for merit or ability. When remonstrated with he promised that he would alter this system in the future, but that it must remain as it was now, as he had made his appointments. In the year A. D. 488 Ming Ti began to have suspicions about the fidelity of his commander-in-chief, Wang-king. This man had formerly been governor of Hwai-chi, Chehkiang, but had been raised to his present important post by the Emperor after he had seized the throne. Although he had sworn allegiance to the present dynasty his heart went out towards the Sung, and he longed to have it restored. Ming Ti, though suspicious, still kept him in office, for he had a great affection for him, and besides he thought that as he was so dear to him, and he had frequently to be in the palace, he would not dare to carry out his treasonable thoughts into action. One day Ming Ti made a present of a harpsichord to a son of Wang-king, who was a great musician, and asked him to play upon it. As he listened to the air that he played and the words that he sang he was alarmed to find that they both belonged to the music of the Sung, and that he found sarcastic references in both to himself and his dynasty. Soon after this the young man returned to his home in Hwai-chi, but Ming Ti, who was greatly distressed at his disloyalty, sent a high official after him to keep his eye upon him and report his conduct to the throne. His father was no sooner informed of this than he sent a letter to his son-in-law Sieh, saying that the hour was come for him to rebel, and calling upon him and all his family that could take up arms to hasten to his side. Sieh, who had no thought of rebellion, at once had the messenger seized and carried before Ming Ti, to whom he revealed the plans of Wang-king.

In the meanwhile, the latter was marching as fast as he could with ten thousand men towards the capital. On his way he passed by the great city of Hangchow, whose governor resisted his entrance, but who was defeated and compelled to fly. Marching on after his victory he came up with the royal army commanded by Siau-i, who defeated and slew him, and thus the incipient rebellion that might have ended disastrously for the Ts'is was crushed. The Emperor wished to reward Sieh with high honours in the State, but he resolutely refused to accept them. He evidently felt that private life was the safest position for a man who in these troublous times had any regard for his life.

This same year Ming Ti became very ill. He wished to hide this from the world, but the disease became rapidly more serious, and in a short time he was compelled to drop the sceptre which he had grasped through bloodshed and murder. He was succeeded by his son Pau-kwan, who is known in history by the title of Tung Hwun Hau, which, being literally interpreted, means "The Addle-pated Eastern Viscount."

Tung Hwun Hau—A. D. 499-501.

This man was of a light and frivolous disposition, and did not seem to have the mental capacity to understand the dignity and responsibility of the high position to which he had been elevated. It is said that when his father was being buried, and the high mandarins and nobles were engaged in weeping and mourning for the dead, Tung Hwun was so tickled at the sight of a bald-headed official that was engaged in noisy lamentations for his late father that he startled the crowd of mourners by loud and boisterous laughter, whilst he kept calling out, "See! the bald-headed is crying!"

Almost immediately after his accession an army was led against the forces of Wei, but they were defeated and compelled to retreat in disgrace to their own territories. During the campaign the king of Wei died, and was succeeded by his son Suan Wu Ti (A. D. 500). During the second year of Tung Hwun's reign the palace at Nanking was burnt, when the Emperor built another and much more magnificent one. No expense was spared in producing a building, or rather a series of buildings, that should rival in splendour anything that had ever preceded them. The walls were rendered perpetually fragrant by being plastered with a substance that was impregnated with musk that had been extracted from the musk bags taken from the deer that were found in Sz-chwan and other Western provinces. The floors were covered with the most beautiful designs taken from nature by the most celebrated artists of the day. One room the Emperor ordered to be paved with golden lilies that had been made with the utmost care by the best goldsmiths of the capital. This was a favourite resort of his, and here he used to sit with his beautiful concubine Pan-fei.* To carry out these expensive designs of his Tung Hwun had to resort to the most extreme measures for raising funds from the people. The exactions were

* Pan-tei is celebrated for her gracefulness and beauty. It has been asserted, though without sufficient proof, that the artificial cramping of the feet of the women of China commenced with her.

This idea has no doubt arisen from the tradition that one day, when she was walking before him in this golden lily chamber, Tung Hwun was so charmed with her exquisite grace that, enraptured, he cried out, "See! every step she takes makes a lily to grow!" and as the polite term for the cramped foot is "Golden Lily," it has therefore been supposed that this unsightly custom originated with Pan-fei. It is more likely that it commenced with Yau-niang, another famous beauty, and a concubine who lived about the year A. D. 970, and who, according to a tradition, was said to have arched her feet to the semblance of the new moon.

so severe, and the distress caused by them so unbearable, that it is said the people could be seen weeping as they walked along the roads, so dire was the misery that was brought upon them by the cruelty of this unreasonable tyrant.

At last, driven to despair, application was made to Siau-i, one of the great mandarins, to undertake to rid the empire of such a profligate monster. This high-minded noble refused to sully his name with the crime of treason, but one of the creatures of Tung Hwun, who had heard of the affair, represented to him that Siau-i had actually consented to put him out of the way. Enraged at this, he immediately sent an officer with an urgent command that he should at once drink of a poisoned cup that he had forwarded to him. Before the messenger could reach his house a friend of his rushed headlong into his presence and urged him to fly at once to Yangchow, where his brother Siau-yen was governor, and thus escape the death that was now imminent. Siau-i refused to do this. "I am not afraid of death," he replied. "From ancient times men have had to die, and no man may escape death; I shall die sooner than I expected, but what matters that, for, after all, it is a mere question of time." When the officer arrived with the fatal draught Siau-i received him smilingly, and drinking it down he said, "I am afraid that when my brother hears of this there will be such trouble in the palace that the Emperor will find his throne in danger." This prophecy was literally fulfilled. When the news of this tragedy reached Siau-yen he instantly summoned his captains and leading men, and boldly proposed that they should march upon the capital and rid the empire of a monster that was a terror and a sorrow to the whole nation. Not a dissentient voice was raised against this, and preparations were at once made. Troops were gathered from every direction throughout his large province, and proclamations were issued and posted up in all the prominent cities of it, declaring the reasons why this armed insurrection was being made, and showing that the time had come when the empire should be delivered from a burden under which all classes of the people were groaning.

In the meantime, Tung Hwun, who had got information of this movement, sent orders to his brother Pau-fung, who was governor of Kingchow, to advance at once with all the troops he could collect and destroy Siau-yen. The latter managed to intercept this man, and putting him to death, sent a message to Pau-fung, telling him that Tung Hwun was meditating his death, and strongly urged upon him to join his forces to his own and seize the imperial power for himself. This he consented to do, and in A. D. 501 he assumed the title of Ho Ti, and issuing a decree, he declared that Tung Hwun, because of his vices, was no longer Emperor of China. Ho Ti, who was only sixteen years of age, continued to reside in Kingchow, whilst Siau-yen, by his orders marched on Nanking with full powers to act precisely as he considered best. He reached this city in November, and after a siege of two months he entered it with his victorious troops, when he found that the miserable Tung Hwun had been murdered by the populace, who had been driven to desperation by their sufferings, and who, conscious that they never would be called to account by the enemy outside the gates, had avenged themselves for the sufferings they had been called upon to endure.   When Pan-fei was brought before Siau-yen he was so much struck with her beauty that he was inclined to take her into his harem, but one of his officers protested against this, as she was just the person, he said, to be the destroyer of a dynasty.   So she was at once led out to execution.   With the coming of Siau-yen to Nanking the extinction of the Ts'i dynasty may be said to have been consummated, for although Ho Ti was still alive, and had the nominal rule, the sceptre he wielded was but a shadowy one, for the real one was now in the grasp of one who, though he still pretended to rule in the name of another, was determined never to abandon it as long as he lived.

CHAPTER XVII.

EPOCH OF DIVISION BETWEEN NORTH AND SOUTH.

THE LIANG DYNASTY (A. D. 502-557).

Wu Ti—A. D. 502-550.

NO sooner had Siau-yen gained possession of the capital than he determined to seize upon the imperial power and found a dynasty of his own. At first he dissembled, in order that he might feel the pulse of the people, and especially learn whether the nobles were prepared to stand by him in case the adherents of the Ts'i disputed his attempt to usurp the throne. His captains and leading men strongly urged him to become Emperor, but he at first refused and took simply the title of prime minister to Ho Ti. His next step was to proclaim himself Duke of Liang, and finding that this produced no commotion amongst the high mandarins and nobility he took the higher title of the Prince of Liang. Ho Ti, who had been advancing towards Nanking, arrived at the town of Ku-shu, when he heard of the ambitious schemes of Siau-yen and the high titles he had assumed, which he had no right to take without the special permission of the Emperor. He very wisely, however, avoided a collision with him and the horrors of civil war by resigning his throne and appointing Siau-yen in his place. No sooner had the latter received the important document that made him Emperor than the question had to be decided where Ho Ti should be allowed to reside and what title should be given him now that he had resigned his throne. It was unanimously agreed that he should be called prince of Pa-ling, but there was extreme difficulty in settling where it would be for the safety of the new dynasty that he should be allowed to live. Wu Ti was for having him transported to Canton, as being the most remote from the scene of his former greatness, and where it was less likely that he could conspire by and by to regain his lost power. Wiser heads than his, however, showed the folly of allowing a man who had been Emperor to be so far removed from the control of the central authority and the danger of insurrection being planned and suddenly bursting upon the empire without any preparations being made to meet it. It was finally agreed that he should be made to reside at Ku-shu, and there await the final decision of the high authorities, in whose hands his fortunes now lay. It was soon discovered that there was no longer any place in the empire, large as it was, where he could be allowed to remain, so Wu Ti sent him some gold to swallow, and thus put an end to his life. When the messenger arrived with the order Ho Ti said, "Far rather give me some strong spirits to drink instead of this gold." His request was complied with by the officials who had to see that his death was compassed. A quantity of the spirits he liked best was given him, and when he had drunk himself into a stupor he was strangled.

Wu Ti called his dynasty the Liang, from the territory over which he ruled as Duke. He began his reign with best intentions of governing his people well and wisely. He had come to the throne with comparative ease. There had been little bloodshed and less of the clearing off by murder of the adherents of the former dynasty than usual, and therefore there were no powerful clans who owed the new ruler a grudge for the destruction of their leaders, and who consequently would be ever on the watch to find a fitting occasion on which to wreak their revenge. He caused two large wooden boxes to be made and fixed in a public place near the palace into which men who were suffering from a failure of justice, or from powerful enemies, or from causes that were oppressing them, could place their complaints with the certainty that they would be brought before the notice of the Emperor and be dealt with in the most impartial and summary manner.

In the year A. D. 503 the kingdom of Wei was terribly afflicted with a severe famine in Shen-si. The soil of that province consists mainly of loess which, under favourable circumstances, produces fairly good crops. There is always a certain peril about it, however, that must make the farmers in it feel uncertain whether the seed they sow will ever gladden them by producing an abundance when the harvest time comes round. When the rains are plentiful and regular everything goes on smoothly, but should these fail, then sorrow is imminent, for the ground is of such a nature that it cannot long retain the moisture that the clouds have sent down, but it allows it to drain below the point to which the labours of the agriculturist have reached. The Emperor sent special officers from Lohyang to the districts affected, with full powers to help the needy and to redress any wrongs from the magistrates that might be the means of aggravating the sufferings of the people. One of these Imperial deputies, though a man in high position under the government, distinguished himself by the unswerving loyalty and fidelity with which he carried out the difficult task that had been assigned him. It is pleasant to think that in those far off times, when corruption abounded in high places, there were still here and there men who were influenced by higher motives than the mere desire to enrich themselves at the public expense, and whose hearts were set upon the noble task of succouring their fellow-men.

In two districts that he visited his integrity was severely tested. The chief mandarins in these were men that it was difficult to deal with, one of them being an uncle of the Queen, and the other a relative of his own. They had both been unfaithful in the discharge of their public duties. When the royal deputy arrived, they each in turn invited him to a great dinner, hoping to propitiate him and make him lenient in judging them.   During the feast each began to beg him to be kind in his treatment of him, but they were immediately silenced by being reminded that this was a time for enjoyment and not for the discussion of public matters.   Next day each one was dismissed from his office, and his name reported to the king for him to deal with each as he might think best.

About this same time an incident occurred in the kingdom of Liang that not only illustrates one of the peculiar customs of those early days, but which shows that the doctrine of filial piety, which is so much revered and honoured by the Chinese of to-day, was one that was practised by many an heroic sacrifice by the men and women of those times.   A mandarin holding a position equivalent to that of the district magistrate of to-day, who is really the chief executive officer in a whole county, was falsely accused by his superior officers of misdeeds, for which he was thrown into prison and condemned to death.   His son, a lad of fifteen years of age, determined to save him by the sacrifice of his own life.   He accordingly proceeded to the capital, and striking the great drum, which was suspended at one of the city gates, he was led at once into the presence of Wu Ti, who asked him what urgent matter had made him take the liberty of beating the drum instead of going through the formal process of law, which was the common way, and which was open to every citizen who had any complaint to make or grievance to be redressed.*   The lad replied that his case was one that would brook no delay.   His father, he said, had been condemned to death, and would soon be executed.   He had come here to offer himself as a substitute for him, and he wished the Emperor to accept him and order the stay of proceedings against his father. Wu Ti was much struck with this heroic resolve of the young fellow, but he was somewhat suspicious that this was simply an ingenious plan to touch his heart, so that, moved by the devotion of the son, he might be induced to pardon the father.   He accordingly ordered one of his nobles to take the boy aside and question him as to his motives in making the appeal he had made to-day.   When they had reached another room he was asked who had suggested to him the idea of offering himself for his father, and was it really true that he was prepared to die.   "What I have done to-day is entirely the result of my own thoughts," he replied.   "No one put

---

* The drum at the gate of the capital seems to have been analogous to that which is found at the entrance of every prominent mandarin's court throughout the eighteen provinces of China at the present day.   In cases of great urgency, where immediate aid is required from the magistrate, and where delay would cause great loss or suffering, men are allowed to strike this, when their cases are at once attended to.   If it is found, on investigation, that this drum has been struck without any adequate justification severe punishment is at once the consequence.   Men have the ordinary forms of law through which they may appeal for protection, and, except in special cases, these must be gone through.   It is only in extreme circumstances that any one may summon the mandarin to his court at irregular hours by the use of this drum.

it into my head to offer my life for my father's.   Death is too
serious a matter to be trifled with.   There is none in all the world
that is not afraid to die, and if I did not wish to give my life away
there is none that could persuade me to do so.   It is for my father
only that I would make such a tremendous sacrifice."   When Wu
Ti heard these words he was deeply moved, and at once ordered
the father to be released, whilst he dismissed the son with many
commendations for his filial piety.

During the next two or three years both the rulers of Wei and
Liang were absorbed in fostering and caring for the religion of
Confucius.   Schools of learning were opened, wherein the sacred
writings of the great sage were studied, and Wu Ti spent large sums
of money in building temples to his honour.   The result was that
large numbers of highly cultivated men were to be found scattered
throughout the two kingdoms, who were prepared to render service
to the state whenever it should be required.

In the year A. D. 508 the king of Wei, ambitious of extending
his territories, secretly equipped a large army and sent it under the
command of two of his best generals to invest the important town of
Tsung-li, in Kiangnan.   In order to reach the city, which was
protected by a river that flowed not far from it, a suspension bridge
was hastily thrown across, and the place was surrounded by the
soldiers of Wei.   Wu Ti, at the first news of the hostile movement,
sent orders to the commanders of his troops in different parts of the
empire to hurry forward with all speed and relieve the town.
Considerable time was lost in carrying these out, during which the
Wei troops were making serious advances towards the conquest of
the city.   When Wu Ti's troops arrived the first thing they did was
to destroy the bridge, which the Liang general Wei-jui did by filling
boats with combustibles and sending them down the Hwai and
burning it, which was accomplished, in spite of all the efforts of the
enemy to prevent it.   The retreat of the investing army being thus
cut off, and a rapid stream rolling between the soldiers and their
homes, they became demoralized, and in consequence suffered a
terrible defeat, in which a large number of men were killed, and the
remainder were glad to escape simply with their lives.   Wei-jui
pursued the beaten enemy up to the borders of Wei, and would have
followed them further, but Wu Ti, with a great want of confidence
in his own soldiers, forbade this, and consequently the full benefit of
the great disaster at Tsung-li was, in a great measure, lost.   Wei,
who, according to the author of the "Former Five Dynasties," had
fifty thousand men captured and over four hundred thousand slain,
was at this time completely prostrated, and would have become an
easy conquest had more courage and statesmanship been shown.
These unauthorized histories, however, are given to exaggeration,
and no doubt their statements have to be vastly discounted.*   In

* See "Former Five Dynasties" *in loc.*

the year A. D. 510 Wu Ti endeavoured to make a treaty of peace with the great northern power, but his advances were repulsed, as the king of Wei never abandoned the dreams that had been entertained by its successive rulers, that they would in time become the masters of the whole of China. It is noticeable that from about this time Wu Ti seems to have abandoned his faith in the Confucian doctrines and to have become a profound believer in Buddhism. He not only built a famous monastery in the capital, but actually himself became a preacher of the religion he had adopted.

He sent messengers to the West for teachers to instruct his people in Buddhism, and the result was that in the course of time over three thousand bonzes arrived and took up their abode in the capital. Before many years had elapsed more than thirteen thousand Buddhist temples had been built in different parts of the empire.

In the year A. D. 513 Fu, the son of Suan Wu Ti, the king of Wei, was publicly acknowledged as the heir to the throne. According to the custom of the country his mother should now have been put to death, but for some reason, not stated, her life was spared, which in after years was the cause of most serious evils, not only to the kingdom, but also to her son. Three years after the king died, when Fu, under the title of Hiau Ming Ti, succeeded him. His first act was to put to death his father's widow and appoint his own mother to be Queen-dowager and to make her regent during his minority. This was a very high and illegal position for one who had simply been a concubine.

Wu Ti, who was always ambitious of extending his empire at the expense of Wei, as the latter was of doing the same at his, made a determined effort to gain possession, if possible, of the important town of Shenyang, situated on the river Hwai. It had been represented to him by his ablest generals that the city could be gained without any fighting whatever. He had simply to dam up the waters of the river, and the place would become so inundated that the troops in possession would have to surrender at discretion, or they and the inhabitants would be drowned like rats. An immense force was sent to carry out this plan, evidently too large for the soldiers of Wei to attack, and for over two years they were engaged in building an immense embankment, which it was believed would stem the fiercest current that the Hwai in its most flooded time could show. It was certainly a most gigantic affair. It was three miles long, fourteen hundred and forty feet at the base, which gradually narrowed up to four hundred and fifty at its summit, and it was raised considerably higher than the city walls it was intended to flood. In spite of all the care that had been taken to ensure success the whole ended in the most miserable failure. After the last gaps had been closed, and the river was fairly imprisoned, it seemed determined to show the haughty invader that it was stronger than any power that he and his hundreds of thousands of armed men could bring to oppose it. As the waters rose higher and higher and began to climb up the city walls, where the terrified inhabitants were gathered, and fear began to paralyze the more timid, a sound like thunder was heard, and instantly the solemn march of the waters was stayed. The people were delivered. The friendly river that had rolled by them so many years, had shattered the embankment, and it had disappeared with fifteen thousand of the enemy, who would never again take up arms against the city.

Both Wu Ti and Hu-shih, the queen regent of Wei, became more and more absorbed in their devotion to Buddhism. The latter built a magnificent temple close by the palace, where she could worship at all hours of the day, and as a work of merit she erected a pagoda ninety feet in height, which could be seen for a long distance in every direction, and which reminded the people of the hold that Buddhism was taking upon those in high position in the land. Wu Ti, in order to carry out to its extreme limits one of the essential doctrines of the new faith that he had adopted, viz., that men should under no circumstances deprive anything of life, issued an edict throughout his empire that no figures of animals should in future be embroidered on any silk or satin, because the tailors, in cutting up such for dresses, were compelled to cut through them, and in so doing they were in danger of becoming accustomed to the idea that animal life, after all, was not so precious as it was, and they would thus be made more cruel in their treatment of it. He also ordered that in the Confucian sacrifices only vegetables should be used, and that figures of the animals that were usually offered in them should be made of flour and presented to the spirits of the dead. This latter order caused an immense commotion throughout every grade of society. Whatever faith they might have had in any other form of religion, the one cherished belief that swayed and dominated the heart of every grown up person in the land, just as it does to-day, was the conviction that the spirits of their ancestors in some way or other controlled the fortunes of each one, and that no sacrifice would be acceptable to them that did not contain the flesh of animals. Men began to fear that sorrow would come upon their homes, and misery and ruin and disaster upon all they engaged in. This decree was looked upon as one of the signs of the speedy decay and extinction of the dynasty. The Emperor heard of the dissatisfaction of his people, but he was too true a Buddhist to give way, and the obnoxious law remained in force.

For nearly ten years the condition of the kingdom of Wei was anything but satisfactory. Even since Hu-shih had been appointed regent the discontent of the nobles and the people had been steadily growing. Not only was she a very ambitious woman, who was determined to make her will felt in the kingdom in every department of its politics, but she was also most immoral and profligate, so that the great mandarins rebelled against the thought of being under the control of such an unprincipled ruler. There were popular risings and intrigues in the palace, one of which was headed by a brother-in-law of the queen regent, who was so shocked at her open wickedness that he managed to deprive her of power and have her confined to her own apartments for more than three years, whilst he himself became the leading spirit in the kingdom during that time. Whilst she was under restraint there appeared on the frontiers of Shansi the first signs of the storm that was soon to come upon the kingdom and cause it to be broken up amidst war and bloodshed. In the year A. D. 525 Ur-chu-ying was the general in command of the forces that were stationed on the borders to keep back the irruption of the northern barbarians. This position of his was a hereditary one, and up to this time the responsible duties belonging to it had been loyally and faithfully carried out. Influenced, no doubt, by the prevailing discontent, and the disorders that were everywhere prevalent, Ur-chu-ying deemed that the time had come when he, too, had as good a chance as many of the competitors that were in the field for advancing his family to supreme power in the state. He accordingly began to make preparations for holding the country he now governed in his own right, and not in the name of another. Next year, by an intrigue, Hu-shih got free from her confinement, and once more seized the reins of power. She had learned no lesson during her forced retirement, but acted in the same shameless manner that she had previously done. The consequence was that incipient rebellions began to spring up throughout the country, and one specially serious one burst out in Chihli. It was found exceedingly difficult to raise the requisite forces to suppress these. The finances were at the very lowest ebb, and in the present condition of the country it was difficult to find any new source from whence they could be recruited. In this extremity an edict was issued that there should be an immediate collection of the land tax for the next six years. Even after these were collected there remained a most serious deficiency. The allowance of spirits and flesh that were granted to the officers in the army was then reduced, and an ordinance was passed that every person who went to market to purchase anything should pay a cash every time he went, no matter how often during the day.

The year A. D. 528 witnessed the remarkable spectacle of the voluntary withdrawal of Wu Ti from his palace and from the direction of public affairs to spend his days as a common bonze in the monastery of "Harmonious Peace" that he had built at a great expense in the capital. Whilst he was chanting the Buddhist prayers, and sometimes occupying the post of preacher for the day, the state of things in Wei was becoming more and more serious. Ur-chu-ying had been maturing his plans, and he now awaited but the arrival of some man of superior genius at his camp to assist him to carry them out. He had not long to wait, for the famous Kau-hwan, who was to play so prominent a part in the stirring events of the next few years, was introduced to him as the very man he was in need of. On his first appearance Ur-chu-ying was greatly disappointed in him. He was very lean and sallow, and looked altogether a very common-place looking individual, so that he had no faith in him whatever. He was told, however, that he was a very uncommon character, with a mind that had the peculiar art of governing others. In order to test this strong will of his he sent him into his stables to see what he could do with one of his horses that was exceedingly vicious and that no one had been able to control. Kau-hwan, without any hesitation, obeyed the request of Ur-chu-ying, when, to the astonishment of everyone, the animal seemed at once to recognize its master, and submitted like a lamb to be handled and moved about, completely conquered by this quiet, self-contained man. When this trial of his skill was over, Ur-chu-ying asked him what he should have done if the horse had not obeyed him. He replied, with a wintry smile on his firm self-restrained features, "There was no possibility of anything of the kind happening, for I have tried the same system on bad men, and I have never known it to fail, even with them." Ur-chu-ying's mind was greatly influenced by this incident, so sending every one out of the room, except themselves, he asked his advice as to what action he should take in the present circumstances. Kau-hwan said, "I hear that you have thousands of horses that you are rearing upon twelve mountain districts within your jurisdiction : what is your object in having so many?" Ur-chu-ying replied, "I don't want you to ask me any questions : what I require is your definite opinion as to what I should do now in the present state of the Wei kingdom?" Kau-hwan then said, "The king of Wei is young ; he is surrounded by faithless and corrupt ministers, and besides, his mother, who is the real ruler, is a profligate woman, whom neither the people nor the nobles respect. You have soldiers in abundance, and you have horses in any number at your command : why not rise now and march on the capital ? Ur-chu-ying gladly accepted this advice that was so in harmony with his own wishes, and the details of the campaign were at once planned and agreed upon.

In order to conceal the true motives for this act of rebellion, and to enlist the sympathies of the nation on his behalf, Ur-chu-ying sent a memorial to Hiau Ming Ti, telling him that he was greatly distressed at the unhappy condition in which he was in. He was surrounded by traitors, whose only object was their own ambitious schemes. His mother had usurped all the power of the state, and her character was so infamous that she would certainly wreck the dynasty, and, moreover, the country was distracted by so many popular risings that the lives of honest people were in constant danger. He had raised an army, he said, and was now on his march to Lohyang to deliver the king from his bondage and to save the kingdom from destruction. By the time the memorial reached the capital Ur-chu-ying, with his army, was half way on their road to it. The king was exceedingly glad when he heard of the force

that was on its way to rescue him. He had been exceedingly
grieved at the immoral conduct of his mother and at the miseries
she was bringing on the country, but he was completely helpless
to do anything to remedy this unhappy state of matters, as she had
not only grasped all power in her own hands, but she had also filled
the palace with men who were creatures of her own, and who would
obey none but her. He at once replied to the intimation of Ur-chu-
ying and ordered him to come on with his army and deliver him
from the bad men that were plotting against his life and against the
welfare of his kingdom. Hardly had his command gone forth than
he began to be apprehensive lest the vengeance of his mother would
be wreaked upon him for this act; so he issued another order that
Ur-chu-ying should retire with his army to his own jurisdiction on
the borders of Shansi. This miserable vacillation did not save him,
however. His mother got to hear of what he had done, and feeling
that her life was in danger she sent her son a poisoned cup, which
he was compelled to drink. She then issued an edict informing
the country that her son had died, and that another had been
appointed in his place. As this one was only three years of age she
said she would still hold the office of queen regent, and she called
upon the subjects of Wei to loyally submit to her authority.

Ur-chu-ying was terribly incensed when he heard of the murder
of Hiau Ming Ti, and hurried on the march of the soldiers to the
capital to avenge his death. Hu-shih, who did not lack in energy,
sent an army under two generals of distinction to meet him, but no
sooner had they come near the approaching force than they went
over to Ur-chu-ying, and their own troops marched side by side
with his towards Lohyang. When this news reached the palace the
traitors immediately fled, and Hu-shih, seeing herself entirely
deserted by the bad men in whom she had trusted, had her head
shaved, and entered herself as a nun in one of the large nunneries
in the city. She hoped thus to get the shield of the Buddhist
church to save her from the vengeance of Ur-chu-ying. In this
she was mistaken, however. This general had no faith in the
Buddhist religion, and moreover, he was come to execute justice
on a woman who for years had outraged and defied it. No sooner
had he taken possession of the city than Hu-shih and the infant
king were seized and brought before him, when they were both
tied and thrown into the Yellow River. He then caused the nobles
and mandarins, to the number of over two thousand men, to be
arrested and brought into the capital. These he had surrounded
by his troops, when he reproached them for the disorders of the
kingdom and for their want of loyalty in tamely standing by and
allowing a vicious woman to rule the country for so long a time.
He then gave a signal to his soldiers, who fell upon them and
massacred every one of them.

As the time was not yet ripe for him to seize the throne for
himself, Ur-chu-ying made the Prince of Chu-yeu king, under the

title of Hiau Chwang Ti, in the place of the child that had been drowned, and who was known as Prince Lin-tau.

Not long after the new king had been settled on the throne, and Ur-chu-ying had retired with his army to the frontiers, a sudden danger threatened to overthrow the new régime that had been so happily inaugurated. A prince of Wei, thinking himself wronged, fled to the court of Wu Ti and begged assistance from him to re-establish the former house upon the throne. The Emperor, glad of any opportunity of attacking his hereditary enemy, at once granted his request and sent an army with him under his general, Ch'en King-chi. Great success attended him at first, and several cities were captured, and he reached the neighbourhood of Lohyang without any one being able to resist him. Hiau Chwang Ti fled incontinently and left his capital to be occupied by the successful Liang commander. The prince that had claimed the aid of Wu Ti was set upon the throne, whilst Ch'en was made prime minister.

Hardly a month, however, had passed before Ur-chu-ying had arrived with his powerful legions. In an engagement with Ch'en he completely routed his forces. The upstart king was slain, and Hiau Chwang Ti was again restored to power. Ur-chu-ying was made commander-in-chief of the armies of Wei, whilst Kau-hwan was employed by him in the capacity of political adviser.

Whilst these things were going on in Wei, Wu Ti had again entered the monastery of "Harmonious Peace" as a common bonze, and resigned the luxury and power of political life. He put off his royal apparel and donned that of an ordinary monk. He slept on a poor bed, and had an earthen pillow on which to rest his head when he slept. and he rigidly obeyed the laws by which the rest of the bonzes were regulated. He seemed to find more happiness in the seclusion of the monastery and in the obedience of its rules than he did in his magnificent palace. After a short time his ministers, who found it difficult to carry on the business of the empire without him, came and begged him to resume his duties as Emperor. This, however, the heads of the establishment refused to consent to until a considerable sum had been paid out of the national treasury for his ransom. When this had been given the royal devotee was absolved from his vows and allowed once more to become a citizen of the world.

Scarcely more than a year had elapsed before Hiau Chwang Ti, forgetful of the great benefits he had received from Ur-chu-ying, began to plot against his life. It is true that the leader had become more and more ambitious as he felt that the stability of the government depended upon himself, and that the craven spirits in the palace began to fear lest in a revolution their lives might be endangered. The secret plots of the conspirators became known to a cousin of his, who informed him of them. Ur-chu-ying was foolhardy, and instead of taking advantage of the warning he went about as usual, fancying himself too strong for even the king to dare to attack. In this thought he was grievously mistaken. Being summoned to the palace, he went, attended only by one of his generals, when they were set upon and murdered as soon as they had entered the hall of audience by the hand, it is said, of the very man whom he had placed upon the throne. The political sagacity of the king was not great enough to allow him to perceive that with the death of the man he had slain was sounded the knell of his own tenure of power as a sovereign. No sooner was the murder of this great man accomplished than the palace resounded with rejoicings as though some great event that ought to be celebrated with songs and mirth had happened, and Hiau Chwang, in order to commemorate it, ordered a general amnesty to be proclaimed throughout the kingdom. In the meanwhile Ur-chu-shih-liang, the cousin who had warned the murdered general, fled with his forces to Ho-yin, and raising the standard of rebellion, proclaimed Prince Tung Hai to be the ruler of Wei. He soon found himself at the head of such an army that he was able to march on Lohyang, which he entered victoriously and put to death the slayer of his cousin. These successes had been gained mainly through the ability of Kau-hwan, who determined not only to avenge the death of his patron, but also at the same time to secure for himself a position that might in the end lead to a throne, either for himself or his family. For his services he was rewarded by being given the command of a large district, with all the emoluments connected with it.

Prince Tung Hai was soon superseded by Tsieh Ming Ti, who, in his turn, was displaced by Kau-hwan, who had rebelled against the new régime, and having gained so many successes with his troops that the fate of each successive ruler was practically in his hands, put prince Ngan Ting on the throne. Finding this man not according to his anticipations he deposed him after a few months and elevated Hiau Wu Ti in his place, whilst he himself possessed the real power, and in order to secure it more permanently for his family, compelled him to marry one of his daughters.

The year A. D. 534 was an eventful one in the history of the great northern power, for in it, it was rent in twain, and from the division there were constituted the Eastern and Western Wei. This disastrous state of things arose mainly from the ambition of two men,—Kau-hwan and Yu-wen-t'ai. The latter, who is now destined to play a conspicuous part in the stirring events of the next few years, was the general of the troops under Ho-pa, who was governor in Shensi. Both of these men were distinguished for their ability, and the latter, who was of the royal lineage of Topa, was terribly annoyed at the conspicuous part that Kau-hwan had taken in setting up his own nominee as king, and he publicly announced to Hiau Wu Ti that he intended to kill him. The latter, who was feeling the galling restraint under which he was kept by Kau-hwan, secretly rejoiced at this and gave him the command of twenty districts. Whilst Hu-pa was collecting his forces for the campaign he was killed by his officers, when all his power fell into the hands of his ambitious general, Yu Wen-t'ai. A few months after this Kau-hwan openly rebelled. Hiau Wu Ti fled to Shensi, when Kau-hwan put Hiau Tsing Ti on the throne and constituted himself prime minister. As the young king was only eleven years of age it can easily be understood that all the power of what was now called the Eastern Wei fell into his hands.

Hiau Wu Ti soon discovered that in being freed from the control of his former minister he had but increased his misery and danger by placing himself in the hands of Yu Wen-t'ai. By the close of the year he had been poisoned by him, and another ruler, the name of Wen Ti, governed in Shensi, the first of the new dynasty of the Western Wei.

During these momentous changes in the north Wu Ti was still absorbed in his purpose of advancing the interests of the Buddhist religion. In the year A. D. 538 he was made happy by the receipt of some of the nails and hair and bones of Buddha. For the reception of these he built a magnificent temple and proclaimed an amnesty throughout his empire.

The two rival dynasties of Wei were now bent on the destruction of each other, and the two men who were the real, though not nominal rulers of them, were ever on the watch how they could injure each other. Yu Wen-t'ai seems to have been the better statesman of the two, for he appears to have had the good of the country at heart, in spite of all his ambitious schemes for the elevation of his own family. On one occasion he had an edict published throughout the country, calling upon the mandarins of all degrees to seriously consider the following subjects: That the magistrates in their administration should not accept bribes; that the education of the people should be attended to as well as their morals; that every effort should be made by those in authority to ascertain what were the natural resources of the country and to develop them to the utmost; that only able men should be employed under government; the enactment of milder penal laws; and that there should be one method in the collection of the land tax, and that no one should be charged more than what was due.

As the years went by the condition of things in the empire became more and more serious in consequence of Wu Ti's devotion to Buddhism. In the earlier years of his reign he had been distinguished for many noble qualities, which the historian delights to recount. He was benevolent, and filial, and noted for his modesty. He was also learned, and a statesman of no mean ability. He had a keen perception of men's characters, and knew how to select the best men to help him in his government. The consequence was that for many years his rule was a most wise and beneficent one, and shed a glory upon his country that gave it a reputation far and wide. In later years his judgment was warped by his faith to such an extent that the administration of law was seriously interfered with. For example, his observance of the Buddhistic doctrine that a true believer must refrain from causing the death of anything living, very often saved the lives of criminals who had been rightfully adjudged to die. Indeed, it was only in cases of high treason that Wu Ti would consent to a person's death, and then he did so amidst weeping and lamentation. The consequence of this was that crime rapidly increased throughout his dominions. Men felt sure of their lives, no matter what wrongs they committed outside of rebellion : and the law had no other terrors to restrain the violence of such great transgressors. The year A. D. 548 saw the death of the famous Kau-hwan. At the close of the preceding year he had raised an army and proceeded to besiege the city of Yupi, belonging to the Western Wei. All his efforts to capture it had proved unavailing, and he was compelled to retreat with disgrace from before its walls. Whether it was chagrin, caused by his failure, or the fatigues of the campaign that affected his health, we do not certainly know, but soon after he was seized by a mortal sickness, of which he soon died. On his death-bed he called his son to his side to give him some counsel as to how he should act after he was gone. After naming certain persons, whom he believed would prove faithful to him, and whose counsel would be an advantage to him, he solemnly warned him against one of his commanders by the name of Heu-king. "This man," he said, "is most ambitious and unscrupulous. He is also exceedingly clever, and a true soldier. The only man he dreads is myself, and I fear that when he hears I am dead he will despise your authority and begin to plan for his own elevation. He told me some time ago that if I would give him but only thirty thousand soldiers he would pledge himself to capture Nanking and carry off Wu Ti to Lohyang, where he would make him a bonze in one of the Buddhist temples there. You must conceal my death until you get the reins of power into your own hands and can dispose of him, so that he will not be able to do you any harm."

Somehow or other the news of the death of Kau-hwan got abroad, when Heu-king passed over with all his men into the service of the ruler of the Western Wei. Not satisfied with the position that was given him, only one month after he sent a memorial to Wu Ti, offering to surrender to him, and stated that he would not only bring an army with him that would loyally fight his battles, but he would also hand over to him thirteen large districts in Honan, which should be annexed to the kingdom of Liang. When this tempting offer reached the Emperor it filled him with the greatest delight. The ambition of his life had been to reconquer Honan and to add it to the empire. Every attempt that he had hitherto made to carry out this design had failed, and now when it had seemed impossible of ever being accomplished Heu-king comes and makes this splendid offer. His mind was all the more influenced to accept it because he had lately had a dream in which he saw a person standing before him and offering him the whole of the long-coveted province.

When the proposition was laid before his ministers, they were nearly unanimous in advising him to reject it. They said, "We are now at peace with the people of Wei, and we have no just cause for taking their territory, and besides, Heu-king is a traitor, and it is a dangerous thing to have anything to do with a man that changes sides so readily as he has done." One of the nobles present, wishing to flatter Wu Ti and to gain his favour, advised that Heu-king's offer should be accepted. "It is evidently the will of Heaven," he said, "that Honan should come to us, and why should we endeavour to resist that? Besides, we must consider that if we reject this offer now, who in the future will ever dare to think of surrendering to the Emperor and of acknowledging his sway?" This argument pleased Wu Ti so much that he not only decided to accept Heu-king's submission, but he also made Chu-i, the noble that had just spoken, Prince of Honan, as a reward for his loyalty in agreeing with him when all the rest dissented. Thirty thousand soldiers were at once despatched to take over the new territory and to assist Heu-king in his rebellion.

This same year, A. D. 548, Wu Ti again entered the monastery of "Harmonious Peace," and for the third time declared that he was determined to spend the rest of his days in the service of Buddha. The ruler of the Eastern Wei was in the meanwhile suffering severely from the tyrant Kau-ting, who was determined, not merely to hold all the power of the state in his own hands, but also show the nominal king that he was merely a puppet in his hands to do simply as he was bidden. One day at a feast at which the two were present with other guests Kau-ting filled a large goblet to the brim with spirits and requested Hiau Ching to drink it. The latter protested that it was beyond his ability to consume so much at one time. Kau-ting at once rose, and by the aid of his attendants, forced it down his throat. Hiau Ching was exceedingly indignant at this shameful treatment, and declared that he would resign the kingdom, as he would rather live as a private person than have constantly to suffer such indignities. Two of the chief mandarins of his court, aroused to anger by what they had seen, plotted with the king how they might murder the imperious minister. Unfortunately this came to his ears, when he determined to execute a terrible vengeance upon them. Hiau Ching was imprisoned, and the two conspirators were boiled to death in the cauldron of oil.

It was at this juncture that he heard of the march of the imperial soldiers into his territories to aid Heu-king in his rebellion. Following the advice of his father as to the particular men he should employ in times of great emergency, he appointed Niu-yang to the command of the army that was to meet the allied force. No sooner did Heu-king hear that he was the general in command than he was filled with the greatest alarm, for he knew that he was a commander of consummate ability, before whom he would never be able to stand. The result proved that his fears were not groundless. Niu-yang advanced with a hundred thousand men against the combined forces of Heu-king and the generals whom Wu Ti had sent to his assistance, and in a terrible battle that ensued he was everywhere victorious. The allied army was entirely dispersed, and Heu-king fled for his life with only about one hundred men that escaped with him out of the bloody field. Niu-yang, who was determined to capture the traitor, immediately followed with five thousand of the bravest of his cavalry, who were called "The Iron Soldiers," and pressed him so hardly that he was almost in his grasp. Upon this, Heu-king sent him a letter in which he said, "Why is it that you are so determined to seize me? What will my death profit you? Don't you see that your value to Kau-ting depends upon my living, not upon my death? As soon as I am dead you will be of no further use, and your power and your office will be gone. Take a hint, even from an enemy." Niu-yang did so, and having learnt a lesson in statesmanship he quietly ordered his soldiers to cease from pursuit and return to the capital.

Heu-king now continued his retreat to the city of Sheu-yang, from which place he sent a memorial to Wu Ti, telling him of his disasters and requesting, as a punishment, that he be degraded from his present rank. In spite of the urgent entreaties of his ministers, who now advised his downfall, Wu Ti not only did not comply with his request, but made him governor of a district in Kiangnan.

Kau-ting, who was indignant both with Heu-king and Wu Ti, determined to have his revenge upon them both. He accordingly professed himself very anxious to be at peace with the latter, and wrote to him declaring that there was no reason why the two kingdoms should be at war with each other, and proposed certain very favourable conditions which, if agreed to, would bind them together in friendship. He also communicated with one of his generals who had been taken prisoner in the recent battle and proposed that he should be exchanged for Heu-king. Desirous of regaining his liberty and returning to his home, the former wrote urgently to Wu Ti, praying him to consent to Kau-ting's proposals and make a treaty with him. When the proposition of Kau-ting was laid before the great council the majority were strongly of the opinion that it should be peremptorily rejected. "There is no genuine desire for peace," they said. "There is a plot to embroil the empire in trouble. Kau-ting knows that Heu-king will never consent to be given up to his enemy, and will again rebel as soon as peace is declared." Wu Ti, who was tired of fighting, and who was supported by the more able of his ministers, agreed to the proposal of Kau-ting and consented to the conditions he had drawn up. No sooner did Heu-king hear of what had been done than assembling his men he consulted with them as to what ought to be done in this crisis of their lives. "It is now a matter of life and death with us all," he said. "We can no longer rely upon Wu Ti for protection, for he is bound by his treaty with Kau-ting to hand us over to him. That would mean death to us all ; so I propose that we again set up our standard of rebellion and see what luck it may bring us." These words were listened to with pleasure by his followers and instantly agreed to. What else indeed could they do? They were in a most desperate condition, and the only means of escaping the axe that was held over their necks, ready to destroy them, was the method that their leader had suggested. In this emergency Heu-king looked around to see what ally he could secure to help him in carrying on the war with Wu Ti. Fortunately, there was then one most powerful and important one just ready to second him with all his resources, and that was Ching-tuh, the Duke of Lin-ho, in the present province of Kwangsi.* Heu-king, knowing the character of this man and his inveterate hatred of Wu Ti, wrote him a letter, reminding him of his grievances and of the honours of which he had been unjustly deprived. He then offered him his own sword and those of his followers to put him on the throne. "Wu Ti," he said, "is old, and he is surrounded by traitors that warp his mind, so that he cannot act justly according to the dictates of his heart. You are the rightful heir, and ought to be Emperor after his decease. Say but that you agree, and I will march my men to your support, and you shall soon be recognized as the ruler of China." Ching-tuh, who was delighted with the receipt of this communication, at once agreed to everything that Heu-king had proposed, and in his reply to him, concluded by saying, "You shall work from the outside whilst I plan from the inside, and between us both we must succeed." Heu-king was too good a general not to know that delay in carrying out any of the measures that he had planned would have been fatal to him and his undertaking. He gathered his men together and marched rapidly towards the capital. His secret ally, Ching-tuh, had prepared a number of boats, so that when he reached the Yangtze there was no delay in crossing it. Wu Ti had no sooner received intelligence of his movement than he summoned his forces from different parts of the country to come to the relief of the capital. These, however, were defeated by Heu-king, and Nanking was speedily invested. Ching-tuh was proclaimed Emperor, who appointed Heu-king to be his prime minister, and gave him

---

* Ching-tuh was an adopted son of Wu Ti, who was made heir to the throne when he had no hope of having a son of his own to succeed him. After a time, when one was born to him, Ching-tuh had to resign his position to the real heir. He did this only under pressure, and never forgave Wu Ti for the supposed wrong he had done him. On one occasion (A. D. 523) he meditated rebellion and fled to the King of Wei for aid. He was, however, so badly treated by the people of Wei that he was glad to return home without having accomplished his traitorous purpose. He appeared before Wu Ti, and wept before him, and confessed his wrong. With his usual large-hearted generosity, he not only forgave him, but he also put him in a very high position, making him governor of an important district. How he repaid the kindness and forbearance of his adopted father, may be seen by the story that is now being told.

his daughter to be his wife.   As no preparation had been made
for a siege, Nanking was soon reduced to the greatest extremity.
Provisions became so scarce that the people endured the severest
sufferings.   Many of the soldiers boiled the leather of their armour
and ate it.   Rats and mice were eagerly sought for and devoured
by the starving populace.   Even Wu Ti had to suffer with the rest,
and he was so driven by hunger that he was compelled to eat some
eggs that one of his nobles presented to him, though in doing so
he was violating the vows that he had made when he became a
Buddhist.   Whilst the people of the city were enduring the horrors
of starvation the condition of things in the camp of Heu-king was
exceedingly distressing.   All the country round about was held by
the generals of Wu Ti, who, whilst they dare not come to close
quarters with the rebels, were yet able to prevent any provisions
reaching them.   The prospect before them was not cheerful.   If
they did not soon capture the city they would die of starvation, for
they could not retreat in the face of the enemy that occupied the
country through which they would have to pass.   In this difficulty
Heu-king resorted to a ruse to save himself and his army.   He sent
in a messenger to Wu Ti, proposing terms of peace, one of which
was that he should order the withdrawal of the forces outside that
were waiting an opportunity to relieve the city.   The Emperor,
with his usual good nature and implicit trust in his fellow-men,
agreed to them, and soon the country was available for Heu-king's
foragers to supply themselves with provisions.   Having obtained
these he disregarded the agreement he had made with Wu Ti and
pressed the siege more vigorously than ever, knowing that it was
now merely a matter of time when the capital should be in his
possession.   The sufferings of the people and the army from this
time became almost unbearable, and besides, they had now lost all
heart, as they saw no means of deliverance.   In a short time the
city was taken by storm (A. D. 550), and Heu-king marched in with
his victorious troops.   When Wu Ti heard the news he exclaimed,
"I obtained the kingdom through my own efforts, and through
me it has been lost, so I need not complain."   Heu-king at
once proceeded to the palace with five hundred of his bravest men,
dressed in armour.   When he entered into the presence of Wu Ti
he was so overcome with the calm, majestic appearance of the
aged monarch that a fear came over him, and kneeling down he did
obeisance to him.   The only remark that the Emperor made to him
was, "I am afraid you must be very weary with your long stay
in the camp and the great labour it has cost you to destroy my
kingdom."   Heu-king felt the reproach contained in these words,
and with his eyes upon the ground he retreated from the presence of
Wu Ti.   When he got outside he remarked to one of his officers,
"I have led thousands of men into battle, and I have charged
the enemy at the head of my cavalry, and I never felt the least
fear.   To-day I was in terror when I got into the presence of the

old man, and could not restrain the feelings of fear that came over me. Truly he is awe-inspiring, and I'll never venture into his presence again.''

He immediately ordered a universal amnesty in the name of Wu Ti, in commemoration of the great victory that he had gained over the illustrious man by whom it was said to be issued. Not long after Heu-king had left the presence of the Emperor the miserable Ching-tuh came in, and falling down before him began to weep and sob. The old man, who had been his benefactor, and had generously spared his life when he had been guilty of treason before, looking down upon him with pity simply said, '' Your tears come too late,'' and dismissed him without taking any further notice of him.

And now Heu-king determined to show everyone that the real power was in his hands. The aged ruler was treated with the greatest indignity and kept a close prisoner in his own palace. This worked upon his spirits to such an extent that he fell ill of a fever, and his mouth and throat became parched, so that he could not swallow anything. When Heu-king, who superintended the diet of the household, and who had studiously not allowed a sufficiency to satisfy the hunger of Wu Ti, was appealed to for a little honey to mix with the water he drank he rudely refused the request. This so irritated him that he almost immediately after died, in his eighty-sixth year, only just two months after the capture of his capital. One month after this Ching-tuh was put to death by Heu-king, because he had been found in correspondence with the enemy out-side, with whom he was planning the deliverance of himself and Nanking from the tyranny of the cruel conqueror.

The time was now come when the field, having been cleared of all the more important competitors, it would have seemed that this crafty adventurer would have seized the throne for himself. He was too wise, however, to take such an unwise step yet. He had possession of the capital only, and even there he was hated for his oppression by everyone in it except his own army. The empire was in arms against him, and only a few miles from the city the country was occupied by imperial troops. He deemed it wiser to rule through another, whose right it was to reign, until such time as he had firmly secured the power for his own family. He accordingly made the third son of Wu Ti Emperor, whose dynastic title is

Kien Wen Ti—A. D. 550-551.

Whilst these important events were going on in Nanking another tragedy was being enacted in Lohyang. Kau-ting, in a campaign in Hwan, had managed to capture two governors of districts in that province. In order to show his contempt for them he treated them in the most insulting manner and made them cooks in his household. Determined to be avenged for this they plotted the tyrant's death, and one day one of them, when carrying in some dishes which they had cooked, hid a knife under one of them, and whilst Kau-ting was not observing him, he stabbed him to the heart and killed him on the spot. He was instantly killed by his brother Kauyang, who ordered the body to be cut into mince-meat. By the advice of his officers he set aside Hiau Ching and assumed the title of Wen Suan Ti, giving the new dynasty that he had founded the name of the Northern Ts'i.

Heu-king meanwhile found that his act of usurpation had not brought him the peace or satisfaction that he had expected, but that it had rather called into existence powerful enemies, with whom he would soon have to battle for his very existence. One of these was the commander of the imperial troops in Kwang-si and Canton, of whom we shall hear more by and by. Another was Ch'a, the grandson of Wu Ti, who claimed the throne by right of descent. As he was unable to enforce his claim by an adequate show of strength he appealed to Yu Wen-t'ai, the all-powerful prime minister of the king of the Western Wei, to help him. This ambitious noble was only too glad of the opportunity given him of interfering in a cause which he hoped would give him an excuse for annexing the empire to his own territories and of thus becoming Emperor of China.

Heu-king, who seemed determined to defy not only the opinion of the world, but also the very first principles of justice, made no efforts to use the great power that he had obtained, either to satisfy the people or to atone in some measure for the great evils of which he had been guilty. Before long he deposed and murdered Kien Wen and his son and put Prince Yu Chang on the throne.

Yu Chang—A. D. 551-552.

Another competitor for the crown appeared in the field, viz., Yih, the seventh son of Wu Ti, who was supported by the forces of the famous commander Ch'en Pa-sien, above referred to, who had a large body of soldiers under his control. His troops, who were anxious to meet those of Heu-king, marched with the greatest enthusiasm against the murderer of kings, and in the engagement that took place the latter was signally defeated and fled to Soochow, where he was captured. The intense hatred that was shown to this violent usurper was manifested in the indignities that were heaped upon his dead body. His head was cut off and placed over the gates of the city of Wuhing, in Kingchow. His hands were taken to Lohyang to be nailed up in a conspicuous place there, and his body was salted and carried to Nanking. There it was placed in one of the most crowded of the thoroughfares, and slices were cut off it and eaten by the enraged people. It is said that even his wife, the daughter of Ching-tuh, whom he had murdered, full of bitterness for the treatment that her family had suffered at his hands, joined in the terrible orgy of the Nankinese and swallowed mouthfuls of his body, to show the utter detestation in which she held his memory. With the disappearance of Heu-king, Yih quietly ascended the throne. His dynastic title is

Yuan Ti—A. D. 552-555.

This ruler established his capital at Kiangling, in Kingchow, but very little is known of him beyond the closing scenes of his life, which have become famous. He resembled his father in being a very religious man, but instead of adopting Buddhism as his faith he found the greatest comfort in Taoism. His belief took a very practical form ; for he very frequently abandoned his palace and took up his residence in one of his favourite temples devoted to Taoism. There he studied the books of that system, and he himself became a preacher of it. He was a great scholar, and had accumulated an immense library, and it was his delight, in the quiet and retirement of the temple, to dream away his days in musing over the mysteries of the faith he so much loved. Whilst he was lost in study the affairs of the empire were going on badly. Siau-ch'a, who had applied to Yu Wen-t'ai, the prime minister of the Western Wei, had at length moved that ambitious man to collect an army and join with him in marching on Kiangling, where Yuan Ti resided. So little did the latter know of what was going on in the world that the hostile forces had actually come into the neighbourhood of the city and crossed the Han before he came out to meet them. He was defeated and driven back into the town, which was soon captured. When the news was brought to Yuan Ti that the Wei troops were almost on the point of taking his capital he seems to have lost all hope and all heart, for he ordered that his library of one hundred and forty thousand books should be burnt, and breaking his sword in two he sent his submission to the conqueror. After his capture he was confined in one of the tents of Yu-wen. Here one of the officers on guard asked him why he had destroyed his library. "What use have my books been to me?" he replied. "All my reading and study have availed me nothing. They have not been able to help me in the hour of my extremity, and so I committed them to the flames, because I felt that all was over, and my life would soon terminate."

His forebodings were only too soon verified. In less than a month he had been executed by the order of Yu-wen, and Siau-ch'a was appointed in his place, with the title of Suan Ti, and his dynasty was called the Later Liang. Ch'en Pa-sien refused, however, to accept this disposition of the imperial succession, and so he placed the ninth son of Yuan Ti on the throne, who is known in history under the title of King Ti.

King Ti—A. D. 555-557.

The ruler of the Northern Ts'i, however, did not acquiesce in this arrangement, for he thought he had as good a right as any one else to determine who should be the sovereign of the country. He accordingly marched with a large force to Nanking and set

Cheng Yang Hau on the throne (A. D. 555). King Ti, who was the nephew of the new ruler, was compelled to give up his royal assumptions, and was made heir to the throne. As he was a lad of only fourteen years of age he had to quietly submit to these arrangements. Ch'en Pa-sien, however, was a very important factor now in the nation's history, and he refused to acquiesce in the high-handed proceedings of the uncle. He accordingly hastily marched with his army and reached Nanking before anyone there knew that he had started. Cheng Yang was compelled to retire into private life, and King Ti was restored to power, whilst his deliverer was made generalissimo of all the troops of the empire.

Whilst these revolutions were going on in Nanking important events were transpiring in the neighbouring kingdoms. Wen Suan Ti, fearful of the growing influence of his powerful neighbour, the ruler of the Northern Chow, built a wall more than three hundred miles in length, extending from Chihli to Shansi, to protect himself and his people from any possible inroad that any ambitious man might make upon them. It is said that nearly two millions of people were engaged on this stupendous work, and that the resources of his kingdom were severely taxed to carry it out. The great undertaking, however, was accomplished, but it could not stay the misfortunes that were impending over the dynasty.

Whilst his subjects were toiling in building this great rampart the question as to the relative importance of Taoism or Buddhism was being discussed in the capital. The Emperor did not think there was any need of both of these systems, for it was impossible for both of them to be right. He therefore called the chief of each side and allowed them to bring forth all the arguments they could on behalf of their own faith. The best of these having been found on the side of Buddhism he ordered the Taoist priests, on pain of death, to shave their heads and become bonzes. They do not seem to have had any very profound convictions of the eternal truth of their own system, for we are told that only four of them became martyrs for their faith, who preferred to lose their heads rather than their hair.

With the capture of Kiangling by Yu-wen, and the establishment of Siau-ch'a on the throne, the troops of the Western Wei were relieved from their arduous duties, and preparations were made for their return home. Yu-wen determined that he would now inflict a serious punishment upon the enemy, and at the same time reward his soldiers for the severe toils through which they had gone. He accordingly distributed more than thirty thousand men and women amongst them, who were to be their slaves, and whom they could sell or dispose of as they liked. These unfortunate people consisted of the soldiers and officers, together with their wives and families, who were found in the city when it was taken by storm. When Ch'ang-ngan was reached the great majority of these wretched captives were sold as slaves throughout the country and treated in the most cruel way imaginable. One of the officers having fallen into the hands of Yu-wen, he was so much struck with his intelligence and his knowledge of astronomy that he gave him a position under government. This man, whose name was Yu-kwei, was so distressed at the sorrows and sufferings of his comrades that out of his own private means he redeemed a considerable number of them and sent them back to their homes. Yu-wen having heard of this ordered him into his presence and asked him what he meant by his conduct. Yu-kwei replied, "From time immemorial it has been the custom with nations that when a kingdom has been defeated the conqueror should respect the officers of the state who have been loyal to their country. Now this has been violated in your case, but being a stranger in your dominions I have not dared to make any complaint. You have crushed Yuan Ti, but what wrong have these that have been sold into slavery done, and why should they suffer such great injustice? My heart has been broken with sorrow when I have seen their sufferings, and I have tried to alleviate the miseries of some by redeeming them and sending them to their native land." Yu-wen was deeply moved by the eloquent words and noble conduct of Yu-kwei. "I have done wrong," he said, "and I thank you for speaking so plainly to me. Had you not done so I should never have known the extent of my misdeeds, and the great empire of China that may be even now looking to me as its saviour from the misrule of kings, would have lost faith in me and hope for themselves." Before long he gave orders that all the captives, with only a few exceptions, should be released and allowed to return to their several homes.

The year A. D. 557 saw two very important events take place. The first of these was the death of Yu-wen. Before he died he committed his son to the care of Yu Wen-hau, his nephew, with strict injunctions that he should defend and protect him, and see also that he succeeded to the power that he himself had possessed as mayor of the palace. Having received his promise that he would faithfully carry out his injunctions, and also that he would be a father to the lad, who was then only fifteen years old, Yu-wen quietly breathed his last. The second was the usurpation of Ch'en Pa-sien. Seeing that the dynasty was near its end the nobles of the palace urged him to take the supreme power into his own hands and found a stronger one of his own. King Ti, who saw how events were turning, anticipated the action of his prime minister and resigned the throne to him, and was rewarded by being made the Duke of Kiangyin. Thus, without a blow, and with scarcely a ripple upon the surface of the life of the capital, the Liang dynasty passed away, only seven years after its illustrious founder had died broken-hearted in his palace in Nanking.

CHAPTER XVIII.

EPOCH OF DIVISION BETWEEN NORTH AND SOUTH.

THE CH'EN DYNASTY (A. D. 557-589).

Wu Ti—A. D. 557-560.

CH'EN PA-SIEN reigned only three short years, when he passed away without having accomplished anything that the royal historian deemed worthy of record. There is one act, indeed, with which his memory is stained, and that is the murder of the poor young man King Ti, who had resigned his crown to him. History leaves no stigma on his name for this cruel deed, because it was then considered politically necessary that any one who might possibly be a danger to the new *régime* should be got rid of.

The same year that witnessed the extinction of the Liang dynasty, saw also the extermination of the Western Wei. Yu-wen's son, Chiau, deposed Kung Ti, and founding a new dynasty of his own, which he called the Northern Chow, he reigned under the name of Hiau Min Ti. With this act finally disappeared as a ruling power the great house of Topa, that had reigned for over a hundred and seventy years over the northern division of China, and which had exercised a commanding influence, not only within its own jurisdiction, but also over the short lived dynasties that had ruled in Nanking. Before Hiau Min Ti had been long on the throne Yu Wen-hau killed, not only him, but also the late King Kung Ti, and appointed a brother of Hiau Wen to succeed him, who reigned under the appellation of Ming Ti (A. D. 557). In A. D. 560 Wen Suan Ti, the ruler of the Northern Ts'i, determined that he would cut off every member of the reigning house that he had usurped, so that his son should not be disturbed by rebellions after his strong arm had ceased to defend him. He accordingly seized seven hundred and twenty-one of the descendants of Topa and had them all executed. There was one more, but he escaped by abandoning his own surname and taking that of the clan to which the murderer of his kinsmen belonged. This wholesale butchery was soon avenged. A few months after he fell ill, pursued, as he supposed, by the infuriated spirits whom he had so ruthlessly hurried out of life. Shortly before his death he said to his wife, "I am not afraid of death. What troubles me now is the thought of my son. He is still young, and I greatly fear that after I am gone men will endeavour to seize the kingdom, and of course if they succeed they will murder him." He then summoned his younger brother Yeu to his bedside and said to him, "Now that I am about to die I want to ask you whether you

would not like to succeed me in my kingdom. If you really are
anxious to be king I shall now consent, and I'll call the nobles to
acknowledge you as such. One thing only I request from you
is that you will not murder my son." The brother, who was
of an ambitious disposition, and who had made up his mind to
obtain the kingdom at any cost, was afraid to accept of this
offer, lest when Kau-yang saw what was in his mind he might
order him out for execution, so that he might not interfere with
the prospects of his son after he was dead. He was therefore
silent, and stood with humble, downcast eyes before his dying
brother, apparently not caring for the proffered honour, whilst
his heart was filled with the most daring schemes for his own
advancement.

Kau-yang now called one of his most trusted ministers, and
telling him to save his son, and be a defender to him, passed away
with the group standing around him. The anticipations of danger
that filled the mind of the late king were speedily realized. In a few
months the son, whose royal name was Fei Ti, was deposed by his
uncle, who ascended the throne under the title of Hiau Chau Ti
(A. D. 560), and shortly after was murdered by him.

A speedy retribution followed this most unnatural crime. One
day, when he was out hunting, he was thrown from his horse, and
suffered such severe injuries that he died from the effects of them.
Before his death a scene similar to the one in which he had acted
a conspicuous part, took place by his bedside. The actors were
changed, but the play was the same. He summoned his brother
and asked him whether he would like the kingdom for himself or
not. "You shall have it," he said, "on the one condition, that
you promise not to murder my son, whom I love so dearly, and who
has no one to protect him unless you consent to do so." The
brother was silent, just as he himself was a year ago, and the
sorrowful, suffering man died without a reply. No sooner was he
gone than his brother ascended the throne, under the title of Wu
Ch'eng Ti, whilst the son was made the Prince of Lok-ling, to be
murdered three years hence, because there were unlucky omens in
the sky that it was believed portended disturbance to the kingdom,
which might possibly endanger the dynasty.

This same year (A. D. 561) saw the death of Ch'en Pa-sien.
This man was an able general, and one who would be sorely missed
at this crisis of the new dynasty's history. He possessed many of
the virtues that stand high in the estimation of the Chinese. He
was a man of great ability, a daring soldier, and yet full of concern
and sympathy for his subjects. His rule was an exceedingly mild
one, and he had already endeared himself to the nation. In one
respect he was very different from the rulers that had preceded him.
Instead of the lavish expenditure in the palace, the utmost economy
was practised. His table was of the simplest, whilst the dress, both
of himself and of the ladies of his household, was plain in the

extreme. He was a Buddhist by faith, and had dedicated himself to the great goddess Kwanyin in the most famous temple in Nanking, in the hopes that she would bring him happiness when he came to die.

He was compelled to appoint his nephew to succeed him, for his two sons, who had been captured by Yu-wen when Kiangling was taken, were still held captives in Ch'ang-ngan, and there was no hope that they would ever be permitted to return to their native land.

Wen Ti—A. D. 560-567.

Wen Ti had hardly been seated on the throne before tidings came that the eldest son of Ch'en Pa-sien had been released by Yu-wen, and would soon be on his way to claim the inheritance of his father. These tidings were confirmed by a letter from his cousin, who demanded that the throne should be surrendered to him, and threatened all kinds of penalties in case he should refuse to do so. Wen Ti was so alarmed by the tone of his demands that he sent orders that the prince should be murdered at a certain place on the road, which was accordingly done, and the country was relieved from the perils of a civil war. Two years after the second son returned, but being of a mild and generous disposition he immediately gained the favour of Wen Ti, who made him a prince of the empire and gave him a position in which he could live in great comfort and elegance.

This year (A. D. 560) Yu Wen-hau added to the atrocities of which he had been guilty by causing Ming Ti to be poisoned and by placing the brother of the latter, Wu Ti, on the throne. This man seems to have been a remarkably fine character and to have exhibited many traits that showed he was fitted to govern. He was a distinguished scholar, and yet he was willing, king though he was, to be taught by others. On one occasion, anxious to be guided as to the best way in which to rule his people, and at the same time to give the scholars a lesson in humility in their treatment of their teachers, he entered the class-room of the university in his capital. Instead of sitting down he acted just like any scholar would have done who wished to pay special respect to his professors. Standing with his face to the north, whilst the master sat facing in the same direction, he asked him, in a reverential manner, what lesson he had to give him to help him in his government of the kingdom. After a moment's thought the teacher rose, in deference to his exalted pupil, and replied that there were four things that he thought essential to the right government of any people. First, that the sovereign should be willing to listen to the advice of his faithful ministers instead of always acting on the impulses of his own mind : just as the carpenter would never succeed in getting a perfect line on his wood without the aid of the inked string, so his conduct would not be correct unless it was guided by their advice. * Secondly, the sovereign ought to be very careful about his people and see that they had enough to eat, and that they should not be distressed by hunger. He was also to make arrangements that his soldiers should be well supplied, and that the commissariat should never be deficient. These two things, he said, he might not be able to accomplish, as circumstances beyond his control might happen that would render all his plans unavailing. There was one thing, however, in which he ought never to fail. He should so live as never to lose the faith of his people in him. Thirdly, he ought to reward the good and punish the evil, so that the good might persevere in virtue and the wicked be deterred from continuing in evil. Fourthly, he ought to be especially careful about his life. A king doing wrong, he continued, is different from an ordinary person, because of the conspicuous place he holds in the state. When the sun is eclipsed every one sees it, and so when the sovereign does evil the people mark it, and are either grieved about it, or are led to imitate him.

Wu Ti was deeply moved as he stood with bowed head and listened to these words of the teacher. When they were ended he acknowledged his thanks for the service he had done him, and then, each bowing to the other, the king departed with his train.

In the year A. D. 566 the ruler of the Northern Ts'i, who was an exceedingly superstitious man and deeply moved by anything extraordinary in nature, was terrified by the appearance of a comet. He thought that, as it foreboded war and revolution, it must have reference to him personally.

He accordingly consulted with his ministers how he could avert the coming storm. They were greatly perplexed at first with the profound problem, for they never doubted for a moment that the comet had taken the trouble to come out of its way to give a hint to the king of the disasters he might expect. They were equal to the occasion, however, only the remedy they proposed was a very heroic one. It was no less than that the king should resign the throne to his son, and thus cheat the coming troubles of their prey. This he consented to do, when his son took his place, under the name of Wen Kung.

In the seventh year of his reign the Emperor Wen Ti became very ill, and as there was no hope of his recovery he began to plan

---

* It is interesting to find from the illustration here used by the Chinese scholar that the custom of the carpenters of to-day in getting a perfectly straight line on their wood, is no merely modern one, but was used so far back as these early times. A small wooden bottle is used in which are two or three yards of string wound round a moveable bar running through the middle. This is filled with ink, which saturates the thread. When a straight line is desired to be got this string is unrolled. At the outside end there is a sharp awl, which is stuck into the plank from the point where the proposed line begins, and with the finger the thread is carried to the spot where the line is to end. When it is properly fixed the carpenter takes hold of the line in the middle, and lifting it up carefully lets it rebound back again on to the board. The result is that an absolutely straight line is obtained between the two points where the awl is stuck in and where the finger holds the other end of the cord.

with regard to the succession. His own son was weak and feeble, both in mind and character, and he was afraid that to make him his successor, would only be to incite revolution in the palace and cause some one of his strong-minded nobles to plot treason, which might end, not only in the murder of his son, but also in the overthrowing of his dynasty. He therefore called the Prince of Ngan-cheng, the second son of Ch'en Pa-sien, and informed him that he was going to appoint him his successor. He refused the honour, though he longed for it, and was even then planning how he should obtain it in the future. Wen Ti then summoned his nobles to attend him. He represented to them that they needed a strong ruler who could firmly grasp the reins of power. The country, he said, was in a disordered condition, and military adventurers everywhere were contending with each other for dominion. As his son was utterly unfit to cope with the responsibilities the throne would bring him he had urged upon his cousin to become Emperor after his death, but he had refused. What then did they advise under these circumstances? One of the ministers present said, "Why not let your son reign? Time will cure the difficulty of his youth, and in the meantime let the prince help him with all the ability and experience he has, and we will loyally do our utmost to assist him in the government of the empire." This seemed a very happy solution of this difficult question. Soon after Wen Ti died, when the son reigned under the title of Hwei Ti, whilst the prince became his prime minister. The arrangement, however, did not last long. The prince in a little over a year deposed him and gave him the title of Lin Hai Wang, whilst he himself assumed the position that he had long desired to have. He is known in history as

Suan Ti—A. D. 569-583.

From this period the chief interest centres around Wu Ti, the wise and intelligent ruler of the Northern Chow. The Ch'en dynasty had now but a few more years to run its course, when it would ignominiously disappear from the world. In A. D. 573 Yu Wen-hau, the slayer of kings, was put to death by Wu Ti, a just retribution for the many crimes he had committed. This was one of the righteous acts that marked the reign of the latter, and which showed that he was not afraid to vindicate the majesty of the law when the occasion required him to do so. He was a very shrewd man, and in many respects far ahead of his times in his disregard for the superstitions that influenced many in those comparatively dark ages of the world. His son went one day into the hills to hunt, and whilst there caught a beautiful white stag. He brought it to his father, saying that it would bring him good luck. "No," said Wu Ti, "that is not so. The only thing that will bring fortune is a virtuous life."

In the year A. D. 575 he issued an edict forbidding the exercise of both the Taoist and Buddhist faiths, and commanded that all his subjects should be content with the teachings of Confucius. He also ordered that all the temples of both the sects should be demolished, and that the priests should return to the duties of ordinary life and conduct themselves as good citizens. This same year his mother died, when he showed the depths of his filial piety and his affection for her by mourning for her three years.

In the kingdom of the Northern Ts'i matters were going from bad to worse. Wen Kung's mind, that had always been of a feeble character, did not grow stronger with his increase of responsibility. He was timid, too, and exceedingly frivolous. He stuttered in his speech, and was afraid to meet his ministers and consult with them about the government of his people. This led him into the most childish and most undignified habits. To solace himself he was continually singing the most merry songs that could be collected for him, and playing on the guitar. From his continually indulging in this habit the people of the capital called him the "Merry Monarch." If his tastes had been confined simply to his indulgence in music men might only have laughed at his folly, but unfortunately he developed habits that showed him to be utterly unworthy of the exalted position he held as head of the state. He had a beggars' village built in the royal gardens, where the mendicants of the city were at liberty to come and take up their abode after the business of the day was over. A beggar's calling seemed to have a wonderful fascination for the royal mind. He dressed in rags like the meanest of those that wandered through the narrow streets of the neighbouring city, whining out his cry for alms, and he carried the straw wallet, which in China is the beggar's badge, into which he might put the gifts he received in charity. He would sally out in the morning and make his rounds amongst the mandarins of the palace and the ladies of the royal household and beg for alms. Whoever gave him any he would invariably reward with some special gift,—the men, by making them officials under the government. When this became known they vied with each other to be present when he made his rounds, so that they might be made mandarins.

This farce was varied in A. D. 576 by his sending an army into Shansi to attack the territory of his neighbour, the Northern Chow. At first it obtained a decided success in the capture of P'ing-yang, but the city was shortly retaken, when his forces had to beat a precipitate retreat. Wu Ti pursued him with such vigour that he dared not stop at Lohyang, but continued his flight to Yeh.

The people of the capital, seeing themselves deserted by their ruler, appointed Ngan-teh (A. D. 576) as their king, but both he and the city were taken by Wu Ti in the beginning of the next year.

Wen Kung, finding himself placed in desperate circumstances, resigned in favor of his son Yiu Chu, but nothing now could save the dynasty. Wu Ti, with his victorious soldiers, marched on Yeh, when both father and son were made prisoners and summarily executed. With their death the power of the Northern Ts'i was completely annihilated, and the country was added to that of the conqueror.

In the following year Wu Ti died, and was succeeded by his son Pin, who is known in history by the name of Suan Ti.

The first act of this gentleman was to circumvent the death of his uncle by a false accusation of treason. He fancied that his power was excessive, and was endangering the stability of his throne, and therefore affection and all sense of justice and honour must be sacrificed rather than that his own miserable life should be put in jeopardy. The poor old man was suddenly accused by the witnesses that Suan Ti had himself suborned, and standing in the presence of his nephew, and with no opportunity allowed him of clearing his character, he was condemned to death on the spot and strangled in the audience hall, right in the presence of his royal relative.

The next important act of the king was to appoint Yang-kien as his commander-in-chief. Next year, A. D. 580, he resigned in favour of his son, Tsing Ti, and in A. D. 581 a marriage was arranged between Suan Ti and a daughter of Yang-kien, who was made prime minister and created Duke of Sui. These important acts had scarcely been transacted when the eyes of Suan Ti were opened to the want of wisdom he had displayed in elevating such an ambitious man as Yang-kien to a position of such power. He showed his want of discretion in openly expressing his dislike to him and in his repeated assertion to his wife that he would exterminate the whole house of Yang. Seeing his danger, Yang-kien determined to take the initiative. An opportunity soon occurred. Suan Ti became ill, and one day, after a visit of Yang-kien to him, the sick man was found dead in his bed. There was no positive proof that he had been murdered, but the absence of any comment by the royal historiographer on this most suspicious circumstance shows that he must have had grave suspicions that he was killed by his father-in-law.

As Tsing Ti was but a baby, Yang-kien acted as though he were the sovereign of the nation. No man better fitted for exercising the royal functions could have been found at this particular crisis. He was not only a soldier, but also a statesman of the very highest ability. He showed this by a revision of the criminal laws. This had been exceedingly severe and oppressive. He had then altered for milder ones, to the great joy and comfort of the people. He also restored both the Taoist and Buddhist religions and made offerings to the idols and prayed them to prosper and preserve him. In the beginning of the year A. D. 582 he assumed the manners of a king. Tsing Ti was sent to a distant part of the country with the title of the Duke of Chieh. His own father was honoured by posthumous honours, whilst his wife was styled queen and his eldest son proclaimed heir to the throne. By the advice of one of his generals he put to death every member of the family of Ch'en Pa-sien, excepting Tsing Ti, so that he or his descendants might have no rival in the possession of the throne.

About this time a famous scholar of the name of Su-wei appears upon the scene, who is destined to have a great influence over Yang-kien and his plans for the government of the country. He originally came from a highly cultivated family. His father had been a mandarin, and evidently a man of thought and gifted with the power of wisely ruling the people under him, for his son remembered some of his maxims, which were now valuable to him in guiding the opinions of Yang-kien. He advised that the land tax should be more equally adjusted, and that the penalties for all kinds of offences against the laws should be made lighter. "They are excessive now," he said, "and instead of restraining the people from evil they had the opposite effect of making them desperate." He recommended that Yang-kien should study the work of Confucius styled the "Filial Classic," for it contained, he declared, the whole method of government, not simply of a family, but of an empire as well.*

This year, A. D. 582, Yang-kien conceived the design of conquering Nanking, and by the advice of Kau-king, another famous scholar at his court, an army under Han-ch'in was sent to occupy Kwangling and Luchow, whilst another, under Ho Joh-pi, marched into Yangchow and encamped there, ready for the coming campaign against the Ch'en dynasty. His young grandson, who was only seven years old, was now put to death by his order, and the colour of yellow, which has been the royal colour ever since, became the distinguishing mark of the new dynasty.

After serious consultation with regard to the mitigation of the penal laws it was decided that the five great punishments for heinous offences, which had been, cutting off the nose, branding on the face, breaking the legs, castration and death, should be replaced by strangling, banishment to long distances—say of six hundred to a thousand miles—banishment to short distances and for terms varying from one year to three, beating before the magistrate—from ten to ninety blows—and a milder flagellation, in which the extreme number of strokes that could be given was fifty.

In the year A. D. 583 the Emperor Suan Ti died, and after a struggle with his younger brother, who made an effort to gain possession of the throne, the eldest son, Shuh-pau, succeeded him, under the title that history has given him of

---

* Filial piety, which is discussed in his famous book, is held to be at the root of all that is excellent, both in private and public life. A young man, for example, who is filial, will abstain from every kind of evil, because it is opposed to the wishes of his parents, whom he desires to honour. He will be a loyal citizen, a faithful minister and a king that desires only to rule his people wisely and lovingly. There is hardly any duty in social life, indeed, which this virtue, so highly honoured by the Chinese, does not touch.

How Chu—A. D. 583-589.

The last ruler of the house of Ch'en was a fit one with which to end a dynasty. He began his reign by a system of extravagance and debauchery that would have imperilled the strongest government in the world. He built three immense buildings for his favourite concubines, the chief of whom was Chang Li-hwa, who exercised a fatal influence over this dissipated monarch.* Although there were abundant signs that the empire was in a most critical condition immense sums were lavished upon these. The rooms in which they lived were made of lign-aloes and sandal wood and inlaid with gold, jade and pearls. A miniature hill was constructed in the garden that surrounded them, and the waters of a distant stream were made to flow into it, where an artificial lake was formed. All kinds of rare and expensive trees were sought out and brought to be planted in this wonderful garden, where the infatuated How Chu was spending the most of his precious time, whilst Yang-kien was marshalling his forces for the overthrow of his house. This astute ruler and general, by the advice of Kau-yang, adopted a system of warfare with the Ch'en people that in the end secured him the victory over them. Sudden raids were made into their territory by small bodies, who burnt their wooden houses and laid waste their fields, and then as suddenly retreated to their own country. These were repeated so often that the impression got abroad that there would be no serious effort on a large scale to conquer their country, so that no adequate preparation was made to repel the large armies of the invader when they finally marched upon the capital. At length, everything being ready for the great enterprise, and boats having been built to cross his immense army over the Yang-tze, Yang-kien, in the year A. D. 589, gave orders for the march upon Nanking. His entire force, which consisted of five hundred and eighteen thousand men, was under his oldest son, Kung, who was appointed commander-in-chief. The news of the movement of this immense body of soldiers was concealed from How Chu by the unfaithful ministers, who preferred to enjoy themselves with him than to prepare to save the country in its imminent peril, and it was not till it was about to cross the great river that he was informed of the peril that now menaced his kingdom.

The only reply that How Chu gave to the alarming communication that was made to him was, "Never mind, don't let us be alarmed at the attempt that Yang-kien is going to make to destroy

---

* Chang Li-hwa was renowned for her surpassing beauty. Her hair was long and glossy, and was said to be more than seven feet in length. Shuh-pau was so enthralled with her charms that he gave up all care for the government of his people and entrusted the administration of the empire to eunuchs and men of unworthy characters. His whole time was spent with her and two others, of the name of K'ung Kwei-fei and Kung Kwei-fei, and every remonstrance that was made to him by the ministers that remained faithful to their responsibilities was unheeded by this dissipated ruler.

our dynasty.   Many have tried to do so before, but they failed. The Northern Ts'i tried three times to advance upon Nanking, and the Northern Chow twice, but each time their plans were frustrated, and they had to retire unsuccessful.   The same will be the case again; so let us enjoy ourselves and be merry.''   No preparation, accordingly, of any kind was made to strengthen the capital, or to collect the forces of the empire for the coming struggle, and Nanking stood like a doomed city, whilst those who should have protected it were plunged in dissipation and revelry.   Although How Chu is still the acknowledged ruler of the empire, the Chinese historians place the close of the Ch'en dynasty at this particular point, and date the commencement of the Sui dynasty from this period.   To prevent confusion of dates we follow their example and pass on to the story of the new house that is now to rule over a united China.

CHAPTER XIX.

THE SUI DYNASTY (A. D. 589-618).

Kau Tsu or Wun Ti—A. D. 589-605.

YANG-KIEN was forty-eight years old when he became Emperor over a territory that until but recently had been divided between three rulers. He gave his dynasty the name of Sui, from the dukedom of that name, which had been bestowed upon his father for services rendered to the dynasty of the Northern Chow. The feeble and dissipated How Chu was doing literally nothing to contest the claim that Yang-kien was now making for the kingdom, and whose armies were advancing rapidly upon Nanking, simply to take possession of a throne that was slipping away from the grasp of a man that had no moral or physical qualities to retain it. How Chu had indeed been roused somewhat when he heard that Yang-kien's soldiers had crossed the Yang-tze, and he had sent three of his generals with what men they could collect to oppose them ; but these had been quickly defeated, and no further efforts had been made to stay the progress of the advancing foe. Han-ch'in marched from the south, and having captured some of How Chu's officers, he pushed forward with five hundred men, and under their guidance he entered the capital. Search was everywhere made for the Emperor, but he could at first be nowhere found, till at last it was discovered that he and his three favourite concubines had been lowered into a well, where they hoped to escape being captured by the enemy. They were speedily drawn up, amidst the derision and scorn of both the people of Nanking and the soldiers of Han-ch'in, and committed to safe custody.

A few hours after Ho Joh-pi arrived with his army from the north, and found, to his chagrin, that the honours of the capture of the city and of How Chu belonged to Han-ch'in, whose soldiers opened the gates of the town to admit him. Two days after Kau-king came up with his force and encamped without the city. The commander-in-chief, who was advancing with his army, sent special orders that Chang Li-hwa should not be killed, but be reserved for himself. Kau-king, who feared for the effect that this celebrated beauty would have upon the mind of Yung, and that the new dynasty might run the risk of being wrecked at its very commencement, determined to disobey his commands, and gave orders that she should be immediately executed, which were at once carried out. His superior was exceedingly irate when he found out what Kau-king had done, and from that moment a deadly hatred sprung up in his mind towards him, and he mentally vowed that he would pay him out at the very first opportunity he could get for the slight that he had put upon his authority.

How Chu was carried prisoner to the capital in Shensi, and after a month's journeying arrived there in safety. His reception was anything but flattering to a man that had been brought up amidst the greatest luxuries, and who had been accustomed to be bowed down to and honored as the head of the empire. Yang-kien instituted a solemn service in the hall of his ancestors as a thank-offering for the signal service they had rendered him in enabling him to so gloriously overcome his enemies. How Chu was compelled to be present and to stand by reverently and respectfully whilst the spirits of the dead were addressed. Yang-kien told them how his troops had marched on Nanking, and how they had overcome every one that had opposed them, and how they had seized the Emperor and brought him a captive for them to feast their eyes upon and to rejoice in the prowess and prosperity of their children.

The great question that Yang-kien had now to decide was the distribution of honours amongst his successful generals. This was no easy matter, because there was a division of opinion between Ho Joh-pi and Han-ch'in as to who was entitled to the greater honour for the services they had rendered in the brilliant campaign so lately concluded.

Ho Joh-pi claimed the highest for himself. "I met the armies that opposed me on the way," he said, "and I not only defeated them, but I also took prisoner one of the most distinguished and valiant of How Chu's generals. It was really through me that the victory over Nanking was gained, for through the bravery of my men the enemy was so terror-struck that resistance was abandoned, and now to-day Your Majesty," he said, addressing Yang-kien, "is Emperor of China." Han-ch'in, on the other hand, contended that he was the one that struck the decided blow that ended the campaign so quickly. "With a handful of men," he said, "I advanced rapidly upon Nanking. I took possession of the city and I seized the Emperor, and was ready, when Ho Joh-pi arrived in the afternoon of the same day, to open the gates and let him in." Yang-kien, with ready tact, settled the matter in a way that was satisfactory to both. "I am exceedingly gratified with you both," he graciously interposed, "and I know not how to reward you sufficiently for the exalted services you have rendered me and the state. Your merit and your deeds are both extraordinary, and therefore are entitled to the highest honours." He then gave Han-ch'in the title of "the Supreme Pillar of the Kingdom," with emoluments sufficient to enable him to maintain with dignity such a distinguished title, and he created Ho Joh-pi Duke of Sung.

Turning now to Kau-king, Yangkien said to him, "and now what do you consider to be the quality of your merit as contrasted with those of Ho Joh-pi? Do you think yourself entitled to as great a reward as he, or what?" Kau-king, who was really superior to the ambitious general, and who by his statesmanship had contributed largely to the successes that had been obtained, modestly replied, "I do not for a moment compare myself with him. I am not a soldier. I am a scholar, and therefore I am content that he should receive higher honours than I can aspire to. Besides, he exposed his life in common with his soldiers and showed the highest generalship by the way in which he led them to victory." Yang-kien, who knew his great ability and his devotion to himself, was exceedingly pleased with his reply, and at once created him Duke of Ts'i, whilst Yang-su, who belonged to the same clan as himself, and had distinguished himself in the late war, was made Duke of Yueh.

This year, A. D. 590, ambassadors came to congratulate Yang-kien from the Turcoman tribes that inhabited the country to the north and north-west of the empire. During the times of the Wei and Ch'en dynasties these people had been a source of terror to the Chinese living on the frontiers. On one occasion they had actually invaded and kept possession of territory belonging to the Wei, and it was only by the diplomacy and tact of Yu Wen-t'ai, who concluded a treaty of peace with them, that they were prevented from over-running and ravaging the whole of the kingdom. After an audience with them Yang-kien, who wished to impress them with a sense of his power, so that they should carry back a report to their people that would restrain any warlike impulses in the future, caused them to be led to the place where How Chu was confined. They were told that this was the late Emperor of China, a name which had always been to them associated with ideas of magnificence and military power, and that he had been overcome by Yang-kien and his dominions absorbed in his own. After the sight of the captive monarch had been allowed to make its due impression on their minds they were next brought into the presence of Han-ch'in, who had been duly notified of their intended visit. They found him sitting in state, surrounded by his chief officers, and with the air and look of a conqueror about him. They were politely told that this was the man that had penetrated into the capital of the Ch'en and had seized the Emperor right in the midst of his people and had brought him away captive to grace the triumph of the redoubtable Yang-kien. The effect of these two realistic scenes upon their minds was to fill them with terror, and the report that they took back to their own people of the power and invincibility of Yang-kien was such as to prevent any hostile demonstrations by them for a considerable time.

Now that peace was proclaimed throughout the empire, Yang-kien, who was even more of a statesman than a general, set himself seriously to legislate for the happiness of his people, and in order to make this more practicable he ordered that every hundred families should have a head man appointed over them who should be responsible for their conduct, and also that over every five hundred a superior officer should be set to whom the heads of each might report in any difficulties that might arise. With great generosity he determined that the conquered territory of Ch'en, and especially Nanking, should be treated with special leniency. Considering that the latter, together with the large district around it, had suffered exceptionally from the large number of troops that had been congregated in it, he gave orders that the land tax should not be collected in it for ten years, and that the rest of the country should be exempted for the period of one year. It is pleasing to note that Yang-kien was seconded in his benevolent efforts, in many places, by mandarins of a superior type, whose hearts were moved by love to the people under their charge rather than by the meaner motives of selfishness and avarice. One of these is worthy of being mentioned. His name was Sin-kung, and he was governor of Min-chow, in Shensi. It happened during his term of office that a terrible plague broke out in his district. It was so infectious and so fatal that men fled in terror, even from their nearest relatives who were attacked with it. When one member of a family was seized every other rushed incontinently away and abandoned him to his own fate. Sin-kung was distressed not only at the misery of the unfortunates who were left to perish, but also at the utter want of humanity shown by the people at large, and he determined to give them an object lesson in heroic kindness that he hoped would touch their hearts and make them ashamed of their conduct. He ordered that all the sick who had been deserted by their friends should be carried to his official residence. He had beds prepared for them, and he procured food and medicines for them out of his own salary, whilst he ministered with his own hands to their wants. The great majority, in consequence of this careful attention, recovered. Sin-kung then sent for their relatives and handed them over to them and said, "Life and death are in the hands of Heaven. Why are you afraid of infection? There is no such thing; for if there were how is it that I have escaped, although I have had so many in my own house with the disease. You must be kind to those who are bound to you by the ties of nature, and not be so selfishly bent in caring for your own lives." The peoples' hearts were greatly moved by this noble conduct. They no longer abandoned the sick, but remained by them in generous emulation of the example set them.

Sin-kung had an exalted idea of the responsibility of his office. When he reached the capital of his district he found the great jail filled with prisoners, many of whom had languished there for years, and who had lost all hopes of ever being free again. Unfortunately this was not an exceptional occurrence. Justice in China walks with slow and leaden steps that can never be hastened, except under the powerful impulse of a bribe. Sin-kung needed no such incentive to make him examine into the stories of the men that were immured within the filthy cells of the prison. He boldly took up his abode within the precincts of the dismal abode of misery and injustice, determined that he would see for himself the rights and wrongs of every one imprisoned within it. Every case was examined with the most

patient care and settled at once.   Those who were wrongfully
detained were released ; others who were breakers of the law, were
punished in the summary method that Chinese rulers well know
how to use with the most satisfactory results.   At the end of a
fortnight there was not a single person confined within the prison,
and the jailers were left with the most delightful freedom to enjoy
themselves.   The only drop of gall that was left in their cup of
bliss was the deprivation of their perquisites which they had been
accustomed to wring out of the unhappy prisoners.   The speed with
which justice was administered astonished and delighted the people.
Never in the history of the oldest inhabitant had such scenes been
witnessed.   The moral effect upon the whole of his district was
most beneficial.   Men saw how much Sin-kung had at heart the
good of those he came to rule and how he was spending his strength
in their service.   The result was there was a general effort to bring
as few cases as possible before him, in order to save his strength.
Slight quarrels were made up, old grievances were adjusted by each
side making concessions, and it was only in grave matters, where
the decision of a judge was required, that litigants appeared in
court.

Unfortunately for himself and for those immediately connected
with him Yang-kien was of an exceedingly passionate temper,
which was rendered all the more irritable by his tendency to suspect
every one with whom he had any dealing.   He was especially severe
on the mandarins, and if they were anything like those of to-day
there is no doubt but that he had good reasons to be so.   He used to
send out messengers to investigate and report to him with regard to
their official conduct.   In order to see whether a certain judge was
taking bribes or not he would send him a present of money when
a lawsuit was going on, as if from the defendant.   If he declined it
he rose in his estimation, and after a short time would find himself
promoted to a higher post.   If, however, he fell into the trap, he
was at once summoned to the palace, deprived of his office and
executed on the spot.   Such scenes as these were very frequently
witnessed by the astonished nobles, who had not been accustomed
to such summary and excessive punishment as this.

As the result of his efforts to improve the morals of Nanking,
and the lately conquered country generally, an insurrection broke
out against his authority, which had to be put down with a strong
hand.   Under How Chu the people had become demoralized.   The
profligacy of the court, and the venality of all in power, had told
with fatal effect upon the whole nation.   Yang-kien, to bring the
people to a better state of mind, gave orders that the mandarins
should see to the education of the masses in the doctrines of
Confucius.   This was something that the public did not relish, and
they showed their distaste by refusing to have anything to do
with the new regulations.   Discontent quickly spread throughout
every class, and as the leaders of the opposition did not dare to

give out that to be taught the doctrines of their sacred books was a sufficient reason for rebellion, they spread abroad the report that Yang-kien was going to forcibly compel the removal of the people of Nanking to Shen-si. The news spread with great rapidity, and formidable risings took place in Chehkiang and Soochow. Yang-su, the Duke of Yueh, was sent with a sufficient force to put these down, which he did promptly and thoroughly. The leaders were seized and executed, and large numbers of the rank and file were put to death by the victorious army.

This year, A. D. 593, the famous Han-ch'in died, when Kau-king and Yang-su were made prime ministers. Ho Joh-pi was exceedingly annoyed that the Emperor had not selected him for one of these important posts. The estimate that he had of his own ability was so overweening that he deemed himself competent to fulfil the highest offices of the state. He vented his anger in reproaches against Yang-kien, who, having been informed of them, deprived him of all his honours. This enraged him still further, and instead of having learnt wisdom by his downfall he became more severe in his criticisms of him. He was now seized and committed to prison. A cabinet council discussed his offence, and he was unanimously condemned to die. He was brought before the Emperor to be told his sentence. As he kneeled in his presence Yang-kien thought of the distinguished services he had rendered him and how he had performed his part in putting him on the throne of the empire. Instead of hurrying him off to the executioner he said to him, "You have been guilty of high treason in slandering me. Have you any reason to give why your life should be spared? Speak now and I will listen to what you have to say." Ho Joh-pi replied humbly, "My life is in your hands, and I pray you to spare it. I have nothing to plead but my poor services, which I had the honour of performing for you and your family. In remembrance of these let me live." "But I gave you exceptional honours for all that you did and suffered for me," replied Yang-kien, "so that I feel you have no further claim upon me in regard to them." "Then let Your Majesty to-day grant me exceptional mercy, and you will add to the lustre of your name." This plea succeeded with the Emperor. His life was spared, and at the end of the year all his titles and honours were restored to him, and he was again placed in a high position under the government.

In the year A. D. 595 Shensi was afflicted with a most grievous famine. The common people were reduced to the verge of starvation, and even the highest classes had to undergo considerable privations. Yang-kien heard of the sufferings his subjects had to endure, and it is said that on one occasion, when an officer of the palace, who was sent out for a sample of the food that the poorer classes of the capital were using, brought in for his inspection a bowl of the wretched stuff they were compelled to eat, he wept for grief at the terrible condition to which they were reduced. The state of things became so serious at last, that to escape destruction Yang-kien and nearly all his army, with a very considerable part of the population, were compelled to emigrate to the present province of Honan, where there was an abundance of provisions. In this long and painful journey the Emperor showed the greatest humanity to his suffering people. The soldiers helped the very old and young along the road and over the difficult passes amongst the mountains they had to cross. As Yang-kien felt that this terrible visitation upon his kingdom was a manifestation of Heaven's anger for the sins he had committed, he determined to make a pilgrimage to the great T'ai-shan mountain, in Shantung, and there, on the top of it, worship God and confess his wrongs to the great Being whom he had offended.*

This he did at the beginning of A. D. 596, and in the third month of the same year he and those of his people who desired it returned to their homes in Shensi. The harvest of the past autumn had been abundant, and food had again become plentiful.

On his return he found that the magnificent palace of "Long-lived Benevolence," so celebrated in history, and which had been commenced two years before, was just completed. To accomplish this, whilst the famine was in existence, entailed great sufferings on the people. Yang-su, who had the superintendence of the work, must have been a hard and unpitying master, for the historian tells how when he came to inspect it, before the Emperor came to live in it, the roads for miles around were strewed with the dead bodies of the workmen, who had died from exhaustion in consequence of the severe toil that had been exacted from them. Anxious to hide this terrible sight from Yang-kien he ordered the bodies to be burnt. When the Emperor appeared upon the scene, and saw the enormous pile of buildings that he had erected for him, he was filled with the greatest anger. Pointing his finger to him he said, "In this extravagance you have committed you have given reason to the people of my empire to hate me with the bitterest hatred," and as his passion rose he launched against him the most terrible invectives, till Yang-su trembled with fear, not knowing but that this fierce anger of the passionate monarch might mean destruction to himself. One of his officers, who was standing by, comforted him after the Emperor had withdrawn, by saying to him with a very significant look, "Don't be afraid, for to-morrow something very pleasant will happen that will be a source of great pleasure to you, and that will make you forget your fears of to-day." Yang-su was so

---

*There are five great mountains in China which are celebrated from the fact that the ancient kings of China were accustomed to ascend them when they wished to pay special homage to God and make confession of their sins to Him. The eastern, called the T'ai, is in Shantung ; the southern, Heng, lies to the west of the river Siang, in Hunan ; the western, Hoa, rises to the west of Singan Fu, in Shensi ; the northern, Hang. is in Tat'ung Fu, in Shansi, and the central, Sung, lies on the watershed between the Yellow and Han Rivers in Honan.

absorbed with his apprehensions that he took no notice of these words, but on the next day true enough a happy surprise that he had never thought of occurred to him. When the queen joined her husband she was in raptures with the palace, and immediately calling for Yang-su, she, in the presence of her husband, said to him, " You deserve the greatest credit for the thoughtfulness with which you have provided so fine a place for us old people to live in. It shows how loyal you are, and how worthy you are of the highest honours your sovereign has to bestow." Instead of having his head taken off Yang-su found himself literally burdened with the presents that the grateful queen showered upon him.

Yang-kien became more lenient in his disposition as he grew in years, and he passed a law that no one should be put to death before the case had been reported to him three times. He also commanded that no artisans or merchants should be made mandarins, and that the honour should be reserved for scholars or men engaged in agriculture. The consequences that resulted from the leniency with which criminals in capital cases were treated led to the greatest confusion in society. The inferior mandarins defied their superiors and committed the gravest offences in their official capacity, as they knew that before they could be convicted for any capital offence their case would have to be stated three times to the Emperor. The difficulties connected with this were almost insuperable, and consequently society was demoralized, as well as the official class, and the administration of the law for the graver offences was rendered impossible. When this state of things was represented to Yang-kien, with his usual impetuosity, he passed from undue leniency to excessive severity. Mandarins were given the most absolute powers to deal with those below them in rank. For the offence of stealing a single cash the person was to be put to death. If three men combined to steal a fowl the whole party were to have their heads cut off. This new law was a terror to honest men, whilst rogues and thieves enjoyed it immensely. All business at early hours, or late in the evening, was completely stopped. No man durst go out in the early morning hours, lest he should be accused of being abroad for some unlawful purpose. Much less could he venture out after dark, for his danger would be intensified should some rogue accuse him of some evil design against the property of honest men. At last this miserable state of things was put an end to by a secret committee of the citizens of the capital. These assembled in force, disguised as thieves. They then managed to seize a prominent member of the Board of Punishment, and they threatened that if he did not memorialize the Emperor and have the late obnoxious law repealed they would put him to death. This high official, afraid for his life, did as was demanded of him, and the foolish law was allowed to drop out of public notice.

The year A. D. 601 was an unhappy one for the prosperity of the house of Sui. Unfortunately for the heir to the throne, his mother took a dislike to him. This was caused by the death of his wife, of whom she was very fond, and the immediate elevation of one of his concubines to her position. The queen held that she had been murdered by her son, because he wished to get rid of her as his affections were centred on her more beautiful rival. The second son, who was ambitious, and a master in deception, saw that there was a way now through the disgrace of his brother to the elevation of himself to the throne. He affected to live a most simple and virtuous life, and to be a pattern of filial piety. On one occasion, when his father came to his house to visit him, he had all his concubines hidden away in remote parts of the house, and only his wife was present to receive the Emperor. The servants, too, about the house, were old and ugly looking, and everything was severely simple, both in his wife's dress and in the furnishing of their home. Yang-kien was delighted with this, and mentally contrasted all this with the mode of life of his eldest son, who was straightforward and open in his conduct, and lived in a manner becoming the heir to a great empire. The young man was cunning enough, moreover, to gain the powerful advocacy of Yang-su by lavish presents to him and by paying court to him and treating him as though he were his patron. Through these means, and by the powerful influence of his mother, who kept the Emperor constantly irritated by reports of the misbehaviour of Yung, Yang-kien at length determined to appoint the second son his successor instead of him. This determination was publicly carried out, and Yung was stripped of every title that he had and made a commoner.

On the day on which this notable act was performed Yang-kien appeared in the hall of audience, dressed in complete armour, as though he were going to meet an armed foe. Yung, who had prepared no plan of defence against the charges that had been so skilfully made to assume so serious an aspect, was completely paralyzed, and seemed all the more guilty to his father, because he had nothing to say for himself. Yang-kien upbraided him with his unfilial conduct, his lavish expenditure and the evils of his life. He then declared him unfit for the high position he had intended for him, and stripping him of all his honours and dignities which, as heir to the throne, he had possessed, he reduced him to the rank of the common people. He then summoned the officers of Yung's household and condemned them, because they had not warned their master to desist from the evil life he had been leading, and to live one more befitting the son of a king. Last of all he called the teacher of his son and publicly rebuked him, because he had not used his position to lead him into virtuous habits. This gentleman had more courage than all the rest, and was not going to be silenced, even by so great a man as the Emperor. In a loud voice he indignantly repelled the accusations that had been made against Yung. "Every one here," he said, "knows that you have done a great wrong in disinheriting your son, but there is no one that has the courage to tell you so. I have, however, for I am not afraid of death, or of anything you may do to me. Your son is not by any means so bad as you have represented. He is a straight-forward man, neither very good nor very bad. You are surrounded by traitors, who have inflamed you against him, and to-day you have done a grievous wrong to him. If you had only a better knowledge of men, and had taught your son more wisely, things would not have come to the pass they have done to-day. I pray you to reconsider your determination and give back to Yung the honour of which you have deprived him, for remember that the history of China, from the remotest times till the present, bears witness to the fact that wherever there has been a setting aside of the true heir to the throne the dynasty has ere long perished and a new one taken its place.'' This bold speech of the scholar had a marked effect upon Yang-kien, and made him thoughtful. There was a ring of truth about it that impressed him deeply, and had he not been surrounded by traitors that were determined upon the destruction of Yung he might have restored his unfortunate son to the position of which he had first deprived him. Unfortunately for himself he was. Under the influence of his wife, and that of Yang-su, who was working vigorously against Yung, only a month after the famous scene described above the second son was appointed successor to Yang-kien. Immediately after this fatal act was committed the historian records that earthquakes took place throughout the empire, as if to show that the very earth reeled at the iniquity that had been done, and that the dynasty of Sui was doomed to destruction. Yang-kien, however, did not seem greatly moved by these signs that struck terror into men's hearts, and that to nearly every one but himself foreboded sorrow and calamity to the empire. He had done the deed, and he was not going to reverse it. This year the Turcomans, forgetting the treaty of peace they had made not many years ago, began to ravage the frontiers of the country. They had latterly grown greatly in power, and had begun to have ambitious views about the conquest of China. Other barbarian tribes had been able to stand face to face with the rulers of that country and had held sway in it, and why should not they, they thought. They were mistaken, however, in the times. The empire was too strong for them yet. Shih-man, a general of distinction, was sent against them, who signally defeated them and returned to Ch'ang-ngan with great honour to himself and the army he commanded. Yang-su, who was jealous of the distinction he had won, as though it reflected upon himself, so represented the matter to Yang-kien that Shih-man was deprived of the rewards that were due to him. This so enraged him that he appealed to the Emperor, who, however, still influenced by the evil report given him by Yang-su, refused to do him justice. Angry expostulations were uttered by the disappointed general, when Yang-kien ordered his officers to seize him and have him executed at once.

In the year A. D. 602 Yang-kien issued a command that all the schools in the district, prefectural and departmental cities should be given up, and the only one left should be the Imperial College at the capital. This order was given, no doubt, for two reasons. First, because Yang-kien, being an uneducated person, did not value instruction as a man in his position ought to have done. He had a perfect contempt for the high classical education which constituted the curriculum which every scholar had to pass. The elegant phrases and the refined sentences of the literary class were an abomination to him. "If a man wants to write anything," he said, "let him do it in the most direct and forcible language he can find, and don't let him waste his time in searching the Classics, or in wandering up and down amongst the books of the learned for some phrase that may express his meaning, perhaps with more elegance, but with a great deal less force than the common words of his own mother tongue can do." A second and more powerful reason was no doubt his desire to save expense. He was of a naturally saving, thrifty disposition, and he could not endure the thought that his people should be taxed for what, after all, he considered to be needless and superfluous.

Next year the third son of Yang-kien, who was a prince in Szchwan, was recalled to the capital by his father to answer a charge of high treason, and for plotting to seize the throne for himself He was condemned, and deprived of all the privileges of sonship, and reduced to the rank of the common people. A short time after, the queen, who had such a pernicious influence on her husband, and who had been the means of destroying the harmony and peace of the family, died. Yang-kien did not elevate any of his numerous concubines to take her place. The favourite that now usurped his affections was a lady of the name of Suan-hoa. This woman had a great influence over him for she was both young and beautiful.

In the sixteenth and last year of his reign he became very ill, and was confined to his room, where he was attended by Suan-hoa and her attendants. Three nobles, of whom Yang-su was one, remained in an apartment close by where the Emperor lay sick, in order to be ready for any commands he might have to give and to watch over the interests of the State. Kwang, the second son, anxious lest any change might take place that would interfere with his succession to the throne, hovered about the palace, and kept up a correspondence with Yang-su and urged him to be faithful to his promise to see that he should become Emperor after the death of his father. One of these fell into the hands of one of the ladies of the palace, who took and showed it to Yang-kien. The sick monarch was exceedingly indignant when he heard it read. "What!" he exclaimed, "is he plotting for my death, this son of mine? I am laid aside with a slight illness, and he begins to talk of becoming Emperor. He had better mind what he is about, or he may never have the opportunity of succeeding me." A short time after this matters were brought to a crisis. Suan-hoa had occasion to leave the room, when she was met by Kwang, who was rude to her. To escape him she rushed back into the Emperor's room. Yang-kien, seeing her flushed and excited, asked her what was the matter with her. She replied by telling him how improperly she had been treated by the prince. Excited beyond measure at his conduct he exclaimed passionately, "Beast that he is, he is utterly unworthy of the honour that I have given him," and then it flashed upon him that he had been systematically deceived with regard to the character of this man. As the truth dawned upon him he cursed his dead wife for the part she had taken in alienating his heart from his eldest son and in causing him to make Kwang his heir.

When his passion had somewhat cooled down he summoned two of his nobles and gave orders that they should immediately send for Yung. The edict was drawn up and signed with the royal seal, and messengers were about to be sent to the residence of the prince to bring him to the bedside of his father. Before they could leave the palace Yang-su came in, and seeing at a glance that unless prompt and decided action was taken Kwang's chances of becoming Emperor would be lost, stopped the issue of the edict, and calling a high mandarin of the palace, named Chang-heng, to his counsels, consulted with him as to what ought to be done in this emergency. Chang-heng was a confederate of Kwang and a man who was not troubled by qualms of conscience to be prevented from the perpetration of the most desperate deeds. By his advice an order was issued in the name of Yang-kien that Yung should be seized and imprisoned. Meanwhile Kwang had joined the conspirators, and everything that was done from this time may be said to have been carried out under his immediate supervision. Chang-heng now collected twenty or thirty desperate fellows, who were prepared for murder, and by the prince's command they proceeded to the apartment of the Emperor with the intention, they said, of caring for the sick man. Orders were at the same time given that the ladies who were in attendance upon him should all retire. Not many minutes after this band of ruffians had entered the Emperor's bedroom they came out, declaring that his disease had terminated suddenly and that Yang-kien was no more. Immediately the news spread throughout the palace and the capital, and every one, without a moment's hesitation, ascribed his death to the wicked act of his own son, the future Emperor of China. A few hours after this terrible deed had been committed a messenger was announced from Kwang to Suan-hoa with a casket, which was to be given her. She was full of fright when she received it, for she was convinced that it contained an order for her to put herself to death. She was terribly agitated, and for some minutes had not the strength to open it. When she did at length do so she found, to her amazement and that of her attendants, that it contained what might be termed a true lover's knot, which at a glance she saw was an invitation of Kwang that she should consent to become a member of his seraglio, and thus one of the royal concubines.*

Her first impulse was to reject with scorn the present of the murderer of her husband and of his father, and she threw it down contemptuously from her on the table. She would not even give any answer to the messenger that brought it, but ordered that he should be dismissed without any reply. Her maids gathered round her and besought her to reconsider her decision, and showed her the peril she was putting her life in by thus treating a man who was now lord of the whole empire. After long delay and driven to desperation by the unhappy circumstances in which she was placed, she at length was prevailed upon to send a favourable answer by the messenger, and from this point she disappears from history, where for a short time she had played so prominent a part. Next day Kwang was proclaimed Emperor, and by his order his brother Yung was murdered in his prison. The character of the murdered Yang-kien was one full of contrasts. It had its virtues and its failings, which existed side by side. He was a most diligent ruler of his people, and was continually planning for their interests. He promoted the study of the methods by which agriculture might be advanced, and he encouraged the manufacture of silk. He was economical not only in the management of his own household, but also in the government of the state, with the result that during his reign the taxes were exceptionally light. The effect upon the people was good, and the extravagance that had prevailed amongst the people from the bad example of their rulers was greatly modified amongst every class of society. On the other hand, he was stern and passionate, and too ready to listen to any story that a person had to tell him about another. He treated his own sons as though they were his enemies, with the result that they had no affection for him, and one of them murdered him when there seemed a danger of his losing the throne. He was exacting to a degree from those with whom he constantly associated ; and the men who had distinguished themselves in his services, and had been loyally rewarded by him, rarely kept his favour for very long. On the other hand, he was magnanimous to his enemies, as was seen in his treatment of How Chu, who instead of being put to death after the capture of Nanking was loyally entertained in his own capital and died just about the time that Yang-kien was murdered. It was a true Nemesis that caused him to lose his life in very much the same manner as that in which he had cut short the days of Suan Ti. When the conspirators rushed in to his sick room to carry out their

* The present that Kwang sent Suan-hoa, and which has, in a rough way, been translated by "true lover's knot," was made of silk or satin, and represented two pieces of fruit with only one stone common to them both. It is an emblem amongst the Chinese of devoted affection.

murderous intention there must have flashed across his mind the memory of that day when he paid his solitary visit to that monarch, and the tragedy that followed, and he must have felt that Heaven was about to avenge the crime that he committed then. The new Emperor is known in history by the name of

Yang Ti—A. D. 605-617.

This monarch was twenty-seven years old when he ascended the throne, and he reigned twelve years. His first great act was the removal of the capital from Ch'ang-ngan to Lohyang and his entrusting to Yang-su the building of magnificent palaces for the reception of himself and his immense household. It is said that two millions of men were employed in the construction of these. This estimate is no doubt grossly exaggerated, but we can still believe, after large deductions have been made, that an immense number must have been employed. This is the more to be believed when we consider that Yang Ti was a prince who was wildly extravagant in his ways, and that his harem consisted of over three thousand ladies, who had all to be housed in a right loyal way. In addition to the royal buildings Yang Ti had given orders for the laying out of an immense garden. This was to be of enormous extent and made without any regard to expense. The rarest plants from every part of the empire that would grow in this more northern region were brought and planted in it. The flowering trees and bushes were never without their flowers the year round, for, when nature failed to supply them, skilled workmen were always in attendance who, with silk and satin, made such exquisite imitations of those fallen that from the distance they seemed the very productions of nature. In the centre of it there was an immense lake five miles wide and three artificial islands, each a hundred feet high, with hills and grottoes and valleys in imitation of those to be found on the mainland. Whilst these gigantic works were being carried out Yang Ti gave orders to one of his ministers, named Hong-yu, for the construction of that immense system of canals with which his name is associated and which proved of such great service to the people of the regions in which they were made. One of these extended from the river Pien, a branch of the Han, in Hupeh, to the river Sz, a short stream in Shantung and a feeder at the present time of the Grand Canal. From the Sz another communicated with the river Hwai, a stream that drains Honan and Nganhwuy and then flows into the lake Hung-tsih. He also ordered the existing water courses at Han, in Kiang-ngan, to be widened, so that they should become navigable for boats as far as Kiang-keu.* One of the main objects of this luxurious Emperor in making these canals was, no doubt, his own pleasure and gratification. He had early formed the purpose

---

* As far back as the time of the "Warring States" a canal and city of the name of Kan-keu existed near this place.

of going in state to visit the various parts of his empire, and to do this in the easiest and most comfortable way was certainly by water. He therefore had thirty or forty thousand boats built for his own special service, which were called dragon boats, and which were ever ready to be used whenever he should require them.   As may be imagined, an immense multitude of people were pressed into the service of the state to carry out these gigantic works.   The canals were no mere ditches along which boats might be poled, but works of art upon which the æsthetic eye of Yang Ti could look with pleasure.   They were forty paces wide, and lined with stone to prevent the waste of the banks by the wash of the water.   On the roads on each side of the canal willow trees were planted at regular intervals, which gave a grateful shade to those that passed along them.   As Yang Ti's orders were imperative that both they and the dragon boats should be completed as rapidly as possible, the greatest suffering was endured by those engaged upon them, so that it is stated that between forty and fifty per cent. of the hundreds of workmen employed died through over-exertion.

The first royal journey that the Emperor made was from Lohyang to Nanking, and the immense procession of boats extended for over sixty miles.   Eighty thousand soldiers were appointed to the duty of dragging these, for as it was a pleasure trip and the winds uncertain it was decided that sails should be dispensed with and the boats be towed by men who were under military discipline, and who could therefore be relied on for doing their work in a systematic manner.   The royal barge was two hundred feet long and forty feet high with four decks.   The uppermost one was where Yang Ti held his audiences and met with his great ministers.   The second contained the bedrooms, whilst the third and fourth were for the accommodation of his queen and the more favoured of his concubines.   Every district through which they passed had to provide provisions for this immense host of people, and a continued stream of carts could be seen converging towards the direction of this mighty pageant laden with the luxuries that were demanded for the Emperor's table and those of his household.

During the journey Yang Ti took it into his head to change the character of the dresses of his suite and of the ladies that had accompanied him.   They were too sombre, he thought, and hardly befitting such a joyous occasion as this, when music and laughter and smiles and bright coloured trimmings to their dresses should testify to the happiness and delight that everyone felt.   He accordingly issued his royal commands that the mandarins on shore should provide an abundance of the feathers of all the most beautiful and various coloured birds that were to be found in their districts, for the adorning and trimming of the dresses of all those who had the honour of being admitted into his presence.   At once the people were ordered by their officers to disperse into the woods and on to the mountain sides and trap and kill and slay every bird that they saw with a bright plumage. The consequence was that ere long the districts on both sides of the canal were denuded of any but the very commonest birds. The rest had all been killed to satisfy the whim of this tyrannical and luxurious despot. After an absence of eight months the royal party returned to the capital, and Yang Ti, who was a scholar and took a great interest in everything that concerned the literary class, issued an edict announcing that examinations would be held in Lohyang, when the new degree of Tsin-sze would be conferred on all candidates that passed it (A. D. 607).* For some time there had been a coolness between the Emperor and Yang-su. He had begun to suspect him of disloyalty, but the real reason no doubt was that he had been the main instrument in the murder of his father, and though the chief responsibility rested with Yang Ti himself, who had given the final order that resulted in his death, he could not feel happy in the presence of a man who was a partner with him in such a hideous crime. He was determined therefore to get rid of him as soon as a favourable pretext occurred. One came sooner than he expected, for the astronomer royal announced to the Emperor that from omens he observed in the sky a great man would this year die in the state of Ch'u.† Yang Ti immediately appointed Yang-su to the government of the region indicated, with the title of the Duke of Ch'u. The intention of the Emperor was so manifest to his whole court and to the unfortunate man himself by this action that it struck him with terror. He knew now that his death was desired and would ultimately be accomplished in some terribly cruel manner. This so worked upon his feelings that he lost all interest in life and soon became seriously ill. When his doctor wished to prescribe for him he refused to take any medicine. "I wish to die," he said, "for I have no longer any desire to live now that the Emperor has turned away his favour from me." And die he did in the course of a few weeks.

Whilst the man who had really put Yang Ti on the throne was dying, the latter was absorbed in plans for getting up festivities on a vast and gorgeous scale to do honour to Ch'i-ming, the chief of the Turcomans, who was coming to pay him a visit. This man had married a Chinese princess, and was on terms of the most intimate friendship with him. Whilst the capital was being adorned for his reception, and musicians were being summoned from far and near with their newest tunes and songs to add to the gaieties

---

* There are three literary degrees obtainable by the scholars of China. The first is the Sew-tsai, somewhat like our B.A.; the second the Ku-jin, corresponding to our M.A., and the third the Tsin-sze, a little like our D.C.L. or LL.D. There is a further honour to which literary graduates may aspire, and that is to become members of the Imperial Academy, which may be done only by a very severe examination at the capital, the Emperor being the nominal examiner.

† This ancient kingdom of Ch'u occupied the present Hunan, Hupeh and parts of Honan and Kiangsu. The title, kingdom of Ch'u, is given to the two lake provinces to the present day.

by which the savage mind of the powerful barbarian was to be amused, the Emperor gave orders for the construction of two public granaries where cereals could be collected in seasons of plenty to be used either in distribution to the people in times of famine, or for the use of his armies when engaged in distant campaigns. One of these was to the north of Lohyang, with three hundred pits, and the other in the country city of Kung, situated on the river Loh at its junction with the Yellow River, which had three thousand. In each pit there was stored over a hundred thousand pounds weight of grain.

The year A. D. 608 was distinguished by two royal visitations which Yang Ti made to the northern part of his dominions, during both of which he met Ch'i-ming, and on one of them was entertained by him. Arrangements were made for a closer intimacy between the Chinese and the Turcomans by giving every encouragement to the development of commercial relationships between the two peoples. A superintendent of trade was appointed, who should reside in Shensi and arrange any difficulties that might occur and protect the Turcomans, that might come into China to trade, from the tricks of the more clever and astute Chinese. This officer, seeing that Yang Ti was foreign in his inclinations, took care to present such reports as he knew would be acceptable to him. He had a work in three volumes compiled that described the manners and customs of the Turcomans, and presented it to His Majesty. He represented that the various tribes outside the frontiers of China were anxious to make their submission to him, and were waiting with the greatest impatience for some intimation from him that they would be permitted to do so. This was an entire fabrication of his, as well as the statement that their territories abounded in gold and silver and precious stones, which they were not civilized enough to know how to use.

Yang Ti, whose self-importance was vastly increased by the idea that so many barbarian rulers were willing to throw themselves at his feet, gave instructions to the superintendent of trade to have the ambassadors forwarded to the capital, and also that due honour and respect should be paid them by the officials and people along their journey. The story of the desire of the barbarians to become vassals of China existed only in the imagination of this wily official, and therefore he was greatly perplexed to know how to obey the orders he had received. The Chinese mind is, however, a highly inventive one in emergencies like the present, and shines in overcoming difficulties that would paralyze a Westerner. He easily arranged with a number of these chieftains to send their representatives to the court. This they were assured would commit them in reality to nothing, and besides, they would have their expenses all paid and a considerable sum over, which he promised them as a bribe for complying with his wishes.

They were only too glad to perform the pleasant services that they were asked to do, and before long their ambassadors were on their way to carry out the farce they had been taught. After entering China their journey was one long pleasure excursion. They were loyally lodged and entertained, of course at the expense of the people, and every attention was shown them, for they were the guests of their sovereign, who would resent any incivility shown them.

This year the famous commander and statesman who had been one of the most trusted and loved of Yang-kien's ministers was put to death by the order of Yang Ti. This loyal servant of the state had expressed his concern at the lavish expenditure of the Emperor, and he had also bemoaned the extreme friendship that existed between the chieftain of the Turcomans and his own infatuated sovereign.

"He is teaching him the way to China," he said, "and he is allowing him to see the weak points of the country, and in some time of national difficulty he will come with his hordes of horsemen and sweep away the dynasty before him." These words were reported to Yang Ti, and to show that he would allow no man to criticize him he cut off his head. Future events proved that the fears of the old statesman were well founded, and in the wreck of the house of Yang his words turned out to have been a prophecy of the coming destruction of it.

Whilst Yang Ti was on his visit to Ch'i-ming, he observed amongst the attendants that thronged round the tents of this chieftain a number of men in a strange garb, and with features unlike the rest of the Turcomans. Upon enquiry he found that they were Corean ambassadors that had come to pay tribute to Ch'i-ming. Yang Ti thought it a thing not to be endured that Corea, that had acknowledged the Emperor of China as lord paramount in the times of the Ts'in and Han dynasties, should now be recognizing the supremacy of the barbarian Turcomans, whilst the great empire of China should be considered unworthy of the fealty of the descendants of the men who in the early days had gone forth from that very land to form their kingdom in the east. In due time ambassadors were despatched to the court of the Corean king with a peremptory order that he should send his tribute bearers to Lohyang, and from this time forward consider himself a vassal of the dragon throne. The king refused to do anything of the kind, and an angry feeling was engendered at the court of Yang Ti, whilst one of defiance was the prevailing one at the other.

Four years went by without any action being taken to force the claim, but in the year A. D. 612 a very large army was led by Yu-wen, the Chinese general, to invade Corea. Immense preparations had been made to make the campaign successful. Three hundred ships had been built in Shantung, and fifty thousand carts had been made in Kiangnan for the transport of provisions, which were stored in the great granary at Loh, above described. Men, too, had been pressed as soldiers for a war that was not popular with the nation at large, and consequently the empire was filled with discontent. Not only were the people impoverished by the repeated calls upon them to meet the lavish expenditure of their magnificent Emperor, but their sons were pressed to do work for the state for which they were badly remunerated, and through which thousands of them died in consequence of the hardships they had to endure, and now their children were called upon to fight far from their homes with all the chances against them of their ever seeing them again. This Corean war seemed to have been the last straw that broke down the faith and loyalty of the nation to Yang Ti. Insurrections broke out simultaneously in different parts of the empire. The leader of one of these was named Tow-kien, who had a following of over ten thousand men in Chihli. Songs were made that became popular amongst the lower classes, and were sung everywhere by them. The chorus in many of these was that it was better to become a rebel than be impressed as a soldier and die by the swords of the men of Liau-tung.*

The great army of the Chinese consisted of three hundred and five thousand men, accompanied by Yang Ti, who was always of a roving disposition, and who was determined to be present at the great victory which he had no doubt his troops would obtain over the Coreans. It crossed the river Liau in the middle of July, A. D. 613, and proceeded to invest the capital of Liau-tung, but it had been so strongly fortified that the Chinese could make no impression upon it. Next month a great battle was fought near the river Yalu, in which the Coreans gained a most decisive victory. Of the immense force that marched confidently to battle only two thousand seven hundred men. managed to escape. The Emperor had to fly for his life, and all the baggage and war material of this great host fell into the hands of the conquerors, together with a very large number of prisoners.

When Yang Ti returned to Lohyang he ordered the great mandarin who had the chief management in the equipping of the late army to be put to death, and all the officers that had escaped to be reduced to the ranks. Immediately after this he commanded Chang-heng, the man whom he had employed to murder his father, to be executed. He had long been suspicious that he was meditating rebellion and had employed spies to watch his proceedings and report any treasonable words that he might utter against him. Hitherto he had not been able to gain the evidence he wished, when very unexpectedly a person appeared who gave him exactly the

---

* Liau-tung was that part of Manchuria lying to the east of the river Liau, and now known by the name of Shing-king. In the times of the Sui dynasty it was subject to Corea, but it now forms part of the Chinese empire.

very kind of testimony that he had desired to convict him. This one of the concubines of Chang-heng, who having been ill-treated by him, was determined to have her revenge by informing against him to the Emperor. She declared that he had been accustomed to vilify and speak evil of him and to express his hatred and detestation of him. The process of law was short in this case. The accused was seized and by the imperial commands led to instant execution. When he saw that death was inevitable he cried out that Heaven was just in bringing about the punishment that he was now going to undergo, for his crime in the murder of Yang-kien was such as could be satisfied only by his death. The officers standing by, in order not to listen to a confession that might compromise them, and perhaps lead to their murder, covered their ears with their hands and cried out to the executioner to take off his head quickly. This was done, and thus another of the great actors in the tragedy that had put Yang Ti on the throne disappeared from the scene, no more to trouble his conscience by their presence, or to remind him of the terrible crime he had committed.

In the beginning of A. D. 614 Yang Ti appointed his grandson Yew, the Prince of Tai, to the command of Shensi, whilst another of the name of T'ung, the Prince of Yueh, was put in charge of Lohyang. In the month of April he led a new expedition against Corea. His most faithful minister tried to dissuade him from this enterprise by representing that the conquest of Corea was a matter utterly unworthy of a great ruler like himself, and that he ought not to spend his strength on such a miserable object. "You would never dream," said one of them, "of using a ballista of a thousand pounds weight to shoot a rat, and why should you undergo the fatigue and expense of this long journey to subdue a country that is beneath your notice"? Yang Ti refused to listen to his advice, and the great armament proceeded on its way, but he was destined to return sooner than he had imagined. One of the officers employed in connection with the expedition was Huan-kan, one of the sons of Yang-su. He was a scholar and proficient in all manly exercises, and by his amiability and fine social qualities had gathered round him a large number of friends. Smarting under the injuries that his father had received from Yang Ti he had determined at the first favourable opportunity to rise in rebellion against him. None seemed to him more suitable than the present when the empire was honeycombed with rebellion, and Yang Ti was away with nearly all the forces of the state on a most unpopular campaign. He had charge of the commissariat, and had under his command five thousand men, who were engaged in the transport of provisions for the royal army. These he could depend upon to follow him wherever he should lead them. Sending for a scholar of the name of Li-mi, who was famous as a strategist, and who from this time took a most prominent part in the troubles that distinguished the last days of the Sui dynasty, he unfolded to him his scheme for overthrowing the government, and asked him to act now in the place of a military adviser and tell him what course he should take so as to ensure success. "I have three plans to suggest to you," Li-mi replied, "two of which will certainly lead to success, and possibly the third also. These are : First, let us boldly march and attack the Emperor with the force that you have, and those that will gather round you when it has become known that you have raised the standard of rebellion ; second, march on Chang-ngan, which would be easily captured and held, and from there operate on the rest of the country ; and thirdly, advance on Lohyang and seize it if possible." The last was looked upon by Li-mi as the most unsatisfactory of the three, for he did not know the strength of the defences of the capital. If they were great and could resist long enough, there was danger that Yang Ti might be able to send such a force to its relief as would cause destruction to Huan-kan and his adherents. Contrary to his advice Huan-kan determined to adopt this last plan. He accordingly made forced marches into Honan and besieged the city. Tidings of this outbreak were rapidly carried to Yang Ti, who at once marched a large force to succour it. He arrived in time to save it from falling into the hands of Huan-kan, who was destroyed with all his followers, except such as were fortunate enough to escape. A terrible and bloody revenge was taken upon the people of the district who had shown sympathy to the rebels. Over thirty thousand of them were murdered in cold blood, and, in addition to these, every person who had partaken of the food which Huan-kan had distributed from the imperial granary at Loh was seized and summarily executed. Another prominent figure now comes upon the stage of history in the person of Li-yuan, whose family were destined to be the chief actors in the mighty changes that were soon to take place in the empire. He had been appointed to the governorship of a district in the present province of Shensi. He is represented as being a very generous-hearted man, and one who had gained the respect and homage of a large circle of persons. He was, moreover, of noble appearance and a physique that attracted attention wherever he went. Yang Ti seems to have had his misgivings about him, and these were increased by his being told that there was a prophecy that a man of the name of Li would one day become Emperor. Determined that Li-yuan should not be the man, if he could help it, he sent orders for him to appear at court, as he had important business to transact with him. Li-yuan hastened to obey the summons, but fortunately for himself he fell ill on the way and consequently was delayed in reaching the capital. Yang Ti could not conceal his satisfaction that the man he feared was ill. A nephew of Li-yuan, who was at court, observing this, and fearing that his uncle's death was intended, hurried off to him and warned him of his danger. Having bribed the chief nobles that had the ear of the Emperor they represented to him that Li-yuan was a loyal servant of the state, and that he need have no suspicions about his integrity. Yang Ti was pleased to listen to these representations, and sent him orders to return to his duties in Shensi.

The year A. D. 615 was an eventful one for Yang Ti. Another expedition was led against Corea, but when the army reached Shing-king, ambassaders came from the king of that country with his submission to the Chinese and his declaration that he was willing to become the vassal of the Emperor. The terms having speedily been agreed to, and Corea having been added to the conquests of the empire, Yang Ti returned to his own dominions, but instead of coming to his capital he made one of his luxurious tours through Shensi. Some of his ministers having remonstrated with him, and showing him that the country was in rebellion, and could not stand the heavy drain that was being made upon it by these journeys, he had them put to death, but he soon after returned to Lohyang. Three months after, he started with his immense train for Shansi. He was in extraordinary good spirits just now, for the omens all pointed to the prolonging of his reign and the prosperity of his dynasty. One day two peacocks had flown into the palace. These are most unlucky birds, and presage war and destruction and disaster in the state. One of the courtiers declared that they were phœnixes, which are the harbingers of peace and prosperity, and reported this to Yang Ti. He was extremely delighted, and rewarded with splendid presents and high honours the man that told him.

On his arrival in Shansi, Li-yuan was made governor of a district in that province, and seemed to be in as great favour now as he had once been in disgrace. For several months Yang Ti enjoyed life in a way that a man, whose whole time was occupied in devising new pleasures to make time pass agreeably, knew how to plan.

His dreams of happiness were, however, soon rudely broken into, and he had to fly for his life. The Turcomans hearing that the Emperor was so near them conceived the design of seizing him. Accordingly their king, Si-pi, the son of Ch'i-ming who had died, suddenly appeared at the head of a hundred thousand men, and swooping down on Shansi hoped to get possession of Yang Ti before he knew he was in the field. He had, however, got timely warning, and managed to escape to Yen-mun, in the prefecture of T'ai-yuan. Here he was besieged for nearly a month, but these barbarian hosts, being unskilled in such slow and tedious warfare as the taking of fortified towns, had at length to retreat, as troops poured in from every part of the empire to the relief of their sovereign. They accomplished but little, it is true, but it was a bad sign that these savage hordes had dared to invade Chinese territory and to presume to think of laying sacrilegious hands upon its Emperor. In the autumn Yang Ti returned to Lohyang, when he gave orders for the equipment of his dragon boats, as he intended shortly to make a tour to Nanking. This plan was carried out, notwithstanding the entreaties of the most loyal and faithful of his ministers, who represented to him the dangerous condition in which his empire was, and how he was needed at the capital to preserve it from being rent in pieces. His only reply to this was to order one of them to be beaten to death and another to have his head cut off after he had suffered the cruel torture of having his cheeks excised. In the month of August of the year A. D. 617 this self-willed monarch started on his pleasure trip, and in doing so threw from him the crown that was already slipping from his grasp.

We must now turn to the northern part of the empire where stirring events were taking place. Si-pi, the king of the Turcomans, determined to have a say in the distribution of the empire' which so many rebel leaders were parcelling out for themselves, made Liu-wu to be the khan or chief of that part of Shansi that lay nearest his own territories, and promised him the support of his hardy and numerous horsemen. Li-yuan had been persuaded by his bold and ambitious son Shih-min to rebel. When this idea was first presented to him he utterly refused to listen to it, but he was finally convinced that it was his only course of safety when the matter was discussed with him by his son. "If you wish to be loyal," he said, "you have an unprincipled ruler to serve, who will reward you perhaps by putting you to death as he has done to others. If you oppose the rebels you will certainly be murdered by them, for you have not force enough to contend with them. Take either course you like you must die; why not then set up your own standard of rebellion and claim the throne for yourself? It is the desire of the people that you should do so, and it is the will of Heaven that you should succeed." Li-yuan, after a sleepless night spent in thought, said to Shih-min next morning, "I have spent the whole night in considering what you have said to me. I am convinced that the course you advise is the wisest and safest for us to pursue. I therefore agree to it. If we fail and our family is ruined and destroyed you will be responsible, and if we succeed and the empire becomes ours then the merit will belong to you." By the advice of one of his friends, Liu-wun, application was made to Si-pi for assistance. The Turcomans were only too glad to have an excuse for interfering in the affairs of China, and at once acceded to the proposal, the only stipulation being that Li-yuan should become Emperor. All his own officers were unanimous in persuading him to take the advice of Si-pi, but Li-yuan was too wise a statesman to consent to take such a dangerous step before the enterprise on which he had just embarked was sure of success. He accordingly adopted the more politic course of declaring to the nation that he had risen to avenge its wrongs and to defend it from a sovereign that was oppressing them, and through whose extravagance they and their children were starving. He at the same time gave out that from this time the true ruler of the country was no longer Yang Ti, but his grandson Yew, the Prince of Tai, who was now in charge of Shensi. It is a singular fact that the Chinese historians have acknowledged this act of the rebel Li-yuan and count the reign of Yew from this date, though his grandfather was still alive in Nanking.

Kung Ti Yew—A. D. 617-618.

Although Li-yuan took the virtuous roll of the redresser of wrongs, a shrewd observer would not have failed to notice that his action was very far from being disinterested, and that there was an air of treason about his whole movement that showed that ambition was at the root of all his plans. He refused indeed to become Emperor, but he discarded the imperial flag and adopted a white one in its place, which so satisfied Si-pi that he was quite ready to join his forces to his as a rebel against his sovereign. Yew, who saw through his artifice refused to have anything to do with him, and loyally held Shensi for his grandfather and garrisoned the towns of Hwo and Ho-tung. Success, however, everywhere attended Li-yuan and his barbarian allies, and city after city fell into their hands, and finally at the close of the year A. D. 617 Ch'ang-ngan was taken by storm and Yew made prisoner. To the honour of Li-yuan it may be said that he behaved with the greatest clemency and generosity to the captured town. Yew was formally installed as Emperor of China, and no one suffered death except a number of prominent men who had destroyed the ancestral hall of his clan and dug up the graves of his buried kindred when they heard that he had rebelled. A few months before the seizure of Ch'ang-ngan, Li-yuan had written to Li-mi, who was at Lohyang with a large rebel force under his command, to make his submission to him, and Li-yuan, afraid lest he should take it into his head to march his men and attack him, wrote back and told him that as he refused to serve under him he was quite prepared to give way to him and act as his lieutenant. "If we succeed you shall be Emperor," he said, "and I'll be your minister." Li-mi was so overjoyed at his proposal that he never dreamt of looking closely at it, or of considering whether it was likely that Li-yuan, who had formerly been his patron and far above him in rank, would be content to give up all his plans of ambition and quietly submit to have the empire snatched from his grasp. It was only the man's conceit and an inordinate belief in his own really great ability that made him fall into the snare laid for him by Li-yuan and his advisers. In the meanwhile Yang Ti was filled with gloomy forebodings in Nanking, and to drown his sorrows took to the wine cup. He would, when he was sober, wander about in a perplexed and dazed manner examining the heavens to see if he could get any omens there that would comfort him. One day he came in and said to his queen, "There is some one outside that is looking for an opportunity to kill me," and then taking a looking glass he would gaze in it, and striking his neck exclaim, "I wonder who will be the man that will cut this off." His queen was terrified, and besought him not to say such unlucky things, but his only reply was, "Joy and sorrow both come to every man. Let us then bear each as it comes and make the best of life we can."

Yang Ti was not wrong in believing that there were men conspiring against his life. When rebellion was in the air, and every ambitious man who had any following believed that a crown was within his reach, it was no wonder that the men that surrounded him should dream of usurping his power. He had slain the honest men that would have guarded his throne, and only their spectres hovered round him and tormented him with the thought that he had ruthlessly murdered the only men that could have saved him in this hour of his extreme peril. One of his officers, Yu Wen-hwa, the son of the general who suffered such a crushing defeat in the first compaign against the Coreans, led a party into the palace and dragged Yang Ti forth to slay him. When a sword was lifted up to cut off his head the unfortunate man said to the one that held it, "What sin have I committed that you should wish to take away my life?" "Sin," he replied, "why, what sin is there that you have not been guilty of? You have persistently abandoned the ancestral hall where the spirits of your fathers reside; you have roamed endlessly round your kingdom for your own pleasure ; you went needlessly to war with Corea ; you have lived a licentious, profligate life ; you have despoiled the people of their property to waste it upon yourself, so that now thieves and robbers are as thick as bees about the country, and you have never been willing to listen to the advice of your loyal ministers, but have surrounded yourself with men that have pandered to your vices. How can you say that you have no sin ?" "What you say may be true, and that I have injured my people," replied Yang Ti, "but you cannot say that I have ever wronged you. I have treated you well. You have no reason to give why you personally should carry out this cruel act."

The men, however, would not listen to him. They had not come to reason, but to murder, and once more they were seizing hold upon him to kill him, when wishing to save his body from mutilation, a thing that is abhorrent to every Chinaman, he cried out, let me die not by the sword but by poison. The conspirators were in no mood to wait for the slow process of poison, and yet they sympathized with his desire not to have his head severed from his body, so they compromised matters by strangling him with a piece of cloth that they found convenient for the purpose.

When his grandson T'ung, who was in Lohyang, which Li-mi had been unable to take, heard of this tragedy he was greatly distressed, and being urged by his officers to become Emperor he at last consented to do so, feeling that the title was his by right, and that if he did not claim the succession now he might never have the chance to do so again. He is known in history as Kung Ti T'ung. His reign was a brief and troubled one, for he was murdered the same year as that in which he assumed the royal state. About the same time that T'ung was ascending the throne in Lohyang his younger brother Yew was laying aside the royal dignity in Ch'ang-ngan, and voluntarily resigning it to Li-yuan, who now became the founder of the new dynasty of T'ang.

CHAPTER XX.

THE T'ANG DYNASTY (A. D. 618-907).

Kau Tsu—A. D. 618-627.

LI-YUAN, who is known to posterity as Kau Tsu, signalized the commencement of his reign by the attention he paid to learning. The edict which had been passed by Yang-kien abolishing all the principal schools throughout the empire, and retaining only the imperial college at the capital, was rescinded, and once more pupils were gathered in the old buildings and teachers were instructing them in the books of their sages and great men. At the same time he established the degree of Sew-tsai, a title somewhat equivalent to our B.A., and he announced that scholars could obtain this by competing at the public examinations, to be held once in three years in the prefectural cities throughout the country. He also built four ancestral temples, in which were placed the tablets in which the spirits of his father, grandfather and great-grandfather, and those of his wife's relatives were supposed to reside. His wife, Tow, was proclaimed queen, and Kien-ch'eng, his eldest son, heir to the throne.* Kau Tsu seems to have been of a far less blood-thirsty turn of mind than the founders of the dynasties that preceded him. Instead of murdering every member of the late royal house that he could lay his hands upon, he not only spared their lives, but gave them titles and honours, and made them officials in the service of his government.

Whilst these events were going on in Ch'ang-ngan, others of mighty import were being transacted by men who aimed at governing China just as much as Kau Tsu did. Yu Wen-hwa, who had murdered Yang Ti, felt that he could not remain idle whilst so many strong competitors were in the field. He saw that to remain quietly in Nanking whilst Shensi was held by Li-yuan and Honan by Li-mi and T'ung, would be to risk his chance for power, and might result in his overthrow and destruction if he did not at once try and prove the victor in this struggle for the

---

* Kau Tsu's queen was a woman of remarkable force of character, and was possessed of an intellect far above the ordinary. She seems to have inherited these qualities from her father, Tow-i, who was a man of considerable importance during the closing years of the last dynasty; this man had determined that his daughter should marry only a man who was of a highly martial character, and to secure his object he had two peacocks painted on a screen. He then gave out that any man that could pierce the eye of one of these with any arrow at the first shot should obtain his daughter's hand. Competitors appeared from far and near, but each one in succession went away without his daughter. At last Li-yuan claimed the right of having a shot for the maiden, when he not only hit one of the eyes, but transfixed the other without a moment's hesitation, and thus by a double right obtained the gifted and intellectual woman for his wife. She had four sons—Kien-ch'eng, Shih-min, Huan-pa and Yuan-kien—as well as one daughter, who was married to a man of the name of Ch'ai-shau. The real hero of the family was Shih-min, without whose push and ability the house of Li would never have come to the throne.

crown of China. He accordingly led his forces against Li-mi, whose army was stationed near the great imperial granary of Loh. In the engagement that followed Li-mi was defeated, and in order to save himself from destruction he made his submission to T'ung, and was admitted within the city. He had not been long there before he discovered that treason was at work in the palace, and that T'ung's days were numbered, for one of his prominent ministers was already plotting his death. Withdrawing from the city he made his way with as many followers as he could collect to Ch'ang-ngan, where he surrendered himself to Kau Tsu and asked to be taken into his service, promising him that the fidelity of a life-time should witness to the sincerity of his purpose.

Kau Tsu was exceedingly delighted to see him, not only because one formidable rival was thus removed from the field, but also because he knew him to be a man most fertile in resources, a strategist and one who would help him to win the rest of the empire. In order to bind him closely to him he loaded him with honours and created him a duke. Li-mi, to show that he was in earnest, sent one of his officers to Shantung to the district where his power was most recognized, and gave orders that from henceforward the authority of Kau Tsu should be supreme in it. He had at the same time a report drawn up, showing the taxes that this province produced, the number of towns and villages it contained and an approximate estimate of its population. This was delivered over to the Emperor, in order that he might be able to see the exact size and condition of the territory that had submitted to him.

A short time only, however, had elapsed before Li-mi began to repent that he had given in his adhesion to Kau Tsu. He had tasted the sweets of power when he was in command of a large army, and he ill-brooked it to have to submit to the will of another. He determined to make another attempt for the throne, and accordingly he asked leave of Kau Tsu to return to Shantung, under the plea that his presence was needed there to see that the people loyally carried out the promises of submission they had made to him. The great mandarins and nobles were violently opposed to his being allowed to leave the capital. "He is naturally changeable," they said, "and he will rebel as soon as he gets to Shantung. To allow him to go is just like letting loose a tiger on the hills. You will not easily catch him again." Shih-min, who was a large-hearted generous man, refused to listen to them, and granted his request, not, however, before he had appealed to him to be loyal and had supplied him with a large sum of money to defray his expenses by the way. No sooner had he reached his home than he raised the standard of rebellion, but the royal army was upon him before he could concentrate his forces, and his adherents were scattered and he himself slain.

Kau Tsu felt that it was now time for him to endeavour to conquer Honan, for it was too important a province to be left in the hands of the men that now ruled it. The unfortunate T'ung had been set aside by his ambitious minister Wang-shih, who now, under the name of Emperor, presumed to found a new dynasty of his own. As Li-mi had seen, T'ung was a puppet in this man's hands, and one day messengers came abruptly into his presence with the poison that Wang-shih had ordered him to drink. T'ung knew there was no appeal from this command, but he prayed that before he drank it he might be allowed to see his mother and say farewell to her. The wretches peremptorily refused this touching request. T'ung was deeply moved by the thought that he should never see her again, and kneeling down on a mat before the idol which was in the room he cried in a voice of agony to it, "When I come again into the world never let me be born the descendant of an Emperor," and then rising he drank down the poison.* As it worked too slowly for the ruffians that stood by they strangled him, and soon the empty palace was occupied by Wang-shih, who, however, was shortly to pay the penalty of his misdeeds. In the year A. D. 662 Shih-min was sent into Shansi to subdue it for his father. After a number of battles, in which he was victorious, the whole of that region submitted to him. He then advanced on Honan, and after a desperate battle at Ku-shuy, in which Wang-shih was defeated, he stormed Lohyang, where he captured the rebel king and Tow-kien as well, who had come to his assistance. They were both sent to Ch'ang-ngan, where they were put to death. In this campaign around Lohyang, Shih-min was greatly helped by a hero of these times, named Yu Chin-kung, who has become a prominent figure in the life of the Chinese ever since. On one occasion, when Shih-min was out with five hundred horses on a reconnaissance, he was surrounded suddenly by Wang-shih with a force of ten thousand men. Yu Chih-kung hearing of this broke singly through the enemies' lines and brought him out safely, just as the imperial troops advanced to his rescue.†

Kau Tsu ordered that every man who was of age should pay to the government as a tax every year twenty catties of grain, two pieces of thin silk stuff and four ounces of raw cotton.‡

---

* He here referred to metempsychosis, a prominent doctrine of Buddhism.

† Yu Chih-kung was a man of immense strength, and possessed great skill in the management of his lance, so that he became the undoubted hero of many a well-fought battle. He became very devoted to Shih-min, to whom he had surrendered in the Shansi campaign. It is told that when the latter became Emperor, and the royal apartments were said to be haunted by malignant spirits that sought his destruction, he and his comrade Ts'in-k'iung kept watch over them, so that none could approach him. In commemoration of this service the Emperor ordered the portraits of these two men to be painted on his palace doors, a custom which has been continued to the present day, and they are now worshipped under the titles of the "Guardians of the Door." Not only have they been honoured by a place at the entrance of the palace, but their figures are also seen on the doors of all public offices in China, where they appear as keeping watch over the affairs of state and guarding the interests of the nation.

‡ A catty is equal to 1⅓lb. In the present day a piece of silk contains about eighteen yards. A man is of age when he is sixteen years old.

He also issued an edict commanding that the currency should henceforward consist of copper coins, each of which should weigh the tenth of an ounce. This was a very important enactment, for during the last years of the Sui dynasty the greatest irregularities had arisen in the circulating medium. The extravagance of Yang Ti had caused money to be so scarce that the precious metals had almost disappeared, and pieces of leather and even of paper with their fictitious values stamped upon them were used in buying and selling. Meanwhile the work of pacifying the empire went on. Shih-min was successful wherever he went. Soon Nanking and the region round, as well as the whole of Kweichow, gave in their allegiance to the new dynasty, and if there were any malcontents left they were of too insignificant a character to need any but the local authorities to deal with them. Shih-min therefore returned to the capital and began to give his mind to what was really the most enjoyable thing to him, viz., the study of literature. He had a building of his own, which was specially devoted to this one object. Here were gathered eighteen famous scholars, whose names have been recorded in history, because of their erudition, and scholarly men besides were invited to attend to assist in the discussions that were held between this famous man and his learned friends in their search for truth. At the time that these studies were going on there was a determined effort made by his eldest brother Kien-ch'eng and his youngest, Yuan-chieh, to undermine his influence with his father. They were jealous because Kau Tsu loved him better than any in the family, and also because of his wonderful ability and the success that had attended everything he had undertaken. To carry out their wicked plot they began to insinuate doubts in the ear of their father about his loyalty to him. The royal concubines who had been gained over to their side also took every opportunity of whispering their fears to Kau Tsu about the integrity of the son in whom he so implicitly trusted. His very virtues were distorted, and made the ground of a serious accusation against him. One day he came into the presence of his father weeping. Unforgetful of etiquette, or of the presence of royalty, he allowed his tears to fall as he thought of the death of his mother, whom he had loved passionately. The concubines represented this filial act as an insult to the Emperor and a menace to themselves, because the prince insinuated that they had taken his mother's place in his heart, and for this he would be avenged. The father, who was a weak-minded man, was easily influenced by the gossip of these women, and so his heart became estranged from his son.

In the year A. D. 625 the Turcomans, under the leadership of their chief, Chieh-li, invaded Shensi. Some of the ministers represented to Kau Tsu the advisability of removing the capital to Lohyang. "The reason why these barbarians make so many incursions into our territory is because Ch'ang-ngan is so near them, and they are continually being tempted by its wealth to come and plunder it. Let us burn it to the ground," they said, "and emigrate to Honan, and then the temptation being removed these raids of the Turcomans will cease." The Emperor was about to consent to this pusillanimous proposal, when Shih-min interposed with his advice. "Let us do nothing so disgraceful," he said to his father. "These inroads of the savages are no new things. From the earliest times they have been accustomed to make them. The whole empire would scorn us should we fly before their presence now, and our newly-established dynasty would be endangered." "We are strong," he continued, "and we need not fear them. Give me the soldiers I require, and I guarantee that in a few years I will bring you the head of Chieh-li and lay it at your feet."

These heroic words turned the scale, and Shih-min's request was granted. When his brothers heard of what had been done they went in haste to their father and made him believe that the only object of Shih-min, in requesting an army to subdue Chieh-li, was that he might have the means of rebelling and getting the throne for himself. The weak-minded sovereign accepted their statements as true, and calling him into his presence he scolded him for the treasonable thoughts which it had never occurred to him to have. He also concluded a treaty with the Turcomans, and though the historian does not say so, it is manifest from the rapidity with which they retired beyond the frontiers that they were induced to do so by substantial presents from the royal treasury.

Kau Tsu issued an edict allowing his people to worship Heaven and Earth, and to erect altars to them when they did so. This was a great privilege which had hitherto been the prerogative of the ruler of the nation. He also issued orders to all the magistrates in the country that they should examine into the condition and character of all the Buddhist temples and nunneries throughout the empire, and that wherever they found persons pure in character and earnest in their faith they were to remove such to some of the more prominent temples, and cause that all the rest should be sent back into the world to do their own proper share of work in it. This action was taken mainly because of the irregular lives and bad morals of the great mass of those who had given their lives to the service of the idols. Fully a hundred thousand bonzes and nuns were scattered throughout the country in the various Buddhist establishments, and their bad fame had caused one of the ministers of the Emperor named Fu-yih to petition that they might be dealt with and no longer be permitted to demoralize the people by their bad example. In the document that he presented to Kau Tsu he said, "The idols come from the regions of the West. Their books, when translated into our language, are full of falsehoods and deceive the people. The bonzes give up their parents, and they eat, but they will not work. They are no help to the state, for they claim to be exempt from taxation. We say that life, and death, and riches, and poverty are at the disposal of Heaven.   They say that it is the idol that has the control of these things, and so they would snatch all power from it.   They are a danger to the state.   Before the idols came the Emperors were intelligent and his ministers loyal, but after their arrival the former became stupid and the latter treacherous.   We have evidence of this in the history of the five dynasties.   Let the bonzes and nuns be sent back to their homes, and let them marry and be given in marriage."   All the nobles with one exception applauded these words.   Siau-ho said, "Fu-yih has not spoken the truth, and he ought to be punished. The idols are holy men that have been canonized, and are worthy of the highest honour."   Fu-yih replied, "The relationships between the ruler and his subjects and between parents and their children are the greatest we have in human life.   The idols do not recognize these, and therefore they should be discarded."   The only reply that the angry Siau-ho deigned to give was, "The Buddhist religion has told us of a hell, which has been undoubtedly created for the reception of such men as you."

The jealousy of the two brothers against Shih-min became more and more bitter as time went on, and they laid their heads together to destroy him.   On one occasion they invited him to drink wine with them.   He had not drunk much before he was attacked with pains and violent vomiting.   He knew at once that an attempt had been made to poison him, and as soon as he recovered he went to Kau Tsu to complain of his brothers.   His father was greatly distressed, and said to him, "You know that the whole merit of placing our family in its present position of power and glory belongs to you.   I wished to make you the heir, but you refused.   I see with sorrow that your brothers cannot live in harmony with you. I therefore propose that you separate.   I'll give you Lohyang and all the country east of it, and you shall rule over it as though you were a king."   Shih-min readily agreed to this proposal, but it was thwarted by his brothers, who again got the ear of their father and represented that to allow such power to be given into the hands of a man who was ready to rebel would be to throw away the empire.   But the crisis was at hand.   The eldest son had been appointed to the command of an army that he was going to lead against the Turcomans, who had again invaded Shensi.   A feast was to be given before he started, and Shih-min was bound to be there.

It was arranged by the conspirators that he was to be murdered at the banquet.   Timely information of this reached him, and a council of his officers was called to decide what should be done in this crisis.   They were unanimous that Shih-min should take the initiative and save himself by slaying his brothers.   At first he would not listen to the proposal, but by and by as it became plain that he could only escape death by doing so his mind gradually inclined to the advice of his captains.   At last he said, "Let us divine in order to see whether it is the will of Heaven that I should do this crime." One of his officers cried out, "Men divine about that which is uncertain. There is no uncertainty here. It is either your life or theirs." Immediately a petition was sent by Shih-min to the Emperor, telling him that his life was in danger, and asking his protection. He sent back word that he would summon the brothers before him at the audience he would hold to-morrow morning.* This fell in exactly with the plans of Shih-min and his captains. About midnight they had all the avenues to the palace held by soldiers, who lay in ambush. When Kiên-ch'eng and Yuan-chieh appeared they were set upon by these, and as they turned and fled the eldest was pierced by an arrow. That was shot by Shih-min, whilst Yuan-chieh fell transfixed by one from the bow of Yu Chieh-kung. There was great consternation in the palace when the news of this tragedy spread throughout it, as no one knew what further horrors there might still possibly be in store for those that had been the adherents of the murdered princes. Kau Tsu instantly summoned his ministers and asked them what should be done in this terrible crisis.

They were unanimous in advising him to accept the situation. "Your son Shih-min," they said, " has gained the empire for your family, and he deserves to succeed to it. Appoint him your successor and the nation will instantly be at peace." The Emperor agreed to this, and Shih-min was not only formerly appointed by royal edict the heir to the throne, but he was also given all the power and authority of the Emperor himself, and in a few months after his father formally ceded the throne to h'im, when he became the sovereign of China, under the name in which he is known in history, viz. :—

T'ai Tsung—A. D. 627-650.

One of the first acts that Shih-min performed after the death of his brothers was to put to death their sons also. This of course was in these days considered an absolute necessity not only to preserve himself from their vengeance when they grew up, but also to save the empire from civil war. If it had been left to the dictates of his own heart he would certainly have spared the lads, that is, if we are to judge by the merciful disposition he showed during the rest of his life.

T'ai Tsung began his reign by an act that showed well the character of the man. He dismissed three thousand of the ladies of the palace to their homes. He considered that the expense of keeping them was a burden that the state ought not to be called upon to bear, and moreover that they ought to be sent back to society, where they could become useful members of it instead of wasting their lives in indolence and intrigue within the palace walls.

---

* The Emperor in ancient times, and also at the present day, meets his ministers for the transaction of public business at about two or three o'clock in the morning.

In this wise reform he was ably seconded by his queen, Ch'ang-sun, who was a lady of a very superior character. She was not only exceedingly talented, but she was also modest and refined. She had great power over her husband, who loved her dearly, and though she steadily refused to meddle in state affairs there is no doubt but that by her silent influence and by lofty views of things in general she greatly contributed to the glory of her husband's reign.

He had not come to the throne many months before he had to prepare for an invasion of the Turcomans. At the invitation of Liang-sze, one of the rebels of the late dynasty, two great tribes, to the number of one hundred and forty thousand men, under the leadership of their chiefs—Chieh-li and Tu-li—invaded the Chinese territory and encamped by the river Wei.* From this place they sent an ambassador to T'ai Tsung to demand certain conditions from him, but if they thought that they were going to frighten him they were greatly mistaken. He shut up their envoy in prison, and with six of his great officers and a handful of troops he marched to where the barbarians were awaiting his answer, whilst his main force travelled rapidly behind him. When he came in sight of Chieh-li he upbraided him with his want of faith in coming with such an armed force into his kingdom after a treaty had been only recently made with him and his people. By this time the first lines of T'ai Tsung's army appeared in view, and soon regiment after regiment had taken its position, ready to fight. Chieh-li was perplexed. His ambassador had not returned to give him his report, and T'ai Tsung took such a high hand with him that he could not but believe that he had a larger force than he had believed it possible for him to raise.

He accordingly deemed it prudent to come to terms with him, and confessing his fault and promising to be more faithful in his keeping of treaties for the future, peace was concluded and the terms agreed to at a meeting that was held on the bridge Pien. In a few days the vast hosts that had come to conquer China had melted away and disappeared in their own country beyond the frontiers.

One of T'ai Tsung's nobles being surprised at the ease with which this great invasion was prevented, said to him, "How is it that you refrain from fighting whilst others delight to meet the enemy in battle, and yet you cause your foe to retreat before you?" "The enemy that I have foiled this time," T'ai Tsung replied, "though so numerous is not well disciplined, and consequently they were afraid to meet my men. Besides, I don't want to fight yet. My dynasty is just in the process of being established, and I fear to risk its stability by entering on a campaign in which I might be worsted. Chieh-li will become all the more arrogant and proud because he has been let off so easily, and will imagine himself stronger than

---

* This river is a tributary of the Yellow River, which it joins in Shensi. It is famous for its muddy waters.

he really is. This will lead him to a self-confidence that will cause him to despise us. We on the other hand shall be getting stronger every day, and when the fitting moment has come I shall fall upon him and destroy him."

From this time T'ai Tsung began to bend all his energies to the strengthening of his army and to the perfecting of its discipline, so that no other force would be able to meet it in the field. He felt that the very permanence of his reign depended upon its efficiency, and that in the mortal conflicts that he saw would soon have to be fought with the gathering hosts of barbarians he would have to rely upon it to save the empire from being parcelled out amongst them. In pursuance of this purpose he selected several hundred of the best men from the various regiments and caused them to meet in the palace yard to be exercised in the use of the bow and arrow. When they were assembled he made a speech to them and said, "I have called you together to practice the use of the bow. I don't ask you to build palaces, or lay out gardens. I want you to learn to know how to use your weapons so that no foe will dare to stand before you. I myself will be your teacher, and when we have to go out to battle I will lead you against the enemy." His ministers were opposed to this radical conception of their Emperor and represented to him the danger he ran. "How easy it would be," they said, "for a traitor to get amongst the men you are training, and with the single flight of an arrow you would be slain before anyone could come to your rescue." "I am not afraid," said the heroic monarch. "I look upon the people of my empire as one family. What motive can anyone have to kill me?" "I'll take the risk," he continued, "and go on with my scheme." This fearless trust in his soldiers created the utmost enthusiasm amongst them, and when his speech was reported through the country every heart was turned in loving affection to him.

T'ai Tsung, who was not a warrior, except by necessity now that the empire was at peace, gave what time he could spare from his strictly official duties to the study of literature and to the discussion of questions that had reference to the right government of a nation. Close by his palace he built an immense library, in which he stored over two hundred thousand volumes. Special rooms were provided in this for the reception of the Emperor and the scholars who met him for the discussion of literary questions. Six eminent men were appointed professors in the establishment, and all the mandarins in the capital, from the first to the third grade, were required to come here and study under them. T'ai Tsung spent the most of his time in it. It was his custom after his early morning audience to pass into it, and sometimes the evening shades would have fallen before he left it. He was a most enthusiastic disciple of Confucius, and had studied his works and those of the same school, until he had become thoroughly indoctrinated with his system. That this was so is manifest from the remark he made one day when he and the assembled literati were discussing the doctrines of the great sage. "I have observed," he said, "that those rulers who have been remarkable for their attachment to either Taoism or Buddhism have been the cause of the destruction of their dynasties. As for me I believe in Confucianism. Just as wings are necessary for the birds and water for the fishes, and without which they would die, so I in like manner put my trust in the teachings of the sages of our country." It is interesting to know what kind of subjects engaged the attention of this really great and enlightened ruler. Fortunately the historian has not left us in the dark in regard to them, and a few specimens will be now given. T'ai Tsung propounded the question, "How is it that Yang Ti, who was one of the profoundest scholars in his empire, turned out to be such an immoral man and finally died a miserable death?" Wei-cheng replied, "It is not enough for a king to be clever. He must be of so modest and humble a spirit that men will dare to reprove him when he is wrong." Yang Ti was intolerably proud, and though he studied the words of Yau and Shun his acts were those of Chieh and Chow-sin.*

On another occasion he asked the company what is meant when it says in the Analects, "Gifted with ability, and yet enquiring of those who are not ; having much, and yet asking of those who are poor ; possessing, and yet acting as though he had nothing ; being full, and yet seeming empty."

One of those present explained that these apparent contradictions were exemplified in the conduct of every really modest man. It was only in the character of the haughty man that there were no lights and shadows. In the conversation that ensued it was the emphatic opinion that every one present, including the Emperor, should try and cultivate the virtue of modesty. T'ai Tsung heartily agreed with the speakers and said that this was the aim of his life. "I think over my words," he said, "and do not dare to utter them until I have measured them." "This is right," said the imperial censor, "for you must remember that they are being recorded, and will be read by future ages."

Another time he asked, "What was the best method of ridding the empire of thieves and disaffected persons?" Some of those present had a sovereign remedy in the greater severity of the laws and a more rigorous dealing with such characters. After a number had given their ideas in the same direction the Emperor said very calmly, "I don't agree with your opinion that men are to be reformed by harsh laws. I believe that if the ruler refrains from

---

* The name of Wei-cheng frequently appears in the following history : He was the trusted counsellor of T'ai Tsung, and fearless in reproving him whenever he thought he had done wrong. His wise counsel and his unswerving honesty have made him respected by every succeeding age, and Chinese scholars hold him up as a model of loyalty and fidelity. Chieh was the last of the sovereigns of the Hia, as Chow-sin was of the Shang dynasty. Their memory is infamous, because of the wickedness of their lives.

extravagance, makes the taxes light, and sees that his people have more than is enough for their daily needs, and appoints high-minded magistrates to rule over them, the country will be at peace, and theft and robbery will disappear from society. I mean to try this plan and see how it works."

He did so, and the result was that people felt themselves so safe that they did not trouble to shut their doors at night, and traders who were travelling with large sums about them would rest for the night at any out-of-the-way place without any fear of being robbed.

On another occasion one of his ministers proposed a method by which he could discover those who were loyal to him and those that were not. "If you suspect a man," he said, "pretend to be very angry with him and use strong language to him. If he is an honest man he will dare to confront you and will not fear your anger. If, on the contrary, he is at heart disloyal, he will cringe to you and show signs of fear." T'ai Tsung at once replied and said, "I don't at all agree with your method. It is too treacherous. I am like a fountain, and my ministers the waters that flow from it. If the fountain is muddy you cannot expect the water to be clear. I prefer to use truth in my dealing with men. I dare not for my own comfort and safety use the plan you propose."

This year, A. D. 629, the whole empire was divided into ten circuits or provinces, viz., Kwan-nei, Ho-tang, Ho-nan, Ho-peh, Shan-nan, Lung-yu, Hwai-nan, Kiang-nan, Chien-nan and Ling-nan. About this time a great disaster fell upon the fifteen hordes or great clans into which the Turcomans were divided. The winter had been inclement beyond anything that had been experienced for many years, and the fall of snow had been so severe that the cattle on which they depended for food had been buried beneath it, and vast numbers of sheep and horses had perished of cold and hunger. T'ai Tsung's envoy to this people returned to the capital and told him how they were starving and were in insurrection against his old foe Chieh-li, and urged upon him to take advantage of the distress into which they were plunged and lead an army against him. He assured him that the conquest of these hereditary enemies of China would be very easy now, as they were in no condition to resist a hostile mission. T'ai Tsung was, however, of too noble a character to listen to the advice of this wily diplomatist. "I have a treaty with Chieh-li," he said, "and I dare not violate it ; were I to attack his people now when they are broken down by calamity I should be inhuman in my conduct. Even though they were in a far worse condition than they are now I should never dream of reaping a benefit from their miseries. When they have done anything wrong then it will be time for me to think of conquering them."

This same year that brought sorrow to the Turcomans was laden with suffering that was to fall upon the people of the region in which the capital was situated.

First of all came drought, then famine, and lastly the locusts to eat up all that were edible in nature. In the sad and solemn discussions that were held between T'ai Tsung and his ministers as to the causes of these terrible evils, it was finally agreed that they were sent by Heaven in reply to the tears and complaints of the large number of ladies that were still confined in the seraglio, and who, separated from their friends and destined never to have homes of their own like their countrywomen outside the palace walls, bewailed their sad lot in the solitude of their own apartments. The Emperor was too honest a man to disregard what he believed to be the teachings of Heaven, and he accordingly dismissed three thousand of these unhappy women to their homes.

The year A. D. 630 was a glorious one in the reign of T'ai Tsung. Embassies from a large number of kingdoms, both small and great, appeared at the capital to make their submission and to bring tribute to this Emperor, whose renown had travelled far beyond his western frontiers. Languages that had never been spoken at a royal audience before were now heard for the firs ttime at Ch'ang-ngan. Men remarked upon the large variety of costumes that were seen in the great open space in front of the palace, and how picturesque they looked as the ambassadors moved about with their attendants waiting to be received by the Emperor. One of his ministers was so struck with this spectacle that he suggested that artists should be employed to paint from life the different groups as they brought their offerings to the court, so that future ages might have some idea of the glory and magnificence of T'ai Tsung's reign. This was agreed to, and by the special command of the Emperor carried out.

Another source of rejoicing about this time was the great victory that the armies of China had obtained over the Turcomans. Dissatisfied with the rule of Chieh-li some of the fifteen great hordes came and made their submission to T'ai Tsung. This of course was resented by their king and war commenced. Three armies, numbering together about one hundred and forty thousand men, invaded the Turcoman territory in different directions. The one commanded by Li Tsing routed Chieh-li, who was compelled to flee, but he was afterwards captured and brought a prisoner to Ch'ang-ngan, to the great delight of Kau Tsu, who publicly proclaimed his satisfaction in having appointed his son to be Emperor in his place. The serious question now arose as to what should be done with the conquered barbarians. Some advocated that they should be allowed to remain in their own country, which was adopted with a large modification for the king, and all the chief men with their families were transferred to the capital, whilst large numbers of the fighting men were planted in colonies in different parts of Shensi. The whole of their territories was divided into ten departments with Chinese rulers over each. Chieh-li was made a high mandarin, and lived in the capital. Tu-li was appointed to be a governor in

Kwang-si, whilst those of the officers who had held high rank in their own country were given titles and emoluments under the Chinese government. Never was a conquered people who had been a thorn in the side of the nation more liberally and humanely treated than these were by the magnanimous and large-hearted T'ai Tsung.

The beginning of A. D. 632 found the nation rejoicing. A splendid victory had been given to the Chinese arms, and the hereditary enemies of the empire had been crushed. A harvest, too, such as had not been reaped for many years, had filled the country with abundance, and hunger and want had been driven from the homes of the poorest. It was suggested by the ministers of state that the Emperor should repair to one of the five sacred mountains of China, and there, on its summit, thank Heaven for the mercies that had been showered on the nation. T'ai Tsung refused to do this. He had larger conceptions than any man of his day of the wide scope of Heaven's power, and he felt that the journey to any mountain top was a superfluous undertaking for a man that really wished to worship it. "Shih Wang, of the Ts'in dynasty, acted as you wish me to do," he said, "and before long his dynasty passed away. Wen Ti, of the Han dynasty, never did, and he transmitted his throne to his descendants. Which of these two has posterity decided to be the superior of the other? You need not ascend a hill to worship. Heaven. Sweep not the ground near you, and Heaven will accept the offering you bring to it."

T'ai Tsung sustained an irreparable loss in the death of his queen in the year A. D. 637.

This lady was one of the finest characters we meet with in Chinese history. She was benevolent, modest, and a great student. She was intensely practical, moreover, and it was undoubtedly owing to her commonsense that her husband, who constantly took her opinion, so often passed laws that gained for him the admiration and affection of his people. The heir-apparent was greatly distressed at his mother's illness, and requested his father to publish a general amnesty throughout his empire in the hopes that Heaven might be moved to pity by this act and prolong her life. He also made special offerings to the idols in order to gain their favour. When his mother heard of what he had done she called him to her bedside and said, "Our life is in the hands of Heaven, and when it decides that we shall die there is no mortal power that can prolong it. There is therefore no need to proclaim a general amnesty, as that will not avert the sorrow that you fear, besides a royal proclamation of this kind is one of the imposing acts of a state, and must not be too often or too recklessly done. As for the Taoist and Buddhist faiths they are heresies, and have been the cause of injury both to the people and the state. Your father has a great aversion to them, and therefore you must not displease him by appealing to them on my behalf."

To her husband she said, "I have not been of much use whilst I lived, and therefore I don't want anyone to be made to suffer by my death. Don't make a magnificent grave for me, and then the people will not hate me, because they have not been called to make any sacrifices in building such a one. I don't wish you to put jewels and precious stones in my coffin. All that I want is a tile to be put under my head for a pillow, and my hair fastened up with some wooden pins. Associate with the good and shun the company of the evil. Don't listen to unworthy men, and neither hunt nor build magnificent palaces. If you promise me these things then shall I die happy." Her husband was inconsolable for her loss, and he built a tower near the palace from which he could look at her grave, which was made on the side of a hill, that could be seen in the distance. The Emperor's university at the capital had become famous not only in China, but also in countries beyond its pale. Kings and nobles from Corea and Sin-lo and from T'u-fan had sent their sons to be educated in it, and T'ai Tsung, mindful of his dying queen's last request, had kept up his practice of associating with the best men that used to meet there for the discussion of great moral questions which were to help him in the government of his people. His efforts to lead a noble life and benefit the nation could not, however, avert unhappiness from his own family. His eldest son was a thoroughly bad man, and spent his time in amusement and dissipations. Fearing that his conduct might be the means of alienating his father's heart from him, instead of correcting his conduct he was led by his evil companions to conspire against his life. He feigned sickness, and had men lying in wait to murder him when he should come to see him. T'ai Tsung got timely word of the conspirators' plans, and he had them all apprehended. His son was deprived of all his titles and banished to a distant part of the kingdom, whilst those that had aided him in his treason were put to death.

The year A. D. 645 was a notable one in the history of T'ai Tsung, for in it he led an army to invade Corea. Four years before he had sent an ambassador to that country, who had discovered that a considerable number of Chinese who had been captured during the campaigns of Yang Ti were still living there, and were prevented from returning to China. These made their complaints to the royal envoy, who repeated them to the Emperor when he returned. His heart was moved at the idea of the suffering his countrymen were enduring, and he determined within himself that he would as soon as a fitting opportunity present itself deliver them. Three years went by, and then an embassy came from Sin-lo praying for help, for that Kau-li and Bai-ji had formed a league to plunder and waste her land.* T'ai Tsung sent an ambassador to demand an explanation, when Kai Su-wen, the powerful noble who had

* The country of Corea then consisted of the three kingdoms of Kau-li, Bai-ji and Sin-lo. See Ross's Corea, Chap. VI.

assassinated the King of Corea, and who was the real ruler of the kingdom, sent a quantity of silver as tribute, hoping thus to avert the storm that threatened to burst upon him. By the advice of some of his ministers this was rejected, because it came from the hands of the murderer of his sovereign, and the Chinese army in two great divisions proceeded on its way to the invasion of Corea. The first of these consisted of forty thousand men under the command of Chang-liang, and was carried in five hundred ships from Tai-chow in Shantung to Ping-yang in Corea. The second was a force of sixty thousand men under the command of Li Shih-tsi, which proceeded by land and reached Yan-chow in March. From this he proceeded to Liu-chung and Hwai-yuen, and crossing the river Liau he joined Chang-liang at the city of Gai-mau, now known as Kai-chow. This place was captured next day by the Chinese, who next took by storm the important town of Liau-tung after the most desperate fighting on both sides. Here the Coreans lost upwards of ten thousand men and as many more that were taken prisoners. T'ai Tsung appeared as though he would carry everything before him, when his victorious arms received a check before the city of An-shih ; not all the bravery of the bravest of his battalions led by men who fought under the eye of the Emperor, who himself had been one of the first generals of the age, could avail to capture this town, and finally he had to retire with his army from before it. The campaign so far had been successful. He had taken ten cities, and seventy thousand Coreans had been transferred to Chinese territory, but he had been foiled before An-shih, and in so far his victory had not been complete. That he was dissatisfied with not having thoroughly humbled Kau Su-wen is evident from the remark that he made to his generals as he was returning to China. "If Wei-cheng had been alive," he gloomily said, "he would have prevented me from entering upon this Corean campaign." Two years after, in spite of the remonstrances of his ministers, T'ai Tsung made preparations for another war with Corea. Large vessels were ordered to be built in Kiang-nan and a force of three hundred thousand men to be equipped, in order to crush the little kingdom that had dared to resist the mighty Chinese empire. An army of ten thousand men was actually despatched to begin hostilities, but the Emperor died, with the power of Kai Su-wen still unsubdued, and his son, who succeeded him, reversed the policy of his father, disbanded the Liau-tung armies and stayed hostilities at all points.

This year, A.D. 649, as if in preparation for the giving up of the imperial power which he had used so well and wisely, T'ai Tsung composed a treatise, consisting of twelve sections, on "How a king should conduct himself," for the special benefit of the heir-apparent. His mind at this time was sadly disturbed by prognostications of evil that were declared to be coming upon his house. Li-fung, the astronomer royal, from observations of the planet

Venus, predicted that a queen was about to arise who would rule over China. A prophecy, too, began to be circulated that this woman would appear in the very next generation, and that she would almost exterminate the members of the family of T'ang. When the Emperor consulted Li-fung about this he replied "that it was quite true that the individual was now in the royal palace, and would carry out her purpose thirty years hence." T'ai Tsung proposed to put to death the whole of the ladies of the royal household, in order to prevent the terrible disasters that were said to be coming on the reigning dynasty. Li-fung dissuaded him from this by assuring him that the coming events were ordained by Heaven, and though he might exterminate every individual in the palace it would raise up another to carry out its sovereign will. Next year he was attacked with dysentery, which ended fatally. During his illness his son, who was to succeed him, was most unremitting in his attentions to his father. Day and night he never left his bedside, and so great was his anxiety and distress that for several days he ate no food, and his hair turned white. In spite of all that could be done for him the disease could not be stayed, and he passed away, commending his son to the care and loyalty of his ministers, one of the noblest and most commanding figures that ever occupied the dragon throne of this great Celestial Empire. He was succeeded by his ninth son, who began to reign when he was twenty-two years of age, and who is known in history by the name of

Kau Tsung—A. D. 650-684.

The first acts of the new monarch showed a disposition to reverence his father and to perpetuate his memory by carrying out his benign legislation. A noble presented a petition praying that the custom of burying servants with their dead lord, and which had not been allowed during the reign of T'ai Tsung, should be permitted to those who had the means of affording it. Kau Tsung replied that he could on no account grant it, because his father, just before he died, had charged him never to consent to its being carried out in his dominions.* We have in this slight incident a very touching evidence of the humanity of the great ruler, who, when he was leaving the world, could still let his thoughts be occupied about benevolent schemes for the welfare of a people whom he so dearly loved when he was their sovereign. Kau Tsung, to perpetuate the memory of the great victory that T'ai Tsung had gained over the Turcomans, had the statue of their king, Chieh-li, and thirteen notables, sculptured in stone and placed outside the north gate of the city, where the crowds that passed through it from the northern

* The barbarous practice of burying the attendants of a noble with him when he died is said to have been begun with Duke Ching about B. C. 730. When he died sixty-six people were buried alive with him, and with his successor Muh one hundred and seventy. Some of the names of the men that were entombed with this latter are given in the Book of Odes. See Legge's translation, pages 198-199.

parts of his empire might be continually reminded of the generalship of the great Emperor that had been able to crush the hereditary enemies of the empire.

As his queen Wang-shih had no children a son by one of his concubines, named Chung, was appointed heir to the throne. This seemed to satisfy every one, and for the first five years of his reign nothing happened to interrupt the harmony and peace of the royal household. Then came a turning point in the life of the Emperor and misery to himself, and ruin and death to the best and most loyal of his nobles were to be the result. The Emperor had excited the jealousy of his queen by showing a marked preference for one of his concubines named Siau-shuh. This lady had completely gained the royal affections. The queen, in order to counteract her influence, introduced to his notice a famous beauty, who she hoped would wean his heart from her rival, and perhaps cause him to return to his allegiance to herself. Fatal hope was this! She did indeed succeed in overthrowing the supremacy of Siau-shuh, but it was only to transfer it to Wu-how, a stronger and more unscrupulous woman, and one who was destined to take a foremost place in the history of China for the next forty years.* As soon as the queen discovered this a deadly feud arose between the two women, which ended in the triumph of Wu-how and the disgrace and death of Wang-shih and Siau-shuh. The master stroke that placed the power fully in the hands of the first was the murder of her own child, which she skillfully attributed to the vengeance of the queen. Kau Tsung was so horrified at this that he determined to depose her and put Wu-how in her place.

In spite of the most strenuous opposition of his chief ministers of state, who showed how unseemly it was for him to marry his own father's concubine, he persevered in his purpose, and in November of A. D. 656 Wang-shih was formally degraded and her implacable foe elevated in her place.

No sooner was she installed in her new dignity than she caused the late queen and Siau-shuh to be apprehended and cast into the palace dungeons. Kau Tsung, who seemed to have had some lingering fondness for Wang-shih, visited her there. She appealed to him by the memory of his former love for her to get her out of her prison and "let her see the light of the sun and moon once more." He was deeply moved by her distress, and promised that she should be released. Wu-how, who all her life long was plentifully supplied with spies, heard of this interview, and at once sent

---

* Wu-how was a daughter of the governor of King-chow, and had been taken into T'ai Tsung's seraglio in the year A. D. 638. After his death she retired to a Buddhist nunnery, where she was seen on one occasion by Kau Tsung when he went to worship the idols. As he had known her when she was his father's concubine, and had been greatly attracted to her, he gave signs that his heart was moved by the sight of her. It was seeing this that induced the queen to introduce her to the palace and to take every opportunity of deepening the impression she had already made on her husband's heart.

an executioner, who chopped off the feet and hands of her two rivals and placed them wounded and maimed in great tubs of spirits, where they lingered for several days in the utmost agonies. The historian tells us that for a long time after this Wu-how never went to sleep without seeing her two victims handless and feetless as they writhed in agony, and she was so frightened and terrified with the sight that she went to live for some time in Lohyang to get rid of it. She does not seem to have learned any lessons of kindness, however, from the visions that she saw at night. She was naturally cruel and vindictive, and the very next year she managed to have the nobles that opposed her being made Empress, as well as all the loyal and faithful ministers of the palace, put to death. For the next few years nothing of any importance took place in the history of the country. Wu-how, with her powerful mind and her determined will, was getting more and more the mastery over her husband, and gradually assuming the control of the executive.

In A. D. 662 this peaceful monotony was disturbed by the invasion of a powerful tribe of T'ieh-leh barbarians that lived beyond the western frontiers of Shansi. Over a hundred thousand of them suddenly appeared in that region and spread death and desolation wherever they came. An army was sent against them under the command of Hueh-jin, who defeated them with great slaughter.

His success was largely due to his having been able with three successive shots from his bow to kill three of the leading men of the savage invaders. Three years after this an incident took place which was the means of confirming Wu-how in her power and of preventing anyone from daring to attempt to deprive her of it. Kau Tsung, who began to writhe under her despotic rule, was one day expressing his anger and indignation against her, when he was quietly reminded that his Majesty had it in his power to relieve himself from her control. "How?" he instantly asked. "By abolishing her," was the quiet reply. "Then let the edict be at once made out," the Emperor cried out, "by which she shall be declared to be no longer queen." The writing of this important document was at once begun, when information was hurriedly carried to Wu-how of what was going on. She was a woman of prompt action, so she hastened into the presence of Kau Tsung and asked him for what reason he was going to depose her. The Emperor, who stood greatly in awe of her, seemed to lose his courage and his manliness with her appearance. "I did not want to depose you," he said, "it was this man, pointing to the one that had suggested the idea, who proposed that I should do so." It need hardly be said that the important edict never was finished; but Wu-how realized the extreme peril in which she stood, and she determined never to be caught again in like manner. From this time she made an arrangement that whenever the Emperor held an audience with his ministers she was to be present at it and partake in the consultations and deliberations of that august body. The title that the two now took in this concerted action was "The Two Holy Ones."

In the year A. D. 666 Kau Tsung visited the great T'ai-shan mountain in Shantung, where he worshipped God on the top of it. He then proceeded to the grave of Confucius, and there made offerings to the spirit of the great sage, and afterwards he proceeded to visit a certain great clan that had become famous throughout the empire, because of the harmony that existed between its members. The Emperors of the five dynasties had each in turn come to verify for themselves the remarkable story that had reached the capital, and each one had testified to his belief in it by erecting tablets recording his admiration and respect for such a harmonious community. At the time that Kau Tsung reached the place there were the descendants of nine generations of the clan, consisting of several thousands of people, associated together under the rule of their chief, and no jar or difference was ever heard amongst any of them. Kau Tsung was struck with wonder at what he saw, and enquired from the latter the secret by which this unprecedented harmony had been attained. Taking up his pen he wrote down a hundred characters on a sheet of paper, and handing it to the Emperor he said, "Your Majesty, here in these words lies the secret you wish to know." The Emperor found that the hundred words were all a repetition of the one character which meant forbearance. Kau Tsung nodded his head, and agreed that forbearance in all the acts of daily life would indeed result in the marvellous unanimity that had rendered them so famous.

At the close of the year A. D. 667 an expedition started to invade Corea under the command of Li-tsi and Sieh Jin-kwei. A great battle was fought at Kin-shan, in which the Coreans suffered a great defeat, and this was followed by the storming of Liau-tung. After considerable delay the army crossed the river Ya-lu and proceeded to invest the capital, Ping-yang, which was at length compelled to open its gates to the Chinese army. The king surrendered himself, and the country submitting to the inevitable accepted the rule of the T'angs. The whole country was divided into five great colonies, and Li-tsi, with twenty thousand men, held Ping-yang and appointed both Chinese and native officials to govern the people.

When this territorial division was made there were one hundred and seventy-six towns, large and small, and six hundred and ninety thousand distinct families under the control of the Chinese. In the meanwhile Wu-how had been gradually absorbing all the power of the state in herself till Kau Tsung, feeling that he was but a nonentity, proposed that he should resign the throne and let her be the nominal as well as the real ruler of the country. This his ministers vigorously resisted, and the idea was given up. They both seemed, however, to wish to be exalted in the eyes of the country by the use of the highest titles they could select, and as earth could not supply them with these they usurped the functions of Heaven by styling themselves the Heavenly Emperor and the Heavenly Empress.

There is no question but that the vigorous reign of the latter would have been acquiesced in more heartily both by nobles and subjects if she had not been so immoral in her conduct. She caused her son Fung to be poisoned, because he had remonstrated with her, because of her irregularities, and she deposed and banished his brother Hien for the same reason, though each in succession had been solemnly and legally appointed heir to the throne.

In the latter end of the year A. D. 679 one hundred and eighty thousand Turfans were in arms, led by their king K'un-ling. As such an immense force was a menace to China, an army under the command of Li King-huan marched to try conclusions with it, and a great battle was fought near Ts'ing-hai, the "Azure Sea," or, Kokonor, as it is commonly written. The Chinese general was defeated, but a treaty of peace seems to have been made by which hostilities ceased for the present. The last two or three years of Kau Tsung's reign were disturbed by inroads of both the Turfans and the Turcomans. Eight great battles were fought between the former and the Chinese, in which the imperial general Lu Sze-teh gained the mastery over his opponents, and he was finally able to expel them from Chinese territory.

Kau Tsung died in the year A. D. 684, and was succeeded by his fourth son, Cho, whose dynastic title is Chung Tsung. His rule was destined, however, to be suspended for fully twenty years through an indiscreet speech he made to one of the cabinet ministers, and which was wrongly reported to his mother. On his elevation to the throne he very imprudently announced his determination to make his father-in-law a great noble. This was opposed by the minister above mentioned, on the ground that he had not rendered to the state any service that deserved such an honour.

The young Emperor said, "If I like to give him the empire I can do so if I choose, and why not the lesser honour?" Word was at once carried to the Empress that her son was going to hand over the country to his father-in-law. Wu-how, whatever her other faults might be, was not one that would permit the power she possessed to slip easily through her fingers. She accordingly called a great council of her ministers, at which it was decided that Chung Tsung should be degraded to the position of Prince Lu-ling, and his younger brother Li-tan made Emperor in his place.

This decision was at once carried out, and the new ruler is known by the name of Jui Tsung. As the real sovereign of China, however, was the Empress Wu-how, we shall now consider the events that transpired for the next twenty years as having taken place during her reign.

CHAPTER XXI.

THE T'ANG DYNASTY (CONTINUED).

The Empress Wu-how—A. D. 684-705.

WU-HOW plainly showed that though the legal farce had been played and a state pageantry had been gone through by which her own son had been made sovereign of China, she was the one that held the reins of government, and that hers was the mind that was henceforward to be supreme in the state. Every day in the small hours of the morning, when the rest of the capital were fast asleep, she would appear in the audience chamber, and with her cabinet devise measures for the government of the country. She also dressed herself in the robes which only the sovereign was permitted to put on, and she ordered that the official dresses of the various grades of mandarins should be changed, as though she were the founder of a new dynasty. Indeed it soon became apparent that she was planning for the disappearance of the T'angs and the substitution of her own house in their place. One most significant act that no one could mistake was her abolishing the ancestral temples of the reigning dynasty and the erection of seven magnificent ones to the spirits of her own family for seven generations past. There were symptoms amongst the official class that this daring assumption of power and this manifest purpose of supplanting the great house of T'ang was bitterly resented and one uprising took place, but every manifestation of displeasure was soon crushed in the death of those who dared to show it. Wu-how was a woman of prompt measures, and as her spies abounded everywhere and were liberally rewarded, she always got timely notice of any danger that was likely to threaten her. She also had shown her wisdom in placing around her men of undoubted ability, whose counsels she took and who preserved her from doing anything that might have seriously endangered her rule. Even in the matter of her amour with Hwai-yi, the Buddhist bonze, who now publicly appeared in the palace and who attempted to take a leading position there, she never interfered on his behalf against her prime minister, who one day publicly slapped his face for not paying him the respect that was due to his office.

In the year A. D. 689 two of the princes of T'ang rose in rebellion against her, but they were speedily subdued. It, however, gave her the opportunity she had wished for of crushing the powerful families of the house of T'ang. Under the plea that they were all guilty, though they had not actually joined the rebels, she had between six and seven hundred families, together with their adherents, seized. These numbered in all over five thousand persons, great and small. By the advice of her able statesman, Ti

Jin-kieh, only four of the chief men were executed, but all the remainder were banished from their homes to different parts of the empire. From this time she gradually began, on various pretexts, to get rid of those of the princes that remained, and against whom she had at first no sufficient proof to justify her in apprehending and dealing with them. Large numbers of them perished till it seemed as though the members of the T'ang family would be exterminated. Wu-how, in the year A. D. 694, gave the most profound evidence of her attachment to the reprobate bonze Hwai-yi, who seemed to exercise a special fascination over her. She caused a most magnificent temple to be built for him, of which he was to become the abbot. Ten thousand workmen were employed daily on the works, and an immense amount of money was expended in making it the most famous in the empire. When it was finished Hwai-yi collected ten thousand bonzes, who were to be connected with it, and it was remarked by the high mandarins that these were all stalwart and lusty fellows, who in some crisis at the capital would have been a positive peril to the state. The Empress' attention was drawn to the case, and with her clear and ready mind at once apprehending the gravity of the case she ordered these young men to be banished to different parts of China. Hwai-yi, irritated at this, set fire to the temple, but no reproof did he get from Wu-how, who simply ordered, that it should be rebuilt. Presuming upon his intimacy with her and jealous of a new power that had risen in the palace that was likely to supplant him in her favour, he dared on several occasions to address her in anything but respectful terms. This of course was not to be tolerated, so she gave secret orders that he should be assassinated, which was accordingly done to the great joy of those who had been scandalized by his presence and conduct in the palace.

Two years later, a new enemy that was destined to appear often in the future annals of China, made an irruption into Chih-li. These were the famous Ki-tans, who, after ravaging and plundering wherever they went, disappeared beyond the frontiers with their booty. Three years had scarcely gone by before the same region was again visited by the Turcomans, who reduced the people to such a state of distress that many of them submitted to their rule, whilst others more independent took to robbery in order to be able to sustain life. Ti Jin-kieh, who was sent to report upon the condition of things, advised the Empress to deal leniently with the people. "The Ki-tans and the Turcomans are the least evils we have to contend with," he said in his official despatch. "What we have most to dread is lest the people should rise in rebellion against the government, as there are signs they are intending to do. Their state is indeed desperate. All their property has been forcibly carried off, and some have acknowledged the rule of the robbers in order to save themselves from destruction, whilst others from the same cause have taken to the road. As they know they are liable to severe penalties for both crimes they have become reckless, and are prepared even to try and overthrow the dynasty ; what I advise is that a general amnesty should be issued and that they be commanded to return to their homes and become loyal citizens again, with the assurance that they will never be punished for the past.'' This wise advice was followed by Wu-how, and the threatened rebellion was crushed in the bud.

The Empress, who had been failing in health for some time, was at last compelled by serious illness in the year A. D. 705 to keep to her room for several months. The strong hand that had kept in control those who had been dissatisfied with her usurpation was no sooner rendered powerless to act than a conspiracy was formed against her. The leading men in it, having killed two of her favorites, rushed tumultuously into her bedroom and demanded that she should resign and that her son, who had been deposed by her, but who after all was the real Emperor, should be allowed to reign. Seeing that her day of power was over, that she would only endanger her life by resistance, she conceded the demands of the conspirators and handed over to them the great seal of the empire. It shows the remarkable hold that this woman had gained over the nobles that at this crisis, when it would seem that nothing could save her from destruction, she was not only spared, but special honour was paid to her. A palatial residence was prepared for her, and the high-sounding title of ''The Great and Sacred Empress, the equal of Heaven,'' was given to her. The common title by which she is known in history is ''Wu, the equal of Heaven,'' which was assigned to her when the sceptre had slipped from her grasp, and not when she was in the zenith of her power. She died in the following year at the great age of eighty-one, one of the most remarkable women that has ever appeared in the annals of China.

Chung Tsung, who now resumed the reign that had been interrupted for twenty-one years, was a comparatively feeble-minded, pleasure-loving man, and had the misfortune of having a wife who was both clever and ambitious. They had loved each other with the most devoted affection during their retirement from power, and he had been so much struck with the fidelity with which she had clung to him when his fortunes were at the lowest ebb, that he promised her that if ever he should become Emperor again she should have whatever she liked to demand of him. As her aim was to be a second Wu-how she requested that she should be permitted to sit in the audience chamber and decide with him the great national questions that were there discussed by the privy council. '' His mother had done so,'' she said, ''and therefore it could not be wrong for her son's wife to do the same.'' This request was at once granted, though the most strenuous opposition was given to it by the more faithful of the ministers. One of them was especially strong in urging the Emperor to withdraw his permission. ''From ancient times till the present dynasty,'' he said, ''it has been the custom for the sovereign to manage imperial questions, and his queen has had no ruling voice in regard to them." "When the hen begins to crow," he continued, "it is a certain sign that the family is coming to destruction."

Chung Tsung would not listen to this wise counsel, and ere long the whole power fell into the hands of his queen Wei. It soon became manifest, however, that she had not the ability of Wu-how, for she fell under the influence of San-su, the governor of the palace, who was a bad designing man, and who was accused of being unduly intimate with her, though he had married her daughter. San-su, in fact, became the supreme power in the palace. He got rid of five of the most loyal of the ministers by first of all making them princes and giving them governments in different parts of the empire, and then accusing them of treason, for which they were all executed. At length, when every one of consequence had been swept out of her path, and the throne lay ready before her, the queen forgot her old affection for her husband and the many ties that had bound her to him for so many years and all his generous treatment of her, and she sent him some poisoned cakes, of which he ate and died. She kept this tragic deed a secret until she had got the privy council to appoint her regent and her own son, a lad of sixteen, as successor to the throne. Unfortunately for themselves they were not satisfied with what they had done, but planned for the murder of Prince Li-tan, the fourth son of Wu-how. It was evident from this that they meant the establishing of a new dynasty and the destruction of the T'angs. No sooner had Liu-ki, the son of Li-tan, heard of this design than without waiting even to inform his father, he gathered round him a body of men that were ready to hazard their lives in his behalf, and, forcing his way into the palace, Wei and all her accomplices were ruthlessly murdered.

Jui Tsung once more ascended the throne (A. D. 710-713). His first important act that he had to perform was the settlement of the question of the succession. As a matter of justice his eldest son, Ch'eng-ki, was entitled to the right of being acknowledged the heir, but it was felt that Liu-ki had saved the family from destruction, and therefore had a claim that could not altogether be set aside. Besides, he was a general of ability, and showed he had a mind that could act promptly in a time of danger, and that he was on a whole more suited for the throne in this time of emergency than his brother. The ministers voted in his favour, and one of them said, "The man that has delivered the empire from bad men ought to have the honours that the empire has to give." Fortunately Jui Tsung was rescued from his dilemma by the generosity of Ch'eng-ki, who said, "When the empire is at peace then the eldest should have the preference, but when it is in danger the man of merit should be selected. If at this time the most suitable man is not appointed heir the country will lose hope." These wise and unselfish words solved the difficulty of the succession, and Liu-ki, to the joy of almost everybody, was formally proclaimed the successor to the throne.

In the month of August, in the year A. D. 713, a comet appeared, which portended great sorrow to the reigning Emperor, for its path was right across the royal stars.* The ministers were in great consternation, and they advised Jui Tsung, if he would avoid the calamities that Heaven thus plainly intimated were coming upon him, to resign his throne and hand it over to his son. This he did after a decent show of opposition on the part of Liu-ki, who at the age of thirty-five ascended the dragon throne, and is known by the name of Huan Tsung.

Huan Tsung—A. D. 713-756.

The reign of this Emperor is one of the most celebrated in Chinese history, both because of the splendour with which it began and also because of the disasters that marked its close. No sooner had he ascended the throne than his sister, who was jealous of the honour that had been put upon him, and who wished to play the part of a second Wu-how, plotted against his life and tried her utmost to poison him. There was a moment indeed in which she almost succeeded, for she had managed to gather a powerful party around her that were obedient to her commands, and who were prepared to go any lengths in order to place her in the post of supreme power. Huan Tsung was not the man, however, to submit tamely to the designs of his sister. Besides he had able men around him who were loyal to the throne, and who dreaded another palace revolution that would make a woman the Empress of China. By a sudden movement the leading nobles in her interest were seized and executed. A command from Jui Tsung was then sent to his daughter that she should put an end to her life, which she dared not disobey, and the rest of her faction were then apprehended and mercilessly put to death. Huan Tsung was of an amiable disposition, as was manifested by the tender affection that he manifested for his four brothers. When the imperial duties of the day were over and he was in their company he was no longer the sovereign of China, but their brother and their equal, and all distinctions of rank vanished whilst he was enjoying their society.† He was also easy tempered and inclined to enjoy the pleasures of life. Music seemed to have a special attraction for him, and as he was dissatisfied with the stiff and solemn kind that had been in vogue up to the present, he ordered that a new and more joyous kind should be composed that would express more fully his own happy emotions, and be the medium to his people by which they could give full play to the feelings of joy and gladness that they might wish to give utterance

---

* These are all in the Dipper, as well as other circumpolar stars.

† It is said that on one occasion, when his eldest brother Ch'eng-ki was sick Huan Tsung himself made the decoction that his brother was to drink, and that whilst bending over the furnace his beard caught fire. Some of the attendants expressed their concern about this, but the Emperor said, "Never mind about my beard. It does not matter how that burns, so long as my brother gets well."

to on festive occasions. It was at this time that the famous music called the "Pear Garden" was composed, so called because of the place in which the Emperor taught several hundreds of the ladies of his household to play it. It soon gained a wide popularity throughout the country, the best evidence of which is that it is used to-day by the people of the eighteen provinces on all occasions of merriment and festivity. In addition to the above Huan Tsung was very simple in his tastes, and opposed especially to extravagance in dress. He passed sumptuary laws advising his people to be more moderate in their expenditure, and in order to enforce these he set the example in his own household of rigid economy and simplicity. Only his queen was allowed to dress in silk or satin, and that the other ladies might not be tempted by the profusion of magnificent dresses that abounded in the palace, he had them all collected in a heap in front of it, together with a large amount of precious stones, and the whole set fire to, to the great distress of the ladies but to the joy of those who had the welfare of the kingdom at heart, for they thought they saw in this act an omen of future good to their country. In the early years of his reign the Emperor made the government of the people his chief concern. He instituted regular examinations for the office of district magistrate, the subjects being chosen not as they are in the present day, from the Confucian classics, but from the statute books. A knowledge of the laws and the best methods of government was essential for any man that hoped to obtain the position of a magistrate. He also ordered that the chief mandarins throughout the country should at times invite the elders of the villages, who were over sixty years of age and who were men of good report, to their yamêns and entertain them. At these gatherings they were to instruct them in the principles of loyalty and filial piety, so that they again might teach the young men under their control these important virtues. The nation being thus trained in the very fountain of all that is good and excellent it was hoped that it would grow up in goodness and morality. In the year A. D. 733 the Emperor ordered that Chiang Tai-kung should be the tutelary god of the dynasty, and commanded that temples should be built to him in all the principal cities of the empire, and that regular worship should be paid him on certain specified occasions by all government officials. Next year he divided the country into fifteen circuits or provinces, viz., The Western Capital, the Eastern Capital, Koan-nei, Honan, Ho-tung, Ho-peh, Lung-yew, East Shan-nan, West Shan-nan, Chien-nan, Hwai-nan, East Kiang-nan, West Kiang-nan, Ch'ien-tsung and Ling-nan. About this same time the Turfans sent an embassy to the court at Ch'ang-ngan, begging for a complete set of the Confucian classics. This was such an unusual request that some of the more narrow-minded of the council advised that it should be refused. One of them said, " These Turfans are our most deadly enemies, and are continually harassing our borders. If we give them our books they will become as wise as ourselves, and then we shall not merely have to contend with brute force, but also with generals and officers whose minds have been enlightened by the divine teachings of our sages." To this another replied, "It is quite true that our classics will civilize and increase the intelligence of our savage foes, but it is also true that they will elevate their characters and teach them lessons of justice and morality. We should hope that instead of training them to know how to fight us they would give them such exalted ideas of their relation to their fellow-men that they would confine themselves within their own boundaries and cease to be a terror to everyone outside of themselves." This statesmanlike view of the matter carried the day, and a set of the sacred books was given to the ambassador. The year A. D. 735 is a memorable one, because of the public appearance in the councils of the state of Li Lin-fu. Up to this time Huan Tsung's reign had been a happy and a prosperous one, but with the appearance of this man may be said to have commenced that course of action that led to the disasters that befell China during the remaining years that he ruled the country.* This same year a great battle was fought with the Ki-tans, when their king and the general of his army were killed by the Chinese troops under Chang Show-kwei. A large force had suddenly appeared under the walls of Kwachow, of which he was governor. The garrison was terrified when they saw themselves beleaguered by such large numbers of their formidable enemies, but Chang showed himself a second Chu Ko-liang on this occasion. He made a great feast to his officers, and he managed it so that the sounds of music and revelry reached the Ki-tans outside the walls. The impression they got from these was that Chang had a larger force inside than they were aware of, and that he felt himself competent to meet them in battle. So terrified were they at the unknown possibilities of this festive commander that they incontinently commenced their retreat. Chang pursued after them and gained a complete victory over them. The Emperor was so delighted with his success that he proposed to make him one of his prime ministers. Chang Kiu-ling opposed this. "The office of prime minister," he said, "is one of vast importance to the empire, is not a position to be given away to a successful general; and, besides, if you give him the very highest reward in your power, what will you bestow upon him supposing he should beat both the

---

* Li Lin-fu is one of the most infamous characters in Chinese history and execrated by every reader of it. In the historical plays that are performed throughout the empire he is made to play so despicable a part that his name has become a by-word in the homes of the people for all that is base and dishonourable. He managed to ingratiate himself into the good graces of Huan Tsung by pandering to his evil passions and by suggestions of wrong that finally led him into the most disgraceful courses. Such an influence did he acquire, indeed, over him that he managed to obtain the dismissal of Chang Kiu-ling, the prime minister, who was a loyal noble-minded man and the appointment of himself in his place. The phrase, "His mouth is honey, but his heart is a sword," applied to him by the Chinese, accurately describes the man.

Ki-tans and the Turcomans?"* Next year an army was sent against the Ki-tans under the command of Ngan Luh-shan who, however, suffered such a terrible defeat that his whole force was absolutely annihilated and he himself barely escaped with his life. Chang-show, according to the Chinese usage, was going to put the defeated commander to death, but he pleaded so earnestly for his life that he determined to send him to the capital and let the Emperor decide what punishment should be meted out to him. When he was brought into his presence he made such an impression on Huan Tsung that he not only forgave him, but gave him a position in Shantung. Chang Kiu-ling protested against this leniency. "He deserves death," he said, "because of his defeat, but much more because he is a danger to the empire. His face is that of a traitor, and he ought to be executed." Unhappily for himself the Emperor disregarded the warnings of his loyal minister, and thus became the patron of a man that ultimately rose in rebellion against him. The day of Chang Kiu's influence, however, was destined shortly to cease. In the following year, A D. 734, Huan Tsung determined to depose the heir-apparent and put in his place Prince Show, his eighteenth son. This was strenuously opposed by Chang Kiu, who reminded him of the sorrows that had come upon former Emperors who had made such a change. The Emperor gave up his purpose on his representations, but the faithful noble incurred the enmity of the prince's mother and Li Lin-fu, who had espoused her cause. The royal ear was so filled with complaints by these two against Chang Kiu that he at last dismissed him from court and sent him to take charge of a district in Chihli. With his departure from the palace the reins of power fell into the hands of Li Lin-fu, who was appointed to be prime minister in his stead. From this time forth no one dared to give expression to his honest opinions, for all stood in awe of the man who swayed the thoughts and actions of the Emperor.

Four years after the fall of Chang Kiu the imperial favorite in the harem, Hwei Hwuy, died. It was on this occasion that the Emperor for the first time saw one of the concubines of his son, Prince Show, named Yang Kwei-fei, of whom he became enamoured at first sight. So much was he smitten with her beauty that he forgot the relationship in which she stood to him as a daughter-in-

---

* Chang Kiu-ling is to the mind of a Chinaman the beau ideal minister of state. He was at first greatly esteemed by Huan Tsung, who gladly listened to his counsels. He was a bold outspoken man, and dared to speak his mind in the presence of the Emperor, when all the other high functionaries were silent. By and by as Li Lin-fu gained influence over Huan Tsung the latter became weary of the warnings and reproofs of the man he once looked up to as his political mentor, and he was dismissed the court. The Emperor found when it was too late that he had rejected the one man that could have saved him from the sorrows that embittered his last year. It is said that Chang Kiu-ling used to amuse himself by corresponding with his friends by means of carrier pigeons, which he used to call his "flying slaves."

law, and actually claimed her from the prince, to whom he gave another lady in exchange for her. Yang Kwei-fei at once became the most powerful, as she was the most beloved of all the ladies of the seraglio. The year A. D. 740 is distinguished by the elevation of Confucius to the rank of a Prince. Hitherto in the Confucian temples the famous Duke of Chow had held the first rank and Confucius the second. From this time the duke disappears and the great sage, dressed in the robes of a prince, takes the seat of honour with his face to the south. His chief disciple Yen-hwuy sits on his left hand, and the rest of his seventy-two disciples according to the place that they were supposed to hold in the estimation of Confucius.*

They were all endowed with the titles of dukes, marquises and earls according to their various ranks. In the meantime Ngan Luh-shan, who was a man of profound dissimulation, and who managed to hide beneath an apparently simple exterior an unbounded ambition, managed to gain the favour of the Emperor to such an extent that he was never content unless he had him in the palace. He made him a major-general in the army and gave him command of the troops in Chihli. He was an especial favorite of Yang Kwei-fei, who in the year A. D. 745 had been raised to the position of Kwei Fei, which thus placed her second in rank to the Empress. This was fortunate for him, for the royal favorite was now the greatest power next to the Emperor in the whole country. Huan Tsung seemed completely dominated by his passion for her. He ennobled her father and her three sisters, who were ultimately admitted into the seraglio. The only man that now stood in the way of Ngan Luh-shan's advancement to the highest posts in the gift of Huan Tsung was Li Lin-fu. This man seemed to sacrifice everything to his one desire of possessing power. There was consequently no man so thoroughly hated in the capital as he. He had offended so many and had made so many enemies that he had to take the most extraordinary precautions to save himself from assassination. He had double doors and windows throughout his house, and not even his own servants knew in what room he would sleep on any night. So certain was he of the speedy downfall of his house, were he removed from his position of prime minister, that he adopted the most injurious methods to his country in order to be able to retain it. One of these was specially infamous. Fearful lest some of the imperial generals might win such fame in their wars with the Turcomans and be promoted to high honour in the royal favour as to eclipse his own, he persuaded the Emperor that there was no need of such large Chinese armies on the frontiers as were there now for their protection. He advised that their

---

* The position of Confucius in his temple corresponds to that of the Emperor when he is giving audience to his ministers. He invariably sits with his face towards the south. The civil mandarins are ranged on his left, and the military ones on his right.

defence should be handed over to those of the barbarians that had submitted themselves to China, and the imperial troops withdrawn. Huan Tsung, who was utterly absorbed in the revelries and gaieties of the capital, seemed to have lost all the sense with which he began his reign, and issued an edict ordering the carrying out of this traitorous plan, to the dismay of the loyal captains and soldiers of the army. Against this destructive order, however, there was no appeal, as the Emperor could only be approached through his powerful minister. Five years more passed by when Li Lin-fu died. He had been prime minister for the unprecedentedly long period of nineteen years. Yang Kwoh, a cousin of Yang Kwei-fei, was installed in his place, and he now determined to have his revenge on the man who had thwarted him when he was in power. He got Ngan Luh-shan to memorialize the Emperor stating that Li Lin-fu just before his death was planning an uprising against the government. Such faith had Huan Tsung in this individual, and so easily influenced was he by any plausible story that a clever man might tell him, that he actually believed, without any investigation, this monstrous libel upon a man in whom he had had the most implicit confidence for more than twenty years. He was so transported with rage that he ordered that the coffin of the dead man should be opened, the splendid robes in which he had been dressed torn from his body, the pearls that are usually placed in the mouths of the rich after death taken from within his lips, and the corpse consigned to the grave with every mark of indignity and contumely. He then commanded that every member of his family should be seized and transported to distant parts of the empire, and thus the drama of a great and powerful life ended in tragedy and disgrace. Ngan Luh-shan, now freed from the one man whose power he dreaded, began to take a more independent position and to show the kind of person he was. He utterly despised the new prime minister and refused to obey his commands. Upon this a feud arose between him and Yang Kwoh, which ended in the most deadly enmity. The latter accused him to the Emperor of treasonable purposes, and when by his order he was brought to the capital to see whether the charges were true or not, he managed not only to clear himself, but also to obtain a firmer hold upon the affections of his sovereign.

The first mention of the famous Hanlin or imperial academy is made in the year A. D. 755, although it is more than probable that it existed earlier in the reign of the present Emperor.* It is specially mentioned at this time, because to the members of it was entrusted the writing of the first drafts of the imperial edicts that

---

* The examinations by which men are admitted into this famous academy are held once in three years, and only six out of all the number that appears in the capital from all the provinces can hope to attain to the high honour of being admitted a member. The first on the list gets the title of "Coryphoeus," the second "The Eye of the List," the third "He who has picked the (apricot) Flower, and the fourth, "The one who makes known the Series," because he calls off the names of the graduates. See Williams' Dictionary, page 166

were to be sent throughout the empire. The design of the Emperor in establishing such an institution was his desire to get the best and most reliable information upon any subject that he desired information upon. The first members of it were scholars; Taoist priests, bonzes, artists, musicians, players of chess, etc., but each of them the most renowned in his profession. When Huan Tsung wanted any particular information he had but to step into the building, and he could at once be supplied with it from the very highest living authority. It was one of the rules of the academy that any business transacted in it that concerned the interests of the state was to be kept a profound secret. Next year the formidable insurrection under Ngan Luh-shan broke out. He had intended to wait until the death of the Emperor, but he began to fear that the incessant machinations of the prime minister, Yang Kwoh, would lead to his destruction, so in the last month of the year A. D. 756 he raised the standard of rebellion, and soon found himself at the head of one hundred and fifty thousand men. The greatest consternation and fear were felt wherever he marched. The empire had been at peace for so many years that there were no adequate forces ready to march at once against him. Fung-ch'ang, indeed, led an army of sixty thousand men, and a great battle was fought near K'ai-fung-fu in Honan, in which the imperialists were overthrown with great slaughter. The result of this was that Ngan Luh-shan obtained possession of Lohyang together with the prestige that the command of such a place gave him. The Emperor now wished to go in person against the ungrateful rebel, but this idea was overruled, and two of the bravest generals of the day, Kwo Tze-i and Li Kwang-pi, were despatched into Honan to meet him. Several battles were fought, in which the insurgents suffered defeats, when Ngan Luh-shan, by the advice of his ablest officers, who saw that they could not hope for victory so long as Kwo Tze-i was opposed to them, determined to make a sudden march into Shensi and try and possess himself of the capital. The only enemy that he had to fear on his march to it was Ko Shu-han, who was in command of a large army and who petitioned the Emperor to be allowed to take possession of the defiles that guarded the approaches to Ch'ang-ngan instead of meeting the rebels in the level country. This was most certainly the wisest course to take, but the prime minister thought differently, so a peremptory order came that the royal troops should advance and meet the insurgents. This was done, and the two bodies met at a place called Ling-pau, where Ko Shu-han was defeated and he himself captured. When he was brought into the presence of Ngan Luh-shan he was sternly asked how he had dared to oppose him. He meekly replied, "My eyes are coarse, and they don't know when they are looking upon an Emperor." This politic speech saved his life, and being willing to change sides he was put in command of a part of the rebel force. The greatest dismay followed this defeat; fugitive soldiers who had escaped from the battle kept continually arriving at the capital, who filled the minds of everyone with fear when they told the story of the terrible combat and the treason of Ko Shu-han.

The prime minister, who was concerned for his own life and that of his house, now advised the Emperor to abandon the capital and retire into Sze-chwan, where his soldiers and adherents were numerous. This advice was followed with such haste that no preparations of any kind had been made for the provisioning either of distinguished fugitives, or of the soldiers that accompanied them in their flight. By midday they had reached Hiau-yang, where some coarse rice was cooked for the children, and where it was with the greatest difficulty a very homely meal could be obtained for the royal party. On the morrow they rested at a place named Ma-wei, and here the soldiers—hungry, discontented and mutinous—broke out into open rebellion. They called for the death of the prime minister, who they said had been the cause of their present disasters. The Emperor, who was now completely at the mercy of his subjects, could not protect him, when a party set upon him and murdered him within sound of where the Emperor was staying. The noise in the camp, instead of being allayed by this murder seemed but to intensify, and when Huan Tsung asked of the eunuch Li-tze what was the meaning of it he was told that the soldiers would not be satisfied until the beautiful Yang Kwei-fei also was put to death. The Emperor at first refused to consent to this. He was as deeply enamoured of her as ever he had been in his life. He was told, however, that it was either her life or his that must be sacrificed, and the sooner he decided this question the better for all concerned. After a most painful and agonizing struggle he at last gave the order, and she was taken into a Buddhist temple near by and strangled. Her body was then brought out and exhibited to the soldiers, who seemed perfectly satisfied, and at once returned to their duty and allegiance. Huan Tsung was evidently so overcome by the scenes that he had recently passed through that he no longer desired to be Emperor. He accordingly insisted upon resigning his throne to his son who, however, declined to accept the honour that belonged to his father. He agreed at the urgent request of the people, several thousands of whom had rapidly enrolled themselves as soldiers for the defence of the empire, to remain with them whilst his father continued his journey into Sze-chwan. A month afterwards at Ling-wu, where he had taken up his abode, he became emperor under the title of Su Tsung. Whilst these tragic events were taking place at Ma-wei, Ngan Luh-shan, delighted with the news that the Emperor had so quickly abandoned his capital, hurried forward with a large force and occupied the city. His first act was to put to death the ladies who had been left behind in the palace as well as the families of those that had followed the fortunes of Huan Tsung. The town was then delivered over to the will of his soldiers, who gave themselves up to riot and debauch of every kind.

Su Tsung—A. D. 756-763.

Su Tsung began his reign with every prospect that he would scarcely be able to hold his own against the overwhelming forces that were everywhere in the field against him. There were not more than twenty or thirty great officials at his court who were prepared to aid him in the arduous responsibilities that he had undertaken. The eastern and western capitals were in the hands of the rebels, and their generals were every day adding to their conquests. One of these, Shih-ming, was specially distinguished, and seemed to be able to claim victory to his standards wherever he marched. The towns of P'ing-yuan, Ch'ing-ho, P'o-p'ing, Sin-tu and Jiau-yang successively fell before him, after the most heroic defence had been made by those who were in charge of them. The story of Sui-yang, in the north-east of Honan, is a most thrilling and exciting one. Tze-chi, another of the rebel generals, had surrounded it with one hundred and thirteen thousand men, whilst the garrison consisted of only six thousand eight hundred. Its commandant, Chang-sun, was a man worthy of being classed amongst the great heroes of antiquity, and his men seemed to wish to rival him in his bravery and enthusiasm. Every attempt that Tze-chi put forth to capture the city was defeated. Sudden sallies were made and ingenious devices adopted by which large numbers of the rebels were slain. On one occasion Chang-sun made the night echo with the sound of gongs that were beaten without cessation. The rebels thought that reinforcements had arrived, and so stood to their arms. When the morning light came they saw, to their disgust, that it had been simply a ruse to annoy them. They retired to rest, and soon the whole camp was asleep, when Chang-sun, who had his men all ready, rushed out, and before the enemy could be put in array they were slaughtered in large numbers. The forces arrayed against him, however, were too numerous for him to successfully contend against for ever. No reinforcements came to help these heroic defenders of the city. In time provisions began to fail, and everything eatable within the town was used up. So great was the extremity that Chang-sun actually killed some of his concubines to give to his hungry soldiers. At length only four hundred unconquered men remained in the city, and as they were not enough to man the walls the rebels swarmed over them and took possession of it. When Chang-sun was brought before Tze-chi he was offered pardon for the resistance he had made if he would join the rebels. He haughtily disdained to have his life spared on such conditions, stating that an officer of the T'angs could never descend so low as to desert his sovereign at a time when his services were most essential for him. He was then immediately put to death by being quartered. Whilst these exciting events were going on, Ngan Luh-shan, the cause of all this misery to China, had disappeared from the scene. He was assassinated by his eldest son Ngan K'ing-su, because he had determined that his second son, the offspring of a favoured concubine, should succeed him in the new dynasty of Yen which he had founded, to the exclusion of the one who was his rightful heir. It was now determined, A. D. 758, that an attempt should be made to recapture the capital. Kwo Tze-i had arrived with his forces at Ling-wu. The Turfans had, moreover, offered to come to the help of Su Tsung, and four thousand Ouigors, led by the son of their king, had arrived to give active assistance in this hour of his extremity. Su Tsung was so grateful for this aid that he promised to give them the spoils of the city. "The land and the people shall be mine, but all the rest shall be yours," he said. The heir-apparent fell so much in love with this savage chieftain that they became sworn brothers and vowed to vie with each other as to who should show the bravest front in the attack on Ch'ang-ngan. It was in the month of September that the troops in three grand divisions moved on towards the city. The front division was led by Shu, the heir-apparent, and consisted of one hundred and fifteen thousand men ; the second by Kwo Tze-i, and the third by Wang Sze-li. The rebel forces in the town were commanded by Li Kwei-jin, and consisted roughly of about a hundred thousand men. The royal troops advanced with the greatest steadiness and bravery. They were determined either to conquer or to die. There was no faltering in any one in that great host that moved forward that day for the deliverance of their country from revolution and bloodshed. Rank after rank marched on as though it had been a living wall, before which everything must give way. The battle commenced about twelve o'clock in the day and lasted till six. No thoughts of mercy entered into the hearts of either side, and so the conflict was stern and serious. The rebels suffered a great defeat, and sixty thousand of them lay dead after the fighting was over. Yeh-hu, with his four thousand Ouigors, had specially distinguished themselves during the fight, and it was mainly owing to them that the victory had been obtained. The royal army marched with flying colours into the capital, and Su Tsung took possession of the palace that his father had left in such sorrow and haste. The next day Yeh-hu reminded Shu of the promise that had been made by Su Tsung that the riches of the city should be his if they were successful in driving out the rebels. "That is quite true," replied Shu, "and the engagement shall be kept. I beg, however, of you to consent to a delay in the fulfillment of the promise. If we were now to hand over the city for you to plunder, however, should we expect to gain possession of Lohyang, which is still in the hands of the rebels? They would hear of the way in which the city had been treated after its capture, and they would fight on the side of the insurgents rather than give aid against them if they believed they were to be handed over to the tender mercies of its conquerors." Yeh-hu acknowledged the justice of these remarks, and consented to wait for his reward till after the fall of Lohyang. "But let us away," he said. "My men shall help you to take the place, and we shall have the honour of driving the rebels out of it as we have done from this."

In three days the troops were on their march for the eastern capital. The army advanced against it in three divisions. One of these was commanded by Kwo Tze-i, another by Li Kwang-pi, and the third by Yeh-hu, who was to lead his savage followers by a round-about way and take the rebels in the rear. Ngan K'ing-su, who heard of the intended attack, got all the men together that he could possibly assemble and went out with a considerable force to meet the division under Kwo Tze-i. In the engagement that ensued K'ing-su was getting the better of his distinguished opponent, when the arrows from the Ouigors, who had come up whilst the battle was raging, fell amongst his men. Looking round they saw the barbarians coming on at the run with savage mien and loud discordant cries. A panic at once seized them, and they fled in disorder, pursued now by both divisions. Lohyang was at once occupied, and as Yeh-hu consented to accept its plunder instead of that of Ch'ang-ngan the city was given over to him and his followers. The barbarians were not by any means satisfied with what they got. Too many had been before them who were as skilful as they in discovering the hidden riches of the place, and they gave vent to their dissatisfaction in loud complaints. In order to compensate them Shu ordered that ten thousand pieces of silk should be presented to them in the name of the Emperor for their services. With these their ill-humour disappeared, and they were once more the faithful allies of Su Tsung, ready to help in the deliverance of the empire. Ngan K'ing-su, who had fled to Yeh, became suspicious of Shih Tze-ming, who, with a force of eighty thousand men at his control and the command of thirteen large districts, had stood silently by whilst he was being driven from Lohyang. He sent two officers with five thousand men to capture and put him to death, but having got information of their intentions he seized the whole party and sent in his submission to Su Tsung. The Emperor was warned by those who knew him that there was no dependence to be placed upon him, and that he ought to be on his guard against a man with such a force at his back, and who was known to be such a master of military tactics. He refused to listen to these, and actually made him a prince with large powers of administration, but in little more than six months he had renounced his fealty to Su Tsung, and was again in the field with a large army. In the month of November of the year A. D. 759 two armies under Kwo Tze-i and Li Kwang-pi were sent to invest Yeh and try and capture K'ing-su. The latter in his distress appealed to Shih Sze-ming to come to his help, and he promised that if a successful resistance were made he would resign everything to him and make him the leader of the rebellion and of the new dynasty of Yen. Shih Sze-ming hurried with all his forces to his aid, when Kwo Tze-i was compelled to retreat without fighting. He then entered Yeh, and having killed K'ing-su he became the sole leader of any note that was in arms against the government. Li Kwang-pi now superseded Kwo Tze-i in his command, but he was soon compelled to retreat from Lohyang before the superior forces of Shih Sze-ming, who, however, in his turn in the course of a few months was obliged to abandon it and fly to Tanyang. For the next eighteen months fighting went on with alternate success, but Shih Sze-ming showed that as a commander he was the superior of Li Kwang, for at the end of that time he was in possession of the eastern capital, notwithstanding all the efforts of the imperial general to keep him out of it. There is no question but that at this time the T'ang dynasty was in the greatest possible peril, and it seemed likely that it would have to give way to the new one of Yen, when it was relieved from its danger by the murder of Shih Sze-ming by his son Shih Chow-i, in revenge for the preference which had been shown by his father for his younger brother. After a reign of seven years Su Tsung died without anything very remarkable having been accomplished by him. Unfortunately he had been ruled by a powerful eunuch, who had not added to the reputation of the sovereign. Another of these miserable men, who had a spite against Kwo Tze-i, managed to get him put out of his command for two years at the most critical time of the nation's history, and when his services were most imperatively required to crush a most formidable and dangerous rebellion. His father Huan Tsung died only a short time before him, at the advanced age of seventy-eight. The heir-apparent Shu now succeeded to the throne, whose historic title is

Tai Tsung—A. D. 763-780.

When Tai Tsung ascended the throne there was disorder both in the palace and in the empire. Li Hu-kwoh, the imperious eunuch who had exercised a powerful influence over the late Emperor, now attempted to rule with even greater arrogance, both over the high officials of the palace and also over Tai Tsung. His rule, indeed, became so intolerable that the Emperor sent a body of soldiers suddenly to his residence and had him put to death. The condition of the country, however, was a most serious question that had to be met promptly, for in spite of all the efforts of the imperial generals the rebels were not only holding their own, but actually seemed as though they would in the end gain the mastery in the struggle that was going on for supremacy. In this emergency the help of the Ouigors was solicited by Tai Tsung, and in response a large body of these hardy barbarians marched into Honan, under the guidance of their chieftain Tingli. When they reached that region they were so much struck by the desolation of the country and the poverty-stricken look of the people that they became insubordinate and showed their feelings by plundering and robbing wherever they went. They had expected to be rewarded for their long marches and the dangers of battle by the spoil of rich cities and prosperous homes. Instead of these they were met by ruined towns and half-starved peasantry, and they felt as though they had been cheated by the Emperor of the rewards they had looked for, in this, that used to be, the most fertile and prosperous part of China. Fortunately Tingli had married the two daughters of a Chinese general, and the good offices of his father-in-law having been brought into requisition the disappointed barbarians turned heartily to the performance of the serious duties for which they had been enlisted. From the time of their appearance the fortunes of the rebels began to wane, and in the course of a few months their cause collapsed. Their chief, Shih Chau-i, having been beaten in several battles, and seeing no hope of retrieving his fortunes, strangled himself in a wood in which he had taken refuge, and the great rebellion of Ngan Luh-shan was thus at an end, after vast misery had been inflicted upon the country and countless lives had been sacrificed in the struggle. The desolation of the country, and the reduction of the population from over fifty millions to less than twenty, were not the only evils attendant upon this most bloody and disastrous revolution. In the struggle for life and death the Emperor was compelled to call in his soldiers that were guarding the frontiers, and thus to leave them unprotected.   The barbarians took advantage of the weakness of the empire and determined to combine together and invade it.   The Turfans and three other nations collected an army of over three hundred thousand men and marched on Singan. Kwo Tze-i attempted to collect a sufficient force to meet them, but all that he could manage to gather round his standard were two thousand men. Of course with this small body he could do nothing. He consequently retreated, still hoping that as the news spread of the invasion of the barbarians the loyal men from all parts of the country would rally to his aid.

The barbarians came on steadily, and crossing the Wei, they in due time took possession of the capital, where they remained for over a fortnight. The Emperor and his court fled to Honan, and these savage victors plundered and murdered to their hearts' content. Kwo, who was joined by two thousand more men, kept well within the hearing of the out-post of the Turfans, and kept up such a beating of gongs during the day, and burning of torches during the night, that they became terrified, lest they were going to be attacked by a superior force.   They had such a dread of Kwo and his generalship that they determined to retreat, which they did, with the plunder of the capital. To add to the sorrows of the country at this time Hwai-yen, the father-in-law of the Ouigor king, and who had performed such loyal service in helping to crush the rebellion, now turned traitor, and actually invited Tingli to come with a large force to help him in his rebellion against Tai Tsung. This he very willingly did, and he joined Hwai-yen at T'ai-yuan in Shan-si, who awaited him there with the Chinese troops that had consented to join his fortunes.

Kwo was sent against him, and no sooner had he come near Hwai-yen's camp than the great body of his men, who had formerly been under his command, incontinently deserted their leader and went over to the service of Kwo, and Hwai-yen had to take refuge in the camp of the barbarians, who were compelled to retreat towards their own country. Next year, A. D. 766, Hwai-yen again appeared with nearly one hundred and thirty thousand of his savage auxiliaries, but died very soon after their arrival. The Turfans, after capturing and plundering Fang-t'ien, retreated to their own territories, and the Ouigors, terrified by the appearance of Kwo, made a treaty with him and peaceably evacuated the country. Though delivered for a time from the scourge of the barbarians the people were in a sad state of poverty and distress. Kwo, finding that he had no other way of sustaining his army, turned his soldiers into farmers. After a time they had abundance and to spare, and the sight of so many men cultivating the soil and living in plenty had such an effect on the peasantry, who in despair had allowed their fields to lie fallow, that they returned to their homes in large numbers and resumed the cultivation of their farms. The government at this time was in the greatest possible straits to find funds to pay their soldiers and carry on the work of the country. A decree was issued that the land tax, instead of being collected after the harvest had been gathered in, as was the usual custom, should be delivered to the tax gatherers as soon as the crops had sprouted. Those who had been able to hide their money from the various plunderers that had visited them were able to pay these taxes, but no imperial edict could exact money from those who had been deprived of their all.

This year a magnificent Buddhist monastery was built in the capital by the eunuch Yu, and on the fifteenth day of the seventh moon there was inaugurated a solemn service for the dead ancestors of Tai Tsung for seven generations back. In this service an abundance of food was prepared for the hungry spirits of the dead, whom it was said by the priests the rulers of Hades had let out on this special occasion to partake of the good things prepared for them in the world of men. Since that time the seventh month in China has been specially famous for the offerings that are made to the spirits that have no living representatives in the world, and throughout the eighteen provinces, in every town and district, the dead are remembered by the offerings of food and by theatrical performances. Nothing of importance took place during the remainder of Tai Tsung's reign, excepting that there was a slight rebellion in Chihli, caused by an uprising of one of Shih Sze-ming's lieutenants. Four generals were sent to put it down ; but two of them having been heavily bribed, due punishment was not meted out to the rebel leader, though his cause was completely crushed. The Emperor died after a reign of seventeen years at the age of fifty-three, and was succeeded by his son, whose royal title is Teh Tsung.

CHAPTER XXII.

THE T'ANG DYNASTY (CONTINUED).

Teh Tsung—A. D. 780-805.

THIS ruler was thirty-nine years old when he ascended the dragon throne, and his first acts showed that he appreciated somewhat the responsibilities of his high office, and had thoughts of ruling well and wisely. He sent home several hundreds of the ladies of his harem in order to lighten the burdens of the state. He also sent adrift on the hills a number of elephants that were kept in the royal menagerie, and he passed a law that his ambassadors to foreign countries should not receive presents, and also that tributary states should not be compelled to send strange and wonderful articles to the capital, but the common commodities of their countries. China was fortunate at this time in having two able financiers, who, though they were rivals, had yet the honour of proposing measures which were highly serviceable to the state and were helpful in restoring prosperity to the country. The first of these was Liu-yen, who devised various methods of increasing the revenue. The salt tax, for example, under his skillful management was made to produce ten times as much as it had hitherto done. Unlike the vast majority of men in his position he made nothing for himself by these reforms, for when his property was afterwards confiscated to the state it was found to consist of no other effects than a few books. The next was Yang-yen, who got Teh Tsung to abolish the three existing modes of taxation and service to the state, viz., land tax, compulsory labour, and payment in kind, for a semi-annual collection of a money tax, an assessment that was hitherto unknown in the country. Unfortunately these men were at daggers drawn with each other, and Liu-yen was put to death at the instigation of Yang-yen, whilst he again was banished to Hainan through the intrigues of a privy councillor named Lu-k'i. In the second year of Teh Tsung's reign a formidable rebellion broke out in Chihli. This arose from serious discontent that had arisen amongst certain nobles, because the Emperor refused to allow their titles and honours to be transmitted to their children. Su Tsung unfortunately had given a promise in the first year of his reign that certain men that had come to his assistance, when his fortunes were at a low ebb, should be rewarded by the gift of lands and titles that should become hereditary in the family. Teh Tsung, who saw that this would produce a class of feudal nobles similar to those that caused such wars and commotions at the close of the Chou dynasty, very wisely refused to be bound by this unwise engagement. A number who were concerned rushed to arms and a civil war that might have become formidable broke out. It was soon put down, however, but unfortunately jealousy and discontent amongst those that had been engaged in the suppression of it caused even a more serious danger to the state. Chu-tze became the leader of a new rising, and the numbers of soldiers that joined his standard were so great that the Emperor fled in terror, first to Hien-yang and afterwards to the fortified city of Fang-t'ien. Unfortunately about this time the famous commander and warrior Kwo Tze-i died at the advanced age of eighty-five. It was a sad loss for Teh Tsung, for his name was a tower of strength on the imperial side, and old though he was his mind was clear and active, and would have been of invaluable service at this particular crisis.* It was the misfortune of the Emperor that when the desperate circumstances in which he was placed demanded that he should be aided by men of the highest ability he was left in the hands of those who were either honey-combed with treason or of such poor administrative powers that they were incapable of any great acts of statesmanship to extricate him out of his difficulties.

Chu-tze was certainly a man of action. He declared the T'ang dynasty abolished, and his own, which he called the Han, established in its stead. He next seized upon seventy-seven members of the royal family and had them executed. Knowing that his fortunes depended upon his army he made great exertions to send a large force up to capture Fang-t'ien. This place, however, had been fortified and provisioned for this very emergency that had been predicted by some prophet, and resisted the utmost efforts of the rebels to overcome its valiant defenders. After a time an army under Lu-ch'i came to the support of Teh Tsung, and routing the besieging force delivered him from the pressing danger in which he had been placed. Fighting went on for three or four years more, with varied success, but Chu-tze managed to retain his hold upon the capital, whilst Teh Tsung was compelled to be a fugitive in his own dominions. At length Luh-ch'i, one of the most faithful and outspoken of the royal ministers, advised the Emperor to make a confession of his wrong to his people and to trust himself to their generosity to rally around him and restore him to his throne. Teh Tsung was intelligent enough to see that this was the wisest course for him to pursue, so he issued an edict that was to be read in all the important places of his empire, in which he made full confession of the misdeeds and mistakes he had committed. "In governing

---

*The character of Kwo Tze-i is one of the finest in all Chinese history. He was a man of consummate ability, and had been on the whole very successful in his campaigns. Notwithstanding his successes, and the many devices of the evil coun-sellors of the Emperor to injure his character, no one ever dared to breathe a word against his loyalty. His name is mentioned in the famous Nestorian tablet, which was erected A. D. 781, and in which the story of the progress of Christianity in China, since its introduction in A. D. 635 till the time of its erection, is told. He was blessed with a very large number of sons and grandsons. His eight sons, and his seven sons-in-law, all occupied high places under the government, and at the time of his death the family that had grown up about him that recognized him as the head consisted of three thousand persons, great and small.

an empire," he said, "it is important that the ruler should keep faith with his people, and should correct his faults. I am entirely ignorant of how to rule my subjects. I have never realized the toil and labour that the husbandman has to endure, or the danger and hardships of the soldier. My goodness has never penetrated to the people, and their sorrows have never reached me, and thus doubts have arisen between us because of the wall of separation between us. Rebellion has been the consequence, and my capital has been taken from me and the temples of my ancestors. I confess my wrong, and I announce forgiveness to all the leaders but Chu-tze. He has taken the royal title, and desecrated the graves of my ancestors, and him I dare not forgive." The effects of this edict were most salutary for the royal cause. When the nation became really sensible that the Emperor knew his faults and promised to be led by the counsels of good and honest men, a wave of loyalty swept through the country, and in a few months after it was issued the adherents of Chu-tze began to desert him. Finding his cause desperate he started with a body of men that still remained faithful to him for the territories of the Turfans, but his passage was everywhere obstructed by the royal governors of the districts through which ie wished to pass. At length, seeing that escape was hopeless, and wishing to gain the royal favour, his officers cut off his head and sent it to the troops that were pursuing them, and thus this most formidable rebellion was crushed, and Teh Tsung restored to his capital.

The remaining years of this amiable but weak monarch's reign were passed without anything eventful happening in them. The Turfans were frustrated in a design they had secretly planned of capturing and destroying three of the principal officers of the crown and of afterwards gaining possession of the northern part of the empire. The Ouigors laid aside all their enmity to China, and by request Hien-ngan, a daughter of the Emperor, was given to their chief in marriage. This kept that hardy and vigorous race at rest for many years to come. Floods desolated the country in various parts of the empire and caused great loss of life and diminution of the revenue. In order to provide a fund to meet deficiencies of this kind a tax was put upon tea. Teh Tsung died after a reign of twenty-five years. His end was undoubtedly hastened by grief for his son, who was afflicted with an incurable disease. He passed away suddenly at the last, leaving the throne to Shun Tsung, who, however, occupied it for only a few months, when by the advice of his privy council he abdicated in favour of his son, whose name in history is

Hien Tsung—A. D. 806-821.

Hien Tsung was twenty-eight years of age when he succeeded to his father. The position in which he was at once placed was a very trying one. The eunuchs of the palace had managed to absorb a great deal of power in their hands, and they had sufficient influence to make even the Emperor afraid of running counter to their wishes. Hien Tsung had therefore to be very circumspect in the way in which he conducted himself, even though he was the ruler of the empire. The first real sorrow that met him on his assumption of power was the rebellion of Liu-pi. This man was a governor in Sz-chwan, and because his request that his jurisdiction should be extended over three new departments was refused, he raised the standard of rebellion. The Emperor was in great perplexity of mind, for he was afraid that owing to the great distance and the unfavourable nature of the country to be operated upon, the royal troops would be long in crushing the insurrection. One of his ministers comforted him by saying, "that Liu-pi was only a stupid man of letters and would soon succumb to the first real general that was ordered against him." Kau Tsung-wen was sent with an army to fight him, and in a great battle at Luh-t'eu-kwan he defeated him. Liu-pi with all his family was forwarded to the capital, where they were all executed. Hien Tsung soon began to show the weakness of his intellect by his belief in spirits and supernatural beings and in his endeavours to find the elixir of life. His ministers tried to weaken his faith in such things by a reference to the unfortunate experience of Wei Ti, of the Han dynasty, and to Tai Tsung, who was said to have died through taking some medicine that the bonzes had given him, and for a time he was persuaded to give up the study of these things. A very curious case occurred at this time that illustrates a custom then in existence. A man had slain another because he had killed his father. He was apprehended, and the question now to be decided was whether the avenger of blood should be judged by the teachings of the Confucian classics, or by the law of the land which, however, had no definite ruling for a case like the one in question. The classics in their enforcement of the duty of filial piety seemed to sanction the conduct of the man when he killed the murderer of his father. The case was brought before the famous Han Wen-kung, who stated the case thus, "If we put him to death there is danger that we shall do a grievous injury to the filial sentiment in men and deter them from doing anything to avenge the wrongs done to their parents. On the other hand, if he is not punished we shall encourage violent acts in the community, and men will be taking the law into their own hands and filling society with bloodshed." In order to meet both difficulties the son was banished to the distant region of Canton.

In the year A. D. 816 a formidable rebellion broke out in the district of Hwai-si, in Honan, headed by Wu-yuan, who was dissatisfied because he was not allowed to succeed his father in the governorship of the region over which he had ruled. Unfortunately he was aided by a military commander named Li Sz-tau, who, professing to march against him with two thousand men, joined his forces to his, because a petition which the latter had presented to the Emperor praying him to pardon Wu-yuan had not been granted.

Fancying that the prime minister was the cause of the displeasure of the Emperor, the leaders of the rebellion called for volunteers to go to the capital and murder him. These were soon forthcoming, and stationing themselves in ambush they killed him with arrows as he was entering the palace and wounded a high official named P'ei-tu, who was with him at the time. Hien Tsung, instead of being alarmed by these lawless acts, determined to use all the force that he possessed to put down the insurrection. An edict was issued, ordering that for the future a guard of soldiers should always attend the prime minister, and two generals—Han-yuan and Li-su—were despatched with a large army against Wei-yuan. The former of these was unwilling to act vigorously and crush the rebellion at once, for he saw that with the return of peace his command of power would cease. He therefore did everything he could to fetter the movements of Li-su and to prevent any decisive action being taken. The consequence was that for more than two years desultory fighting went on, but no serious attempt was made to bring matters to a crisis. The Emperor becoming seriously alarmed, and being distressed that the insurrection should foil all the efforts of the royal troops to suppress it, P'ei-tu, the prime minister, undertook that if he were allowed to take command of the troops he would speedily crush the rebellion. "In fact the rebels will be conquered," he said, "before I can reach the army, for the commanders will be so afraid that I shall carry away their laurels that they will have vanquished the enemy before I can encounter him." This prophecy turned out to be true. Li-su determined to act on his own responsibility and gain the victory before P'ei-tu appeared. The rebel army lay before him, and the city of Tsai-chow, when Wu-yuan lived, was distant a little over twenty miles. As soon as the shades of evening fell he called his officers around him and told them of his determination to march at once before the enemy learned his plans and capture this place and seize the rebel chief. Nine thousand men were then despatched in three divisions, and at three o'clock in the morning they were thundering at the gates of the town. No preparation had been made for such an attack, and the place was easily stormed. Wu-yuan was sent in chains to Singan, and with this act the rebellion may be said to have collapsed, for Li Sz-tau, in the course of a few months, submitted and gave his son as a hostage for his good behaviour. Scarcely was the country pacified when Hien Tsung again became afflicted with the craze of wishing to find some elixir that would give him immortality. He issued an edict enquiring if there was any Taoist wizard in his dominions that could give him the requisite information, and commanding his presence at the capital. In response to this Liu-pi appeared, who stated that on the mountain of T'ien-t'ai, in the department of Taichow, in the present province of Chehkiang, there was a marvellous herb that had the power of indefinitely prolonging life. He did not know its exact whereabouts, but he requested to be made the magistrate over that particular district, and he would then order the soldiers under his command to search for it. The Emperor had such faith in this charlatan that he gave him the position he had desired. Next year a memorial was presented to him, telling him that there was a Buddha's finger in the Fa-men monastery in Shensi, and that every thirty years it was the means of bringing good harvests and peace to the district in which it was situated. As this was the auspicious year, the Emperor ordered that it should be brought with all due ceremony to the capital and carried in state to all the monasteries in it. Han Wen-kung presented a vigorous remonstrance against the honours that were being paid to this alleged relic, and this state paper exists to the present day. Hien Tsung was exceedingly angry with him, and proposed to have him put to death, but by the interposition of P'ei-tu he was given a post in the semi-barbarious district of Chau-chow, near Swatow, where he exercised the most beneficent influence over the people entrusted to his care.* After a year's vain search on the sides of the T'ien-t'ai mountain for the herb that was to drive away death, Liu-pi, fearing the wrath of the Emperor, fled from his government, but he was soon arrested and sent to the capital. Fortunately he found a friend amongst the eunuchs there, and between them they compounded a medicine which they declared was the elixir of immortality. Whatever the ingredients of it were, it had a most pernicious effect upon the temper of Hien Tsung. He became irritable to such a degree that he was offended at the least thing that ran counter to his will, and he would for trivial offences order men to be taken out and immediately executed. In this way a large number of the eunuchs lost their lives. One of his ministers observing the baleful effects of this life-giving elixir upon him besought His Majesty to give it up until Liu-pi had tried it upon himself for at least a year. This he refused to do, and one day the news flew through the palace that he was dead. The popular belief was that he had been given his quietus by Ch'en Fung-chi, a powerful eunuch, who dreaded lest he and his fellows might fall a victim to the caprice of the Emperor. He was succeeded by his second son (Hing) through the all-prevailing influence of the eunuchs of the palace, who had power enough to exclude the eldest from the succession. His royal title was Mu Tsung.

Mu Tsung—A.D. 821-825.

His first act was to order the execution of Liu-pi, who had been the cause of the death of his father. The only memorable thing that happened during his reign of four years was the restoration

---

* Han Yu or Han Wen-kung was one of the ablest statesmen and philosophers that the T'ang dynasty produced. In order to reconcile the theory of Confucius, that men are good by nature, with that of Sun-tze, that men are radically bad, he thought out a scheme of his own, by which he endeavoured to prove that both were right, as might be seen from the experience of life. His system was largely accepted by the scholars of China till the times of Chu-hi, when it was discarded for the orthodox Confucian one, the same that is held at the present day.

of Han-yu to favour and the permission for him to return to his home in the north.   Urged by the same mad purpose that resulted in the death of his father of obtaining some medicine that would secure him immortality, he permitted himself to be deceived by a designing charlatan, and drinking his elixir he paid the penalty of his folly with his life.   He was succeeded by his son

King Tsung—A. D. 825-827.

This man soon gave signs that he was utterly unfitted for the position he was called to occupy.   The declining fortunes of the T'angs demanded that a man of strong will and elevated character should ascend the throne to save the reigning house from destruction.   He never for a moment realized the responsibilities that belonged to him as a sovereign.   His whole aim and purpose was to get as much pleasure and enjoyment out of life as possible. He indulged in drinking carouses and played ball, and had musical entertainments with his favourites, whilst the business of the state was almost entirely given up.   He met with his privy council not more than once or twice a month to discuss the condition of the empire.   One of his ministers, Shui-si, was so distressed with this state of things that he formally protested against his conduct. Kneeling in front of him he reminded him that his father was not yet buried, and that it was not becoming that his son should indulge in merriment and noisy dissipation.   He entreated him to give more time to the concerns of the empire.   He got so excited as he went over the various matters that required reform that he knocked his head upon the ground so vigorously that the blood flowed from his forehead.

King Tsung seemed moved for the moment, and dismissed him with a promise of amendment, but the impression was only momentary, for he went on precisely as before.   Li-teh, a governor in Chehkiang, presented a memorial in which six important points were brought before his notice, in which he was prayed to make reformation.   The first of these was that he should get up earlier in the morning ; second, that he should wear dresses more suitable to his exalted condition ; third, that he should not allow his officers to make him expensive presents of curios ; fourth, that he should be willing to listen to the advice of his loyal ministers ; fifth, that he should dismiss all the disloyal and cease to believe so much in his eunuchs ; and sixthly, that he should be careful not to go about at night time, lest he should be assassinated.   Again the Emperor signified his pleasure for the advice that was given him, but he made no change whatsoever in his manner of life.   His intemperance tended to make his temper, which was not naturally good, overbearing and domineering, and in his fits of passion he would insult and ill-treat the eunuchs that were in attendance upon him. One of these, Liu-k'o, had been specially abused by him, and he determined to have his revenge. One evening after the Emperor's return from fox hunting he had drank deeply, and going into a neighbouring room to change his dress he was stabbed to death by Liu-k'o, who was lying hid in it. Some of the eunuchs now attempted to set up a nominee of their own in the person of Prince Li-wu, but one of their own number of the name of Wang-shen, who had a considerable party of his own amongst them, sided with the nobles, and the second son of Mu Tsung was proclaimed Emperor, whilst Li-wu and Li-k'o were ruthlessly put to death. The new sovereign is known in history by the name of

Wen Tsung—A. D. 827-841.

This prince began his reign with every sign that he was going to prove to be the ruler that was specially required at this critical time in the history of the T'angs. He was exceedingly temperate in his manners and opposed to all unnecessary expenditure. He dismissed three thousand ladies from the royal harem, and sent them to their homes. He also gave audience to his ministers every other day, and seemed in earnest that the best measures should be adopted for the government of his people. It was soon discovered, however, that all this excellence was in a great measure counterbalanced by his want of firmness. Plans which had been carefully considered at the meeting of the privy council, and to which he had given his adhesion, would in the course of a short time be abandoned, because he had been influenced by some other person of stronger will than his own.

The usurpation by the eunuchs of all power in the palace became more and more intolerable. That this was so is manifest from an incident that took place at the first examination for the degree of Kujin which the Emperor had just brought into existence by an edict issued A. D. 828. The man that stood first amongst those who had passed successfully was Liu-fan. The examiners had been struck with the great ability that his paper showed, and they were unanimous that his name should head the list. Unfortunately the subject he had chosen was the eunuchs, their misdeeds, with the demand that they should be suppressed in order to save the state from great disorders. So afraid were the examiners of passing a man that had dared to write so boldly about this great power in the palace that they quietly passed him over, and twenty-two other names were selected, to whom the degree was given as well as official positions under the government. The historian tells us that the whole of the twenty-two refused to accept their appointments until justice had been done to Liu-fan, who they declared should have headed the list. Not even the Emperor dared at this crisis to give Liu-fan the honours he deserved for his courage in attacking what was really a national danger. Almost immediately after this, Wen Tsung began to plan with his prime minister for the destruction of his tyrants, but the matter becoming known they brought an accusation against the minister, and in self-defence he was compelled to resign his office and disappear from public life. Six years after this another attempt was made by Wen Tsung to deliver himself from bondage by endeavouring to deprive Wang-shen, the chief of the eunuchs, of the great control he exercised in the palace by appointing another, named C'hen Sz-liang, as his rival in authority. This seems to have succeeded, for, shortly after, the Emperor was able to send a confidential messenger, who managed to get Wang-shen poisoned.

It was now determined that at the funeral of Wang-shen, at which the whole of the eunuchs were ordered to attend, a general massacre of the whole body should be made. The secret, however, was badly kept, and the eunuchs came prepared to meet their foes. Instead of waiting for the attack they fell upon their enemies and slew five great mandarins with fully sixteen hundred of their attendants, whilst only about half a score of themselves were killed in the affray. As they had the command of the household troops, who obeyed them implicitly, they showed their power after this victory by committing the greatest excesses in the capital, murdering every one that they deemed hostile to them and pillaging the houses of the well-to-do. Nothing of any great importance happened during the remainder of Wen Tsung's reign. Shortly before his death, feeling himself too weak to carry on the duties of the state, he wished to appoint the heir-apparent, Ch'engmi, to act for him, but this was opposed by the eunuchs. Dying shortly after, they elevated Wen Tsung's younger brother, Ch'an, to the throne, who at once had Ch'eng-mi, his nephew, murdered, in order that he might not be disturbed by the thought that he had a rival near him that might any day try to claim the power that was now possessed by him.

Wu Tsung (A. D. 841-847)

was twenty-seven years old when he ascended the tottering throne of the T'angs. He was a man of considerable ability, and under more favourable circumstances his fame might have descended to after ages for the ability with which he ruled his people. There was one local rebellion, led by Liu Chan, which was easily suppressed, however, and one invasion of the Ouigors, which was speedily repelled, during his short reign. The one important thing he did was to order that all the Taoist and Buddhist priests and nuns throughout the empire should return to their homes, and instead of living in idleness and immorality engage in the ordinary business and avocations of life. Shortly after this important law had been carried out he was weak enough to believe that though his predecessors had failed in gaining immortality there was no reason that he should not be the lucky finder of the elixir of life. He accordingly began to take the medicine that some quack had prepared for him. From this time a remarkable change came over him. His temper, which had been an easy one before, now became moody and irritable. He would be seized with fits of joy and anon tossed with tempests of passion. When he asked the wizard the cause of this he was told that it was the result of the gradual change of his bones that was going on. They were being etherealized, so that ere long he would be able to pass rapidly through the air as the nimblest of the fairies could do. Wu Tsung believed in this absurdity and continued to drink this life-giving mixture, as he thought, but after a few months' experience of it he died, another victim to the superstition of the age.

Suan Tsung—A. D. 847-860—

the thirteenth son of Hien Tsung, who was then thirty-seven years of age, succeeded him on the throne and reigned thirteen years (A. D. 847-860). This sovereign was the nominee of the eunuchs who now assumed the rôle of king makers. Their minds were inclined towards him, because as a young man he had seemed half-witted, and therefore they deemed that he would prove to be a willing instrument in their hands. In this they were entirely mistaken. He turned out to be a man of intelligence and decision of character, and one who kept the reins of government well in his own hands. He was constant in his attendance at the audiences with his council, and the petitions that were presented to it received his most careful consideration. Many of his utterances were so profound, and he showed such a willingness to listen to the advice of his ministers, that he came to have the title of the second T'ai Tsung.

All his wisdom and sagacity, however, could not save him from the fatal tendency of his house to believe in the charms of famous Taoist wizards for the indefinite prolonging of life. In the year A. D. 857 hearing that there was a celebrated Taoist priest in one of the great temples near Canton he sent for him. When he was brought into his presence Suan Tsung said to him, "My ancestors sought in vain for a medicine that would save them from dying. Is it possible for me to be more successful than they"? The priest replied, "Let the Emperor subdue his passions and live a noble life, and then he will of course obtain the endless happiness that Heaven has to give him. Exemption from death is something that man may never hope to find." This noble answer stopped him for the time in his search for the herb of immortality, but two years after he fell a victim to the craze that had taken hold of him. A Taoist priest, who professed to be able to drive away death, gave him a mixture, which resulted in a carbuncle on his back, of which he died. He was followed, on the throne, by his son

I Tsung—A. D. 860-874.

This young man was only seventeen when he found himself the sovereign of China. He was utterly unfitted by nature for the responsibilities that were thrust upon him at this early age. He was proud and arrogant, and wanting in those commonsense qualities that were especially requisite to enable him to meet the dangers that were now about to come upon the empire. He had hardly been seated upon the throne when a formidable insurrection broke out in Chehkiang, headed by Ch'ui-hu. This man soon found himself at the head of thirty or forty thousand men. He captured the important city of Ningpo and then Shau-hing, where he managed to seize the public treasury. Troops were forwarded with all haste against him, and they were fortunate enough to be able to seize him, when he was hurried to the capital and there beheaded. With his fall the rebellion collapsed.

In the year A. D. 863 the barbarians of the Laos tribes invaded Tonquin, and orders were sent to Kiangnan to furnish two thousand troops to meet them and drive them back. Eight hundred of these were retained in Kwangsi, whilst the remainder, together with the contingents from the other parts of the empire, marched to fight the Laos. The Chinese troops must have found the task of repelling them very difficult, for it was six long years before they returned from the far south to their homes in the north. The contingent which had remained in Kwangsi expected to rejoin their regiments on their march home, but they found that they were to be detained for another year. Disappointed beyond measure they broke out into open mutiny, which soon resulted in a widespread rebellion, and ere long twelve thousand men marched throughout the country, capturing towns and pillaging and ravaging wherever they went. Nearly a year elapsed before the imperial troops could suppress it. These troubles in the empire and the lavish expenditure of the court involved the country in expenses that fell so heavily upon the people that discontent and unrest began to be manifested in every direction. There was an utter want of sympathy between the sovereign and his people. All that he thought of was his own pleasure, never caring how many must suffer in order that his enjoyments might be ministered to. He began to be imperious and cruel in his treatment of those who served him. One of his daughters having died, he immediately ordered that twenty doctors, who had been successively called in to attend her, should be put to death, and three hundred of their relatives seized and imprisoned. When his ministers came humbly pleading for these he drove them from his presence with the greatest indignities.

In the last year of his reign he sent a splendid embassage to bring him one of Buddha's bones that he heard was in a far off distant temple. They took between three and four months in this journey and returned successfully with it. His privy council ventured to remonstrate with him against this folly of his, and showed him how Hien Tsung, not listening to the remonstrance of Han-yu, had insisted upon bringing a relic of Buddha to the capital and how he had soon after died.   To the urgent entreaties of the nobles I Tsung replied, "I am not concerned about the fate of my ancestor.   I am quite prepared to die if only I can get this sacred bone to my capital and I am permitted to see it."   Three months after its arrival at Ch'ang-ngan the Emperor died, and was succeeded by his son, a boy of twelve, whose royal name was

Hi Tsung—A. D. 874-889.

At the time of his succession to the empire the country was in a very depressed and unsettled condition.   In consequence of the disturbances during his predecessor's reign, large demands had been made upon the people and the taxes had been considerably increased.   Great floods too in some places and droughts in others had deprived the people of extensive districts of the means of subsistence.   No measures had been taken by the mandarins to meet this distressing state of things, and consequently large numbers had taken to brigandage, and accepting the leadership of Wang-sien they formed a revolutionary body that menaced the well-being of the state.   Unfortunately the movement was joined by a man of the name of Hwang-ch'au, and from this time it became one of the most disastrous rebellions that devastated China during the whole of the T'ang dynasty.   City after city was taken by the rebels, and though occasionally success attended the imperial arms the cause of Hwang-ch'au generally prevailed.

In the year A. D. 878 Wang-sien died, and Hwang-ch'au became the sole leader.   Three years later we find him flying before the royal general Hau-ping and compelled to take refuge in the far south of China.   A great plague having attacked his men, Hwang-ch'au led them northwards, and reaching Hunan he took Chung-sa. From there he marched into Honan and captured Lohyang.   Giving his victorious troops but a short rest, a month after he had crossed the Hwai and taken possession of Ch'ang-ngan.   The Emperor fled to Hing-yuan, and Hwang-ch'au, after exterminating every member of the royal family that he could lay his hands upon, proclaimed himself Emperor and called his dynasty "The Great Ts'i."

In obedience to the urgent entreaties of the Emperor soldiers poured in from every direction to his rescue, and ere long two armies were in the field, whilst the governor of Sz-chwan sent a force to escort the fugitive sovereign into this province, where he would be safe from immediate danger.   At this particular crisis a famous commander of the name of Li K'eh-yung appears upon the scene.[*]

---

[*] His father was a chieftain of the Sha-t'o tribe of the Turcomans that lived near Lake Balkash.   This man rendered important military service in A. D. 847 in repelling an invasion of Turfans or Thibetans, and in gratitude for the aid he had rendered, I Tsung allowed him to adopt the Imperial surname of Li.

At the head of forty thousand of his countrymen the aspect of affairs at once changed. His men were dressed in black, and they had a savage appearance, so that everybody fled in terror before the "Crows," as they were called. Li K'eh-yung led his men straight towards the enemy, and in one day three engagements took place around Ch'ang-ngan, which ended in the utter defeat of Hwang-ch'au. Finding the fortunes of the day so decidedly against him the rebel leader, having set fire to the palace and all the main buildings of the city, fled to Ts'ai-chow, pursued by "The One-eyed Dragon," as Li K'eh-yung was called, where the governor of that district not only submitted to him, but also joined his forces to his. This temporary success, however, availed him nothing. Li K'eh-yung's "Crows" inspired such terror that the rebels fled from before them, first to Tin-chow in Honan and finally to Yen-chow in the south of Shantung. Just before the victorious allies reached the latter place they were suddenly attacked by a division under Chu-wen. This man had been a general under Hwang-ch'au, but had submitted to the Emperor and had been entrusted with the command of an army. He was an unscrupulous military adventurer, and having a deadly hatred to Li K'eh-yung he could not restrain it when he saw him marching with his victorious force against his late commander. Li was compelled to retreat, but Chu-wen's intervention did not save Hwang-ch'au from the fate that awaited him in the city of Yen-chow. He arrived there in A. D. 884 with only a few adherents. His nephew Liu-yen, seeing that the rebellion had now almost collapsed, and wishing to be able to make terms with the government by which he and his family would be saved from extermination, combined with a few others, and having seized Hwang-ch'au and his family they cut off their heads. The soldiers in the camp seeing them carried on the ends of poles made a desperate effort to obtain them, that they might have the merit of handing them over to the government. In the melée Liu-yen lost his life, and the heads were carried off by some of the soldiers, and the great rebellion of Hwang-ch'au was at an end.*

Li K'eh-yung, angry at the attack that Chu-wen had made upon him, memorialized the Emperor and demanded that he should be punished. The country, however, was in such a disordered state, and so many of the governors throughout it were upon the

---

* Historians consider that the insurrection under this famous leader was one of the most terrible that ever devastated China. He was cruel and sanguinary and seemed to delight in the effusion of blood. In the life of him which has been written it is stated that eight millions of people perished in his rebellion, and that blood flowed for a thousand miles. This of course is a gross exaggeration, still we get from this statement a vivid idea of the terrible slaughter that must have taken place during the time of this sanguinary rebel. The book abounds in the most marvellous and impossible deeds that were said to have been performed by him. It is declared that a "precious sword" had been presented to him by one of the genii with which he accomplished the most wonderful feats. With one stroke of this he could cut off the heads of a whole regiment of soldiers, as though they had been grass falling before the sweep of the sickle.

verge almost of rebellion, that Hi Tsung thought it his wisest policy to temporize for the present. He accordingly issued an edict commanding the two enemies to become friends and to combine their forces and their abilities for the good of the empire.

In spite of all the efforts of the Emperor and his ministers to preserve peace disturbances of a very serious nature soon broke out again. A powerful eunuch in the palace, of the name of Ch'an-ling, planned to deprive a governor, of the name of Wang-chung, of the monopoly of salt which he possessed. This man, who had gained considerable credit for the effective part he had taken in the suppression of Hwang-ch'au's rebellion, protested against this, and when he was transferred from his government in Shansi to another in Shantung he refused to be moved. He at the same time memorialized the Emperor and prayed him to take measures to restrain and punish the eunuch. Of course Hi Tsung had not the power to do either of these things, and Ch'an-ling determined to show him the kind of foe he had dared to measure himself with by sending a force of thirty thousand men to seize him. Wang-chung in this extremity appealed to Li K'eh-yung for help, who replied by marching an army to his assistance. A battle took place, in which Li was victorious, and he pursued the retreating army to the capital. Ch'an-ling finding himself in danger, fled to Fung-siang, carrying the Emperor with him, still pursued by the indefatigable Li. Here the soldiers of Ch'an-ling went over in a body to their conqueror, when the baffled eunuch with Hi Tsung further fled to Shan-kwan. Again Li K'eh-yung memorialized the Emperor to punish Ch'an-ling, assuring him at the same time that he had the most loyal intentions towards himself, and wished only to free him from the dominion of the bad advisers by whom he was surrounded. Hi Tsung seems now to have been in a position to act independently, for the ambitious eunuch was banished to Canton, and the gates of Shan-kwan having been opened he was led back in triumph to Ch'ang-ngan. Next year he fell sick and died, when he was succeeded by his brother Chau Tsung.

Chau Tsung—A. D. 889-905.

This man began his reign with the best intentions of governing his kingdom well, and had he come in an earlier stage of the T'ang's history he might have been distinguished as one of the rulers of China that deserved the praise of posterity. He came too late, however, to avert the storm that was about to sweep away his house for ever.

One of his first acts was to make Chu-wen a prince. This must have been to propitiate what was then a growing power that threatened to be dangerous to the monarchy, for he had not performed any public service that deserved to be rewarded with such a dignity. He at once showed that he was not going to let his new honours become rusty for want of use, by impeaching his enemy, Li K'eh-yung, for having dared to be the means of causing the late Emperor to fly from his capital and take refuge in the city of Shan-kwan. The privy council was divided in its views as to what action should be taken in the matter. The majority held that he had done on the whole such good service to the state that his wrong should be forgiven. Two dissented from this view, and insisted upon it that he should be punished. The Emperor very unwisely yielded to their opinion, and gave them authority to levy troops and proceed against Li K'eh-yung. A battle was fought in Shansi, near P'ing-yang, when the Imperial forces were routed with great slaughter. Chau Tsung wisely bent before the storm, for he banished the two men that had advised the expedition to a distant part of the empire, and at the same time he confirmed Li K'eh-yung in all his appointments and honours.

Five years later Wang-chung died, and a contest arose between his two sons as to which of them should succeed their father in the government that he had held. The eldest had married a daughter of Li K'eh-yung, and therefore had his support. The second was upheld in his pretensions by three governors, who promised to maintain his rights with all the forces at their command. They memorialized the Emperor, and because he would not grant their request they marched with several thousand men to Singan, and believing that the prime minister was the one that opposed their wishes they murdered him and forced Chau Tsung unwillingly to grant the investiture of their candidate. Li K'eh-yung was not the man, however, to stand tamely by and see his son-in-law's rights overridden. With the permission of the Emperor he marched against the rebellious governors and defeated them, and in gratitude for this service he was made Prince of Tsin.

In the 12th year of Chau Tsung's reign a conflict ensued between the eunuchs of the palace and the high mandarins in it. The former of these was headed by Liu-kwei, whose object was to set aside the Emperor and put his son in his stead. Both sides summoned all the aid they could get from outside, and they prepared for a desperate struggle. One evening Chau Tsung after his return from hunting got drunk, and in his blind fury killed several of the ladies of the harem. Liu-kwei took advantage of the dismay and confusion caused by this to lead a thousand of his followers into the palace and to seize the Emperor and his queen and confine them in a certain room in it. In order to prevent their escape he had the outer walls encased in iron and a hole knocked in them, through which their food was passed in to them. Ts'ui-yin, one of the great mandarins in the capital, sent an urgent message to Chu-wen that he should come at once to the aid of the Emperor. After some hesitation he did so, and his soldiers soon freed him from his iron prison after a large number of the eunuchs had been slaughtered.

A contest now arose between Chu-wen and Li-mau, the governor of Fung-siang, for the possession of the person of the Emperor. The latter prevailed, much to the discontent of Chu-wen, who proceeded to besiege the city to which he had been carried. Li-mau, who was the real master of Chau Tsung's actions, caused him to issue a decree commanding Li K'eh-yung to come to his rescue. Chu-wen, hearing of the advance of the latter, hurried forward to meet him, and a battle was fought, in which the good fortune of Li K'eh-yung deserted him, for he was defeated and shut up by Chu-wen in the town of Tsin-yang in Shansi.

After this decisive victory Chu-wen returned to the siege of Fung-siang with the determination, he said, of delivering the Emperor from the hands of the eunuchs, by whom he pretended he had been carried off. In the beginning of the next year, finding that the besiegers could not be kept out, one hundred and sixty-two eunuchs were murdered, and then the city gates were thrown open, and Chau Tsung came forth and delivered himself into the hands of Chu-wen, who, with a great pretence of loyalty, threw himself at the feet of his sovereign and begged for forgiveness. This was graciously accorded him by Chau Tsung, who at the same time took off the jade girdle that he wore and gave it to him. On their arrival at Singan several hundreds of the eunuchs were put to death, so that only twenty or thirty boys were left to do service in the palace. This almost utter destruction of this influential class that had used their power so cruelly and so relentlessly seemed a just retribution for the misery and sorrow they had brought upon so many.

A little more than a year had passed by when Chu-wen determined to carry out the ambitious plans which he had been silently maturing for some time. Fearful lest the mandarins would oppose his usurpation he had a number of them killed, and others he banished to different parts of the empire. He then memorialized the Emperor that he should move his residence to Lohyang. This he was compelled to consent to, though he felt that in doing so he was delivering himself to destruction. The people along the road felt the same, for they wept and lamented for him as he passed away from his capital. On his arrival in Lohyang he secretly sent orders to a number of the governors to immediately arm and come to his rescue. "This communication," he said, "is the last you will ever receive from me unless you do so. I am in captivity, and any edicts from this time forward that may be issued in my name you must not accept as from me. They will have been forced from me by the rebel that holds me prisoner."

. In September, A. D. 905, troops began to march from every direction towards Lohyang to deliver Chau Tsung. Chu-wen, knowing that the crisis had now come in which he must act boldly, prepared his army to go out and meet them. Before doing so he sent Li-tsin with a number of soldiers to murder the Emperor.

After the fatal deed was done Chu-wen pretended to be afflicted with the greatest sorrow. He upbraided the men he had employed for what he called their mutiny and for their daring to take the life of their sovereign, and he ordered them all to instant execution. They were thunder-struck at the villainy of Chu-wen, and declared loudly in the hearing of the bystanders that they had been commanded to do the deed for which they were now going to suffer.

The ninth son of Chau Tsung, whose dynastic title is Chau Soan Ti (A. D. 905-907), was now appointed Emperor, and as he was only fourteen years of age it may be easily imagined that the real ruler was Chu-wen, and that he was now only waiting for his opportunity, when he would destroy the youthful ruler and found a dynasty of his own. That this was his intention was manifested by the fact that he put to death the other nine sons of the late unfortunate monarch, whose bodies were thrown into the lake near which they were living, after they had been strangled at a feast to which they had been invited.

These were not the only cruelties that Chu-wen was guilty of. One of his chief adherents, Lin-ts'an, was at serious enmity with a large number of the leading nobles at the court, and sought for some means of destroying them. Fortunately for his purpose a comet was seen in the heavens. The royal astronomer, after due investigation and divination, predicted that this meant evil to some of the leading dignitaries of the empire. Lin-ts'an reported this to Chu-wen, at the same time giving him a list of the most conspicuous men in the palace who, he declared, had been expressing their dissatisfaction at his acts of usurpation. Chu-wen, jealous for the position he occupied just now, ordered them all, to the number of over thirty, to be strangled and their bodies thrown into the river.

Vengeance, however, soon fell upon Lin-ts'an. The Empress-Dowager, knowing the power that he had, sent a messenger to him, pleading with him to use his influence with Chu-wen, when the latter became Emperor, to spare her own life and that of her son Chau Soan. Some one that had a grudge against Lin-ts'an went at once to Chu-wen and told him that his trusted minister was in secret correspondence with the Empress-Dowager, and was plotting for the restoration of the T'angs. There is nothing that makes a man so suspicious as an evil conscience. He believed the story, and immediately issued an order for the execution of both, which was carried out without delay.

In the third month of the year A. D. 907 Chau Soan-ti, feeling the danger of his position, and wishing to propitiate the usurper who was the real ruler, sent an imperial edict to him, containing his resignation, together with the great seal of the empire. Chu-wen was graciously pleased with this farce that was being played, and made the young ruler Prince of Ts'i-yin, but he took care to have him sent to a safe place in Shantung, where he was carefully guarded by a strong detachment of soldiers.

And thus fell before a common adventurer, and one with no special genius or ability, the great T'ang dynasty, after governing the country for two hundred and eighty-nine years. Its influence on this nation is not to be surpassed by any other in its long history, and one reads the records of what was accomplished by it with admiration and profound respect. That there were great errors committed, and that many of its sovereigns were men of weak and feeble characters, it is true. It is equally a fact, however, that the genius and virtues of T'ai Tsung, one of the greatest and most statesmanlike of all the rulers that ever sat on the dragon throne, impressed themselves upon the nation and gave it a reputation that spread far beyond the confines of China and made the barbarians look up to it with fear and respect. What the opinion of the men of to-day is respecting this famous dynasty is seen in the fact that the common colloquial name for the Chinese, in the Fuhkien province at least, is "The Men of T'ang."

CHAPTER XXIII.

THE ERA OF THE FIVE DYNASTIES.

(A. D. 907-960.)

The After Liang Dynasty.   T'ai Tsu—A. D. 907-913.

CHU-WEN'S conduct was evidently not a subject of congratulation to the members of his own family.   On his ascending the throne his younger brother addressed him in these words : " You were not long ago just one of the common people, and you took it into your head to become a rebel and follow the fortunes of Hwang-ch'au.   Our Emperor forgave you and made you a governor of four districts.   You were in a position of great honour and comfort, and His Majesty was continually showering his favours upon you.   Why then have you destroyed the house of T'ang, which for a period of three hundred years has reigned over China ?   Alas ! I fear that as you have overthrown the royal family, so others in like manner shall completely destroy us."

Whatever feelings of compunction these words may have caused in the breast of Chu-wen it was too late for him now to retrace his steps.   The T'angs were gone, and were he to retire from his present position it would only be to leave it to be seized by some other adventurer who would mercilessly massacre him and all connected with him.

The governors throughout the country were by no means unanimous in acknowledging the new Emperor.   Amongst those that refused to accept the new *régime* were Li K'eh-yung, the Prince of Tsin, and Li-mau, of Fung-kien, in Sz-chwan.   Li-mau wrote a letter to Li K'eh-yung counselling him to take the royal title and rule over his own region as he intended to do in Sz-chwan.   Li K'eh-yung, for reasons of policy, refused to accept this advice, and determined to bide his own time, when he would overthrow Chu-wen and seize the throne for himself.   It was well for him that he had not acceded to the advice of Li-mau, for shortly after over three hundred thousand Khitans, led by their famous leader Apanki, invaded the territories over which he ruled.   Li found the marauders too strong for him to cope with, so he came to terms with them and concluded a treaty with their chief, which bound the latter to join him with all his forces in a campaign against Chu-wen.   Whilst the negotiations were going on some of Li's officers assured him that the Khitan chief was not sincere, and that he should take advantage of the opportunity, when he visited him in his camp, to put him to death.   Li refused to do this, as he had implicit faith in him, but he soon discovered that the wily Khitan had been making terms with Chu-wen at the very time that he had been arranging with him to lead an army to attack him.

Next year Li K'eh-yung became dangerously ill, and despairing of life he called his officers around him and commended his son Ch'un-hu to their care and affection as his successor in the princedom of Tsin. He also strictly charged his younger brother to use his influence in defending his son in his rights and to stand between him and any enemy that might wish to wrong him.

All promised to be as loyal and faithful to his son as they had been to himself, but he was scarcely dead before his brother began to plan the death of his nephew, that he might gain his title and his inheritance. The young man, however, who was now twenty-four years of age, showed the metal of which he was made by ordering his uncle to be executed, for his treasonable secret had leaked out, and he was not going to stand quietly by and allow himself to be murdered by any one.*

After these preliminary obstacles had been removed out of the way, Li Ts'un-hu began to look abroad for wider fields of action and to determine with himself that he would try issues with Chu-wen as to who should rule over China, the usurper or himself. He accordingly made up his mind to attempt to recover the important city of Chia-chai, in Luchow, which had been taken from his father some years before. Chu-wen had been so pleased with the taking of this town that he had determined to make it impregnable against any assault that might be made upon it. He accordingly had another wall built outside the old one, and both fortified in the strongest manner possible, so that any one that thought of attacking this place must be prepared to find two cities frowning down upon him. He had also well provisioned it, so that it could stand a long siege.

All these difficulties only whetted the appetite of Ts'un-hu for the conflict. Having made all his preparations, he led his soldiers, who were as sanguine of success as himself, against this strong fortress, which soon fell before the impetuous assault of men that were fighting under the leadership of their own prince, for Ts'un-hu delighted ever to be in the forefront of the battle. Ten thousand of the garrison were slain, and all the provisions and arms that it contained became the property of the victors. When the news arrived in Lohyang, Chu-wen was struck with terror, for he no doubt saw in Ts'un-hu a rival before whom he would find it difficult to maintain his power. Sighing deeply, he said, "I see that Li K'eh-yung is not dead, but lives in his son. If a man would have a son he should have one like Ts'un-hu." "As for mine," he

---

* Li Ts'un-hu from this time became one of the leading spirits in the contests that now ensued for supremacy during the period of the five dynasties, after the final fall of the house of T'ang. He was a man of great military capacity and a true soldier that loved fighting for its own sake. From a lad he had that martial air about him that attracted the attention of all that looked at him. When he was only eleven years of age he was brought to the court of Chau Tsung, and that Emperor, struck by the extreme intelligence that he displayed, patted him on the back and declared that one of these days he would become one of the pillars of his kingdom.

continued, "they are like pigs or dogs, and are utterly useless." After his return from this great victory Ts'un-hu had an inspection of the troops that had been engaged, when he gave rewards and honours to those that had specially distinguished themselves. He also showed his pleasure by making the taxes in his territories lighter; by caring for orphans; by vindicating those that had been oppressed, and by passing laws against adultery and robbery.

In the year A. D. 912 Liu Shen-kwang, who had been an adherent of Li K'eh-yung, but going over to Chu-wen, had been made Prince of Yen, now proclaimed himself Emperor. When Ts'un-hu heard of this he laughingly declared that in ten years all he had would belong to him. Partly in derision he sent an officer to congratulate him, but the ambassador refusing to kneel before him and pay him the honours which he believed were due to one of his exalted position, he cast him into prison, thus offering a slight to Ts'un-hu that he was not soon likely to forget or forgive.

In the year A. D. 913 Chu-wen led an army into Yiuchow, in Chihli, to fight Ts'un-hu, but he was compelled to retreat with great speed to his capital. On his arrival there, dispirited and losing all hope, he fell ill, and unburdening himself to one of his ministers he said : " I have been fighting now for thirty years to obtain the empire, and I never dreamt that there was such peril coming to me from Shansi. When this army of Ts'un-hu arrives in my dominions there will be great danger to my throne. The ambition of the Prince of Tsin is very great, and he has wider aims than merely ruling in Shansi. Whilst I am alive I can successfully contend with him, but Heaven is going to take my life, and then there is no one left of my family that is competent to meet him in the field. Alas! when I die there will be no place left even for my body to rest in."

It now became certain that T'ai Tsu was going to die, and he finally determined that his second son, whom he loved dearly, should succeed him. The third, however, had other views of his own, and he determined that he should be the successor on his father's throne. He was a bad man, the son of a prostitute, and Chu-wen had always looked upon him with aversion. In the dead of night, when the palace was hushed in profound quiet, he stealthily led a number of soldiers that were devoted to him into his father's room. T'ai Tsu woke up with a start and saw his bedroom filled with armed men. Sitting up in his bed he cried out, "Ah! I knew that you were a useless character, and I should have killed you long ago. If you murder me remember that the vengeance of Heaven and earth will fall on you."

There was evidently no love lost between these two, for the son replied, " You old rebel and thief, you deserve to be cut into ten thousand pieces." One of the soldiers hearing these words drove his lance through his body, so that he died in great agonies in a few moments. A hole was immediately dug within the precincts of the palace and his body ignominiously thrown into it.   Before the news of his death could reach the outside world the son sent orders, as if from T'ai Tsu, to his younger brother, who had command of the troops that guarded the city, to proceed at once and put to death the heir-apparent, as he had been found guilty of treason.   This command was obeyed, and now Yiu-kwei found himself master of the situation.   His term of power lasted, however, only a few months, for his reckless, vicious life disgusted everyone, even the very soldiers that had helped to lift him into power.   A plot was formed by a son-in-law of the late Emperor, and in conjunction with the younger brother, who had unwittingly slain the one who should have been reigning, put him to death.   Some of the great nobles having been induced to give their support, a body of men proceeded to the palace to perform the same kind of tragedy that had been enacted there only a short time ago.   They found, however, that Yiu-kwei and his wife, having been informed of their coming, had committed suicide, and so they were saved the horrible scenes that otherwise would have filled the palace with bloodshed and murder.   The fourth son, Yiu-ching, whose dynastic title was T'ien, and who is also known as Mo Ti, now ascended the throne.

T'ien, also Mo Ti—A. D. 913-923.

This same year, A. D. 913, Ts'un-hu led an army against Liu Shen-kwang and completely annihilated his forces.   He also took him and his son prisoners, when he commanded their hearts to be cut out, and taking them into the ancestral temple of his father, Li K'eh-yung, he offered them to his spirit, in order that he might be gratified with the vengeance that he had executed upon those who had dared to rebel against his authority.   A little over two years afterwards he marshalled his forces for that deadly struggle with the soldiers of Liang, which was to end in the overthrow of that ephemeral dynasty.   He was greatly assisted in his first movements by the submission of the people of Siangchow, against whom the Emperor had ordered sixty thousand men to be led, because they had refused to obey one of his commands.   In the first campaign Ts'un-hu was successful, and the imperial general had to retire before him.   At the end of the next year both the Emperor and Ts'un-hu led their armies against each other.   The winter had been an exceptionally severe one, and the Yellow River was frozen over so hard that the Prince of Tsin, with his usual dash and gallantry, marched both his infantry and cavalry across it.   The fortune of war was decidedly in his favour, and many places in the imperial territory fell into his hands.   There is no knowing how far his successes might have reached had he not been interrupted by the news that was brought him that the Khitans had made an irruption into China and were marching into Shansi.   The reason of this was that a brother of Ts'un-hu had been murdered by one of his officers, who had fled to Apanki, the Khitan king, and not only prayed for his protection, but also solicited him to invade China, assuring him that in the present disturbed state of the country it would become an easy prey to his hardy warriors. Apanki, nothing loath to lead his men wherever there were any hopes of plunder, listened to the advice of the traitor and so appeared at this critical time when Ts'un-hu seemed to have his hands so full that he would find it impossible to contend with him. Apanki was mistaken in this, however, for Ts'un-hu was a true soldier, and the more enemies he had to contend with the better he seemed to like it. Dividing his forces he sent a half of them under Li Sz-yuan to meet the Khitans who were besieging Yiuchow in Chihli.* This general, who was as much a soldier as his adopted brother, soon caused the barbarians to return to their own dominions with a great deal more speed than they had left them, and ere long there was not a single hostile Khitan on Chinese territory. Ts'un-hu continued his warfare with the troops of Liang for nearly a year, when he returned to his own principality, east of the Yellow River.

The year A. D. 919 saw Ts'un-hu in Shantung with a large army, where he captured Yunchow and Puh. The Emperor, at the earnest solicitations of his Privy Council, who were alarmed at the repeated defeats that the royal arms were suffering, collected immense forces and sent them to meet the invader in Shantung. Ts'un-hu had also exerted himself to the very utmost to bring all the men he could collect into the field. Not only had he the soldiers of his own state, but he had also a goodly number from some of the barbarian tribes that had settled within the Chinese territory to the north of Shansi. When the two armies came near each other they lay entrenched for some time watching each other's movements, neither side daring to begin the attack. During this time Ts'un-hu showed his usual daring and intrepidity in repeatedly going out, in spite of the remonstrance of his officers, with a handful of men and challenging the other side to come out and fight him. On one occasion he sallied forth with about two hundred men, when he fell into an ambuscade of five thousand of the enemy, by whom his party was surrounded. Every man of his escort fell fighting, and he alone escaped with the utmost difficulty to his camp. In the first engagement that took place Ts'un-hu suffered a reverse, but in another battle that was shortly after fought he obtained a great victory, and the Liang soldiers were glad to escape into Honan.

The great seal of the empire, which had been lost during the rebellion of Hwang-ch'au, was recovered this year (A. D. 922) by Ts'un-hu. This was interpreted by his officers and ministers as an omen that Heaven intended to bestow upon him the empire. With the assumed modesty of men that resolutely refuse what they are

---

* Li Sz-yuan was originally a Turcoman orphan, whose parents were unknown. He was adopted by Li K'eh-yung, who gave him his name and treated him like his own son.

longing for, and ultimately intend to accept, Ts'un-hu declined at
first to listen to his counsellors, but after a few months' solicitation,
in the fourth month of the year A. D. 923, he laid aside his title of
Prince and took that of Emperor, whilst he called his new dynasty
the After T'ang, and he is known in history by the name of

Chwang Tsung—A. D. 923-926.

The new Emperor made his capital in Weichow, in Chihli.
In the summer of this year he led an army into Shantung to meet
the forces of T'ien that still maintained his authority in that region.
The Liang general, feeling that the old dynasty could not be
revived, submitted with all his men and ranged themselves on the
side of Ts'un-hu. This latter was so delighted with this that he
took his girdle from his waist and gave it to him. He also made
him large presents and gave him a high command. He then asked
him what plan should be adopted for the future. His reply was in
the following words: "The country that still acknowledges T'ien
is very extensive, his soldiers too are very numerous, but on the
other hand he is a man of small understanding, and is ruled by
traitors. He has, besides, no generals of ability. There are several
armies collecting now that are intended to combine and attack you.
United you will be no match for them. What I advise is that
whilst your main army remains here you should send a flying
column of five thousand men into Honan and seize upon T'ien. In
less than a month this may be done, and then the whole empire is
yours." Ts'un-hu was pleased with this advice, but before it could
be carried out the Liang troops arrived, and a great battle was
fought, in which they were defeated and the commander-in-chief
was captured and put to death, because he refused to change sides.

Immediately after the battle Li Sz-yuan assumed the command
of five thousand men and started at once for Lohyang. He arrived
at Ts'auchow before any one knew of the disaster that had happened
to the Liang army. When the news of it reached T'ien he took no
active measures to repair the mischief that had been done, but spent
his time in weeping and bemoaning his unhappy condition. Knowing that the conqueror would soon be at his gates he determined to
commit suicide, but he found that he had not the courage to do so.
Calling one of the high officers of the palace to his side, and
presenting him with a sword, he asked him to slay him with it.
He refused to do so at first, but when pressed, he first slew his
master, then himself. Scarcely was this tragedy enacted when
Li Sz-yuan appeared before the city, the gates were thrown open by
the people, and he was rapturously received by them as though he
had been their saviour instead of their conqueror. On the evening
of the same day Ts'un-hu arrived with the advanced guard of his
army and took possession of the capital. All the vengeance that he
took upon the fallen dynasty was to order that the ancestral temples

of the house of Chu should be burned, the posthumous honours of
the dead taken away from them, and the whole reduced to the rank
of the common people.   He would have unearthed the body of
Chu-wen, but he was prevented by his ministers; so he contented
himself with having the trees on his grave cut down and molten
iron poured over it.

It is a very extraordinary fact that from the time that Chwang
Tsung was firmly seated on the throne his character began to
degenerate.   Instead of being chivalrous and warlike he began to
develop low and vicious tastes.   His great delight was to associate
with play actors.   He made them his companions and introduced
them into his palace, where he and the ladies of the household
frequently joined with them in taking part in the plays that were
performed.   All this had a demoralizing effect upon his life, for the
actors in China are usually a vicious, dissipated class of people with
whom no one associates that has any respect for his reputation.

Next year, A. D. 925, the Khitans again made one of their
usual plundering forays into Shansi, but they were soon vanquished
by Li Sz-yuan, and peace was restored in that direction.   Hardly
had the Khitans been driven back when an army had to be
equipped for an expedition into the province of Sz-chwan.   The
governor of that extensive territory had assumed to himself the airs
of an independent prince, and so it became necessary to show him
that he could not do this with impunity.   Kwo Ch'ung-t'au was
sent at the head of a well-appointed army, and so rapid were his
movements, and with such military skill did he act against the
enemy, that in seventy days the objects of the expedition were
attained and Sz-chwan became a peaceable province of the empire.
Through some miserable cabals of the queen and the palace eunuchs
the general, instead of being rewarded, was put to death with his
two sons, on the alleged ground that he was going to rebel and hold
the conquered province for the benefit of himself and his family.
In the third year of Chwang Tsung's reign a formidable mutiny
took place amongst the army stationed in Yeh, in the north of
Honan.   Li Sz-yuan was sent with a sufficient force to quell it,
but his soldiers, instead of carrying out his orders at once, joined
the rebels and declared that they would make common cause with
them.   The whole then tumultuously demanded that he should be
their leader, and that he should become Emperor instead of Chwang
Tsung, whom they were determined they would no longer acknowledge as soverign of China.

The general pretended to agree to the demands of the men, but
said that they must allow him to go and collect soldiers to enable
him to fight for the new dignity they had conferred upon him.
This they consented to do, but no sooner had he got beyond the
influence of the mutineers than he hurried to the capital and
demanded an audience of his adopted brother.   Certain traitors in
the palace managed to prevent this by representing to Chwang

Tsung that Li Sz-yuan had already rebelled, and that he only sought an opportunity for putting him to death.   Finding his own life in danger, and that rebellion was the only safe course left him, he hurried back to the camp and led the men into Honan in the direction of the capital.   In the meanwhile serious events were transpiring there.   One of the actors, Kwo Ch'ung-k'ien, with whom the Emperor had associated, thought that whilst rebellion was abroad he had as good a chance of being Emperor as anyone else.   He therefore collected a number of soldiers and fellow-play-actors and marched upon the palace.   Chwang Tsung no sooner heard of this than, assembling as many followers as he could hurriedly collect, with a revival of his old dash and gallantry, he issued from the palace gates to meet the traitors who would deprive him of his throne.   A fierce hand-to-hand conflict took place, during which the Emperor was struck by an arrow and killed.   His old comrades, the actors, threw their musical instruments on his body until it was covered by them.   They then set fire to the whole, and in a short time the pile was reduced to ashes.   And thus perished in an ignoble fight a man who, if he had not allowed his vices to degrade him, might have long retained his power and become famous in the annals of his times.   He was only thirty-five when he came to his untimely end.

In a very short time after Li Sz-yuan arrived upon the scene. All the high mandarins besought him to become Emperor.   This he refused to do, but he consented to act as regent until the succession should be decided.   A month after, however, at the earnest solicitation of the ministers, and because he saw it was the only safe course for himself, he consented to become sovereign of China.

Ming Tsung—A. D. 926-934.

No sooner was this sovereign settled on the throne than he executed a terrible vengeance upon the play-actors, and a large number of them were massacred. About the same time that Chwang Tsung was killed, Apanki, the Khitan king, died, and was succeeded by his second son, Teh Kwang, of whose doings we shall hear more by and by.   The Emperor gave the command of all the imperial troops to his son, whilst his son-in-law, Shih King-t'ang, was appointed his lieutenant.   The year A. D. 932 is a famous one in the annals of China as being that in which the art of printing was first discovered.   The Chinese historian, with true philosophic calmness, relates this event as though it were one of the most commonplace in the world, and he makes no mention of who the original genius was that first invented it.   There is simply a bare statement that the nine classics were printed by imperial orders from wooden blocks and sold to the public.   No name, no date, and no circumstances connected with this momentous discovery are left on record for the benefit of the curious of future ages.

Two years after, Ming Tsung was compelled to put his son Ts'ung-yung to death, as he found that he was conspiring to dethrone him. This distressed him greatly, for he was naturally a gentle, peace-loving man, and to have to perform such an act of justice on one whom he loved filled his mind with distress. This intensified the disease from which he was suffering, and a month after he died, leaving his third son to succeed him, who is known in history by the title of Min Ti. His eldest brother, Li Ts'ung-k'o, however, refused to acknowledge him as the rightful heir to the throne and marched from Shensi to seize it for himself. Min Ti, hearing this, fled in great terror to Weichow, in Shantung, but he was intercepted on his way by Shih King-t'ang, who killed every one of his followers and spared only the life of Min Ti. Soon after, Li Ts'ung-k'o arrived in K'ai-fung-fu, when the Queen-Dowager and all the officials at once recognized him as the successor to Ming Tsung, and having gone through the prescribed ceremonies he ascended the throne under the title of Fei Ti.*

Fei Ti—A. D. 934-936.

Almost the first act of the new Emperor was to reward Shih King-t'ang for the service he had rendered him by making him a governor in Shantung, and the next was to send a special express to Weichow to order Min Ti to poison himself. As he refused to do this he was strangled. In the second year of the new reign Shih King-t'ang, fearing that the Emperor had designs upon his life, made up his mind to rebel. Before doing so he determined to try the temper of Fei Ti. He therefore sent in his resignation of his governorship. If he accepted it he would collect his forces and proclaim himself Emperor. If he declined it he would reconsider his position and wait for the development of events. When Shih's letter was read before the Privy Council there was considerable discussion as to how it should be answered. They were unanimous in their opinion that he was determined upon rebellion, and that it was a mere question of time as to when the treason would be carried out. It was therefore decided to temporize with him.

His resignation was accepted, but he was given another similar position in a different part of the same province. When the reply of the Emperor was received all Shih's officers advised him to raise the standard of rebellion at once if he would save his life and those of his followers. A council of war was accordingly assembled, at which his chief advisers, Liu Chih-wan and Sang Yu-i, were present. It was then decided that the assistance of the Khitans should be

---

* Li Ts'ung-k'o was only an adopted son. As such he and all his suite had to kneel in deep mourning before the coffin of Ming Tsung, and after worship was paid to the spirit of the departed they all rose, and changing their dresses for those more suitable for such a festive occasion he was proclaimed Emperor of China. This is a custom that every adopted son has to go through before he can be acknowledged to be the rightful sovereign of the people.

invoked, and to induce their chief, Teh Kwang, to come to their aid they promised allegiance to him, and that they would address him by the name of Father, whilst they would call themselves his sons. An additional inducement was held out by the promise of sixteen departments in Shansi, which were to be handed over to him in case they were successful in their efforts to overthrow the T'ang dynasty. Liu Chih-wan was the only one that opposed the decision of offering such liberal terms to the Khitan king. "All that he would promise him," he said, "would be large sums of money such as he believed would be enough to arouse the cupidity of the barbarians and bring the clans to their side." His advice, however, was rejected, and an ambassador was despatched with the above-mentioned terms. His reception at the court of Teh-kwang was most flattering, and an agreement was soon come to that a large Khitan force should enter Shansi and assist Shih in his scheme for founding a new dynasty.

No sooner had his ambassador returned with this good news than Shih sent a memorial to Fei Ti, reminding him that as he was only an adopted son he had no right to the throne, and demanded that he should resign his position and give it to some one who had a better claim to it. When this document was read before the Privy Council the Emperor was so indignant at it that with his own hands he tore it in pieces. Orders were given for the advance of the royal army to meet the insurgents, and a great battle was fought in Fan-ch'u, in Shansi, when the combined forces of Shih and the Khitans gained a great victory. The vanquished troops retreated to Tsin-yang, which was soon invested by the enemy.

Fei Ti was greatly distressed with the tidings of disaster that reached him, and advanced towards the borders of Honan as if with the intention of succouring Tsin-yang. His courage, however, failed him, and he stopped short before he reached the frontier. His officers remonstrated with him and urged him either to advance or to return to his capital, but he refused to listen to them, and spent his time in drunken bouts and lamentations over his miseries.

By the advice of Teh-kwang, Shih now proclaimed himself Emperor and called his dynasty the After Tsin. He also handed over to the Khitans the districts in Shansi which had been promised them, and he agreed to give besides three hundred thousand pieces of silk annually. After the lapse of several months the commandant of Tsin-yang, finding that no succours came to him, surrendered the city to Shih. This relieved the besieging force, and accordingly another forward movement was made to Luchow, where the imperial army was again met, and in another great battle that was fought Shih and his allies were once more successful. Teh-kwang now addressed Shih and said to him, "You must at once pursue the beaten army and give the troops of T'ang no time to collect and rally again for another fight. Victory is certainly yours. I'll send a detachment of five thousand men with you, but I'll encamp my main army here till I hear from you. If I receive good news I'll return to my own dominions, but should you not be able to hold your own I'll come to your rescue with every man that I have. I would accompany you now, but I am afraid it would prejudice your cause, as the people would not like to be beaten by a foreign force." Shih agreed to this, and the two commanders separated from each other with mutual regrets. The last words that the Khitan king uttered were injunctions to Shih not to forget the kindness he had done him, and not to prove ungrateful when he was firmly seated on the throne, to which the valour of his men had raised him.

As the victorious army drew near the capital Fei Ti, seeing that all was lost, and that the entrance of it into the city would be the destruction of himself and his family, determined to anticipate the vengeance of his enemy. He accordingly ascended a high tower, with his wife and his mother and his children, and with the great seal of the empire in his possession he set fire to the place, when they all perished in the flames. The people of K'ai-fung-fu, with their usual fickleness, threw their gates open to the conquering army and welcomed it with loud and joyful acclamations. Shih now ascended the throne and gave his dynasty the title of "The After Tsin." His dynastic name is Kau Tsu.

Kau Tsu—A. D. 936-943.

The new Emperor Kau Tsu did not find that universal submission to him that he had expected, for even those that outwardly acknowledged the new dynasty were by no means hearty in their professions of loyalty. Great distress prevailed amongst the people, especially in the regions where the fighting for so many years had been carried on, and money was exceedingly scarce. There is no doubt but that the pecuniary demands made by the Khitans for the services they had rendered were a severe tax upon the nation. Presents of money and of valuable goods were being constantly demanded, and these could not be refused without a serious rupture in the relations between Teh-kwang and the ruler that he had put upon the throne. The high mandarins were exceedingly indignant at having to be in such subjection to the barbarian king, and especially that their sovereign should have to address him as Father, whilst he took the lower title of Son, and they would have gone to war, but they were restrained by the wiser counsels of Sang Yu-i. Two events of importance took place this year. One was that the Khitans gave their dynasty the name of Liau, and imitated the manners of the Chinese in their appointment of officers and in their mode of carrying on their government. The other was the rebellion of Su Chih-kau, in Hwainan and Kiangnan, who called himself king and gave his dynasty the title of the Southern T'ang. In the year A. D. 941 a plan was organized by the great military commanders, headed by a general named Ngan-chung, to shake off the yoke of the Khitans, and war would most certainly have ensued had it not been for the strenuous exertions of Liu Chih-wan, who now came to the front and opposed a movement that would have brought disaster upon the empire. "You must not be ungrateful," he said to the Emperor, "to the man that made you a ruler. Ngan-chung is a fool and does not understand what he is doing. Men complain of having to pay money and silk to the Khitans, but think how much more we shall have to expend if we have to fight for a few years with such a powerful enemy. My advice is, bear for the present; teach the people to engage in agriculture; train your soldiers in the art of war; be careful of the interests of your people, and when the empire is in a better condition then we can consider the question of war with the barbarians."* This advice was taken, and for the present peace was preserved.

Kau Tsu died in the seventh year of his reign, his death being hastened by the angry reproaches of Teh-kwang for his having dared to enter into treaty relationships with another tribe of barbarians without first consulting him. Before dying he entreated his ministers to protect his young son and help him in his government. Some were willing to do so, but others declared they would have no minor as their Emperor at this critical time in the nation's history, so it was finally decided that his nephew should succeed him, which he did. His dynastic title was

Ch'uh Ti—A. D. 943-947.

The reign of this unfortunate sovereign was an exceedingly uneventful one, excepting for the sorrows that he brought upon himself by his unwisely endeavoring to match himself with the warlike Khitans. His first important act was to order the murder of every Khitan in his dominions that had come for purposes of trade, etc. This of course aroused the anger of Teh-kwang, and early in the year A. D. 944 he sent an army into Chihli with orders to lay siege to the important town of Pei-chow. Ch'uh Ti, who was not wanting in courage, led his men against the enemy, who were discomfited and had to retreat to their own country. Liu Chih-wan, who had been made commander-in-chief, was exceedingly opposed to the policy of the Emperor, because he saw that he had not the ability to oppose such a man as the Khitan king successfully. He therefore refused to obey the royal command to lead his armies, but stood quietly by waiting to see what the issue would be, and then to decide what action he should take. In this procedure he had the advice of one of the ablest of his captains, Kwo-wei, who finally became the founder of the After Chow dynasty.

---

* Liu Chih-wan was noted for being a large-hearted generous man. He was originally of a poor family in Tsin-liang, in Shansi, and when he was a lad he had the care of horses. One of these one day strayed into the pasture land of a bonze, who caught him and gave him a good thrashing. In after years he was made governor of his native district. When he took his command he sent for this same bonze, who came with fear and trembling, as he expected to be repaid with interest for his ill-usage of him, but instead he was courteously received and sent away with presents.

The year A. D. 946 was spent in fighting with the Khitans. In the early part of it Ch'uh Ti was again victorious, but towards the close of it dangers began to gather thick and fast about him. He sent a large army to meet another inroad of his implacable foes, but it was defeated and had to surrender to the enemy. The victorious Khitans now entered Honan, and Ch'uh Ti, finding that he could no longer contend with Teh-kwang, sent word that he was prepared to submit to him, and not long after he and his mother and his wife and relatives entered his camp bound with ropes, in token that they submitted unreservedly to him, and were prepared to be treated by him as he thought best. Teh-kwang accepted his submission, and giving him the title of "The Ungrateful Marquis," banished him and his family to Hwang-ling, in Tartary. The Khitans now entered K'ai-fung-fu and commenced a system of plunder that greatly distressed the people. The hatred against their oppressors became so intense that plans were formed for a universal rising against them, but ere long, having satiated themselves with murder and rapine, the barbarians withdrew from China without having appointed any one to succeed Ch'uh Ti.

Liu Chih-wan, who had fifty thousand troops under his own command, stayed quietly in his territory whilst these exciting events were going on at the capital. After the Khitans had withdrawn, the ministers who were still left in K'ai-fung-fu, feeling that he was the best man to mount the throne, and the most powerful of all the governors, invited him to become Emperor. As this accorded exactly with his wishes there was no difficulty in getting him to consent, and he accordingly became sovereign of China, and called his new dynasty the "After Han." History tells us that his dynastic name was Kau Tsu.*

Kau Tsu—A. D. 947-948.

Kau Tsu had hardly got settled on the throne when he heard that the formidable warrior and vanquisher of the Chinese, Teh-kwang, was dead. His death happened on the return journey to his own dominions, to the great joy of the Chinese, who were never sure, whilst he lived, that he would not suddenly surprise them with his hardy soldiers and ravage and destroy everything before him. The next year Kau Tsu became ill, and after a very short sickness died. Before his death he left his son, who was only eighteen years old, in the charge of Kwo-wei and three other ministers, with strict injunctions that they should be loyal in their support of him, and also that they should be on their guard against the governor of Tu-wei, who had given in only a feigned submission to the new dynasty, and who, he declared, would rise in rebellion at the first good opportunity that occurred. His son is known in history as

---

* This appellation means the illustrious founder of the dynasty, and is frequently met with in history.

Yin Ti—A. D. 948-951.

Before the death of Kau Tsu could be known the four nobles that had received his dying charge issued an edict in his name, declaring that as the governor of Tu-wei had dared to vilify the Emperor he must be put to death. This order was carried out, and thus one of the dangers to the dynasty was averted. Not many months after the accession of Yin Ti the news reached the capital that those inveterate marauders and disturbers of the peace of China, the Khitans, had made an irruption into Chihli. Kwo-wei was immediately despatched with an army to meet them. The fullest powers were given him by the Emperor to act on his own responsibility in regard to the way in which he was to treat with them. Some of the members of the Privy Council, who were enemies of his, objected to a subject having such plenary authority as was entrusted to him, whilst others, who knew his great military abilities, highly approved of the action of the Emperor. Kwo-wei soon proved to the satisfaction of every loyal Chinaman that he was the right man in the right place, for in the course of a few months he returned with his army, having compelled the Khitans to retreat into Tartary. About this time the royal household was alarmed by the presence of evil spirits that acted in the most irregular and fantastic manner. They opened doors at pleasure and raised great storms of wind that would tear up great trees by the roots. They were considered to be signs of ill-omen that portended mischief to the dynasty. A great consultation of wise men was held, when the question was discussed how this dangerous state of things might be remedied. With all his superstition, the Chinaman is an exceedingly practical person, and it was decided that these spirits had dared to invade the royal home simply because there was some misgovernment of the nation. No ghost would ever dare to show itself when the sovereign was a wise and faithful ruler of his people. It was therefore determined to examine the book that had been written by the great T'ai Tsung, of the T'ang dynasty, on the "Proper Government of a Nation," and see in what points the empire might be ruled in a better way than it was at present. History does not say what was the result of this investigation as far as the ghosts were concerned. It soon turned out, however, that there were more hurtful things in the palace than they, and that was Yin Ti himself. No sooner was the empire at peace that he became restive under the restraint of the four nobles whom his father had left in charge of him, and, listening to the advice of the bad companions with whom he associated, he determined to have them put to death. An ambush was accordingly laid, and the three that were in the capital were murdered one morning as they entered the palace to attend the audience. Yin Ti also sent an officer to the camp of Kwo-wei with orders that he should be put to death. This man, fearful for his own life, and not daring to attack this famous general in the midst of his own officers and soldiers, by whom he was greatly beloved, took the order of the Emperor and showed it to him. Kwo-wei saw the extreme peril in which he stood, but he was a man of decided action, and he took his measures at once for bringing matters to a crisis. Calling his chief officers together he told them of the order of Yin Ti, which had just arrived. "The three nobles," he said, "that with myself were entrusted with the charge of the young Emperor have been ruthlessly murdered. They were men that had done great service to the state, and besides, they were instrumental in raising Kau Tsu to the throne. They deserved a better fate than that of being slain by a band of soldiers in the dark. Not content with their death Yin Ti longs for mine too. If you think I ought to die, I am ready. Kill me; here is my neck," and he bared it as he spoke, "and I shall not resist if you think I ought to perish."

These words excited the utmost enthusiasm in the council, which soon spread to the camp. They all declared that their general should not die, and that if he did they would know the reason why. "Lead us back," they cried impetuously to their general, "that we may slay the traitors that have dared to give such base advice to our Emperor. We will rid the world of them, and then Yin Ti, freed from their evil influence, will govern his people with justice." In a few hours the army was on its march to the capital. As it got nearer and nearer to K'ai-fung-fu the report was spread amongst the people that Kwo-wei had rebelled, and the news being carried to the palace the greatest consternation was produced there. All the forces that could be hastily collected in the city and from the places near, where troops were stationed, were hurriedly collected and sent out to meet the rebel army. They were no match, however, for men led by such a commander as Kwo-wei, and who, moreover, were now fighting for their lives. The fugitives of the beaten army soon brought the ill-tidings to the foolish young Emperor, who made instant preparations for flight. In his endeavours to escape, he somehow or other got mixed up amongst Kwo-wei's soldiers, who slew him without being aware that he was the Emperor.

When Kwo-wei appeared in the presence of the Empress-Dowager he asked her to appoint a successor to her late son. After considerable discussion it was decided that a son of Liu-tsung, a nephew of Kau Tsu, was the most suitable of all the eligible candidates to ascend the throne at this crisis.

Kwo-wei agreed to this, and shortly after he marched his army back again to meet the Khitans, who he had heard had captured the city of Sun-teh-fu in Chihli. They had not advanced many days on their journey when the officers refused to march any further, and gathering round their general demanded to be led back again to the capital. "The empire is yours," they said, "and why should you abandon it to another. The Emperor is young and knows nothing of us, and will not be able to discriminate as to which of us shall be rewarded for distinguished services. You know us, for you have fought by our side, and we demand that you become our Emperor," and in a few minutes the camp resounded with the cries, "Ten thousand years! Ten thousand years."*

The return journey was soon made, and Kwo-wei, presenting himself before the Queen-Dowager, informed her that his soldiers demanded that he should become Emperor. Of course resistance was out of the question. The young ruler, to whom history does not give a royal title, was deposed and sent to Hunan under the name of the Duke of Shang-yin, where he was soon after murdered by the order of Kwo-wei. The dynasty that was now set up was called the "After Chow," and the new ruler is known by the name of T'ai Tsu, or the founder of the dynasty.

T'ai Tsu—A. D. 951-954.

T'ai Tsu was fortunate when he came to the throne that there was none of the governors or princes throughout the empire to oppose him. The Prince of the Northern Han did indeed meditate using all his forces against him when he first heard of the death of Yin Ti. When he found, however, that his own son was elected to become Emperor, he laid aside his hostile intentions and remained quietly within his own jurisdiction. By and by, when the news of his murder reached him, he was greatly enraged against T'ai Tsu, and raised the standard of rebellion, though he refrained for the present from active hostilities.

Kwo-wei, who had risen to military command from a very humble condition in life, was illiterate, but he seemed determined to fulfil the duties of a ruler to the best of his abilities. On one occasion he said to his ministers, "I have passed through almost every experience of life. I have known what want is, and hunger too, and therefore I can all the more sympathise with the people I have to govern. I desire to live plainly and simply, both in regard to food and clothes, so that I may have the more to give them. I want you all to assist me to the utmost of your powers to govern the country well, and therefore I request you to put down your ideas in writing so that I may be able to study them carefully." During his reign he made a visitation to Shantung, and of course he went to do honour to the memory of Confucius and worship at his grave. Some of his attendants remarked to him that he was demeaning himself by kneeling before the tomb of the great sage, for as Confucius had been an officer of the empire it was unbecoming for an Emperor to pay such reverence to him. "By no means," he replied, "for Confucius is the master of a hundred generations of Emperors," a saying which posterity has retained, and which is applied to him to the present day.

---

* Long live the Emperor.

Shortly after his return, and in the third year of his reign, T'ai Tsu became seriously ill, and had to give up the management of affairs to his son, the Prince of Tsin, who was then thirty-three years old. His sickness grew more and more serious, and he died at the comparatively early age of fifty-three, and he was succeeded by his son.

Shih Tsung—A. D. 954-960.

No sooner had the news gone abroad that Kwo-wei was dead than Liu-tsung, the Prince of the Northern Han, moved forward his own army of thirty thousand men, and a considerable force of Khitans as allies with him, and began the siege of the important city of Luchow. When the Emperor heard of this he insisted upon leading his own army to the scene of warfare, though his generals strongly dissuaded him from doing so. When he arrived there he at once marched to where the enemy was and engaged with him, but his troops were not successful. A series of engagements took place, which were all disastrous to Shih Tsung, and things began to look serious for the royal cause. At last he was surrounded by a large force of the enemy, and his fate seemed to be sealed, when one of his captains, Chau Kwang-yin, cried out in a loud voice to his men, "Those who are willing to die for their Emperor follow me." His words flashed like lightning amongst those of his own command, and in a few minutes two thousand soldiers, prepared to sacrifice themselves, followed him to where the great fight was raging around Shih Tsung. In a short time the tide of battle turned, for nothing could withstand the impetuosity of this devoted band. The Emperor was rescued from his perilous position, and the enemy was soon flying in great disorder before the imperialists, whose enthusiasm had been excited by the gallant rescue, and who were now sweeping everything before them. The enemy was compelled to retreat in every direction. Liu-tsung made his way back to Tsin-yang, and his allies hurriedly retired to their own territory. For the signal services that he rendered on this memorable occasion Chau was made a marquis, and was appointed commander of the palace guard, a position that put him in the way of further preferment.

In the second year of his reign Shih Tsung, sincerely anxious about the condition of the empire, addressed his privy council as to the best way of pacifying and uniting it. At that time a large part of Shansi was held by Liu-tsung; Kiangnan by Li-king; Szchwan by Ming-ying, and Chihli or Liau-tung by the Khitans. Each of his ministers was requested to put his ideas in writing and submit his thoughts to him, to see if there were any that could be carried into action and the unity of China thus be effected. Only one of the essays, viz., that by Wang-p'oh, was of sufficient merit to deserve commendation. He was made a high mandarin for it, but we have no record of its having been adopted as a state paper and carried into practice.

A great scarcity of copper money was experienced at this time. So many copper utensils had been made for common use by the people, and so much had been employed in the casting of idols, that there was actually a dearth of the metal for monetary purposes. An edict was issued commanding the people to carry their copper utensils to the nearest mandarins and deliver them up to them for imperial uses. Anyone after this that was found with as much as five catties weight in his house would render himself liable to the punishment of death.*

The copper idols also were ordered to be broken in pieces and handed over to the royal mints, to be made into cash. Some one ventured to remonstrate with His Majesty about this last order, on the ground that many would be afraid to take such liberties with their gods, and would not dare to carry it out. Shih Tsung replied to him in these memorable words, "The man that does right and benefits his fellow-men is a true reverencer of the idols. The gods," he continued, "have the good of mankind at heart, and therefore they will be quite willing to have their images broken up. For myself, if my death would bring happiness to my people, I would willingly give up my life for them."

Towards the end of the year (A. D. 956) a military expedition was sent against the Prince of the Southern T'ang, as he termed himself, but it was not entirely successful. Next year another army, under the command of Chau Kwang-yin, again entered his territories, when a decisive victory was gained, but not sufficiently so to make the prince submit to the Emperor. It was not till the beginning of A. D. 959, after a series of disasters had been experienced by him, that he consented to be called an official of the Chow dynasty and to surrender some of the country he had claimed to govern to Shih Tsung.

After his return from this successful expedition the Emperor began to busy himself about agricultural matters. He had maps drawn up of all the cultivable lands in his empire by thirty-four officials who had been appointed for this special business, and who travelled through the country, and with the aid of the local authorities obtained the information that was necessary for such an important undertaking.

In the following year he led an army against the Khitans for the purpose of demanding the restoration of the sixteen departments that had been given to Teh-kwang for the services that he had rendered to Shih King-t'ang. He succeeded in rescuing some of them, but after he had been away sixty days he became seriously ill and had to return to K'ai-fung-fu. In three months this kind-hearted and generous sovereign was dead, and his son, who was only seven years old, became Emperor in his stead. The dynastic title of this latter was

---

* A catty is 1⅓ lbs. English.

Kung Ti—A. D. 960.

The young Emperor had not been long seated on the throne when the news reached the capital that the Khitans were again on the move. Chau Kw'ang-yin, who by this time had become commander-in-chief, was sent with an army to meet them in the field and to drive them from Chinese territory.

Even before starting there had been considerable dissatisfaction amongst the officers and soldiers at the present political state of things, and this did not disappear as they marched further from the capital. "What have we to hope," they said, "from this boy Emperor of ours? He does not understand what campaigning means and what dangers we have to pass through, and therefore he will not know how rightly to reward those who have ventured their lives, or have done heroic deeds. The man who ought to be our ruler is Chau Kwang-yin, and we will acknowledge none other as our sovereign." Very soon matters came to a crisis. One morning, shortly after midnight, whilst the army was halting at "The Bridge of Ch'en," and Chau was still under the effects of the liquor he had been drinking the previous evening, a party of his officers tumultuously broke into his tent, and hastily wrapping him in a yellow robe, which none but an Emperor was allowed to wear, they woke him out of sleep with the cries, "Long live the Emperor! Long live the Emperor!" Soon the cry spread throughout the camp, and every soldier in it knew that a revolution had been accomplished, and that night the After Chow dynasty had ceased to exist.

Next morning Chau agreed to become Emperor on certain conditions. These were that the lives of the royal family should be spared, as well as those of the ministers in the palace, and that there should be no robbing of the treasury, but the question of rewards to those that had been faithful to him should be left to his own discretion. These were agreed to by acclamation, and in a few hours the army was on its return march to K'ai-fung-fu, and from that moment the great Sung dynasty was virtually established.

CHAPTER XXIV.

THE SUNG DYNASTY (A. D. 960-1127).

T'ai Tsu—A. D. 960-976.

THE first act of Chau Kwang-yin when he reached K'ai-fung-fu was to depose Kung Ti, and, giving him the title of Prince Ching, have him removed to Fang-chow, where he was treated with the greatest kindness and consideration. He then called his dynasty the Sung, from the district of which he had been governor in Honan, and ordered that the royal colour should be brown.*

From the moment that T'ai Tsu grasped the reins of power his mind seemed to become absorbed with one great thought, viz., that it was his supreme business to overcome the princes that in various parts of the country maintained an independent rule and to restore the unity of the empire. That this was no easy task may be imagined when it is understood that the Prince of Han in the north, and the chief of the Southern Han in the south, as well as the rulers in Sz-chwan and in Kiangnan, paid no allegiance to him and did not recognize him as their feudal lord. In addition to these were the war-like and powerful Khitans, who were ever ready to lead their forces into the field to the assistance of the Prince of Han, or in an independent foray of their own to measure their swords with the soldiers of the imperial dynasty.

T'ai Tsu had not long to wait for the carrying out of his purpose, for the gauntlet was thrown down by Li Chun, the governor of Chau-yi, in Shansi, who was determined, not only not to submit to the new rule, but also to take the field in active opposition to it. For this purpose he entered into a correspondence with the Prince of Han, who gladly agreed to join forces with him in the attack upon the common enemy. Dissensions, however, arose between the two, and when the imperial army arrived only a small division of the Prince of Han's troops appeared ranged on the side of Li Chun. In the battle that ensued the Sung soldiers were everywhere successful, for they were led by the Emperor in person, who impressed a spirit into his men that nothing could resist. Li Chun fled to Tsochow, and finding that everything was lost, he shut himself and his family in his house, and setting fire to it everyone perished in the flames.

The next competitor that ventured to enter the lists against T'ai Tsu was his old military comrade Li Tsung-sin. They had

---

* The historian tells us that the birth of the founder of the Sung dynasty was marked by very unusual natural phenomena. Immediately after he was born the sky was filled with reddish clouds that overhung the house where the child was, and for three days the dwelling was pervaded by a most fragrant odour. People at the time remarked to each other that all this portended a great future for the boy, and his mother believed that he would one day occupy a distinguished position amongst his fellow-men.

been officers together, and had cemented a great friendship for each other in the wars in which they had both been engaged.   When he became Emperor, T'ai Tsu did not forget his friend, but made him governor of Kwang-ling, in Shantung.   Li could not forget, however, that he was the destroyer of the Chow dynasty, of which his uncle, Kwo-wei, had been the founder, and though he accepted the office he gave him he felt bound by his duty to his family to raise the standard of rebellion and try to restore the fortunes of the fallen house of Chau.   For this purpose he sought the aid of Chun, but the letter to him was handed to T'ai Tsu instead, who, with his usual generosity, forgave him.   He then applied to the Prince of T'ang, who refused to have anything to do with him, and who informed the Emperor of the application that had been made to him. T'ai Tsu, finding that leniency was thrown away in this case, led his forces against him, when he was defeated, and flying to Kwang-ling he imitated the example of Li Chun and perished with his whole family in the flames.

In the second year of T'ai Tsu's reign his mother, to whom he was devotedly attached, and whom he had always honoured with the most perfect filial piety, became alarmingly ill.   Feeling that she was about to die she summoned her son and his prime minister Chau-p'u to her bedroom, in order to convey her dying wishes to the Emperor.   Addressing herself to him she said, "Have you ever thought how it is that you were able to obtain the throne of China?"   He meekly replied "that it was no doubt owing to the powerful protecting influences of his ancestors, but especially to hers."   "No, it has not been so," she promptly answered.   "It has been entirely due to the fact that Kung Ti was a child.   If he had been a full grown man you would not be Emperor to-day.   I want you now, therefore, to promise me that after your death your younger brother Kw'ang-yi shall succeed you, and your third shall occupy the throne after him, and then your own sons shall come next in the succession.   Your dynasty will then avoid being ship-wrecked by having boys, who don't know how to rule an empire, on the throne."   T'ai Tsu at once agreed to this proposal of his mother, who ordered Chau-p'u to draw up a document containing an account of this singular agreement and to sign it as prime minister. It was then put away in a golden casket, to be produced at some future time when the occasion might require it.

As a reward for the services which many of his generals and captains had rendered him in making him sovereign of China, T'ai Tsu had bestowed upon them titles and positions which gave them the command over considerable bodies of troops.   In the present transition stage of the country this was a dangerous state of things to be in existence, and none was more conscious of it than T'ai Tsu himself.   He felt that his throne was unsafe so long as so many military adventurers had the means at their command of initiating a rebellion whenever their ambition prompted them to do so, and he determined by a vigorous stroke of policy to put an end to a danger that threatened the state.

He invited them all to a great dinner in the palace, and when the meal was over he said to his assembled guests, "If it had not been for you my captains I should never have been Emperor. It was your valour and fidelity that raised me to the high position I now occupy. You must not think, however, that it is an easy thing to be a king. I sometimes think I should be happier if I were only a governor. Now lately I have not been able to sleep at night for thinking of the great military power that each of you possess." At these words a shade of anxiety flashed across the faces of his hearers, and voices were instantly heard exclaiming, "The empire is at peace. Who dares think of rebellion now?" "You are true men I have no doubt," he continued, when the excitement had abated, "and I don't question any of you. I myself was as loyal as any of you, till the yellow robe was thrown around me when I was asleep, and then I became a rebel." "The life of man," he continued, "is short at the best, and the great object of us all is to gather riches and to live happily, and then leave what we have to our children. Now what I propose is that you should all resign your military appointments. I'll give you positions where you can make money, and where you can buy lands to leave to your posterity, and in the meantime you can enjoy life to the fullest and drink day and night. Any man that is willing to accept my proposal I shall treat as my friend, and our families shall intermarry." This generous speech touched the heart of every one present, and one by one they resigned their commissions into his hand, and thus the great danger that had threatened the stability of his crown passed away.

The next great reform was in reference to the governors throughout the country. He took away from them the power of life and death and handed it over to the Board of Punishments, without whose consent no one could be executed. He also erected a new tribunal that had cognizance over them and also had authority to enquire into their conduct and to see if they were loyal to the throne or not. In the autumn of the year A. D. 963 T'ai Tsu, who constantly kept before his mind his purpose of subduing the princes that refused to acknowledge his supremacy, sent an army under Kwo-tsin to attack the Prince of Han.*

---

* Kwo-tsin was distinguished for the severity of his discipline. Before the army started on the campaign the Emperor, in the speech he made to the troops, reminded them of this saying, "You might hope for mercy from me if you transgressed the rules, but none from him." Shortly after some of his men accused him to T'ai Tsu of wrong treatment of them, who replied by simply sending their names to the general. Calling them before him he sternly rebuked them for their audacity and said, "There are many of my men that dare not even look upon me as I review them, and yet you have had the temerity to prosecute me before the Emperor. I shall therefore make an example of you. In our first engagement with the Khitans I shall put you in the front rank of the army. If you conquer I shall forgive you. If you do not you shall all die." It is needless to remark that in the first battle with their fierce foes these men fought like heroes, and so distinguished themselves that every one was made an officer.

It succeeded in capturing the important city of Loh-p'ing, in Shansi, and though the Prince of Han made the most desperate efforts to retake it, and even called in the help of the Khitans to assist him in his endeavours, the place remained in the hands of the imperialists.

Two years passed by, and again T'ai Tsu meditated a further attack on the Prince of Han, but he was dissuaded from doing so by his intimate friend and Prime Minister Chau-p'u, who advised him first to conquer Sz-chwan and Kiangnan, and leave this the more easy task of the three to the last.*

In pursuance of this advice T'ai Tsu began to make his preparation for an invasion of Sz-chwan. He first of all sent officers to examine the roads that led through that great province and report upon which was the best for military operations. They were also to investigate the condition of the people and see whether the popular verdict was in favour of the royal dynasty or of the prince that was in rebellion against it. News of what he was doing having reached the prince, he at once wrote to the Prince of Han asking him to cross the river with his troops and create a diversion in his favour. The messenger, instead of carrying the letter into Shansi, brought it to T'ai Tsu, who despatched without delay an army of sixty thousand men into Sz-chwan, under the command of Wang-ch'uen. Although it was the depth of winter, and unfavourable for military operations, he was determined that no risks should be run by allowing the prince time to organize his forces, or by leaving the soldiers of Han free to fight, whilst the great contest for Sz-chwan was going on. His last words to the general as he rode away to join his army was, "Remember that all the gold and the plunder belong to the soldiers. I only want the land."

In the first battle that was fought the Sung troops gained the victory, and in the beginning of the next year (A. D. 966), in a second engagement, they captured the enemy's general and routed his forces, whilst they carried by storm the important town of Kwei-chow. The prince now became alarmed at the condition of affairs, and sent forward another army under the conduct of his own son, but having heard that the strongly fortified town of Chien-mung had been captured by the imperialists he retreated to the capital, Ch'eng-tu. Seeing that it was hopeless to carry on the struggle any longer, the prince surrendered himself and family to Wang-ch'uen, who sent them under a strong escort to the capital, where they were received and kindly treated by the Emperor. Thus, in the short space of sixty-six days, the extensive territory covered by the large province of Sz-chwan was added to the imperial dominions. The

* Chau-p'u was a man of strong commonsense and indomitable will, but wanting in those more sterling qualities that would have made him distinguished as one of the great men of the past. The Emperor was a constant visitor at his house, where they used to discuss affairs of state till late in the night. As he grew in power he became domineering and rapacious, so that he had at last to be dismissed from the court.

effect of these rapid successes was most injurious, however, to the morale of the army. The commander-in-chief was so intoxicated with the victories he had gained and the complete subjugation of the country that he gave himself up to drinking and the wildest excesses, which were of course eagerly imitated by his army. Instead of treating the people with kindness and consideration, which they had done when they first entered the province, they mercilessly plundered and maltreated them. The indignation which this cruel conduct aroused amongst all classes of society was so great that a determination was come to that it would be better to fight the royal troops than suffer the indignities to which they were daily exposed. Silently but swiftly messages were sent from district to district, and from village to village, and in an incredibly short space of time over a hundred thousand men had surrounded Wang-ch'uen, who was on his return march to the capital. Unable to cope with such a large force, he was compelled to retreat to Ch'eng-tu, and there await reinforcements. It was not till the close of the next year (A. D. 967) that he was extricated from his difficulty, and Sz-chwan was once more a peaceable province of the empire.

T'ai Tsu now turned his thoughts towards the subjugation of the Prince of Han and the recovery of the remaining departments that Shih King-t'ang had given the Khitans for their aid in placing him on the throne of China. He began to exercise his army for the expected campaign, and he had a miniature lake made not far from the palace, were his soldiers could be trained to be able to cross the rivers that might meet them in their advance on the Khitans. The success that he obtained was, however, comparatively trifling, and though he gained several victories over the Prince of Han, and twice besieged T'ai-yuan, he was finally, after more than a year's struggle, compelled to withdraw, because the troops that the Khitans brought into the field to the help of the Prince of Han were too strong for him to resist. He had the satisfaction, however, of subduing the Prince of the Southern Han, who held Kwangtung and Kwangsi (A. D. 972), and of adding those two important provinces to his empire. No sooner had the Prince of the Southern T'ang heard of this than he hastened to make his submission to T'ai Tsu. In his communication with him he said, "I give up the title of Prince from this time forward, and only ask to be addressed by my own name when you send your orders to me." The Emperor granted his request, although he had afterwards reason to consider that he had been rather hasty in giving his consent to a proposition that really left him an independent prince in his own estates. He was so convinced that he had been unwise that three years after (A. D. 975) he determined to have the question settled in a more satisfactory manner, and as he had no valid excuse for going to war with him he determined to make one that would bring the matter to a crisis. He sent orders to him that he should appear at the capital and present himself to the Emperor as his superior lord and suzerain. Being badly advised by his leading men, he pleaded sickness and refused to come. Imperative commands were now issued, but these were again disregarded. T'ai Tsu then collected an army of one hundred thousand men, and putting them under the command of Ts'au-pin and P'an-mei, launched them against the recalcitrant prince. True to his kind and generous nature, his last orders to Ts'au-pin were those of mercy to the conquered. "Don't hurt the people," he said, "and when you capture a city let there be no indiscriminate slaughter of the inhabitants, and if the prince submits to you spare him and his whole family." The army travelled by land to a certain point where it reached the Yangtze, when it was conveyed in ships down the river to Nanking. The Prince of T'ang sent ambassadors twice to T'ai Tsu, remonstrating against his being attacked, but the Emperor had a great and imperial purpose in view, and he was not to be stayed in his execution of it. The city was now closely invested by the besieging army after the forces of the prince had suffered a great defeat outside the town. It was exceedingly well fortified, however, and withstood the fiercest assaults of the enemy, and it was not till it had been besieged for twelve months that it was finally captured. When Ts'au-pin saw that the city must fall he sent in a flag of truce and demanded its surrender and promised the most favourable terms to all within it. These were rejected by the besieged, who declared that they would fight to the bitter end and perish in the ruins of their town rather than submit to the will of the conqueror. Ts'au-pin, who saw that the fall of Nanking was inevitable, and that the long struggle had embittered the hearts of his men, and that consequently there would be a tremendous slaughter when the infuriated troops rushed into the city, had recourse to a ruse to avoid what he knew would be exceedingly disliked by the Emperor.

A day or two before the final assault he suddenly became, to all appearance, very ill. Consternation spread throughout the camp, for it was felt that without the skill and genius of their commander-in-chief their whole enterprise that had involved them in such great toil and suffering might possibly end in failure. Ts'au-pin, calling his chief captains to his bedside, said that his disease was a mental one, and that there was no medicine in all the world that would cure it. "I believe," he continued, "that if you would solemnly swear to me that when we capture the city there shall be no bloodshed I should soon get well again." With loud voices they declared that they were willing to do anything that lay within their power to bring about such a happy result, and they proceeded to take the oath required. No sooner were the solemn words uttered that bound them to be merciful to the fallen foe than Ts'au-pin rose from his bed and declared that he was completely recovered. The city was soon after taken by storm, and the territory that had been ruled by the Prince of T'ang became incorporated in the royal dominions.

After this signal success T'ai Tsu went to his native place to worship at the grave of his ancestors and to thank them for the glorious victory they had given him. He also repaired to Lohyang and offered up sacrifices to Heaven and earth at the great altar that had been built outside the south gate of the city. Whilst here he discussed with his brother the advisability of removing his capital either to this place or to Ch'ang-ngan, as being more suitable and central than K'ai-fung-fu. Hw'ang-yi was exceedingly opposed to this idea, and after some discussion the matter was dropped, and they returned to the capital.

At the beginning of autumn (A. D. 976) T'ai Tsu sent an army against the Prince of Han, which gained a victory, but the practical results of it were of little service, for the Khitans coming to the rescue, the Sung troops had to retreat within their entrenchments and defend themselves behind them. Soon after the news had been brought to the Emperor of the want of success in this campaign, he became seriously ill. As he approached his end he sent for his brother to give him his last instructions, for in obedience to the promise exacted from him by his mother he had appointed him to succeed him on the throne. What these last words were the royal historian has not been able to record, for there was no one present to witness the interview. No member of the privy council, or even of his own family, was called to hear the last words of the dying sovereign. What is known with certainty is that when Kw'ang-yi emerged from the sick chamber his brother was dead.*

T'ai Tsung—A. D. 976-998.

Nothing of special importance happened during the first three years of this monarch's reign, with the exception that in A. D. 979 he ennobled the past descendants of Confucius for forty-four generations, and thus made the honours of the family hereditary. In the following year, in pursuance of the policy imitated by T'ai Tsu, he made extensive preparations for the subjugation of the Prince of Han, and a large army under the command of the veteran P'an-mei marched against him. In great alarm he sent messengers to

---

* Chinese scholars maintain that there is a mystery about the closing hours of the founder of the Sung dynasty. As no one was allowed to enter the sick chamber but his brother some of the ladies and eunuchs of the royal household peered through the crevices in the partition wall to try and see what was going on within. The words were too low for them to catch, but by and by they saw the sick man rise and seize an axe, and then there was the sound of it, as it clanged to the ground. and one sentence was heard distinctly, "Very well, I'll let you be it," and he dropped back on his bed and was dead. T'ai Tsu was a man whose character contained many loveable features. He was manly and straightforward. He was also tender-hearted and careful of human life. He seemed to have a deep sense of the responsibility of his exalted position. One day he was observed to be very sad and cast down. One of the mandarins spoke to him about it and asked him the reason. His reply was, " Do you think it an easy thing to be a king? I remember that in my audience with my privy council this morning I decided a case wrongly. I have just found out that I did so, and I am grieved." He died at the early age of fifty.

the Khitans, begging them to hasten to his assistance, which they were nothing loath to do. In order to prevent their junction with the Han troops Kwo-tsin was sent forward with a large force to intercept them. The two armies met at "White Horse Ridge," when the Khitans suffered defeat and were compelled to retreat. P'an-mei, zealous of the glory which his lieutenant had obtained by this victory, determined to outshine him by the capture of T'ai-yuan, which he was then besieging. Extraordinary measures were taken to cause it to fall, and the enthusiasm of the soldiers was excited to the highest pitch, as it became evident that this city, that had so often defied the armies that had besieged it, would soon succumb before the valiant soldiers that were attacking it. The Emperor, who was present, personally superintended the operations of the troops and encouraged them in their toils and dangers. At length it became evident that the city could hold out no longer. There was not a stone in the great walls that was not broken and battered. T'ai Tsung now offered favourable terms to the besieged, with threats of terrible vengeance if they refused to capitulate. Then Prince Liu, seeing that the defence was no longer possible, opened the gates and admitted the Sung troops. He was made Duke of Kiang-ngan and sent with his family to his dukedom, so that he might be far removed from his adherents and thus be less able to raise the standard of rebellion again.

T'ai-yuan was reduced in rank and made a district city, and the whole of the inhabitants were transferred to Pingchow, in the S. W. of Chihli, whilst the people of that city were removed to T'ai-yuan. No more effectual plan could have been adopted than this to utterly crush out the spirit of rebellion which had caused its people to be so often arrayed against the forces of the crown.

T'ai Tsung was rendered so confident by the double victory that his arms had achieved that in an evil hour he determined to measure his strength with the Khitans and see whether he could conquer a foe that had always been the persistent enemy of the Chinese. The royal troops therefore advanced into Liau-tung and prepared to battle with them in their own territory. The Khitans, seeing that the invasion had come to their own doors, rallied all the forces they were capable of collecting, and led by the famous captain Yeh-luh Hiu-ko advanced to meet the Sung army. A tremendous battle took place at Kau-liang, in which the Khitans were everywhere successful. The Sung army was utterly routed and fled in utmost disorder. The Emperor was amongst the fugitives, and had to abandon everything in the effort to save dear life. The household troops that should have guarded His Majesty during the retreat were dispersed by the repeated charges of cavalry, and for a long time it was not known where T'ai Tsung was. Some thought he had been slain, and men began to discuss whether Teh-chau, the eldest son of T'ai Tsu, should not be proclaimed Emperor. This unfortunate rumour proved fatal to the young man, for it reached the ear of the Emperor and aroused his jealousy of him as a possible competitor for the throne.

After the return to the capital there was nothing but mourning and discontent, because of the great disaster that had happened to the royal army, and the Emperor refused to distribute rewards of any kind, even to those who had most conspicuously distinguished themselves. As this caused considerable dissatisfaction, Teh-chau ventured to remonstrate with his uncle, and showed him that though the army had been defeated at Kau-liang they had vanquished a Khitan force and captured T'ai-yuan. T'ai Tsung, whose mind was still filled with jealousy of his nephew, angrily replied, "When you become Emperor you can distribute your rewards." Teh-chau saw that mischief was intended him, so he went home and cut his throat. Two months after, the request that had been so ungraciously refused was carried out, and amidst the many honours bestowed Yang-yeh was made commander of T'ai-yuan.*

The year A. D. 981 saw the Khitans again on the move, and a hundred thousand of them were marching on the city of Yen-mun. Yang-yeh, who had heard of their design, placed himself with several hundred horsemen in ambush in an advantageous position near a difficult place where they had to pass, and falling upon them routed them, so that they fell back precipitately and gave up their purpose in regard to Yen-mun. This victory was counter-balanced, however, by a defeat that the Sung army suffered the same year at Wa-ch'iau from the hands of Yeh-luh Hiu-ko. The following year is distinguished by two important events. The first of these was the appearance at court of a deputation from the Nu-chen Tartars for the purpose of paying tribute and formally acknowledging the supremacy of China over them. The second was the settlement of the succession. According to the agreement made with the Emperor's mother his next brother, K'wang-mei, ought to come to the throne after the death of T'ai Tsung. There were unequivocal signs, however, that the latter meditated keeping the succession in his own family to the exclusion of the elder branch that had the legitimate right to it. He consulted Chau-p'u, who had lately become a member of the privy council, as to what course he should take in the matter. His reply was pithy and to the point. "The deceased Emperor made a mistake," he said, "and don't you fall into the same error." This settled the question, and his son was appointed heir-apparent. Almost immediately after, by a singular but suspicious coincidence, it was reported to the Emperor that Kw'ang-mei was meditating rebellion, and he was at once banished to Fang-chow, where he died two years afterwards of grief and terror lest he should lose his life by foul means.

---

* Yang-yeh was a famous hero of this period. He had been one of the captains of the Prince of Han, but after his surrender he entered the service of T'ai Tsung and became conspicuous for his daring and gallantry. He was perhaps the one man that the Khitans feared, for he was so invariably sucessful in his fights with them that he was popularly known as "Yang the Invincible."

During the intervals of his wars with the Khitans the Emperor became a great student and spent about six hours a day in study. There was one treatise of a thousand volumes called "The Emperor's Guide for Pacifying his Empire," which he read with the greatest avidity and set himself to master three volumes a day. So impressed was he with the value of the books that he ordered the mandarins throughout the empire to send collections of them for the imperial library. Any person that presented three hundred copies would be made a mandarin. It was also ordered that all rare copies that the owner was unwilling to part with should be copied and sent to the capital.

In the year A. D. 986 hostilities were again begun with the Khitans. The Emperor had observed that they had been grievously molesting the Coreans, and he had advised the latter to raise troops and join with him in punishing them. After considerable hesitation they consented to do this. T'ai Tsung then sent four separate armies against them, one under Ts'au-pin, another under P'an-mei, a third under T'ien-chung and a fourth under Mi-sin. The first successes were with the Sung armies, for the Khitans were not prepared to meet them, and Ts'au-pin took the city of Cho-chow, P'an-mei Hwan-chow, and T'ien-chung Wei-chow. No sooner had the Khitan forces, however, taken the field under the command of Yeh-luh Hui-ko than fortune seemed to desert the imperial cause. This famous commander marched straight for Ts'au-pin, whose fame had made him the most formidable of all the Sung leaders, and a great battle was fought under the walls of Cho-chow, close by the river Cho. Ts'au-pin suffered a terrible defeat and lost thirty thousand men, who were either slain in the combat or were drowned in the river that flowed by as they endeavoured to escape from their ferocious enemies. The next to feel the power of the enraged Khitans was P'an-mei, whose army was routed in a great battle at Ch'en-chia-ku near Hwan-chow. The loss of life was great, and here the invincible Yang met his death whilst bravely contesting with overwhelming numbers, whom he strove to keep back, so as to preserve the army from utter destruction. One by one the other two armies were defeated, and soon there was not a single Sung soldier left in the Khitan territory.

T'ai Tsung was terribly distressed when the disastrous tidings reached him, and he ordered that all the officers engaged should be punished for the shame that had been brought upon the empire by being degraded a certain number of steps according as it might be proved by investigation that they had acted inefficiently in the late battles. The Emperor felt the loss of Yang-yeh, for as a warden of the marches he was the most efficient commander that he had. In his audience with his privy council he demanded who there was that could adequately succeed him, when the prime minister Chang Ts'i-yen volunteered his services. These were accepted and another army was collected, of which he was made commander-in-chief, with P'an-mei as his second in command. It took up its quarters at Tai-chow, in Shansi, and in an attack that the Khitans made upon it these latter were defeated and two thousand horses and all their baggage were captured by Chang Ts'i-yen. The next three years are remarkable only for the border warfare that was continually kept up with varying success. In one of the battles that was fought at Su-ho, in Chih li, the famous Yeh-luh Hiu-ko suffered a serious defeat at the hands of a general named Yin Chi-lun, and so strikingly were his great military abilities shown in his conflict, where his forces were inferior to those of the enemy, that orders were issued to all the Khitans that they were always in the future to avoid fighting with him.

In the year A. D. 992 the celebrated scholar and statesman K'ow-chun first appears upon the stage of history. He was a man of sterling integrity, of great determination of purpose and of unswerving loyalty. His counsels were destined to have an important effect in the management of the nation's affairs. This year the country was terribly afflicted with drought and locusts. The Emperor offered up his petitions to Heaven to have these evils removed, but no answer came back to his prayers. At last, in desperation, he declared to his council that he would try once more, and if the rain failed to come he would burn himself to death. He was saved, however, from this terrible alternative, for next day it poured in torrents. Shortly after this the Nutsin Tartars, who had made submission to China, sent word that if the Chinese would only conquer the Khitans they would continue their allegiance to them, but if not they would transfer their fealty to the latter. As T'ai Tsung was not in a position to make war upon his formidable neighbours they became the subjects of the Khitans.

A formidable rebellion broke out in Sz-chwan in A. D. 994, headed by a man of the name of Wang-siau. The cause of this was the misery and sorrow that abounded amongst the common people ever since they had been conquered by the Sung troops.

At that time a great deal of the gold and silver in the country had been carried away to K'ai-fung-fu and placed in the imperial treasury. The result was that there was a dearth of the precious metals throughout the province. Again, the mandarins appointed by the Emperor to govern the people seemed to have got the idea into their heads that their main business was to fleece the people, and they proceeded to carry out this idea in that thorough way that long experience had taught them to do so effectually. In addition to these troubles they had others of even a more severe character. The rich bought the lands of the poor, and putting men in the farms to till them for them, they stored the crops, and waiting for a rise in the market they sold out at exorbitant prices. The sufferings of the poor were consequently very great, and large numbers were on the verge of starvation. Wang-siau, sympathizing with them, advised them to rebel and execute vengeance on those that were oppressing them. Influenced by his words, and most of all by their miseries, they collected in large numbers and marched upon the district city of P'ang. The chief magistrate of this place had been most rapacious in his treatment of them, so they seized him, and cutting him open they filled his stomach with cash, declaring that he should have his fill of it.

The news spread with lightning rapidity, and robber bands desolated the country, and law and order practically ceased to exist. T'ai Tsung sent Wang Chi-yin, one of the eunuchs of the palace, with a considerable army to put down the rebellion. This he succeeded in doing very quickly, but because he was not given the high honours that the Emperor deemed it unsafe to bestow on a eunuch he took to drinking and allowed his troops to ill-treat and rob the people. The disaffection again broke .out, and the rebels began to assemble at various points in force, when another general arrived to supersede Wang, who managed by his wise measures to restore order to the country.

The question of the succession again came up for decision.* By his father's wish and the consent of the high officials his third son, whom he greatly loved, was appointed heir-apparent. He was at once led to the ancestral temple of his fathers, where he thanked the spirits of the dead for the favours they had bestowed upon him, and he prayed them to use their unseen power to protect and defend him in the future.

The last important act that T'ai Tsung performed was the division of the empire into fifteen provinces.† Shortly after, T'ai Tsung died, when there was an attempt made by Wang Chi-yin to set aside the third son in favour of the first, but Lu-toan, the prime minister, acted with such promptness in the matter that the schemes of the conspirators were thwarted, and the third son, who was thirty years old, ascended the throne. As the Empress-Dowager had showed a disposition to hold the reins of power in her own hands the nobles were determined to resist this, especially as the Emperor was old enough to govern for himself. Accordingly, on the day when all the great dignitaries came to make their obeisance before the new Emperor they determined that there should be no mistake as to whom they were going to honour. Chen Tsung and his mother were seated behind a curtain, and the great nobles stood waiting for the signal for them to kneel down. Lu-toan cried out, "Raise the curtain and let us see before whom we are going to prostrate our-

---

* The eldest son had been disinherited A. D. 986, because of his disapproval of his father's conduct in his treatment of his brother K'wang-mei. The banishment and death of the latter had so worked upon the young man's mind that he had become insane. During one of his fits he set fire to part of the palace, and for this he was stripped of all his honours and reduced to the ranks of the common people.

† The names of these were Eastern Capital and Western Capital (both in Honan), Ho-peh, Ho-tung, Shensi, Kwai-nan, Hunan, Hu-peh, Foh-kien, Kiang-ngan, Sz-chwan, Kwang-tung, Kwangsi and the two Cheh-kiang.

selves." Slowly it lifted, and the only one that was seen was Chen Tsung sitting on his throne, for his mother had wisely vanished and left the government to him.

Chen Tsung—A. D. 998-1023.

The commencement of this Emperor's reign was marked by an unlucky omen, namely, the appearance of a comet. Chen Tsung was distressed with this, for it was a manifest token to him that Heaven considered that there was something wrong in the government of the country. He accordingly invited a free expression of opinion from his nobles as to what should be done to avert the judgments that this comet portended. One proposed that the taxes that had fallen in arrears to the amount of ten million ounces of silver, through the poverty of the people, should be all remitted. History does not inform us whether this suggestion was carried into effect or not: what we are told is, that over three thousand prisoners were released from confinement and allowed to rejoin their families.

The year A. D. 1004 is an important one in the history of this reign, for in it the Khitan king, accompanied by his mother, at the head of an overwhelming force, entered the Chinese territory. City after city fell before them, until at last they came into the neighbourhood of the strongly fortified town of Tanchow. Despatch after despatch was carried by excited couriers to the capital praying for immediate help, and no fewer than five arrived in one evening to be read by the privy council that sat in constant session to debate what should be done under the present alarming circumstances. The minds of all were highly excited, the only exception being K'ow-chun, who drank and laughed, and declared that the matter was so trifling that he guaranteed he could settle it in five days. "You must implicitly follow my plan, however," he said to the Emperor, "and come with your army to Tanchow." All the rest of the council were aghast at this proposal. "What! walk into the very camp of the Khitans," they exclaimed. "That would never do." Chen Tsung was about to retire into his own apartments, but K'ow-chun detained him and said that this question must be settled at once, as delay meant danger. He then withdrew with the rest of his council to discuss this most startling proposition. One was in favour of removing the capital, which they considered in peril, to Ch'ung-tu, Sz-chwan. Another favoured Kin-ling, in Hu-kwang.* When the Emperor rejoined K'ow-chun and told him the plans that had been discussed he was beside himself with indignation. "Let me know the names of the men that have dared to suggest such a cowardly proposal," he cried, "for they ought to be put to death as traitors to their country." "Let us march," he continued, "and save the empire. To fly would be the ruin of everything."

---

* Hu-kwang is represented by the present provinces of Hunan and Hupeh.

The enthusiasm of K'ow-chun overcame every obstacle, and ere long the Emperor had started on his way. As he got near to where the enemy was encamped the fears of his officials again recurred, and once more Chen Tsung was urged to fly to Kin-ling. K'ow-chun besought him not to listen to the words of men that wished to destroy him and his dynasty. "You may advance a .foot," he said, "but you must not retreat a single inch. Your soldiers are on the frontiers, and day and night with longing eyes they are watching for your arrival. The bravery of the soldiers will be intensified when they see you in their midst, whilst their hearts would grow weak and they would fly in disorder if they heard that you had deserted them. The Khitans would then pursue, and you would never be able to reach Kin-ling." This spirited appeal was seconded by those who heard it, and again the royal party advanced.

As they got near the banks of the Yellow River they began to have a glimpse of the Khitans beyond, and, terrified by their great numbers, some advised the Emperor to encamp the force that was with him on this side of the river. "No," exclaimed the valiant K'ow-chun, "we must cross and show them that we don't fear them, besides, we run no risk in doing so, for reinforcements from all parts of the empire are marching to the aid of your Majesty." No sooner had the royal party crossed over than the cry of "Ten thousand years! Ten thousand years!" was raised by the joyful soldiers, who saw that their Emperor was amongst them. At once it spread from camp to camp and from soldier to soldier, till tens of thousands of voices were shouting the glad sound and startling the astonished Khitans with its echoes. Chen Tsung now entered Tan-chow, which was besieged by the enemy. K'ow-chun, to whom the supreme command was now given, was not the man to allow this to be done with impunity. An attack was made upon them, in which they were badly defeated and lost a large number of men.

The Khitans now sent an ambassador to make a treaty of peace with Chen Tsung. The conditions they insisted upon were that Tan-chow should be delivered over to them, with the territory that lay to the south of it. The Emperor, in discussing the matter with K'ow-chun, said he did not object to paying a large subsidy to the Khitans, but he certainly would not consent to giving up any land that belonged to China. K'ow-chun was opposed to giving them anything, and advised that an unconditional surrender should be insisted upon, but this Chen Tsung would not agree to, as it might make the Khitans desperate and cause them to renew the war. He therefore instructed his ambassador to offer them a million ounces of silver in case he could not get off with less. Just before leaving the camp K'ow-chun threatened this man that if he agreed to more than three hundred thousand he would take off his head. When he returned, it was found that peace had been concluded on much less severe conditions than had been anticipated, namely, one hundred thousand ounces of silver and two hundred thousand pieces of silk to be paid annually. Great rejoicings now took place throughout the empire, and a general amnesty was proclaimed. Half of the soldiers on the northern frontier and two-thirds of those in the direction of the Khitans were withdrawn and sent home to till the soil. The troops still in garrison were ordered to cultivate friendly relationships with their late deadly foes ; the horses and oxen that had been taken away from them in the late struggles were restored to them, and the traders from both peoples began to cross the border and enter into commercial relationships with each other.

The reputation of K'ow-chun was now very great, and deservedly so. He had saved the empire and concluded a peace that had turned the implacable foes of China into friends. He had reached the very highest pinnacle of fame, and there seemed to be years of prosperity and honour before him, but this was not to be his experience. It has always been the curse of China that its Emperors have been easily led by the words of some wily traitor to distrust the very men that were essential to the welfare of the state, and these have been driven away into comparative exile, whilst their more plausible enemies have been retained in high official positions to work mischief by their counsels. The very next year after the conclusion of peace Wang K'in-joh so worked upon the mind of Chen Tsung that he actually persuaded him that the treaty was a disgraceful one, and reflected upon his honour, and that K'ow-chun, instead of being rewarded, ought to be punished. These words sunk deep into the mind of this weak monarch, and he sent K'ow-chun to be commandant, first of Shan-chow, in Honan, and then of Tai-ming, in Chihli. When the Khitans saw the low rank to which he had been reduced they were astonished, and said to him, "How is it that a man of your great reputation is in this small place, instead of being in the privy council managing the affairs of state ?" "There is nothing for me to do there," he replied. "My position here is a more important one, for I have been placed here to guard the frontier."

With the prevalence of peace throughout the empire, and the absence of the continual anxiety that the possibility of attack from the Khitans had produced, Chen Tsung did not improve in character. It became manifest that his nature was a deeply superstitious one and liable to become the dupe of any crafty designer that might gain an influence over him. Unfortunately for him, Wang K'in-joh was the man that was now high in the royal favour, and of all men in the court he was the most unsuited to be near the royal person. In the year A. D 1009 the Emperor had a dream which he told to this unscrupulous courtier. He said, "Last night I saw in my dream a spirit descending from Heaven. It was dressed in a green hat and a red garment, and it told me to employ a Taoist priest to perform certain religious rites, and that I should build a temple. It also promised to give me three heavenly volumes that were never made by human hand." This was an opportunity that Wang K'in-joh was determined to make the most of. A few days after, the commander of the city guard reported that outside the walls there lay three books that had fallen from Heaven. The Emperor, at the head of a number of his courtiers, walked to the place where they lay, and after prostrating himself before them he had them reverently brought into the palace. When opened, the first volume was found to be filled with praises of the Emperor for his virtue and filial piety; the second commanded him to be pure in heart, to be contemplative and to be more economical, and the third contained a promise that his dynasty would be a perpetual one. They were carefully put away in a golden casket, and in token of his thankfulness for having received them the Emperor ordered a general amnesty throughout his empire. He also commenced the building of a magnificent temple, which it took seven years to complete, and upon which such immense sums were lavished that some have dated the commencement of the decline of the Sung dynasty from this period.

In the year A. D. 1013 the Empress died, and Chen Tsung, in spite of the protests of his ministers, made Liu, a favourite concubine, queen in her stead.* She was a woman of great intelligence, and studied politics so thoroughly that her husband used to constantly consult her on questions of importance. During his illness, indeed, it may truly be said that the whole government was practically in her hands.†

Two years before his death the Emperor became so seriously ill that he could not look after the business of the state, and handed over everything to the management of his queen. This was greatly resented by the great mandarins, who petitioned that the heir-apparent, Ching, in conjunction with the privy council, should perform these state duties. The queen and Ting-wei, the prime minister, who were unwilling to lose the great power they possessed, interfered and prevented Chen Tsung from acceding to their wishes. The Emperor never recovered from his sickness, and in the twenty-fifth year of his reign, and at the comparatively early age of fifty-nine, he died. His son succeeded him, and Queen Liu was appointed regent during his minority, for he was only thirteen years old. The dying command of the Emperor was that K'ow-chun should be made one of the members of the privy council.

---

* There is quite a romantic story about this famous Empress. Her father was a soldier, and dying on the road of wounds that he had received in battle, his little daughter was left without any one to care for her. She wandered up and down, gaining her livelihood in a most precarious fashion, and calling the attention of the people to her by the sound of a rattle. A goldsmith, seeing her desolate and forlorn condition, adopted her, and when she was fifteen, finding that she had developed into a great beauty, sold her to Chen Tsung, who was then heir-apparent, to be one of his concubines.

† During this same year the famous poet Liu-ho was summoned to court, and presents were bestowed upon him by the Emperor. His poems that have come down to the present day show that he was a man of genius and of most vivid imagination. He was very fond of flowers and birds, and he called the flower of the plum his wife and the crane his son.

CHAPTER XXV.

THE SUNG DYNASTY (Continued).

Jin Tsung—A. D. 1023-1064.

AS K'ow-chun was obnoxious to Ting-wei, whose patron he had been, and through whose influence he had risen to power, he was banished to Lui-chow, in the Canton province. A speedy nemesis followed, however, for in the course of the same year Ting-wei suffered the same fate, being transported to a city beyond the one to which K'ow-chun had been sent.

The fourth year of Jin Tsung's reign was distinguished by a remarkable flood that prevailed over Honan, Kiang-ngan and the country to the north of the Yellow River. The greatest distress prevailed and vast multitudes were made homeless. The Emperor, considering that this calamity was caused by some mismanagement or misdeed of his, fasted and gave orders that the homeless should be supplied with food out of government funds, and that all taxes should be remitted in the districts to which the flood had extended.

This same year Teh-ming, the son of the rebel Chau-pau, who had given in his submission in the eighth year of Chen Tsung, again raised the standard of rebellion, and sent his son Chau-yuan with a large force to besiege the city of Kan-chow.*

In the year A. D. 1033 the regent died, having kept the whole power in her own hands, though she ought by rights to have resigned it some years previously to Jin Tsung. Immediately after her death rumours began to be bruited about that she had caused the death of the Emperor's mother, who had been one of the concubines in the harem of Chen Tsung. In order to verify these Jin Tsung had the coffin opened, in order to see if her death had been really caused by some foul play. To his delight he found that it had not, for the prime minister at the time she died suspecting that some difficulty like the present might arise in the future to tarnish the good name of the regent, had himself superintended all the arrangements for her funeral. The body was found dressed in royal robes, fit for the mother of an Emperor, and quicksilver had been poured into it, so that it retained its freshness, though four years had gone by since it was buried. These were decisive evidences that she had died a natural death. Not only was the character of the regent vindicated, but also his own heart was set at rest, for she had acted to him all his life as though she had been his real mother, and he still retained for her the deepest affection.

---

* Chau-pau was governor of Hing-chow, in Shensi. His grandson, Chau-yuan, was a man of distinguished abilities. He knew the Chinese and Khitan languages: he was an artist, and he was a brave and able commander.

For seven years the reign of Jin Tsung was marked by nothing special excepting a severe earthquake, A. D. 1037, that affected Honan and Shansi, and caused the death of twenty-two thousand people and the wounding and maiming of between five and six thousand more. At the end of this time Chau-ming, who had succeeded his father, Teh-ming, impelled by ambition, determined to extend his dominion at the expense of the Empire, and he accordingly led his forces to the county city of Pau-ngan and captured it.

Ti-ts'ing, a renowned border captain, led what forces he had under his command and defeated him, so that he had to retreat. The victory, though an important one, does not seem to have broken the spirit of Chau-yuan, for in the following year he led an immense army and met the one under Han-k'i at San-chwan, where, after three days' stubborn fighting, the advantage remained with Yuan. During the fighting Han-k'i one evening sent a force of seven thousand men under his lieutenant Jin-fu, who, after a forced night march, reached Hia-chow, which had been left unprotected, and took it. He slaughtered a large number of its people and destroyed the military stores it contained, and then rejoined the main army. Next year Yuan, with increased forces, met Han-k'i, when the latter suffered a severe defeat. It was at this disastrous battle that the brave Jin-fu was slain. Being grievously wounded with over a dozen arrows he was entreated by his soldiers to withdraw, but this he would not consent to do. "I am a high officer," he replied, "and it is my duty to give my life for my country." He then advanced against the foe, when he was killed by a spear being driven through his throat. In this battle ten thousand three hundred men were slain, and a large number of officers. The Emperor was so displeased when the tidings of disaster reached him that he took away the command from Han-k'i and gave him an inferior position in Ts'ui-chow. Shortly after Fan Chung-yen, who had been placed in command in Si-ngan, was also sent away, because he tore up a letter from Yuan containing terms of peace which he proposed they should agree on, instead of forwarding it to the Emperor for him to decide upon.

The evil results in removing two such able commanders were soon apparent in the increased activity of Yuan, who soon after took the important city of Fungchow. The Emperor was therefore obliged to recall them and reinstate them in their commands. In order to crush the rebellion four distinct armies were assigned separate districts in Shensi, each one under its own commander. To Fan-chung was assigned Ch'ing-chow; to Han-k'i Tsu-chow; to Wang-yen Wei-chow, and to P'ang-tsih Yen-chow. This last named district, which had previously been in the possession of Yuan, was found to be in a sadly desolate and ruined condition, and showed how terrible is war in its power to turn the most populous and thriving region into a wilderness. The county city was in ruins and its walls cast down. P'ang-tsih set his army to work, and not only rebuilt them, but also ten others that had been levelled by the rebels.

Fan-chung found his district in a somewhat better condition. He determined, however, to build a city at Ta-shun, on the extreme boundary of his district, for it was so situated that Yuan must pass through it in order to get into it. It required great secrecy on his part to do this without the knowledge of Yuan, who, had he known of the intention, would have at once occupied it in force. Fan-chung had the bricks to build the walls quietly collected, and employing every soldier he had to carry them he made a rush for the place, and the foundations were laid before Yuan could get information that the work had been begun. Soon Yuan appeared with thirty thousand men, but by the time he had arrived the walls had risen to such a height that the Sung soldiers could fight behind them. Finding that he had come too late, he withdrew with his men.

The Khitans, seeing the difficulties in which the empire was placed, determined to take advantage of them to advance their own interests. An ambassador was sent to Jin Tsung demanding that ten counties should be handed over to them, and threatening him if he refused that war would be declared against China. The Emperor was quite decided that he would never consent to alienate Chinese territory, still, rather than go to war, he was prepared to pay the Khitans increased sums of money, and even to allow one of the royal princesses to be given in marriage to their king. Fu-pi was selected by the Emperor as his ambassador to the Khitan court to explain the terms he offered, in order to avoid a collision with them. These were indignantly refused at first, but Fu-pi, by wonderful diplomatic tact, overcame all the arguments of the king, and finally a treaty of peace was ratified by the payment of one hundred thousand ounces of silver and a hundred thousand pieces of silk annually, in addition to what had been agreed upon in the previous treaty nearly forty years ago. This treaty, although it averted war, was a most humiliating one for China, for Fu-pi, with all his diplomacy, could not keep the word out of it that showed that this payment to the Khitans was a tribute that was being paid by an inferior to a superior power.

The war between Jin Tsung and Chau-yuan came to a sudden termination in the year A. D. 1043, the latter submitting terms of peace to the Emperor, which were accepted by him. The principal of these were that Yuan was so far to recognize Jin Tsung that in addressing him he was to style him Father Emperor. It was to be distinctly understood, however, that he was not an officer of his, but to all intents and purposes an independent prince, whose royal name should be Uh-tsu, and the title of his kingdom Ni-ting. Fan-chung and Han-k'i now returned to the capital amid the rejoicings of the people, and were appointed to high positions in the palace, where their great abilities could be utilized by the Emperor in the government of the country. An immediate change come over the spirit of the palace, for the leading men in it were not only distinguished scholars, but they were also profound statesmen and animated by the sincerest loyalty to their country.   Fu-pi was entrusted with all matters that concerned the Khitans, whilst the same responsibility was thrown on Fan-chung in regard to Chau-yuan.

By the advice of Ou Yang-siu commissioners were appointed whose business it was to visit the officials throughout the empire and to report to the capital whether they were faithful in the discharge of their duties or not.   They were invested with large powers, for even the governors were obliged to submit their official conduct to their scrutiny.   This was a most dangerous power to give any set of men in such a country as China, as it opened up the way for the most unlimited bribery and corruption.   One suspects from the silence of the historian in regard to the success of this new movement that it must have been an utter failure.

By the advice of Fan-chung colleges were opened in every district throughout the empire, where students could live and study. Professors were appointed and regular examinations were held. Before a student could get his diploma he would have to pass in three subjects, viz., history, writing an essay on some famous historical personage, and a poetical composition.   The college in the capital was an exceedingly spacious one, with accommodations for a very large number of students.   It was opened by the Emperor in person, who prostrated himself twice before the image of Confucius, which was placed in a conspicuous place in it.

The reforms introduced by Fan-chung and Han-k'i raised a storm of opposition from the more conservative in the palace, and in order to destroy their influence it was said that they were purposing to do away with the Emperor.   Jin Tsung did not believe this, but these two statesmen, seeing that suspicion had been implanted in the mind of the sovereign which in time might involve them in ruin,   petitioned to be allowed to go and investigate into the condition of the Khitans and Chau-yuan, who were reported to be going to fight with each other.   This was granted, and after they had gone the evil reports grew in intensity, so that the Emperor ordered Fan-chung to be degraded and sent to Pin-chow, Han-k'i to Yang-chow, and Fu-pi and Ou Yang-siu, who had been associates with them, to Yun-chow and Su-chow.   The colleges remained, but the new system of examinations was abolished.

In the year A. D. 1048 Chau-yuan died, and as his son was only a year old, his widow acted as regent for him, appointing three of her relatives to assist her in the government.   An ambassador was sent to the court of Jin Tsung to inform him of the decease of Yuan, and some of his ministers advised him to advance the three nobles to positions of great power and authority in the hope that they would quarrel with each other and thus subserve the interests of China.   Jin Tsung was not the man, however, to listen to such a diabolical scheme. "I cannot take advantage of their sorrow," he replied, "to engage in any plan that will injure the bereaved family." He sent messages of condolence instead, and bestowed upon the infant son the title of "Lord of Hia."

A rebellion broke out in Cochin China in the year A. D. 1049, headed by Nung Chih-kau, who entered Kwang-si and committed excesses there. Three years were allowed to pass before any effective measures were taken to suppress him, and even then he might have been let alone, but he had the audacity to memorialize the Emperor, requesting to be made governor of that province. Jin Tsung, with his usual good nature, was inclined to grant his request, but his ministers vigorously opposed this, and Ti-ts'ing was appointed commander of an expedition to put an end to his rebellion. The general in charge of the troops in Kwang-si, hearing that he was coming, and anxious to obtain for himself a reputation that he knew would never be his after the arrival of Ti-ts'ing, led eight thousand men against Nung, and a battle was fought at "The Pass of K'wen-lun," in which he suffered a severe defeat and fled in the direction of Ti-ts'ing. The latter, who was a man who exercised a severe discipline in the army, at once investigated the cause of the disaster and ordered the defeated commander and thirty-two of his men to be executed for mismanagement and incompetence.

He then circulated a report, which he took good care should reach the camp of the rebels, that he was going to give his men ten days' rest after the fatigues of their long journey. Next morning, however, before daylight his army was on the move, and in the early dawn they reached the scene of the late defeat and found the enemy totally unprepared for them. Nothing daunted, however, they speedily put themselves in battle array and fought most stubbornly, but they were no match for the Sung troops, led by such a famous commander as Ti-ts'ing. Several thousands of them were killed, and five hundred were taken prisoners. Amongst the dead there lay one body dressed in royal robes, which his officers declared was that of Nung Chih-kau. Ti-ts'ing disbelieved this and supposed it to be a ruse of the rebel chief to prevent pursuit. In this he was right, for two years after it was discovered that he had died and was buried in Yunnan, when his body was exhumed, and his head being struck off, it was hung up in a conspicuous place, a warning to all who meditated the crime of rebellion.

In the year A. D. 1055 there was a terrible flood of the Yellow River. Six great water courses were opened to drain off the waters and three hundred thousand men were employed in this gigantic work ; but everything failed, for the banks of the six new water-ways gave way before the great pressure of the waters upon them, and the flood spread still further and still wider, and countless people were sent adrift without a home, and large numbers died of starvation and suffering. Five years later Ou Yang-siu, with the aid of Sung-k'i, brought to completion his "New History of the

T'ang Dynasty,'' in two hundred and twenty-five volumes, which was intended to supercede the one made by Sieh Ku-cheng, and which had been unsatisfactory, because of its incompleteness and diffuseness.

In the year A. D. 1063 Jin Tsung died, and was succeeded by his second cousin, whose dynastic title is Ying Tsung. His long reign of forty-one years, if not remarkable for any great event that took place in it, is memorable in Chinese history for the large number of scholars and statesmen that adorned it. This period may in truth be termed the golden age of Chinese literature. There is a perfect galaxy of poets and historians and profound scholars to be found at this time, whose writings have not only remained to the present day, but have also tinged and moulded the literature of succeeding ages.*

Ying Tsung—A. D. 1064-1068.

This Emperor was thirty-two years old when he ascended the throne. A few months after he began to reign he became so seriously ill that he had to invite the Empress-Dowager Ts'au to act as regent for him. This she did, and in order to hold her audiences with the privy council without being seen by them she sat behind a curtain whilst business was being transacted, and a eunuch attended to carry documents backwards and forwards for her to examine. After the recovery of Ying Tsung, which was in the course of four months, the prime minister Han-k'i was exceedingly anxious that she should resign her position and hand over the government to the Emperor. She seemed unwilling to do this, so he determined to adopt a plan that would compel her to do so. One day, at a public audience, after a dozen questions had been settled by the Emperor and the documents had been carried to the regent for approval, Han-k'i rose and said, as Ying Tsung was again restored to health and was capable of transacting public business, he begged leave to resign his office as prime minister. The regent saw at once that this speech was aimed at her, and she knew that one of them would have to yield. With great good sense she determined to be the one to do so. She accordingly called out and told him that the Emperor could not dispense with his services and that he must not resign. She also declared that the power that had been vested in her as regent she handed back to Ying Tsung. ''Then wind up the curtain,'' Han-k'i cried out, ''and as it was slowly rising, the vanishing garments of Ts'au could be seen as she disappeared in the apartment beyond.''

In order to be ready for any movement that might be made by the Lord of Hia, a law was passed at the instigation of Han-k'i that

---

* A few names of the more distinguished scholars are here appended, viz., Ou Yang-siu, Fan Chung-yen, Han-ki, Su-sim, Su-shih, Sze-ma-kwang, Ch'ang Ming-tau, Wang Ngan-shih, Chu Show-ch'ang, Lu-hwei, Lu I-kien, Fan Shun-jen, Pau-ching, Shau-yung, Sung-k'i, Chow Fun-i, etc.

every family that had three sons should give one of them to be a soldier to the state, and that one of his hands should be branded with a word to show he belonged to the state. This caused great dissatisfaction amongst the people, but on the assurance that they would be employed simply to protect their own districts, the discontent subsided. This new law resulted in providing one hundred and fifty-six thousand militia for service when needed. After a brief reign of four years Ying Tsung died, and was succeeded by his eldest son, whose title in history is Shen Tsung.

Shen Tsung—A. D. 1068-1086.

The commencement of this reign is distinguished by the coming into power of Wang Ngan-shih, a man who was destined to play a prominent part in the history of this period. He had been made prefect of Kiang-ning, but his great abilities becoming widely known, he was sent for by the Emperor, who, being only twenty years of age, was soon fascinated and controlled by this singularly talented man. Han-k'i was violently opposed to his elevation, as he predicted that he would bring great calamities on the country, but his advice being rejected, he resigned his high position, and was made a governor in Honan. In A. D. 1069 Wang Ngan was made a member of the privy council, whilst Fu-pi became prime minister, though it soon became evident that the former was the ruling spirit in the counsels of the state. The Emperor asked him one day, "If I were to make you chief minister of state. what would you do?" "I would change the customs and institute reforms," he promptly replied. As a result of this speech a new Board of three high officials was formed for the purpose of examining into the condition of the country and of suggesting where improvements might be made and where better regulations might take the place of the old. Officers were sent by it throughout the country to report upon the nature of the soil, where watered and where not, where it was rich and where it was poor, with any other information that would help the Board to legislate for the farmer, so that his condition might be alleviated.

In the summer of this year Wang Ngan brought forward the first of his great reforms by which the commerce of the country was to be carried on by the state instead of by the people. His proposition, briefly stated, was this: The taxes for the future should be paid in the produce of the district where they were levied, and the state should furnish funds to buy up what was left. This should be transported to different parts of the country where a good market could be found and sold at a reasonable profit. Thus would the state be benefitted and the poorer classes be saved from the oppression of the rich, who had been in the habit of buying cheaply and selling at exorbitant prices.

This scheme was vigorously opposed by Su-cheh, who showed the abuses that would be created by the new system. The expenses that would be incurred in carrying out this vast measure, he said, would be enormous, and besides, there would be a total loss of the customs' dues that were now paid to the government. But the most serious difficulty of all, he continued, was the bribery and corruption that would certainly exist amongst the host of employés throughout the country. The sufferings of the people, he held, would be eventually greater from these causes than those they had endured from the avarice of the rich. The Emperor, who was earnestly desirous of advancing the good of the people, was fascinated by the bold and daring genius of Wang Ngan, and consented to try his scheme.

The next great reform that was carried out was called "The State Advances to the Cultivators of the Soil." The original idea was not Wang's, but Li-ts'au's, an official in Shensi. A memorial had been presented by the latter to the Emperor, in which he represented that the very large number of soldiers that were in Shensi to guard against the invasion of the Lord of Hia could not obtain sufficient provisions from the districts in which they were stationed, in consequence of the poverty of the farmers, who had not capital enough to work their farms, to the full extent of their producing powers. He therefore proposed that the government should advance certain sums to the farmers, to be repaid in the sixth and tenth months, after they had gathered in their crops, and that an intereset of twenty-four per cent. should be charged for all such loans. Wang was charmed with the idea, and, making it his own, proposed to Shen Tsung that it should be adopted for the whole empire. A meeting of the privy council was called to discuss it, when Su-cheh again led the opposition to the proposed innovation. He showed the sorrows that would come upon the people when the time came round for payment and when they had no money to satisfy the officials that were to collect it, and how they would be imprisoned, and squeezed, and tortured by men who thought of nothing but their own interests. In spite of all that could be said against it the eloquence and enthusiasm of Wang prevailed, and the new ordinance became law.

Another famous law that was passed through Wang's influence was the "Militia Enrollment Act." This divided the people of the whole empire into divisions of ten families, with a head man over each. Above him was another officer who had the control of fifty families, and still another higher who was responsible for five hundred. Every home with more than one son was bound to give one to serve the state. In times of peace these militiamen could pursue their ordinary avocations, but when the enemy threatened the country they were called to arms through the head men above mentioned.

The law relating to state labour was what might be termed the last of the great reforms that were carried by Wang in spite of the most strenuous opposition of Sze Ma-kwang and other great statesmen. This was an act for taxing every family for the construction of public works, instead of the compulsory labour that had hitherto been exacted when such were being carried out. In order that the rich should bear this burden equally with the poor each family was rated according to the property it possessed. To find out this was an extremely difficult thing, for everyone would naturally try and make it appear that he was poorer than he really was. Wang adopted an ingenious experiment for finding out the truth, but it was one attended with much trouble and sorrow to the people. Orders were issued that everyone should make a declaration to the mandarins of the precise value of his property. Anyone that understated the sum was to be fined in the exact amount to which he had endeavoured to cheat the state. Every informer was to receive one-third of that, and the rest was to go to the government. The immediate result was that the needy, and the vicious, and the unprincipled became suddenly zealous on behalf of the state. Accusations, sometimes true, very often false, were made by them against persons in the community, and as the mandarins and the hosts of hungry officials connected with their courts were always on the look-out for a squeeze from those that had broken the law, it may easily be conceived what misery and disorder were caused by this new law.

Sze Ma-kwang had spoken strongly against the passing of it. "Hitherto the labour of the people," he said, "had been employed only when their services had been required. They were called upon, too, when they could best afford the time, viz., after they had gathered in their harvests." "Now," he said, "you want to introduce a permanent tax upon the people, whether there are any government works going on or not. This is unjust, and I predict there will be universal discontent." Wang refused to listen to his protests, and as the Emperor was under his spell his new scheme became law.

In the third year of Shen Tsung's reign another law was passed at the instigation of Wang, the benefits of which he predicted would be of immense service to the agricultural class. This was a law for state advances to the cultivators of the land. The truly patriotic statesmen and rulers throughout the country were exceedingly opposed to this measure, which was intended to be a compulsory one, and the advances to be made at the exorbitant rate of thirty-three and a third per cent. per annum. Han-k'i presented a petition to the Emperor against it, on the ground that the rich did not want any state aid, and the poor, oppressed by the heavy interest, would never be able to pay the debt they had been forced to contract. The Emperor showed this to Wang, who defended his system and threatened to resign if his plans were not carried out. His own party, who saw a danger to themselves, prayed the Emperor to reject the advice of Han-k'i and adopt the wise policy of Wang. This he did, to the disgust of the loyal party in the state, and Han-k'i, in order to relieve himself from responsibility in measures that posterity would be sure to condemn, resigned his office as Viceroy of Hu-peh and became simply Prefect of Tai-ming. Wang, in order to give a stimulus to the study of history, arranged for examinations in it at the capital, but the scholars would not attend, and so the plan fell through. Difficulties, too, began to arise in the militia law which he had introduced. It was exceedingly unpopular, and in order to secure exemption from its provisions, men all over the country resorted to all kinds of plans to prevent themselves from being enrolled. They voluntarily maimed themselves and cut off their arms or their legs or wounded themselves in such a manner that they were not fit subjects to join the ranks of the army. When the Emperor became alarmed at the terrible mutilations that the people were inflicting upon themselves, and consulted with Wang about modifying the law, he frustrated the humane intentions of the ruler by insisting that it should be carried out to the very letter. "What does it matter," he said, "what the thoughts of the people are? Your wish ought to be supreme in the state. Is it the business of the Emperor to ask the people what they desire? If it is so, then all legislation on the part of the executive would be at an end. Let the law be carried out in its entirety, and soon the nation will be a martial one and the enemies of the empire will tremble before us."

In the year A. D. 1074 the Khitans sent ambassadors to China and demanded the cession of two hundred *li* of Chinese territory that lay along their S. W. boundaries. Instead of sternly refusing such an audacious demand Wang advised compliance with it. "Give it them," he said, "in order to avoid a conflict now. When my measures have had time to work, and the nation has become strong, we shall then demand it back again with a considerable addition to it from the lands of these barbarians." There was great indignation amongst the bolder spirits at this dismemberment of the empire, and when a severe drought affected the whole of the northern part of the country, and no rain fell for ten months, it was considered that this was an indication of the displeasure of Heaven at the disloyalty of the prime minister. Wang thought otherwise, and declared that droughts were the result of natural laws and had nothing to do with men's actions. Whatever were the causes of the drought, it produced widespread distress through the country. The crops failed, and consequently the people could not pay the interest on the money they had received from the state. The officials, who were bound to deliver the sums due into the imperial treasury, were most cruel in their methods of raising them. Sorrow and lamentation filled the country. Tidings of this state of things reached the ears of the humane Emperor, who, acting on his own instincts, issued a decree suspending the operation of the law that was causing such distress. Immediately heavy rains fell throughout the empire and the whole of the people were filled with a double joy.

In the year A. D. 1082 General Ch'ung-ngoh, who had suffered a defeat at the hands of the men of Hia, determined to build an immense fort on the borders of China, in order to be prepared to meet any army that might be marching to invade it. Permission being granted by the Emperor, a hundred thousand men in fourteen days raised the walls sufficiently high to make it a very formidable barrier to the inroads of Hia. This latter power was evidently impressed with the danger that this virgin fortress of Yung-loh was to the country, and orders were issued that every available man should hasten to his colours and march to the attack of the place. The Chinese generals, conscious of the peril in which they stood, despatched urgent requests that additional men should be sent to their assistance. These were at once complied with, and before the Hia men could arrive more than two hundred thousand men stood behind the walls of this mountain fortress to meet the attack of the coming foe. If the Chinese had been officered by able generals, the strong position they held would have enabled them to have resisted any attack that might have been made upon them. Unfortunately they were not. At the foot of the hill on which the fort was built ran a broad mountain stream. It was strongly urged by some that the inner bank of this should be held by a powerful force in order to contest the passage of it by the enemy. The general in command refused to listen to this advice, deeming himself strong enough to defy any force that might dare to attack him. He paid most dearly for his folly. A regiment known by the name of the "Iron Kestrels" led the van of the Hia army. These men, somewhat like Cromwell's Ironsides, were conspicuous for their valour and their contempt of danger. Rushing into the stream, which to their amazement was left undefended, they soon crossed it, and with a shout that paralyzed the Chinese they drove them helter skelter behind their works. The rest of the army followed quickly behind them and completely invested the fortress. In time the provisions of the invested began to fail, and as no succour could reach them, they began to suffer severely from hunger. One night a terrible storm blew, accompanied with a perfect flood of rain. The walls that had been thrown up hastily began to crumble and fall before it. The Hia troops, who were on the alert, rushed through the gaps that had been made by the rushing streams and captured the place. No thoughts of mercy entered the hearts of either officers or men, and nearly the whole of the Chinese force was massacred by them. It is estimated by the historian that nearly two hundred thousand men were put to death, and that only a few hundreds were carried away captive by the victorious army. When the news of this terrible disaster was brought to the Emperor it so affected him that he contracted a disease of the heart, which finally led to his death.

In the year A. D. 1085 posthumous honours were bestowed upon Mencius, who was created Duke of Tsow, and his statue placed in the temple of Confucius, as were also the images of Han-yu and Yang-hiung, which were deemed worthy of this exalted and honoured place.*

This same year Sze Ma-kwang finished his famous history. It consisted of three hundred and fifty-four volumes, and told the story of the nation from the twenty-third year of Wei Lieh, of the Chow dynasty, to the end of the five dynasties. It is entitled "A Comprehensive Mirror for the Aid of Government." Next year Shen Tsung died at the early age of thirty-eight years, and was succeeded by his son Cheh Tsung.

Cheh Tsung—A. D. 1086-1101.

This prince, being only ten years of age when he ascended the throne, his mother, the famous Empress Kau, was made regent during his minority. She was a woman of such remarkable virtues that she was called Yau and Shun amongst women. No higher distinction than this could have been accorded her, for these two worthies stand in the very forefront of Chinese history as the very embodiment of all that was excellent, both in public and in private life. She chose Sze Ma-kwang to be her prime minister, to the great joy of her loyal subjects, because he had always opposed the reforms of Wang-ngan as dangerous to the state. Great changes were looked for on his appointment. He was, however, a true statesman, and he knew that too sudden a reversal of his great opponent's policy would have been detrimental to the interests of a large number of people in the empire. He therefore determined to proceed with great caution. The most unpopular and widely hated of all Wang's measures was the universal militia enrollment bill. This was first dealt with, and by royal decree abrogated. Next year the laws concerning state aid and state labour were abolished, and further improvements would have been made, but Sze Ma-kwang died, to the great sorrow of the regent and the grief of the people of the capital, who manifested it by closing all their places of business and by having his image placed in their house and worshipping it.

---

* Mencius, second only in reputation amongst the Chinese to the great sage Confucius, lived B. C. 372-289. His writings form part of the Chinese classics, the most revered and most studied of all the books in the literature of this country. In addition to the honours granted him by Shen Tsung he was subsequently invested with the title of "Duke Second Sage" by the Emperor Wen Ti in the year A. D. 1330. His tomb is still in existence in the province of Shantung, close to the city of Tsow-hien.

Han-yu was a distinguished philosopher of the T'ang dynasty, A.D. 768-824. He took a middle position between Mencius, who held that human nature was innately good, and Sun-tze, who maintained that it was radically bad. Han-yu believed that life was composed of three classes—those innately good, those innately bad, and those that shared the qualities of both. He was a most violent opponent of Buddhism, and his state paper on this subject is one of the most famous in all Chinese literature. For his protest against idolatry he was banished to Ch'au-chow-fu, near Swatow, of which place he was made governor.

Yang-hiung (B.C. 53—A. D. 18) maintained that human nature is made up of both good and bad qualities, and what a man shall become depends upon education.

His loss at this time was a serious one for the nation, for there was no one to take his place at the helm of affairs that could undo the evils that had been brought upon society by the legislation of Wang-ngan. The friends, indeed, of the latter, who had died the same year as Sze Ma-kwang, began to combine against the regent and to insist that there should be no further abolishing of the reforms of their great leader. Though she was firm in maintaining the policy with which she had entered upon her high office, she found it advisable not to come into collision with the advanced party. The state, indeed, was in too critical a condition for her to do anything that might endanger its present stability. The Hias were ever on the alert for any opportunity to attack the empire, and it required a good deal of diplomacy to avoid a rupture with them. It is true, indeed, that in A. D. 1090 they restored one hundred and forty-nine officers and men, who were the sole survivors of the immense army that had occupied the fortress of Yung-loh, but they demanded in return the delivery up to them of four forts in Shensi, under the threat of immediate hostilities if this were not granted them. The regent found herself compelled, for the sake of peace, to comply with these haughty demands of her powerful enemy.

In the year A. D. 1093 the regent died, and now Cheh Tsung, who was a weak-minded, vacillating monarch, took the reins of government into his own hands. His accession was signalized by a terrible flood that desolated the provinces of Honan and Hu-peh, and that caused the destruction of an immense number of his subjects. Instead of calling to his aid the best men in the country, he employed ten of the eunuchs of the palace and placed them in important positions about him. It was in vain that his ministers protested against this unwise action of his. Like all men of weak intellect, he could be very determined when his mind was made up on a point that could not possibly benefit any one. He naturally fell into the hands, too, of the more daring and progressive party, and soon, under the leadership of Ts'ai-king, who acquired a great ascendancy over him, he began to overthrow the new system of government that had been commenced by Sze Ma-kwang and his colleagues. The first step in this retrogressive policy was the issuing a decree for the re-establishing of state labour as first inaugurated by Wang-ngan. This necessarily led to the disappearance from the court of men who believed in the new order of things. The next act in his life that gave great offence to the nation was his divorcing his queen and raising one of his concubines to her position. When a censor protested against this act, Cheh Tsung replied that he had a precedent for what he had done in the lives of some of the Emperors that had preceded him. "You imitate the evil in the lives of your forefathers, whereas it would best become you to copy their virtues," the sturdy preserver of the royal morals said in reply. The Emperor was displeased with his fidelity and banished him to Canton. Not many months after this

Cheh Tsung died of grief in consequence of the death of his infant son, and was succeeded by the eleventh son of Shen Tsung, Prince Twan, whose royal title was

Hwei Tsnng—A. D. 1101-1126.

This Emperor was twenty-nine years old when he ascended the throne. He was a man of naturally good abilities, but was wanting in that broad commonsense that was especially demanded from the ruler at this special crisis of the nation's life. He was very fond of music, and had an inordinate passion for articles of *vertu*, which he collected from all parts of his empire and placed in a museum which he had built specially for their reception. His whole energies seemed to be bent on adding to this collection, and men were particularly favoured that informed him of any curiosity that they had discovered. In consequence of this, any one that was possessed of any article of antiquity either at once gave it up or hid it in the ground, for no home was safe from the spies that were in the employ of Ts'ai-king, whose aim it was to please his royal master. This man was raised to a high position at the court on his assurance that he was thoroughly acquainted with the reforms of Wang-ngan, and was capable of carrying them out in the country. In order to show his appreciation of Wang-ngan, the Emperor caused a stone tablet to be erected at the door of the palace, on which had been cut a decree in which the memory of Sze Ma-kwang was assailed and his deeds condemned. The statue of the latter was broken and his books burned, and all the foremost men of the day that were disciples of him were banished to distant parts of the empire. Not content with this, he had the image of Wang placed in the temple of Confucius, and by a royal statute ordained that he should be elevated to an equal position with that of the great sage. Two years after, a sudden stop was put to these vagaries by the appearance of a comet in the sky. This has always been considered in China as a menace to the reigning dynasty. Hwei Tsung was terrified, and ordered that the stone tablet at the palace gates and all the others which he had caused to be put up throughout the country in honour of Wang should be taken down, and also that Ts'ai-king should be deprived of his rank.

The year A. D. 1111 was an important one in the history of the Sung dynasty, for it was in it that the first measures were taken that led to the long series of campaigns with the Kins that brought so much disaster upon China. Influenced by the representations of a disgraced Khitan official, Hwei Tsung, in opposition to the advice of his counsellors, entered into a treaty with the Kins for the destruction of the Khitans. His one motive that led him to do this was the hope of recovering the sixteen districts that had been wrested by them from China. This was the price the Kins were willing to pay for his alliance, by which they hoped to relieve themselves from a power that had always been oppressive to them, and whom they were compelled to acknowledge as over-lord. Preparations were silently made by the Kins, and though the chief of the Khitans, T'ien-cha, got information of this he took no notice of it, for he never dreamed that the Kins would dare to rise in rebellion, so insignificant had they been as a military power up to this time. In the year A. D. 1114 Akuta, who had succeeded to the chieftainship of the Kins, marched with his troops into Liau-tung and captured the city of Ling-kang-chow, and a few months after, with a force of ten thousand men, he almost destroyed the army of the Khitans that met him in battle. A month after this Akuta, who was a man of great daring and ability, took the title of Emperor, and gave the name of Kin, which means gold, to his new dynasty instead of that of Nu-chen, by which these Tartars had hitherto been known.

From this time forth a fierce conflict went on between these rival Tartars till the year A. D. 1125, when the Kins became completely victorious and crushed out all opposition by the complete extinction of the Liau dynasty. It is true, indeed, that Yen-k'ing refused to submit, and assuming the title of Teh Tsung, founded the feeble line of the Western Liau dynasty, but his power and that of his successors was not considered of any importance in the great struggle that was now about to be entered on.

If Hwei Tsung had hoped for any advantage in the destruction of the Khitans he was soon taught in a very severe way by his Kin allies that he was gravely in error for doing so. Whenever he attempted to get back any of the Chinese territory that had been seized by the Khitans he was met either by evasions, or by demands for large supplies of money and silk, for when they were asked to restore the district of Yen they said they would do so on condition that a million ounces of silver and a million pieces of silk were given them in return for it. The Emperor agreed to this, but the compact was never carried out, as the Kins felt that the riches of China would in a few years be theirs without the necessity of ceding any of the conquered country in exchange for them. Indeed, constant causes of irritation were arising that were making it more certain that before long the great struggle between these two powers for mastery would soon commence. In the year A. D. 1123 the Kins captured Hong-liang-fu, the capital of the Khitans, and T'ien-cha fled for his life to Ying-chow, in Shansi, which, however, was captured by the victorious Kins, whose general at once ordered that all the well-to-do people of the city should be removed to Kin territory, so as to take away from them the power of plotting against their new masters. In this extremity one of their leading men, Chang-kwoh, was persuaded to raise the standard of rebellion against the Kins, and ambassadors were sent to Hwei Tsung, offering him the submission of the Khitans if he would send troops to their assistance and help them to drive the Kin soldiers from their territory.

Contrary to the advice of the sagest of his counsellors, he agreed to this, and made Chang-kwoh an officer of high rank. The Kins sent three thousand men against the latter, but they were compelled to retreat, but shortly after he was defeated by a superior force that had been marched with great haste into the conquered country. Chang-kwoh fled to the Sung capital, but the Emperor was compelled to comply with the stern request that his head and those of his two sons should be forwarded to the irritated Kins.

Next year the Kins demanded from Hwei Tsung a large supply of provisions which had been promised them by treaty. These he refused to give, and consequently a fierce feeling of indignation arose in the mind of these haughty Tartars, and preparations were openly made for securing by force of arms what they considered to be their rights. The seizure of T'ien-cha, and the virtual extinction of the great Liau kingdom in A. D. 1125, freed the Kins from the fear of any danger from hostile forces in that direction and left their armies free to carry out the great schemes of conquest that they had been silently maturing ever since the commencement of their struggle with the Khitans, in which they had proved their superiority over an enemy that had shown itself more than a match for China.

Towards the end of the year two armies under the command of two of the most famous generals that the Kins possessed—Nien-mo-ho and Koan-li-pu—marched to the conquest of the empire. No preparations had been made for such a contingency, and consequently they were victorious wherever they came. The greatest consternation now prevailed at the Sung capital, but there was no man of commanding ability there to help the feeble monarch to devise measures to save the country or to summon her armies, scattered throughout the provinces, to save her from the ruthless and barbarous foe that was marching upon her. The weakness of the dynasty was now shown in the craven spirit of the man who unfortunately was at the head of the Chinese nation. Instead of manfully standing forth as the champion of his people, and rousing the country by a spirit of heroism that would have brought countless myriads from every part of the empire to the succour of their country, he meanly evaded the dangers he had brought upon it by his bad statesmanship, and abdicated the throne in favour of his son

K'in Tsung—A. D. 1126.

The first act of the new Emperor was to send an embassage to Koan-li-pu to negotiate for peace. Some of the Kins at headquarters, who thought that the Yellow River should be the boundary of the conquered territory, were inclined to enter into terms with the imperial ambassadors. Others again, and these the more numerous and influential party, were bent on further conquests. The proposals therefore of the Emperor were rejected, and the Kin army advanced to the banks of the great river. To the surprise of everyone not a single soldier was in view on the opposite side to oppose their crossing. In five days all the horses and men had passed over in the small boats they had been able to capture on the river, without the loss of a single man. Koan Li-pu was amazed that no opposition had been made during the transit of his men. "Surely," he exclaimed, "there cannot be a man left in China, for if only one or two thousand soldiers had been here to oppose me I should never have been able to have got across." The Kins now marched with all speed for K'ai-fung-fu. Upon their approach Hwei Tsung fled to Nanking, whilst his son was left to make preparations to meet the coming foe. A spirit of terror seems, however, at this critical time, to have paralyzed the hearts of the bravest. The people of the capital, knowing the sufferings they would have to endure if the barbarians captured it, were mad with terror. The mandarins fled wholesale, and no wonder, therefore, that the young Emperor should have been terrified and unfit to cope in a manly and dignified way with the great crisis that was threatening his country with destruction.

When Koan Li-pu arrived before the walls of K'ai-fung-fu he sent a messenger into the city to inform K'in Tsung what were the terms he proposed, in order to the cessation of the war and his own immediate return to his own country. "I could easily capture the city," he said, "if I liked, for the Emperor is young, and he has no forces that could hope to hold out against those that I now command. I shall be satisfied to make peace if the Emperor agrees to what I have proposed." The terms were very severe, but K'in Tsung was compelled to accept them, for a successful resistance was out of the question at present. They were—five million ounces of gold, fifty million ounces of silver, ten thousand oxen, and the same number of horses, and one million pieces of silk. It was also stipulated that the Kin ruler should be allowed the title of Emperor; that T'ai-yuan, in Shan-si, and Chin-tung and Ho-chien, in Chihli, should form part of the Kin territory, and that the imperial troops should escort them to the banks of the Yellow River, so as to preserve them from attack till they had crossed it. These humiliating conditions were agreed to, and Prince K'ang, one of the brothers of the Emperor, was handed over to the Kins as a hostage to secure that they would be faithfully carried out.

And now began the weary task of collecting the immense indemnity that had been demanded. The rich were almost stripped of their wealth, and the houses of the common people invaded by the officers of the crown in their search for money. Only two hundred thousand ounces of gold and five million ounces of silver could be collected which were paid to Koan Li-pu as they were handed into the treasury. Widespread dissatisfaction existed amongst every class, because of the excessive demands of the Kins. "There is not enough money in China to satisfy the greed of these savage barbarians,'' some said.   In this miserable state of things, when the grip of the enemy was on the throat of the empire, it is satisfactory to find that there were some brave men, whose advice, if carried out, might still have averted the sorrow and disgrace that the Kins were about to bring upon the country.   These advised delay before yielding to all the demands of the foe.   ''Temporize,'' they said, ''and in a short time our succour will arrive, and then we shall march out and fight the enemy that has dared to desecrate our soil.''   Li-kang, who thus far had valiantly conducted the defence of the city was for bold measures, and he pledged himself that when the troops that were marching to their aid arrived he would engage the Kins and drive them back, scattered and defeated to perish in the Yellow River.

The Emperor unfortunately refused to take the bolder course, and so agreed to every condition that the Kins liked to impose upon him.   Before long Ma-tsung arrived with his force from Kiang-si, and knowing nothing of the agreement that had been made, broke through the Kin lines and entered the city.   Another under Ch'ung Sz-tau arrived from Fan-shwuy.   K'in Tsung was so pleased when he heard that the latter had got safely through the foe that he came out to meet him.   Telling him of the terms he had agreed to with Koan Li-pu, he asked him what he thought ought to be done under the present circumstances.   ''Think !'' replied the sturdy soldier, ''I think we ought to fight.   I am not good at making treaties, but if you only give me the order I shall lead my men against the robbers that are encamped outside our walls.''   One of the officials named Li-pang, faint-hearted as the Emperor, advised the carrying out of the treaty, and accordingly the silk and gold, as they arrived from the interior, were sent into the camp of the Kins.   The receipt of these precious things only seemed to rouse the cupidity of the Kins, for instead of observing the treaty they began to plunder the people in the region around.   Li-kang now urged upon the Emperor the advisability of attacking the enemy.   ''We have over two hundred thousand men,'' he said, '' whilst they have only sixty thousand.   Their provisions, moreover, are getting low, and there is no doubt they are becoming anxious about their condition.   To attack now is to gain the victory.''   K'in Tsung gave his consent, and the Sung forces were at once let loose against the enemy.   That night a force of ten thousand were sent out to surprise the Kins, but they were routed and driven back.   Li-kang went out to its aid, but he could make no impression on the foe, and had to return unsuccessful.

Koan Li-pu bitterly upbraided Prince K'ang for the breach of faith of his brother, but no threats or invectives of the Kin general could terrify him.   He accordingly returned him to the city and demanded that Li-kang, upon whom the Emperor had thrown the blame of the attack, should be sent into him instead. The former, irritated at this request, which, however, was not complied with, issued a general order that everyone that brought him in the head of a Kin would be rewarded. From this time there was no more talk of peace. The city was closely invested, and every attempt that bravery could suggest was made to capture it, but in vain. The forces inside were too strong and too well-handled to allow of this. At length, in the month of April, the Kins, terrified by the scarcity of provisions in their camp, began to retreat. Ch'ung Sz-tau now entreated the Emperor to allow him to attack them whilst they were in this dispirited condition. "Now is the time," said this spirited commander, "to destroy this robber host. If we allow them to escape now we shall have them back in increased numbers in the winter, when it will be more difficult to cope with them." K'in Tsung refused his consent, and the golden opportunity thus lost never came back to him again. With the return home of Koan Li-pu there also arrived there Nien Mo-ho from Shansi, where he had been everywhere victorious. He had taken T'ai-yuan and all the country round, and returning with great spoil he had filled the Kin capital with rejoicing. From this time forward the conquest of China and the plunder of its rich provinces became the theme and the hope of all the daring spirits in the Kin dominions.

Two months after the departure of Koan Li-pu, Hwei Tsung returned to the capital. In spite of the urgent entreaties of the generals, no steps were taken to assemble the forces of the empire to be ready for the next invasion of the Kins, nor was the capital strengthened. The only thing that was done was to despatch Li-kang to the frontiers with a small force to watch the movements of the Tartars and to report to the throne.

In November Koan Li-pu again returned, and, as before, crossed the Yellow River without opposition and invested the capital. The greatest fear fell upon the inhabitants, and the royal counsels were distracted by the various kinds of advice that K'in Tsung received in this emergency. Some advised the flight of the Emperor to Sz-chwan, whilst a few of the bolder spirits held that the seventy thousand soldiers that garrisoned the town were sufficient to meet the more numerous Kins, if they were only properly led by officers in whom they had confidence. In the end nothing of importance was done to meet this crisis, except to hold out against the assaults of the besiegers. Three months went by, when Prince K'ang, who had collected ten thousand men, advanced to the relief of the capital. With such a small force he could of course accomplish little against the larger army of the Kins. K'in Tsung, seeing that any further resistance was useless, issued orders to his brother to retire, whilst he, carrying the document that announced his surrender, repaired to the camp of Koan Li-pu and formally gave in his submission.

Koan Li-pu demanded that China should pay him ten million ingots of gold and twenty millions of silver, each containing ten ounces; also ten million pieces of silk, and that the territories of Ho-tung and Ho-peh should be delivered over to him. Though these terms were utterly beyond his power to carry out, the unfortunate monarch was compelled to consent to them. The Kin general, who had larger views with regard to China than even this immense indemnity indicated, demanded that when the first installment came to be paid it should be brought in person by the Emperor himself. Even this he promised to do, but he found, to his dismay, that when he would return to his home he was a prisoner in the hands of his conquerors. Koan Li-pu was not going to be satisfied, however, with anything less than the capture of the whole royal family, in order that the throne of China might be at the disposal of the Kin nation. He therefore demanded that Hwei Tsung, his queen and all the members of the royal household, should repair to his camp. This they did to the number of three thousand persons. Having got possession of them, he appointed Chang Pang-ch'ung a vassal Emperor of the Kins, in the place of the one he now deposed, and abolishing the name of Sung he gave the new dynasty the title of Ch'u.

Prince K'ang, seeing his relatives in captivity and the empire about to be wrested from his family, now seriously took up arms in defence of his rights. With his ten thousand men he attacked the enemy, but he was of course defeated. He then retreated south-wards and set himself to increase his army to such an extent that he could hope by and by to meet on equal terms with the forces of the invader. In the month of June in the following year the Kins retired to their own country with the immense plunder which they had seized and with their three thousand captives, very few of whom would ever have the happiness of seeing their homes again.* With this sad procession of Emperors, nobles and ladies of the royal household, led by a savage and victorious enemy into a strange land, ends the first drama of the great Sung dynasty.

---

*Hwei Tsung died A. D. 1135 and K'in Tsung A. D. 1156, many unsuccessful efforts having been made to induce their captors to set them free. Both these Emperors were weak and vacillating and unfit to hold the reins of power at this time, when a strong and powerful hand alone could have guided the ship of state through the storms that threatened its existence. The one notable thing that Hwei Tsung did that has lasted down to the present day was the deification of Chang-yi, a hero of the Later Han dynasty, with the title of the "Pearly God." This creation of his has become so popular amongst the Chinese that he now stands at the head of their pantheon and usurps the place held by the true God.

CHAPTER XXVI.

THE SOUTHERN SUNG DYNASTY (A.D. 1127-1280).

Kau Tsung—A. D. 1127-1163.

PRINCE K'ANG was the ninth son of Hwei Tsung and just twenty years of age when, seeing the throne vacant through the capture of his father and brother, he became Emperor under the title of Kau Tsung. His first important act was to remove the capital from K'ai-fung-fu, which had been again occupied by the Chinese forces after the departure of the Kins, to Nanking. This was a great sign of weakness, and was the first step that ultimately led to the extinction of the dynasty. There were no doubt strong reasons which induced the newly-made Emperor to adopt a plan that must have struck the hearts of his subjects throughout the empire with consternation. His forces were weak and inadequate to meet the stronger hosts of the Kins. There must have been an empty treasury, too, for the expenses of the war and the heavy indemnity they had been compelled to pay their conquerors had been a severe drain upon it; still, a man of more heroic mould would have hesitated before he made such a public confession of weakness as to abandon thus easily the capital where his fathers had reigned. The latent strength of the empire had never yet been fully called forth, nor had the patriotism of its people even had a chance of showing to what extent they were willing to suffer for their fatherland. Men would have been forth-coming and money, too, if time had only been given for the nation to have gathered itself together, and competent leaders, in whom the people had confidence, had been ready to arouse them.* Shortly after he ascended the throne Koan Li-pu died. Just before his death he recommended that peace should be made with China and the royal captives restored to their country. Some were in favour of this, but the bolder and more martial spirits who were looking forward to another successful campaign opposed it, and so the idea was given up.†

---

* The Emperor had a vast resource in the paper money which the government were in the habit of issuing. Even the Kins knew the value of this mode of currency, savages as they were in comparison with the Chinese, who had used it for fully three centuries before this time. See Yule's Marco Polo, vol. I., page 380.

† It is said that after Hwei Tsung and his family reached the place of their captivity he managed to send a messenger from amongst his followers, dressed in one of the garments he used to wear, to his son, Prince K'ang; when he reached Nanking he gave this dress to Kau Tsung, who, upon examination of it, found that his father had written on the inner lining, telling him to become Emperor and beseeching him to use every effort in his power to effect their release. Kau Tsung's wife, who had also been carried away by the Kins, managed to send a bracelet by the same messenger, and besought him to deliver her, so that as there was no break in the bracelet, there might never be any interruption to their union as long as they lived. Kau Tsung, who was passionately fond of his wife, wept when he saw this token from her loving hand, but he was destined never to see her again, for she died in the land of her captivity.

In October the Kins were on their return march to China with overwhelming forces. All the towns on the north of the Yellow River fell into their hands. Two months after, the Emperor, terrified by the reports of the fearful ravages committed by them, fled to Yangchow, on the Yang-tze, where he supposed he would be more safe. His generals, who were more anxious to take the bolder course and advance against their savage foe, remonstrated with him and urged him, instead of running away, to march north with his troops and occupy the old capital and show the Kins that he was ready to fight for his empire to the very last extremity. He refused to consent to this heroic course, though there was no doubt but that if he had it would have been the turning point in the history of the dynasty. There were emphatic signs throughout the country that the people were being roused by a national fervour to come to the help of the empire in this extreme hour of its peril. Large numbers had already taken arms, and to distinguish themselves as volunteers in their country's cause they had adopted a red turban as a sign of their loyalty. Their numbers were growing every day, and the enthusiasm was spreading, which before long would have touched every class till the entire nation would have been in arms. With the news of the Emperor's flight the whole movement collapsed, and golden opportunity for deliverance from the ruthless enemy never came back again. Meanwhile the Kins, under the command of Nien Mo-ho and Wuh Shu, were marching on K'ai-fung-fu, which was held by the imperial troops under the gallant Tsung-tseh. Not content with guarding the city only, he marched out and met the Kins in the open field. In the great battle (A. D. 1128) that ensued, the Kins suffered defeat, and in every succeeding engagement the military skill of Tsung-tseh made him victorious over an enemy that was hitherto considered invincible. Disappointed in their expectations of capturing K'ai-fung-fu, the Kins retired west in the direction of Lohyang. At the beginning of next year, laden with the booty which they had collected from the cities they had taken, they crossed the Yellow River and returned to their own country.

During the disorders consequent upon the invasion of the Kins, rebellions had broken out in different parts of the country. These Tsung-tseh proceeded to deal with, and so successful was he that he managed by force of arms and the generous way in which he treated the leaders to gain them to the cause of loyalty, so that both they and their men offered their services to him to fight against the common foe. These he at once accepted, and proposed to utilize them by leading them across the river and driving the Kins out of Chinese territory. He at once drew up a memorial to Kau Tsung and entreated him to return to his capital, whilst he, with the brave men under his command, marched against the enemy that had brought such desolation upon China.   His words have a noble ring about them and are worthy of record.   "The heritage of your fathers ought to be very precious to you.   Your parents, your wife and your brother have been carried into captivity, and every day they turn with longing eyes to you to deliver them.   The western capital (Lohyang) contained the graves of your ancestors, but they have been dug up by the robbers.   This year, when the feast of tombs comes round, there will be no offerings to the spirits of your dead.   East and north of the Yellow River every home has been ravaged.   Your subjects are in the very midst of fire and water. You are detained by traitors in Nanking.   It is because they fear the enemy, and because their families are in the south, that they persuade you to live there.   The capital is now strong and secure. We have abundance of arms.   Our troops are numerous and well disciplined.   Come to us, and don't disappoint the longing expecta- tions of your people."   This pathetic appeal touched the heart of the vacillating monarch, and he was on the point of acceding to it, when, hearing that the Kins were on the march again for his dominions, he countermanded the orders that he had given for his journey to Honan.   Twenty times did Tsung-tseh repeat his entreaties to the Emperor to come and take charge of the capital whilst he crossed the river, but without success.   Finding his hopes of saving the empire to be in vain he fell ill and died ; his last words being, "Cross the river, cross the river."

His death was an irreparable loss to the country, for he was the one man that had gained the affections of the people and that had inspired his troops with the certainty of victory.   When another general was sent to take his place the soldiers refused to serve under him, and the old rebel elements that had become loyal under Tsung- tseh silently melted away from the city and took up arms again in defence of their own interests.

At the close of the year the Kins, under their famous leader, Nien Mo-ho, marched south and entered the province of Shantung. Rapidly passing through that they proceeded direct for Yangchow, in hopes of capturing Kau Tsung.   Instead of listening to the voices of those that urged him to make a stand and fight the coming enemy he fled with the utmost precipitation to Hangchow.   The Kins entered the city not long after he had left it, and five hundred of those who had the fleetest horses were sent in pursuit of him.   He managed to escape them only by the devotion of the followers that accompanied him, but everything he had was abandoned, and it is recorded that even the ancestral tablets that were said to contain the spirits of some of his fathers, were dropped on the road and picked up by his savage pursuers.

This disgraceful flight had a very disastrous effect on the spirits of his people, and two generals that represented the popular opinion demanded that the Emperor should resign his throne to his son, who was only three years of age, and appoint Kau Tsung's mother to be.

regent during his minority.* This he consented to do, but there was only a temporary suspension of the royal functions, for the famous generals Chang-tsun and Hau-shih, hearing of the troubles in Hangchow, marched their armies to that city, and having put to death the two generals they reinstated Kau Tsung on the throne.

It seemed at this time as though the Sung dynasty had fallen to the lowest possible condition, and that it would soon disappear before the victorious march of the Kins. Three times in one year (A. D. 1129) did the Emperor write to them and offer to hold his empire as a fief of theirs, but no reply was vouchsafed to his humble and suppliant words. The tramp of their soldiers was heard in the distance, and the frightened monarch fled to Lin-ngan, then to Shau-hing, then to Meng-chow, and after that to Wenchow, and finally he crossed the arm of the sea to the T'aichow group, where the impetuous enemy following him were defeated by the imperial men-of-war and compelled to retreat.

Whilst these disasters were occurring in the south, the Kins were ravaging the country in the north and carrying everything before them. The city of Shen-chow, in Honan, suffered especially from them. In their first attack upon it they were repulsed with loss by its brave commander, Li-yen. Additional forces having come to their aid the city was again assaulted, but once more they were driven back, shattered and broken by the besieged, who pursued them in the precipitate retreat they were compelled to make. Exasperated beyond measure, they summoned all the forces they could collect, until a hundred thousand warriors stood before the doomed city. Li-yen was then called upon to surrender, with the most fearful threats if he refused. The commander was a man of heroic nature, and scorned the idea of giving up what had been entrusted to him by the Emperor. The assault immediately took place. The city was taken, and all the soldiers in it, with a large number of the citizens, were massacred.

The Kins, having burnt Hangchow and collected the immense booty that they had plundered from the regions they had conquered, proceeded north on their way to their own country. When they reached the banks of the Yang-tze they found the river guarded by a fleet commanded by Han Shih-chung, waiting to dispute their passage. Wuh-shu, the general of the Kins, sent a challenge to Han, and asked him when he would fight. "To-morrow," was the prompt reply. Next day, when the Kins attempted to force the passage, a most bloody engagement took place, in which they suffered a great defeat, large numbers being not only killed and wounded, but also taken prisoners. The imperialists behaved with great heroism, and though the enemy were a hundred thousand strong, whilst they numbered only eight thousand, they never doubted for a moment but that victory would be the result of the

---

* Kau Tsung was not the son of the queen who was in captivity amongst the Kins, but of a concubine who was with him in his flight from Yangchow.*

battle. Han's wife took a most conspicuous share in the desperate struggle for mastery. Seated near the head of the mainmast of her husband's vessel she shouted down to him below the movements of the enemy, and thus enabled him to manœuvre his ships to the very best possible advantage. With the close of day the Kins were found beaten at every point and the broad river still flowing between them and their road to their homes. So utterly discouraged were they that they offered to resign to Han the whole of their plunder if he would allow them peaceably to cross the river. This he refused to do, and fighting was again resumed, but with the same result, for at the end of forty-eight days they still found themselves on the southern bank. In this extremity a traitor suggested a way out of their danger. He advised Wuh-shu to wait for a perfectly calm day, and then cross over in their smallest boats, which the large ships of Han could not follow. He also counselled that a few of the fastest and lightest of them should be manned with the bravest men in his army and approaching the largest of Han's ships should fire burning arrows into their mat sails. This idea was eagerly seized by the general, with the result that the whole of his army passed safely over without any serious molestation, for the Sungs were too busy endeavouring to save their vessels from being burned to be able to molest them in their passage.

In the year A. D. 1131 the statesman Ts'in-kwei, who had been captured by the Kins about four years before, made his appearance at the court of Kau Tsùng. He declared that he had killed his keepers and made his escape from captivity, but as none had noticed him by the way, and as his wife accompanied him, there were grave suspicions that his story was a made up one. The Emperor, however, put implicit trust in him and listened with great attention to his advice that he should make peace with the Kins. In the following year he made him prime minister, because he professed to have a plan by which he could save the empire from the difficulties that now threatened it, if only he had the power to carry it into execution.* An opportunity soon occurred of testing his powers in this respect. Towards the close of the year Wuh-shu, at the head of over a hundred thousand men, was on his march south. When he arrived at the river Wei† he began to make a bridge of boats to enable his men to cross over it. The famous Chinese general Wu-kiai was waiting for him, however, with an army which had entrenched itself on the opposite bank. They fought with such vigor that the Kins were unable to make good their passage, and had to retreat to their encampment. That night Wu-kiai managed to cross unobserved with a large force, and

---

* The Chinese historians believe that this man was a double-dyed traitor, and that his escape and appearance at the court were all planned. His aim and purpose, they declare, from this time was to betray his country and play into the hands of its savage enemy.

† The Wei is a large tributary of the Yellow River, which joins it near the great bend in Shensi.

attacking the sleeping Kins, routed them with great slaughter. Wuh-shu received several arrow wounds in the face and body, and his army was completely disorganized and scattered. It was with the greatest difficulty that he himself escaped, and in order to avoid detection he had his whiskers shaved off, whilst he skulked across the country by the least frequented ways till at last he reached the encampment of his friends.

This great defeat of the chief leader of the Tartars gave the Emperor a breathing space, and next year he returned to Hangchow. Two years after (A. D. 1134) Wuh-shu was again near the Yang-tze with a hundred thousand men, and Kau Tsung, terrified by their rapid approach, began to make preparations for flight. These were disapproved of by Chang-tsun, who pertinently asked, "Where will you fly to?" "Stay and fight the enemy is what I advise," said this sturdy general. The imperial forces were commanded by Han-shih, and under him were Chang-tsun, Yoh-fei and other distinguished men. Wuh-shu, who seemed undeterred by the terrible defeats he had suffered, no sooner came in sight of them than he challenged them to come out and fight him. Permission having been obtained from the Emperor, Han-shih gladly led his men against the hated foe, and once more the Tartars were flying in confusion before their conquerors. The sufferings the vanquished endured were exceedingly great. The ground was covered with snow, their provisions were exhausted, and the enemy was close behind them, determined to avenge the injuries and insults of years. Vast numbers of them perished by the way, and Wuh-shu hurried home without having accomplished anything worthy of the great armament with which he had set out. When he reached his own kingdom he found that the king, Wu Kin-mai, was dead, and was succeeded by his cousin, Ho-tz, whose royal name was Hi Tsung.

The year A. D. 1135 was an important one in the story of this period. The captive Emperor Hwei Tsung died, and was buried in the land of his captivity. But an event still more important than this and fraught with mighty consequences to both the Kin and Sung dynasties now occurred. This was the appearance of the Mongols on the Kin frontier and their conflict with the Kin power, which they were destined ultimately to destroy. For the next three years nothing of any great importance took place. The puppet prince whom the Kins had set up in Shensi was quietly set aside, because in his encounters with the Sung armies he had been invariably defeated, and he had shown no ability for the high position that had been bestowed upon him.

At the close of A. D. 1138, by the advice of Ts'in-kwei, a treaty was made with the Kins, by which they agreed to return Honan and Shensi, whilst they were allowed to retain all the rest fo their conquests for themselves. The chief counsellors of the Emperor were opposed to this dismemberment of the empire, and Chang-tsun and Yoh-fei resigned their offices, as well as many

others, rather than share in the responsibility of such a measure.
Kau Tsung would have listened to their remonstrances had not
Ts'in-kwei threatened to resign if he did so. So completely was
the Emperor under the control of this man that this threat at once
decided him to agree to the treaty. In the month of May Wuh-shu
began to evacuate Honan. He himself first returned to his own
country, leaving the rest of the troops that were in it and in Shensi
to slowly follow him. Hardly had he reached the capital when a
tragedy took place, which changed the whole aspect of affairs. The
completion of the treaty above mentioned was mainly through the
influence of the eldest son of the late ruler, Wu Kin-mai. This man
was discovered in a plot to murder the king and ascend the throne
of his father. He was seized and put to death, and the cession
of territory, which had been exceedingly distasteful to Wuh-shu, was
at once stopped and the latter marched back again into Honan and
re-occupied the country that had been vacated, and an order was at
the same time issued to all the generals to stay their homeward march.

The year A. D. 1140 was a glorious one for the arms of the
Sungs. Wu-kiai obtained great victories over the Kins in
Shensi, and Yoh-fei thoroughly routed them in Kiangsi. He
pursued the flying hosts as far as K'ai-fung-fu, and there again
they suffered a great defeat. He was preparing to pursue them,
when imperative orders came from Ts'in-kwei for him to repair
to the capital, as a treaty of peace, he said, had been made with
the Kins, and he was therefore to stay all hostile proceedings
against them. The indignation of the army was great beyond
measure when the tidings of his recall reached them, especially
when the rumour passed throughout the camp that this had
been effected through the demand of Wuh-shu, who was in
secret correspondence, it was declared, with Ts'in-kwei. No one
was more affected than Yoh-fei. It was not simply that his
honour was at stake and that his life would be imperilled if he
obeyed the urgent orders, twelve of which, it was said, reached him
in one day to repair to Hangchow ; he felt that a great opportunity
would be lost of freeing his country from the dominion of the Kins.
He had so crushed Wuh-shu that the absolute expulsion of the hated
enemy from Chinese territory was now simply a matter of time.
Even the Tartar general felt this, for he was so humiliated by his
late defeat that he was on the point of cutting his throat and ending
his shame in death, when his hand was stayed by some Chinese
scholars that were in his camp. " Don't despair," they said, "there
is treachery in the palace, and no amount of devotion outside will
be able in the end to countervail that." In spite of the entreaties
of his captains and soldiers, who urged upon him to disobey the
orders he had received, Yoh-fei set out for the capital, but the
immediate return of Wuh-shu to the neighbourhood of K'ai-fung-fu
opened the eyes of the Emperor to the dangers of the case, and he
was ordered back to meet the Kins. This he did, and another

great engagement took place, when they were once more defeated with great slaughter. Wuh-shu now wrote in great indignation to Ts'in-kwei and told him that if he really wished for peace he must manage to stop Yoh-fei from fighting with him by compassing his death. "There will be no peace," he said, "between the two kingdoms as long as he lives, and therefore it is for your interest to deprive him of the power of prolonging the enmity that now exists between the two nations." Ts'in-kwei upon this bribed some of his officers to present a memorial to the Emperor, in which they accused Yoh-fei of sedition and of aiming to become Emperor instead of Kau Tsung. Ts'in-kwei eagerly seized upon this infamous accusation and issued a pretended decree from the Emperor, summoning him to the capital to answer the grave charges that were laid against him. When he arrived there he was thrown into jail, and the governor, who was commissioned to examine him, asked him if he were a traitor. Taking off his clothes he turned his back to him and asked him to read his answer there. The governor looked and saw four Chinese characters tattooed on it, which meant "Loyal and faithful, because grateful for the Emperor's favours." On further examination of him he found him a loyal and devoted servant of the crown. When he reported this to Ts'in-kwei the unscrupulous traitor replied simply by removing him from his post and by appointing another more subservient to his wishes in his place. Yoh-fei was put to the torture, but nothing could be extracted from him to show that he was guilty. Hau-shih memorialized Kau Tsung and declared that Ts'in-kwei was a villain and deserved to die. As the Emperor refused to listen to him, he resigned his command and retired into private life. Shortly after, Yoh-fei, at the early age of forty-nine, was put to death in his prison, and this through the weakness of Kau Tsung ; and thus the two men that could have saved the empire were irrevocably lost to it.

A new treaty was now signed, A. D. 1142, with Wuh-shu, in which it was stipulated that Shensi should belong to the Kins, and besides, a yearly payment of two hundred and fifty thousand pieces of silk and the same number of ounces of gold should be paid to them. In the document that was drawn up by Ts'in-kwei the Emperor was styled the vassal of the Kin nation. Wuh-shu in return agreed to allow the bodies of Hwei Tsung, as well as those of his queen and the wife of Kau Tsung, to be taken to the capital to be buried in Chinese territory. He very graciously also returned four districts in Shensi, which he permitted to remain under Chinese rule, and he allowed Kau Tsung to retain the title of Emperor of China. For the great services that Ts'in-kwei had rendered in bringing all this about he was elevated to very high rank, and great honours were heaped upon him, instead of which, if the historian has been true to facts, he should have suffered an ignominious death.

The military glory of Wuh-shu, which had been lately tarnished by the crushing defeats they had received from the Chinese generals, was still further eclipsed this year, A. D. 1147, in the war which he waged with the Mongols. The Kins had previously, in the year A. D. 1135 and A. D. 1139, come into conflict with these ambitious foes, and on both occasions had to retire discomfited before them. This year, however, the result of the campaign was more disastrous. Not only was Wuh-shu thoroughly beaten and his army driven in confusion before the Mongol cavalry, but he had to consent to terms of peace which were exceedingly humiliating to his country. Thirty-seven fortified places belonging to the Kins had to be handed over to them, besides an annual payment in kind of oxen, sheep, rice and beans. The haughty conquerors of Northern China must have been driven to great straits when they consented to such a public confession of weakness. After the treaty had been signed the Kins offered to recognize the Mongol chieftain Kabul Khan as king, but he haughtily refused to acknowledge their right to give him any title, and he himself assumed the high sounding name of the First Great Emperor of the Mongols.

Next year Wuh-shu died, and was succeeded in his command of the armies of the state by Wan Yen-liang, who in the succeeding year murdered the Kin Emperor and ascended the throne in his place. He commenced his reign by the murder of seventy of the relatives of the late Emperor and over thirty of the kindred of the distinguished general Nien Mo-ho. This barbarous conduct roused the indignation of the people in the capital to such an extent that he became apprehensive lest his life might be endangered. This idea took such a deep root in his mind that he finally removed his capital from Wu-kwuh-ch'ung to Shun-t'ien-fu, in Chih-li.

Several years went by without any interruption to the peace that had been secured by the last treaty, but Wan, either moved by ambition, or restless under the stings of conscience because of the murders he had committed, began to prepare for war with the Chinese. Kau Tsung, after a good many entreaties by his high officials, who showed him the danger of being unprepared for his restless and unrelenting foe, began also to arm.* At length the Kins were ready for the conflict, and in the month of July, A. D. 1161, a formal demand was made by them for the cession of Hunan and Kiangnan, and at the same time explanations were required

---

* It was during this year, A. D. 1159, that the famous Chu-hi made his appearance upon the scene. He was a man of profound erudition. He had distinguished himself in the literary examinations of the empire, and had at a very early age passed two of these and taken the degree of M.A. Although he subsequently held high official rank, he managed to pursue his studies with such good effect that he has left his mark on Chinese history. With the help of the numerous disciples that flocked to him to be taught by such an eminent master he recast the great historical work of Tze-ma-kwang, and has left us the writings known as the Standard History of China. His most famous productions, however, were his Commentaries on the Classics. These have superseded all others, and are recognized as the only authorized ones by the scholars of China at the present day. His influence on the minds of thinking men has been immense, and his views upon the difficult problems that the sages hinted at, but left unsolved, have modified the opinions of the scholars of China ever since he propounded them.

why the Chinese were arming themselves for war. The Kin ambassadors were treated with the greatest politeness, though they intentionally behaved with the utmost rudeness to the Emperor, in order to obtain some plausible pretext for their country's breach of faith. The demand for territory was refused absolutely, upon which a declaration of war was made, and in October an enormous force of six hundred thousand men were on their way south to the conquest of China. Yu Yun-wen, a distinguished statesman who had been appointed comptroller of the army for the defence of Nanking and the south bank of the Yang-tze, met the forces under the command of Wan and routed them with great slaughter at Lai-shih. Twice after this did the Kins advance bravely against the Sungs, maddened by the thought that the soldiers they had so often conquered, and upon whom they were accustomed to look with contempt, had at last proved themselves the better men ; but all in vain.

Wan's position was now an exceedingly unenviable one. Behind him were the victorious Chinese, and at home a revolution, which had placed a descendant of Akuta on the throne, and which showed him that he would have to fight against his own people should he return there. If he had been popular with his army he might have done this successfully, but he was not. He was naturally of a cruel and tyrannical disposition, and his late defeats had only rendered him still more brutal. Floggings and beheadings were the order of the day throughout the camp, until a spirit of fierce resentment was excited in the hearts of both men and officers. A plot was finally formed against him by the latter, and he was put to death in his tent by one of his generals. The army then retired to K'ai-fung-fu, which Wan had made his capital, and his unfortunate son was murdered by a party that had been hurriedly sent ahead to seize him. The new ruler of the Kins now proposed to make another treaty with the Sungs, but the attempt failed, because the Chinese demanded the return of Honan. Instead of peace, therefore, war was again determined upon, and in July of A. D. 1162 the Kin army had entered Kiangnan, but was once more repulsed and driven back with great slaughter. Two months after this defeat of his persevering and unrelenting foes Kau Tsung abdicated in favour of a royal prince, a descendant of T'ai Tsu, the founder of the dynasty, as he had no son of his own to succeed him.* The title by which he is known in history is

---

* The reign of Kau Tsung was marked by a series of disasters, which were in a arge measure due to the weakness of his own character and to the facility with which he was duped by clever and designing men. In his early years he seemed to have been a man of bold and fearless bearing, and just the one to come to the helm of affairs in the great crisis when his father and brother were carried away captive by the Kins After years did not carry out the promise of his earlier ones, and vacillation and cowardice became marked features in his government. It is true there was a decided revival of the military spirit during the latter years of his reign, but this was not due to any influence that he exerted. It was rather the result of the heroic spirit and the fine military qualities of the distinguished generals that came into prominence during that time. After his abdication he lived for twenty-five years, dying in A. D. 1187 at the ripe old age of eighty-four.

Hian Tsung—A. D. 1163-1190.

The first acts of this monarch were the elevation of Chang-tsun to high rank and the redeeming the memory of Yoh-fei from disgrace by publicly decreeing him posthumous honours and the appointing of his six sons to official positions under the government. Scarcely had he got settled on the throne when war once more broke out between him and the Kins. In the first encounter the Chinese army led by Chang-tsun inflicted a terrible defeat upon their fierce antagonists, but subsequently returning with increased forces this famous general found himself out-generaled by his opponent, and the result was disaster to the imperial army. An attempt was now made to bring about peace, but the demands of the Kins that the old *status quo* should be made the basis of the new treaty, and that in addition the four districts in Shensi which Wuh-shu had ceded to Kau Tsung should be returned to them, made it difficult of accomplishment. Hian Tsung was determined that there should be no cession of territory. An ambassador was sent to Liau-yang to treat with the Kins and to state the terms on which the two nations might be reconciled. Either through fear, or because of the superior diplomacy of the Kin statesmen, this man, Lu Tsung-hien, yielded the very points that he had been instructed to resist. When he returned to China the indignation at the court was intense, and speedy punishment followed his dereliction of duty. Many insisted that he ought to be put to death, but the Emperor, more merciful, was content with banishing him to a distant part of his empire. The Kins were speedily informed that China refused to ratify the treaty that had just been made, and that hostilities would be resumed unless better terms were conceded.

Preparations were now made by Chang-tsun to place the country in a fit condition for the next campaign, which he was sure was not far distant. Unfortunately he died in October (A. D. 1164), and there was no one with the commanding abilities that he had to take his place. Two months after, the Kins were once more on their march south, where they obtained a victory over the Chinese army and took possession of the district of Hwai-ngan, in Kiangnan. Again ambassadors were sent to treat with them, and as the ruler of that people was an enlightened and generous spirited man who was more concerned for the welfare of his own subjects than in the subjugation of the Chinese, a treaty was soon concluded, which, though it did not concede the long desired province of Honan, was still more favourable than some previous ones, in that it arranged that the annual subsidies by the Chinese should be considerably reduced. The Kin troops then retired to their own territories, and peace was formally established between the two countries.

Nothing of importance happened till A. D. 1170, when Yu Yun-wen, the prime minister, urged upon the Emperor to make a demand upon the Kins for the restoration of Honan. Nearly all the great ministers were opposed to this, and the son of Chang-tsun came specially to court to use his influence to prevent it. When he appeared at the audience the Emperor said to him, "I hear that the Kins are at war with their powerful neighbours, and that a famine is desolating the people. Don't you consider that this would be a favourable time for us to demand our rights?" "The time is good as far as they are concerned," he replied, "but it is not for us. We are not prepared for a campaign, and besides, our people are in great misery from the long wars that have ravaged the country. Let us wait until we are in a better condition, and then we shall be able to make our demand with a more reasonable hope of obtaining what we desire." The Emperor refused to listen to this sensible advice, and an embassy was sent to the court of Shih Tsung ; but a peremptory refusal was given to the request, and for want of force to back it up the matter was necessarily allowed to drop.

After Hian Tsung had reigned twenty-six years he resigned the throne in favour of his third son and retired into private life, where five years after he died, greatly regretted and beloved by his people. He had not shown any great or commanding abilities, neither had he performed any brilliant actions by which his reign might have been distinguished. He had been a good ruler, and had done everything in his power by wise legislation to increase the happiness of his subjects, and to do away with the miseries that war had brought upon them.

It was a singular coincidence that the Kin ruler, Shih Tsung, died this very same year, and was succeeded by his grandson, Chang Tsung. His death was a national loss. He was a man of exceptional abilities and of high moral qualities. He was so wise and beneficent in his rule that he was compared to the ancient sages of China—Yau and Shun—who were supposed to have exhibited in their lives every virtue and every excellency The whole nation had been touched and moulded by his example, and crime diminished to an amazing extent. It is said that during his reign of thirty-one years only seventeen criminals were executed throughout his whole dominions, thus proving the marvellous influence that this noble ruler had upon the conduct of his people.

Kwang Tsung—A. D. 1190-1195.

This monarch was thirty-nine years old when he ascended the throne, and he reigned but five years. The only thing that history has to record about this man is his miserable weakness of character which made him a slave to the imperious will of his queen Li. She was jealous and overbearing, and executed terrible vengeance upon any of his concubines that her husband seemed to show any preference for. One of these ladies, who one day had brought in some water for the Emperor to wash his hands with, incurred her hatred. Next day before dawn, whilst he was holding audience with his ministers, he was horrified by one of the attendant eunuchs of the queen bringing in a pair of bleeding, mutilated hands and presenting them to him with his consort's compliments. He recognized them as those of the unfortunate woman who had done him the slight service the day before. She very soon took the government of the country into her own hands, and utterly ignored her husband in the decision of state affairs. There was one thing that she was determined upon, and that was that the late Emperor should have no voice whatever in the councils of the nation. The fact was she had taken a most undisguised and bitter hatred against him, so that when he fell ill of the disease of which he died she would not allow his son to visit him or be present during his last moments on earth.

Some of the great officials about the court were so shocked at the want of filial piety that they resigned their offices and left the court. Two others that remained—Han-ni and Chau-jù—memorialized Kwang Tsung that he should abdicate the throne in favour of his son. The poor man, who was under the tyranny of his wife, and felt himself a cypher in public affairs, gladly acceded to this request, and his son, who was twenty-seven years old, became Emperor, under the title by which he is known in history of

Ning Tsung—A.D. 1195-1225.

The first year of this reign was marked only by the ambitious conduct of Han-ni, who was determined to elevate himself to a pinnacle of power that was hardly consistent with loyalty to the throne. Because Chau-ju refused to co-operate with him he compassed his exile to Fuchow, and there he was put to death by his orders. The famous Chu-hi, who had been appointed royal preceptor, after a stay of only forty-six days in the palace, was dismissed for the same reason. Not content with this he got the queen-dowager, who still continued to hold the reins of power, to issue an edict forbidding the use of the latter's commentaries on the classics by the scholars of China, and as many as fifty-nine of his adherents were dismissed from the government service.

Nine years went by, and peace still reigned in the Sung dominions, for the Kins were engaged in a struggle for dear life with the new Mongol power that threatened their very existence. The fortune of war had been against them, and the people began to realize that in this new conflict they had a different kind of people to contend with from the inhabitants of the Chinese empire, and that in their campaigns with the hardy warriors from the steppes of Mongolia there were no wealthy cities to be plundered and no treasures to be brought home to enrich their own country. At the close of the year A. D. 1203 Han-ni, hearing of the straits to which the Kins were reduced, began to prepare for war, believing that the time had come when China could again by force of arms recover all she had lost in her struggle with them. Materials of war were gradually collected, gunboats were built and the army largely strengthened.

The Kins, who were informed by their spies of what was going on, began to get ready for a campaign, which they saw was inevitable, and in the month of December of A. D. 1204 they strengthened the garrison of K'ai-fung-fu, and at the same time sent ambassadors to Ning Tsung to demand an explanation from him as to the reason of his arming, since there was a treaty of peace existing between him and them.

The Emperor, who was not yet in a condition to fight, replied that he was not thinking of war. Some of his officers, indeed, had, without his knowledge, been enlisting soldiers, and otherwise putting their troops in a condition to commence a campaign, but he had dismissed them from his service, and he assured the Kin messengers that he had no thoughts but those of peace with their country. Satisfied with this reply, the troops were withdrawn from K'ai-fung-fu, and the Chinese were left in peace to silently strengthen themselves for a conflict which the more eager spirits of the country believed they could successfully wage.

A year later the mask was withdrawn, and four armies, under four distinct generals, were led against K'ai-fung-fu. The Kins, who heard of this movement, at once hurried on reinforcements, and a great battle ensued, when the Chinese were thoroughly discomfited. The victorious enemy now advanced south and took three important cities, but their further progress was stayed by the ratification of a treaty on the old terms, and the Kin troops retired to Honan.

The year A. D. 1206 is a famous one in the history of the times that is now being narrated, for in it Te Mu-jin was made the supreme Khan of all the Mongol tribes.* His fame had gone abroad throughout them, and there was none so famous as he. At a great council of the Mongol chiefs held at Onan Kerule he was raised by acclamation to the supreme dignity amongst them, and from this time he dropped the name of Te Mu-jin and assumed the prouder title of Genghis.

Meanwhile, the war had been resumed in the west by the Kins. Wu-hi, the governor of a region in Sz-chwan, had turned traitor

---

* This famous conqueror was born, according to the Persian accounts, in A. D. 1155, but by the Chinese his birth is said to have happened in A. D. 1162. His father was named Ye Su-gai. He had greatly distinguished himself by the victories he had gained over the Keraits, the Naimans and over the people of Tangut, or Hia, and had shown his consummate generalship in his overthrow of Aung Khan, or Prester John, as he has been wrongly styled, and the occupation of his territories, the capital of which, Karakorum, subsequently became that of the Mongol rulers. See Col. Yute's Marco Polo.

and handed over four large districts to them. Many of his officers refused to be faithful to him in his treason, but the Kin forces had already taken possession of the country and held them till they were driven out by the Sung troops that had been sent from the capital. Fighting still went on for some months between the two armies in this province, which was at length put an end to by Ning Tsung agreeing to one of the terms of the enemy, viz., that the head of Han-nı, the cause of all the disturbance between them, should be given them.

In the month of August, A. D. 1208, the Kin troops retired to their own territories, and thus practically ended their great contest with their powerful Chinese neighbours, for such stern work lay before them for very life with the Mongol conqueror, Genghis, that for the future all their resources and military strength and generalship would have to be put forth, but in vain, to avert their coming doom.

Unfortunately for the Kins their ruler now died, and was succeeded by his brother Wei-shau, a very incompetent and useless character, who was thoroughly unfitted to take the helm of affairs at this time when the nation was in great peril. What the Mongol ruler thought of him may be learned from the way in which his ambassador was treated by him. When he asked him the name of his sovereign, and learnt that it was Wei-shau, he scornfully spat on the ground, as though to show his disgust at the man, and declared that he was not the person that was worthy to occupy the throne of the Kins.

Not long after this the Mongol warriors appeared in the west and noth-west of the Kın dominions, plundering and conquering wherever they appeared. The Kin soldiers were invariably defeated by them, and not all the generalship of their best leaders—Hu Sha-hu and Kau-ki—could stay the devastating march of these savage hosts. After lading themselves with plunder, they retired to their own country, only to appear next year and go through the same sanguinary process. In A. D. 1213 the Kin ruler was slain by Hu Sha-hu, and Shan Tsung was placed on the throne by him. This same year the Khitans, seeing that the power of their conquerors was waning, rose in rebellion under the leadership of Yeh-luh Liu-kau, and the latter took up his residence in Tungchow and assumed the title of king. In order to make his position more secure, he sent messengers to Genghis and placed himself and all his followers at his disposal and declared that he submitted entirely to his rule. His proposals were gladly accepted, and titles of high rank were bestowed upon him, and he was classed amongst the nobles of the Mongol power.

This same year Hu Sha-hu was murdered by Kau-ki, who was made commander-in-chief in his place, and thus the Kins were deprived of the services of a general who could have helped them in this crisis more than any other that the country possessed at that time.

In order to avert the danger that was now threatening his country Suan Tsung opened negotiations for peace with Genghis, and finally terms were come to by his giving him in marriage a daughter of the late Wei-shau and a great quantity of precious things, which for the time satisfied the cupidity of this rapacious conqueror. Suan Tsung, however, who was in mortal dread of the Mongols, spoiled all these pacific arrangements by moving his capital from Yen-king, in Chihli, to K'ai-fung-fu, in Honan. He thought that the further he got away from them the safer he should be, but this show of fear only precipitated the danger he sought to escape. When Genghis heard of the step he had taken his anger was excited. "What!" he said, "does he doubt me? If not, then why has he moved his capital south. No terms must be kept with a man that thus shows such want of faith in me that he cannot trust my word." The Mongol forces were at once set in motion towards Yen-king, and as they advanced, considerable numbers of the influential Kins, disgusted at the cowardice of their ruler, submitted themselves to them. Although troops were called in from every possible direction to the succour of the late capital, every effort failed to preserve it from capture, and the Mongol general Min-gan, in spite of the most heroic defence of the city by its commander, took it by storm and added it to the dominions of his master in the month of July, A. D. 1215. With the usual ferocity of the Mongol at this period of their history, the garrison was put to the sword, as well as a large number of the inhabitants, and the palace was ransacked and plundered, and an enormous quantity of booty was carried off by the victors. So indignant were the Kins at the Chinese government, because they had taken advantage of their distresses to refuse the annual subsidies they had been accustomed to pay, that they sent three small armies into the Sung territories to punish them. The days of their supremacy, however, were at an end, and they soon returned in disgrace, having to fly before the Chinese armies that inflicted a crushing defeat upon them.

Genghis, who was determined to be satisfied only with the complete submission of the Kins, sent an army of ten thousand men under San-kau-pa-tu to enter into Honan and capture the city of K'ai-fung-fu if possible. His most direct route was by the way of the famous Tung Kwan pass, a place strong both by nature and by art, lying between Shensi and Shansi, and which he hoped would be so negligently guarded that he could take it by the way. In this hope he was grievously mistaken, for he found it so strongly occupied by troops that he saw it would be madness with his small force to attempt to carry it. In this dilemma he made a detour through the mountains, over hills and through deep ravines and across mountain torrents that would have frightened men less valorous and daring than these wild horsemen of the steppes. At one time the men were climbing the almost inaccessible sides of mountains where only the wild beasts felt themselves at home : at another they came to the edge of foaming streams, far too deep to be forded, but which they managed to cross on bridges made out of their long iron lances. After incredible suffering, and the loss of many men, who were dashed to pieces on the rugged mountain sides, or drowned in the raging torrents, San-kau-pu-tu managed to get within six or seven miles of K'ai-fung-fu.

The Kins, however, had not been asleep during his march, and troops had been hastily gathered together for the defence of this famous city. The Mongol general soon found himself confronted with a host that his men had no chance of defeating. In the engagement that took place he was overcome by the Kins, but he evaded utter destruction by a masterly retreat that he made in the direction of the Yellow River. Fortunately for him the cold at this time was so intense that it was frozen over, and he made the passage over on its surface, thus avoiding the capture of his force by the victorious Kins. The Kin ruler now sent ambassadors to the court of Genghis desiring peace. Personally he was willing to agree to this, but his counsellors advised otherwise by showing him that the strength of the enemy had been so reduced that he had but to continue for a short time in the present policy, when the whole of their country would become subject to him. He accordingly replied that he was quite willing to consent to peace, but only on the condition that the Kin ruler should consent to be his vassal and hold his kingdom as a gift from him. This, of course, could not be consented to, and so the war was to be conducted to the bitter end.

The campaign of A. D. 1218 was entrusted to the charge of Muh Hoa-li, perhaps the most distinguished and trusted of the commanders of Genghis. The vast powers that he handed over to him are seen in the parting words of the great warrior to him as he started with his chosen band for the conquest of China. "To the north of the Tai-hing mountains my rule everywhere extends, but to the south of them I put everything into your hands." That this confidence was not misplaced is seen by the splendid results that were achieved. Not only were a number of cities and important towns captured in Shansi and Chihli, but what was of still more importance, they were retained by the conquerors instead of being abandoned after they had been plundered. At the end of the year the Kins sent ambassadors to the Mongols, begging for peace, but no reply was given to their entreaties, and it now became apparent that their aim was the entire subjection of the Tartar power. Before this could be accomplished, however, a great deal of hard fighting would have to be gone through, for the Kins were by no means a vanquished foe. In order to demonstrate this, they sent a large army into the Sung dominions in order to show that they still considered themselves the masters of the Chinese, but though it obtained some successes at first it was ere long compelled to flee before the superior generalship of the Sung commander Meng Tsung-chin. Although the success of the latter was most decided, he durst not follow the flying Kins too far, for the remembrance of the prowess of their foe in many a hard fought fight was still strong in the minds of the Chinese, and operated to restrain them from following up their victories to the extent they would otherwise have done.

The next four years were spent by the Mongols in subjugating the country north of the Yellow River, under the leadership of the famous general Muh Hoa-li, but a stop was put to this work by his death in A. D. 1223. Genghis, who had been occupied in the conquest of Western Asia, and who, it is stated, had conquered no fewer than forty kingdoms, great and small, and had subdued the great Mohammedan powers with whom he had come in conflict, now returned, to continue in person the war with the Kins. This same year Suan Tsung, the Kin ruler, died, and was succeeded by his son Ngai Tsung, and in the following one the Sung Emperor passed away, and through the intrigues of Shih-mi, the prime minister, was succeeded by Kwai-seng, instead of Kwei-ho, the real heir to the throne.

CHAPTER XXVII.

THE SOUTHERN SUNG DYNASTY (CONTINUED).

Li Tsung—A. D. 1125-1265.

THIS prince was a descendant, in the tenth generation, of the founder of the Sung dynasty, and was only twenty-two years old when he ascended the dragon throne. He reigned for the long period of forty years. The most important event in the early part of his reign was the death of Genghis Khan, A.D. 1227, a man who had achieved more victories, and had conquered over a wider range of country than almost any one that had ever preceded him.* He died at the age of sixty-six, and bequeathed the conquest of the Manchus to his sons, the third of whom—Okkodai—became his successor on the throne. It was fully two years after the death of his father, however, and after he had been recognized by the chief of the nation as their supreme ruler, that he took the title of T'ai Tsung and acted as sovereign of the Mongols.

During this interregnum the war with the Kins had been carried on with less vigor, and, indeed, on one occasion they had obtained the victory in a small engagement they had had with a detachment of the Mongols, the first that for many years had happened to their arms. With the return of Okkodai, however, from his installation, matters assumed a different complexion. Energy and activity began to be displayed in the preparations that were made for the prosecution of the war. His first act was to divide the territories that had been conquered from the Kins into ten great departments, and the next was to organize his forces for the struggle that was to end in their overthrow. With him had come his brother, Tu-li, and the famous statesman Yeh-lu-ch'u-ts'ai.†

---

* Genghis left four sons—Tuli, Chagatai, Okkodai and Juji. His death occurred in his camp at Luh-p'an, in Shensi, as he was on his way to Honan. He died, we believe, from natural causes, though some writers have stated that he did not. Marco Polo speaks of the place where he was buried in common with all the Mongol Khans. He also says, " When they are carrying the body of any Emperor to be buried with the others the convoy that goes with the body doth put to the sword all whom they fall in with on the road, saying, 'Go and wait upon your Lord in the other world.' They do the same with the horses, for when the Emperor dies they kill his best horses, in order that he may have the use of them in the other world, as they believe, and I tell you, as a certain truth, that when Mongou Kaan died more than 20,000 persons, who chanced to meet the body on its way, were slain in the manner I have told." Col. Yule's Marco Polo, I, 216-217.

† Yeh-lu-ch'u-ts'ai was of the royal family of the Western Liau, or Khitans. On the appearance of Genghis he took service under him, and subsequently he became the confidential adviser of his son Okkodai. He was a man of distinguished learning and performed a noble service to the more illiterate Mongols by persuading their rulers to encourage the study of Chinese literature. He introduced the use of the calendar (A. D. 1220) and got the Mongols to adopt a system of paper money (A. D. 1236). His death is stated to have been caused by the sorrow he felt at the ambitious schemes of the widow of Okkodai, which he had endeavoured, but in vain, to oppose. He wrote the history of the Tartar dynasties. See Mayer's Chinese Reader's Manual.

In A. D. 1231 the two brothers, each commanding a separate army, started for the conquest of Honan. The one led by Okkodai took the more direct route south, whilst the other, under Tu-li, travelled through the southern district of Shensi, called Han-chung, and after surmounting incredible difficulties from the mountainous character of the country, over which his troops had to construct a road, he joined his brother in the neighbourhood of K'ai-fung-fu. Several severe engagements, however, took place before this was accomplished. One of them, which was fought in the Yu mountains, was at first decidedly in favour of the Kins, but their general did not know how to take advantage of the victory he had really gained, and all its fruits were lost to him. Another battle, which was fought at San-fung to the south-west of Yu-chow, ended disastrously for the Kins. The soldiers who were in great distress, for want of food, were routed with great slaughter, and the commander-in-chief, with two of his generals, were killed. No obstacle now lay in their way, and in the month of February, A. D. 1232, the city of K'ai-fung-fu was beleaguered by the Mongols.

This magnificent city, the last great stronghold of the Kins, made a stout and desperate resistance, and for months defied all the efforts of the besiegers to capture it. Su Pu-tai, the Mongol general, used every artifice known in war to break down the great walls that resisted every assault that the bravest of his men made upon them. His strongest batteries of cannon were pointed against them, and great stones weighing one hundred and fifty or sixty pounds were hurled against them or flung into the city, and watch-towers and buildings were laid in ruins to the consternation of the inhabitants, but still after three months' incessant attacks no impression seemed to have been made on the town.

It seemed, indeed, that the Mongols began to despair of taking it at all, for at this juncture the Kin ruler proposed an armistice, which was agreed to by them, and they actually withdrew their troops to Ho-loh, where they remained for nine months, and where Tu-li died. That they were not eager to fight may be learned from the fact that though in the month of August thirty Mongols, who had been going backwards and forwards to K'ai-fung-fu, negotiating with the Kins, were murdered by a Kin general, no immediate rupture took place. The Kin ruler thought there certainly would be, for though he had not ordered the murder, he at once began to arm and train the able-bodied men in his capital. Still the Mongols made no movement for five months more, when they sent an embassy to Li Tsung and asked him to ally himself with them and join in the destruction of their ancient foes, the Kins. This he consented to do, on the express condition that the province of Honan should be returned to the Sungs. The Mongol ambassadors readily agreed to this, and great rejoicings filled the Sung capital at the prospect of the speedy vengeance upon an enemy that had brought such disgrace and sorrow upon China.

In the meanwhile, and before the intentions of Li Tsung could have been ascertained, the Mongol army, which had been largely reinforced from every possible direction, began its march on K'ai-fung-fu, and ere long an impassable ring of valiant and heroic warriors surrounded the doomed city. Before this had been done Ngai Tsung, who had lost heart and faith in the power of his people to sustain the siege, fled with a large escort to Kwei-teh, and though the Mongols pursued him, and cut to pieces a thousand of his rearguard, who were detained in the crossing of a river, he himself escaped in safety to that town.

And now the siege began again in real earnest, and once more the cannons thundered, and great stones flew into the city and crushed the citizens to pieces, and crumbled great buildings into ruins, and filled many a home with sadness and despair. Still there was no talk of surrender, though the desertion of their sovereign had cast a blight over the hearts of the most faithful of his subjects. Day after day went by, but no word from him, and no sign that the outer world cared for them in this the greatest strait in which men could be placed. Outside, the enemy, by deeds of daring and valour, worked for their destruction, and though vast numbers of them perished in the frequent assaults, in which Mongol and Manchu met in a death struggle, their ranks were soon filled up with warriors that came from the great steppes to join in the mighty contest for a new empire.

Three months had elapsed, and the fighting was as fierce as ever. Both soldiers and citizens had vied with each other in deeds of heroism, and if they had had a man of nobler build than their commandant they might have held out still longer. Ts'ui-li, however, was not the man to perish at his post, or surrender his life rather than the city that had been consigned to his care. He opened negotiations with Su Pu-tai, and, without asking for terms, he declared that he was ready to open his gates and hand over the town to him. In order to propitiate him he delivered over to him five hundred ladies of Ngai Tsung's harem, as well as thirty-seven chariots that belonged to the royal household. The defenders then descended from the walls, and the citizens laid aside their arms, and the great city waited in anxious suspense to know how their savage conquerors would treat it after the stern resistance that had been given them. Su Pu-tai wished to follow the Mongol custom, which was that no mercy should be shown to a place that had long held out against an attack. "This city," he said to Ok Ko-dai, "has resisted long, and vast numbers of our soldiers have been slain and wounded. My advice is that we should slaughter every one in it."

Yeh-lu-ch'u-ts'ai, hearing of this savage counsel, sought the Emperor and besought him to spare the people. "The land must have people on it," he said, "for if there are no inhabitants in a country it becomes valueless to the sovereign." At first Ok Ko-dai refused to listen to his appeal, but this generous statesman was not to be refused. A second time he pleaded for the unhappy people, and this time he was successful. Their lives were to be spared, but their property was to be at the mercy of the conquerors, and everything they possessed was considered to be at their disposal. And thus this great city of fourteen hundred thousand families, with its magnificent buildings and its great wealth, fell into the hands of the Mongols, and with its fall the Kin dynasty practically was destroyed.*

Ngai Tsung, not feeling himself safe in Kwei-teh, fled to Ts'aichow, where, with all the soldiers of the falling dynasty, he made a stand. There is no doubt but that if he had had only the Mongols to contend with he might have considerably lengthened the days of his house, and thus have postponed the tragedy that was soon to be enacted. The Sung troops, however, who had marched in obedience to the invitation of the Mongols, had now arrived and joined themselves to those of Ok Ko-dai, and the united armies were on their way to endeavour to capture the last refuge of the Kins.†

Early in December, A. D. 1233, Ts'ai-chow was completely invested, and with such rigour that all communication with the outer world was completely cut off. Ngai Tsung, seeing that all hope of deliverance had vanished, and perhaps hoping to touch the hearts of the enemy outside the walls, resigned the throne in favour of his kinsman, Ch'eng-lin, who is known by his royal title of Mo Ti, the last Emperor. His reign lasted but for a few days, for the city fell before a grand assault of Mongols and Sungs. Ngai Tsung and his commander-in-chief fell bravely fighting against the infuriated soldiers that had entered this his last stronghold, and the young Emperor disappeared amongst the slain that died on that fatal day. With this great disaster perished that remarkable dynasty that, rising from small beginnings, had gradually attained to such a power that they had been able to conquer the warlike

---

* It seems impossible that such an enormous population as that given by the historian could have been assembled in any one city, however great. There is no doubt but that vast numbers had flocked into it from the country as the Mongols advanced, and thus the native population had been greatly increased. Still it requires a great stretch of imagination to conceive of a town where over eleven millions could be collected within its walls, for, as the Chinese reckon eight to a family, the fourteen hundred thousand families would mean 11,200,000 people. The way in which the average of eight is assigned to each household is as follows: Husband and wife, their father and mother, two brothers and two children. From a Chinese standpoint, and with their system of not breaking up the family on the marriage of the sons, this does not seem an excessive estimate. There must have been some mistake made, however, in the number of the families.

† Ngai Tsung had sent ambassadors to Li Tsung, beseeching him to refuse to ally himself with the Mongols. "These enemies of mine," he said, ' have already conquered forty kingdoms, and last of all they have attacked me; when they have overcome and destroyed me then your turn will come next. Rather join your forces to mine and we will thus render important service to each other by opposing an enemy that is hostile to us both." Li Tsung refused to listen to these prophetic words, so fierce was the hatred of the Chinese for the men that had so deeply wronged them.

Khitans, and so completely subdue the northern part of China that the Chinese with all their vast resources and their almost unlimited command of soldiers had not been successful in any of the efforts they had made to wrest it from them.

Their fall was no doubt a nemesis for the cruel and unsparing way in which they had, with but few exceptions, treated the people of China, and more particularly those unhappy sovereigns that had had the misfortune to fall into their hands. Had there been more generosity shown by them after their victories, and more clemency to the vanquished, and less haughtiness to the Emperors of China, who often humbled themselves by the most abject submission to them, the Sung soldiers would not on that day of their fall at Ts'ai-chow have been amongst the numbers that rushed side by side with the Mongols to avenge the wrongs of more than a century. Unfortunately for themselves, several of the Kin generals were taken prisoners by the Sungs, and their fate was a terrible one. They were sent to Hangchow and taken into the great temple that contained the ancestral tablets of the ancestors of the dynasty. There, in the presence of these, the story of the fall of the Kins, who had brought such disgrace upon their descendants, was rehearsed. They were then slain before them, and thus their spirits were supposed to be appeased by the slaughter of their unplacable but now fallen foes.

Great were the rejoicings in Hangchow at the fall of their inveterate enemy, but there was at least one prophet, Hung-tsu, at the court, who predicted sorrow from this event, and who warned the Emperor to prepare for war with the victorious Mongols. The latter, after their conquest, had withdrawn their troops to the north. The Sung soldiers marched in July to take possession of K'ai-fung-fu, and the gates were opened to them by the captains of Ts'ui-li, whom they had murdered, and thus, without striking a single blow, this great city was recovered. Lohyang was next attacked and captured, and the famous Tung-kwan pass, which had been left unguarded, passed into the hands of the Sungs.

The Mongols, who had not anticipated such prompt action on the part of their allies, now despatched a force to attack the Chinese. In the battle that ensued the later were defeated and had to fly in confusion before the Mongols. They, however, managed to retain the towns they had taken, and in February, A. D. 1235, Li Tsung sent Meng-kung with fifteen thousand men to K'ai-fung-fu, whilst at the same time ambassadors were ordered by him to repair to the Mongol head-quarters and demand an explanation why they had attacked his soldiers, seeing that he was simply carrying out the treaty between them, that Honan should be his. if he helped to overthrow the Kins. The Mongols brusquely replied that they had no explanation to make, as they were determined to make Honan part of their dominions, and that if the Chinese wished for peace the sooner Li Tsung ordered his men to withdraw from it the better it would be for him.

To enforce this argument five Mongol armies were at once set in motion. The first, under Ku-tan, a son of Ok Ko-dai, marched into Sz-chwan ; the second into Kiangnan ; the third into Hu-kwang ; the fourth, under Man-gu, into the western part of Honan ; whilst the fifth was sent against Corea. Li Tsung now began to realize his danger and to repent of his precipitate action which had involved him in a conflict with such a powerful foe as the Mongols. At the beginning of the campaign in Sz-chwan, Ku-tan was successful, for he took Ch'ungking and other important places, but when Meng-kung reached that province with his army the towns were recovered and the Mongols were compelled to retreat from it. For the next two years desultory fighting was carried on, but the balance of success was on the side of the Sungs. Wherever Meng-kung appeared the Mongols had to give way, and in A.D. 1238 they had disappeared from Kiangnan, and though they came in force again next year they received three crushing defeats at the hands of this famous general. In the meanwhile Ok Ko-dai, influenced by his prime minister, Yeh-lu-ch'u-ts'ai, made arrangements for the better government of the vast territories that had fallen to him by the conquest of the Kins. He issued a decree inviting the scholars of China to appear at his capital for examination in the classics, and promising that all that passed should be made mandarins in the conquered country. Large numbers responded to this appeal, and no fewer than four thousand and thirty were found competent, and swearing allegiance to the Mongols became officials under them.

At the same time many reforms were introduced that tended to assimilate the Mongol rule to that of China. The weights and measures of the latter country were adopted, and no doubt in imitation of the Chinese the issue of paper money was now commenced (A.D. 1237).*

Ok Ko-dai died in A.D. 1241, and desired that Shih La-wun, the eldest son of his fourth son, should succeed him on his throne. His queen, however, who was ambitious of power, refused to consent to this, and acted herself as regent of the kingdom, in spite of the advice of Yeh-lu-ch'u-ts'ai, who urged her to carry out the will of her late husband. This same year the Mongols sent ambassadors to China to enter into a treaty of peace, but they were unfortunately murdered by the general in command of the Chinese frontier, to the great indignation of their countrymen. To avenge this wrong an army under Hung-shih was sent into Sz-chwan, when Ch'ungking was captured through the treachery of one of the officers in the city, and a large number of minor places in the same region.

In A.D. 1246 a great council of the Mongol nation was held, in which it was decided that a ruler should be definitely appointed

---

* Paper money had been used by the Chinese from at least the beginning of the 9th century. Their conquerors, the Kins, had also adopted this kind of currency, and Kublai, when he became Emperor of China, used it on a large scale. See Yule's Marco Polo. I. 381.

to reign over the empire. The rule of the queen regent had been unsatisfactory, especially since the death of Yeh-lu-ch'u-ts'ai, that took place three years previously.*

They were determined that the interregnum should last no longer, and Ku-yuk, the eldest son of the late Emperor, who was now forty years of age, was elevated by the suffrages of the chiefs of the nation to the throne. Shortly after this event Meng-kung died, and Kia Sz-tau, a brother of one of the ladies of the harem, was appointed generalissimo in his place. Ku-yuk's reign was very brief, for he died in A. D. 1248, and his queen became regent. Some were for having Shih La-wun made Emperor, but there were so many influential persons opposed to this that the proposal was never carried out, and in A. D. 1251 Man-gu, the eldest son of Tu-li, was raised to this exalted position.

The first act of Man-gu was to seize Shih La-wun, who had not asquiesced in the nation's choice, and his adherents, and place them under restraint. The next was the appointment of his brother, Kublai, to the command of the forces that were sent into Honan for the subjugation of that province. This latter was not merely a great soldier, but he was also a statesman, and fortunately for him he had as his guide and adviser Yau-chu, a man of distinguished ability and broad and liberal views.† He not only gave him sound advice in regard to the regulation of his conduct, but he also wrote down what he considered had been the evils that had brought sorrow upon the Kin ard Sung dynasties and showed what were the principles upon which a state should be rightly governed. Kublai was so pleased with his views that he had a book specially composed of the words and thoughts of this eminent man, which he kept constantly by him that he might consult it on all occasions. He also took his advice in every important affair of state and religiously carried it out whenever possible.

Next year, A. D. 1253, Man-gu added Shensi to the territory over which he ruled, and for the next few years his time was spent in devising plans for the welfare of the people and in advancing the prosperity of the regions that had been desolated and wasted by the ravages of war. The Sungs, with unaccountable negligence, were content simply to guard their own frontiers, and seemed never to dream that the day was not far distant when this statesmanlike ruler, that appeared content with the society of literary men and in winnirg the hearts of his people, would pour down upon them with

---

* He is said to have died of sorrow, because T'u-li-ki-na refused to listen to the remonstrances that he addressed to her. After his death some one represented to her that he had died immensely rich. She at once sent officers to examine whether this was true or not. All that they could find were some musical instruments, pictures and several thousand volumes of books, but absolutely no money.

† Soon after taking the position of confidential adviser with him, Yau-chu said to him, "If you want to gain the hearts of the people over whom you rule there are eight things that you must be careful to carry out: Cultivate virtue; be studious; respect men of superior intelligence; love your relatives; reverence Heaven; love your people; delight in good, and keep yourself aloof from disloyal advisers."

his warriors and claim China for himself. The only military achievement that he in the meanwhile performed was the subjugation of the aborigines in his own district and the conquest of a portion of Yunnan (A. D. 1255). There, with his famous lieutenant Vriang Kadai, he compelled three of the fiercest tribes to make submission to him, whilst several more, hearing of his success, voluntarily acknowledged his sway. He captured Ta-li and four other prominent towns and returned to Honan to carry out the reforms he had already commenced there.

A sudden stop was put to these in A. D. 1257 by the news which reached Kublai from Karakorum that his brother was harbouring jealousy towards him under the suggestion of some ill-minded advisers that too much power had been entrusted to him, which might possibly endanger his own position. Cut to the heart by the suspicions of Man-gu he consulted with Yau-chu as to what he should do to vindicate himself. "The best way for you to place yourself right with your brother," he replied, "is to at once move with all your family to the capital and stand face to face with him. He will know by this action that you are loyal to him, and the old confidence will be restored." Kublai immediately acted on this advice, and handing over his authority to the commissioner that had been sent to watch his movements he set out for Kara Korum. Arrived there, the two brothers met, and silently looking at each other for a few moments they burst into tears. No word of explanation was given or offered, but from this time their hearts were united, never again to be divided by any suspicion. Shortly afterwards Kublai returned to his command, and Man-gu started for a campaign in Sz-chwan, whilst the fourth brother, Arikbuga, was left in charge of the capital.*

At first, Man-gu obtained considerable success in Sz-chwan and took several cities, but on the arrival of two Chinese armies, the Mongols found themselves very much restricted in their operations, and after one encounter, in which victory was not granted to either side, they attacked Yun-chow, which they captured. Next year, A. D. 1259, Man-gu laid siege with all his forces to Ho-chow, the modern Ch'ungking, but he met a most stubborn resistance. The commander of it, Wang-kien, was a most valiant and loyal soldier, and foiled every attempt to capture it. The bravest of the Mongols, stimulated by the presence of their sovereign, advanced boldly up to the walls and endeavoured to scale them, but they were met with such showers of stones and arrows that large numbers of them were slain or wounded, and no impression could be made upon the valiant defenders. After the siege had lasted six months it was suddenly put an end to by the death of Man-gu in his camp. The Mongols now withdrew, carrying his body with them, and returned to Kara Korum.

---

* Hulaka, the son of Tu-li, had started three years before this for the conquest of Persia, and became the founder of the Mongol dynasty in that country.

Kublai, who had received no news of the death of his brother, had led his army into Kiangsi, where he had captured several cities. Li Tsung now became thoroughly alarmed. He summoned some of his generals to the capital with their forces and ordered that soldiers should be enlisted and drilled, so that they could help in the defence of the country. Kia Sz-tau was sent with all the forces he could collect to meet the Mongols, but he was a coward at heart and dared not face Kublai. Instead of fighting he resorted to underhand measures, which were ultimated most disastrous to his country. He privately sent messengers to Kublai, proposing terms of peace, viz., that the Emperor should pay him an annual subsidy of silk and consent to call himself the vassal of the Mongol Emperor. No reply was returned to these propositions.

Shortly after, Kia Sz-tau heard of the death of Man-gu, when he sent other messengers, saying that in addition to the terms already proposed the Emperor would be willing to pay him annually two hundred thousand ounces of silver, and also give him part of the territory of Kiangnan. Kublai, who by this time had also heard of the death of his brother, accepted these conditions. The reason for his doing so was because the news had been brought to his camp that Arikbuga was plotting in the capital with those that were hostile to him to deprive him of his succession to the throne and to become the chief of the Mongols. As the presence of himself and his army were needed in the capital to secure his rights, he concluded a peace with Kia Sz-tau and began his march to the north.

The Mongols had not advanced far upon their journey, when Kia Sz-tau basely ordered an attack upon their rear, and several hundreds of them were killed. He then retreated, not daring to bring on a general engagement, and immediately despatched an officer to the Emperor with a flaming account of the great victory he had achieved over Kublai. He was careful, however, not to say anything about the secret treaty he had concluded with him. Li Tsung was in raptures, and ordered him to the capital in order that he might adequately reward him for his services. When it was known that he was nearing Hangchow a great number of mandarins of high rank were sent out to meet him and to escort him to the palace.

Kublai, who knew the temper of his men, and that they were prepared to defend his right to the throne, determined not to wait till he reached Karakorum, and meet the assembly of the chiefs there and get their votes for his succession to his brother. He decided to settle the matter more summarily and seize the power whilst it was within his grasp. Having reached Hwan-chow, he summoned a council of his great officers and disclosed his plan to them. As he had expected, they were delighted with it, and carrying out their unanimous wishes he proclaimed himself the great Khan, to the unbounded delight of his whole army.

Kublai was a man of action. He had been exceedingly annoyed at the conduct of Kia Sz-tau, and was determined to bring him to book for it. Ambassadors were sent to the court of Li Tsung, demanding that the treaty that had been made with him should be carried out. These no sooner reached the capital than they were seized and imprisoned by Kia Sz-tau, and others that were sent after the lapse of several months to demand an explanation of this insult to him were similarly treated.

Kublai vowed with himself to exact a terrible vengeance from the Sungs for this dishonour that had been put upon his envoys, but in the meantime he had the serious business of conquering his brother and of firmly establishing his own authority over the Mongol nation before he could move in the matter.

In the month of November, A. D. 1261, Kublai led his army to Karakorum, and there, in an encounter with Arikbuga, obtained a great victory. His brother fled with the remnants of his beaten army, and Kublai's supremacy was acknowledged by the Mongols. Subsequently Arikbuga returned and made his submission to his brother, who, with great generosity, forgave him and gave him a position in his government befitting the rank of a prince of the blood. He took severe vengeance, however, on the leading men that had supported him in his rebellion and mercilessly put them to death.

The year A. D. 1262 was marked by two events of considerable importance. The first of these was the arrival of an embassy from Cochin China with offers of submission to Kublai. This of course was exceedingly pleasing to him, as it showed that his reputation had extended beyond the limits of his empire, and that distant peoples were prepared to acknowledge his supremacy. The second was the defection of one of his lieutenants, to whom he had entrusted the command of Shantung and some districts in Kiang-nan. This general, whose name was Li-tan, transferred his allegiance from Kublai to Li Tsung, and after massacring the Mongol garrisons scattered throughout the country, fortified the cities Tsi-nan and Tsing-chow. Two Mongol princes were soon in the field, and in a battle with Li-tan they defeated him and drove him into Tsi-nan, which they captured after a siege of four months. Li-tan was put to death, and the authority of the Mongols once more re-established throughout Shantung.

Great preparations were made during the whole of the next year for the reception of Kublai and his court in Peking, which he had decided to make his capital. Palaces were built, and ancestral halls, where the tablets which were supposed to contain the spirits of his ancestors could be placed. These were removed with magnificent ceremonies, which large numbers of bonzes performed, to their place of honour in these halls, and in the beginning of A. D. 1264 the Emperor and all the great officers of state removed to the new capital. Towards the close of this same year Li Tsung died, and was succeeded by his nephew, who was forty-three years of age, and whose dynastic name is

Tu Tsung—A. D. 1265-1267.

Immediately on his accession to the throne the new Emperor issued a general amnesty throughout the country, and at the same time bestowed still further honours on Kia Sz-tau, by making his voice the supreme one in the councils of the nation and by following his advice in every matter of importance that affected the welfare of the state.

Kublai, in the meanwhile, was steadily making preparations for the invasion and conquest of the Chinese dominions. He was wise enough to see that this would be a matter of great difficulty and one which ought not to be undertaken rashly. At length, at the beginning of the year A. D. 1268, everything was ready, and by the advice of Liu-ching, the former governor of Lu-chow, in Sz-chwan, who six years before had gone over to the Mongols, the first important step in the campaign was the siege of Siang-yang, a city on the Han river, in Hupeh.

This town, with Fan-ching, on the northern bank of the river, was a strongly fortified place, with a large population, and from a strategic point of view valuable to those who held it, for it commanded the chief road to and from Shensi. When the governor, Lu-wun, heard of the approach of the immense army that was coming to capture the two cities under his control, he sent urgent messages to the capital, praying that large reinforcements should be sent to help him to fight the Mongol hosts. Kia Sz-tau made light of the matter, and Lu-wun was left to his own resources. The Mongol commander, Ashu, found that without a fleet his army would never be able to make an impression upon Siang-yang. He at once set to work, and in a very short time a considerable number of junks of larger size than those belonging to the Sungs was afloat and ready for action. His difficulty now was about the men to man them, for the Mongol soldier was of no service in a case like this. Notices were sent abroad that men accustomed to the management of vessels were required, and rewards were offered to such as were willing to enter the Mongol service. Tempted by these, more than seventy thousand men, with an utter absence of patriotism, in the course of a few months enlisted under the banners of Kublai.

In spite of all the efforts of the Mongols, both by land and by the use of their ships, they made scarcely any impression on Siang-yang. The garrison and the citizens had caught the enthusiasm of their great commander and repelled all the attacks that were made upon it. Although they knew the fate that awaited them, if they refused the offer of the terms that were generously made them, they persisted in their purpose of dying rather than surrendering, and when threats were held out they replied only by taunts that must have cut to the quick the renegade general Liu-ching, who directed the siege in conjunction with Ashu.

Next year reinforcements reached the Mongols from Kublai, and seeing no prospect of taking the city by storm the generals determined to build military lines that would serve the purpose of preventing any relief getting to Siang-yang, and also of acting as a defence to the besiegers in case they were attacked by superior Chinese forces. They intended also by these to isolate the besieged, so that no provisions could reach them, excepting through the Mongol entrenchments. This plan they carried out, and in the beginning of A.D. 1270 Fan-ching was also closely invested. News of this disastrous state of things reached Tu Tsung, who was greatly distressed, and appealed to Kia Sz-tau to know if it were true. "It is utterly false," replied this traitor to his country. "The Mongols have retreated long ago to their own territories, and Siang-yang has been relieved." Upon the Emperor informing him that one of the ladies of his harem had positive information to the contrary Kia Sz-tau had her put to death, and from this time no one dared to let him know the truth about this famous siege.

Another year went by, but still the besiegers were as far off as ever apparently from getting into Siang-yang, although they fought with the heroism and valour with which the Mongols were wont to carry on their campaigns. As brave men as they, however, stood behind those famous walls, and for the honour of their country, and for the welfare of those dear to them, they were determined there should be no surrender. The year A.D. 1272 dawned darkly upon the besieged, and the hopes of success grew more faint as the long-looked-for succours failed to reach them. The one great fact that had hitherto sustained their spirits was the abundance of food with which the city had begun the siege. It is stated that there was enough to last them for ten years. At this juncture, however, it was found that the supply of salt began to fail them. Despatch after despatch from the governor to the Emperor had been carried through the Mongol lines, but they had been invariably suppressed by Kia Sz-tau. Now at length he saw that this policy could be carried on no longer. He accordingly sent an army under Li-ting to the relief of the city, but it was so closely beleaguered that it could not come near it.

The commander now called for volunteers to break through the line of junks that guarded the approach to the two cities by the river. Two brothers—Chang-shun and Chang-kwei—offered their services, declaring they were ready to sacrifice their lives in the attempt to succour the besieged. A hundred boats were given them, laden with the necessary stores, and they waited till midnight, when the Mongols were not on their guard, to make the bold attempt. Each one was furnished with a red lantern, so that they might be able to distinguish each other from the Mongol junks, which would be sure to contest the passage with them.

At the appointed hour the junks moved silently up the river till they reached the place where the Mongols lay moored. A rush was now made to break through before the enemy was thoroughly aroused. Chang-kwei, leading the van, broke through the line and passed on. The Mongols, however, by this time were at their posts, and a fierce encounter took place, in which the success of the attempt was seriously imperilled. Chang-shun, who brought up the rear, now determined to receive the attack of the whole of the Mongol ships, and so engage their attention till his brother had succeeded in getting safely past. He succeeded in his purpose, but it cost him his life. His body was found next day in the river, transfixed with four spears and six arrows. The joy of the citizens of Siang-yang at the arrival of Chang-kwei with the needed supplies was unbounded, especially when they heard that Li-ting, with a large force, had come to their assistance.

Their newly raised hopes were, however, destined to be speedily dashed, for a new power was soon to come into force that would reduce the valiant defenders of the two cities to subjection. A Uighur general, who was engaged at the siege, had represented that there were great cannon in the west, superior in use to those known by the Chinese, which, if brought to the camp, would soon change the aspect of affairs. Kublai ordered that the suggestion of Alihai-yai should be carried out, and the latter at once wrote to his nephew in Persia to forward him as speedily as possible a certain number of large guns with the necessary officers and men who understood the working of them. Their arrival at this time produced a most profound change in the condition of affairs. The great stones of over a hundred and fifty pounds that they threw smashed the bridge that connected the two cities and demolished the outer of the two walls of Fan-ching and shattered the buildings within the town, so that the hearts of the soldiers and of the citizens sunk within them, and when a rush was made by the victorious Mongols the walls were scaled and the defenders driven back. Even then, however, the place was not surrendered. From house to house and street to street the besieged fought with the greatest courage, and it was only at last when they were overpowered by the hosts that rushed into the ruined city that all defence of the town ceased, and the Mongols became masters of a place that had defied their utmost efforts for four years.

The fall of Fan-ching really involved that of Siang-yang, for the whole energies of the besieging force could now be concentrated on it. Su-wun, who had fought nobly and waited patiently for the re-enforcements that never reached him, still maintained the struggle, but there was no longer the hope of success to stimulate him and his gallant soldiers in this unequal conflict. In the month of April, A. D. 1273, the Mongol general, who looked with respect upon him as a model warrior, sent in a flag of truce and promised that if he capitulated he should be rewarded with high honours, and his officers and men be taken into the service of the Emperor Kublai. Seeing no prospect of relief, and knowing that he could not finally hold out against the Mongols, he opened his gates and allowed the enemy to march in and take possession. He was at once given the rank of commander of Siang-yang and Fan-ching, in consideration of his great military ability, and also in recognition of the great service he had rendered the Mongols by not prolonging his defence of the city. In September of the next year Tu Tsung died, and was succeeded by his second son, who was only fourteen years of age, and who is known in history by the name of

Kung Ti—A. D. 1275-1276.

The capture of Siang-yang not only freed the immense forces that Kublai had concentrated before it, but also opened up the way for the further conquest of China. It happened, too, by a most fortunate coincidence, that one of the most famous generals of his day, and a man of princely Mongol birth, viz., Bayan, who had served with great distinction under Hulaku, Kublai's brother in Persia, should now appear upon the scene. The chief command of the invading army was entrusted to him, and under him were Ashu and Alihaiyai, together with Liu-ching and Lu-wun, as well as a number of more or less distinguished captains. The whole army numbered fully two hundred thousand men.

A detached force, under Liu-ching, marched direct upon Yang-chow in Kiangnan, whilst the main body kept the lines of the rivers Han and Yang-tze. The first important place that it encountered was Wuchang, which stood at the junction of the two rivers and was well manned and officered, and should have been strong enough to have kept the Mongols engaged for a long time. The general-ship of Bayan, however, was conspicuous for the ability with which he manœuvred his men and his fleet, and soon this famous place was in his possession, where, leaving a garrison under Alihaiyai, he proceeded on his way down the great river.

The consternation at the capital when the news reached it of the fall of Wuchang and the neighbouring cities of Hanyang and Hankow, was great in the extreme. A memorial was presented to the Emperor that either he or Kia Sz-tau should head a force to meet the Mongol army. Upon this, Kia Sz-tau issued an order for all the soldiers of the empire that could leave their posts to assemble at the capital for the defence of their sovereign and their country. The result of this call was the appearance of one hundred and thirty thousand men at Hangchow. Kia Sz-tau, who had heard of the recent death of Liu-ching in Kiangnan, and who was relieved from the dread he had of meeting him in the field, now led this great body of men to meet the Mongol forces. In addition to them he had an immense fleet of war junks that stretched for fully thirty miles along the Yang-tze, laden with money and all manner of precious things which the officers had brought with them, in order to be under their own protection in case of the capture of Hangchow before they returned. Kia Sz-tau, having reached Wuhu, entrenched himself there and sent messengers to Bayan, offering the same terms that had been formerly agreed upon with Kublai. Bayan's reply was brief and to the point: "Your offer that China should become the vassal of my Emperor would have been discussed if it had been made before I crossed the river. Now that I have passed it, and the country is in my hands, further negotiations will be required. If you want peace come personally to my camp, where we can talk over the matter more easily." It is needless to say Kia Sz-tau did not accept this polite invitation.

Bayan now moved on to the important town of Chihchow. The commander of this was named Chau Man-fa, a patriotic and high-minded officer. When called upon to surrender he indignantly refused, though advised to do so by the officers immediately under him. One of these, disgusted perhaps at the miserable state of things at the capital, or perhaps influenced by the well-known generosity of Bayan, entered into a correspondence with him, and finally opened one of the gates for the entry of his soldiers. When Man-fa heard of this he summoned his wife to the great reception hall and said to her, "It becomes me as a loyal officer of the Sungs to die, for the city that was entrusted to me has been delivered to the enemy. With you it is different, and you must now flee if you would save your life." His noble partner, Yung-chi, replied, "If you are going to be a loyal officer of the crown then I shall be an affectionate wife and die with you." They then strangled themselves together in the hall, and thus in death this loving couple were not separated from each other. Bayan was so impressed with the chivalrous action of them both that he ordered that a grand funeral should be accorded to their remains.* Kia Sz-tau, hearing of Bayan's success at Chihchow, determined to try issues with him, and so led his immense fleet in the direction of it. It consisted of two thousand five hundred ships, small and great, but unfortunately that of the Mongols was equally numerous. The result of the engagement was disastrous to the Chinese. The heavy guns of the Mongols told fearfully on the ships of their enemy. Large numbers were sunk, whilst many more were disabled. The loss of life was most grievous, and the killed and wounded were so numerous that the great river ran red with blood, whilst crowds of men and officers in their dread of capture by the Mongols threw themselves into the swift flowing waters and were drowned.

---

* It is said that Man-fa, just before he committed suicide, wrote an ode of four lines, which roughly is as follows: "I must not be a traitor to my country, neither must I surrender my city. If husband and wife die together then both loyalty and affection have their perfect work."

The immediate result of this great victory was that all the region round about submitted to the conquerors, and the garrisons of cities far off that heard the news fled in consternation from them, a state of things that was not improved by the speedy capture the important town of Jau-chow. At this juncture Kia Sz-tau memorialized the Emperor to seek refuge in flight, but the Empress Dowager opposed this, as did also the members of the great council, especially as at this time Wen Tien-siang arrived from Kiangsi with ten thousand men, and another general with three thousand, for the defence of the Emperor. And now the day of reckoning came for the wretched Kia Sz-tau. One of the palace officials, named Ch'en-yi, presented a petition to the Emperor, in which he declared he ought to be put to death, because he had made a secret treaty with Kublai, and also because he had detained his ambassadors without the knowledge of his sovereigns, both of which acts had been the direct cause of the present miseries that had been brought upon the dynasty. The reply to this was that Kai Sz-tau should be banished to Changchow, in Fohkien, and that Sung-heu, with a sufficient guard, should conduct him there. No sooner had they got to their destination than he was put to death by the orders of the man that had escorted him there, and thus ended a life that had been most powerful in hastening the fall of the great dynasty of the Sungs.

The next movement of Bayan's was against Nanking. Fortunately for him at the time of his arrival a terrible pestilence was raging amongst the people of the city and a famine had added its miseries to the plague. The city surrendered almost without any show of resistance, and Bayan's heart was so moved by the miseries of its citizens that he at once ordered that provisions should be distributed amongst the starving, and measures taken to stop the ravages of the terrible disease from which they were suffering. No sooner had he been settled in the place than Kublai, who seems to have been desirous of peace, sent orders that military operations should be entirely suspended. Bayan, who saw that victory was within his grasp, and that with a few more bold strokes the Chinese empire would be at his feet, wrote urgent remonstrances against this course of action. He showed Kublai that to stop now would be to lose all, for never again would such an opportunity occur to the Mongol forces of gaining possession of a territory that far surpassed in excellence anything that they had ever conquered before. The reply promptly came that the previous orders were countermanded, and as Bayan was on the spot, and knew the condition of affairs better than he did, he was at liberty to take whatever action seemed to him the best.

Bayan was not slack in taking advantage of this permission, and in the month of April the important towns of Ch'angchow and Suchow were successively taken. That Kublai, however, was in earnest to arrange terms of peace with the Chinese, is manifest from the fact that about this same time ambassadors had well advanced on their way in the present province of Kiangsu to the capital to propose terms to the Emperor, when they were unfortunately murdered by the Sung soldiers, and the last chance for the deliverance of the house of Chau from destruction vanished. Nothing now was thought of but the complete subjugation of the Chinese.

Orders now reached Bayan and Ashu to repair to Peking to consult with Kublai and to give him more precise information concerning the state of things in the south than he could get from their despatches. The absence of these famous commanders was soon felt in a very unmistakable way in the region they had quitted. Victory, which had hitherto deserted the Sung standards, now began to incline towards them once more. Various trifling successes showed that the Mongols, without their great generals, were not invincible, and men began to hope that a new era had begun, and China should yet be able to drive the barbarians from her soil.

Liu-sz led a considerable force in July and recaptured the city of Ch'angchow, but these triumphs were but momentary gleams of light that flashed over the land before complete darkness enshrouded it. With the return of Bayan everything was changed. His first business was to recapture Ch'angchow. He accordingly appeared before it with an imposing army and summoned it to surrender. Being refused admittance, Bayan became exceedingly incensed against the city, and vowed a terrible vengeance upon it. He built a huge mound of earth outside level with the city walls, and it is said that large numbers of the unhappy country people whom he caught were thrown into it to augment its size, and that the fat of human bodies was used to grease their mangonels. After about a month's siege the place was taken by storm, and Bayan, contrary to his usual humane dealing with conquered cities, ordered the whole of the inhabitants to be massacred. *

The Mongol forces were now divided into four commands. Bayan with his army had his head-quarters at Nanking; Ashu marched to the siege of Yangchow; Alihaiyai led his men into Hunan, and another marched into Kiang-si. In the meanwhile there was the greatest alarm and confusion in Hangchow. A levy was ordered of every male over fifteen for the defence of the capital, and every spare soldier that could be met with was utilized for the same purpose. An embassage, too, was sent to Bayan to supplicate peace, but they were murdered by the way by their own countrymen, who were not yet prepared for this indignity. Immediately after this tragedy was enacted news reached Hangchow that Alihaiyai was carrying everything before him. Changsha, the capital, was taken, and soon every place submitted to him. Great

---

* Marco Polo gives the account of how Ch'angchow was first taken by a company of Alan Christians in the service of Kublai, and that becoming intoxicated through excessive drinking of some good wine that they found in the city they were slain to a man by the citizens, who recovered their town. See Col. Yule's Marco Polo, II., 140.

suffering had accompanied his successes, and immense numbers of people preferred to commit suicide rather than trust themselves in the hands of the Mongols. Again the Emperor and his mother were filled with alarm, and fresh messengers were sent to Bayan, praying for a stay of hostilities and offering to resign to him all the conquests he had made, if he would only leave the royal house a small portion of their territory that they could call their own, and where they could worship the spirits of their ancestors.

Bayan in reply requested that commissioners should meet him at Chung-ngan, a place that lay to the north-west of Hangchow. When he arrived there he found no one to meet him, as the great officials had been opposed to the concessions made by the queen-dowager, and consequently refused to attend. The Mongol general, indignant at this treatment, moved his forces nearer the capital, when Wen Tien-siang begged the Emperor to fly, whilst he remained to hold the city against the Mongols. The queen's mother refused to consent to this, as she declared that she was going to submit to Bayan, and as an evidence of her purpose she sent the great seal of the empire to him. The messengers that conveyed this to his camp brought back word that he wished the presence of the prime minister to discuss the terms of surrender. Upon this Wen repaired to his head-quarters, but the demands of Bayan being too severe he refused to agree to them, and as no argument could be found to move him he was put in close confinement and treated as a prisoner.

The state of things at this time in the capital was most deplorable. The two brothers of the Emperor had fled, and the commanders of the troops had disappeared in various directions with their men, so that the city lay at the mercy of the Mongols. Bayan sent a considerable force to occupy it, and seized the treasury and the money it contained, as well as the persons of the Emperor, his mother and his queen and all the members of the royal household, and with a large and well appointed force he accompanied his noble prisoners to Peking. Wen managed to escape from confinement, and making the best of his way to Wenchow he joined the royal brothers, who had escaped the close pursuit of the Mongols. At Wenchow the elder of the two had already been proclaimed Emperor in place of his unhappy brother, who was on his way to exile.

Twan Tsung—A. D. 1276-1278.

The court of the new Emperor was now removed for safety to Foochow, in the Fohkien province, and there his great captains and the relics of the Sung armies gathered around the young sovereign, who was only eight years old, to endeavour, if possible, not only to stem the tide of Mongol invasion, but also to recover the territory that had been seized by them. His mother was made queen regent, and three armies were equipped, one to recover Shau-wu, in

Fohkien ; a second to attack Jau-chow, in Kiangsi ; and the third to capture Cheh-tung, in Chehkiang. In the meanwhile Kung Ti was being conveyed to Peking, where in spite of the efforts made by the way to rescue him by a force that was led by a general of the name of Li-ting, he arrived in safety, and being deprived of his royal title he was degraded to the rank of a duke.

The cause of the Sungs from this time grew still more desperate ; for the Mongols were successful in the province of Kwangtung as well as in Fohkien, where the Sungs suffered a defeat before Shan-wu and had to retreat in disorder to Foochow. Chang Shih-kieh, one of the faithful generals that remained loyal during this terrible crisis, seeing that he would not be able to hold out against the coming foe, embarked his men to the number of one hundred and seventy thousand and sailed south for Chin-chew, but he was denied admittance by the commandant of that city, who had declared for the invaders. The fleet then held on its way still further south, when it anchored in the harbour of Swatow and awaited the development of events.

The victorious march of the Mongols was now unstopped, either in Fohkien or in Kiang-si, in which latter province Alihaiyai had greatly distinguished himself and had reduced nearly all the large towns to submission. It seemed indeed that with the close of A. D. 1276 the prospects of the Sungs was at the very lowest ebb, and that any serious fighting was now over for ever. There is a vitality, however, and a spirit of indomitable perseverance in the Chinese that prevents them from abandoning a purpose that to a weaker race would seem impossible of being carried out. Wen Tien-siang recaptured Canton, which had been taken by the Mongols, as well as Hing-hwa, whilst Chang Shih-kieh succeeded in capturing Shau-wu. Six months after, in the month of August, A. D. 1277, the Mongols recovered all the places they had lost. The slaughter at the town of Hing-hwa was terrible. Angered with the gallant defence that the Chinese had made, they ruthlessly massacred nearly the whole population of the place. The loss of life was so great and the blood spilt so copious that the Chinese historian, in order to give a vivid picture of the awful scene, describes how the sound of the latter could be heard as it rushed gurgling and bubbling into the river that ran by.

The advance of the Mongols compelled the young Emperor to fly once more, and he made his way to Tung-au, in the Kwangtung province. Whilst sailing towards the south they encountered a violent storm, and the ship carrying the royal fugitive was wrecked and Twan Tsung fell into the sea. It was with the greatest difficulty that his life was saved. So grievously did he suffer from this mishap that he became seriously ill, and in a few months died at the early age of eleven, on the island of Wang-chow, whither he had been compelled to fly.

The close of A. D. 1277 and beginning of A. D. 1278 were marked by Mongol successes in the far west. An expedition that had been sent against Burmah, that had not only refused to pay tribute to Kublai, but had even dared to encroach on Chinese territory, was most successful in its results, for more than three hundred military posts in the occupation of the Burmese troops were stormed and their garrisons made to fly. In Sz-chwan, too, success had attended the operations of Kublai's soldiers, so that now the whole empire belonged to him, with the exception of the small corner into which the descendant of a long line of royal ancestors was now crowded.

With the death of Twan Tsung it was believed by many that the resistance to the Mongols would have ceased, and the whole body of loyal men that had risked their lives for their country would have disappeared to their homes. Luh Siu fu thought differently, however, and addressing his comrades he said: "Whilst there is still another son of Tu Tsung alive let us not give up the struggle for our freedom. In ancient times five hundred valiant men have been able to found a kingdom. We are more than that, for we number several tens of thousands, and our officers are numerous. If Heaven has not determined upon the destruction of the Sungs then we may still devote our lives to the defence of our country." These stirring words found an echo in the hearts of all that heard him, and it was unanimously decided to continue the struggle. The youngest son of Tu Tsung, who was only eight years old, was then raised to the throne, and in him we have the last of the Sungs, known by the title of

Ti Ping—A. D. 1278-1280.

In order to be able to meet the advancing hosts of Mongols with a greater chance of success, it was decided to remove their forces from the island of Wang-chow, where they were now concentrated, to Yai-shan. This latter possessed a harbour of special excellency in the present exigency. It could be entered only at full tide, for at low water it was left completely dry. It was so shaped, moreover, that it could be very easily fortified. Thither, then, Chang Shih-kieh and Luh Siu-fu removed their ships and men, and as the former were insufficient to contain the whole of their troops, which consisted of over two hundred thousand men, they proceeded to build more.

In the beginning of A. D. 1279 the Mongol general, Chang Fung-fan, who had discovered the position of the Sungs, proceeded with his immense fleet to blockade Yai-shan. Chang Shih-kieh now saw that the final struggle would soon take place, and he accordingly made such disposition of his forces as would enable him to present the best front to the enemy. His ships, that numbered more than a thousand, were anchored in lines across the harbour and tied to each other by ropes, so that the Mongols could not easily break through them. Chang Fung-fan used every artifice possible to destroy his enemy, but without avail. Fire ships were sent in with the flood tide, but the Sung ships, being very wet, would not ignite. He then resorted to diplomacy. Amongst his officers was a nephew of Chan Shih-kieh. Three times he caused him to appeal to his uncle to surrender, promising him pardon and high honours if he did. These appeals having had no effect, he next asked Wen Tien-siang, who had been captured a few months previously, to write and persuade his friend to abandon a falling cause and take service with the Mongols. At first he refused to do so, but being hard pressed, he wrote a note which, when Chang Fung-fan saw, he laughed and tore it up as useless for the purpose he had in view. The letter contained the following words, "Death is a thing that no man may avoid. The great thing, however, is to leave a name that may be recorded in history with honour."

The blockade was carried out with such severity that the Sungs began to suffer, both from the want of provisions and also of water. For many days they had nothing to drink but sea water. The result was that dysentery largely prevailed throughout the army. By this time the Mongols had got all their arrangements made for attack, and entering the harbour a tremendous battle ensued, in which the Chinese were utterly defeated and the whole of their fleet captured, with the exception of sixteen that Chang Shih-kieh managed, under cover of a fog, to escape with. When Luh Siu-fu saw that the day was lost, and that there was no escape from the Mongols, he first drove his wife and family into the sea, and then taking the young Emperor on his back, jumped in after them, where they were all drowned. A large number of those most loyal and devoted did the same and perished with those that were slain in the battle. A more disastrous day had not been seen for many a long year in Chinese history, for more than a hundred thousand corpses covered the surface of the sea, amongst which was that of Ti Ping, which was afterwards picked up and honourably buried by the Mongol general. Chang Shih-kieh made his way with all despatch to Wang-chow to impart the tidings of disaster to the queen-dowager and to enquire of her if there still remained any prince of the royal blood that could be raised to the throne. The poor mother was too distressed at the loss of her son to listen to any plan for continuing the struggle with the Mongols. Her heart was broken, and life had become a burden to her, so she threw herself into the sea and was drowned. He accordingly sailed to Cambodia, in hopes that the ruler of that country would assist him in the recovery of China for the captive monarch. His reception there, however, was anything but flattering; indeed, he was told by some of the wealthy men of the place he visited that he had better depart, as his presence there might involve them in difficulties with the Mongol Emperor. He accordingly returned to the islands off the coast of Canton and rendezvoused at the island of Hai-ling. After some little time passed in organizing his forces he set sail for the mainland, with the object of attacking Canton. They had hardly sighted the land when undoubted signs of an approaching typhoon appeared to the affrighted mariners. They implored Chang to draw near the shore and land if possible. This he refused to do. Nothing in the world, he declared, should stay him in his enterprise. Instead, he ascended a platform that had been erected high up on one of the masts. There he burnt incense to Heaven, and whilst the offering was slowly burning he said: "I have served the house of Chau to the utmost of my ability. When one Emperor disappeared I set up another, and he also has perished, and now to-day I meet this great storm; surely it must be the will of Heaven that the Sung dynasty should perish." He descended, and soon the storm grew apace, until it was blowing a fierce and terrible hurricane, before which all the ships but one or two succumbed. Chang went down in his, and thus the last famous defender of the fallen dynasty perished in his heroic efforts to save it.

The contest having ended in complete victory, the troops returned to the capital, and Wen Tien-siang was carried prisoner with them. His great wish was to die, for he did not desire to survive the noble men that had fought and died in so gallant a manner. For eight days he would not eat anything, hoping to die of starvation, but he was frustrated in his purpose by his guards, and he arrived in safety at his destination. Kublai, who had an intense admiration for him, had him brought into his presence. He used every possible argument to induce him to become a servant of the new dynasty, and even offered him the post of prime minister, but in vain. Nothing could make him swerve from his devoted allegiance to the Sungs, and Kublai had no resource but to commit him to prison, in hopes that longer thought on the subject might make him change his mind.

And thus, after the lapse of three hundred and twenty years, the great Sung dynasty ceased to exist. With the exception of the Chow, it was the greatest that ever ruled in China. The names of its great scholars and statesmen stand out brilliantly in its history, and the words they wrote and the great thoughts that they conceived have left an impress on the Chinese nation that will never pass away until a new era, that Christianity alone can introduce, will give a nobler and higher tone to the civilization of this remarkable people. That the house of Chau possessed some specially fine qualities for ruling a people is manifested by the long lease of power that it held for so extended a period in China. It was not because the majority of its rulers were possessed of great executive ability or of military genius. A Chinese writer dealing with this very subject gives the true reason. "The Sungs," he says, "gained the empire by the sword and kept it by kindness. Their goodness to the people was not tinged enough with severity, and so the kingdom was snatched from them. Still, through it the empire was maintained for one hundred and fifty years after it seemed to have slipped from their grasp, and it caused such men as Chang Shih-kieh and Wen Tien-siang to cling to them to the very last, and finally to give their very lives for them."

CHAPTER XXVIII.

THE YUAN* DYNASTY (A. D. 1280-1368).

Kublai—A. D. 1280-1295

THE first important act of Kublai, after he had become Emperor of China, as well as of Mongolia, was to despatch a commission of the best men he could select for the purpose, to examine into the sources of the Yellow River and its subsequent course, in order, if possible, to devise measures for avoiding the sorrow and desolation caused by its frequent overflows. Kublai was not merely a savage warrior who was bent simply on gaining renown and enriching himself on the spoils of the conquered. He was a statesman with large and liberal views, and he had been so fascinated with the learning and civilization of the Chinese that his ambition seemed to have been to assimilate himself and his people to them.

Towards the close of the year ambassadors were sent to Japan with the demand that he should be acknowledged as lord paramount by that country.† That proud and haughty people, who held themselves quite strong enough to cope with the Chinese, were by no means prepared for such a claim on the part of the Chinese Emperor, or to pay the tribute he demanded. In order to show their views on the subject they murdered the Mongol envoys and awaited with calmness the development of events. In order to avenge this insult to his authority Kublai ordered the collection of an immense fleet from the chief coast ports of his dominions, but more especially from those of the Fohkien province. Two admirals—Aleuhan and Hoan Wen-hu—one a Mongol and the other a Chinese, were put in command of the expedition. Unfortunately the former died at sea, but the fleet reached Japan in safety, and over a hundred thousand men landed from the ships. Scarcely had this been accomplished when a tremendous storm arose, which shattered the greater part of the fleet and left the army on shore without any possibility of getting away from the country. Hoan selected the best of those that had survived the storm and set sail for home for the purpose of getting a fresh supply of ships, but he was never heard of again, so that he and all the rest with him must have perished at sea.

---

* Yuan means first, or original, and was the name that Kublai gave his new dynasty in the year A. D. 1271.

† Kublai had on several previous occasions sent ambassadors to Japan, demanding submission, but they had been dismissed with slight ceremony. In A. D. 1274 he had despatched a fleet of three hundred vessels, carrying fifteen thousand men, to enforce his demands, but they had been defeated by the Japanese and had been compelled to return in disgrace.

The soldiers and sailors who were on shore now began to build ships in order to get away home again, but the Japanese forces, both naval and military, now arrived, and attacked them with such vigor that they suffered a total defeat. A hundred thousand men were put to the sword, whilst ten thousand Fohkien men were spared and made slaves. The reason why they were not massacred with the rest was because the Japanese ships had been in the habit of visiting Fohkien for the purposes of trade, and consequently a friendly feeling had arisen between the two peoples.

Kublai, who was a great believer in Buddhism, ordered that an examination should be made of the Taoist writings to see whether there was any truth in them. The report was made to him that with the exception of the classic named Tau-teh (The Way of Virtue) they were all corrupt, and therefore injurious to mankind. He at once gave an order that they should be summarily burnt, which was accordingly done throughout the empire, with the exception, of course, of those that the disciples of the Taoist faith managed to conceal.* This same year, A. D. 1282, a great minister of state, named Ahmed, came to a sudden and tragic end. He had been entrusted with great power by Kublai and had managed to enrich himself at the expense of others. The heir, Prince Ching-king, was thoroughly opposed to him, and on several occasions high Chinese officials had insinuated their doubts of him to the Emperor, but no notice had been taken of them. These failures only tended to encourage this man in his wicked ways and to make him believe that he was utterly beyond the reach of any one to harm him. His oppression and vices became at length so intolerable that a conspiracy was entered into to murder him. Taking advantage of the absence of Kublai at Shang-tu, Wang-chu, a chief officer of the city, concocted a story that the prince imperial had arrived in the city and wished to hold an audience. This was late at night, and as Ahmed hurried to the palace, Wang-chu killed him with a blow of a heavy iron mace. Kublai was exceedingly angry when he heard of this, and had Wang-chu and some of the other conspirators executed. Subsequently, on the whole story being told to the Emperor by Marco Polo, he had the body of Ahmed exhumed and beheaded and four of his sons and a large number of his adherents put to death, whilst all the immense wealth that he had so wrongfully accumulated was confiscated to the state.

Shortly after this, rumours began to be circulated through the capital that there was to be an uprising of the Chinese in order to

---

* Kublai, from the accounts we have of him, seems to have been a man greatly given to the external performance of religious services. In A. D. 1263 he introduced into his own family the practice of ancestral worship. It is also said that he greatly favoured the Christian religion. Any careful reader of Marco Polo's narrative will perceive, however, that his religion was simply a matter of state policy, as he hoped through it to gain a power over the hearts of his people which he could not have got otherwise so easily. See Col. Yule's Marco Polo, I, 310 and 348.

rescue Kung Ti and Wen Tien-siang. Kublai ordered the latter to be brought into his presence and asked him if he knew why there was discontent abroad. " The reason of the discontent," he replied, " is because the people are unwilling to submit to you." The Emperor then urged upon him the duty of transferring his allegiance to him, and promised to make him a high official in the palace if he consented to do so. The only reply of this great states-man was, " If you really wish to do me a favour put me to death, as I do not wish to live now that the Sung dynasty exists no longer." Kublai, who had an intense admiration for him, hesitated at first to comply with his request, but finally, considering it necessary for the welfare of his empire, he did so, and thus, in the forty-seventh year of his life, perished one of the most patriotic men that China has ever produced.*

One of the most important acts of Kublai's reign, and one that has been of lasting benefit to the Chinese empire, was the construc-tion of the Grand Canal. This great national work was commenced in A. D. 1282 and completed in seven years. The service it was intended to accomplish was the carrying of the tribute rice from Kiangnan to the capital for the use of the people in Peking and of the troops in the northern provinces. The transmission hitherto had been slow and uncertain, but with the opening of the canal, which was gradually utilized as the labourers proceeded with their work, the supplies of rice reached their destination with more regularity.† Whilst Kublai was taking measures for the develop-ment and prosperity of his empire he was also alive to the necessity of protecting his subjects from the encroachments of their enemies on his extreme western frontiers. He accordingly sent a large force under the command of Neseradin to Yunnan, in order to defend his territories from evil-disposed men that were accustomed in a most lawless manner to cross the borders from Burmah to harass and plunder the people of Yunnan. The king of Burmah, being informed of the arrival of the Chinese troops, was filled with alarm, lest they should after a time be used to operate against his own country. In order to gain the advantage of striking the first blow, and also to intimidate Kublai from sending any such forces in the future, he determined to attack the Chinese with such numbers as he believed could be sufficient to completely annihilate them. He

---

* His death made a great impression, and relics of his dress were eagerly taken possession of as mementos of this great man. On his robe he had written two sen-tences from the Chinese classics. The first was a saying of Confucius, " The scholar and the virtuous man will not desire to live at the expense of their virtue. They will, on the contrary, willingly give up their lives to preserve it." The second was a quotation from Mencius, who said, " I am fond of fish, and I am also fond of bear's paws. If I cannot get them both I will dispense with the fish and take the bear's paws. In like manner, I have a desire for life, and I also love righteousness. If I cannot retain them both, I will sacrifice life and hold on to righteousness."

† This canal is not used now to the extent it was formerly, as the great mass of the tribute rice is despatched in steamers along the coast to the port of Tientsin, from whence it is forwarded to Peking.

accordingly ordered an army of sixty thousand men, horse and foot, as well as two thousand elephants, each carrying from twelve to sixteen men, to cross into Yunnan and attack the force under Neseradin. This latter was a man of metal, and desired nothing better than to see the faces of his enemy, and though he had only twelve thousand horsemen under his command he advanced with the greatest boldness against the well-equipped Burmese army.

The hostile forces met in the plain of Yung-chang. At first the advantage was decidedly in favour of the Burmese, for the horses of the Tartars took fright at the appearance of the elephants and refused to advance in their direction. The general, upon this, ordered his men to dismount and tie their horses to the trees of the forest that stood near by. He then commanded that they should shoot their arrows against the elephants, in order to throw them into confusion, for he felt convinced that the chief danger to him and his men lay in them. This they did with such success that in a short time these great, unwieldy animals, wounded and terrified by the flights of arrows that were poured in upon them, turned tail and fled in the utmost disorder. No sooner was this perceived than the Mongols mounted their horses and rushed impetuously on the enemy. The Burmese received the charge of these wild warriors with the greatest courage, and a fierce and deadly strife ensued, in which a large number of the former were slain. Finally, they were compelled to retreat, when they were pursued by the enemy, who mercilessly cut to pieces the flying foe and made prisoners of a considerable number, whom they used to care for the elephants that they had captured, and which from this time they began to use as an engine of war.

The ease with which the Burmese were defeated by a far inferior force led to serious consequences. Neseradin represented to Kublai that the conquest of Burmah was a very easy matter, and a force was accordingly sent into that country, which carried everything before it. Though the Burmese made a stout resistance at Bamo they were compelled to retreat to the hill of Male, which had been strongly fortified. A great battle took place, which ended in the rout of the Burmese army and the advance of Kublai's men on Tai-kung, the capital.* This place they held till they were compelled by a scarcity of provisions to abandon it, when they returned laden with booty to Yunnan. The same year that witnessed the triumph of Kublai's arms in Burmah saw them considerably tarnished in the inconsiderable country of Cambodia. This place had been a vassal of China, but had recently thrown off its allegiance, and when imperial envoys had been sent to demand a reason for this they had been ruthlessly murdered. General Soto, with a sufficient force under his command, was despatched with all due speed to the off

---

* This Tai-kung is, according to Sir A. Phayre, identical with Ta-gaung, which place was a royal residence at the time of the invasion of the country. See Col. Yule's Marco Polo, II, 76.

vassal to bring him to reason, and the army had got within a short distance of the capital when unexpected difficulties were encountered. A small force of one or two hundred men were sent in advance to reconnoitre, but they were set upon by the Cambodians and slain to a man.

Soto, who now determined to carry the city by storm, hurried on his approach to the capital, but the roads were bad and the ambuscades numerous, so that advance became almost impossible. The Cambodian forces, moreover, that had concealed their movements in order to deceive the Mongols, now converged upon the foe, and in the severe engagement that took place they were everywhere victorious, and the unusual spectacle was witnessed of the ignominious flight of the Mongols before an enemy that they had hitherto held in contempt.

When Kublai heard of this defeat he was exceedingly annoyed, and sent his ninth son, T'o-hoan, with a body of troops to co-operate with Soto. As the bad roads of Cambodia had been a very large factor in his defeat, the latter determined to advance through Annam and thus avoid the disasters that might be repeated were they to attempt to reach the capital by the way they had originally tried. There was another reason for this resolve. Though a vassal of China, Soto had reason to suspect that the king of Annam was in league with the Cambodians and was secretly helping them in their resistance against China. He was determined therefore to find out the exact position he held in this matter, and he accordingly sent in a demand for a supply of provisions for his army and a right of way through his territories to Cambodia. Both of these were refused, and not only were troops sent to the frontier, but armed boats were also equipped and placed on the river Fu-liang to oppose the passage of the Mongols. The Annamese, however, were no match for their foes, and soon the former had crossed the river and defeated the army that had dared to stand in its way. The king fled, and his brother made his submission to Soto and agreed to all his demands ; but this unfortunate general's difficulties that now seemed in a great measure overcome were really only commencing. The march across the country during the great heat of August and September tried the troops, who were more accustomed to the snows of the far north than to the burning sun of the south, most severely. Sickness prevailed amongst the men, which soon developed into a plague, and great numbers of them died. A retreat was then commenced, but the Cambodians, who had been biding their time and allowing nature to fight for them, attacked the Mongols, and Soto fell, bravely fighting, whilst another of his generals, Li-heng, died from the effects of a poisoned arrow.

T'o-hoan succeeded in escaping with a remnant of the army and returned to Peking. Kublai, smarting under the disgrace, made plans for avenging the defeat, but he was induced by his ministers to give up the idea, and the Cambodians were allowed to enjoy the triumph they had won without any further molestation from the Mongols. The same was the case with Japan, for though three years were spent in building ships and making preparations for another invasion of that country, the influence of Li-suan, the prime minister, prevailed, and the expedition never sailed.

In A. D. 1285 the heir-apparent, Chin-kin, died, to the great grief of those that knew him, for he was a man well worthy to succeed his father. He was intelligent and upright and a great student of the literature of China. His father showed his grief by the magnificent funeral services that he had performed for him after his death. Forty thousand Buddhist priests chanted the prayers for the dead, and went through the ceremonies that were believed to be requisite to deliver his soul from purgatory and land it in the abode of happiness. Kublai had never been satisfied with the way in which Annam had treated his army in its campaign with Cambodia, neither had he been pleased with the pretended submission that had been made after the victory that had been gained by Soto. In the beginning of A. D. 1287, therefore, he despatched an army, consisting of three great divisions, whose object was the complete subjugation of that country. Seventeen engagements were fought between the Mongols and the Annamese, in which the former were victorious and the king was compelled to fly from his capital. Apatsi, the general in command, now advised Kublai's ninth son, who had accompanied the expedition, to give orders for the withdrawal of the force during the extreme heat of summer. "The enemy," he said, "are now waiting for the hot months to see our men laid low by fevers and dysentery. What I advise is that we should retire for a time, and when the cool weather comes, return and complete our conquest." This prince had learnt nothing by experience, and hesitated to accept the advice so wisely given him. Unfortunately, at this juncture the king of Annam sent ambassadors to the Mongol camp with offers of submission. These were not honest, but were intended to have the very effect that Apatsi had warned the prince against. This latter fell into the trap, and negotiations were carried on which were purposely lengthened by the Annamese until sickness broke out in the camp. Then they were suddenly broken off, and an army of three hundred thousand men appeared on the scene. The Mongols, being in no condition to fight, were compelled to retreat. The enemy, however, were too numerous to be evaded, and so a battle was fought, in which the Mongols were defeated with the loss not only of Apatsi, but also of a large number of men and officers. The remnant escaped from the country by avoiding the great roads, but in the end only a very few were ever permitted to return to their homes from this fatal expedition. Kublai was so angry with his son that he refused to see him, and ordered him to take up his residence at Yang-chow on the Yang-tze. This defeat rankled in his mind, and six years after he had serious thoughts of again invading the country, but his purpose was not carried out, because his death happened before the expedition could be fully organized.

In A. D. 1288 Kublai ordered that the unfortunate Kung Ti, who had been kept a prisoner all these years, should be conveyed to Thibet and there become a Buddhist priest in one of the monasteries of that country, and three years after his mother was compelled to become a nun, and sixty acres of land, free of all taxes, were assigned for her support. He hoped by these acts to banish the members of the royal family of the Sungs into oblivion and thus secure for his own successors uninterrupted enjoyment of the throne he had usurped. A less kindly ruler would have found an easier but more tragic method of solving the difficulty.

During the remainder of Kublai's reign nothing of special importance took place. In the northern part of the empire plagues of locusts and consequent famines seriously distressed the people, whilst as many as nearly half a million of people were drowned in the great floods that took place in Kiangnan. Kublai, with his usual kindness of heart, issued orders for the distribution of food from the royal granaries, but the evils were too widespread to be fully met by the royal munificence. He died at the good old age of eighty, in the year A. D. 1294, and through the influence of Bayan, Timour the Third, of Chin-kin, was elevated to the throne. Kublai was one of those remarkable men that have appeared in the history of China and whose name stands out prominently amongst those that have influenced the destinies of this great empire. He was a man of great ability, but it was as a warrior that his fame has been handed down to us. His conquests extended not simply over the surrounding tribes, but into the remotest countries. His armies were led to victory across the Persian Gulf and even into Europe to the confines of the present Austrian empire. So wide was the terror excited by the battles that he had won that nations spontaneously offered to submit themselves to him. He is the first foreigner that was able, not only to conquer China, but also to sit upon the dragon throne as the ruler of the vanquished people. This is a proof, not merely of his genius as a warrior, but also of his administrative ability as a statesman, for the Chinese were essentially different both in education and civilization from any of the peoples that had as yet submitted to his arms. He was sincerely desirous of advancing the happiness of his subjects, and if there was any failure in this great purpose the fault was not his, but lay rather with the officials to whom had been entrusted the carrying out of the orders of their imperial master. One great mistake that he made was that in the appointment of his ministers he invariably selected them from foreigners, who of course were lacking in sympathy with the people and who, from the absence of public censors, whose duty it is to warn the sovereign of evils that might be going on in the state, felt themselves free to oppress and harass the Chinese. Such painful incidents of the misconduct of some of the high officials in the palace as we have a record of would never have happened had some of the Chinese scholars and men of ability that lived at his court had also been employed in the high offices which were then filled by Mongols and Saracens. In spite of all this Kublai appears before us as a mighty warrior, an undoubted statesman and a generous foe, either to those who had risen in rebellion against him or had resisted his arms. Although there are serious blots in his social life, and a good many of his barbaric habits followed him to his new capital of Peking, he is on the whole worthy of being the founder of the new dynasty that was transferred from the steppes of Mongolia to the civilized land of the Middle Kingdom.

Ch'eng Tsung—A. D. 1295-1308.

Almost the first act of this new ruler was to issue an edict commanding both the Mongols and the Chinese to hold the memory of Confucius in the highest reverence. To the student of Chinese history this is a remarkable and interesting fact. That a fierce and uncivilized people like the Mongols should so soon recognize as the great hero of the nation a man who had never been distinguished for feats of arms, but simply for his scholarship and his ethical teachings, shows a wonderful change in them since they became the masters of China. He will see in it the first step in the process by which the conqueror in the battle field will ere long have his victory snatched from his grasp, and he shall be so assimilated to the people he has triumphed over that he shall lose his own identity and be merged in them. Such has been the fate of the peoples of the east, whether conqueror or conquered, that have come within the personal influence of the Chinese race.

At the time that Ch'eng Tsung ascended the throne the empire was at peace, and even Annam had sent in its submission in the form of tribute to the capital. The waters, too, of the Yellow River had suddenly become pure and limpid, a sure sign that a great sage was about to appear and that war was going to cease throughout the wide dominions of China. Unfortunately the omen was not verified, for the sage did not make his appearance, and an outbreak took place in Burmah, which finally affected the western part of China. The cause of the disturbance was the murder of the Burmese king by a rebel Shan, who gathered such a force about him that none could compete with him. Not content with his successes in Burmah, Papesifu crossed over into Yunnan, but hearing that a Mongol force was on its way to fight with him he sent his submission to the Emperor, and the threatened campaign was for the time being averted. Subsequently, however, the forces came in collision, for the Mongols who had crossed the border into Burmah suffered so severely from the heat and want of provisions that they were compelled to retreat. On their way back they were intercepted by the enemy, and in the battle at Sung-liang which ensued they were defeated with great slaughter. The people of Kweichow, seeing the turn that affairs had taken, unfurled the standard of rebellion, and ere long city after city was captured from the imperialists.

That Ch'eng Tsung was sincerely anxious about the happiness of his people is proved by the fact that he reduced the land tax to one-thirtieth of the existing one ; also that in the fifth and ninth years of his reign he sent round special commissioners to examine into the conduct of the mandarins and to see whether they were administering the laws with justice. In the latter year it was found that eighteen thousand four hundred and seventy-three had been guilty of bribery and oppression, and they were in consequence dismissed from their posts.

During the later years of his reign the country was afflicted by severe earthquakes in T'ai-yuan and Ta-tung in Shansi. In the former town over eight hundred houses were thrown down and a large number of people were killed. Ta-tung, however, suffered still more severely. There five thousand houses were shattered into ruins and two thousand people were buried beneath them. The only important event that took place during the remaining years of the reign of Ch'eng Tsung was the death of his son and heir, Teh-siu. This was a great grief to his father, who was not only distressed at the loss of one he loved so dearly, but was also made miserable by the thought that he had no child of his own to succeed him on the throne. He died in the thirteenth year of his reign, and was succeeded by a great grandson of Kublai, named Ai-yu-li. This young prince and his brother, Hai-shan, had been removed from the capital, one to the north and the other to the south, by the late Emperor, lest they should mar the succession of his own son to the throne.

On the death of Ch'eng Tsung, A-hu-tai, the prime minister, plotted the elevation of Ananta, the prince of Ngansi, and made the queen-dowager queen regent. Another high official, however, disapproved of this action, and seizing the treasury sent off post haste for the two brothers. Ai-yu-li, who was nearer at hand, arrived first. He at once gave orders that both Ananta and the queen regent should be put to death, and sending fresh messengers for his brother, he ascended the throne.

Wu Tsung—A. D. 1308-1312.

This sovereign seemed to be a kind and genial man, if we consider the two chief things that the Chinese historians have recorded of him. The first of these was the order that the Confucian classic on "Filial Piety" should be translated into the Mongol language, and that a copy should be given to each of his relatives, in the hope that the refining influence of this celebrated work might elevate and purify their minds, and thus make them better citizens of the new empire that their house had acquired. The second was the edict that he issued commanding that funds should be supplied from the royal treasury to buy back again the children that their parents had been compelled to sell in consequence of the great distress occasioned by the floods in Honan, Shantung and Chihli, and by the earthquakes in Shensi.

After a peaceful reign of four years he died, and was succeeded by his brother, Hai-shan, whose dynastic title is

Jen Tsung—A. D. 1312-1321.

This ruler was a scholar, and was so diligent in his habits that he had no delight in the ordinary pleasures, such as hunting, etc., that other Emperors had been wont to indulge in. He was exceedingly filial in his conduct and kind and generous to all, but especially to his near relatives. It is recorded that he never signed the death warrant of a criminal without being deeply affected with sorrow, and that it was the constant aim of his life to have universal peace throughout his dominions. In order to encourage the higher study of literature Jen Tsung ordered that the examinations for Chin-sz, or third degree, should be held triennially, and that in cases where Mongols and Chinese came out evenly the former should take the precedence of the latter, and that in case of their being appointed to official positions the Mongols should always be given one step higher than the Chinese. He also passed a decree that no eunuch should be appointed to any civil post in the empire, and that any mandarin that was convicted of bribery should be branded on the face.

In the year A. D. 1315 Ho-shih, the son of Wu Tsung, was banished from the capital and sent to Yunnan with the title of Prince of Chow, and in the following year he was transported to a place north of the desert of Gobi. This was to secure the succession to his own son, Shu-teh-pa-tz, and was in direct violation of the solemn agreement made with his brother before his death that Ho-shih should become Emperor after his (Jen Tsung's) death. This must have been done after a severe struggle, for he was of a generous disposition, and simply from the ambition of continuing the royal line in his own family. The one important event that took place during his reign was the great fire in Yangchow, where twenty-three thousand three hundred houses were burnt and a large number of people lost their lives. After an uneventful reign of nine years he died, and was succeeded by his son,

Ying Tsung—A. D. 1321-1324.

This sovereign was remarkable for the misfortunes that befell him and for the tragic manner in which his reign ended. He was noted for the great love he bore his father. When the latter lay ill with his mortal sickness his son burnt incense to Heaven and requested that he might be allowed to die in his stead. Unfortunately for him his prayer was not granted. His first step in bringing calamity upon himself was the appointment of Temudar as prime minister. This man was exceedingly unscrupulous and had a following of such magnitude that he was able to have all the loyal ministers of the court put to death. He oppressed the people with his exactions and grew rich by his official robberies. In the following year, after his death, his misdeeds came to the ear of Ying Tsung, who deprived him of his posthumous honours and confiscated his property. He also gave out that he intended to put to death all those that had been implicated with him in his wrongs. A censor of the name of Tieh-shih, who had reason to fear an investigation, became alarmed and plotted with a number of others to murder the Emperor. This they were able to accomplish in September A. D. 1323, whilst he was travelling with his prime minister, Pai-tsu, to his summer residence at Shang-tu. Both sovereign and minister were despatched by the swords of the conspirators, who the same night sent off messengers to bring Yesun Timour, a great grandson of Kublai, from the north of the desert of Gobi to come to the capital to become Emperor.

Tai Ting Ti—A. D. 1324-1329.

Although this sovereign reached the throne through the murder of his predecessor he soon showed that he had no sympathy with the murderers, for he had Tieh-shih and the whole of the conspirators put to death. He also recalled from Canton the second son of the late Wu Tsung, who had been banished there, and sent him to reside in Nanking and gave him the title of Prince of Hwai. In order, too, to prevent the recurrence of the murder of the sovereign by his ministers he issued an edict in A. D. 1325 that for the future no high court official should have any control over the troops. He was evidently a man of decision and imbued with statesmanlike views, but his reign was brief, and in August A. D. 1328 he died at Shang-tu, and was succeeded by his young son, who was only nine years old.

The prime minister, however, who saw there was now an opportunity for advancing his own fortunes, seized the supporters of the young Emperor, and putting them in prison sent for Prince Hwai in Nanking and offered him the throne. He gladly listened to the summons that was at length to give him and his brother their rights. Arriving at the capital he seized the chief men at court who were opposed to him and put them to death. He then sent a force to Shang-tu to seize the Emperor. The place soon fell into their hands, and the latter disappeared, and was never heard of again. It is supposed that he was slain in the capture of the place, and that his body had been hurriedly buried with those that had fallen.

The prime minister now urged the prince to become Emperor. This he refused to do at first, as he wished to wait for the arrival of his elder brother to hand over the throne to him. It was shown to him, however, that delay meant danger, as the power that was now within his grasp might at any moment slip away from him, and the chance of becoming sovereign of China never return to his family. Influenced by these arguments he consented to assume the royal authority, and at the close of the year he became Emperor under the title of Ming Tsung (A. D. 1329-1330.) When the news reached Ho-shih, who was then at a place north of Ho-ling, in Mongolia, he was evidently displeased that his brother had usurped the position that by rights belonged to him. He therefore refused to listen to the summons that had been sent him to hurry with all speed to Peking. After the lapse of some months he began his journey towards China, and in September he met his brother on his way to Shang-tu. They treated each other with every sign of affection, and for three days they spent the time in feasting and rejoicing. On the third day, however, at the close of one of their feasts, after Ho-shih had left the tent of his brother, when the attendants entered it was found that Ming Tsung was dead. No explanation of this tragic event has been given by the historian, and it is but reasonable to conclude that he was murdered by his brother.

Wen Tsung—A. D. 1330-1333.

In order to show his joy at his accession, and also that the nation might share it with him, Wen Tsung issued an edict declaring a general amnesty throughout his dominions. Whilst he was still residing at Shang-tu the Grand Lama of Thibet sent messengers announcing that he was on his way to visit the Emperor. In order to do him honour he ordered a large company of high officials, both civil and military, to go a considerable distance to meet him. When they encountered him on the way they treated him with the most profound respect and knelt in his presence. Instead of responding to their civilities in a becoming manner he treated them with the greatest rudeness and remained sitting in his chair and acted as though he were a god and the mandarins were his worshippers. The great question with the leaders of the Confucian party now was, how this man should be received, so that they should not lose their self-respect, and yet should do due honour to one whom the Emperor had given orders to treat with the greatest possible courtesy. Lu-ch'ung, the president of the Hanlin Academy and the head of the Confucianists, solved the difficulty in a very happy manner. Advancing into the room where the Grand Lama was haughtily sitting, and with a glass of wine in his hand, he said to him, "You are a disciple of Sekya Mouni and the head of all the Buddhists in the empire. I am a disciple of Confucius and the chief of all his followers in China. There is therefore no need of ceremony between us.'' The Grand Lama had the wit to see the point in this speech, so rising from his chair he smilingly took the proffered cup and drank its contents, and then the two great chiefs of the rival systems sat down to friendly intercourse.

Wen Tsung, in order to ingratiate himself with the scholars of the country, ordered that additional honours should be given to the parents of Confucius and also to those of Mencius. He treated the two sons of his late brother with great kindness, and gave both of them the title of prince. In the third year, however, of his reign he died. His widow, who was an ambitious woman and eager to possess power, set aside her own son, who was an infant, and proclaimed as Emperor the second son of the late Ming Tsung, who was only seven years old, and appointed herself regent. After the lapse of a month, however, the young ruler died, when she placed his elder brother, Tsing Kiang, on the throne. Messengers were at once despatched to Kwangsi to escort him to the capital, but in consequence of the intrigues in the palace it was fully six months before he was formally recognized as Emperor, and it was only upon the distinct understanding that after his death the son of the queen-dowager should succeed him that all opposition to his ascending the throne ceased.

CHAPTER XXIX.

THE YUAN DYNASTY (CONTINUED).

Shun Ti—A. D. 1333-1368.

NO sooner had this sovereign become possessed of the royal authority than he handed over all authority and responsibility to his prime minister. He thus demonstrated the essential weakness of his character and proved himself to be worthy of being the last of the Mongol line. Sad disasters gave their ominous signs that the dynasty was near its close. A terrible flood in the capital, that inundated some parts of it to the depth of ten feet and caused a considerable loss of life as well, and similar calamities in Shansi and Honan, brought widespread sorrow over the most populous parts of the empire.

In the following year, A. D. 1334, earthquakes and landslips and showers of rain, so red that men said it was blood, excited the minds of the people with alarm and made them look anxiously for the disasters which they believed were presaged by these unusual phenomena. Shun Ti seemed more concerned about his own pleasures than he did about events that were arousing fears in the minds, not only of the superstitious, but also of the more enlightened of his subjects. He issued an edict that extended even to Corea, that no maiden over sixteen should be allowed to marry until the royal selection had been made that should make up the complement of the Emperor's harem.

About this time Bayan, an ambitious and cruel man, was acting as prime minister. He had complete control over the Emperor and used his power in a most unscrupulous and tyrannical manner. The influential Chinese, seeing no hope of redress from Shun Ti, entered into a conspiracy to dethrone him, as with his fall the obnoxious minister's power would be at an end. Unfortunately for them a knowledge of this came to the ears of Bayan, so that when the conspirators marched with their troops into Peking they were seized by the soldiers that lay in ambush within the city. The brothers of the queen were implicated, and they fled to her for protection, but they were pursued and wounded at her very feet, their blood spurting on the garments of their sister. Bayan declared that because of the treason of her brothers the queen was worthy of death and must therefore die. The unhappy woman appealed to her husband to save her, but the craven-hearted monarch refused to listen to her cry, and she was abandoned to her fate.

The next few years are mainly distinguished by famines and earthquakes and small rebellions in different parts of the country. In the prefecture of Changchow, near Amoy, a number of men rose in opposition to the government, and were so strong in their organization that the mandarins found themselves unable to cope with them. The country people, who saw that sorrow would come upon themselves if order was not restored, banded themselves together, and attacking the malcontents routed and dispersed them.

During all this time Bayan continued his high-handed proceedings and showed by his actions that his ambition had crushed all loyalty out of his heart, and that he kept continually before his gaze the vision of a throne. In A. D. 1339 he had a Mongol prince put to death, and two others, nearly allied to the Emperor, were sent into banishment without the royal permission being asked. About the same time he appointed his nephew, To-tu, to the command of Peking, and made him colonel of the guards. Next year his suite had become larger than the Emperor's, and To-tu, apprehensive of the terrible destruction that would fall upon his family were his uncle's treasons not successful, appealed to the Emperor to use his authority to prevent the outbreak that he saw would speedily take place. Shun Ti, who could hardly believe that a nephew would thus betray an uncle, and who suspected a deep laid plot that would place him more thoroughly in the hands of Bayan, than he was now, refused at first to act. He was soon, however, convinced that there was a genuine desire to free him from the tyranny of Bayan, and so he entered into the plans for his delivery. One day when Bayan was out hunting the city gates were closed against his return ; his followers were overawed, and he was exiled to Kiang-si, where he died not long after.

Shun Ti, now freed from the tyranny of his late prime minister, began to act with more independence. He had the murderers of his father punished, and he issued an edict that the ancestral tablet of the late Wen Tsung should be removed from its place in the hall of ancestors ; that the queen-dowager should be exiled to Tung-ngan, and the crown prince, her son, to Corea. These last two measures were carried out, in spite of the remonstrances of the censor, who reminded the Emperor that he owed his throne to the queen-dowager, and ought therefore to treat her with consideration. To-tu as a reward for his conspicuous services was made prime minister. For the next few years rebellions throughout the country became more prevalent, and there were signs that the Mongols were gradually losing their authority over the Chinese. In A. D. 1343 the histories of the Liau-kin and Sung dynasties were published, and in A. D. 1345 an edict was issued forbidding the manufacture of spirits, in consequence of the prevalence of the famines and the scarcity of grain. In A. D. 1348 we have the first mention of Fang Kwoh-chin, who afterwards gave the dynasty so much trouble.*

* He was originally a dealer in salt, and was represented by an enemy of his to the authorities that he was in collusion with the pirates that infested the coast near the Tai-chow islands, in Chekiang. An order was issued to apprehend him, and so to save himself from imprisonment, and perhaps death, he joined the free-booters and became a leading man amongst them.

He was a bold, determined fellow, and had a few ships under his command, with which he ravaged the coast. Some war junks were sent against him, and he had to fly to Foochow, defeated by the imperialists. He managed, however, to collect another fleet, with which he sailed out and attacked the enemy. They were completely defeated, and the captain in command was captured. On his being brought before Fang he was reproached for having pursued him. "I am a good man," he said, "and unless you promise to represent me as such, and have me made a government officer, I shall at once put you to death." The captain gave the desired promise. He was then set free, when he faithfully fulfilled his part of the bargain, and Fang was made a small mandarin. The office, however, was too small for him to accept, so he again hoisted his pirate flag and attacked Wenchow.

At the close of this year there was a great flood of the Yellow River, and a special commissioner, named Ku-lu, was sent to examine into the nature of the disaster, to draw up a map of the region affected and to report to the Emperor. In the beginning of A. D. 1351 the report was handed in, and Ku-lu advised that the present course of the river should be altered and that it should be made to flow into the Gulf of Pechili, as it used to do in the times of the Sung dynasty. It was represented that unless this was done continual inundation would take place, and the people would suffer in consequence.

To-tu concurred in the views of Ku-lu, and strongly represented to Shung Ti the propriety of accepting his recommendations. The Emperor gave his royal assent, but in order to have the fullest information on such an important subject another commissioner, Ch'eng-tsun, was appointed to still further investigate the matter. This man seems to have been a very trustworthy official and to have done his work in a thoroughly business-like manner. He visited Shantung, Chihli and Honan and made enquiries from the heads of the people as to their opinion of the feasibility of the plan proposed to the Emperor, and he found a universal opposition to it.

On his return to the capital he gave in his report and stated in a very able paper the reasons why he disagreed with the views of Ku-lu, and he advised that the river should be allowed to continue to flow in its present course. "The people of Shantung," he said, "are so poor now that in some places they are actually devouring each other. To burden them with the taxes that would have to be raised to carry on such an immense undertaking would be to crush them under a load that would be intolerable to be borne. Besides," he added, "what will be done with the two hundred thousand men employed on the works after they are completed? They will only be a source of trouble to the government, and in the end the cause of rebellion. I advise therefore that the Yellow River be let alone." To-tu, who had already compromised himself in the matter and had advised the Emperor to adopt Ku-lu's recommendations, endeavoured to dissuade Ch'eng-tsun from making such an adverse report, but he was not to be moved. "If you were to take off my head," was his spirited reply, "I should still declare that the course of the river should not be diverted." To-tu, seeing that he could make no impression upon him by argument, got him out of the way by having him appointed salt commissioner in Ho-chien, in Chihli.

By the end of May all the arrangements for the great undertaking were completed. The Imperial edict commanding it had been issued. Ku-lu had been appointed superintendent of works, and one hundred and seventy thousand workmen, consisting of soldiers and common people, were ready to commence operations. The first opening was made at a place to the north-east of Hwang-ling, which was to be continued through Kwei-leh and thence on to the sea.

In six months the new branch was completed and ready for the passage of ships, and in two months more the banks had been put into such a state that they could stand the pressure of the river that now flowed between them.

In the meantime, whilst the works were progressing, revolutions were breaking out throughout the country, and especially in Kiang-nan. The immorality of the court and the lavish expenditure that was practised there created the widest dissatisfaction throughout the country. The taxes were increased and a thousand plans for the raising of money were devised by which the people were oppressed. An impetus to rebellion was given by a popular prophecy that declared, "That when the stone man with one eye disturbed the Yellow River revolutions would break out throughout the empire." Singularly enough, when the ground was opened at Hwang-ling, it was reported that a stone image with one eye was found in the ground, at the very point where the river would enter its new course.

The most formidable elements, however, that the dynasty had to contend with were the secret societies that existed throughout the country. That such should have been formed at all was a sure sign that the people were dissatisfied with their rulers, and were endeavouring by these to find some bent to the discontent that was prevalent amongst them. Conspicuous amongst these societies was that of the "White Lily," whose moving spirit was a man of the name of Hai-shan. The ostensible purpose for which its numbers enrolled themselves was the worship of the idols, and more especially of the Goddess of Mercy. The real object, however, was a political one. The agitated state of the country seemed to Hai-shan a sufficient reason why the standard of rebellion should be raised. At a great meeting of the initiated he declared that the goddess was about to come to the earth in human form to deliver them from their oppressors, and that now was the time for them to declare themselves against the Mongols. This proposition was received with the utmost enthusiasm. A white horse and a black cow were sacrificed to Heaven in order to secure its intervention on their behalf, and having adopted a red scarf to be wound round their heads as their distinctive mark, they broke out in rebellion against the government. The imperialist soldiers managed to seize Hai-shan and put him to death, but they could not stay the course of the rebellion. His son, Han-lin, at the head of a hundred thousand men, was prepared to carry on the struggle in conjunction with his general, Liu-fuh. At first they were everywhere successful, and city after city was captured by them.

In the meanwhile two other independent leaders of revolt had appeared in the field, viz., Li-urh and Siu-hwui, who, with their followers, made war upon the Mongols and endeavoured to drive their garrisons out of the cities that were held by them. The imperial troops by this time found themselves fully occupied in resisting the numerous leaders that with powerful numbers were threatening the very existence of the empire. Fang Kwoh-chin was at the head of a large fleet near Tai-chow, and was complete master of all the southern coast. The Mongols collected a considerable number of war junks and proceeded south to encounter him. Unfortunately for them they were not sailors, for all their training in war had been on land, away in the remote interior, far from the sea. Fang, on the other hand, was a thorough seaman. He attacked the Mongols by night and gained a decisive victory. Large numbers in their fright threw themselves into the sea and were drowned. The admiral was seized, and Fang gave him the alternative of either reporting him to the throne as a loyal citizen or of being at once put to death. He chose the former, and the result was that Fang was made a high mandarin and his brothers also were given posts under the government.

In another direction the Mongols were more successful. In an engagement with Liu-fuh the large force under his command was completely routed and the general killed. This success, however, was of but temporary value, for the spirit of revolution pervaded the entire country, and it was with that the government had to reckon. At the close of this year, in which so many disasters had occurred, Siu-hwui proclaimed himself Emperor and captured several cities, the chief amongst which was Han-yang. Shun Ti now gave orders that all cities should be strongly fortified, so as to guard against being taken by surprise, and as the rebels all gave themselves out as being relatives of the late ruling house, all the descendants of Kung Ti were banished to Sa-chow. All these precautions were, however, in vain. Events had progressed with such rapid strides towards revolution that no steps could now be taken that would stay their progress. Not only did Fang throw off his allegiance and take to his more lucrative business of buccaneering, but Kwo Tz-hing, a military commander, also raised the standard of rebellion and became a new competitor for the

throne of China. Two slight successes, indeed, marked the year
in the victory of To-tu over Li-urh and the capture of Ho-chow
from the rebels, but the impression that these made was soon
obliterated by the appearance of other leaders of rebellion, who
soon took a prominent part in the disorders of the country.

At the close of the year A. D. 1353 Chu Yuan-chang became
conspicuous as a leader under the banner of Kwo Tz-hing, and
showed by his generalship that he was a man that would soon
make his mark amongst the many leaders that were contending for
supremacy.* Unfortunately for the stability of the dynasty these
latter, instead of diminishing, kept still further increasing in
numbers. In the autumn of A. D. 1354 a new adventurer, named
Chang-show, found himself at the head of an imposing force, when
he at once proceeded to invest the important town of Yangchow.
To-tu marched against him with all the forces he could collect, and
in the battle that ensued the Mongols gained a most decisive
victory. Whilst the whole army was rejoicing at the defeat of
the enemy a despatch arrived from the Emperor depriving To-tu
of his command and ordering him into exile to Hwai-ngan.

It seemed that after the latter had left the capital the members
of the privy council, led on by Ho-ma, represented to Shun Ti that
To-tu was a man unfitted for the high position he now held, and
that he had appropriated to himself the public moneys that should
have been spent in the defence of the empire. Three times did
the censor make these representations to Shun Ti, but he refused
to listen to them, as he had great faith in him. At last he gave
the order that was to deprive him of an able and loyal minister.
When the edict reached the camp, his captains, who suspected its
nature, advised him not to open it until he had finished his campaign, and by his success frustrate the designs of his enemies.
This he refused to do. He reverently opened the royal missive,

---

* Chu Yuan-chang, the founder of the Ming dynasty, came from Fung-yang,
a town lying to the N. E. of the province of Ngan-hwui. His father was named
Shih-chin, who had four sons. On the birth of Yuan-chang it is said that the
house was illuminated with a light so bright and red that the neighbours thought
it was on fire, and rushed hastily to put it out. When he became a young man the
whole of his family, with the exception of himself, died of a plague, and he was
left alone in the world. Deeply impressed with the calamity that had come upon
his home he determined to become a priest and dedicate himself to the service of
the idols. For this purpose he went and became a bonze in the temple of Hwang-
chiau-sz, in Fung-yang. He was then seventeen years old. Not long after rebellion
broke out in this region, and sympathizing with the national movement against
the Mongols he felt that he should like to join it. Before doing so he determined
to consult the idols and get their opinion as to what course he should take. The
reply was to doff his priest's robe and become a soldier. This harmonized exactly
with his own feelings, so he bid good-bye to the temple and joined Kwo Tz hing,
who, struck with his martial bearing, not only enrolled him amongst his men, but
also gave him his adopted daughter in marriage. Yuan-chang soon proved that
the soldier's profession was one that suited his abilities, for he was successful in
almost every enterprise that he undertook. He was soon put in command of seven
hundred men, and not long after, of thirty thousand, when he was joined by Su-ta,
Li-shan and Ch'ang, men that afterwards became famous in helping him to found
the new dynasty of Ming.

and handing over his command to his successor he submissively went into exile. The Emperor was so absorbed in the amusements and revelries of the capital that he had no time to examine into the characters of the men that were essential to him at this supreme time when the stability of his house was at stake. It seemed, indeed, as though he had purposely set himself to hasten the downfall of his dynasty by pursuing a course that must inevitably alienate the hearts of his subjects from him. At the very time, for example, that a severe famine was desolating part of his very capital, and people in their hunger were actually devouring each other, the Emperor and his court were indulging in all kinds of feasts and plays, in which money and food were used in the most lavish manner.

In July, A. D. 1355, Kwo Tz-hing died, and Chu Yuan-chang succeeded to the supreme command of all the rebel forces that had been commanded by him. He now came to the determination that he would take a more decided step in advance than any that had so far been thought of, and that he would endeavour to capture the city of Nanking. The possession of this place would add to his prestige, and besides, it would be a centre from which he could operate in his conquest of the other provinces. Extensive preparations were accordingly made for the passage of the Yang-tze. In this emergency he was greatly assisted by a pirate, who lent him a thousand boats, small and great, to carry his army across.

His daring venture was completely successful: indeed it turned out to be a more easy undertaking than he had anticipated. No enemy appeared to stay his progress, and no fleet guarded the approaches to this important town, so that it fell easily before his army. In commemoration of his victory he changed the name Tsiking, which it was then called, to Ying T'ien-fu, and styling himself the Duke of Wu, he made his new conquest for the present time at least, his capital.

That his success was acceptable to the people is evident from the fact that a deputation, headed by a great scholar named T'aungan, waited on him to congratulate him on his victory. The fact is, Chu was not like the other adventurers that were now striving for mastery throughout the country. Most of them were robbers on a large scale. and sought but to enrich themselves and their followers at the expense of the regions they had occupied. Chu was a statesman, and desired not to rise to power through the miseries of the people. After his occupation of Nanking he issued proclamations through the country, telling the people that his mission was to put down rebellion and restore peace to the empire. He advised all classes of men to attend to their business and not to be alarmed by groundless fears. "The good," he declared, "should have his protection, whilst the evil would find in him a most determined enemy." Happy would it have been for Shun Ti had he been gaining the same kind of reputation that was even now securing the throne for his rival. Instead of that, a conspiracy was being formed in the palace for his deposition by Ho-ma, the same that had caused the disgrace and subsequent death of his benefactor, To-tu. Disgusted with the disgraceful conduct of the Emperor, he plotted with the crown prince for the removal of his father and the elevation of himself to the throne. The conspiracy became known, and both were banished from the capital.

In the beginning of A. D. 1357 Han-lin made an attempt to capture Shang-chow, in Shensi, but he was foiled by the Imperial troops, who compelled him to retreat. In April of the same year Chang-sz made preparations to march on Nanking. Chu, hearing of this, sent Su-ta against him, and a battle ensued, in which Chang-sz was routed with great slaughter. Su-ta pursued him as far as his capital, Ch'ang-chow. Arriving there, he sent out his brother with thirty-five thousand men to meet him. In the battle that took place Su-ta was once more victorious, and the brother was made prisoner. Chang-sz now sent officers to the camp of Su-ta to propose that there should be a treaty of peace agreed upon between them. He promised if he would release his brother to give Chu annually two hundred thousand bushels of grain and five hundred ounces of gold. Su-ta demanded five million bushels, but whilst the negotiations were proceeding Chang-sz received a private letter from his brother saying, "Make no terms with Su-ta. If you really mean to capitulate do so to the Mongols." In consequence of this Chang-sz refused to have any further communication with Su-ta, who then stormed the town and captured it; Chang-sz escaping with a remnant of his army, with which he repaired to the Mongols and surrendered to them.

The fall of this town was followed by the capture of Ling-kwoh and Yang-chow, every step thus marking a decided advance towards the goal that Chu ultimately reached. Rebellions, however, were the order of the day, and two adventurers appeared in Sz-chwan—Ch'en Yiu-liang, who styled himself King of Shuh, and Ming-yuh, who called himself King of Han. Han-lin made an attempt on K'ai-fung Fu, but he was defeated and driven back. In the year A. D. 1358 he sent a large force into Shantung under the command of Man-kwei, who took the important town of Tsi-nan Fu, and proceeding with his victorious force he captured Tientsin and advanced with his troops towards Peking. When the news of this hostile movement reached Peking there was the greatest consternation and confusion in the palace, and Shun Ti was in the greatest perplexity as to what course he should take in this unexpected emergency. Some advised him to escape to Mongolia, whilst others advised him to go to Shensi. The prime minister urged him to remain where he was, which advice, after considerable hesitation, he finally decided to carry out.

Urgent commands were at once issued for the advance of all available troops to the capital, in order to save their Emperor in this time of extreme need. Fortunately a considerable army was got together before the arrival of Mau-kwei, who was defeated and had to retreat to Shantung. This bold movement of Han-lin's general on to the capital showed the weakness of the government and the contempt in which it was held by men who were mere adventurers, and who had no hold upon the country beyond the men that had enlisted under their flags. Han-lin avenged himself for his non-success here by capturing K'ai-fung Fu, which he made his capital, and by leading a considerable body of troops, before any one was aware of his purpose, to Shang-tu, the old summer residence of Kublai, which he reduced to ashes.

In the meanwhile Chu was making decided headway in Cheh-kiang, and by his wise and generous treatment of the vanquished he established a reputation that was more serviceable than even his victories for the accomplishment of the purpose he had in view. His instructions to his generals that they should use moderation in their treatment of the people were explicit and definite. "When you take a city," he said, "you have to use force, but afterwards if you would give these people confidence you must treat them with kindness. When I captured Nanking I acted in this way, and the result was that I gained the affections of the inhabitants. The true way to obtain the sympathy of the conquered is to treat them with generosity. Any general that refrains from reckless slaughter after he has taken a city shall have my highest approbation." Chu now summoned the pirate Fang Kwoh-chin to surrender. Calling a council of his captains he asked them what reply he should return to this demand. After considerable discussion it was decided that, for the present at least, they should give in their allegiance to Chu, especially because it was seen that the Mongol power could not last long, and he seemed to be the most powerful of all the rival leaders now in the field. A message to this effect was sent to Nanking, and Wen-chow, Tai-chow and Ningpo were declared to be ready to be handed over to him, whilst Fang sent two of his sons as hostages to prove his sincerity in the submission that he was now making. The former, with a deep knowledge of human nature, returned the young men to their father, with the message that hostages were unnecessary where people were in earnest and had faith in each other. As was natural, Fang was deeply touched by this very practical display of confidence in him, and shortly after sent him a present of a horse and a magnificent saddle adorned with precious stones. Chu returned them with the declaration that he had no desire for luxuries. "My great aim," he said, "is to give peace to the empire. For this purpose I require able men, both civil and military, to assist me, and I also need corn and cloth for the use of my soldiers." In July, A. D. 1359, Ch'en-yiu captured Sin-chow, in Kiang-si, and in the beginning of the following year made an effort to gain possession of Nanking. He had a friend in the city who pretended to be a traitor, and who promised that if on a certain day he came with a sufficient force during the night he would open the gates and let them into the city, which he ought to have no difficulty in holding. He eagerly fell into the trap, but instead of having the promise fulfilled he was attacked by a body of men that was lying in ambush waiting for him, and it was with the greatest difficulty that he managed to escape with his life. Nearly about this same time Shun Ti found himself threatened with an invasion of the Mongols. Prince Ali-kwun, a descendant in the eighth generation of Og-dai, at the head of a considerable army, advanced on Peking. As he drew near he sent an officer with a message to the Emperor, saying, "Your empire belongs to your ancestors, who gave it you to be preserved intact for them. Already you have lost more than a half of it, and I now demand that you hand over to me what remains that I may govern it more wisely than you are doing now."

Shun Ti replied to this bold demand, that the empire was not at the disposal of their ancestors, but of Heaven. " If it is the will of the latter that you should be the ruler come then and take possession if you can." That he doubted that this was the case is manifest by the fact that he at once despatched all his available troops against him, and in the battle that was fought Ali-kwun was defeated and fled to Shung-tu. Next year a force of one hundred thousand men marched against him, when he was again discomfited, and being betrayed by some of his own officers he was delivered to the Emperor, who ordered him to be executed.

Chu had been so continuously successful, and had gained the hearts of the people to such an extent that he now felt able to devote more attention to the coping with the other rebel leaders that still held the field. He accordingly advanced to the attack of Kiang-chow, in Kiang-si, which Ch'en-yiu held, and after a vigorous siege carried it by storm, but he failed in getting hold of his rival, who fled to Wuchang.

During this time Ming-yuh was still playing the king in Sz-chwan, and generally extending his conquests into Yunnan. One is struck, in reading the history of these times, with the apathy that characterized the government of Shun Ti, in view of the rebellions that were rending his country from him. Instead of vigorous measures being taken, and all the forces of the empire being concentrated, in order to crush those that had risen in revolution, he seemed to be more concerned about the pleasures and enjoyments that occupied the minds of himself and his courtiers, and that were such a scandal to his people in this critical time, when every nerve should have been strained to defend his authority against those that were in arms against him. His action, too, as a ruler, in this emergency was utterly wanting in common sense. Instead of massing his troops and launching them against the enemy of his house he sent them off in expeditions in which they should never have been engaged. An instance of his folly occurred at the end of

A. D. 1362. The family of the queen, who was a Corean, was a very powerful one, but it had gained the reputation of being lawless and unruly. The king of Corea having heard of their evil practises, gave an order that a number of the worst of the clan should be put to death. News of this tragic event was brought to the queen by her brother, who had escaped the massacre. Shun Ti was induced by her to issue an edict depriving the king of Corea of his throne and giving it instead to her brother. This was done, in spite of the remonstrances of the wisest of his ministers, and ten thousand men were given to the latter, with which to enforce his claim to the throne that had been bestowed upon him. The Coreans, however, were determined that he should never reign over them, and gathering in their thousands they marched to the Ya-loo River, where they engaged the Chinese army and defeated it with such a terrible slaughter that only seventeen men escaped alive from that fatal battlefield.

In the beginning of A. D. 1363 Han-lin, who was in Shen-chow, was attacked by Chang-shih. Seeing that he was no match for him he wrote to Chu, urging him to come to his aid. This he did, but before he could arrive the city had fallen. He still continued his march, however, and recovered the town and defeated Chang-shih. Upon this Han-lin submitted to Chu and joined his forces to his. In August of this same year Chu was called upon to wage a terrible combat with the most formidable of all his rivals in the field, viz., Ch'en-yiu. The latter, who had determined to try issues with him, led his immense forces to the siege of Hung-tu. Messengers were sent post haste from that place, praying Chu to come with all speed to their rescue. Chu was a true warrior, and he knew, moreover, that before he could gain the throne of China, he must prove himself to be the superior of the only man that now could really hold the field against him. He accordingly gathered all his available forces, both of men and ships, and set out for the Poyang Lake.

Ch'en-yiu, hearing of his arrival, at once abandoned the siege of Hung-tu and hastened with his immense army and flotilla to meet him there, and for once and all settle the question which of the two was the better man. He had with him six hundred thousand men, whom he divided into eleven divisions. His large fleet was ranged in the most advantageous position, and in order to prevent their line being broken by the enemy the ships were fastened to each other by iron chains.

In spite of all the generalship of Chu and the undaunted bravery of his men they were foiled in their first attack and had to retire discomfited. They were so discouraged with their defeat that they could not be induced to engage their formidable foes again. Fortunately, soon after, a violent north-west gale began to blow, which drove the rising waves right upon the anchored fleet. Chu took advantage of the confusion that ensued and sent down

fire ships that ignited some of Ch'en's vessels.   Immediately every
nerve was strained, both by soldiers and seamen, to save their fleet.
The situation was indeed alarming.   The gale was blowing with
perfect fury, and it shrieked and howled above the swish and
roar of the waves that it sent tumultuously on the heaving ships.
To add to the terror of the scene the flames began to spread
from vessel to vessel.   The men became paralyzed, for death stared
them in the face, for the ships being lashed to each other, and the
storm being right in their teeth there was little possibility of escape.
Chu saw that the critical hour had arrived when fortune had
thrown the victory within his grasp.   Sailing down upon the
enemy with all his force he attacked him at this terrible disadvantage and gained a complete victory.   Ch'en, with some of his ships,
managed to escape to an island in the lake, where he was strictly
blockaded by Chu.   Ere long, pressed by famine, an endeavour was
made to break through the besieging force, but the attempt was
foiled, and Ch'en fell fighting, killed by an arrow that pierced one
of his eyes.   His eldest son died by his side, but the second one
was saved by Ch'en's general and carried in safety to Wuchang,
where he was proclaimed king of Han by him as successor to his
father.   The victorious army advanced on Wuchang, which they
proceeded to invest.   Chu, however, returned to Nanking, leaving
the army in charge of his generals.   After a few months' rest he
came to the relief of the besieging army with reinforcements, when
the city capitulated, and the rebellion that was begun by Ch'en
from this time practically collapsed.

About this time, viz., in the spring of A. D. 1364, to add to
the sorrows of the reigning house, serious complications took place
in the palace, caused entirely by the folly and hot-headedness of the
crown prince.   He had taken a dislike to some of the nobles in the
capital, and in order to wreak his vengeance upon them he accused
them of having entered into a conspiracy to murder the Emperor.
These men were at once seized and examined, and, Chinese-like, in
order to free themselves from suspicion they made serious charges
against each other.   The result of the investigations, however, was
to prove that there was no plot against Shun Ti, and the son
was ordered by him to let the matter drop.   This he refused to do,
and the consequence was that the greatest unrest prevailed amongst
those officials and their adherents that had unfortunately incurred
his hatred.   Amongst those accused by him was a prince of the
blood named Polo Timour, who was in command of all the troops
in Shansi.   To defend himself from this false accusation he sent a
petition to the Emperor assuring him that he was a loyal man and
true.   This enraged the prince so much that he accused him and
another prince of intriguing together against the state, and Shun Ti
was so unwise as to deprive Polo of his command and order him
into exile.   Instead of obeying this command he proceeded to lead
all his forces against the capital to settle matters with the Emperor

at the head of his soldiers. The crown prince, who had been informed of his movements, sent an army to meet him, and the two forces joined issue at the fortress of Ku-yang, when the rebels gained a decided victory, and the prince, terrified at the result, fled in consternation from the capital to Zebol. Polo now hurried on his troops to Peking, where the greatest consternation prevailed. The city gates were closed and guarded by soldiers, and the people were in a state of constant alarm, not knowing what might happen to them were the town stormed.

A high official was sent by the Emperor to the camp of Polo to ask an explanation of this armed advance on the capital. He replied that two traitors in the palace had incited the crown prince to falsely accuse him and Prince Tusin of treason, and he declared that there could be no peace until they had been sent into his camp to be punished. After some demur this was done, and the two men were executed ; the honours of which the two princes had been deprived were restored to them, and the troops were marched back again to Shan-si and the revolution was over.

Shun Ti's son now returned to the capital, but with more fierce hatred against the men that had foiled him than ever, and ere long a hundred and twenty thousand men, that would have been better employed in fighting Chu, were on their march in three great divisions to crush Polo and Tusin. In the great battle that ensued the royal army was again defeated, and a second march was made on Peking, from whence the crown prince had again fled. When they appeared in the presence of the Emperor they upbraided him with his folly, but the weak and luxurious monarch could only reply to them with tears. Polo was made prime minister, and the whole executive power committed to his hands. His first acts were to have the adherents of the prince executed and the bonzes deprived of the special privileges that Shun Ti had accorded to them. Shun Ti's son, though baffled and defeated, and an exile from his home, had not given up all hope of yet succeeding in his purpose. He was able to collect sufficient soldiers to form three distinct armies, which he proceeded to launch against the capital. Polo strained every nerve to meet his inveterate foe, but the numbers he could collect were so far inferior to those in the field that they were compelled to retreat. Fortunately for him the rainy season came on, which compelled a cessation of hostilities for several months. In the meanwhile, Polo, by his arrogance and misconduct, had raised up numerous enemies against himself, who were determined upon his destruction. These finally got the Emperor to consent to his death, and a body of soldiers having been placed in ambush, they slew him, and in October, A. D. 1365, the crown prince returned to Peking. The following year was one full of incidents and adventures of the deepest importance. During the month of March a serious overflow of the Yellow River took place, which caused an immense amount of destruction and sorrow. Tsi-nan Fu suffered especially, and its people were reduced to the direst distress by the inundation that deluged it and the region around, and which destroyed the crops, so that large numbers died from want of food. The court at Peking was too much occupied with its own intrigues and vices, either to care for calamities that were crushing the suffering, or to devise remedies for their alleviation. The Emperor, indeed, and his family seemed fatuously indifferent to the serious danger that was impending over them, not only because of the alienation of the hearts of the Chinese from them, but also because of the successes that were being achieved by Chu in the south. The latter had indeed succeeded in all the enterprises that he had undertaken. Having captured the towns of Hochow, Hangchow and Shauhing he laid siege to Suchow, where his rival, Chang-shih, was entrenched, and after a vigorous assault the place was taken by storm, and Chang-shih, having been made prisoner, was carried to Nanking, where he committed suicide. The whole of Kiangnan * thus came under his control, and as Ming-yuh had died in Sz-chwan a few months previously two formidable opponents were removed out of his way.

From this time Chu began serious preparations for the sub-jugation of the whole empire to himself and the expulsion of the Mongol dynasty from the throne of China. For this purpose he organized three powerful armies : one to operate in the south, another in the northern provinces, and the third, consisting of two hundred and fifty thousand men, under the command of the distinguished general Su-ta, to advance through Shantung on the capital. His progress through that province more resembled the triumphal march of a conqueror than a serious campaign where the opposing forces of the empire contended with him in a fierce struggle for the very existence of the state. Everywhere the cities opened their gates and submitted to the rising power. Whilst Su-ta was thus distinguishing himself in his famous march on Peking Chu's power was being conciliated in the south.

Fang Kwoh-chin, who had turned traitor and joined his forces to the Mongols, was attacked by Chu's lieutenants and suffered a severe defeat, and Wenchow and Taichow were wrested from him. Seeing no hope of success, he once more surrendered and handed over the towns of Yen-ping, Kien-ning and Fuchow to Chu's generals, whilst at the same time he sent his son as a hostage to Nanking. With the performance of these acts he vanishes from our sight and ceases for the future to have any political significance in the history of his times.

In the meanwhile the forces of Chu were everywhere victorious. Thirty-four captured cities in the province of Kwang-tung, the seizure of the capital of Kwang-si, and the triumphant entrance of Su-ta into K'ai-fung Fu, showed plainly that all serious resist-

---

* Kiangnan comprehended the two provinces of Kiangsu and Nganhwui.

ance on the part of the Mongols was no longer to be expected. The leading men about his court now insisted that he ought to take the title of Emperor. He pretended at first to be opposed to the idea, but, as may be imagined, his scruples were easily overcome, and with affected reluctance he took the coveted title and called his new dynasty the Great Ming, whilst at the same time he called himself Hung Wu. His devoted wife, who had shared his fortunes thus far, was made Empress, whilst post-humous titles and honours were accorded to his parents. All this took place in the early part of the year A. D. 1367.

As soon as Hung Wu received the joyful intelligence that K'ai-fung Fu was captured he hastened with a large body of troops to this city, for it was felt that the last act in the drama that had been played for fourteen years was now about to be enacted, and that nothing more was left to be done, excepting the march on Peking. Great was the rejoicing when Hung Wu arrived with reinforcements. The troops were filled with enthusiasm and were eager for the orders that would launch them against the Mongols. Before the army started Su-ta was called into the presence of Hung Wu to receive the final words that were to remind him of his master's wishes in the important campaign upon which he was about to enter. "The people of China," he said, "are in a great sorrow, and I wish to deliver them. They are now, as it were, in the midst of fire and flood, so dangerous is their position. The founders of the Mongol dynasty deserve remembrance for their kindness to the Chinese, but their descendants have acted so tyrannically that Heaven has cast them off, and they are hated by mankind. When Kublai took a city he destroyed all in it, but this is not my method ; you are now going to march north. Don't slaughter recklessly. Don't burn the houses of the people. Don't even think of slaying the Mongol nobles unless they resist." Su-ta bowed his head to the ground and reverently received the orders of Hung Wu. He then led his army to the bank of the Yellow River, and immediately crossed to the other side, the Mongols, to his astonishment, having made no preparations to resist him. The fact was, the ancient valour and dash that had gained them the empire had deserted them, and at this critical moment there was no general of ability who could stay the force that was marching with irresistible steps for their destruction. The greatest consternation now existed in the capital. Shun Ti, who could with difficulty drag himself away from the pleasures of the palace, sent an army against the approaching foe, but in its first encounter it was defeated with great slaughter. The Emperor now made preparations for flight, though he was advised by some of the bolder spirits to remain and fight for the inheritance that had been bequeathed to him by Kublai. At the dark hour of midnight one of the northern gates was opened, and he fled with his retinue towards the region from whence his victorious fore-fathers had come. In a few days after, Su-ta, with his immense force, approached the city, which, after a nominal resistance, was captured. Those that refused to surrender were cut down, whilst those who were content to become the subjects of the new dynasty were spared. The vast majority of the people submitted to the conqueror. There was no pillage and no unnecessary bloodshed, for the orders of Hung Wu were implicitly obeyed. Proclamations were issued throughout the city, informing the people that they and their property would be protected so long as they were quiet and remained obedient to the new masters that were now in occupation of the place. They were only too glad to be let off on such easy terms. In a few days the town resumed its old aspect, and business was carried on just as though no enemy held it, and Sung Ti was still in his palace.

As soon as the news reached Hung Wu he left K'ai-fung Fu and marched with the army he had in reserve for Peking. With his arrival the reign of the Mongol dynasty may be said to have ceased in China and that of the Ming to have commenced. That the former fell so easily can be accounted for by the fact that its rulers were men of no ability or character, but chiefly because the Mongols had never gained the confidence or respect of the Chinese. Coming from the steppes and wilds of the northern regions they had never known how to adapt themselves to the higher civilization they met in China. Overcome by the wealth and luxuries they had never been accustomed to in their own homes they became depraved and effeminate, and so by degrees they lost the bold and daring spirit that had made them victors in many a well-fought battle-field, and which, if they had still possessed, might have kept them longer on the throne of China.

CHAPTER XXX.

THE MING DYNASTY (A. D. 1368-1644).

T'ai Tsu—A. D. 1368-1399.

T'AI TSU, or as he is more familiarly called, Hung Wu, was forty years old when he obtained the empire. His first prominent act after he returned to Nanking was to constitute that city his capital, whilst K'ai-fung Fu was decreed to be the northern one. His wife, Ma-chi, in conformity with his previous decision, was announced to be empress, and his ancestors for four generations were ennobled by a royal edict that gave them titles and honours of distinction. For the better government of the country he created two additional Boards, thus increasing the number to six, the same as exist at the present day.

Hung Wu was not simply a warrior ; he was also a statesman. With his grasp of the reins of power he saw that if the country were to be made prosperous important reforms must be instituted throughout almost every branch of the public service. The Mongol rulers, unmindful of the example set them by Kublai, had spent the resources of the state, either on their own sensual indulgence or on objects of no general utility. Literature had been almost entirely neglected by them. Hung Wu began by cutting down all unnecessary expenditure. He largely reduced the number of ladies connected with the royal household, and he sternly forbade the use of public money for anything excepting what was to benefit the people.* He also gave his attention to the encouragement of education. The common schools that had been allowed to fall into decay were again re-established throughout the country, and a system was set in operation by which a supply of competent teachers could be obtained. The Hanlin Academy, too, was taken under the special protection of the Emperor, who gave its members privileges and honours that tended to elevate it in the eyes of the people and to stimulate the scholars everywhere to aim at becoming members of it. To encourage study he founded libraries in all the provincial capitals and in a good many of the other large cities of the empire. In addition to all this he appointed a commission, consisting of the most eminent members of the Academy, to write the history of the late dynasty.

---

* The Mongols had erected a magnificent tower in the city of Peking. Hung Wu went to inspect it. For a time he was silent, and then he said to the officers that followed him, " If the Mongols had paid as much attention to the comfort and happiness of their people as they did to building such costly but unnecessary structures as this they would still be the rulers of China to-day." He then gave orders that it should be razed to the ground, so that not a single trace of it should be left by which posterity could distinguish it.

To show that he was grateful to those that had distinguished themselves in the campaigns that had ended in his gaining the throne Hung Wu had a magnificent hall built in Peking, in which were placed twenty-one statues of the most famous of his generals, while vacant places were left for those who might in the future win for themselves such a name as might entitle them to a place in it. Amongst these Su-ta took the first rank, whilst Ch'ang Yu-ch'un stood second. He also selected seven scholars of great ability, who had rendered special services to the state during the revolution, and had their images placed in his own ancestral temple, where their spirits were worshipped regularly once a year.

Whilst these things were going on Su-ta, who had marched against the Mongols soon after his occupation of Peking, was gaining great successes against the Mongol Prince, K'u-k'u Timour, who by the end of A. D. 1368 was compelled to retreat into Kan-suh, leaving the whole of Shansi in the hands of the conquerors. The Japanese thought that the country was now in such a troubled state that they could easily take advantage of it for their own advantage. They accordingly landed a force on the coast of Shantung, and after ravaging the country withdrew to their ships and sailed again for home. A Mongol ex-prime minister also led a body of ten thousand men as far as T'ungchow, near Peking, but he was compelled to retreat without having accomplished anything of importance. Su-ta, with his accustomed dash and valour, decided to attack the forces that were under the command of Li Sz-chi, in Shensi. He accordingly crossed the Yellow River in April, A. D. 1369, and advanced with rapid marches against Fung-siang, which was the head-quarters of Li. Terrified by the approach of so formidable an opponent Li abandoned the city to its fate and fled to Lin-tau. Having occupied the town, Su-ta was again on his track, and capturing the cities that lay on the way, he soon appeared with his victorious soldiers before Lin-tau. Again Li's heart failed him, and preferring to surrender rather than to fight, he delivered up the town and was sent prisoner to Nanking. Whilst Su-ta was thus distinguishing himself in Shensi, Ch'ang Yu-ch'un * was gaining no less honour in the campaign that he waged with Shun Ti. With ninety thousand men he marched to T'ai-ping, where the latter was entrenched. In the battle that ensued Ch'ang seized a number of Mongol princes and slew them. He also took ten thousand soldiers prisoners and captured ten thousand chariots, three thousand horses and fifty thousand oxen, whilst the late Emperor fled to Ho-lin, in Mongolia. Two months after the unfortunate Shun Ti made another and final attempt to regain the power he had lost, and sent an army to Ta-tung, but this was routed with the loss of over ten

---

* Ch'ang Yu-ch'un at the end of the campaign returned to Nanking, where he died soon after at the early age of forty. He was a general of consummate ability, and knew better than even Su-ta himself how to handle a large army in the field. His cognomen of Ch'ang, " the Hundred Thousand," perpetuates his memory in this respect.

thousand men. The only important events that took place during the remainder of this year were the return of Su-ta from the pacification of Shensi, the receiving of tribute from the ruler of Corea, who was confirmed in his title of king, and the appointing of Fang-yang, in Nganhwui, to be the central capital of the empire.

The departure of Su-ta from the north-west provinces led K'u-k'u to believe that with his absence victory might be brought back again to the Mongol standards. He accordingly led a large army to the siege of Lanchow, where Chang-wun had been left with a comparatively small garrison. The news of this movement spread, and Yu-kwang, the commander of Kung-ch'ang, hastened with all the men he could collect to his assistance. Unfortunately, they were captured by the Mongols, who led them to one of the gates of the city and threatened Yu-kwang with immediate death if he did not pretend to the defenders that he had just got through the besieging army, and that he wanted them to open the gate and allow him to enter the city. When he got within hail of the soldiers on the wall he cried out with a loud voice, " Don't be deceived, I am a prisoner in the hands of the enemy, but you must not be discouraged, for a large army is now on the march to your deliverance. "

He was at once cut down by the enraged Mongols, but this heroic man had accomplished his purpose, for the garrison, inspirited by the news that relief was coming, fought with such vigour that the besiegers could make no impression on the city.

Not long after, Su-ta, with his famous lieutenant, Li-wun, arrived with large reinforcements, but K'u-k'u did not dare to await his approach, but retreated to the river Ch'au-url. There Su-ta came up with him, and in the great battle that took place K'u-k'u was utterly defeated with the loss of eighteen hundred officers and over eighty thousand men. He himself narrowly escaped with his life, and crossed the Yellow River on a tree that happened to be floating by. Li-wun was now sent to engage Shun Ti, who had made Ying-ch'ang his residence, but on his arrival there it was found that he was dead, and had been succeeded by his eldest son. The city soon fell before the vigorous onslaught of Li-wun's troops and became the prey of the conqueror. Though the son escaped, his wife and concubines and eldest son, Mai-teh Lipasu, as well as hundreds of mandarins, were captured, whilst amongst the booty were the great seal of the dynasty and all the regalia. The royal family were all sent prisoners to Nanking. The summer of A. D. 1370 was distingushed by a terrible drought in the north of China. The Emperor, assuming that this was due to some misconduct on his part, reformed his household and went and remained for three days by the Altar of Heaven and Earth, sleeping at night on the straw by it. As the rain did not come he set free a number of prisoners that had been unjustly accused, after which a copious downfall rejoiced the hearts of his subjects.

Towards the end of the year Su-ta and Li-wun returned to Nanking. The Emperor did them the honour of coming out to the river to receive them. A great feast was then given them, and in a set speech Hung Wu gratefully acknowledged their services and declared that it was through the instrumentality of his generals that he had been able to succeed where all his other rivals had failed.

In the beginning of A. D. 1371 Fuyuta set out with a large force for the pacification of Sz-chwan. Instead of going by the direct road he led his men through Kiaichow, which he took. He successively captured Wenchow, Mienchow and Kweichow, and finally, after incredible difficulties, Chen-tu, with which successes the contest was ended in this province. In June of next year the Mongol prince, Liang, who still ruled in Yunnan, was summoned by Hung Wu to submit. He would have done so, but for the intervention of K'u-k'u, who strongly urged him to hold out. Su-ta and Li-wun were in consequence of this sent with two distinct armies and by different routes to attack him. The results were not at all in accordance with the anticipations of every one that knew the military fame of Su-ta. At first the Mongols were everywhere successful. Twice did Su-ta attempt to carry the Mongol entrenchments, and twice was he repulsed. Compelled by the want of provisions in this desert country he had divided his force, one division of which he put under the command of T'ung-ho, which was surprised and cut to pieces in the desert. Li-wun was a little more fortunate, but still far from accomplishing the purpose for which he had come, and for the next few years incessant warfare went on, the Chinese simply holding the cultivated country, whilst the desert beyond remained in the hands of the Mongols.

The year A. D. 1373 was spent by Hung Wu in legislating for the prosperity of his people. He gave orders to the mandarins throughout the empire that kindness and justice should be conspicuous in their government of those under them. He also issued an edict that for the future men should be appointed to public offices who were known for their high character, as well as their intelligence, and who had shown themselves filial and submissive to their superiors. As a corollary to this he put a stop to the public literary examinations, as he was determined that the usual custom of giving appointments only to those who had graduated in them should cease from this time.

He soon after appointed a commission of learned men to draw up the laws of the new dynasty. As he wished these to be as brief as possible, in order to facilitate the administration of justice, they consisted of the small number of six hundred and six. In the early part of A. D. 1374 the Japanese again made a descent on the coasts of China. A fleet was sent after them under the command of Wu-ching, who pursued them as far as the Loochow islands and managed to capture a number of them. This so terrified them that they ceased their depradations, and for a long time they made no more descents on China.

For the next few years the empire remained comparatively at peace. K'u-k'u, the great leader of the Mongols, died, but still the latter kept up their periodical incursions into China, only to return, however, with their plunder when the Chinese armies appeared on the field. In A. D. 1381 the invasion became so serious that Su-ta and Fuyuta were both despatched against them, when they were once more driven back into their savage wilds utterly defeated. After this decided success Fuyuta was sent into Yunnan against Prince Liang with a force of three hundred thousand men. In three months the campaign was over. The defeated prince fled into Burmah, where he committed suicide. With his death the whole of Yunnan came under the control of the Ming dynasty. The early training of Hung Wu seems now to have had a baneful influence on his mind, for in spite of the protests of his ministers he began to employ Buddhist priests in his great councils and in the government of his people.

His wife, who had always exercised a happy controlling power over her husband, died in September, A. D. 1382. On her death-bed she warned him against faith in the idols, and urged him to follow the advice of the loyal men that had the interests of the empire at heart. A great funeral was given her, and all her sons came to the capital to be present. When they returned to their governments Hung Wu gave each of them a bonze to be their confidential advisers, thus showing how little he remembered the warning that his wife had given him.

In the beginning of A. D. 1385 Su-ta died. The Emperor was deeply affected, and for several days mourned and wept for him. He was the greatest of the generals that had helped him to the throne, and he was in every respect worthy of the admiration and esteem in which he was universally held. He was not merely a general of the highest ability ; he was also a scholar. The disorders of the times had not spoiled him, nor had his successes inflated him, for the historian is careful to record that he was a singularly modest man and one that had no love for money.

At the close of this year the Burmese renounced their allegiance to China, and to show that they were in earnest they despatched a hundred thousand men into Yunnan and commenced to take possession of that province. The imperial troops were totally inadequate to cope with such an immense force, and they were defeated with great loss. Three years later, however, this disgrace was avenged by the complete overthrow of the Burmese, with the loss of forty thousand men and the immediate payment of tribute to the Emperor as an acknowledgment of the supremacy of China. A formidable invasion of the Mongols under the leadership of one of their chiefs, named Nakochu, now took place (A. D. 1386). They marched into Manchuria and began to ravage the country and capture the cities that came in their way. A force of two hundred thousand men was hurried forward to meet them under the supreme command of Fuyuta. One of his generals, Lan-yu, having marched to within a short distance of the Mongols with the division under his command, Nakochu, under the pretence of submitting to him, but really for the purpose of seeing for himself the strength of his enemy, came into his camp with a few of his officers.

A few words dropped by him to one of these let out his secret to Lan-yu, who understood Mongol, and who suddenly drew his sword and wounded him in the shoulder. He was at once made prisoner and sent to Fuyuta. The Mongols now surrendered to the number of two hundred thousand men, whilst an immense booty of money and horses fell to the victorious Chinese.

In order to make the victory more complete Fuyuta determined to capture, if possible, the son of Shun Ti, and at one blow crush the one power that had any semblance of right to compete with the new dynasty. He accordingly sent Lan-yu with a large force to Payu-url, where he heard he was encamped, but when he reached there no traces of him could be found.

He was thinking of returning unsuccessful, but was prevented by one of his captains, who represented the disgrace of such an action and the shame that would come upon him and his large army if he did so. A further advance was made, but this time more cautiously. He travelled only by night, and during the day the fires required for cooking were made in holes in the ground, so that no ascending smoke might let the enemy know where they were. In this way they surprised the large encampment they sought. In the engagement that took place the Mongols were defeated, but Shun Ti's son, Oyusili, managed to escape. His wife and concubines, however, were captured, as well as seventy thousand Mongols and one hundred and fifty thousand horses, oxen, camels and sheep. The royal prisoners were sent to Nanking, and Oyusili, having been murdered shortly after by one of his officers, the Mongol dynasty came to a disastrous end.

The year A. D. 1390 saw the enactment of a terrible tragedy in the capital. Li-shan had been one of those that had helped the Emperor to his throne and had performed such signal services that he was made a duke, and a daughter of Hung Wu had been given in marriage to his son. He was now old, and his soldiers, taking advantage of his age, became overbearing in their treatment of the people.

Some one who had a grudge against the old general whispered into the ear of the Emperor that he was meditating rebellion. Without investigating his case he was seized and put to death, as well as over seventy of his clan, whilst his son was sent into banishment. He was, however, recalled upon the discovery that the information that had resulted in the death of so many innocent persons was false.

The Emperor now thought of removing his capital to Peking, and sent his son to examine into its feasibility and report to him.

This he did, and returned to Nanking with a plan of the city, but in the course of a few months he died, to the extreme sorrow of his father and the regret of the nation. Hung Wu now made a vigorous effort to have his fourth son, the Prince of Yen, recognized as his heir, but the opposition of his ministers and leading men was so decided that he had to give up his purpose, and his grandson was appointed instead. The Prince Yen, who was an exceedingly ambitious man, and aimed at succeeding his father, determined to have his revenge upon those who had thwarted his plans. He accordingly made a special journey, from his government in Chihli to the capital, to see his father. Knowing his jealous disposition he whispered into his ear his suspicions of the loyalty of the great generals and statesmen that had helped to found the new dynasty. He represented them as being proud and arrogant and ready to rebel as soon as he was dead, indeed, even before then, if severe repressive measures were not speedily adopted. The old man nodded his head to his crafty son, thus intimating that he was determined to be on the watch against a foe that he had not suspected before.

An opportunity only too soon occurred for the display of that vengeful passion that had been awakened by the prince. Lan-yu, who had not been rewarded sufficiently, as he thought, for the distinguished services he had performed, had for some time meditated disloyal thoughts. He became imperious, and trusting to his power over the soldiery, seized upon some land belonging to a citizen. When remonstrated with by the censor for his unjust and arrogant conduct, he drove him from his house with blows and insults. This was reported to the Emperor ; orders were at once issued for his seizure. When he came to be examined he showed his craven spirit by implicating sixty or seventy of the old comrades in arms of the Emperor, though very few indeed had ever thought of rebellion. He was explicit in his statement that they had all agreed to murder the Emperor when he went out in spring to perform the royal ceremony of ploughing. In the suspicious mood of Hung Wu the guilt of all was at once accepted, without any care being taken to investigate the charges that had been so recklessly made by an unscrupulous man. Lan-yu, with all his relatives, as well as the implicated men, with all the members of their clans that could be seized, were put to death ; so that fully fifteen thousand men and women died a horrible death, mainly to appease the jealousy of an old man, whose fears had been kindled by the cunning hatred of a disappointed son.

In consequence of the discovery of this supposed plot to overthrow the dynasty an order was issued throughout the empire that all military weapons should be handed over to the government, and that those who refrained from doing so, or who were found in possession of such after a certain date, should be held guilty of high treason and be liable to be treated as rebels and traitors.

So completely had the belief taken hold of Hung Wu's mind that a widespread conspiracy actually existed that not very long after the terrible tragedy above described had been enacted, Fuyuta and eleven other eminent officers, who had performed distinguished services for the Emperor, were put to death by his orders.

In the year A. D. 1395 Hung Wu composed and issued a treatise, consisting of thirteen different subjects, which he hoped would be of service to his children in the government of the empire after he was gone. It was printed and distributed amongst the officials of the eighteen provinces, who were all required to master its contents and to carry out all its requirements, as far as they were concerned, under penalty of the severest punishment should they neglect to do so.

A hostile movement in A. D. 1396 amongst the Mongols was sternly repressed by Prince Yen, who moved across the frontiers with a formidable force and obtained a great victory over their army before they could reach Chinese territory. Another in Kwei-chow, two years later, of the aborigines of the soil was also crushed by two of the Emperor's sons, who were sent against the rebels and who completely routed them and recovered the two cities that had been captured by them. A rebellion, too, in Burmah, which caused its king to fly into China and demand protection from the Emperor, was successfully overcome by the intervention of the Chinese, who placed the fugitive sovereign again upon his throne and put to death the traitor that had dared to assume the royal title for himself. In the month of June, A. D. 1399, Hung Wu became very ill, and in a month he was dead. Before he died he made a will, leaving his throne to his grandson and forbidding his sons, who might come to his funeral, to enter the capital. He was fearful that disorders might arise if they came, and that with his strong hand absent to restrain them the ambition of some of them might precipitate a contest that might be injurious to the interests of his house. He was buried in the country of Shang-yuan, in Kiang-nan, at the age of seventy-one.

Hwei Ti—A. D. 1399-1403.

Unfortunately the young Emperor, who was only sixteen years of age, had not sufficient experience or ability to cope with Prince Yen, who still entertained the ambitious thought of possessing the throne for himself.

He was, moreover, of a filial and affectionate disposition, and felt himself utterly indisposed to treat his uncle with any kind of harshness. When the president of the Board of War advised that some of the troops under his command should be sent to other parts of the empire so that he should have less power to rebel, Hwei Ti refused to take any action in the matter, and desired that all reference to the subject should be avoided.

Unfortunately the young sovereign adopted as his advisers two men who were totally unfit for such a responsible position, and who were the sources of infinite trouble and sorrow to him. These were Tsi-tai and Wang Tze-ting. By their advice his uncle, Prince

Chow, was seized and deprived of all his titles and reduced to the level of a common citizen. Prince Yen, who was own brother to Chow, encouraged by his confidential adviser, To-yen, began now to make vigorous preparations for the conflict that he saw was inevitable, and trained his soldiers day and night, so that they might be efficient when they took the field. The Emperor got information of this, and sent a high mandarin to his residence to watch his movements, whilst at the same time some of the prince's soldiers were ordered away from Peking to Shansi.

The year A. D. 1400 was a troublous one for Hwei Ti. News was brought that his uncle, Prince Shang, was about to rebel in Kiangnan. He was seized, and in order to avoid the disgrace of an examination he threw himself into the fire and was burnt to death. Two other uncles—Tsi and Tai—were stripped of their titles and deprived of all their honours. Prince Yen, who was not quite ready to begin the contest, dissembled, and in order to remove suspicion sent three of his sons to Nanking.

Their kind-hearted cousin, instead of detaining them, sent them back with presents to their father, who, instead of being moved by his generosity, was confirmed in his purpose of rebellion, as he considered the return of his sons an indication from Heaven that his designs were sanctioned by it.

In the month of August, finding that events had transpired that made it impossible for him to dissemble any longer, he raised the standard of rebellion, and with between thirty and forty thousand men marched into Shantung. An army of three hundred thousand soldiers was immediately sent under the command of King Ping-wun to meet these, but in the engagement that took place the royal troops found they were no match for the rebels, who were led by more skilful generals than they possessed. As a punishment for his want of success Ping-wun was displaced in his command by Li King-lung, who, seeing himself at the head of six hundred thousand men, led them into the province of Chihli and encamped at Ho-chien. Prince Yen was delighted beyond measure when he heard that this huge army was under the control of a man that had never learned the art of war, and who consequently was utterly incompetent to manœuvre such a large body of men in the presence of an enemy, and he felt that victory was as surely within his grasp as though he had already obtained it.

Li advanced with his immense force to the attack of Ying-ping, which the prince had left in the charge of his son, with strict orders to act on the defensive only. The assault on the city, which was made by a captain named Ku-nung, was so vigorous that it was about to fall, when Li, jealous of his success, ordered him to retire from the attack. Most fatal for him was this ungenerous treatment of his lieutenant, for soon after the Prince of Yen advanced with all the forces he had been able to collect, and launching them upon the imperial army a terrible conflict ensued.

Whilst the fighting was going on the gates of Ying-ping were thrown open, and every soldier that could be spared from the defence of the city was marched out to assist in the battle that was being fought.

Li, who lacked all the qualities of a true general, was utterly unprepared for this, and the result was his army was thrown into confusion. His men and officers, who had no confidence in him, lost heart, and in order to save the entire army from destruction a retreat was ordered. This movement in the face of an enemy so well officered and already flushed with success was most disastrous. When Li reached the city of Teh-chow it was found that two-thirds of this immense force had disappeared, whilst the loss of his enemy had been but comparatively slight.

The prince now sent a demand to the Emperor that his two advisers, who had shown such implacable hostility to him, should be put to death. Hwei Ti promised to comply with this request, but with fatal persistence he still continued to confide in them and to be guided by their advice. Eight months after the defeat at Ying-ping Li had been so largely reinforced that he felt strong enough to advance from Teh-chow to the river Peh-keu, near which the prince's forces lay encamped.

The latter crossed with a large division of his troops, but they were repulsed with great slaughter, and he returned with only three men, who with himself managed to escape alive from the conflict. At this juncture his son arrived with large reinforcements, when the battle was once more resumed. In order to disconcert the imperialists burning arrows were shot into their encampment, which set on fire their tents, and as a great storm was blowing at the time they were soon in a blaze. A panic now seized upon the army, so that every semblance of discipline was lost in the mad endeavour of each man to save his life by escaping from the advancing foe. The soldiers trod upon each other in the fierce struggle to flee, and vast numbers perished. The prince's soldiers had simply to slay, for excepting in individual cases, where the captains did not lose their heads, and had managed to hold together the men under their command, there was no resistance made to them. Amidst the wildest confusion the beaten army fled to Teh-chow, followed by the prince, and so great was the terror inspired by him that Li immediately evacuated it, and when he found he was pursued, retreated still further on to Tsi-nan-fu. Teh-chow, which was well provisioned, fell into the hands of the victorious army, after which an immediate pursuit was made after Li, who was so terrified when he heard the news that he abandoned Tsi-nan-fu, though strongly fortified, and leaving it under the charge of a brave captain, named Shing yang, he fled to Nanking.

In the meanwhile the prince had arrived before the walls of the town, which he expected would at once capitulate to him. In this, however, he was mistaken. Shing-yang was a man of mettle and not so easily terrified as his commander-in-chief. When summoned to surrender he replied that he would do so if the prince would come personally with his staff and take possession of the town. This he consented to do, and part of his escort had already passed over the drawbridge, and the fore legs of his horse were actually on it, when it was suddenly lifted up, and he and it were thrown violently to the ground. By some mistake the bridge had been raised too soon, and the stratagem of the commander to seize the prince was thus foiled. In revenge for this a fierce assault was kept up on the city day and night, and it would undoubtedly have fallen, but news was brought that an army under Ping-ngan was on its way to the attack of Teh-chow. The prince at once broke up his camp and marched to its relief. The valiant Shing-yang followed with all his forces, and attacking the retreating army, gained a decided victory over it, and Teh-chow being thus left to its fate speedily surrendered to the besieging force.

The prince now led his army against Tong-chang, but the two generals in charge—Chin-yung and Tieh-huen—so manœuvred the forces under their charge that they managed to surround the prince, who was thus placed in extreme peril. In the battle that ensued he suffered a great defeat, and if it had not been for the positive orders of the Emperor that his life should be held sacred, he would have been slain at this time.

As soon as Hwei Ti heard of these signal successes he recalled Tsi-tai and Wang Tze-ting to the palace, and once more submitted himself to their guidance. The prince of Yen was so discouraged by the ill-fortune that he had met with that he proposed to give up the contest and retire from the field. In this, however, he was opposed by To-yen, who predicted that from this time victory would certainly attend his arms. He accordingly made preparations for another campaign and marched to meet Chin-yung, who had two hundred thousand men under his command.

In the battle that ensued the prince on the first day again suffered a severe repulse, and would have been slain but for the orders of the Emperor that restrained the hands of his generals. On the morrow, however, when it was renewed, the tide of fortune completely changed. A storm was blowing that drove the dust into the faces of the imperialists. This greatly distressed them. The prince's soldiers being northern men were well accustomed to such experiences, and therefore fought as well as usual. As the storm continued to rage the imperialists soon lost all heart for battle, and they began to fly before their enemies. Soon all order and discipline were lost, and a panic having seized upon the men, they fled precipitately towards the river Hu-to, in which a large number of them were drowned.

Chin-yung, with a division of the troops that he had been able to hold in hand, fled to Teh-chow, and so demoralized had his men become by the crushing defeat they had suffered that they did not feel themselves safe until they stood behind the protection of its walls.

When the news of these disasters reached Hwei Ti he dismissed his two unpopular advisers and publicly proclaimed that all their estates were confiscated.

This, however, was not true, but was meant only to propitiate his uncle and incline him to leniency in the use of his victory. At the same time he sent urgent messages thoroughout his dominions for the advance on the capital of all the soldiers that could be spared from the various provinces in which they were stationed. In the month of April, A. D. 1402, Ping-ngan arrived with reinforcements from Shensi, but unfortunately he had to retreat again to the same province with the loss of sixty thousand men, for the same reason that had brought such disaster on Chin-yung. The prince, who had heard of the dismissal of Tsi-tai and Wang Tze-ting, sent an ambassador to his nephew, proposing that they should both withdraw their armies from the field and sign conditions of peace. The Emperor, who seemed to be the sport of ill-advisers, instead of frankly accepting this proposal and carrying it out, dissimulated, and whilst professing pleasure at the conditions suggested, sent secret orders to Ping-ngan to hurry on with a considerable division of the troops under his command by bye-ways and unfrequented roads to Peking, and, menacing the prince's dominions, compel him to retreat. At the same time he sent a letter to the prince, declaring that he fully forgave him and his son for the rebellion they had been engaged in, and ordered him to return to his own government. The prince, suspecting the honesty of his nephew, and seeing no movement amongst his troops to return home, instead of obeying this command, organised a movement to cripple his enemy by the destruction of his supplies for the army. He had six thousand of his men dressed in the clothes of the imperialist soldiers that he had captured, and boldly advancing to the river where the boats lay, he was able to set fire to the whole and destroy all the provisions they contained. This was a great blow to the enemy, who were dependent on them for very existence ! Soon after this news arrived of the raid of Ping-ngan on Peking, and of his defeat by the garrison of that city and his retreat into Shansi.

The prince, now convinced that no terms could be kept with one that was so insincere as the Emperor, gave orders to his troops to march south (A. D. 1403).

General Su was sent to Shantung to oppose this movement and in a battle that took place the prince was defeated. His soldiers now became dissatisfied, and insisted upon being led home, and it required the exercise of all his authority to prevent them from deserting their colours and giving up a struggle in which they had suffered so many reverses.

In order to divert their minds from their present sorrows he led them to Pu Tze-keu, where Chin-yung was encamped, and boldly attacked him. The result was unfavourable, and would have ended in a great disaster, but his second son fortunately arrived at this critical moment with large reinforcements, which enabled him to retrieve the fortunes of the day and defeat the almost victorious enemy. Now confident of success he marched his troops, flushed with victory, against Ho-fuh, the successor of General Su, and routed his army with great slaughter. Without permitting any delay he crossed the river Hwai and captured the important city of Yang-chow. When the news of these rapid successes reached Nanking the utmost consternation prevailed in the palace. Orders were hurriedly sent in every direction commanding the great mandarins to hurry up all the troops under their command to the help of the capital. Hwei Ti, too, despatched the prince's sister to meet him on his march and to endeavour to get him to come to peaceable terms with him, offering him as an inducement a considerable amount of territory, over which he should rule with independent powers. The prince rejected all offers of accommodation and declared that he would not rest until he was in Nanking.

Hwei Ti was now in despair and thought of flight, but Fang Hau-vu dissuaded him from this and advised him to wait for the troops that were being sent to his relief. The prince, however, was determined that he would reach Nanking before they did, and so he pressed onward with the most urgent haste. Victory attended his arms whenever he engaged with the enemy, and Mei-yin and Chin-yung had to retreat in disgrace before his victorious troops. Nothing could stay his march, and in the month of August he was before the gates of Nanking.

Li-king, the general in charge of these, at once opened them and surrendered the city to him. His first order was that the palace should be set on fire. This was done, and the queen and a considerable number of the ladies of the household perished in the flames. Search was made for the body of the Emperor, and at last a charred and disfigured corpse was brought, which was declared to be his. The prince, on beholding it, burst into tears, and commanded that a royal funeral should be given it. That this was not the body of the unfortunate Emperor is evident from the fact that he escaped to Sz-chwan and lived there as a Buddhist priest for many years. *

---

* The story of his escape is as follows : On the approach of the prince's army the Emperor proposed to get out of the difficulty by cutting his throat. This was opposed by a eunuch of the name of Wang, who declared that his father, Hung Wu, had left a chest in his charge, with orders that it should be opened should any great crisis occur during the life-time of his son. " Let us open it at once then," cried Hwei Ti, " and see what my father would do were he here now." When the lid was lifted up it was found to contain the full dress of a Buddhist priest, a diploma, a razor and ten ingots of silver. The young ruler at once took the hint, and escaping by an underground passage with about a score of attendants he reached a temple outside the city. There he was shaved and arrayed in his new robes, and a boat having been prepared for him, he sailed away up the Yang tze and never stopped till he had found refuge in the obscurity of a temple in Sz chwan. There he lived for forty years, till discovered by some poetry he had made he was brought to Peking during the reign of Ying Tsung and died a state prisoner in the palace shortly after.

The Prince of Yen now behaved with the utmost cruelty and barbarity to those who had been loyal to his unfortunate nephew, and pursued them with the most retentless savagery. All the great men that had helped Hung Wu to the throne were sought out, and those that had not already committed suicide, to avoid an ignominious death, were slain in the most cruel way. Not content with the murder of these individuals who had committed no crime except that of being faithful to the new dynasty, he ordered that all their relatives, both by the father's and mother's side, should be seized and executed. Fang Hau-yu, for example, whose life would have been spared had he been content to serve the prince, was put to death because he refused to write out the edict that declared his accession to the throne in the place of the late Emperor, and eight hundred and seventy-three of his relatives and some of his scholars perished at the same time.

At length, wearied of this wholesale butchery, and finding no more prominent subjects on which to wreak his vengeance, he stayed his hand. His friends now urged upon him to proclaim himself Emperor, and after going through the farce of pretending that he had no desire for such an exalted position, he at length allowed himself to be proclaimed sovereign of China.

Ch'eng Tsu—A. D. 1403-1425.

Amongst the first public acts of the new ruler was the restoration of his brothers—Chow, Tsi, Tai and Min—to their former rank and honours from which they had been degraded by their nephew. He also elevated to high positions and gave splendid presents to thirty of those who had fought by his side and had helped him to final victory over his late foes. Li-king, who had opened the gates of the capital for him, was also rewarded with high office. This, however, proved his ruin, for some of the officials, jealous of this, whispered into the Emperor's ear that he was meditating rebellion. Suspicious and cruel by nature he listened with avidity to these slanders. He had him seized and cast into prison, and in spite of his entreaties for mercy he was put to death within the precincts of it.

The empire was now practically at peace, for though the Mongol tribes on the north had shown themselves restless during the time the revolution was going on, the Chinese forces had been quite competent to keep them in restraint.

In the year A. D. 1406 a tragedy took place in Tonquin which finally led to intervention by the Chinese and the march of their troops into that country. An ambitious minister, of the name of Li-kwei, had first killed his king, and shortly after his son, whom he had put on the throne in succession to his father, and had then become sovereign himself.

In order to divert the anger of the Chinese Emperor he sent an embassage to him, declaring that the king had died, and having no one to succeed him the people had desired him to become their ruler, and he humbly prayed that imperial consent should be given to this. Ch'eng Tsu, unsuspecting, at once gave his permission, but next year a grandson of the murdered king arrived at the capital and implored him to redress the wrongs that his family had suffered at the hands of the usurper.

The Emperor, indignant at having been deceived, sent a large escort with the young prince to Tonquin, but every man in it was slain by a body of troops that Li-kwei had ordered to intercept them. Ch'eng Tsu was highly enraged when the news of this tragedy reached him, and he despatched a large army under the command of Chu-nung and Chang-fu to avenge the insult that had been offered to his authority. The former died on the way, so that the expedition finally remained under the orders of the latter.

When he reached the river Fu-liang he found it filled with stakes which the enemy had stuck in it, so as to prevent its being crossed by the Chinese. These he burnt by means of fire rafts, and finding no further opposition from the enemy he and his army passed over in safety. In a great battle that subsequently ensued the Tonquinese were routed with great slaughter, and the usurper was made a prisoner. Search was now made for the heirs to the throne, and as none could be found it was determined to annex the country to China. Thus, after the lapse of many ages, viz., since the time of the Han dynasty, Tonquin became once more a dependency of the Chinese empire.*

The following year, A. D. 1408, was distinguished by a raid which was made by the Japanese on the Chinese coast and the despatch of a fleet under the command of Chen-suan to meet them ; and also of an insurrection of the Tonquinese. The leader of the latter declared he was of royal blood and entitled to the throne. He took several cities, and it was not till the close of the following year that peace was again restored to the country. In the meanwhile there was a movement amongst the Mongols that boded no good to the empire. Though Ch'eng Tsu had rewarded those who had sided with him in his great struggle for power, there were still amongst them leading men of great ambition who looked upon the throne of China as belonging to their nation. It was found necessary this year to send an army of one hundred thousand men under general Kiu-fuh to engage the Mongols who were gathering in force with the evident intention of crossing the frontiers over into China. This man allowed himself, either through want of generalship, or through contempt of his enemy, to be surrounded by them, and he and nearly all the men under his command were massacred. The Emperor was exceedingly indignant at this, and as he could not wreak his vengeance on the unfortunate general, he banished his

---

* The country was now divided into fifteen prefectures, forty-one departments, and two hundred and eighty hiens or counties. The population was then estimated at thirty-one millions two hundred thousand.

widow and her children to a distant part of the empire. Next year he himself led an army of five hundred thousand men into Mongolia and obtained a great victory over the combined forces of the Mongols in the western part of the country. He then marched eastwards and engaged the army under Alutai, when success again attended his arms. He then returned to Peking, his army laden with plunder, where he rewarded those that had shown conspicuous valour in the late campaign.

The disasters that had occurred to the Mongols had so crushed their spirits that for four years no military movement threatening China was observed amongst them. At the end of that time, however (A. D. 1414), such strong symptoms of rebellion were manifest amongst them that the Emperor, leaving the control of affairs to his eldest son, led an army against them, when they were once more defeated, and a great number of their warriors slain.

Family troubles now began to disturb the concluding years of Ch'eng Tsu's reign. His brother Hwei raised the standard of rebellion (A. D. 1417), but was seized and reduced to the rank of a common citizen. His second son, too, by name Kau-hu, behaved in the most reckless manner, and allowed a body of soldiers, whom he had privately enlisted in his service, to plunder the people. When a high mandarin, who was appealed to on the subject, asked him for an explanation, he struck him dead with the blow of a hammer, and going from the presence of the murdered man assumed the title of Emperor. His father would have put him to death, but his eldest brother interceded for him, and he was banished from the capital to Yo-ngan, in Shantung. News soon after this reached the capital that another revolution had taken place in Tonquin, and once more an army had to be despatched to that distant dependency to reassert the royal authority. Next year, A. D. 1419, the Japanese sent a force into Liau-tung, but they were compelled to retreat without effecting anything worthy of the attempt that had been made by them.

The Emperor, who had long contemplated the removal of the capital to Peking, carried out his purpose in A. D. 1421. Great opposition was made to this in various quarters, but especially by the inhabitants of that city. They had been greatly impoverished by the incessant wars that had been carried on around it, and they felt themselves inadequate to sustain the burdens that would be laid upon them in the erection of the palaces and other royal buildings that would be required for the use of the Emperor and the government officials. Their opposition, however, was speedily over-ruled, for in a despotic country like China it is the will of the sovereign that is supreme, and not that of the voice of the people.

Hardly had Ch'eng Tsu got settled in his new capital, when he had to lead an army into Mongolia to chastise Alutai, who refused to recognize him as his suzerain, and who declined paying the customary tribute to him. The Chinese forces soon brought him to reason, and a serious reverse made him for the time submit to the conqueror. A year hence, however, the lesson had again to be repeated, and though another disaster attended his conflict with the Chinese power, in the beginning of A. D. 1424, not only had he gathered a large army about him, but he actually led it across the frontiers into the very territories of the man who had so often inflicted defeat upon him. The Emperor, though afflicted with a grievous malady, led another army against his indomitable opponent, and once more gained a decisive victory over him, and caused him to retreat into his own country. On his return from this successful campaign he became so ill that he was unable to proceed home, and he died at Yu-muh-ch'wan at the age of sixty-five, after a reign of twenty-two years. Before his death he gave orders that his eldest son should succeed him on the throne, and that he himself should be buried in the same manner as his father had been. These two directions were carried out in the manner he desired, and the heir became Emperor and reigned in his father's stead.

Jen Tsung—A. D. 1425-1426.

This prince was forty-seven years old when he came to the throne, and he reigned only a little over nine months. This was unfortunate for his people, for he was a man of rare virtues and full of tenderness and sympathy.

It was said at the time that if Heaven had but increased the number of his years he would have been equal in character and reputation to the greatest of China's sages. He died during the absence of his eldest son, who had been sent to Nanking for the purpose of making arrangements for the transfer back of the capital to that city. Hearing of his father's death he returned with all haste to Peking, when he ascended the throne without opposition, though at one time it seemed as though his uncle, Kau-hu, the second son of Ch'eng Tsu, was preparing to claim this honour for himself.

Suan Tsung—A. D. 1426-1436.

The first and most pressing question that the young Emperor, who was only twenty-seven, had to deal with was Tonquin, where another revolution had broken out. Some argued that China should cease to rule it directly ; that it should be handed over to native rulers and a tribute be received from it. The difficulty of governing a place so far removed from the seat of power had been found very great, besides it had always controlled its own affairs, excepting during the Han dynasty. Others again held that after so much blood and money had been expended in conquering it, it would be a great disgrace to retire from the field so soon and give up so large and important a country. The Emperor was in favour of the former proposition, and his mind was still further confirmed in his opinion by three successive defeats that happened to the royal forces. Accordingly, when the army returned to China from the last campaign, about the close of the year A. D. 1427, orders were given that the government of the country should be handed over to the natives, and that China for the future should simply act as overlord and receive tribute from it.

Kau-hu, the Prince of Han, who had been secretly meditating rebellion for some time, now began to show his hand. He had been slowly gathering around him a body of soldiers that had gradually become very considerable in numbers. He sent a confidential agent to Peking, and requested Chang-fu to open the gates for him, with the promise that he would make him a high mandarin. This general, instead of listening to this traitorous suggestion, handed over the letter he had received to the Emperor, who led an army to Yo-ngan against him. Instead of fighting with the courage of a brave man he showed the craven spirit and deserted his followers, who urged upon him that he should now fight to the very death, whilst they would do the same for him. He gave himself up to the Emperor, who made him prisoner and carried him to Peking. No fewer than six hundred and forty of his adherents were put to death, whilst over fifteen hundred were sent into banishment. Shortly after the prince was executed in prison, and the rebellion, which might have assumed most dangerous proportions had he possessed the ability and daring of his father, was crushed at the very commencement.

The Emperor now decided upon a most important step that was destined in days to come to have the most disastrous effect upon the fortunes of the dynasty, and that was the education of the eunuchs. He commanded four of the most eminent scholars of the academy, with assistants of less celebrity, to become their teachers and take charge of the education of all those in the palace under twelve years of age. The numbers at first were between three and four hundred, but by and by they increased to nearly five hundred. They received, of course, first-class instruction, and many of them, having good abilities, were able, when they grew up, to take a commanding position in the palace, which was used not for the interests of the nation, but for themselves and their class.

The next few years of Suan Tsung's reign were marked by no event of any great national importance. The most striking thing in the life of the Emperor was his putting away his queen, who was childless, and the elevation of a favourite concubine, who pretended that she had had a son born to her, and whom she got Suan Tsung to recognize as his own. His ministers were exceedingly opposed to the deposition of the empress, but the Emperor, influenced by love for the beautiful woman, who he believed had brought him an heir to the throne, was determined in his purpose, and had it carried out. He died in the early part of the year A. D. 1435, greatly regretted by his people and all that knew him. He was a man of excellent abilities and of good character.   He was both a statesman and a scholar, and ruled the country well and wisely.   He appointed the son, whose birth had brought such happiness to him, his successor, and he died, leaving his country in peace and prosperity, mainly through his wise government during the ten years he had been permitted to reign over it.

Ying Tsung—A. D. 1436-1450.

It was supposed by every one that the mother of the late Emperor, whose influence was great in the palace, would set aside his will and place her second son on the throne instead of the boy about whose birth there was such doubt and suspicion.   When the ministers approached her to learn her will in this matter she distinctly declared that she had no intention of doing any such thing.   They then invited her to act as regent during the young Emperor's minority.   This she consented to do, but only in conjunction with five of the great ministers who were to act as her great council, one of whom, Yang Sz-ch'i, was to be prime minister.   Under the present circumstances this was no doubt the best possible arrangement that could have been decided upon.   Chang-chi was a woman of specially good abilities and of a high moral character and of great determination of mind. It very soon became manifest that, however she might be willing to admit others to a share with her in the executive, the supreme power should always remain in her own hands.   She plainly showed this by her treatment of Wang-chin, a eunuch who was greatly beloved by the young prince.   Presuming on his influence with him he began to interfere in matters of state, so as to incur the resentment of the prime minister.   At an audience presided over by her, she addressed the young Emperor and said, "These five great officers were chosen by your father for their wisdom and fidelity.   When-ever you want advice appeal to them, but be sure to avoid having anything to do with Wang-chin."   This latter was then called into her presence, when she proceeded to tell him that he was worthy of death for his daring to meddle in state affairs.   Waxing more furious as she continued to dwell on his wrongs she declared he should die then and there.   Calling the ladies of her household she told them to arm themselves with knives and fall upon him.   The Emperor, seeing the danger of his favourite, knelt down and besought the regent to spare his life, and the other members of the council joining their entreaties to his, the eunuch was dismissed with the command for the future to confine himself to his own business.

During the year A. D. 1440 an old bonze, ninety years of age, declared that he was the Emperor Hwei Ti, who had escaped from Nanking when it was surrendered to his uncle, the Prince of Yen. On investigation of the matter he was found to be an impostor, but the result of the searching enquiries that were made was that Hwei

Ti was discovered to be still alive, and that he had been living all these years in a monastery in Sz-chwan. Orders were at once despatched to the viceroy of that province that he should be escorted with all honour to Peking, and when he arrived there apartments were given him in the palace, which he occupied till his death. In the middle of A. D. 1441 a rebellion took place in Burmah, and an army of one hundred and fifty thousand men was despatched there, which speedily suppressed it, and thus peace was restored to the country. In the meantime Wang-chin seems to have forgotten the severe lesson that had been given him in the palace, and using his growing influence with the Emperor, had the hardihood on one occasion to imprison the governor-generals of Shansi and Honan, because they did not pay him proper respect when they came to the capital to have an audience with the Emperor.

Next year the Emperor married, and rejoicings were made throughout the empire. The close of it was marred by a great sorrow that afflicted the people of the capital, caused by the death of the regent, who had been ailing for some time. Wang-chin, who had been kept in some restraint by her, now began to act in the most imperious and domineering fashion. A member of the academy, who dared to suggest that the temple of Heaven and Earth had been struck with lightning as a reproof for the iniquities perpetrated by him, was imprisoned and murdered within the jail.

Several years passed by without anything of importance happening in the country. The year A. D. 1449, however, was destined to show a different record. The Mongols, who for a long time had been comparatively quiet, crossed over the border in great force under the leadership of Wei-la-teh into Kansuh and began to ravage the country.* An immense army of over half a million of men was despatched under the command of Wang-chin to meet the enemy, and the Emperor, in spite of the remonstrances of his council, was persuaded to accompany him.

The movement by this time had become more general amongst the Mongols, and other bannerets, excited by the prospect of plunder, had led their forces into China. A large body under the command of Ye-sien had advanced as far as Ta-tung, in Shansi, but they gradually retreated as the Chinese drew near. The condition of things in the imperialist army was wretched in the extreme. Wang-chin was not the man to know how to handle such an immense force, and by the time it came within the region of the enemy it had become disorganized to such an extent that it was ready for the

---

* The person that was really responsible for the movement was Wang-chin. The Mongols had been accustomed to pay their tribute in horses, and the embassy with their attendants were wont to receive presents of silk, together with all their expenses in return. This year over two thousand persons accompanied the tribute, who waited for the expected goods and money that they had annually received. Wang-chin objected to the amount demanded, and gave them less than they thought their due. Burning with indignation they returned home, when the call to arms was immediately issued throughout the bannermen.

disaster that was impending over it.   A further advance was made
to Suan-hwa, when the sad intelligence reached Ying Tsung that
the advanced division of his army had been literally annihilated by
the Mongols.   A retreat was now decided upon, and the army
reached T'u-muh, when suddenly it found itself surrounded by the
Mongols.   Contrary to the advice of his most skilful generals,
Wang-chin encamped instead of fighting his way through the
enemy, a piece of folly that insured the destruction of the whole
force.   The place was totally unsuited in every way for such a large
body of troops to rest in, for there was absolutely no water anywhere
near.   For two days both men and horses suffered severely from
drought, and though vigorous efforts were made to break through
the enemy, they all failed.   They had, however, entrenched themselves so strongly, and their numbers were so great that the Mongols
could make no impression upon them.   Ye-sien now resorted to a
ruse.   He sent in messengers proposing that hostilities should cease
and terms of peace be agreed upon between them.   Wang-chin, in
spite of his captains' urgent entreaties not to listen to any proposition
of the kind, fell into the trap so skilfully laid for him, and articles
were agreed upon that put an end to any further hostilities, and the
Chinese army was allowed to proceed on its way.   It had hardly
marched two miles, however, when the Mongol hosts swooped down
upon it, when a scene of indescribable confusion ensued.   Some of
the captains held their men well in hand and bravely withstood the
assaults of the enemy, but a panic soon seized upon the majority of
the troops, who, mad with fear, lost all discipline, and throwing
their weapons to the ground fled for dear life.   Soon all resistance
ceased, and the wild Mongol cavalry had but to slay the great army
that had now become a disordered rabble.   Immense numbers
perished, amongst whom was Wang-chin, the real cause of this
disaster.   In the disorder and confusion the Emperor was deserted
by his guards and attendants, and he was left solitary and deserted
by the panic-stricken soldiers.   A Mongol horseman, attracted by
his dress, rushed up to him, and was about to slay him when
another interposed, and he was led a captive to Wei-la-teh's brother.
    The Mongols were delighted to find that they had got possession
of the person of the Emperor.   They led him up to the gates of
Suan-hwa, and in his name ordered the commander of the garrison
to open them to them.   This he refused to do, as he knew that to do
so would be simply to hand over the city to the enemy.   The
unfortunate captive was next carried to Ta-tung, but with the same
result.   The Mongols now gave out that they were willing to let the
Emperor go, if a very large sum of money were paid for his ransom.
Messengers at once started for the capital to inform the authorities.
They reached Peking at midnight, and great was the sorrow in the
palace when the sad news flew through it of the misfortunes of Ying
Tsung.   Every possible effort was made to collect the large amount
demanded.   The queen-dowager and the high mandarins devoted all

their energies to the task, and soon eight great wagons were filled with the treasure of the capital and the jewels and ornaments of the queen, which she threw into the common stock, and officials were despatched with them to the Mongol camp to bring back the Emperor, but though his captors received the treasures that had been sent for his ransom they treacherously retained him a prisoner and refused to liberate him.

When the news of this breach of faith reached the capital the greatest consternation prevailed amongst all classes, and the rumour went abroad that the Mongols were advancing and would soon be at the gates. Some advised that the capital should be removed to a safer place further south. General Yu-ch'ien stood bravely forth and advised that an order should be issued by the executive, commanding that any one that should again dare to make such a proposal should be put to death.

The queen-dowager now summoned her high officials round her, and troops were ordered to Peking, and Yu-ch'ien was made commander-in-chief. As an act of severe justice the whole of Wang-chin's family was exterminated, and his immense wealth, which filled sixty large treasure rooms, was confiscated to the state. In order that the empire should not be without a head in this great crisis the younger brother of Ying Tsung was elevated to the throne, and soldiers and people sternly waited for the struggle that was now imminent.

King Ti—A. D. 1450-1457.

The Mongols continued to invest Ta-tung without any success, and once more they announced that they were willing to accept a ransom for Ying Tsung. After the experience of their treachery the Chinese refused to listen to any overtures that were made by them. Seeing no more hope of any gain through their captive they advanced towards the capital, everywhere using the name of Ying Tsung to induce the cities that fell in their way to surrender to them. Very little advantage, however, was gained by this manœuvre, for Yu-ch'ien had sent strict orders that no command of his was to be obeyed. As they drew nearer the capital Yu-ch'ien asked to be allowed to lead his forces out and meet them in the field. Permission was granted, and the result of the battle that took place was the utter defeat of the Mongols, who fled in great confusion across the frontiers. For this signal service Yu-ch'ien was offered a marquisate, but he refused to accept the honour. Ye-sien was so annoyed at the failure of all his plans that he determined to put his royal prisoner to death, but he was stayed in his purpose by a flash of lightning that killed his horse. This was considered by him as a hint from Heaven that he was to do nothing of the kind, so he offered him instead his sister in marriage, whom Ying Tsung prudently declined.

Early next year (A. D. 1450) Ye-sien, at the head of his warriors, again appeared on Chinese territory. Twice defeated, he retired in disgrace to his own country, where he found ample employment in striving to quell the storm that raged amongst the allied bannerets in consequence of his refusing to divide fairly the spoils that had fallen to them in their late campaign. Seeing that no further profit could be obtained by detaining his royal prisoner, Ye-sien sent ambassadors to Peking, desiring peace and offering to set him free. King Ti was opposed to any negotiations being opened on the subject, as he was determined not to resign the position he had obtained. His ministers represented the disgrace it would be to China to leave his brother in bondage, and they assured him they had no intention of depriving him of the throne. With this assurance he reluctantly gave his consent, and an escort was sent to receive his brother from the hands of the Mongols, who had done their utmost to make his return as splendid and honourable as possible. King Ti was determined not only to keep the throne for himself, but also to secure it for his children, for in A. D. 1452 he had his own son appointed heir, whilst Ying Tsung's son, who had been acknowledged as such up till this time, was rudely set aside, and honoured only with the title of prince. He was a very superstitious man, and had great faith in the Buddhist religion, and about this time he built the temple of "Great Happiness" at an enormous expense, where he and the empress worshipped the idols enshrined in it. If he had hoped that this act of devotion would be rewarded by securing the succession in his own family he was mistaken, for shortly after his son died.

In the year A. D. 1454 Ye-sien, who had seized the supreme power for himself only the year before and proclaimed himself khan, was killed by Ala, who was ambitious, and who wished to be second in rank to Ye-sien. Being denied this honour he revenged himself by leading his horde to the attack of Ye-sien, who in the conflict that ensued was defeated and slain. In the beginning of A. D. 1457 King Ti fell ill, and though he endeavoured to hide the seriousness of his case from his ministers, it soon became known that his disease was a mortal one.

A council was called, in which the question of the succession was discussed. It was then decided to invite Ying Tsung to resume the throne, which he consented to do. The dying Emperor was informed of this transaction by hearing the firing of cannon and the beating of drums that announced the accession to the people of the capital. King Ti eagerly asked an attendant, "Who is the new Emperor? Is it Yu-ch'ien that has usurped the throne"? "No," he replied, "it is your brother that succeeds you." "That is well," he said, and seemed satisfied with what had been done.

Ying Tsung—A. D. 1457-1465.

The resumption by this Emperor of his former position and duties was signalized by the execution of a number of those officials that had shown zeal in the service of the late sovereign. Amongst those that were apprehended was Yu-ch'ien, who was falsely accused by his enemies that he refused to acknowledge the new *régime*. His death speedily followed his seizure, and his whole family were banished to a distant part of the empire.* This gross injustice, done to a man who had rendered such signal services to his country, was speedily avenged in the sorrows that were inflicted by the Mongols on China, and which would have been averted had he been alive. These restless warriors, led by Pau-la, twice made a considerable invasion, and though they did not succeed as far as they had hoped, they were able to inflict a vast amount of injury and sorrow on the people.

Rendered more confident by the partial success they had obtained, they began from this time to make more frequent incursions into China.

The remainder of Ying Tsing's reign was not distinguished by anything very special or important. One act of his showed his extreme credulity. Notwithstanding all he had suffered through the folly and incapacity of Wang-chin he still considered that he had been a loyal and faithful servant to the throne. He had therefore a wooden image of him made, and buried with great honour, and he had a temple built where sacrifices could be offered to his names. An insurrection in the palace, headed by the eunuch Ts'an-kieh, took place in A. D. 1461, but it was speedily suppressed by the royal guard on duty, so that no serious consequences ensued from it. The Emperor fell ill at the beginning of A. D. 1464, and died in a few days.

Before his death he gave orders that none of the ladies of the harem should be buried with him in his tomb, as he could not endure the thought that any one so intimately connected with him in life should have to undergo such terrible sufferings with him in death.†

Hien Tsung—A.D. 1465-1488

This prince succeeded his father when he was seventeen years old, and he reigned twenty-three years. He was not a strong man mentally, as is manifest by the fact that he allowed himself and household to come under the severe control of one of his concubines— Man-kwei—whom he loved with undue devotion, and who used her power to distress every other woman in the palace that appeared likely to prove a rival to her. One act of justice he certainly did, that was the restoration of the family of Yu Ch'ien to their homes

---

* It is said that when he was executed the sky was clouded in dense darkness, thus testifying to the displeasure of Heaven at this official murder. The whole capital mourned for him, and Ying Tsung's mother was filled with grief. When his home was searched it was found that his ent re property consisted of simply one box that contained the presents that had been be stowed upon him by King Ti.

† During this reign the famous work entitled Tai Ming Yih T'ung Chi, consisting of ninety volumes, was published. It was prepared by Li-hien in conjunction with distinguished members of the academy, and contained a history of the Ming dynasty up to date.

and their property and the issuing of an edict in which he defeated his memory and heaped posthumous honours upon him.

For several years insurrections occurred throughout the country, in Honan, Kweichow, Sz-chwan and Shansi, but they were in time suppressed. An irruption of the Mongols was also successfully met, and Ha-mi was captured, and came under the control of China, A. D. 1473.*

Two public works of great importance were carried out, viz., the repair of the Great Wall, which secured the cultivation of a large area of land within it, and deepening of the Grand Canal from Peking to the Peiho, so that boats carrying the tribute rice could travel along it. The Emperor showed his weakness, not simply in the matter of Man-kwei, but also in coming under the control of a eunuch named Hung-chih, who for five or six years exercised great authority in the palace and assumed a power that was a danger to the state. The eyes of Hien Tsung at last having been opened, he was dismissed to the interior of the household to perform the duties there that specially belonged to him.

In the twenty-third year of his reign Man-kwei in the beginning of the year died, to the great grief of the Emperor, who loved her with the most devoted affection. So overcome was he with grief that for seven days he held no audience with his ministers and took no interest in the concerns of his kingdom. He never got over her loss, but gradually pined away, and eight months after her death he also died, leaving the empire to his son, who was then in his eighteenth year.

---

* Ha-mi has always been a town of great importance, as it is a great centre of trade, in consequence of the roads that lie to the north and south of Tien-shan mountains converging here.

CHAPTER XXXI.

THE MING DYNASTY (Continued).

Hiau Tsung—A. D. 1488-1506.

HIAU TSUNG was fortunate in possessing an able and loyal minister in Ma Wen-chin to assist him in the government of the empire. Various abuses that had crept in were remedied, to the great benefit of the state. The chief of these had been the sale of government offices, which was now prohibited.

Again, too, Ma Wen-chin showed himself to be both able and vigorous in the measures he took for the repression of disturbances throughout the country. A Tartar chief named Ahamateh, inspired by the thought that being far removed from Peking he was beyond the reach of the Chinese government, swooped down upon Ha-mi and captured it. Before long a Chinese army was on its march westward, and the town was retaken and a Mongol prince, a descendant of the family that had ruled China, was put in command. Again Ahamateh captured it, but once more he had to make his humble submission, and the prince was left in peaceable possession of it.

The only other event of this reign worthy of being recorded was the suppression of an insurrection in Hainan, which at one time threatened to be formidable.* After a reign of eighteen years Hiau Tsung died, to the great regret of his people, for he was a kind and gentle sovereign, and had made himself loved through the amiability of his character. Before his death he committed his son, who was then only fifteen, to the care of his ministers, who promised to be loyal to him.

Wu Tsung—A. D. 1506-1522.

Scarcely had this prince been raised to the throne when it was seen that serious troubles were impending over the country. He was a child both by years and by nature, and if his father had been wise he would have appointed a strong regency until his son was old enough to understand the responsibility of ruling so large an empire as that of China. Unfortunately at this time there was an ambitious, intriguing eunuch, named Liu-kin, who, with seven others of kindred mind, were determined to seize the present opportunity and acquire a predominating influence in the capital. These set themselves out to meet the tastes and enjoyments of the young Emperor, so that under the teachings of these men state affairs were entirely neglected.

---

* Hainan is an island attached to the province of Canton. Latterly the trade there has largely developed, and now promises to be of importance.

The nobles to whose care he had been entrusted, as well as the six Boards, remonstrated with him, but in vain. Two royal eunuchs secretly informed Wu Tsung of the disloyal aims of Liu-kin, and warned him against being led by him. Instead of listening to these he handed over complete authority to the latter to act in his name. The old officials of the palace were dismissed, and only the creatures of the disloyal eunuch employed, and fifty-three high mandarins were put to death by him.

In the beginning of A. D. 1508 the Emperor decreed that all petitions to him must first pass through Liu-kin, and if he disapproved of any they must be dismissed. One day at the audience a petition containing the most grievous charges against the eunuch was found on the floor. The Emperor suspected some of the great mandarins, but none would confess. He therefore caused three hundred of them to kneel in the open courtyard in front of the palace until they did. Every man was compelled to remain there until some one acknowledged that he had written the document. For five days and nights they were kept in that position. Several died, and many became seriously ill, but no voice of confession was heard from any one of them, and at last they were dismissed to their homes. From this time Liu-kin's power immensely increased, and he and his seven confederates formed a kind of Star Chamber, that, irresponsible to any, judged and condemned without any semblance of right.

A nemesis, however, was soon to fall upon this wrong-doer. Insurrections broke out in several parts of the empire, viz., in Hunan, Hupeh, Sz-chwan and in Shensi, the one in the last being headed by the Emperor's uncle, Ngan-hoa. Troops were sent in large numbers to put them down, in which they were successful. When General Chang returned from Shensi he told the Emperor that unless Liu-kin were killed the whole country would be in revolution. After considerable hesitation he gave his consent to his being apprehended and brought to trial. After he was in prison his home was searched, and an immese amount of treasure was found in it and suits of armour and royal robes, showing that he had meditated making himself Emperor. Sentence of death was issued against him, and so great was the fury of the people whom he had oppressed that they seized his body and struggled with each other for bits of his flesh, which they tore and mangled with their teeth, in order to show their detestation of so wicked a tyrant. A large number of his adherents suffered death, whilst others were banished to distant parts of the kingdom.

No sooner was the empire at peace, and the insurrection put down at an immense sacrifice of life, especially in Kiangsi and Honan, than Wu Tsung, who seemed incapable of choosing the right kind of men to assist him in the government of his people, selected another favourite, who was in every way unworthy of so high an honour. This was a military adventurer of the name of Kiang-pin, who was admitted to his closest intimacy, and became the commander of his bodyguard, and in time gained such an ascendancy over the royal mind that he became a danger to the state.

In the autumn of A. D. 1513 Ha-mi was once more lost to China, and as the Emperor was too busy looking after his own amusements no steps were taken to recover it. The prince who had been put in command of it by Ma Wen-chin died, and was succeeded by his son Pan Ga-chi. This man treated the people of the place with such cruelty that plots were formed to deprive him of his life. Terrified by the fear of assassination he offered to hand over the place to Ahamateh, who was only too glad to be reinstated in his old position of power and honour.

Wu Tsung, instead of growing in wisdom as he became older, only developed a more vicious and dissolute taste, which was encouraged by his favourite Kiang-pin. Influenced by him he made an expedition to Shansi, and though the loyal commander of the fortress of Chu-yang would not open his gates to let him pass he speedily overcame that difficulty by degrading him and appointing a eunuch in his place, who was more compliant in his obedience to the royal commands. On one of these wild excursions a large army, led by Ahamateh, advanced into Chinese territory as far as Ta-tung and invested it. In a succession of encounters, fighting every day for five days, the imperialists could make no impression on these Mongol foes. The Emperor then sent for General Chang, who inflicted a severe defeat upon them and compelled them to fly in disorder. Wu Tsung was so pleased with this victory, the credit of which he took to himself, that he ordered the Board of War to give large presents to the soldiers that had fought.

Having made several expeditions north he was planning another south, when his ministers interfered by showing him the danger he ran from the soldiers of Prince Ning, who had raised the standard of rebellion in Kiangsi. Persisting in his purpose, General Chang remonstrated with him, but he was cast into prison, where he shortly after died. Others of the great mandarins, who had dared to oppose the royal will, also suffered, for ten or twelve of them were beaten to death, whilst a number were banished.*

In the meanwhile, in the summer of A. D. 1519, Prince Ning, at the head of a hundred thousand men, was on his way towards the capital. Considerable success attended his arms, for he had captured the important towns of Nanking and Kiukiang. Wang-shen, who had been quelling local risings in Fukien, no sooner heard of his

---

* The year A. D. 1516 is a memorable one, from the fact that during it the first vessel that we have any record of flying a European flag arrived at Canton. It was commanded by a Portuguese of the name of Rafael Perestrello. Next year Ferdinand Andrade came with four ships, accompanied by a special envoy sent by the governor of Goa, who was received with due honour by the high authorities at Canton. In time others of the Portuguese followed, who traded on the coast and established themselves at Amoy and Ningpo. In A. D. 1537 there were no fewer than three Portuguese settlements near Canton.

movements than he led his forces into Kiangsi and laid seige to Nanchang. The former, hearing of this, retraced his steps to succour the beleaguered garrison. A pitched battle was fought, in which the prince was defeated and captured. He was sent to the royal army, which by this time had reached the confines of Kiangsi, and forwarded to Peking, where he was executed in November of the next year.

With the suppression of this revolt in Kiangsi, Wu Tsung felt that he had more leisure and disposition for the frivolities that had hitherto been a characteristic of his reign. Arriving at Nanking he gave himself up to a course of vicious pleasure that would have disgraced one of the meanest of his subjects. But the end was near at hand. In September, A. D. 1520, under the guidance of Kiangpin, who had had thoughts of murdering him and possessing himself of the throne, he set out for Peking. On his way he stayed at the house of one of his eunuchs, and whilst sailing in a boat on a lake near by he fell into it. He contracted a cold that developed into something more serious, for at the beginning of the next year, whilst engaged in the worship of Heaven, he had a violent fit of blood-spitting. Three months after he died, confessing his wrong and his sorrow for his past wickedness.

As he left no heir to succeed him, his mother, the empress-dowager, called a council of the ministers, when they unanimously decided to appoint a grandson of Hien Tsung to the throne, who accordingly was summoned to the palace to be invested with the supreme authority.

Shih Tsung—A. D. 1522-1567.

This young prince, who had been living in Hunan, arrived in Peking in May, and was formally recognized as Emperor of China. Before this took place summary vengeance had been meted out to Kiang-pin for the wrongs he had committed in leading Wu Tsung astray. Being ordered to appear at the palace he was slain, as he was about to enter, by a party of soldiers that lay in ambush for him. His wife and children were also put to death, and all his property confiscated. The next few years were remarkable for nothing, excepting the risings that took place in Kansuh amongst the soldiers, and in Honan, Yunnan and Shantung amongst the people, which, however, were suppressed without any difficulty. In August, A. D. 1524, Ahamateh led a body of twenty thousand Turfans to the attack of Suhchow, but he was compelled to retreat, as also three years later when he had the hardihood to advance as far as Suan-hwa-fu and lay siege to that important city. A second attack on Suhchow, in A. D. 1528, in order to seize an ally of his who had given in his allegiance to the Chinese, was equally unsuccessful. His offer to surrender Ha-mi, if the man he was after were given up to him being refused, he retreated with his army, and from this time we hear no more of him in the struggles that were going on along the frontiers.

In the year A. D. 1536 Shih Tsung, who was a devoted Tauist, and therefore looked with aversion on Buddhism, pulled down all the temples in connection with the latter system in the capital, and melting down the gold and silver idols in them, he built his mother a palace with the money they realized. As there were one hundred and ninety-six of pure gold, and over three thousand of silver, it can easily be imagined what a substantial building he was able to place at her disposal.* Whilst engaged in this transaction ambassadors from the king of Cochin China arrived, urgently requesting assistance from the Emperor in a great crisis that had occurred in that country. The story that was told by them was that Li-li, who had usurped the throne, had been murdered by Moh, a scion of a former royal family, and though he had set a son of Li-li on the throne he retained all the power in his own hands, and was in reality the true ruler of the country. An army was at once despatched to that distant region, when Moh, dreading a conflict with so formidable a power as China, made his submission, and was given a command over thirteen circuits in the kingdom, with a certain defined authority over all the officers in it, whilst the supreme authority was restored to the young ruler, who gladly paid tribute to Shih Tsung as over-lord.

The Mongols, who had kept up an incessant raiding on the borders, now began (A. D. 1542) to assemble in more formidable numbers under the banner of An-ta, who led them up to Ta-tung, in Shansi. The commander of that fortress went out to meet him, but he had to retreat discomfited, whilst the victorious enemy devastated all the surrounding country. Laden with plunder, and dragging many of the people into captivity, they retired unmolested to their own territories. Towards the close of A. D. 1544 An-ta again appeared with a still more numerous host, and penetrated as far as Wei-chow, which they captured, causing the utmost consternation amongst all classes in Peking.

Two of the chief commanders of the frontiers were ordered to the capital, and one of them was beaten to death and the other banished for not defending them better. General Chang-han was sent against the invaders, who retired as his forces drew near. For two successive years, viz., A. D. 1546, and A. D. 1547, An-ta again led his horsemen into China, and found none that could successfully cope with him, for the generals that led the Chinese troops were all wanting in the ability to give their men confidence in meeting a foe that had showed himself so brave and so full of daring. At length,

---

* Macao was occupied at this time, A. D. 1537, by the Portuguese, on the pretext of drying goods that had been injured by a storm. They took up their permanent abode, and in A. D. 1573 the Chinese built a barrier across the isthmus that joined Macao to Hiang-shan, and at the same time appointed mandarins to rule the Chinese residing in the place.

in A. D. 1549, when the usual foray was made as far as the gates of Ta-tung, its commander, Chow Siang-wen, inflicted a defeat on An-ta, who was compelled to retire without the booty and prisoners that had usually graced his triumphal return to his own home.

This same year the heir to the throne died, and his next brother was formally appointed instead. A serious trouble now arose between the Japanese and the people of Chehkiang. For many years trade had been carried on between the two peoples, but as the former found great difficulty in getting payment for their goods they determined to reimburse themselves by plundering the towns and villages on the coast. The governor of the province, in order to stop this state of things, forbade all trade between the Chinese and the Japanese. This, however, did not suit the ideas of the former, so they impeached the governor to the Emperor and declared that he had taken bribes and had recklessly injured the trade of the province. The Emperor, listening to the advice of some of his high mandarins who had been bribed by the merchants, put the governor to death, and ordered that trade should be carried on as before.

In the month of September, A. D. 1550, An-ta again appeared at the head of an immense army, and was everywhere victorious. He penetrated as far as T'ungchow, where the graves of the relatives of the Emperor were, and dug them up. Orders were sent in all directions for troops to hasten to the support of the capital, and men were rapidly recruited for this service. Between fifty and sixty thousand men arrived from Shansi, but they were so deficient in the materials for war and provisions that they durst not attack the Mongols, who accordingly plundered and slew the people as they liked, and returned home in perfect security without being molested by any of the imperial forces. In order to stop these continual incursions Ch'eu-loan petitioned the Emperor that horse fairs should be opened at Ta-tung and Suan-hoa, where the Mongols could bring their horses, and where the Chinese and they could get better acquainted with each other, and thus become more friendly in their relationships the one with the other. Shih Tsung agreed to this, but the Tartars brought such miserable animals for sale and raised such disturbance when the exorbitant prices they demanded for them were not given them, that in less than two years they had to be closed. The Emperor was so angry with the author of this experiment that though he had died in the meanwhile he ordered his body to be exhumed and his head to be cut off as a great criminal. To anti-cipate the invasion of the Mongols, which was sure to take place with the stoppage of commercial relationships, Shih Tsung had another wall, five miles in length, built outside of the weakest part of the existing one of the capital, and had both strengthened and fortified so as to be able to resist any attack that might be made on Peking. Whilst these works were being carried on, the Japanese came with a formidable fleet and captured Ningpo, Shanghai and Suchow, and after plundering to their hearts' content they retired to their ships and returned to Japan. Two years after they came again in force, but none of the troops that met them in the field could stay their progress or prevent them plundering the country around Shanghai and Sungkiang.

Whilst these exciting scenes were being enacted in the south, An-ta, influenced by two Chinese traitors that visited his camp in August of A. D. 1553, led his horsemen as far as Ta-tung, where he destroyed the army that had been sent against him and once more retired when it suited him. About the same time a most formidable rebellion broke out in Honan, led by Sz-shang, who had more than a hundred thousand men under his command. A large tract of the province was subdued by him, and it took the royal army that was sent against him forty days of severe fighting before it could restore order and give back peace to the people.

Chang-king, finding that he could make no headway against the Japanese with the troops under his command, petitioned the Emperor that soldiers from Canton and Kiangsi, who were noted for their fighting qualities, should be ordered to his assistance. This request was complied with, but he was handicapped by the silent intrigues of the prime minister, Yen-sung, who disliked him, and who was bent upon his destruction. At his instigation Chau Wen-hwo was sent to the camp to watch his movements and report to Peking.

On his arrival at the seat of war he ordered Chang-king to attack the Japanese, but he refused to do this till the troops promised him had reached him from the south. He at once reported him to the Emperor as a coward that was not fit for his command. A few days after the troops arrived, when Chang at once engaged the enemy and defeated them with great slaughter. Chau was now in mortal dread, so he sent a despatch post haste to Peking, saying that he himself had led his troops against the invader and had gained a great victory. Yen-sung, on being appealed to, confirmed the statement of his creature. The Emperor, indignant at the cowardice of his general, ordered him to the capital, and in spite of all his assertions that the charges brought against him were false had him and another officer, Yang-kwo, executed for cowardice.

Chau-wen was now elevated in rank for the services he had claimed that he had performed, but his honours remained with him only a short time, for in A. D. 1557 the Emperor discovered he had been imposed upon by him, and he banished him to the extreme north. He never reached his destination, however, as he miserably died on the road.

About this time there was another invasion of the Chinese territories by An-ta's son, Sihlina. The wife of the latter, having misbehaved herself, had fled across the border into China to escape the immediate vengeance of her husband, who followed her with a considerable force, and by way of making the pursuit as profitable as possible to himself and his followers he took the towns of Ying-chow and Sohchow, in Shansi, after which he proceeded to invest Ta-tung, whither his miserable wife had taken refuge. Failing in his immediate capture of this city he opened negotiations with the Chinese authorities, and promised that if his wife were delivered up to him he would not only withdraw from China, but he would also hand over several Chinese traitors that were then with him in his camp. These terms having been agreed to, the unfortunate woman was led back to the camp of her countrymen, where she was barbarously executed. Sihlina, however, declined to carry out the promises he had made, and so a battle ensued, in which he was defeated, and he was compelled to retreat across the borders.

The Japanese still continued to harass the southern coasts with their ships that came over partly for trade and partly for plunder. They occasionally joined themselves with the Chinese pirates that infested the region between Wenchow and the Chusan group, and worked havoc, both amongst the trading junks and the villages on the mainland. Vigorous efforts were made by the government to suppress these, but they were only partially successful, for though defeated at one time they would, after a while, when the vigilance of the cruisers was relaxed, again appear in force to carry on their work of destruction as before. In the year A. D. 1559 they again appeared with a huge fleet, consisting of several hundred vessels, and resumed their systematic plundering of the villages and towns on the coast. They were, however, interrupted in their ravages by the appearance of a strong force of Chinese men-of-war, which, attacking them, gained a decisive victory over them and compelled them to fly in disgrace to their own country. Once more, in A. D. 1563, they again terrified the Chinese by coming in increased force, but mindful of their former defeat they avoided the northern coasts and began operations on the shores of the Fohkien province. They were most successful in this enterprise, and captured Amoy and Tung-ngan, as well as the important city of Hing-hwa. The imperial authorities were roused, and large forces were sent against them. In the conflict that ensued all the places that were taken by them were recovered, and between two and three thousand of the Japanese were slain. So disastrous had been the campaign to them, and so severe had been their losses, that their periodic visits to the coast were given up, and we hear no more of them for a long time to come.

The last few years of Shih Tsung's life were not spent with a due regard to the interests of his people. His great thought was how to amuse himself and how to get as much pleasure out of life as possible without any regard as to what the people of his empire would say about him. He was exceedingly superstitious, moreover, and put himself into the hands of ignorant Tauist priests, who promised to give him the elixir of immortality, so that he should never know the pains of death.* Every effort, however, of himself or friends to postpone the final call that would hurry him out of life, was ineffectual, and he died at the close of the year A. D. 1566, confessing his follies and ordering that all the Tauist altars in the palace should be destroyed. He was succeeded by his third son, who was then thirty years of age.

Muh Tsung—A. D. 1567-1573.

The first years of this Emperor's reign were greatly disturbed by the irruptions of the Mongols under An-ta into Shansi. After murdering large numbers of the people and plundering the country, they returned, near the close of the year, to their own territories. In the following year, immediately after his third son had been appointed heir, an edict was issued by the Emperor, commanding Tsi Chin-kwang to take command of a large army and proceed to the frontiers to anticipate any movement that the Mongols might have been intending to make. This general, knowing the war-like character of the foe he had to contend with, took every precaution to ensure success in case of a conflict. He had his men trained in the severest discipline, and he made them build a long chain of forts, to the number of twelve hundred, which he had provisioned and garrisoned. In a great battle that took place near Suan-hwa the Mongols were completely routed, and had to fly before the Chinese.

The memory of this great defeat kept them quiet for two years, but in October, A. D. 1570, An-ta, with his son Sihlina, invaded Liau-tung, and at first gained some success. The Emperor then sent a very able general, named Li Ch'eng-liang, who compelled the invaders to retreat. Shortly after a grandson of An-ta came with a large number of his bannermen and placed himself under the protection of China. The reason for this was that his grandfather had carried off a beautiful woman that he had married in order to make her his concubine. An-ta in a great rage demanded him from the Emperor, who undertook to surrender him to him if he gave up the Chinese traitors in his camp, who had been the cause very often of the inroads that had been made upon Chinese territory. This being agreed to a treaty of peace was ratified, and at his earnest request An-ta was made a prince and acknowledged

---

* A member of the Board of War, named Hai-jui, a bold and fearless scholar, had the courage at this time to hand in a remonstrance to the Emperor, condemning him for his conduct. "You only," he said, "think of how you shall prolong your life, and nothing of your country. You ill-treat your ministers and show slight affection to your sons. You are perpetually planning for your own pleasures and drinking mixtures which you think will insure you against death. Cannot you see that all those men, in any age, that have encouraged such a belief have long since died? What is the good then of their elixirs of immortality?" The Emperor was exceedingly indignant when this document was read to him, and he ordered that the greatest care should be taken that the man that wrote it should not escape. "There is no danger of that, your majesty," exclaimed one of the eunuchs, "for the man has brought his coffin with him, and has bidden farewell to his relatives" The Emperor was deeply moved, and though he imprisoned him at first, after a time he pardoned him.

as the head of all the Mongol tribes. This arrangement proved a
fortunate one for China, because for more than twenty years these
restless foes of China honourably observed the agreement that had
been made, and thus the inhabitants on the borders were saved the
sorrows and disasters that always attended the raids of these savage
horsemen.

In the beginning of A. D. 1572 Muh Tsung fell ill, and two
months after he suddenly passed away. One morning, whilst holding an audience with his privy council, he fell from his seat on to
the ground. Being carried to his room he had but strength to
commend his son to the care of Kau-kung and Chang-chu, two of
his ministers, when he breathed his last. He was succeeded by his
son, who was only ten years of age.

Shen Tsung—A. D. 1573-1620.

The first years of the reign of this ruler, who is more familiarly
known by the name of Wan-li, the title of his reign, were not distinguished by anything special that happened in them. The great
source of trouble and annoyance to the Chinese, viz., the Mongols,
were at peace with the empire, and there was no other power that
had any desire to come into collision with China. Wan-li was a
youth of an affectionate and loving disposition, and he willingly
submitted himself to the guidance of the men to whom he had been
entrusted by his father. Chang-chu, who was of an ambitious turn
of mind, soon managed, by an intrigue with the chief of the
eunuchs, to get Kau-kung dismissed from all his offices and to
absorb all the power into his own hands. A formidable insurrection
took place in the summer of A. D. 1577 amongst the aborigines in
the province of Kwangtung, which, after a conflict of four months,
was quelled after some desperate fighting. Five hundred forts were
taken, and over forty thousand of their wretched defenders were
slain by the imperial troops. In the following year a Tartar chief,
named Tumuhteh, led a force of thirty thousand men into the
neighbourhood of Yau-chow, but he was driven back by Li-ch'eng
with the loss of nearly a thousand men and nine of his chief officers.

In the beginning of A. D. 1580 Chang-chu, who had hitherto
been acting with all the authority of a regent, resigned his powers
into the hands of the Emperor and begged him to assume the
government himself. This he was unwilling to do, and insisted
upon his allowing things to remain as they were. Being requested
by the queen-dowager to consent to this, and to remain in office
till her son was thirty years of age, he took back his resignation,
no doubt glad to resume a position that he had gained after a vast
amount of diplomacy and intrigue.

The country in the meanwhile had greatly prospered, for the
Tartars, with the exception of Tumuhteh, were quiet, and the empire
throughout all its borders was at peace. A very large extent, too,

of new ground had been brought under cultivation, and the taxes from it and the other customary ones had been paid so regularly that the royal exchequer was in a most flourishing condition. The Emperor accordingly issued an edict that all taxes not fully paid up during the first seven years of his reign should be remitted, and the debtors should never be required to pay up what was due to the government. There was great rejoicing over this, for the clemency of their sovereign affected that class of people who, through poverty or other causes, had been unable to pay, and who were therefore always at the mercy of the mandarins' underlings as fit subjects for annoyance, whenever they thought fit to oppress them.

In July, A. D. 1582, Chang-chu died, to the great sorrow of Wan-li. but to the joy of those who had the welfare and honour of their country at heart. Posthumous honours were lavished upon him, but only a few months had elapsed when startling revelations of his true character having been made, these were all withdrawn and every title that he had originally possessed taken from him. At the same time serious charges were laid against his confederate, Fang-pu, the chief of the eunuchs, who was banished from the country, and his immense wealth confiscated to the state. All the property, too, of Chang-chu was seized by the government, and thus the iniquities of two men, who had enriched themselves at the expense of the state, and in defiance of all principles of right, brought public odium on them both, and a warning was given to wrongdoers to avoid the evils that had brought upon them well merited disgrace.

The year A. D. 1583 is a distinguished one in the history of these times, for in it appeared the famous Noorhachu, the founder of the present Ts'ing dynasty.* The immediate cause of his emergence from obscurity, and his becoming a famous historical personage, was the action of Ni-kan, the ambitious chief of Tu-lun city, who, with a body of soldiers, lent him by Li Ch'ung-liang, the Chinese commander of Liau-tung, marched against Gu-lo, the city of Ua-tai Jang-jing, who was married to a cousin of Noorhachu.

---

* Noorhachu belonged to the Nuchen Tartars, and was born in the year A. D. 1559 in Hotuala, at the southern extremity of the Long White Mountains. Some two hundred years previously it was said that three maidens were bathing in the lake Burhuli, when a divine bird, the magpie, dropped some red fruit into the dress of the youngest, Fokulum, the consequence was that she had a son named Bukuli Yung-shun, with the surname of Aisin Gioro, who became the head of the family that two centuries after produced Noorhachu. Aisin Gioro became the chief of three clans of Tartars who had been at variance, but who recognized in him a man that was worthy to be their leader. Several generations passed by, when the people rose against his family and killed every one of them, excepting Fancha, who, flying before his pursuers. escaped only by a magpie alighting on his head, and thus causing him to be passed by as a tree by those who thirsted for his blood. Fancha fled across the Long White Mountains to Hotuala, and there founded a power, which, after a while, had Shing-king as its chief city. In course of time the ruling family rose in power, and from it there came sons that became the chiefs of small clans who exercised power till the time of Noorhachu, who, by his great ability and courage, made himself the ruler of a considerable number of the Tartars, so that at length he felt himself able to measure swords with the Chinese, who had taken sides with the enemies of his house.

Pressed by superior numbers, the besieged sent urgent messages to Huen, the grandfather of Noorhachu, to come to their assistance. Impelled by a sense of honour as well as by the ties of kindred, Hu-en with his son set off with what forces they could hurriedly collect to the aid of Ua-tai. On their arrival at Gu-lo they tried to persuade their relative to remove with them to a place of safety, but this Ua-tai forbade, and consequently they remained to be beleaguered by the allied army. Finding themselves too weak to make a successful resistance, Ua-tai agreed to surrender, on condition that their lives should be spared. This being agreed to, the place was delivered up, when, in defiance of the stipulation that had been made, a general butchery ensued, and Hu-en and his son were slain amongst the rest.

Noorhachu, who had been at a distance whilst these great and startling events had taken place, was horrified when he heard of the terrible tragedy that had ended in the death of his father and grandfather. He vowed that he would have an ample revenge on Ni-kan, the author of so much sorrow to him and his clans. His first act was to demand the bodies of his relatives from the Chinese, who readily granted his request. His next was to require that Ni-kan should be surrendered to him, but they not only refused, but they also had the folly to appoint him lord over all Manchuria, which thus included Hotuala. The indignation of Noorhachu was extreme against this fresh indignity, and he vowed that he would have satisfaction, not only from Ni-kan, but also from the Chinese. Various attempts were made by him to wreak his vengeance on the former, but without success. At last the Chinese, tired of defending him, handed him over to Noorhachu, who at once put him to death. The determination with which the former had carried out his purpose raised his fame amongst his countrymen, which thus gave him a position amongst them that ultimately led to his family being seated on the throne of China.

For the next few years nothing of any special importance took place within the empire. In A. D. 1587 a great flood in the capital caused the death of a large number of the inhabitants, and in the following year an extensive famine brought great suffering upon the peoples of the northern provinces. The Emperor, too, did not seem alive to the responsibilities of his high office, and neglected the business of the state. One of the censors had to reprimand him for drunkenness, bad temper and licentiousness, but it is not said whether the admonitions of this brave official were attended with any very great success or not. It is to be feared that they were not.

In A. D. 1591 the Tartars had frequent collisions with the Chinese. Towards the end of the year Li-Ch'ung suffered a defeat at their hands. For this he was degraded. This victory over such a distinguished commander added to the fame of Noorhachu, and enabled him to take another step in his victorious progress, and that was the annexation of the Yalukiang district that lay to the east of

Hotuala. Next year a serious military insurrection broke out in Shensi, headed by an officer high in the service, named Pa-pai. He was a Mongol who had fought well for the empire, and had been rewarded by being placed in command of a considerable force, that guarded the north-western frontiers. The Chinese officers, who were jealous of his success, plotted for his disgrace, and they so managed to inspire him and the large number of the Mongols who were in the Chinese service with an idea that they were in danger that they raised the standard of rebellion and flew to arms. A large force, under Li Jio-sung, was sent against him, when he was defeated and fled to Ning-hia. Thither he was followed by Li, but the town was so well defended that the latter could make no impression upon it. Determined to succeed, he diverted the waters of the Yellow River against the city. They rushed into it and filled it to the depth of nine feet. Famine ensued, and the city walls gave way. Pa-pai, seeing that there was no hope of deliverance, committed suicide, and the insurrection was at an end.

This trouble was scarcely ended when another, more formidable one, arose in connection with the Japanese. Fashiba, seeing that through the vices of Li-yen, to Corean king, that country was in a state of disorder, led a large force in one hundred ships to the conquest of Corea, and landed at Fusan.* From there he advanced upon Seoul, the capital, and defeating the force that opposed his onward march he captured the city, after he had besieged it a month, and obtained a vast amount of plunder. Li-yen, in the meanwhile, had fled to Yalukiang, from whence he sent messengers to Peking, imploring assistance from Wan-li.

An army was despatched with all haste against the Japanese, but it was beaten, and a wholesome fear came over the Chinese soldiers for the invaders. Not content with the victory they had gained over the Coreans, the Japanese had the hardihood to advance into Chinese territory and to hold themselves in readiness to dispute with any force that might be sent against them.

Wan-li now sent ambassadors to Fashiba, nominally to arrange terms of peace with him, but in reality to get information as to his strength and position. As neither party was in earnest, a battle soon ensued, in which the invaders suffered a great defeat and retired before the Chinese. Li Ju-sung pursued, but elated by his success, and despising the enemy, he allowed himself to be led into an ambuscade, and was overthrown by the Japanese, and barely escaped with his life. He was able, however, to retreat with the greater part of his army

Li Ju-sung, hearing that the Japanese had stored a large amount of provisions for the use of the army at Liang-shan, sent a force and succeeded in burning the whole, thus leaving them without any supplies upon which they could rely. Under these circum-

* Fashiba is known to the Chinese by the name of Ping Siu-kieh, but to the Japanese by his more popular name of Hideyoshi.

stances they were compelled to retreat from Seoul and retire to
Fusan. As their communications with Japan were easy and secure
from this place, they were left in undisturbed possession of it, and
fighting for the time being ceased.

Four years passed by, marked only by minor irruptions of the
Mongols, in which they were defeated, and also the opening of
silver mines in various parts of the empire, in order to supply the
deficiencies in the exchequer that the extravagance of the court and
cost of the war had created.

In A. D. 1597 the government had its hands full, for not only
did hostilities break out again with the Japanese, but an alarming
insurrection in Sz-chwan, amongst the aborigines, threatened the
rule of the Emperor in that distant province. It seems that in the
drawing up of the treaty of peace with Japan expressions had been
used in the documents that had been sent to Peking that gave
umbrage to that haughty court. These had implied that Japan
was an equal with China, and not a tributary that owed allegiance
to it. As the Japanese refused to modify their language war was
again commenced. Chen-yin was sent with an army to convince
them of their mistake, and in a battle that was fought he came off
victorious. His superior, Yang-kau, jealous of the fame that his
subordinate had gained, took command, and in a great battle
suffered a terrible defeat. The slaughter amongst his soldiers was
very great, and besides he lost all his baggage and the whole of the
provisions upon which the army depended. When news of this
disaster reached Wan-li, Yang-kau was recalled to give an account
of himself. Fighting, however, still continued without any decided
success on either side till news arrived, at the close of A. D. 1598,
that Fashiba, who in the meanwhile had become Tycoon of Japan,
had died. With his death hostilities, after they had been waged for
seven years at a terrible expense, both of life and money, ceased,
and the Japanese returned home, though they still continued to hold
Fusan, which they do to the present day.

The Emperor, who had long delayed in appointing his heir,
was now compelled, through the pressure of public opinion, to do so,
and his eldest son, Ch'ang-lo, was formally recognized, though
Wan-li would have much preferred, had state etiquette allowed it,
to have had his second son, Prince Fuh, succeed him. This partiality of Wan-li for the latter was attended with unhappy results in
the domestic life of the Emperor. He was not a high principled
man, however, or one that took a lofty view of the responsible
position he held as the head of a great empire. His time was much
occupied in pleasures of a character quite unsuited for the ruler of a
people whose ideal of their sovereign is such an exalted one. The
immediate result of his behaviour was great sorrow to the people, for
the taxes had to be increased to meet the heavy expenditure of the
court. These were all the more difficult to be borne, as droughts
and floods had largely prevailed in different provinces of the empire

The marked preference that was shown for Prince Fuh led the latter to enter into a plot with his mother and some of the eunuchs of the palace for the destruction of Ch'ang-lo, and an attempt to murder him in the palace was frustrated only by the bravery of the eunuchs who were on duty at the time. In the investigation that took place positive evidence was obtained from the would-be assassin that Fuh's mother, Ching-kwei-fi, was the instigator, and in order to avoid the indignation of the Emperor she had to beg of the injured prince that he would intercede with his father for her and obtain his forgiveness. This he did, and the matter was allowed to drop.

At the close of this year, A. D. 1615, the Mongols, with a hundred thousand men, under forty-two banners, invaded China. At first they obtained considerable success, but in a great battle that was fought they were defeated and driven back into their wilds. With the death of Ni-kan (A. D. 1586) Noorhachu took up the role that had ended so fatally for his rival, and made it the purpose of his life to make his own tribe the supreme one in a grand confederation of the Nu-chen. His first important step, as mentioned above, was his sudden attack of Ya Lu-kiang and his annexation of that district. His next was the defeat of seven chiefs who had joined their forces to crush him. Advancing at the head of thirty thousand men they attacked Noorhachu, who routed them at Gu-lo Hill with great slaughter, killing four thousand of them and capturing three thousand horses. After this decisive action he felt that he had considerably strengthened his position, and in A. D. 1599 he annexed Ha-do, an important district that lay to the north of his own. The Chinese remonstrated against this, but Noorhachu felt himself strong enough to disregard their threatenings, and from this time to refuse payment of the tribute that he had been accustomed to render to China.

Notwithstanding all these successes Noorhachu still considered himself far from the goal he had placed before him. In A. D. 1613 the district of Wu-la, having been already added to those he had conquered, he advanced at the head of forty thousand men to the attack of Ye-ho, "the last and most powerful of the southern or civilized independent Nu-chen principalities."* The news of this invasion spread with lightning rapidity throughout the whole of the Ye-ho district, and preparations were made to resist it, and at the same time urgent requests were sent to the Chinese commander at Kai-yuen to come to their assistance against a foe that would not be content to rest satisfied with the conquest of Ye-ho.

Noorhachu proved his power by taking seven cities and nineteen stockades, but on the arrival of the Chinese troops he was compelled to retire from Ye-ho with the loss of all the places he had captured. He now saw that if he were ever to succeed in attaining to the supreme control over all the Manchu bannermen he must

* See Ross' "The Manchus."

inevitably come in collision with the Chinese, and by some great and decisive defeat prevent them from interfering in the affairs of Liau-tung. He accordingly desisted from his attacks on Ye-ho and began his preparations for the great campaign with his powerful foe. By the year A. D. 1616 he had succeeded in establishing his power so thoroughly over the chiefs he had conquered that they looked upon him as a man whose authority was not to be disputed, and they actually urged upon him to assume the title of the Emperor Ying Ming, which, being translated, means the "Brave and Illustrious Emperor." This he consented to do, and from this year he dated the first of his reign and assumed the name of T'ien Ming, or "By the Decree of Heaven," which was the title by which he was known to his people. About the same time he set about the formation of the Manchu characters from the Mongolian and adopted twelve root symbols, from which all the other words in the language were to be formed. He also divided the whole of the Manchus into eight banners. The colours were yellow, red, blue and white, and each one of these, bordered with another, made up the eight.

Noorhachu, having made all his preparations for the great campaign against the Chinese, led twenty thousand men in the spring of A. D. 1618 against the city of Fu-shan that lay about seventy miles to the east of Moukden. In order to justify his action in the sight of Heaven and of the world he had a document drawn up which recorded seven great wrongs that he had suffered at the hands of the Mings. This he caused to be read in the presence of his army, and then burnt, believing that the story would thus ascend on high and influence Heaven to prosper the mighty enterprise that he was now about to undertake.* The city was easily captured and garrisoned by the Manchus, and a force of ten thousand men that had been sent against them from Kwangling was almost annihilated. In the autumn of the same year the important town of Ts'ing-ho was carried by storm, and nearly all the Chinese that defended it were slain.

The greatest consternation now prevailed in Peking, and troops were collected from all directions, and before long Yang-kau found himself at the head of four hundred and seventy thousand men, ten

---

* The seven grievances roughly translated are briefly as follows: 1. Though he had never invaded Chinese territory the Mings had slain his father and his grandfather. 2. That after the bodies of his relatives had been given up to him an agreement had been made that neither party should invade each other's lands. The Mings had violated this by their coming to the aid of Ye-ho. 3. That every year lawless Chinese had come into his territories and plundered and slain his people. 4. That through the influence of the Mings a horde, to whose chief he had betrothed his daughter, had rebelled against him, and he had been compelled to give his daughter to another. 5. The lands around the river Ch'ai, and about San-pun and Fun-gan, had been wrested from the Manchus, and their owners dispossessed of their homes. 6. That the Chinese believed the misrepresentations of the people of Ye-ho and had sent insulting letters to him. 7. That the Mings had prevented Hada from remaining in its allegiance to him after he had twice conquered it, and that they had thus run counter to the manifest will of Heaven. "For this cause," he continued, "I hate you with an undying hatred, and I am now ready to risk my life in the struggle in which I am now about to engage."

thousand of whom were Coreans who came to take part in the campaign. Yang-kau, having arrived at Moukden, unwisely divided his force into four great divisions. The first he sent under Tu-sung, along the bank of the Hwun, to attack Fu-shan ; the second, under Ma-lin, marched north to Kai-yuen to encourage the people of Ye-ho ; the third, under General Li, advanced along the Ching river, and the fourth under General Liu, set out from Kwan-tien towards Shing-king.

Noorhachu at once abandoned all the places he had taken and concentrated all his forces, which amounted to more than sixty thousand men, at Shing-king. His plan was now to conquer in detail the divisions of the enemy, and in pursuance of this he attacked and routed Tu-sung at Sar-hu hill. He next advanced against Ma-lin, who had entrenched himself at Shang-jien and gained a complete victory over him. He then threw himself against Liu's division and routed him, so that at last there was no enemy left in the region of his capital, for General Li, hearing of the disasters that had occurred, retreated with all speed to a place of safety. Thus in five days three decisive victories had been obtained with the loss to the Chinese of forty-five thousand eight hundred men and three hundred and ten superior officers.

When the news of these disasters reached the Emperor he was exceedingly displeased with Yang-kau, and recalled him, appointing General Hiung in his place. In the meanwhile Noorhachu, taking advantage of the terror that had seized upon the Chinese, advanced rapidly against Kai-yuen, where the remnants of Ma-lin's army had concentrated and captured it. He then took the city of Tieh-ling and defeated the Mongols of Kar-ka, who had come to its aid. By the beginning of the winter, A. D. 1619, Gen. Hiung had reached Liau-yang where he organized his plan for meeting the Manchus. These were of the most vigorous and active kind, when, unfortunately for the cause of the Ming dynasty, he was recalled to the capital to defend himself from serious charges that had been made against him by a faction that were opposed to him in the capital. Before he could reach that city the Emperor Wan-li had died, and was succeeded by his son, Kwang Tsung, who, however, held the reins of government only about a month, when he died, and was followed by his son,

Hi Tsung—A. D. 1621-1628,

a youth of only sixteen years of age, whom his dying father commended to the care of his ministers, imploring them to befriend him and to be loyal to him in the great crisis in which he was coming to the throne.

In the meanwhile matters had been becoming more serious in Liau-tung Yuan Ying-tai, who had succeeded Hiung, was a thoroughly incompetent general, and no match for Noorhachu. The latter led his forces against Moukden and captured it. He then marched against Liau-yang, and after a terrible conflict, in which there was great loss of life, he entered triumphantly into the city, Ying-tai perishing in the flames of a tower over one of the city gates, which his own hand had set fire to.   The fall of Liau-yang gave the conquerors complete possession of Liau-tung, for seventy walled cities, small and great, at once opened their gates and admitted the soldiers of Noorhachu.

The greatest alarm was felt in Peking when the news of these disasters reached it.   Hiung, who had been declared guiltless of the charges that had been brought against him, was reinstated in his command, whilst his accusers were deprived of all their offices and reduced to the rank of common people.   He proceeded at once to the seat of war and made his head-quarters at Shan-hai-kwan.   When he reached that important stronghold he found that Wang-hoa, who had succeeded Ying-tai, had disposed his force in six different camps along the west bank of the Liau.   Hiung remonstrated against this, and urged that they should be concentrated near the important town of Kwan-ling.   Wang, who was strong in the support of the eunuch Wei-chung, who at that time controlled the councils of Hi Tsung, refused to obey, and declared that with his sixty thousand men he could disperse and destroy any force of Manchus that dared to attack him.

His refusal to obey his superior officer was soon attended with the most disastrous results.   The Manchus, who saw the mistake Wang had made in having his men so dispersed, swooped down upon Kwan-ling and captured it, and forty cities, large and small, at once submitted to the conqueror.   Both Hiung and Wang were recalled, and both subsequently were beheaded, though the former was in no manner responsible for the disasters that had occurred.

The year A. D. 1622 was a stirring one in the annals of the empire.   A formidable rebellion broke out in Kwei-chow, and three armies had to be sent into that province before peace could be restored.   In Shantung, too, the members of a secret society called the "White Lily" found their members so great that they felt themselves able to come in collision with the imperial forces.   Their success at first was very great, and they captured several important cities.   Their main idea, however, was plunder, and so in time they lost the sympathy of the masses, who would have helped them if they had given any promise that they would secure them a more just form of government than the one under which they had been oppressed.   In seven months the revolution collapsed, and peace was once more enjoyed throughout the whole of the province.

Next year the imperial troops were engaged with a foe that they had never before met in actual warfare, and these were the Dutch.   During the last year of Wan-li's reign these had come in their ships to Formosa, where they made a settlement.   They then took possession of the Pescadores and landed at Amoy, from whence they penetrated as far as Chang-chow and Hai-ting.   In the engagements that took place the Dutch were worsted on the mainland, and

were compelled to retreat to Formosa.* The condition of things at
the capital was becoming more serious every day. Under the leadership of Wei-chung the eunuchs were absorbing all power into their
own hands. They had recklessly driven from the court all those
who dare to protect, and a loyal censor, named Yang-lien, was
imprisoned and put to death in his cell. In the meanwhile the
course of events in Manchuria was all in favour of Noorhachu, who
in A. D. 1625 removed his capital to Moukden. The two Chinese
generals now opposed to him were Chung-hwan and Kau-ti, the
latter of whom held the craven policy that the Chinese should not
hold any territory beyond Shan-hai-kwan. To give emphasis to this
he retreated with his army to this place and ordered all under his
command to retire within the Great Wall. Chung-hwan refused to
obey, and declared that he would hold Ning-yuen till he and every
man under his orders were slain in its defence. The Manchus,
hearing of the retreat of Kau-ti, advanced in force against Ning-
yuen, but after repeated assaults they were compelled to retire after
an enormous loss of life. This repulse so affected Noorhachu
that he fell ill and died in September, A. D. 1626, in the sixty-
eighth year of his life. He was succeeded by his son, to whom we
shall give the Chinese appellation of T'ai Tsung. Condolences and
congratulations poured in upon the latter from many directions, and
even Chung-hwan sent in a very guarded and cautious letter to him,
expressing his sympathy. The new ruler, who seemed really desirous
of coming to terms with the Chinese, sent back a very courteous
but firm reply, stating that if the Emperor were really anxious for
peace he was equally so, and he only waited for conditions to be
proposed, by which hostilities might be put an end to as speedily
as possible. Chung-hwan was a warrior rather than a statesman,
and failed to grasp the situation. The idea of making terms with
rebels was to him a ridiculous one. He therefore sent the letter
back to the writer, without any comment or remark of his own, a
most discourteous and unwise proceeding, and one destined to have
a disastrous effect upon his country.

The year A. D. 1627 was spent by the Manchus in an invasion
of Corea, which ended in the submission of that country and the
removal of an enemy that had always been faithful to the Mings,
and that might have proved most dangerous in case of future hostilities with China. After their return from this successful expedition
the Manchu forces in the month of August were led again to Ning-
yuen to endeavour to capture it. Chung-hwan, however, who was
still in command, gave them such a warm reception that they had
to retire in disgrace and give up all hope of obtaining this city, for
the present at least. A month after this Hi Tsung died. His last

---

* This statement of the Chinese historian differs from the accounts given by
foreign writers, who make the Dutch to have seized upon the Pescadores in A. D.
1622, and then to have retired to Formosa two years after. See Williams' Middle
Kingdom, Vol. I., 141.

words showed the weakness of his character and the way in which he had been deceived and cheated by those who had helped materially to bring the empire to the sorry condition in which it then was. Calling his ministers round his bed he commended Wei-chung, the traitor eunuch, who was at that time actually planning rebellion and the seizure of the throne, to their care, as a man who had the best interests of China at heart. These words had hardly escaped his lips when he fell back dead, at the early age of twenty-three. As he had no heir he was succeeded by his brother, Ts'ung-ching, whose dynastic title is

Chwang Lieh Ti—A. D. 1628-1644.

The first act of the new ruler was to banish Wei-chung, who, however, committed suicide on the way to his place of exile. His body was brought back to Peking and beheaded, and his head was stuck up in a prominent place as a terror and a warning to all traitors. His next important step was to invest Chung-hwan with full powers to act as seemed best to him in his conflict with the Manchus, and with his commission he sent him a magnificent sword, a significant hint as to the kind of method he was to employ in dealing with those hardy warriors. Chung-hwan was delighted with the confidence that was reposed in him, and undertook that in less than five years he would restore Liau-tung to the imperial rule. Full of these hopes he communicated with T'ai Tsung, who curtly replied, that for the sake of peace he was willing to rank second to the Emperor and receive from him the title of Khan, but that he would never consent to return a single foot of land that the will of Heaven and his own good sword had secured for him and his people. Where such a decided difference of aim existed, it is not surprising that all correspondence between them ceased from this time.

In A. D. 1629 T'ai Tsung, at the head of over one hundred thousand men, began his march on China. Wisely avoiding Ning-yuen he concentrated his eight banners, who had entered China by different directions, near the city of Han-url-jang, from whence he proceeded to invest Tsun-hwa. Amongst this large army was a considerable force of Mongols, who, through not receiving their subsidies regularly, had revolted and joined the Manchus. Tsun-hwa having fallen before the arms of T'ai Tsung, the Manchus proceeded to Tung-chow, where they encamped. From this place a proclamation was issued to the Chinese people vindicating this advance into their territory and recapitulating the wrongs the Manchus had suffered at the hands of their rulers. T'ai Tsung then led his army to the north of Peking and encamped not far from the city walls. The danger that threatened the capital soon brought succour to the beleaguered city. Man-kwei first arrived with five thousand men, who, coming beneath the walls, were assisted by the cannon from it and forced the Manchus back.

Other forces kept continually pouring in. Amongst these were Chung-hwan, whom T'ai Tsung hated and dreaded most of all. In order to get rid of him he devised a most cunning scheme, which, if successful, would end for ever the warfare of his distinguished opponent. He arranged with some of his officers to hold a conversation near two of the palace eunuchs that had been taken prisoners. In whispers they spoke to each other of how Chung-hwan had turned traitor and offered to open the gates of Peking to the invading army. The eunuchs were allowed to escape next morning, who hurried with all speed to the palace and told the Emperor the terrible news with which their hearts were bursting. Chung-hwan was at once seized and thrown into prison; from which he never again came forth, for in August of the following year he was executed within its walls.

Instead of attacking the capital T'ai Tsung sent in proposals of peace, which, however, were rejected. Fighting still continued with very undecided success on either side, but it was apparent to the Manchu leader that he was not strong enough to invest the city, so in February, A. D. 1630, he retreated with all his forces to his own territories. The Chinese troops that had been daily augmented followed fast in the steps of the retreating foe and recaptured the important towns of Yung-ping, Tsun-hwa, Ts'ien-ngan and Lan-chow.

About this time news of that terrible rebellion in Shensi, that was destined to shake the empire to its very centre, and finally to overthrow the dynasty, reached the capital. The two principal leaders in this great revolt were Chang Hien-chung and Li Tsi-cheng, the latter of whom, however, was fated to be the one that was to bring such dreadful calamities on his country. An army was sent against the rebels, who feigned submission, but shortly after it was found necessary to despatch another under General Ts'au-wen, who gained a decided victory over them, which caused them to flee into Shansi. This lull in the storm was but temporary, for again the rebels collected in vast numbers, and though more than once again defeated by Ts'au-wen their organization spread throughout the important provinces of Hunan and Hupeh.

In A. D. 1634 the imperial forces had so far gained the upper hand over the rebel chief Li that if a vigorous policy had been then employed the rebellion would have entirely collapsed. General Chen had several times routed the rebel forces, and had driven Li into a cul-de-sac in the mountains where it was evident no human power could save him. In this extremity Li sent to Chen, intimating his willingness to lay down his arms and submit to the government, on condition that he and his followers were allowed to depart whither they liked. The general very unwisely, without making any investigation into the actual condition of affairs, granted this request. When the rebels marched out their numbers were found to be far in excess of what Chen had any conception they were, and to amount to as many as thirty-six thousand men, who no sooner found themselves free than they at once returned to their old style of living, and in the course of a few months their numbers were augmented to two hundred thousand.

In the meanwhile the Manchus had not been idle. Determined to be in a position to meet the Chinese more evenly in A. D. 1631 they cast their first cannon and called it the "Great General." They also attacked a fortress that General Tsu was building on the bank of the river Ta-liang to the east of King-chow, and captured it. A most important conquest that they effected during this time, when their armies were not engaged with those of China, was that of the entire districts of Cha-har, which thus rendered the whole of Inner Mongolia subject to their sway. The possession of this region was invaluable to them in case of a march on Peking, for experience had proved to them that it was impossible to advance by the way of Shan-hai-kwan. Frequent raids of the Manchus had been made into Shantung and Shansi, and cities had been captured, but they could not be retained, because of the existence of that formidable fortress in their rear. T'ai Tsung saw that there was no hope of his successfully attacking it so long as the four strong cities that lay to the north of it were unconquered. He therefore determined to deal with King-chow, the nearest one to it. After a terrible siege the city was captured, and shortly after Hing-shan. T'ai Tsung now felt that he was in a position to assume a more regal style than he had hitherto done, so in May, A. D. 1636, he gave the name of his dynasty the Tai Ts'ing, the same as it is to-day. He also built an altar to Heaven and an ancestral temple, and honoured his father with magnificent posthumous titles.

The great rebellion, with the lapse of time, was gradually assuming large proportions, and in spite of successes here and there of the imperial armies, and of the exhibition of most heroic courage of the part of individuals and cities, the royal cause was declining. The Ming dynasty had lost the confidence of the nation, and Ts'ung-ching, through weakness of character, was not the man to inspire enthusiasm or to devise some great scheme that would have brought the best men of his empire about him to help him to crush the revolution that was rending his kingdom from his grasp.

The rebels, under Chang Hien-chung, had gained immense successes in Honan, whilst the arch rebel, Li, was all-powerful in Shensi and the neighbouring province of Shansi. In spite of occasional successes on the part of the imperialists the rebels on the whole were decidedly in the ascendancy. The most remarkable thing in the desultory warfare that desolated the country was the singular changes of fortune that attended the rebel leaders. At one time they would be at the head of great armies, and shortly after they would be flying before their conquerors with but a scattered remnant of their large forces. For example, Chang-hien was defeated in the beginning of A. D. 1640 by Liang-yu, and lost ten thousand men. A year after we find him in possession of the important city of Hiang-yang and captor of one of the royal princes, whose large wealth he appropriated to himself. Shortly after Liang-yu, who had gained a decided success against Li, suddenly marched south, and attacking Chang-hien, routed him, taking ten thousand of his cavalry prisoners and causing a large number of Li's men to desert to his side. In A. D. 1641 Li advanced to the attack of K'ai-fung, in Honan, but he was forced to retire. Chang-hien, on the other hand, captured the city of Siang-yang, where he found his wife and children, whom he had lost in an engagement in which he had been worsted ten months before. Success followed all his movements, and in a short time, through treachery in the city, he gained Wu-chang (A. D. 1643), and from that place operated with such vigour that he soon had the control of the Yang-tze.

At the close of A. D. 1641 Li captured Nan-yang and again invested K'ai-fung, but having lost an eye by an arrow he withdrew, once more baffled in his attempt to obtain this important city. Next year, after having gained possession of over a dozen neighbouring towns, he again invested the place. For nine months it held out bravely, when Li, who was determined to have it at any cost, opened a passage from the Yellow River and allowed its waters to inundate the city. The destruction of life was terrible. It is said that over a million people were drowned in the waters that stood as high as twenty feet. Li himself lost ten thousand men, and was compelled to flee to avoid greater loss.

By this time the fortunes of the royal house were becoming desperate. Chang-hien was victorious in Kiangnan, and Li took the title of king and appointed officers who should rule over the districts he had conquered. He was indignant with Chang-hien for taking the same liberties, and sent special messengers to him to warn him against his assumptions. In November, A. D. 1643, Li captured the famous fortress of Tung-kwan. The commander of this, Sun-ch'wan, had gone out with a large army to meet him, but he suffered a most disastrous defeat. Fully forty thousand of his men were killed, and in the pursuit that ensued the remnant of the army was dispersed, so that the officers in Tung-kwan, seeing no hope of being relieved, opened its gates and admitted the conqueror.

In February, A. D. 1644, Li took the style of Emperor and called his dynasty "Tai Shun." He also appointed six boards for the government of the country, established orders of nobility, and rewarded with titles and emoluments those who had distinguished themselves in the campaigns that had ended so successfully for himself.

Li, now considering that the empire lay within his grasp, determined to march on Peking and claim it for his capital. T'ai-yuen and a number of other cities that lay in the line of his march were successively captured. At Ning-wu, however, the resistance was most desperate. Ten thousand men fell before it, and the place was left a heap of smoking ruins by the inhabitants, who set fire to their houses and perished rather than submit to the rebels. Li was concerned at the great loss of his men, and called a council of war "If all the cities on the way fight like this," he said, "we shall certainly fail in our enterprise." Whilst they were deliberating letters were received from the fortified towns of Ta-tung and Suan-hwa, the very places he most dreaded, surrendering themselves to him. Great was the joy on the receipt of these, and an immediate advance of the army was ordered.

The Emperor was greatly troubled when he heard of the loss of these two cities. Some of his ministers advised his flight to Nanking, but he refused to do this. "Better die," he said, "when the empire is gone." He was silent when some one suggested that his family at least should be sent there for safety. Li had taken the precaution of preventing any communication with the capital, so that no news reached it of the movements of the rebels. Before the Emperor was aware, therefore, Li, with his immense army, was before its walls. The provision that had been made for such a contingency was of the scantiest possible description. Nominally there were one hundred and fifty thousand men to guard the nine gates and the extensive walls, but there were not in reality more than fifty or sixty thousand, and these not of the stuff to save a dynasty in its fierce struggle with a powerful foe.

The Emperor now ordered his son-in-law to take the house-hold troops and lead his son to Nanking, but this was found an impossibility now, as was also his proposal that he should head his troops and go out and fight the rebels. In point of fact there were hardly any soldiers to lead, for large numbers existed only on paper, and those that might have been available had fled in terror from the city. To add to the calamities of this time Ts'an-hwa, who had command of one of the southern gates of the city, turned traitor and opened it for the entrance of Li's men. The Emperor was terribly distressed, and that night, in company with his faithful eunuch, Wang, he ascended Mei-shan hill, from whence he had a complete view of the city. The flames that rose in every direction showed him how fully it was in possession of the enemy and with what ruthless savagery they were wreaking their vengeance on the inhabitants.

He returned to the palace in great distress, when the saddest scenes were enacted between him and some of the members of his family. Next morning, before daybreak, he again ascended Mei-shan hill in company with Wang, for all the great officials had fled to find safety elsewhere. He there wrote a note with his own blood, in which he said, "My virtue is small, and therefore I have incurred the anger of Heaven, and so the rebels have captured my capital. Let them disfigure my corpse, but don't let them kill one of my people." After composing this pathetic letter he hung himself with his own girdle. Wang, determined not to outlive his royal master, also committed suicide, and his body was found close to that of the Emperor.

Li now took possession of Peking and issued orders that all mandarins should present themselves before him, under pain of death, within three days. Search was made for the Emperor, and a reward of ten thousand taels, and the title of count, was promised to anyone that would produce him. It was not long before the dead body was found, and the uneasy feeling that Li had experienced up till then vanished, for he now fully believed that the empire was his own. But whilst the prize was actually within his grasp he was destined to have it rudely snatched from him by the new actors that now appear upon the scene. Amongst the host of high officials that made their submission to the rebel chief was Wu Siang, whose son, Wu San-kwei, was in command of the important fortress of Ning-yuen. The latter had been summoned by the late Emperor to the defence of the capital, with the order to abandon all the posts beyond Shan-hai-kwan. He had already reached the town of Fung-yun, when he heard of the capture of Peking and the suicide of the Emperor.

Distressed and perplexed by the terrible news he decided to stay his advance, and wait where he was until he could decide what was the best course for him to take under the unlooked for circumstances. Whilst waiting a letter reached him from his father, urging him to proceed to the capital and submit to Li. The latter had threatened unless he did so to order the execution of himself and all the members of his family. Impelled by the desire to save his father, and feeling perhaps that submission was the wisest course at the present crisis, he signified to the messenger that he accepted the terms that had been offered him by Li. Whilst they were conversing about the state of things in Peking he learned, to his horror, that a beautiful young slave girl that had been given him by a high official before he left for his command at Ning-yuen, had been seized by the rebels, and was now in possession of one of them. Enraged beyond measure at this news, for he was desperately in love with the woman, who was named Ch'en-yuan, he at once wrote to his father an indignant letter, reproaching him for the loss of the lady, whom he averred he had made no efforts to save, and declared that he renounced him for ever, and that he would fight the rebels as long as he had a single soldier remaining under his banner. To show that he was in earnest he at once broke up his camp and marched back to Shan-hai-kwan, from which place he wrote his famous letter to the Manchus, asking for help to drive out the rebels from Peking and save the dynasty from being exterminated.

The Manchu rulers had been no uninterested spectators of the terrible civil war that was destroying the empire, and they had been steadily arming and waiting for the time when it would be safe for them to act in their own interests. They had captured Sung-shan, and the general in command of that place had gone over to them with all his soldiers. After the evacuation of Ning-yuen they immediately occupied it, and thus possessed the fortress they had often attempted to capture, but without success. The regent,* who was on the western bank of the Liau, with an army ready to march on China, no sooner received San-kwei's letter than he at once replied that he was coming to his assistance, and with the departure of the answer his soldiers were on the move. The distance to Shan-hai-kwan, which was about two hundred and seventy miles, was accomplished in eight days.

San-kwei was delighted with their arrival, for Li was approaching with an immense army to conquer the last enemy that he supposed he had to meet before the empire was his own. Dor-gun encamped on a hill a little over three miles away to the east of Shan-hai-kwan, where he could see all that he was going on without being observed by the enemy. Hardly were these arrangements made when twenty thousand of Li's picked cavalry advanced towards the east gate of the fortress, whilst Li, at the head of two hundred thousand men occupied the country between it and the sea. In order to strengthen his position Li had brought with him the father of San-kwei, as well as the son of the late Emperor. The former was led in front of the fortress, where he implored his son to surrender, and thus save his life. San-kwei declared that he was a loyal minister of the dynasty, and would never surrender his command to rebels. Upon this Wu-siang was executed in the presence of his son, who became more than ever fully determined never to surrender to such relentless foes.

San-kwei determined to take the initiative, and so he first attacked the cavalry and drove them back on the main army, leaving his rear open. Next day, in consequence of orders received from the regent, he marched out of the west gate and made straight for the centre of the huge army of the rebels. The fighting was terrible, for the bitterest feelings animated the imperialists. A fierce storm was blowing at the time, which screamed and roared above the clang of arms and the cries of the wounded. Still San-kwei made no impression, for the rebels far outnumbered his forces, and if left to himself he would certainly have been vanquished. Never for a moment, however, did he dream of retreat, but fought on as though victory were certain to come to his arms. At last the Manchus, who had been watching the unequal contest, drew themselves up, ready to take a part in the battle. Steadily and slowly at first twenty thousand iron breast-plaited horses came down the hill and marched to the battle. Quicker and more quick became the motion as they advanced, till at last, with a rush and a shout, they madly galloped into the midst of the rebels, who were shattered and broken by his irresistible onset.

---

* T'ai Tsung had died in October, A. D. 1643, leaving the throne of his ninth son. As he was only five years old his uncle Dor-gun was appointed regent to govern till he became of age.

They were completely taken by surprise, for they never dreamt of a foe being so near them. The first to take to flight was Li. In his terror he leaped from his horse and fled on foot by unfrequented paths from the scene of conflict. Soon the whole rebel army was in a disordered flight, pursued by San-kwei and the Manchus, who slaughtered them in vast numbers. For fourteen miles the pursuit was kept up, when the regent returned to Shan-hai-kwan, which he took possession of whilst he ordered San-kwei to continue to follow the flying foe. The first place that Li rested at was Yung-ping, but the approach of San-kwei, with whom he had in vain endeavoured to open negotiations, caused him to continue his flight to Peking. Here he gathered all the valuables that his men had plundered, executed all the relatives of San-kwei, as well as of the Ming princes, and setting fire to the palaces, set off with his immense army for the west. San-kwei, whom the politic regent had placed at the head of the pursuing force, advanced by rapid marches after Li, his great object now being to prevent him from strengthening himself in the famous fortress of Tung-kwan, which would have enabled him to have indefinitely prolonged the conflict.

The regent entered Peking in June, A. D. 1644. He at once issued a proclamation to the inhabitants, telling them that he had come to deliver them from brigands, whose only objects were plunder and murder, and that therefore they might dismiss all fears from their minds, and go about their ordinary business without any anxiety. He then caused the bodies of the late royal family to be interred in a suitable manner, and gave the name of Chwang Lieh-ti to the late unfortunate Emperor. Considering that China now practically belonged to the Manchus, by a wise stroke of policy he determined to remove their capital from Moukden to Peking. As he was a man of prompt action he sent orders that his nephew, escorted by a suitable force, should come to him as speedily as possible, in order that he might take possession of the vacant throne. His commands were implicitly obeyed, and in October the young Emperor, who was then six years old, reached his new capital, and the reign of the Ts'ing dynasty was formally inaugurated. Thus amidst bloodshed and disorder the Ming power vanished before its conqueror. It at first owed its rise to the same unhappy forces that finally caused it to disappear. We have no pity for the family that has just fallen. It had never proved by its purity or statesmanship that it had a divine commission to rule the empire. As the years went by it showed by its reckless and lavish expenditure of the revenues of the country, and by the licentious habits that turned the palace into a pandemonium, that it was unfitted for its high position. It fell as other dynasties did before it, because of the inherent want of moral qualities, without which no power will ever be long tolerated by a people like the Chinese, who demand so high an ideal in their sovereign.

CHAPTER XXXII.

THE TS'ING DYNASTY (A. D. 1644—).

Shun Chih—A. D. 1644-1662.

A FEW days after the young Emperor reached Peking he held an audience. The first to approach and pay their respects to him were the eunuchs. The high officials of the Board of War were indignant at this, and, remonstrating with those who had charge of the ceremonials of the court, declared that they were only fit to sweep the floor and not to have access to a monarch. The result of this remonstrance was that an order was issued forbidding the eunuchs for the future to hold any official posts under the crown, an injunction that is in force at the present day.

The greatest unanimity seemed to prevail amongst the nobles and leading men, both in the army and the state in and around the capital, to acknowledge the new dynasty, and the regent must have been surprised at the easy victory that brought to his family an empire so renowned as that of China. News of the accession of his nephew was at once forwarded to Mongolia and Corea, and commands were issued that the same loyal obedience should be paid to the Manchus as had been rendered to the Mings.

In the meantime stirring events were taking place in the south. There, at least, the people were not prepared for a foreign power to take possession of the country, and they were determined to remain loyal to the royal house that had fallen on such evil times. Shih K'o-fa, who was president of one of the boards in Nanking, was a man of high reputation and a scholar of the first rank. In these times of perplexity the eyes of all were naturally turned to him as the one best fitted to take the lead in affairs at this critical time, when the fate of the nation was at stake. Unfortunately the one who had the best right to the throne was Fuh Wang, a grandson of Wan Li. He was not a favorite with the people, for he was ignorant, drunken and dissolute, and they would infinitely have preferred Ch'ang Wang, a grandson of Muh Tsung. True, however, to the instinct that is deeply rooted in the Chinese, the nobles insisted that Fuh Wang should ascend the throne, and K'o-fa gave his consent.

The regent, who knew how powerful was the influence that was wielded by K'o-fa, wrote him a letter, in which he attempted to show that the only objects for which the Manchus were in China was the avenging the late Emperor's death and the destruction of the robber Li. "Come now," he continued, "and submit to us. We are not the usurpers of the Mings, we take but the place that the rebel Li seized for himself. I have fought with the destroyers of your dynasty, and you ought to be grateful to me for so doing.

Do you think it was right to sit still while the fighting was going on, and not to come to the aid of your sovereign? Don't think for a moment that we cannot cross the Yang-tze to you ; that is a simple matter for my troops to perform. Come, therefore, and submit, and you will have large rewards given you.''

To this K'o-fa replied, "The late Emperor was one that rever-enced Heaven and followed the teachings of his ancestors. Having been killed by the rebels I felt obliged to appoint someone to succeed him. This is what has been done in all previous dynasties. When we heard that you had fought with Li and entered the capital, and not only buried with funeral honors the royal dead, but also went into mourning for them, our hearts were filled with gratitude. Now your letter has arrived, and you blame me for appointing a successor. Why should you ? You have ever been tributary to China, and you have received money and silks from it. Who ever dreamt that you wished to rule it? Your action at first was noble ; now it is selfish. You surely don't mean to carry out this latter policy. Let us both combine to punish Li, and whether it be land or money that you want you shall certainly not be without your reward.''

The regent had the wisdom to see that there was no use carry-ing on any further correspondence with a man of such exalted character as this, and so he determined to use the severer method of arms. He accordingly sent an army, under the command of his brother, to proceed to Kiang-nan, where it captured Hai-chow and other cities. K'o-fa, who had advanced to meet the Manchus, recovered Hai-chow and showed so bold a front to them that they were for the time stayed in their victorious march.

In the meanwhile San-kwei had pursued Li with the greatest activity, and in every engagement was successful. Immense spoils fell to his men and vast numbers of the rebels were slain. Li, who saw that the contest with his relentless enemy was a hopeless one, endeavoured to amalgamate his forces with those of his former colleague, Chang-hien, who had proclaimed himself king in Sz-chwan and ruled that province with the most sanguinary despotism, but all his advances were repelled. One after another the great fortresses that were held by the rebels were captured by the pursuing army. After the fall of Tung-hwan he took his army, which still consisted of five hundred thousand men, into Shensi, where he hoped the avenging enemy would stay its advance. In this, however, he was deceived, for the Manchus were determined never to be satisfied with anything less than his total destruction. In eight great battles he was routed, and large numbers of his men slain. Gradually his forces dwindled down to twenty men, by the time he had reached the mountains of Kiu-king, thirty miles to the south of the district of Tung-shan. Here, without food or necessaries of any kind, they were compelled to plunder the peasantry. These gathered in large numbers, and with their hoes struck down the robbers. When the Manchus came up they handed over the body of Li to them, and thus this great rebellion, that had overthrown a dynasty and been the means of the destruction of millions of lives, was in this region, at least, crushed, and its savage leader came to the miserable and ignoble end that he deserved.

The forces that had been engaged in the suppression of the rebellion now found themselves free for the sterner and more momentous struggle that was going on in the south. Fuh Wang had proved his utter unfitness for the critical position that he held in this most perilous time when his country was in danger. His days were spent in revelry and licentiousness, and he was more concerned about his pleasures than he was about his empire. One day a eunuch heard him sigh. "What is it that troubles you," he asked him. "I am sighing to think that it is impossible to obtain a first-rate actor," replied this true descendant of the Ming family.

The regent, who was well informed of the state of things in the south, hurried forward his troops for what he was convinced would be a crowning victory. Wherever they advanced they were successful, and city after city opened their gates to receive them. At length, crossing the Hwai river by night, they found themselves near the important town of Yang-chow, the gate of Nanking. This place was under the command of K'o-fa, who originally had thirty thousand men to defend it. Unfortunately, however, he had weakened himself by the despatch of twenty thousand of them to protect the war material which he had been compelled to leave behind him in his ineffectual endeavour to relieve Suchow.

The Manchu general concentrated his forces about six miles from the town and waited for his heavy guns. K'o-fa was advised to open a canal from the river and swamp the Manchu camp, but this he refused to do, on the ground that more of the Chinese would perish than the Manchus. He held that the interests of the people were to be considered superior to those of the dynasty.* Seven days and nights of fierce fighting, in which the losses of the Manchus were most severe, passed by, and Yangchow was taken by assault. K'o-fa made an unsuccessful attempt to commit suicide by cutting his throat. In his flight toward the north gate he was met by the victorious enemy and slain. By the middle of June (A. D. 1645) the conquerors were on the bank of the Yang-tze. In order to find out the plans of the enemy they set adrift a number of boats on it with lights on them. These were fired into by the Chinese, and as they were picked up next morning quite empty they claimed a victory and sent special messengers to Nanking to inform the authorities. Next night the Chinese, fancying the Manchus would refrain from a second attempt to cross the river, made no preparations to resist an advance. At midnight, accordingly, the latter passed their whole force over, and pushing on rapidly, they arrived before the walls of Nanking. Fuh Wang, in a drunken condition,

---

* See Ross' "The Manchus," page 257.

was hurried from the city and fled towards Wuhu, whilst the Manchus entered and took possession of his capital. When it was discovered that the prince had succeeded in escaping, a body of horsemen was at once despatched in pursuit. Deserted by his men and officers, he was speedily captured and brought into the presence of the Manchu commander, Yu Wang, who sent him a prisoner to Nanking, where he was subsequently executed.

Fuh Wang being a prisoner in the hands of the Manchus, it was necessary to appoint another to occupy the vacant throne of the Mings. Ch'ang Wang, the one whom K'o-fa would have recognized instead of Fuh Wang, was accordingly named Emperor, and took up his residence in Hangchow. Either he was wanting in daring, or he saw the hopelessness of his cause, for when the enemy appeared before the city he at once opened the gates and made his submission to them. His reign was an exceedingly brief one, having lasted but three days.

The next to assume the imperial role was T'ang Wang, a descendant of Hung Wu in the ninth generation, who set up his authority in Fuchow and invited all who remained loyal to the old dynasty to rally round him and drive out the invaders of their country. In was in vain, however, that he hoped to retrieve the fortunes of his family. Wherever the Manchus marched they gained victories over the forces that dared to encounter them. In the beginning of the year A. D. 1646 an army was sent against Ch'ang-hien, in Sz-chwan, and that cruel and blood-thirsty rebel in his first engagement with it was defeated with great slaughter, and being discovered in the hiding place under a bush, whither he had fled, was put to death by his captors. The result of this engagement was to give the Manchus complete possession of Sz-chwan.

T'ang Wang, in order to be nearer to Hangchow, moved his residence to Yen-ping, and had it not been that his generals were at variance amongst themselves, and more concerned for their own interests than his, he might have accomplished more with the large forces he was able to collect than he did. It was in consequence of this serious state of matters that the Manchus met with no serious resistance when they advanced to attack T'ang Wang. An engagement near the river Ts'ien-tang proved most fatal to the Ming soldiers, and the fall of Ningpo, Shanghai, Wenchow and T'aichow followed the disaster that had occurred there. Soon the whole of the Chehkiang province was in the hands of the invaders, and their armies were liberated for their advance on the province of Fuh-kien. In the beginning of November (A. D. 1646) the Manchus were at the gates of Yen-ping, which they took by assault, and then rapidly pursued T'ang Wang to T'ingchow, where they captured him, and having sent him to Fuchow, he was excuted there. The consequence of this was most disastrous to the Ming cause. The important cities of Changchow and Chinchew were lost and passed within the control of the Manchus, whilst Ching Chih-liang, the commander of the fleet, made his submission to the conquerors, and was sent to Peking, where he had been promised that high honours would be bestowed upon him.   His son, the celebrated Coxinga, refused to follow the example of his father, and setting sail with the ships that were under his own immediate command, he proceeded to sea, and making the region of the Pescadores his point of rendezvous he commenced that system of warfare which has made his name so famous in the history of that period.

T'ang Wang having disappeared from the scene, Kwei Wang, a great-grandson of Wan-li, aspired to succeed to the now vacant throne of the Mings.   He was proclaimed Emperor in Chau-k'ing, in the province of Kwangtung.   His reign was soon disturbed by the march of the conquering Manchus, whose arms were successful wherever they met any body of troops that dared to engage them. Kwei Wang fled into Kwangsi, still pursued by the enemy, and rested not till he brought up at Ch'uenchow, though the commander of Kwei-lin endeavored to induce him to make a stand at that strongly fortified town.   It was not long before the Manchus appeared before it, but its commander, Ch'ü Shih-sz, was a brave and high-spirited man, and refused indignantly the terms that were offered by them.   Determined to have the town, if possible, the besiegers made assault after assault, but every time they were repulsed with great loss to themselves.   This was all the more creditable to Ch'u, for whilst the struggle was going on a mutiny took place amongst his soldiers, because their pay had not been given them, and they declared they would fight no more till their arrears had been paid.   Ch'u ordered that all the gold and silver ornaments of his wife should be sold and the proceeds handed to the men.   This so touched their hearts that they flew to arms, and joining their standards drove back the Manchus from the walls. Finally the siege was abandoned and the liberated Ch'u was able to lead out his troops and give aid to the cities that needed assistance. Ping-lo was retaken by him, and in fact all the places that had been captured by the Manchus, till the whole of Kwangsi province had been recovered to the rule of Kwei Wang.

The fortunes of the Mings, which had seemed to have fallen to the very lowest ebb, from this time began to be more favorable. In Kiangsi, Kin-shing, a general that had submitted to the invaders, gave up his allegiance to them and fought on the side of Kwei Wang, with the result that the whole of that province acknowledged his rule.   In Kwangtung, too, Li Ch'eng-tung, animated by the same reason, viz., unjust treatment from his new masters, rebelled and gave up the city of Canton to the Ming soldiers. Thus, in a very brief space of time three important provinces, in which there had been severe fighting and great loss of men to the Manchus, were lost to them.   This defection proved a most serious matter to the latter, for it meant not simply that so much conquered territory had been wrested from them, but also that fully two hundred thousand men had been added to the existing forces of Kwei Wang.

The Manchus, however, were not the men to stand idly by and let the empire, which they had won with such hard service, slip from their grasp without a struggle. An army was sent into Kiangsi, and Kiukiang was recovered and Nan-chang besieged. In the meanwhile Ch'eng-tung entreated Kwei Wang to come to Canton, but Ch'u, insisting that Kwei-lin was the more suitable place as a royal residence, with a wavering and undecided mind that was destructive of the later members of the royal family, he halted at Chau-k'ing, and could not be induced to move further. In February (A. D. 1649) not only was Hangchow relieved, in which the Manchus had been beleagured, but Nan-chang was captured and King-shing slain. These two successes were followed by the recovery of the whole of Kiangsi. The Manchus now turned their arms against Ch'eng-tung, who was defeated and his army dispersed, whilst he himself was drowned in crossing a river during his flight from his pursuers. They then proceeded to invest Canton, which, after a siege of ten months, again became their own. Victory after victory succeeded, and even Kwei-lin, from want of proper support, fell into their hands. Kwei Wang was now compelled to fly, for the victorious enemies were on their march to Wuchow, where he was ; so he retreated to Nan-ning.

About this time the regent died. His death happened whilst he was out hunting, at the early age of thirty-nine. The Emperor was deeply moved by the news, and went out to meet the body on its approach to Peking. He ordered that a royal funeral should be accorded it, and at the same time he issued an edict in which he extolled the virtues of the illustrious dead and declared that he owed all the power that he possessed to him. He also bestowed posthumous honors upon the deceased. Eight months after two of the royal princes severely criticized this action of Shun Chih, because they avowed that the regent had meditated rebellion and had intended deposing the Emperor after his return from this very hunting expedition, in which he died. An investigation proved that these charges were true, so the honours that had been assigned him were revoked, but the Emperor refused to proceed to further extremities against his family, because of the distinguished services his uncle had rendered to himself and to the state. From this time Shun Chih ruled by himself, and amongst the first laws that were passed by him were the regulations that no man could become a bonze without an order from a mandarin ; that the public examinations for degrees should be carried on in a certain manner (which manner they retain to the present day), and that mandarins might retire from the public service in such a way as was then prescribed by him.

The affairs of Kwei Wang becoming desperate in Kwangsi, he sent Sun-k'o, a former general of the rebel Chang-hien, who was in great power in Yunnan, a patent of nobility, giving him the title of prince or king. This had been long and anxiously wished for, not simply through loyalty to the Ming cause, but because he believed it would add to his power and give him a standing amongst the large numbers that were drawn to his standard, partly through the hopes of plunder and partly through dislike to being ruled by a foreign power. Five thousand men were sent by Sun-k'o to escort him from Nan-ning to a place of safety in Yunnan, but he found the commander such a rough, fierce individual that he feared to entrust himself to him, and so preferred to remain where he was.

Fate, however, was against the Ming cause, for the Manchus were everywhere victorious in the north, and so in the beginning of A. D. 1651 Kwei Wang accepted the guard that was sent him and came to the place of residence appointed for him by Sun-k'o at Ngan-lung, where a house had been prepared for him, and a yearly income of eight thousand taels (or ounces) of silver allowed him for the maintenance of his household. That he was not altogether a welcome guest is proved by the scant courtesy with which he was treated by those who were sent to be a guard of honor to him.

During his stay here fighting was going on vigorously in the south and west of the empire. The Manchus managed to get control over the whole of the Kwangtung province, but Li Ting-kwoh, an adventurer who was fighting for his own hand, got several cities in Hunan and Kwangsi. A great battle was fought in the former province between him and the Manchus, in which the former suffered a severe reverse, but the commander of the victorious force, pursuing without due caution, was led into an ambush and experienced a great defeat, and one of the royal princes who was present, to escape being captured, committed suicide by cutting his throat. After this unexpected success Ting-kwoh was again victorious in his engagements in different parts of Kwangsi, and captured the cities of Liu-chow and Chau-k'ing. Kwei Wang, unhappy under the protection of Sun-k'o, who was making preparations for becoming Emperor, sent messengers to Ting-kwoh to come and save him. When Sun-k'o heard of this he was greatly enraged, and seizing a number of his officers that waited near his person, put them to death. Unfortunately Tin-kwoh had his hands too full to obey the summons he had received, and shortly after he was defeated with great slaughter by the Manchus, and was compelled to fly to Nan-ning. The city of Canton, which he had captured, and other important towns, he was compelled to abandon.

In the summer of A. D. 1654 Sun-k'o sailed with a force of sixty thousand men in a thousand vessels of all sizes to the attack of Wu-chang, but he was met by the Manchus, who overthrew his army and destroyed a large number of his ships, compelling him to retreat to Kweichow. The war was going on vigorously in the meanwhile around Amoy and Quemoy. Coxinga's general, Hwang-wu, had treacherously betrayed Hai-ting to the Manchus, but his leader had compensated himself for this by taking Fuchow, Wenchow and

T'aichow. This year was distinguished by the appearance of a Dutch embassy at Peking, which came to beseech the Emperor for special trading privileges for their countrymen. Though they remained three months in the capital and allowed themselves to be treated as officials of a vassal state, kneeling before the Emperor and knocking their heads upon the ground, the utmost they could gain from him was the privilege of being allowed to come to China once in eight years with their merchandise, with which they might trade with the Chinese.

The next two years were important in their issues. Ting-kwoh in the beginning of A. D. 1655 came to the aid of Kwei Wang in Ngan-lung, and both fled to Tienchow, in Yunnan. Sun-k'o was annoyed, but it was not till the end of next year that he was able to take adequate steps to resent what he considered as a blow struck at his pretentions to supreme power. In the beginning of November he led a large army to chastise Ting-kwoh, but he himself was utterly defeated and his soldiers dispersed. In order to save himself from capture he went over to the Manchus and surrendered himself to them. There was great rejoicing at the capital when the news arrived, for he had hitherto been the most formidable enemy that the new dynasty had been compelled to reckon with. He was sent on to Peking, where, instead of being punished, he was highly honoured, and received the title of prince.

By the middle of next year (A. D. 1657) the Manchus had three armies on the march, each consisting of fifty thousand men, and all converging on Kweichow, to crush out the rebellion that had raged so fiercely there and in Yunnan for so many years. Ting-kwoh summoned all his available forces to meet the coming foe, but the response to his call was not as enthusiastic as he had expected, and the army with which he marched was too small to venture to cope with the combined forces of the enemy. By the close of the year one of the divisions entered Yunnan, and Ting-kwoh had but thirty thousand to oppose it ; still he bravely went forward, hoping to be joined by reinforcements ere the collision took place. These expectations were not realized, and in the battle that was fought on the bank of the river that acts as a boundary line between Yunnan and Kweichow, he was defeated and had to fly for his life.

The effect of this disaster was soon seen in the submission of all the eastern cities of Yunnan and the occupation of Yunnan-fu, the provincial capital, by the combined armies of Manchus. Ting-kwoh and Kwei Wang made their escape to Ying-chang. Expecting that they would be pursued, Ting-kwoh prepared a series of ambushes amongst the hills they would have to cross. Part of the Manchus, amounting to twelve thousand men, had fallen into these, and would have been slain, but before they could advance far enough a deserter from Ting-kwoh revealed the danger. The men, abandoning everything, retreated in disorder, but the artillery stood its ground, and firing into the place where the men in ambush lay, made havoc amongst them. A general battle now took place, which was fought with the utmost desperation, but numbers were bound to prevail, and soon the adherents of the Mings were flying in disorder from the last battlefield on which they were ever to fight for the old cause. They were pursued for a distance of forty miles to T'ung-yueh, which lay near the Burmese frontier, and whither Kwei-wang had fled for refuge. The larger proportion of the Manchu troops was marched back to Peking, and Yunnan was left in charge of San-kwei, who made the amplest preparations for preventing the return of the fugitive prince from Burmese territory, into which he had crossed, and of even marching into it himself and seizing him there.

Whilst these disasters were going on in the west Coxinga was moving into the Yang-tze with his large fleet, in order to attack Nan-king. There the Manchus met him, and in a great naval fight were completely victorious, and burning five hundred of his vessels they compelled him to retreat with the loss also of all the towns he had captured on his way up.

In the meanwhile, Ting-kwoh had been gradually gathering a small army about him, and hearing that Kwei Wang was detained a prisoner in Ava, desired to advance to his aid, but was prevented by the Burmese, for though successful in his engagement with them Kwei Wang was kept so close a prisoner that he could not be got at, so Ting-kwoh had to withdraw without effecting his purpose.

His bitter enemy, San-kwei, was destined to be more successful. With an immense army he advanced close to the Burmese capital and demanded Kwei Wang, threatening that if he were not given up he would attack the place. The king, terrified by the formidable forces arrayed against him, consented to the demand, and handed over the prince, his family and all that was left of his retinue, to San-kwei, who at once started for Yunnan with his royal captives, and reste not till he reached Yunnan-fu, where they were kept in close guard. Here Kwei Wang, despairing of life and hopeless of mercy from the Manchus, in May A. D. 1662 strangled himself with a silk cord, and thus escaped from the cruel hands of those that had captured him and from the sorrows that had embittered the closing years of his life.*

After a reign of eighteen years Shun-chih died, leaving the throne to his young son, who was only eight years old. He entrusted him to the charge of four of his ministers, who, in order

---

* The cruel way in which San-kwei hunted Kwei Wang until he at last got him within his power, is one of the serious blots on his character. When he was on his last march to demand him from the Burmese he received a most pathetic letter from him. In that he reminded him of the honours he had received from the last Ming Emperors and the high position he formerly held in the state, and appealed to him to have pity upon him, and instead of hunting him to death come and deliver him. No reply was sent to this touching letter, and San-kwei marched, as though he had never received it, to the capture of the unfortunate prince.

to prove the sincerity of their intentions, went into the royal
ancestral hall and swore before the spirits of the dead that they
would be loyal to the trust imposed upon them.

K'ang Hi—A. D. 1662-1723.

The boy that now succeeded his father was one that was
destined to be amongst the most famous of those that have ever sat
upon the dragon throne.   As a child he was very attractive.   He
had a very pretty face and engaging manners.   He was, moreover,
exceedingly truthful, clever and fond of study.   This love of books
began when he was only five years old.   He became Emperor at a
most auspicious time.   His dynasty was acknowledged almost
throughout the eighteen provinces, for all the most formidable
enemies to it had been overthrown.   Kwei Wang died shortly after
he came into power, as did also a few months later Ting-kwoh,
whose son submitted to the Manchus, and nearly at the same time
Coxinga, irritated at the unfilial conduct of his son, Ching-chin,
became mad and injured himself, so that he died. *

On the death of Coxinga, at the early age of thirty-eight, the
chief officers in Formosa elected his brother to succeed him, but
Ching-chin had sufficient influence to maintain his own rights, and
defeating his uncle, who fled to the Manchus and submitted to
them, he became the acknowledged head of the forces that had been
commanded by his father.   In A. D. 1663 the Chinese, in conjunction with a Dutch fleet that had come to make reprisals for the loss

---

* It will be remembered that when Coxinga's father submitted to the Manchus
the son sailed away south with his fleet and declared he would never yield to the
invader of his country. Failing in all his efforts to overthrow their power, and
discouraged by the disasters that had happened to him in A. D. 1658, when he
endeavored to capture Nanking, he now looked around for some place where he
could concentrate his forces, and which he could safely make his head-quarters for
the larger fleet under his command. Formosa seemed to be exactly the place that
was best suited to meet all the requirements of his case. As it was occupied, however, by the Dutch, it meant that he would have to expel them before he could take
possession of it. How they happened to come to the island may be here explained.
Anxious to have commercial relations with the east they appeared before Macao in
A. D. 1624 with a fleet of seventeen ships. Being unsuccessful in their attempt on
this place they sailed to the Pescadores, which they took possession of, and built a
fort, in order to be ready for any attack that the Chinese might make upon them.
The latter, being unwilling to give up the islands, fought and parleyed with the
Dutch, with the result that they were induced to withdraw to Formosa, which then
happened to be in the possession of the Japanese. Having made satisfactory
arrangements with these latter, who abandoned the island to them, they built the
fortress of Zelandia in A. D. 1626. The rule of the Dutch was not acknowledged
very far beyond the guns of the fort, but they seem to have done a great deal for
the moral and spiritual welfare of those under their rule. Missionaries arrived in
due time, and no effort was spared to teach them Christianity.
  Coxinga, finding that Formosa was just the place that suited his needs in June,
A. D. 1661, landed twenty-five thousand men and began to blockade the Dutch in
their forts. Being entirely unprepared for such an emergency, the latter were
finally overcome. Zelandia was compelled to surrender after a siege of nine
months, during which sixteen hundred of the Dutch had been slain, and those that
remained of the garrison and the inhabitants were taken prisoners and treated with
great cruelty by Coxinga.

of Formosa, made an attack on Ching-chin, and so thoroughly defeated him that he was compelled to fly to T'ung-shan, leaving Amoy and Quemoy in secure possession of the Manchus. Pursuing their advantage, they attacked T'ung-shan, which surrendered to them, and a large number of ships fell into their hands. Ching-chin, feeling that he had lost all hold upon the mainland of China, retired to Formosa, there to maintain the struggle with the new dynasty for some years to come. In the following year the Dutch were again solicited to assist the Manchu General, Shih-lang, in an attack on Formosa. They consented, but a contrary wind prevented them reaching their destination, and so they were obliged to return to Amoy and leave Ching-chin in undisputed sway and with the power to harass and annoy the Chinese trading junks that travelled up and down the Formosa channel and to levy black-mail upon the trade carried on by those that lived near the sea-coast.

Quarrels and divisions having arisen between the four regents that Shun Chih had deputed to care for his son whilst in his minority, K'ang Hi, in September, A. D. 1667, took the government into his own hands, and from this time forth ruled China in his own name. The assumption of power by the Emperor was a most fortunate matter for the Roman Catholics, who had suffered great hardships under the rule of the regents. Shun Chih had shown himself specially well disposed towards them, and had lavished unusual honours on Adam Schaal, with whom he was peculiarly intimate. This latter had been appointed tutor to the young monarch, but the regents caused him to be thrown into prison, and they had even condemned him to be cut into a thousand pieces. This punishment, however, was not carried out, and he was simply kept in confinement till his death, which happened in his seventy-eighth year.

Two years after Kang Hi took the government into his own hands a dispute arose as to the correctness of the calendar that had been issued by the Astronomical Board. The Emperor carefully examined the statements made by the Chinese officials and those of the Jesuit Verbiest. He found the knowledge of the latter so far superior to that of the former that he made him President of the Board and dismissed the others in disgrace. A new calendar was also ordered to be issued, and though the disgraced officers besought Verbiest not to expose their ignorance to the nation he very unwisely refused to make any compromise in the matter, and the one that he drew up and sent forth throughout the eighteen provinces by command of K'ang Hi, was minus an intercalary month, which his predecessors, through their ignorance, had inserted. This conduct of Verbiest was destined to bring terrible sorrow and suffering upon the church he represented in future years, in consequence of the enmity he incurred by his unyielding attitude.

In August, A. D. 1669, K'ang Hi issued an edict, ordering that all taxes due to the end of the 17th year of his father's reign should be remitted ; that for the future all taxes should be collected twice a year, viz., in July and August, and again in September and October ; and that all lands unjustly taken from the Chinese by the Manchus should be restored to them. K'ang Hi, who was a man that had the interests of his people at heart, was greatly distressed at the large number of serious cases that were reported to him by the Board of Punishments, and ordered an investigation of the whole subject, and a report to be made to him as to the causes. He was certain, he said, that misgovernment by the mandarins was the reason why such disorders existed in the empire, and he was determined that those who were the efficient cause of so many crimes should be severely dealt with. He discovered at this time (A. D. 1670) that large numbers of criminals, who were being banished to the north, died on the way through the privations they endured and the hardships and sorrows of the journey. He gave an order that this state of things should be altered, and that no criminals should be transported between the months of July and November until, in fact, the great heat had considerably diminished.

The Emperor, though still young, had studied the condition of the country, and he had been considering, now that the empire was at peace, what were the best plans for its government, so as to prevent rebellion against the new dynasty as well as to secure the attachment of the people to his house. There was one feature of the present system that gave him considerable anxiety. When the war closed those that had been most distinguished for the assistance they had rendered the Manchus in their conquest of China had been rewarded with the title of prince and appropriate territories to command, with large forces under their own control. Three of these were conspicuous for the large powers they possessed and for the importance of the districts over which they ruled. These were Prince Wu San-kwei, whose command extended over Kwei-chow and Yunnan ; Prince Shang Ko-shi, who ruled over the provinces of Kwangtung and Kwangsi ; and Prince Kang Ching-chung, whose dominion extended over Fuhkien and Chehkiang. K'ang Hi was statesman enough to know that there was extreme peril to the empire so long as these men exercised such large powers, and therefore it was of the utmost importance that these should be restricted as speedily as possible. As a commencement to this it was decided that the title of prince, which had been bestowed upon Sun-k'o when he submitted to the Manchus, and which was now held by his grandson, should be changed for that of duke. The question came up in the form of a memorial from a censor, who held that a man who had been a rebel and a robber should never have had such high honors granted to him, and therefore the Emperor ought to reconsider the question and bestow upon his descendant a lower rank. K'ang Hi agreed to this, as well as to the suggestion that the services of an officer specially employed by the Emperor should cease after a period of five years.

Not long after this the question that had been agitating K'ang Hi's mind came up in a very unexpected way. Prince Shang Ko-shi was a loyal and faithful subject of the Emperor. Unfortunately his son Chi-sin was a man of fierce and drunken habits, and restrained in his life by no principles of right or reason. His father was in constant dread lest some outbreak should involve him with the Emperor; so to save himself from possible disgrace, in A. D. 1673 he petitioned the throne to be allowed to retire to his home in Liau-tung. The request was placed in the hands of the officers of the Board of Rites, who, after considerable discussion, agreed to his petition, at the same time deciding that his troops should be recalled and disbanded. News of what was going on was regularly transmitted to San-kwei by his son, who was resident in the capital. In order, perhaps, to see what the real intentions of the Emperor were in the proposed disbanding of Ko-shi's soldiers he also sent in his resignation and induced Kang Ching-chung to do the same. After a long discussion, in which the members of the Board were by no means unanimous, it was agreed to accept the resignation of San-kwei, who was appointed to the command of Shan-hai-kwan, and officers were sent to occupy the positions vacated by the three princes, as well as provisions, boats, etc., to be used by them on their journey home. San-kwei, who now saw that it was the design of K'ang Hi to rid himself of a powerful vassal, raised the standard of revolt, about the beginning of A. D. 1674, killed the governor of Yunnan, and sending proclamations throughout his wide territories, declared that a new dynasty, even the Chow, was now established, and that all patriotic Chinese should rally round him and drive the hated Manchus from the soil of China.

A war council was immediately summoned when tidings of this revolt reached the capital, and orders were sent to the princes in Canton and Fuchow to remain at their posts until the pleasure of the Emperor should be made known to them. A large army was ordered to march as soon as possible to occupy Kingchow and Ch'ang-teh before they could be seized by the rebels, and vigorous preparations were made for the assembling of all the disposable troops of the empire to meet an emergency which K'ang Hi saw would be fraught with great danger to his dynasty. To add to the difficulties of the situation, an insurrection, headed by Yang Chi-liang, broke out in Peking; but such prompt measures were taken that the revolution was soon suppressed, several hundreds of the conspirators being executed, and Yang compelled to hide himself from the search that was made for him. Meanwhile, San-kwei had made dangerous headway in every direction in which he had advanced. The governor of Kweichow joined his standard and slew all the Manchus in the towns that soon followed his example. The whole of Sz-chwan gave in its adherence to his cause, and Prince Kang Ching-chung, in Fuhkien, rose in rebellion and made common cause with San-kwei. Hunan next revolted, and then the commander of Kwei-lin ; so that in the course of a few months six important provinces were lost to the royal cause.

San-kwei now advanced rapidly towards Wuchang, with the hopes of capturing it, but he was repulsed by the Manchus, and K'ang Hi was so indignant with him that he put to death his son and grandson, who had been imprisoned in the capital. Anxious to gain the powerful province of Kwangtung to his side, San-kwei sent messengers to Shang Ko-shi, inviting him to join the popular cause and help him to drive out the invaders of their country. The only response to this was to arrest the bearers of the letter and to despatch the latter to the Emperor for his inspection.

During all these troubles the Emperor showed himself fully competent to grapple with the terrible crisis that had come upon his dominions. Troops were sent to Sz-chwan and Han-chung, and several other important places were recovered. These successes were, however, only temporary. Provisions failed, and the soldiers had to withdraw, abandoning the places they had captured. Wang-hu, the governor of Shensi, also rebelled, and by the end of the year (A. D. 1674) the whole of that important province had thrown in its lot with the rebels. The year A. D. 1675 passed by, leaving the condition of things very much the same as it was at the beginning of it. On the whole, perhaps, the imperial forces were rather more successful than those of the rebels, for in Shensi, Wang-hu had suffered several severe defeats. In the spring of next year Shang Ko-shi's son, Chi-sin, went over to the rebels, which so enraged his father that he died of vexation. This loss was made up somewhat by the submission of Wang-hu, who was made a general and ordered to atone for past misdeeds by zeal in the royal service. Kang Ching-chung, also, towards the close of the year, after having suffered several defeats, returned to his allegiance, and was forgiven by the Emperor, on condition that he should show his repentance by quelling the pirate Ching-chin. When the latter heard of this surrender of his late colleague he led twenty thousand men to the attack of Fuchow, but he was defeated and pursued for nearly twenty miles by the victorious Manchus. The consequence of this victory was that nearly the whole of Fuhkien again came under the control of the conquerors. Chi-sin, the drunken renegade who had never once been moved by a single patriotic impulse in his defection, prayed to be forgiven by K'ang Hi, and he was taken back into the imperial service. Ching-chin, after his defeat, fled to Formosa, where for the time being he was safe, but not long after he put out to sea again with his large fleet, and first attacked Chusan and then Canton, but in each case he had to retire without any success. He next advanced against Swatow, where he was defeated, but he managed to take possession of Hai-ting and Amoy. San-kwei, in the meantime, had captured Chang-sha, and usually wherever he commanded in person his troops were victorious ; so that the imperialist cause, though successful in other quarters, was

by no means in a promising condition in the region where the
troops were led by himself ; still it was manifest that the Manchus,
with their immense resources, must in the end remain masters of
the empire. To the great joy of the Emperor, San-kwei died in
October, A. D. 1678, of paralysis, and though the forces of the
rebels were still very considerable, the master spirit of the revolution was gone, and there was no mind left to guide it as he had
done. His grandson, Wu Shih-fan, was recognized by the rebels
as their leader, but he was not the man to succeed so brilliant a
commander as his grandfather had been, and the mistake of appointing such an incompetent person was soon seen in the reverses that
followed the rebels in their engagements with the Manchus. The
imperialists, now confident of success, pressed forward with all their
forces, and gradually, after terrible fighting, in which they were
sometimes defeated, drove the enemy out of Hupeh, Honan and
Kwangsi. Then Kweichow was recovered, and Shih-fan, with all
his forces, retired to his capital, Yunnan-fu, which was the only
place left to him in the province. After several months' close
siege, during which severe fighting was carried on, it was captured
about the close of the year A. D. 1681, and with its possession the
great rebellion of the three princes collapsed and K'ang Hi found
himself seated on a throne which no one dared now to dispute his
right to. Shih-fan committed suicide before the city fell, but his
head was sent to the capital, whilst the body of San-kwei was
disinterred and his bones were dispersed amongst the provinces to
which the rebellion had extended. Great rejoicings' were manifested in the capital at the overthrow of the princes ; feasts were
spread and a poem written by the Emperor to commemorate the
great event. Severe measures were also taken towards some of
those that survived. Kang Ching-chung and Lin Ching-chung
were condemned to be sliced, whilst the descendants of San-kwei
were forever debarred from going in for the literary examinations of
the country, or from becoming mandarins.

It was now decided that vigorous measures should be taken to
suppress the robbers of Formosa and reduce that beautiful island to
the rule of the Manchus. One of the royal princes, named K'ung,
who was in command of Fuchow, ordered Wan-ching, with a force
of thirty thousand men and three hundred ships, to attack Ching,
who had possession of Amoy and Hai-ting. The imperialists gained
a decided victory, and Ching, abandoning all his conquests on the
mainland, sailed away, with all that were left of his men and ships,
to Formosa. Six months after his arrival there he died, and was
succeeded by his son, Ko-tsang. This man, who was the son of a
slave woman, was a person of great ability, and had been so fully
trusted by his father that he had been left in charge of Formosa
whilst he was away in Amoy. In the exercise of his authority he
had been compelled to use severe measures with some of the more
unruly subjects of Ching. The consequence was that he incurred

their deadly hatred, and they were therefore determined not to submit to his rule. Backed by his family, who disliked him on account of his ignoble birth, the conspirators determined on his death. He was seized by Fang Si-fan and strangled, and Ko-shwang, the second son of Ching, became chief of the robbers.

Preparations were now made by the government for an attack on Formosa, and three hundred ships and twelve thousand men were got ready for this great undertaking. The Dutch had been invited to join their forces, but as they did not arrive in time the fleet sailed without them. They started July, A. D. 1683, under the command of Shih-lang and Yau K'i-sheng, for the Pescadores, which it was determined should be first conquered. On their arrival there a typhoon began to blow, so they were compelled to anchor. Before the storm had fully abated Shih-lang got his vessels under weigh and advanced towards the enemy. Liu-kwoh, who was the rebel commander, had, with the twenty thousand men under his charge, made ample preparations to resist the enemy, and had built an embankment along the bay and armed it with cannon. Shih-lang boldly advanced with the van of his fleet, but through the force of the gale, which was still blowing, his ships became disordered. Liu, seeing this, put out to meet them, and in the confusion gained a temporary advantage, Shih-lang being wounded in the eye. The latter, far from being discouraged, got his ships together and ordered them to attack in fives ; each set engaging one of the enemy. All that day the battle raged furiously, as well as the next, and the result was the total defeat of the pirates. Over a hundred of their ships were burnt, and fully twelve thousand of their men were slain. Liu escaped in one of his ships to Formosa, and the rest of his men submitted to Shih-lang. As soon as possible the latter was in pursuit of the flying enemy, and arrived shortly after him at Lur-mun. The water was so low that his ships were obliged to anchor some distance from the land. After a delay of twelve days an unusually high tide raised the sea so high that all his vessels could come close in to the land. A similar event happened when Coxinga made his famous descent upon the island and became the conqueror of it. As it was looked upon as a special sign from heaven that he was to be the possessor of it, so now it was considered as an indubitable evidence that it was the will of the same great power that the Manchus should be the rulers of it. An immediate submission was made to Shih-lang by Ko-shwang, who handed over to him the gold and silver seals that had been given to Coxinga by Kwei Wang. He was sent to Peking, where he was created a duke, and where he lived the rest of his days. Shih-lang, for the distinguished services he had rendered, was created a marquis, and others of the inferior officers were rewarded according to the degree of merit they had gained during this brief but most successful campaign. Formosa now came under the formal rule of the Manchus, being divided into one prefecture and three *hien*, or counties, and thus the whole empire was at peace and K'ang Hi ruled with undisputed sway over the vast territories he and his race had conquered.

In the year A. D. 1686 we find difficulties arising between the Russians and the Chinese in the neighbourhood of the Amoor. The former were inclined to encroach upon the territories of the latter, and frequent collisions were the result between them and the frontier guards. At length, in A. D. 1689, a treaty was concluded between Russia and China at Nih-chu, in which it was agreed that the country north of the Amoor should belong to the former, whilst all south of it should be governed by China. This was the first treaty that was ever made by China with any foreign country, and in order that there should be no disputes regarding the territories in question, boundary stones were erected with inscriptions, both in Russian and Chinese.*

The year A. D. 1680 is an important one, not only in the history of this reign, but also in that of the empire at large, for in it was commenced a new policy in regard to the treatment of the tribes that inhabited Central Asia that led to their subjugation and to the extension of the Emperor's authority over a vast area that had hitherto been outside his jurisdiction. The occasion of this was the ambition of a young Eleuth chief named Galdan, who, in his desire for power, dared even to come in collision with the great Chinese Empire.†

---

* The year A. D. 1567 is mentioned as the one in which the Russians first visited China. Two Cossacks arrived in Peking, but they were not permitted to see the Emperor, because they had not brought presents, or really, tribute, with them. The same fate happened to Pettlin in A. D. 1619, and for the same reason in A. D. 1653 Baikoff, the ambassador of the Czar Alexis, was not allowed an audience, because he would not prostrate himself before the dragon throne. Trade, however, was not suspended between the two countries, and commercial relationships were maintained to a certain extent between the merchants of both.

† Galdan was the younger son of a powerful Eleuth chief. When his elder brother succeeded his father Galdan, who did not care for a subordinate position, travelled to Thibet. Hearing of his death he speedily returned and murdered his nephew, who had become Khan. A younger brother of the man he had slain fled for protection to K'ang Hi, who listened to his story and showed his sympathy for him in various ways, but took no active steps to redress his wrongs. Galdan now became the acknowledged head of the tribes over whom his father had ruled. He married a daughter of the chief of Tsung-hai, and shortly after slew his father-in-law and appropriated his territories. He then planned a scheme by which the lands of the Khalkans might also come under his sway. He sent a number of his people to their chief, who, under instructions from him, used insulting language towards him. Being put to death for this, Galdan made a formal complaint that reparation should be made him for the murder of his subjects. Whilst negotiations were going on he sent a thousand of his men, dressed as bonzes, throughout the Khalkan states, who were to act when the time arrived. An army was put in motion, the Khalkan territories were invaded, and the Eleuth bonzes opened the gates of the cities that they approached, so that Galdan everywhere obtained an easy victory, especially as the Khalkans were entirely unprepared for such an invasion. The chief, T'u Sieh-tu, and his son fled to the court of K'ang Hi, and laying their grievances before him implored him to assist them against their powerful foe. The Emperor listened to their statements and promised them his protection, at the same time taking them presents for themselves and their attendants and allotting them lands where they might reside for the present. Galdan, who heard of their kind reception by K'ang Hi, at once sent an imposing embassy to Peking with tribute for the Emperor. He expressed his humble submission to him, and at the same time begged him to render up to him the fugitive Khalkan chief and his son, who, he declared, had grievously wronged him. K'ang Hi not only refused to listen to this request, but he also commanded him to retire from his territories and also from Tsing-hai, which he had unlawfully usurped.

Because K'ang Hi refused to deliver up the chief of Khalka, who had fled to him for help, in the month of June he led a formidable force into Chinese territory, hoping, perhaps, that a display of force might intimidate the Emperor into compliance with his demand. Never did he make a greater mistake in his life than when he thought of influencing K'ang Hi by such an argument. His reply to it was the march of a large army in three divisions, one commanded by himself, another by Prince K'ung and the third by Prince Yu. The two hostile forces came into conflict at Wulanputang, when Galdan was defeated and compelled to retire. The latter now sent messengers to K'ang Hi, disclaiming any desire to invade his territories; he was simply in pursuit of his enemies, he said, and with their delivery to him hostilities might cease. No reply was given excepting that of the most vigorous pursuit of the vanquished enemy. When the royal forces came up with him they found his army prepared for battle. They had formed a square with their camels, and the men stood within, ready for action. A more unfortunate disposition could hardly have been made, for the cannon of the Chinese made such havoc amongst the camels that, mad with fear, they broke through the ranks of their owners and caused the greatest confusion, during which the Chinese delivered an attack that ended in their utter defeat. Galdan again sent messengers, entreating peace, but the Emperor, distrusting him, made no reply. Just at this crisis the latter became seriously ill, and had to return immediately to Peking, without leaving orders as to how the campaign should be carried on. The generals, instead of following up the advantages gained by two victories, led back their troops to the capital, where they were greatly blamed for their unsoldierly conduct, and, for the time, Galdan was freed from his powerful enemy. It is interesting to note that two years after these battles were fought (A. D. 1691), and through the experience gained in them, artillery formed a distinct and recognized arm of the imperial army. This same year the Coreans sent three thousand "Black Guns" as a present to K'ang Hi, who was so pleased with them that he excused them from paying him any other tribute that year.

Galdan, who had recovered from the effects of his two defeats, forgot the lesson he had been taught, and felt himself strong enough to measure swords once more with his great opponent. He accordingly led a small force against the city of Kwei-hoa, which he failed, however, to capture, but he seized and killed the messengers that were on their way with presents to his own nephew, whom the Emperor had made ruler of a district in Ili. He also sent emissaries amongst the tribes that had given in their allegiance to K'ang Hi, exhorting them to submit to him. The chief of one of these informed the Emperor of Galdan's doings, who advised him to pretend to listen to his proposals, but to be prepared to attack him when he should arrive in his territories, promising that a sufficient force of his troops should be on hand to assist him.

Galdan, who did not realize the mighty force that he was daring to attack, led an army of thirty thousand men across the Chinese frontier and waited to see what K'ang Hi would do. Before long officers arrived, demanding from him a reason for this invasion. He imperiously ordered them back and told them to tell the Emperor that unless he came to terms he would make an alliance with the Russians, who, having guns, would soon bring him to his knees. K'ang Hi was a man that could be reasoned with, but not threatened. An immense army was organized and set out in three divisions in the beginning of A. D. 1695 to teach Galdan a lesson that he would not easily forget. The division commanded by the Emperor arrived first, for the others had been delayed by the difficulties of the road. His ministers advised him to retreat, but this he refused to do. Galdan, who was completely taken by surprise, no sooner became aware of the presence of K'ang Hi than he precipitately fled. The Chinese crossed the Kerulon and pursued him for three days, getting a large amount of plunder which the terrified enemy had dropped on the road, after which he halted. In the meanwhile, the "Western division," under Fei Yang-kee, came up and continued the pursuit. Galdan had concentrated his forces at Chanmuhto, where ten thousand of his bravest men had gathered and a large number of the families of his men, as well as his own. The enemy occupied so formidable a position that Fei did not dare to attack. He accordingly took possession of a low hill, which he fortified, placed a strong force in ambuscade and waited for the approach of the enemy. The battle that ensued was a long and desperate one, and there was no knowing how it would have ended, when the sagacity of Fei turned the threatened defeat into a great victory. Observing a large body of people on a neighbouring hill that remained stationary he concluded that these must be the women and children that were gathered there to watch the fight He at once ordered the men in ambush to attack them. No sooner was the movement of this force observed by Galdan's men than a panic seized them, and abandoning the contest they flew to the rescue of their families. At once the Chinese swooped down upon the disordered mass, and a terrible slaughter ensued. Several thousand were killed, whilst three thousand laid down their arms and submitted. With this great defeat the power of Galdan was broken for ever. A few months after the Emperor appeared with his army and restored their territories to the Khalkans. The men of Tsing-hai, too, concentrated their forces to recover their liberty. Galdan made an appeal to K'ang Hi to enter into a treaty of peace with him, who replied that he would treat him as generously as he had done others if he would only appear before him and make his complete submission. Refusing to do this the Emperor, in March, A. D. 1696, led another force against him, determined upon his destruction. Galdan, driven into a corner, poisoned himself, and thus ignobly ended his career. His followers, anxious to make their peace with K'ang Hi, were conveying his body to the latter, when it was forcibly taken from them by his nephew, Tseh Wang Putan, who claimed all the merit of his death for himself, and was actually rewarded for it. The Emperor, in recognition of his services, decreed that all west of the Altai mountains should be under his rule, whilst the lands lying to the east should be under his own. The kindness of K'ang Hi's heart was shown in his treatment of the son and daughter of Galdan, who had been taken prisoners. Instead of ruthlessly putting them to death he made the one a mandarin and married the other into a good family.

For the next few years no great event happened in the administration of this wise monarch. He was greatly troubled about the succession. The second son, who had been appointed heir, was found to be out of his mind, to the great sorrow of his father, especially as he believed this had been caused by the wickedness of his eldest son, who, it was said, had engaged a Mongol bonze to bewitch his brother, so that the throne might come to himself. The uncertainty about the health of the heir, who was sometimes well and at others ill, caused considerable anxiety to his ministers, who dreaded a disputed succession, but the Emperor refused to come to any decision till the very day he died.

Seventeen years had gone by since Tseh Wang Putan was invested with such great power by the Emperor, and during that time his ambition had grown till, like Galdan, he believed that he was destined to become the chief ruler in Central Asia, and that all the other tribes and independent hordes should acknowledge his supremacy. His first step to put this idea into a practical shape was the usurpation of Turhuto, his father-in-law's possessions. He next turned his gaze towards Thibet, and though so far distant, he still believed that he had the ability to place it under his sway. The marriage of his daughter to Lah Tsang-khan, the civil and military ruler under the Dalai Lama, helped him in his ambitious projects. Under the pretence of escorting his daughter to her new home, with a sufficient force to protect her from danger by the way, he led an army of six thousand men across the mountains by the most secret ways, in order that his march might be concealed from K'ang Hi, and finally, after months of suffering, reached Thibet. His men seized the town of Kungputalah, and meeting with resistance from Lah Tsang-khan, who suspected the designs of Tseh Wang, they murdered him. The Dalai Lama was then confined in one of the monasteries, and the work of plunder commenced. Having accumulated as much as they could possibly carry away, Tseh Wang placed his son-in-law in supreme authority and marched back to Ili. Intoxicated with this brief but successful campaign, he led his men against the important fortress of Hami. Five thousand Chinese troops having come to its rescue he was obliged to retreat without having succeeded in his attack. K'ang Hi became so suspicious of his intentions that he kept them there for upwards of two years, and when he did withdraw them he simply put them in garrison in Tsing-hai, to be ready for any emergency.

The year. A. D. 1716 was an important one to the Roman Catholic missionaries in China. The Viceroy of Canton, in a memorial to the Emperor, prayed that the foreigners who had come to China for the purpose of preaching their religion, should be forbidden the privilege of living in the empire. "They are in every province," he said, "and their one aim is to seduce men into a belief of their doctrines, which are contrary to those of the great sages of China." K'ang Hi, irritated at the position the pope had taken in connection with the dispute between the Jesuits on the one hand, and the Dominicans and Franciscans on the other, in reference to ancestral worship and the proper name for God, etc., in Chinese, and determined that he would be master over everyone in his empire, issued an edict forbidding missionaries to remain in China without a special permit from himself. For purposes of his own he allowed certain of them to reside in Peking, whilst at the same time he permitted severe measures of persecution to be carried out against those that continued secretly to reside in the provinces.*

Tseh Wang, whose ambitious schemes became more and more pronounced, continued to wage war with the Chinese troops, and though generally unsuccessful, he managed to obtain a great victory over them on one occasion (A. D. 1717) when a battle was fought at Kolawusu. The Chinese were routed with great slaughter and their general killed. This, of course, emboldened the Eleuths to continue the contest with K'ang Hi, believing that in the end he would be wearied with the strife and leave them to achieve universal dominion over the tribes of Central Asia. In reasoning thus they made a mistake in their estimate of Chinese character, and little dreamed of the terrible reckoning that was in store for them when the giant should arouse from his apparent apathy and come to the death struggle with them. News having at length travelled to Peking of the daring invasion and occupation of Thibet by Tseh Wang, a force of ten thousand men was

---

* There is no question but that K'ang Hi for many years showed himself exceedingly friendly to the able Jesuit missionaries that resided at his capital, and that a large measure of liberty was given them in the propagation of their faith. Verbiest was an especial favorite of his, because of his astronomical ability, and because he cast cannon which were of service in his wars. Influenced by the representations of such men he issued an edict of toleration in A. D. 1692, which for a time was a veritable Magna Charta to the Catholic church. The issue of that made the latter very popular, and it became so prosperous that in the provinces of Kiang-si, Kiangsu and Nganhwui alone there were one hundred churches and one hundred thousand converts (see "Chinese Repository," vol. 13, p. 545). There is no doubt that the troubles which came upon the Roman Catholics were of their own creating. The story of their disputes is a very interesting but painful one, and one cannot but come to the conclusion, after reading it, that the Jesuits, by their unscrupulousness and want of Christian charity, were mainly responsible for the wreck of Roman Catholic missions in China in the eighteenth century.

despatched to that far-off country, which soon made short work of those that had dared to overthrow the rightful authorities. Tseh Wang's son-in-law was compelled to fly, the Dalai Lama was restored to power and K'ang Hi's troops remained in the country to preserve it from any possible enemy that might assail it. The military authorities at Peking now strongly advised the Emperor (A. D. 1719) to wage a war of extermination upon Tseh Wang, as he had done upon Galdan. The proposition was favourably received, and the most famous generals in the service was summoned to Peking to consult upon the matter and draw up a plan for the campaign.

Whilst these events were transpiring a formidable rebellion broke out in the south of Formosa, caused by the avarice of the prefect of Taiwan-fu. Oppressed by him, the people rose in insurrection and declared their intention never again to submit to the Manchus. The officials fled in terror to the Pescadores and hardly felt themselves safe there. The authorities in Amoy and Fuchow gathered all the available forces they could collect in the province till in the course of a few months there were no fewer than six hundred ships and twelve thousand troops assembled at the Pescadores ready to cross over to Formosa and attack the rebels. The campaign was a short but very bloody one to the poor people, for both officials and soldiers acted in the most cruel and savage manner to all that fell within their power. Within six months the rebellion was crushed and the imperial rule was re-established.

Again, in the autumn of A. D. 1720, Tseh Wang led a large force against the Turfans, who had originally been tributary to the Eleuths, but who had placed themselves under the protection of China. The Chinese came to their assistance, and in the battles that ensued Tseh Wang suffered a great defeat, and was compelled to flee, with the loss of a large number of horses and materials of war. The Chinese soldiers got to within a short distance of Ili in their pursuit, when they were stayed by the appearance of the head of the Buddhist sect, who prayed for mercy for the flying foe. This being granted the Chinese withdrew to their own frontiers and remained there on guard.

Towards the close of A. D. 1722 the great K'ang Hi became seriously unwell, and after suffering for thirteen days he died. On the very day of his death he called his sons and great ministers of state into the room where he was lying, and there he appointed Yung Ching, his fourth son, to succeed him. This was the last important act of his reign, for that same night, at the age of sixty-nine, he passed quietly away. With the exception of Yau and Shun there are few Emperors in the long history of China that will bear any comparison with K'ang Hi. He was a man of great natural abilities, a wise ruler and a distinguished scholar. His great dictionary, which is the standard one throughout China, and his "Sacred Edict," which is supposed to be read on the first and fifteenth of every month in some prominent place in every town and city of the empire, in order that the people may be instructed by its teachings, are evidences of this. He left his empire at peace, and though the Central Asian difficulty remained unsettled, he had shown the tribes there that it was not for want of power that he had refrained from completely subduing them and from making their territories an integral part of his own dominions.

CHAPTER XXXIII.

THE TS'ING DYNASTY (Continued).

Yung Ching—A. D. 1723-1736.

THE new ruler was forty-four years old when he came to the throne. He was a man of fine presence and good natural parts, and men looked upon him as a fit person to succeed so distinguished a ruler as his father had been. The only shadow upon his life, as he ascended the throne, was the want of harmony that prevailed amongst the royal brothers. Some of them were disappointed at the decision of K'ang Hi, and went so far as to meditate rebellion, and had in consequence to be imprisoned. Others, with less ambition, submitted to the new *régime*, but not with that sympathy which would have secured their hearty co-operation in the government of their brother. Amongst the most important acts that were passed by Yung Ching, after he came to the throne, were the appointing his fourth son to be his successor and the issuing of an edict depriving the Roman Catholic priests, whom he disliked even more than his father in his later years did, of the liberty of living in the interior of China.*

Towards the close of the year an insurrection broke out in Tsing-hai, headed by a chief named Lo-puh Tsang-tan-tin, who wished for more power and distinction than he then possessed. Calling a meeting of the other chiefs he urged upon them to refuse any longer to acknowledge the Chinese Emperor as their lord, but to recognize him as their leader. Some agreed, whilst others strongly dissented, and civil strife was the immediate result. Lo-puh, being victor in the contest, would have shown scant mercy to his opponents, but in the meanwhile they had fled to Peking and claimed the protection of Yung Ching. The latter sent messengers to Lo-puh to remonstrate with him, but he seized and imprisoned them, and knowing that he had a formidable .enemy to contend with, he induced the chiefs of the Buddhist faith to throw in their fortunes with him. The consequence of this politic move was to cause more than two hundred thousand men to rally round his standard. Feeling himself strong enough to take the initiative, he

---

* In the first year of this Emperor's reign the literati presented a memorial against the Roman Catholics, as did also the Governor of Chehkiang, who prayed for the banishment of the foreign priests and the conversion of their churches to other and better uses. These were referred to the Board of Rites, who decided that all missionaries, except those in the service of the Emperor in Peking, should be banished to Macao and be forbidden to propagate their doctrines. More than three hundred churches were destroyed, and over three hundred thousand converts left without their foreign pastors. The priests were conducted to Canton, where they were allowed to remain for the present, so long as they behaved themselves. Naturally, however, they wished to visit their flocks, from which they had been driven away. Having done so in some cases, in A. D. 1732 they were deported from Canton to Macao.

advanced against Si-ning, and defeating the imperial troops, he captured immense droves of cattle from the people of this region. The Emperor, feeling that something decisive must be done to curb the insolence of this rebel, put in motion five strong columns of troops that were to converge on the enemy. Another was sent to Tur-fan to prevent any assistance from Tseh Wang, whilst a seventh guarded the approaches to Thibet. Lo-puh, terrified by these extensive preparations, would have submitted to the Emperor, but all his advances were rejected. The Chinese commander, Nien King-yau, now advanced against Lo-puh, and in a desperate engagement managed to defeat him, when he made a precipitate retreat and did not stay until he had put three hundred miles between him and Si-ning. By the advice of General Yoh, the second in command, the Emperor sent an additional force of five thousand men and ten thousand cavalry, when a rapid march was made upon Lo-puh. The difficulties of the road were very great, but under the inspiration of Yoh the soldiers willingly underwent great privations, —so anxious were they to take their enemy by surprise. Their enterprise was entirely successful. They arrived at Lo-puh's encampment before any news of them had reached him. He himself was in bed, and only escaped by being dressed in female clothes. A vigorous pursuit was made after him, but he escaped to Tseh Wang, who gave him a refuge at his court. General Nien shortly after arrived upon the scene and completed the victory that had already been achieved by Yoh, so that the rebellion was crushed out of existence and peace was restored to the region that had been so recently in arms. The Emperor was so pleased with the successes they had achieved that he made them both dukes. In order to render the pacification of Tsing-hai more complete, the Emperor gave orders that there should not be more than three hundred bonzes in any one monastery in it, and that they should not be allowed to carry arms. This defection of the Buddhist to the side of his enemy had greatly displeased him, and had shaken his belief in a system in which he had formerly had profound faith.

With the close of the Central Asian campaign there broke out a most serious rebellion, in A. D. 1726, of the original natives of the land of the three provinces of Kweichow, Sz-chwan and Yunnan. Ngoh, the viceroy of Kweichow, was commissioned to investigate the cause of this outbreak and report to the throne. He informed the Emperor, in a memorial that he presented to him on the subject, that the system of home rule which had been permitted these aborigines had been the chief cause of the disturbances that had arisen, and he strongly advised that they should come under the direct rule of the Emperor. This report was accepted, and he was invested with full powers to deal with the whole question. After considerable difficulty and severe fighting, in which the Chinese troops displayed great bravery in the way they attacked the natives in their mountain fastnesses, complete success attended the imperial troops, and the Emperor's rule was accepted by those who had lately been in arms against him. Fully three years, however, elapsed before these important results were obtained.

The year A. D. 1727 is distinguished as the one in which Magaillans, the envoy of the King of Portugal, arrived in Peking for the purpose of gaining special facilities for his subjects in their trade with China. The interchange of presents and the quiet assumption by the Court of Peking that the ambassador came for the purpose of paying tribute to Yung Ching, were the only results of this embassy. A few months after this Tseh Wang died, and was succeeded by his son, Tseh Ning, who resembled his father in his high opinion of his own abilities and his power to contend with the Chinese. No sooner was he become Khan than he organized expeditions against the Chinese possessions, and was so persistent in his attacks that two considerable armies were despatched against him in A. D. 1729, under the command of Generals Fu and Yoh. These had arrived not very far from Ha-mi, when they were ordered to return to the capital to consult with the Emperor, and to leave two of their lieutenants in charge till they returned. Tseh Ning, hearing of this change of commanders, led twenty thousand men by forced marches, and suddenly attacking the Chinese, defeated them and captured all their baggage and camels and materials for the campaign, and although a relieving force came up and recovered fully one-half of what had been seized, the victory remained with Tseh Ning. A few months after the army under General Fu suffered a severe disaster, one detachment of four thousand men being slain, and the rest, after a desperate engagement, being compelled to retreat in disorder. Two years after (A. D. 1732), being foiled in an attempt to take possession of some of the territories of the Khalkas, Tseh Ning made a sudden swoop upon a large Chinese force, whose commander happened to be absent, and defeated it, capturing the general's family and killing a large number of the men. When the news reached General Ngoh of the loss of his family and the calamity that had befallen his command, he was distressed beyond measure, and swore a terrible oath that he would never rest until he had avenged himself upon Tseh Ning. Sending urgent orders for all the various detachments of troops to join him, he soon found himself at the head of thirty thousand men, when pressing on day and night he came upon Tseh Ning, who was quite unprepared for his arrival. After two days' fighting Ngoh obtained a decided victory and compelled his enemy to retreat. Mindful of his oath, he pursued the flying foe with unrelenting hatred till two days after he came up with him on the side of a mountain where, from the absence of roads, it seemed impossible that he could escape him. In this emergency Tseh Ning, in order to avoid utter destruction, determined to sacrifice all his baggage, so piling it up across the only way by which he could be pursued, he managed to escape whilst Ngoh's men were occupied with its removal. On the other side of the mountain range was a Chinese force of thirteen thousand men under the command of General Ma, who, despite the positive orders of Ngoh and the entreaties of his own officers, refused to attack the disorganized force under Tseh Ning. The army, indignant that a man who had wrought such mischief upon the Chinese armies, and who could have been crushed had prompt measures been taken, should be allowed to escape, marched out without the consent of Ma and attacked the enemy. A decided victory was the result, but unfortunately Tseh Ning managed to escape, and got safely to Ili.

In the beginning of A. D. 1734, Tseh Ning, having come with a large force to try issues with General Ngoh, and having been defeated, sent messengers proposing peace with China. When his proposition was discussed at Peking some were for a war that should end only with the complete submission of Tseh Ning, whilst others, General Chang-ting amongst them, advised that it should be accepted. The Altai mountains, it was accordingly agreed, should be the boundary separating the Emperor's dominions from those of Tseh Ning, and that military operations should at once cease on both sides and peace be proclaimed. There were great rejoicings in consequence of this agreement, and thus the Central Asian question, though by no means settled, was for the time being quietly dismissed from men's minds.

Shortly after this a great rebellion broke out (A. D. 1735), amongst the aborigines of Kweichow, the immediate cause being the heavy taxes and the cruel way in which they were collected. The rebels advanced from their mountain dwellings in great force and took towns and cities, at one time even threatening the provincial capital. The Emperor, impressed with the seriousness of the uprising, ordered that the troops of six provinces should concentrate in Kweichow and fight the rebels. With the approach of the soldiers these retreated with their plunder to the hills, but returned again and met them in the field. Finding that the aborigines remained unconquered the Emperor sent special commissioners to investigate the true causes of the outbreak. The report given him was that the plan proposed by General Ngoh, not to allow the natives to be ruled by their own chiefs, was the source of all the trouble. Ngoh, who had been created an earl, was punished by having his rank taken from him. In the meanwhile the difficulties of the Imperial armies were increased by the want of harmony between the two generals—Chang-chau and Hoh—who refused to co-operate with each other or even to take action to prevent the enemy from plundering and marauding in purely Chinese territory. There was a serious discussion in the cabinet whether it would not be best to withdraw from the conflict and to allow the natives to have full control in the districts occupied by them, when the Emperor fell ill, and in about a month after died, being succeeded by his fourth son, the famous K'ien Lung, who was then twenty-five years old.

K'ien Lung—A. D. 1736-1796.

The new ruler was a man of great natural abilities, a scholar, and of a strong, decided purpose, that made him just the man to meet the difficulties which were threatening to assume large proportions in Central Asia. His first action in regard to the insurrection amongst the aborigines in the south-west of China showed the character of the man. He recalled the two generals to Peking to be punished for their misconduct and sent General Chang Kwang, with the soldiers from seven provinces, to put down promptly and without mercy the rebellion. His wisdom in the choice of his man was shown by the fact that in four months from the time that the Chinese forces began their work, the insurrection was at an end. About eighteen thousand of the enemy were slain in battle, etc., twelve hundred forts, small and great, were destroyed, and twenty-five thousand prisoners taken, the half of whom were executed, and imperial law again in force throughout all the disaffected districts. Four years after, in another serious outbreak amongst the aborigines of Hunan and Kwangsi, the same general once more distinguished himself by the vigour with which he suppressed it, though, as in the former case, the object was accomplished by a terrible sacrifice of life.

In the tenth year of K'ien Lung's reign Tseh Ning died, and with his death the Central Asian question, which had lain in abeyance for a number of years, came again into prominence. During his life he had been able, by the firmness of his rule, to keep the restless hordes, who owned a nominal allegiance to China, in order. With his removal the tribes that acknowledged his sway broke out into rebellion, and war amongst themselves was the result. He was succeeded by his second son, because the first was by a secondary wife, but in consequence of his being a cruel and licentious man he was murdered at the instigation of his brother-in-law. The first, whose name was Taurcha, then became Khan, but ere long two chiefs—Davatsi and Amursana—grandsons of Galdan, raised the standard of rebellion and proclaimed the third son as the one who had the right to the chieftainship. In the contest that ensued the new rival was killed, and his two supporters were compelled to fly, but gathering a force of fifteen hundred men they made a sudden swoop upon Taurcha, who was slain, and the Khanship was bestowed upon Davatsi (A. D. 1745) and peace for a time was restored to Ili. Next year a formidable insurrection broke out amongst the aborigines in Sz-chwan, near the Great Golden River, headed by their chief, Salopan. General Chang Kwang sent against him, but through the treachery of a man in whom he trusted all his plans were revealed to the enemy, and he was several times worsted. The Emperor, dissatisfied with this, sent Nachin to examine into the causes. The result was a quarrel between the two men, which led to further disasters, and Chang Kwang, being recalled to Peking, was executed, whilst a sword was sent to Nachin with the order to use it upon himself. General Fu, who was sent to take command, having killed the traitor, made his arrangements to suppress the insurrection, which after months of severe fighting he did, and, returning to Peking, was made a duke.

Davatsi was allowed to reign nine years in peace, when the ambition of Amursana threw the tribes into confusion and precipitated war. Thinking that the share of the honours which had fallen to the former was out of proportion to his merits he began to encroach upon his domains. Davatsi resented this, and in the conflict that ensued he was victorious, and his rival fled to the court of K'ien Lung. There he was received with great honour and created a prince. An immense army, consisting of seventy thousand infantry and as many cavalry, was despatched under the command of Panti and Ying to crush Davatsi, whilst Amursana and Salai led the Eleuth contingents to co-operate in the campaign. Davatsi, terrified by these vast preparations, fled across the Tien-shan mountains into Turkestan, where, however, he was seized by the Mohammedans and sent a captive to Peking.

Contrary to Amursana's expectations, the Emperor divided Ili into four great divisions, over each of which he nominated a chief. Amursana wished the whole for himself, and was taking steps to secure it, when he was ordered to Peking to give an account of his conduct. On the way he threw off the mask, evaded the commissioners that accompanied him, and who had orders to slay him if he resisted, and hastily returning to Ili, put to death Panti and the five hundred soldiers who had been left as a garrison there. This treachery towards a man who had really been his benefactor, roused the anger of the Emperor, who despatched an immense army against him with instructions that they were not to rest till they had crushed Amursana. A great battle ensued, in which he was routed and on the point of being captured, when by a ruse he escaped. Sending some of his own soldiers to the Chinese camp, who represented that they were prepared to seize their chief, he escaped whilst they were planning with the general the manner in which he was to be captured. For this piece of folly the two generals in command were recalled to Peking, but on their way they were murdered by brigands. A few months after he again escaped by a similar kind of deception, and once more the officers who had been deceived were summoned to the capital to answer for their credulity.

K'ien Lung, with a purpose as fixed as that of fate itself, and determined that nothing should stand between him and the vengeance he meditated, next commanded Chan-hui, a man who had suddenly manifested great abilities as a general, having with only fifteen hundred men beaten a force of more than a hundred thousand, to take the command of the Chinese forces, and to never rest till he had secured the person of Amursana. Obedient to the Imperial orders, he lost no time in coming to close quarters with his enemy, who a third time sustained a disastrous defeat and fled into Russian territory. There he was attacked by small-pox, a disease then prevalent amongst his people, and of which it was said that four-tenths of them had died, and in a few days succumbed to that fell disease. An officer sent by Chan-hui to demand him from the Russians was shown the body, and a report was sent post haste to Peking to inform the Emperor.

Jungaria and Ili having been thoroughly conquered, it followed as a matter of course, and especially for strategic purposes, that Eastern Turkestan on the south of the Tien-shan range should also be compelled to submit to the Chinese authority. Its ruler, Pulu-tun, with his brother, Hwotsichen, were of a different mind, however, on this subject. When imperial officers reached them demanding their submission they refused and prepared for war. The Emperor no sooner heard this than he set his troops in motion and attacked Kashgar. General Ma, who was in command, failed to take the city, and suffered a decided reverse. For this he was executed, and Chan-hui, who was in charge of Ili, was ordered to take his place. At first this commander was anything but success-ful ; indeed, on one occasion he was surrounded by the enemy, and would have been destroyed ; only reinforcements under Alikwan and Fuh-teh arrived and extricated him from his perilous position.

In the battles that followed the Mohammedans were gradually beaten. Kashgar and Yarkand were carried by assault, and finally the two brothers, with a large following, fled into Bodakshan, the chief of which, however, through fear of the Chinese, dared not receive them. To avoid any collision with the latter he put to death the two chiefs and any of their followers that he could seize, and thus Turkestan became an acknowledged dependency of the Chinese empire. In the beginning of A. D. 1761 Chan-hui and Fuh-teh led their troops back to Peking, and the Emperor, out of gratitude for the services they had rendered him, came out to meet them, rewarding the one with a dukedom and the other with an earldom.

Two years after the conquest of Central Asia was completed a most romantic incident occurred in the return of a Tourgot tribe after an exile of over fifty years from their ancestral home. Galdan had married the daughter of their chief, Ayuki, and as he had been accustomed to do in other cases, proceeded to annex his territory. The horde fled for protection to Russia, where lands were assigned them in the government of Orenburg. Here they lived for many years, till at last, rendered restless by the exactions of the tax-gatherer, and by the best of their men being drafted into the Russian armies, they decided to return to their homes. One fine morning one hundred and sixty thousand people began their march east-wards. After a journey of over eight months they came upon the Kirghis tribes, who opposed their passage to Ili. Compelled to make a detour over the mountains they suffered terribly by the way, and at last only seventy thousand reached their destination. K'ien Lung treated them with great kindness, and not only appointed a district where they might live, but also named a chief who was to be their Khan. They have proved most loyal and faithful to the present dynasty.

The year A. D. 1766 saw the Chinese engaged in a war with Burmah. The reasons given for this are very different from those recorded by the Burmese historian. It seems that some of the native tribes that lay outside the Chinese frontier, and who paid tribute to China, were in the habit, for purposes of security, of doing the same to the king of Burmah. About this time they came to a general understanding that they would cease their payments to the latter. Upon this a Burmese force attacked them, and all but two consented to pay the usual tribute. The chief of one of these fled to the governor-general of Yunnan, who for some unexplained reason put him to death. His wife fled to the chief of another tribe, and so worked upon his mind that he joined his forces with hers and made an inroad upon the Chinese, whom they defeated. The king of Burmah at the same time sent officers to demand the person of the chief who had fled for protection to China, but of whose death he was still ignorant.

When the Emperor heard of the defeat of his soldiers by the aborigines he was highly incensed, and ordered the governor-general to commit suicide, and at the same time he sent Yang-ying to proceed at once and take the direction of affairs. This man proving incompetent, and the Burmese having entered Yunnan, K'ien Lung sent an army in two divisions to the seat of war. The division under the command of General Ming first arrived, and capturing Muh-pang, drove the Burmese before them and captured all their provisions. Leaving five thousand men in charge of the place, and being joined by the troops in Yunnan, they advanced into Burmese territory. Here they had an engagement with the Burmese army, in which they were victorious. Ere long, however, misfortunes began to trouble them. The difficulties of the way were immense, and to crown all, their provisions began to fail. It was now found necessary to retreat, but the Burmese, who had been slowly augmenting their forces, rendered this very perilous. At last the Chinese army found itself completely surrounded by the enemy, and seeing no way of deliverance, General Ming gave orders that in order to avoid complete destruction the soldiers should save themselves the best way they could. Immediately the whole force dissolved, with the exception of several hundred that collected around their commander. These, urged by him to show the enemy how Chinese could fight, displayed the utmost heroism, and every man was slain. Very few escaped from that fatal field, and when the Emperor heard of the cowardice of the commander of the other division, who was afraid to lead his troops to the rescue of Ming, he ordered him to be sliced.

Generals Alikwan and Akwei were now sent to take command of the troops, and after desperate fighting on both sides, in which neither gained any decided advantage, a treaty of peace, at the suggestion of the Burmese, was concluded, in which it was agreed that the latter were to pay tribute to China, prisoners should be released and all territory taken in the war should be returned The Emperor having given his consent (A. D. 1770) the Chinese troops returned to China, burning their boats and melting their cannon, the material of which they carried home with them, and the war was at an end. As the Chinese, however, refused to return three districts that they had occupied, the Burmese retained their prisoners and complained of the breach of faith that the Chinese had been guilty of. K'ien Lung on this occasion did not behave with that magnanimity which one would have expected from him. Annoyed at the fact that the contest with his tributary had been anything but successful, he not only meanly avoided the carrying out of a treaty that he had sanctioned himself, but he also gave orders to Akwei to harass and annoy the Burmese whenever he had an opportunity. Because this general laid before him the difficulties that existed to his doing this he was removed from his command in Yunnan and sent to fight the aborigines in Sz-chwan that lived in the Great and Little Golden River districts. When he arrived there he found the condition of things anything but satisfactory. The two tribes were in active rebellion, and had already inflicted several defeats on the Chinese forces. One detachment under General Kwei-lin, consisting of three thousand men, had been all slain, with the exception of two hundred. Akwei's plan was to conquer the two tribes in detail. He accordingly attacked those in the Little Golden River district, and speedily subdued them, their chief escaping to Solomuh, the head of the other tribe. A demand was made for his surrender, which was refused, whereupon the Chinese marched to attack him. This was a matter of extreme difficulty, for the roads were more inaccessible and the forts and their commanders stronger and more numerous than in the first campaign. Solomuh, too, was a warrior of greater generalship than the fugitive one was, as the Chinese found to their cost. Sending messengers to the men of the Little Golden district he urged them to rise and combine with him for the destruction of their enemies. Moved by his appeals they flew to arms and massacred General Wun-fuh with his detachment of three thousand men, who were taken by surprise. Once more Akwei had to recommence the conquering of the territory he had lost, which, however, he did after five days and nights of hard fighting, and secured it in such a way that there was no danger of his losing it again. He now united his forces for a final struggle with Solomuh. Fort after fort was taken in spite of their strength, till this man, terrified at the successes of the Chinese, poisoned the fugitive chief and sent his body to Akwei, at the same time asking pardon for himself and family. When the request was sent to K'ien

Lung he wrote refusing it, and ordered that no terms should be made with him. Once more the fighting began, and as no mercy was expected the defence was more vigorous and protracted. At length every fortress had been taken, excepting the stronghold, and before this the Chinese forces appeared for a final struggle. After a heroic defence, and finding there was no food left and no water, Solomuh led out his wife and children and surrendered to Akwei. They were put to death, and the garrison sent to Ili to spend the rest of their days there. Akwei returned with great eclat to Peking, where he was made a duke. The expenses of this war had been enormous, being estimated at seventy million ounces of silver, or double the amount that had been spent in the conquest of Ili and Turkestan.

A serious insurrection broke out in Shantung in A. D. 1777, headed by a man named Wang-lun, and another in A. D. 1781 amongst the Mohammedans in Shensi, in consequence of differences in religious views amongst the members of that sect, which were put down by the authorities only after great loss of life and the destruction of property. These were followed by another of a much more serious nature in A. D. 1786 in the island of Formosa. There a man named Liu, taking advantage of his large connections, and especially his intimate relationship with the savages in the mountains, formed a secret society, to which all the riff-raff of the people flocked. This conduct became at last so offensive that the mandarins issued an order for his apprehension. This was a signal for the insurrection that had been anticipated, and it soon spread throughout the island till Liu found himself at the head of one hundred and fifty thousand men. Two generals—Fuh Kwang-an and Hai Lanch'ai—were sent from the capital with twelve thousand men to put down the rebellion. This they succeeded in doing after some severe fighting, in which large numbers of the undisciplined rebels were slain. Liu was captured and sent to Peking, and the imperial rule was once more restored throughout the island.

The year A. D. 1788 witnessed a revolution in Cochin China, by which the king was driven from his throne and compelled to fly to China for aid against his rebellious minister, Yuan. Sun, the governor-general of Kwang-si, to whom he appealed, memorialized the Emperor on the subject and suggested that the present was a suitable opportunity for annexing that country to the Chinese dominions. K'ien Lung's reply was an order to him to raise a sufficient force and replace the fugitive prince on his throne, declaring at the same time that he could never dream of taking advantage of a man's misfortunes to deprive him of his rights. In the month of June, Sun, at the head of twenty thousand men, led back the king and placed him once more on his throne. His rapid success, however, had rendered Sun over-confident, and he had become careless in the disposition of his troops. Yuan, being thoroughly posted in all that was being done, collected a large force, and suddenly attacking the Chinese, they were compelled to retreat in confusion. Reaching the "Rich Dragon" River they found the bridge broken and their retreat cut off, and nearly ten thousand men perished, either drowned in the river which they attempted to cross, or slain by Yuan's men. Fuh Kwang-an was next despatched with a force to retrieve the disaster, but Yuan made such humble submission that the Emperor forgave him, and actually made him king in place of the other, who, he saw, had not the ability to maintain his position without the assistance of a foreign force. Next year, on the Emperor's eightieth birthday, Yuan repaired to Jehol to congratulate him, and was received with great honor by K'ien Lung and formally invested with the title and power of a tributary prince. At the same time ambassadors from Burmah appeared, and the Emperor was so pleased with the messages they bore that he issued an edict permitting trade, which had been stopped since the war, to be once more carried on between the two countries.

In the year A. D. 1790 a force of the Ghoorkas crossed the Himalayas into Thibet on a marauding expedition. Exactly ten years before they had visited that country, and the recollection of the pleasures of that expedition had been a sufficient incentive to bring its hardy warriors across those great mountains once more in the hopes of plunder. On the first occasion they had been invited by Pa-shen, a younger brother of the Dalai Lama, who had visited K'ien Lung, and who had received magnificent presents from him, but who had unfortunately died of small-pox in Peking. His property was appropriated by his elder brother, who refused to share it with another younger one.. Not being strong enough to compel him the latter invited a band of the Ghoorkas to assist him, who only too gladly obeyed the summons, and after accomplishing the purpose for which they had been sent, returned home laden with presents and with the spoils they had been able to appropriate for themselves. On this second occasion they fared even better than they did on the first. The Chinese general, Pa-chung, not daring to fight with them, entered into a convention with them by which he promised them an annual subsidy of fifteen thousand ounces of silver and the same number of pieces of silk. In order to screen himself from the anger of the Emperor he stipulated with them that they should consent to become tributary to China. This, of course, they readily agreed to do. Pa-chung then memorialized K'ien Lung, saying that a band of Ghoorkas had appeared in Thibet with tribute in their hands, and having heard of the power of the Chinese Emperor, wished to be recognised by him as one of his tributaries. This little by-play of Pa-chung was destined to have serious consequences for himself and for Thibet. Next year the Ghoorkas appeared for their money and their silk, but Pa-chung was gone, and the new general knew nothing of the treaty. Upon this the Ghoorkas, nothing loth, began to plunder the rich lamaseries and so rob and murder the people. The general in command sent urgent requests for help to K'ien Lung, and the Dalai Lama, who had dis-approved of the treaty, also sent special messengers imploring help. The two generals—Fuh Kwang-an and Hai Lan-ch'ai—who had distinguished themselves in Formosa, were ordered to Thibet, where thirty thousand men were put under their command to punish the marauders. The generals lost no time in their pursuit of the Ghoorkas, who, conscious of their power, and, moreover, laden with booty, had delayed their return to their own country.

No sooner did Fuh join the army than an immediate advance was ordered, and the returning Ghoorkas were caught up with as they were moving leisurely amongst the mountain passes. A battle took place, in which Fuh was victorious and the enemy obliged to retreat. Flying before him the Chinese general pressed on inces-santly, until at last he found himself amongst mountains high and terrible, and where the roads were well-nigh impassable. As the Ghoorkas fled they cut down the bridges which crossed the mighty chasms, down which roared the mountain torrents, and timber had to be cut, and these re-made to allow his troops to pass. At length the flying foe was once more reached, and they sent into the Chinese camp desiring an armistice. The terms, that all the plunder should be restored, being refused, a series of engagements took place, in which the Ghoorkas were again routed, losing four thousand men. Driven from position to position the defeated hill-men gathered all the forces they could collect for a final stand to defend their capital. A mountain stream lay between it and the Chinese, which the latter attempted in vain to cross, so they encamped on the opposite side. Three times did the Ghoorkas pass over and attack the entrenched camp, and on each occasion they were repulsed with great slaughter. The Ghoorkas were now in a terrible position. General Fuh, in order to keep the neighbouring tribes from coming to their assist-ance, had given out that after he had conquered his foe he would divide his territories amongst the peoples that lay adjacent. Incited by these promises they began active preparations for the occupation of the lands which they saw would soon be wrested from the Ghoorkas by their terrible foe.* Again they appeared in Fuh's camp and begged that favorable terms might be given them, as they were prepared to make full submission. Influenced by their humble appeals, but much more by the fact that the cold weather was coming on, and that ere long the mountain passes and roads would be covered with snow, so that his return home would be rendered extremely difficult, he agreed to stop hostilities if all the plunder were restored, the deed of the treaty made with them by Pa-chung given to him and a tribute of elephants and horses paid the Chinese Emperor once in every five years. These terms were gladly

---

* The "Holy War" states that the English made a demonstration against the Ghoorkas, which terrified them to such an extent that they made the most abject submission to the Chinese. This was remembered with gratitude by the latter two years later, when Lord Macartney appeared in Peking.

accepted, and ere long Fuh, with his victorious army, marched back to Thibet, leaving an impression of China's power on the warlike Ghoorkas that they were long in forgetting.

In the autumn of the year A. D. 1795 Lord Macartney reached the Peiho on an embassy to K'ien Lung to endeavour to arrange with him some system by which more intimate and cordial relationships between England and China might be cemented. According to the statement of the "Holy War" the Emperor, grateful for the part that the English had taken in the Ghoorka campaign, received him with the greatest honour. Twice did he give him an audience in a tent specially set up in the gardens of the palace of Jehol. Although nothing of any importance was the immediate result, the friendly feeling shown by the aged Emperor was not without its effect upon the authorities at Canton in their intercourse with the English. A precedent, at any rate, had been set, which would not be without its value in the future.

The last two years of K'ien Lung's reign were disturbed by risings of the Miautze on the borders of the Kweichow and Hunan provinces. General Fuh was sent against them, but his success was not so great as had been expected, and before the campaign was ended he died in his camp. The Emperor, after a reign of sixty years, resigned in favor of his son, who reigned under the title of Kia K'ing.

Kia K'ing—A. D. 1796-1821.

When K'ien Lung abdicated the throne, the empire, with the exception of the troubles amongst the Miautze, but which were now nearly suppressed, was at peace. Throughout its length and breadth the people were enjoying prosperity, and the wise and statesmanlike way in which K'ien Lung had ruled his people for sixty years, gave the hope that nothing would interrupt the harmony and quiet that prevailed throughout the eighteen provinces. Hardly had Kia K'ing got seated on the throne, however, before a rebellion broke out that gradually spread through six of the richest provinces of China, and for nine years caused infinite sorrow and distress. A secret society named the "White Lily," and composed mainly of Buddhists, was the cause of this. There is no doubt but that the cruel and unwise action of the officials, when the insurrection first commenced, was the direct cause of its spreading as far as it did. Instead of seizing and punishing only the guilty they relentlessly broke into houses to which the least suspicion attached, and without sufficient evidence condemned men and women to punishment and their property to confiscation. This was a fine harvest time for the mandarins who got rich upon the wealth that was seized under the name of law.

The troubles first broke out in Hupeh, and spread with such terrible rapidity that in four months' time the governor-general had decapitated between twenty and thirty thousand people. This fearful severity only seemed to exasperate the insurgents, who met the imperial troops in several engagements and defeated them. Success brought new adherents, and with lightning speed the revolution spread till the whole power of the empire was engaged in a life and death struggle with it. A hundred million ounces of silver and countless lives were spent before peace was restored to the desolated provinces. Kia K'ing was a man thoroughly unsuited by nature for the high position which he now occupied, and he was specially unfortunate in following such a man as his father. His was a selfish, heartless man, and so he gained the love of but few. His treatment of Duke Ho is an instance of how under the guise of zeal for the public service he managed to bring ruin and sorrow upon a man who had been the trusted friend and counsellor of K'ien Lung for many years. When Lord Macartney visited Peking this man, known by the name of Ho-kwan, was prime minister. He made a considerable impression on the embassy by his pleasing and courteous manner. During his long term of power he had amassed an enormous fortune and lived in an almost regal style. Kia K'ing affected to believe that he had treasonable designs against the state, and so he had him tried for his life. Under such circumstances his condemnation was certain. He was thrown into prison, where he died, and his immense wealth was appropriated by the Emperor and used to minister to his own pleasures and passions.

Lest Macao should be attacked by the French it was occupied by the English in A. D. 1802, and the Chinese had barely time to remonstrate against the violation of their territory when they withdrew in consequence of the treaty of Amiens, which restored the place to the Portuguese. Six years later a force under Admiral Drury landed to assist the latter to hold it against a possible attack by the French. The Chinese protested against this, and orders were issued that the English should be driven from the place. The English admiral made use of threats against Cantonese authorities, and even went so far as to make an armed demonstration against them, but fearful of doing injury to trade, he did not proceed to hostilities, but sailed away to India, leaving an impression on the minds of the Chinese that they had gained a victory over the foreigner, to commemorate which they built a fort at the entrance to the river leading to Canton.

In the year A. D. 1806 a famous pirate named Ch'ai appeared on the coast of China and worked havoc amongst the merchant junks that traded north and south. In order to escape being seized these had to pay toll, and all that refused to do this were treated in the cruelest manner. As the government could do nothing to protect them, the merchants of the different ports subscribed a large sum of money and built thirty ships, having four hundred guns. These they put under the command of a valiant sailor named Li, who showed his mettle by seeking out the pirate and fighting him whenever he would stand to his guns. In one of the engagements, when Li had captured all but three of his enemy's ships, and the destruction of Ch'ai seemed imminent, a cannon-ball struck the former in the throat, and he was killed instantly. His men, discouraged by his death, gave up the contest, and Ch'ai escaped. For another year the pirate carried on his work of plunder and robbery, when he was defeated by an imperial fleet near Amoy, and to escape capture he scuttled his ship and was drowned.

A serious rebellion broke out in A. D. 1813 in connection with a secret society named the "Heavenly Reason," in Honan, under a man named Lin, and in Chihli under Li-wun. The former was said to have had more than a million adherents that were ready to obey his commands. He was not content to be merely the leader of a rebellion ; he aimed at being the founder of a new dynasty. He accordingly plotted with a eunuch to take advantage of the absence of the Emperor whilst away on a tour in Shensi, and seize the palace and install himself as ruler of China. The 13th of October was settled as the day on which the deed was to be done, and Li promised to be present with his contingent of men. On the day appointed Lin, with two hundred men, disguised, was all ready waiting for Li, who, however, had been betrayed, and was already in the hands of the authorities. Not daring to put off their plans, Lin, led by two eunuchs, boldly entered the palace and got as far as the study of the princes, when the second son seized a gun and shot two of the conspirators. A cousin who was present killed three more, and by this time the soldiers, hearing the firing rushed in and captured them all. The Emperor was at once sent for, who returned immediately to Peking. He severely reprimanded the officers who were in charge of the palace and ordered that Lin should suffer the cruel death of slicing. Twenty thousand of the rebels were executed and as many more were sent into exile to Ili.

In consequence of complications which had arisen between the English in Canton and the Chinese authorities there, it was determined by the English government to send a special embassy to Peking to arrange with the Emperor some better method of carrying on trade than that at present in existence. Lord Amherst was appointed to undertake this important mission, and he and his suite reached Peking August 28th, 1816. They were, however, summarily dismissed, because the demand of the Emperor that they should see him at once was not complied with. They had just reached the capital after a wearisome and painful journey from Tientsin, and their presents and uniforms were amongst the baggage that had not yet been brought in. It was no wonder that the ambassador, being in such a condition, should refuse to appear before the Emperor. It is also equally not to be wondered at that the latter should feel indignant that this foreigner, whom he considered he was conferring such a favour upon, should dare to disobey the command of such an august personage as he. The whole party was ordered to return immediately to the coast, and thus ended in this inglorious fashion a mission from which so much good had been expected.

The last few years of Kia K'ing's life were not distinguished by anything specially worthy of notice. He died in the 61st year of his age, after a troubled and unsatisfactory reign of twenty-five years, and was succeeded by his second son.

Tau Kwang—A. D. 1821-1851.

This prince, who had been selected by his father, from the time that he began to rule alone, to succeed him on the throne, began his reign with every prospect that he would govern his people with more wisdom than his father had done. In the edicts that were issued by him when the supreme power devolved upon him, he seemed to recognize the responsibility of his position and the duty that was laid upon him to maintain the honour of his empire by a virtuous and dignified rule. That great changes and misfortunes should happen to his country whilst he sat upon the throne, was not so much caused by his misrule as that he had lighted upon times when the haughty contempt of China for other countries could be tolerated no longer, but when she would be compelled to enter the comity of nations and treat with courtesy those she had been accustomed to regard with contempt. The first troubles that disturbed his government came from Turkestan. The causes of these were in a large measure due to the misconduct of the Chinese officials. Many of these had been banished from China for crimes and misdeeds, but somehow or other they had been put into office ; even convicts had been placed in government posts as secretaries, etc. These treated the people with the greatest injustice. They took possession of their lands, and very often broke up their homes, and all under the plea that they were doing these things for the good of the public service. For these and other causes the people determined to rise in rebellion against the Chinese, and they rallied round Jehangir, a descendant of their Khojans,' who they believed was just the man to give them their freedom. *

In the summer of A. D. 1825 Jehangir appeared at the head of a large force, that rapidly grew as he advanced. City after city was taken by him, four being captured in one day. On receipt of the information of this rising Tau Kwang appointed Chang-ling commander-in-chief and Yang Yu-chun general of division, to proceed with reinforcements to Turkestan. They found that the forces of the enemy, when they arrived there, had taken possession

---

* When Turkestan became a dependency of China their own native chief, or Khoja, as he was called, was allowed, for purposes of policy, to still have a nominal control over his people. This plan had not worked well, as serious complications had arisen from it, and consequently, after the close of the last war, it was given up. Jehangir had been residing with the Khan of Kokand, and had been long waiting for a chance to claim his rights to rule over the eight cities that K'ien Lung had assigned to his grandfather, Pulatan.

of nearly the whole country. A great many engagements took place, which ended eventually in the defeat of the rebels and the capture of Jehangir, who was sent prisoner to Peking. There, being questioned by the Emperor, he defended himself on the ground that he had only asserted his rights in the endeavour to recover his inheritance. He was condemned to a lingering and cruel death, and then his head was cut off and exposed in public to be a warning to all intending conspirators. This rebellion proved a very expensive one, both in men and money. The "Holy War" declares that ten million ounces of silver were expended in its suppression, and considering its distance from the capital and the wide extent of country that was in arms against the state, it cannot be considered a very exaggerated estimate.

The next troubles that demanded the attention of the executive arose in Formosa and Hainan, but these were comparatively small when compared with the rising of the Miautze in the provinces of Canton, Kwangsi and Hunan. The immediate cause of this was the high-handed acts of injustice perpetrated by the Chinese, which became at last so intolerable that in self-defence the natives had to rise against their oppressors. This was in the year A. D. 1832. At that time there was a secret society named the "Heaven and Earth," the members of which were very numerous, and whose main purpose was revolution. They were very powerful in Hunan and Kwangsi, and felt themselves strong enough to act in open defiance of the law. As many of them were worthless vagabonds they were unwilling to earn their living by honest work. They accordingly used to rob the fields of the Miautze and carry off their crops. When the magistrates were appealed to for redress they were not listened to, for nearly all the police and under-officials were members of the society. Finding they had to depend upon themselves for redress they united and killed twenty of the officials. Upon this the military officers led out their troops and killed three hundred of the Miautze. News of this disaster flew like wild-fire among the natives, and a general rising under their leader, Golden Dragon, was determined upon. Governor Li, of Canton, was sent against them, but in his first engagement with the rebels he was worsted with a loss of two thousand men. Further fighting took place, which seems to have been favourable to the Miautze, for they advanced and took the town of Ping-tseuen. Here, however, disaster awaited them, for they were defeated with the loss of ten cannon, three thousand small arms, and six thousand men killed and wounded, and a number of prisoners, amongst whom were the two sons of Golden Dragon. The scene of the conflict now shifted from the Hunan province to that of Canton. Here the Imperial troops were again defeated, and Li was disgraced. Two commissioners—Heng-an and Hu Sun-gi—were sent with full powers by the Emperor to carry on the war and to supersede Li. By orders of the former placards were distributed amongst the Miautze, telling

them of the perils they were in if they continued in insurrection, and
how clemency would be extended to all that submitted. The effect
of these was more powerful than all troops that had been led against
them, and the result was that in the course of ten days the rebellion
was at an end and Heng-an was waiting to receive the rewards that
the Emperor was ready to shower upon him, whilst Li set out on
his journey to Peking, there to be tried by the Board of Punishments
for his grievous offence of having failed to conquer the Miautze.*

The year A. D. 1833 is a conspicuous one in the annals of
China, for from it may be dated the change in the policy that had
hitherto guided the English in their intercourse with the Chinese,
and which finally led to wars between the two peoples and the final
opening up of the empire to foreign nations. In order to make the
story more plain it will be necessary to give a brief account of the
way in which English trade had been carried on by the English
previous to this time.† Up to this time commercial dealings had
been managed in a very irregular and unsatisfactory manner. When
a ship arrived she was visited by an officer of the Hoppo, the Chinese
Commissioner of Customs, who had to be propitiated by a valuable
present, for on his report depended the success or failure of the
venture. When this man was satisfied, and all the necessary port
charges had been paid, the ship was allowed to proceed from the
entrance of the river to Whampoa, where, even then, she could only
trade with some officially recognized trader or broker. A change
from this system was made in A. D. 1702, when a chief supercargo,
with the powers of Consul for the whole of China, was sent out by
the East India Co. The Chinese who were determined to ignore
the official character of the man thus appointed, got out of this
difficulty by giving a high officer, whom they selected, the exclusive
monopoly of trade, and who, in addition to the Hoppo, had to be
fed and courted and pandered to before a ship was allowed to trade.
This system continued till the year A. D. 1720, when, instead of one
man, a committee of Chinese merchants, called the Co-hong, was
appointed in his place. These were entirely responsible for foreign
trade. They guaranteed all debts due to the English, the amount
of squeezes to be given the provincial authorities, and the Customs'
dues, as well as the conduct of the officers and men of the ships that
came to trade, etc. Five years after, the authorities in Peking, in
order to get their proper share of the revenue, fixed a tariff, but this

---

* See *Chinese Repository*, Vol. I.

† The earliest notices that we have of English trade in China was the opening
of houses in Zelandia in Formosa and in Amoy by the permission of Coxinga's son
in A. D. 1625. In A. D. 1634, in consequence of "a truce and free trade" with the
Viceroy of Goa, Capt. Weddel appeared at Macao with a number of ships to carry
on trade there. Being repulsed by the Portuguese, who showed in these early days
bitter hostility to the English, he applied to the Chinese to be allowed to trade
with Canton. Influenced by misrepresentations of the Portuguese, these not only
refused this request, but also fired upon his ships. The Bogue forts were then
bombarded by him, after which the English were allowed to participate in the
junk trade. It was not till A. D. 1684 that a footing was got in Canton.

only added to the difficulty, because the officials now had not only to secure a certain definite sum for the capital, but they had also to see that their own gains were not curtailed.

Up to A. D. 1755 the Co-hong system had concerned only the direct import and export trade, but from this date foreigners were prohibited from dealing with native junks or small merchants whilst lying off the Bogue forts at the entrance to the river. In A. D. 1760 the East India Co. petitioned the Viceroy at Canton to do away with the Co-hong system, but their request was denied. In A. D. 1771, however, it was abolished, mainly because some of the members of it became bankrupt and could not pay their debts to the foreigners. Another committee, consisting of twelve officials, who really were merchants, took their place and possessed the monopoly of foreign trade. Things went on in their usual fashion, when great anxiety began to be felt by the Chinese at the very large yearly exportation of silver from the country. The cause of this was the great increase in the import of opium, which was paid for in bullion. Various laws were passed by the Chinese to correct this, and they became so oppressive that the East India Co. formally threatened to suspend business, but finally they had to withdraw their protest and to allow things to go on as they were before. The restrictions, placed on the opium ships, which latter brought in a very considerable revenue to the mandarins, were evaded by their anchoring at Lin-tin, outside of the Bogue forts, where a great deal of smuggling was going on, and by which the official trade monopoly suffered in its revenue, to the great grief of expectant officials, both high and low.*

At length, after more than two centuries of continual conflict with the Chinese mandarins, the trade struggles took a new phase with the abolition (August 28th, 1833) of the East India Co.'s charter and the throwing open of the trade with China to all British subjects, and the appointment of an officer to protect their rights and to insist that they should be tried by their own laws, and not by those of China. This legislation on the part of the English government brought them face to face with a subject that involved continual and fierce conflict with the Chinese, and that was the equality of the Queen of England with the Emperor of China. Such an idea was utterly scouted by the officials of that day. According to their imagination, the Emperor was the great ruler of the world, and all others were inferior to him, and in reality his tributaries, that should be treated as though they were under his rule. To

---

* As early as A. D. 1688 a regular duty on foreign imported opium was levied at Canton, but for seventy-seven years after that the annual import did not exceed two hundred chests. By the year A. D. 1796, however, the annual rate of importation had risen to 4,100 chests, and the rapid spread of a taste for opium smoking, and the consequent demoralization of individuals, who indulged in this vice, attracted the attention of government. Accordingly an edict was published formally forbidding the importation. On this the regular levy of a duty ceased, and for it was substituted, with the connivance of the Cantonese authorities, a system of secret importation under a clandestine levy of official fees. The effect of the imperial prohibition was an immediate rise in the selling price of opium, and a consequently increased supply See *China Review*, Vol. 20, No. 4, page 218.

disabuse the Chinese nation of this arrogant assumption was now the serious business of every representative that Her Majesty should send to China to guard her subjects there. In pursuance of the above act Lord Napier was sent out by the British government at the beginning of A. D. 1834 as chief superintendent of trade, with large powers to deal with the Chinese officials, as well as ample authority over his own countrymen. Without waiting for the passport which the officers of the company had been accustomed to apply for, when they wished to go to Canton, he proceeded without any formality to that city. On his arrival at the city gates he presented a letter that he had prepared and wished the officer on guard to take it to the Viceroy. This was indignantly refused, on the ground that he had no right to address him directly, but should do so through the hong merchants, and also that he had committed a serious breach of etiquette in writing a letter, instead of a humble petition. As Lord Napier could not consent to take any other course than what he had already done, after waiting for nearly three hours at the entrance of the city, during which his party were treated with much indignity, he returned to the factory.*

Viceroy Lu now felt that severe measures must be taken to curb the daring of this foreigner that had assumed a position that no previous officer had ventured to take. These barbarians must be taught a lesson that they should not easily forget. He accordingly issued an order (Aug. 18, 1834) that Lord Napier should leave the neighbourhood of Canton immediately, and at the same time by proclamation he ordered the Chinese to stop all trade with the English, and all servants in their employ to leave them. The hong merchants were also enjoined to forbid the shipping of cargo by English vessels, and to persuade their agents not to listen to the orders of Lord Napier. As these, of course, refused to do this, all trade was put an end to, and the English factories were surrounded by Chinese soldiers, even provisions not being allowed to those who were thus imprisoned. Two frigates, the *Imogen* and the *Andromache*, were then ordered to Whampoa. As they passed the Bogue forts these were fired into, but they were replied to with such vigour that they were speedily silenced, and the ships reached their anchorage in safety. September 11, 1834, finding that trade was being injured, and no satisfactory progress made in this struggle for the rights of England, Lord Napier retired to Macao, where he died October 11, 1834. With the departure of the frigates and his death, the victory seemed to remain with the Chinese. They little dreamed that this was but the first act in a tragedy, the last of which should be played amidst conflict and bloodshed, for war in the future was now inevitable, and though other causes might arise that might seem to be responsible for that, the one disposing force that would bring the soldiers of England and China into the battlefield was the demand of the former for equal rights with the latter.

---

* *Chinese Repository*, Vol. xi., p. 27.

Mr. J. F. Davis succeeded Lord Napier, and he was most urgent in his despatches to Lord Palmerston that no craven policy should be adopted by the English in their communication with the Chinese. He recommended, indeed, that a small fleet should be sent to the Peiho, in order to bring a pressure upon the Emperor, who, he held, was kept entirely in the dark by the officials at Canton as to the true state of affairs there. In this appeal he was heartily supported by the whole of the English community. The government, however, was not yet prepared to take so serious a step, and so matters reverted to the unsatisfactory condition in which they were before the arrival of Lord Napier. That matters would grow worse instead of better was now apparent to every thinking man, and the causes for this were manifest. Trade having been thrown open to all comers, a race of men had appeared in the field who were not disposed to be so narrowly bound down by rules as their predecessors in the East India Co. had been. Some of them even refused to acknowledge the authority of the chief superintendent, on the ground that, as he could not protect them, they must devise means for their own safety. Another source of danger was constantly increasing. The consumption of opium had grown so largely that a vast system of smuggling had sprung up that was entirely beyond the control of either the English or Chinese. Sir G. Robinson, who succeeded Mr. Davis, was so certain that this could not be suppressed that he actually wrote to Lord Palmerston (February 5, 1836) suggesting that the growth of the poppy should be discontinued in British India, as the one certain way in which the difficulty could be met.*

All this time the Chinese, with the dogged perseverance of their race, refused to abate one jot of their claims to be regarded as the superiors of the English, and Captain Elliot, who followed Sir G. Robinson as chief superintendent, seeing himself helpless because of the want of power to enforce his claims, actually consented to petition the viceroy for a passport to permit him to reside outside of Canton, thus giving up the very point that Lord Napier had fought for, and which had been the cause of the struggle between the English and the Chinese. The viceroy was delighted, and in his despatch to the Emperor on the subject he informed him that the trouble with the barbarians was over, and that they would hence-

---

* This opium trade was a source of infinite trouble, both to the chief superintendents in China and also to the English government. Lord Palmerston and all the members of his cabinet disliked it, and they absolutely refused to assist any British subjects in making good any losses they might incur whilst carrying on his business. Capt. Elliot looked upon the whole business as he would upon piracy. There were two difficulties at this time that stood in the way of controlling it. It had grown so immensely and become so mixed up with legitimate trade that no measures for its repression could be passed without seriously affecting this. Again, too, the covetousness of the Chinese officials, both in Canton and in the imperal household, presented an absolutely insuperable difficulty. That these would be willing to forego the large sums that came to them from this illegal traffic was entirely out of the question.

forth meekly occupy the position which they, as an inferior race, ought to be content to accept. Elliot, by consenting to use the word *pin* (humble petition), had in fact fixed his own official status, and once more came under the hong merchants and the Hoppo.

He now removed to Canton (April 12, 1837), when on November 23rd he received an order from Lord Palmerston that he must maintain the dignity of England in his correspondence with the mandarins, and refrain from using the objectionable word *pin*. When the viceroy was informed of this he peremptorily refused to receive any communication from him without it. Upon this Elliot hauled down his flag and retired to Macao. It will scarcely be believed that a year after this dignified action had been taken, though his conduct had been approved of by the English government and a man-of-war had been sent out to back him up, Elliot (December 31, 1838) again consented to use the obnoxious word and to take even a lower position than he had previously occupied, for the viceroy, presumably to punish him, refused to receive any despatches from him through the hong merchants, but ordered that they should be sent through the latter to the local governor's subordinate officers by the prefect of Canton city and the commandant of the city constabulary, thus denying him the privilege of communicating with himself as too unimportant an official to have such an honour. The English community were in arms at this insult, but unless Elliot was prepared for the suspension of all business relationships it is difficult to see how a more resolute attitude could have been taken by him. Besides, the condition of things had become so desperate that he felt himself bound to submit to this indignity, in order to preserve the community from some great disaster, which it was then believed was imminent. During the year in which he had held no official communication with the Canton authorities the opium difficulty had immensely increased. The smuggling at Lin-tin, where the receiving ships lay, had grown into a vast system that no one could now control. Swift cutters and schooners, heavily armed, and most of them English, carried the opium up the river, and continual conflicts were taking place between the Chinese war junks and them, in which lives were lost, and hostile feelings were being engendered between the English and the Chinese.

Unfortunately the imperial government at Peking had not taken a decided position on the question. The statesmen there were divided into two parties. One was for legalizing the drug, and the other was for total exclusion from the country. It is a fact worthy of note that neither of these looked at the subject from a moral point of view, but simply from a fiscal one. They were both distressed that so much silver should be going out of the country in payment of the opium, and the one point they were anxious to settle was how this was to be avoided. At length the anti-opium party in the cabinet became supreme, and in the beginning of A. D. 1839 it was decided that the opium trade should be put an end to.* In order to carry out this decision Lin was appointed special imperial commissioner and high admiral, with large power to act in this emergency. No better man could have been found to execute the policy of his party, for he had an iron will and an indomitable purpose that not any of the officials in Canton who had been involved in the disgraceful traffic dared to oppose. In another sense his appointment was a most unfortunate one. He was proud and overbearing, and had a supreme contempt for the barbarians and believed that he had but to appear upon the scene and he could crush them into submission. He was just enough to consider that a large part of the blame for the disastrous state of things that now existed was due to the officials at Canton, who had been corrupt in the administration of the laws. These were so terrified at the news of his appointment that for several months before his arrival the opium traffic was stopped, and the carrying of the drug between Lin-tin and Whampoa was forbidden. A proclamation was also issued by the viceroy ordering the receiving ships to leave the country, with the threat that, if they did not, trade of all kinds would be stopped.

Eight days after his arrival at Canton (March 18, 1839) Lin demanded from the foreign merchants that all the opium they possessed should be delivered up to him, and in order to secure obedience he surrounded their factories on the land side with lines of soldiers, and on the river by a large number of war junks. At the same time all the Chinese servants were ordered to withdraw, and all supplies of food and water were stopped. It may be imagined what a miserable plight the community, numbering over two hundred people, were now in, as their lives could be saved only by the surrender of the opium. Elliot (March 28) signified that he was prepared to deliver twenty thousand two hundred and eighty-three chests to Lin, and requested that their servants should be sent back to them and food supplies once more permitted. The commissioner replied that these requests could not be complied with until at least one-fourth of the opium had been handed over to him, and it was not till the 17th of April that servants and fresh provisions were allowed to pass the Chinese sentries. By the 4th of May the delivery of the opium was accomplished, and the imprisoned foreigners felt themselves free once more. Lin, however, not satisfied with the severe measures he had adopted, insisted that sixteen of the principal merchants should be detained in custody as a punishment for having engaged in the illegal traffic. This demand, that was resisted, together with the regulations that he made for the carrying on of trade generally, which were hard and oppressive, caused the English to quit Canton, and by the end of May they and their ships had left the scene of

---

* The import of opium had in 1838 reached the large amount of 18,212 chests.

conflict, never again to occupy the same position there that they had held before. *

On the withdrawal of the English community from Canton they proceeded to Macao, which they hoped would prove an asylum in this time of extreme need, and which it was desired might take the place of the former city as a centre of trade. At first they were heartily welcomed by the Portuguese, but Lin, who was anxious that the trade should again return to Whampoa and Canton, so worked upon the mind of Governor Pinto by promises and threats that the English soon found that they were unwelcome guests, and that they must look for some other place of refuge. Things were finally made so unpleasant for them that on the 26th of August, A. D. 1839, they all, with sad and heavy hearts, embarked on board their ships, which set sail and finally anchored in the harbour of Hongkong. Lin, who was still determined to carry his point, entered into communications with Elliot and proposed certain new regulations for the carrying on of trade, which might have been accepted had he not demanded that the English merchants should sign a bond consenting to come under Chinese law and to be tried and punished by it. This of course they could not agree to, when Lin gave the ships three days to leave China, at the same time preparing a number of fire ships to destroy them if they did not. In order to anticipate the Chinese, H. M. S. *Volage* and *Hyacinth* sailed up to Chuen-pi and demanded that all warlike designs should cease. The only reply to this was the getting under weigh of the Chinese fleet of twenty-nine junks and their standing towards the English men-of-war. These at once accepted the challenge, and tacking up and down the Chinese line they poured in their broadside with the most damaging effects. In less than an hour one junk had been blown up, three sunk and several water-logged, whilst the rest had retired in great disorder before the despised barbarians (November 3, 1839). This decided defeat had no influence whatever on the mind of Lin in causing him to look with any less contempt upon his foreign foes or in inducing him to offer them more favourable terms by which trade could be

---

* As is well known, Lin destroyed the opium that had been delivered to him, and he believed that by so doing he had stamped out the trade. He was not statesman enough to know that by this very act he was giving it a new impetus. The owners had been indemnified for their loss by an order on the English treasury for £120 a chest. The market that had been glutted before the delivery now became depleted, and new supplies flowed into an empty market, when high prices were sure of being realized. That Lin was conscientious in the course he took, and that he had a real hatred of opium, there is no reason whatever to doubt. He foresaw the miseries it would entail upon his countrymen, and he was determined by one fell stroke to drive it out of China. That he did not succeed was not his fault, but rather because the forces opposed to him were too strong for him. That the opium question was one employed by him simply to disguise his real purpose of hatred to the English, cannot be believed after reading his proclamation against opium, issued September 27, 1840, in which he reminds the Chinese of the near approach of the period for putting in force the new law against opium smokers, and strongly urges that those who have broken the law should reform, so " that human life may be spared, and those awakened who are still in the deceptive road."

once more resumed. He offered five thousand dollars for Elliot's head, and different sums for those of English officers, varying according to their rank, thus widening the breach and rendering hostilities in the future inevitable.

Whilst these events were taking place, Parliament had discussed the Chinese question and decided to send out an expedition to protect the interests of British subjects in China. By the end of June, A. D. 1840, seventeen men-of-war and twenty-seven troop-ships, carrying four thousand soldiers, reached Hongkong. The troops were under the command of General Bremner, subject to the control of Hon. G. Elliot and Capt. Elliot. General Bremner, having announced the blockade of the port of Canton, proceeded north and occupied Ting-hai, in the island of Chusan, and from thence he went to Tientsin where Lord Palmerston's letter to the Emperor was handed to Ki-shen, the viceroy of Chihli, by whom it was forwarded to Peking. The effect of this, and of the armed force at the mouth of the Peiho, was soon apparent in the active measures that were taken to meet the present crisis. Ki-shen was appointed imperial commissioner to settle the Canton difficulty, and Ele-poo the Chusan one. Lin was degraded and ordered to return to Peking "with the speed of flames," that he might be examined in the presence of his sovereign. A truce was concluded (November 6, 1840) to allow of further deliberation at Canton, and it was agreed that in the meanwhile Chusan should be held by the English till matters had been satisfactorily settled between England and China. Things however, did not move on so smoothly as they would have done if Ki-shen had been left to himself to decide as he wished. Unfortunately another order had come to Lin, commanding him to associate himself with the commissioner in the settlement of the case and there is room for suspecting that he did all in his power to thwart the plans for a peaceful solution of the difficulty. At any rate Captain Elliot, after six weeks of juggling and delay on the part of the Chinese, sent an ultimatum to Ki-shen on the 6th of January, 1841, saying that unless he came to some definite agreement by eight o'clock next morning he should order the seizure of the Bogue forts. No reply having been received, the English moved on the forts Chuen-pi and Tai-kok, and in little over an hour both places were captured, with the loss of five hundred killed and two hundred wounded and the destruction of sixteen war junks to the Chinese and the wounding of only twenty of the English. A flag of truce was sent by Admiral Kwan to Elliott, proposing an armistice, which was at once agreed to, and the treaty of Chuen-pi was concluded January 20, A. D. 1841. In this it was contracted that Hongkong should be ceded to the English, six millions of dollars should be paid for the opium that had been seized by Lin, and that official intercourse should be conducted on terms of equality between the English and Chinese, and that Canton should be opened for trade early in February.

The British squadron was then ordered to withdraw from the Canton river, Hongkong was taken possession of (January 26), and a vessel was despatched to Chusan to recall the troops that were in occupation there. The drama, however, was not yet played out, and many a bloody scene was to be enacted before the objects of the war could be effected. The Emperor disavowed the action of Ki-shen and ordered him to atone for his folly by the utter extermination of the barbarians. As a practical commentary on the treaty so lately concluded the fort on Wang-tong island opened fire (February 18) on one of the boats of the steamer *Nemesis,* and thus declared war against the English. The challenge was at once taken up, and war was proclaimed against China. In reply to this Iliang, the Lieut.-Governor of Canton, issued a proclamation offering $30,000 for the head either of Elliot or Bremner. That he was acting in the spirit of the instructions received from Peking is manifest from the edict which was issued by the Emperor Tau Kwang (January 27), in which he says, "There remains no other course than without remorse to destroy the foreigners and wash them clean away, and thus display the majesty of the empire."

The English forces were again led, the third time, against the Bogue forts, when the batteries of north Wang-tong and Anung-hoi were captured in the course of a few hours. Next day the fleet proceeded to a position near Whampoa, where a force of two thousand Hunan soldiers, with a hundred pieces of artillery, was entrenched, and before the close of the day they were defeated, after a fierce and obstinate struggle, in which there was considerable loss of life. Fort after fort was now taken in rapid succession, till at last the fleet lay anchored close to the city of Canton, which now lay at the mercy of the English. Captain Elliot now issued (March 7, A. D. 1841) a proclamation, informing the Chinese that any resort to force would be answered by the same, and intimating that the city would be spared on the condition that trade should be allowed to go on without interruption. Trade indeed was carried on, but the Emperor had no more idea of peace than ever he had, and consequently the Canton officials continued to make secret preparations for a renewal of the contest. Ki-shen was degraded and ordered to be arrested and carried a prisoner to Peking, there to be tried for his failure in carrying out the policy of the Emperor. Observing the hostile attitude of the Chinese, the English once more commenced operations by taking several forts and by the destruction of a number of junks. This decisive action brought the Chinese to terms, and at the request of Yang-fang, one of the imperial commissioners, a suspension of hostilities was agreed upon and a convention was signed (March 30), in which it was stipulated that the English men-of-war should be allowed to anchor off the foreign factories, that the Chinese should cease arming, and that trade should be opened up once more with Canton. Had the Chinese been sincere in their desire for peace, hostilities would have

stopped from this time, but they were not. Their supreme contempt
for the barbarian, who had hitherto consented to acknowledge the
supremacy of China, and their inborn belief that all nations outside
of their own country were really tributaries to it, operated so forcibly
on the minds of the rulers that they could never honestly come to
the conclusion that they ought to treat them as equals and faithfully
carry out any stipulation that might be agreed upon between them.

Hardly was the ink dry upon the paper which contained the
above agreement before preparations were begun for another trial
of strength with the English. Cannon were secretly cast at Fatshan,
forts were quietly re-armed, picked troops from other provinces
were continually arriving at Canton and a large number of fire
ships were got in readiness to burn the English fleet. At length,
on the 21st of May, Yik-shan, another of the commissioners,
decided to begin the attack. Elliot, however, who had not been
ignorant of the intentions of the Chinese, was ready for it. All
the plans of the enemy failed. The fire ships were repelled, the
batteries were silenced, and the English troops on the 27th of May
found themselves in position before the north-west gate of Canton,
ready to begin the assault of the city. All at once the movement
of the soldiers was stopped by the announcement that a treaty of
peace had been signed, the most important conditions of which
were that all the Tartar troops, and those from other provinces,
should immediately evacuate Canton, that six million of dollars
should be paid for the ransom of the city, and that trade should
be resumed at it and at Whampoa. Capt. Elliot, having been
superseded by Sir H. Pottinger, the latter arrived at Macao August
10th, A. D. 1841, when three days after he notified the high
authorities at Canton that he was vested with plenary powers to
settle all questions in dispute, and warning them that any attempt
to evade the terms of the treaty of Canton would be visited with
the severest penalties. The Chinese, unaccustomed to such language
from the English, were highly excited, and began once more to
arm the Bogue forts, but a visit from H. M. S. *Royalist* convinced
them that they had made a mistake.

The English expedition, under the joint command of Sir H.
Gough and Sir W. Parker, sailed (August 21) out of Hongkong,
and first captured Amoy. It then proceeded north and took possession of Chusan and the port of Ningpo, after a brave resistance on
the part of its defenders. When the Emperor heard of these
reverses he ordered troops from all parts of the empire to march
and recover the places that had been captured, at the same time
appointing Yih-king special commissioner to retake Chusan from
the English. In the meanwhile Yik-shan, in Canton, was making
vigorous efforts to prepare for another attempt upon the English.
Large bodies of volunteers were being drilled, and cannon cast and
money collected to prepare for the struggle. A plan, too, for a
sudden massacre of all the foreigners in Hongkong was devised

and sanctioned by the Emperor, as well as a scheme for the recovery of Ningpo and Chinhai.   The forces organized to attack these two last were defeated with great slaughter, though they numbered from ten to twelve thousand.

Sir H. Gough, hearing that a large body of troops was concentrated at Tsz-ki, ten miles from Ningpo, attacked and overcame them, and about a month after (May 18, 1842) captured the important port of Chapu, together with vast quantities of war material, which was immediately destroyed.   In consequence of these decided successes in the north the intended rising in Hongkong never took place.   Leaving Chapu, the fleet proceeded up the Yang-tze and captured Wusung and Shanghai, after a desperate resistance at the former place.   A large number of cannon was taken, amounting "to the astonishing number of three hundred and sixty-four," of which seventy-six were of brass and chiefly large handsome guns. Many of the latter had devices showing that they had been cast lately, and several of them had Chinese characters signifying, "The Tamer and Subduer of the Barbarians," whilst one particularly large one was dignified by the title of the "Barbarian."*   Having been detained by bad weather and other circumstances, the expedition did not start from Wusung till the 6th of July, but in a fortnight from that time seventy ships lay anchored abreast of Chinkiang, which it was decided should be attacked on the morrow. The troops experienced a more determined resistance here than they had met with at any previous place.   The Chinese troops, it is true, that were encamped outside the city, did not even wait for the approach of the English, but fled in all directions over the country. The Tartars, however, who defended the town, behaved in a very different manner.   They fought in the most heroic manner, and even after they had been defeated, many of them preferred self-immolation to surrender.   Out of a garrison of three thousand, forty officers and one thousand men were killed and wounded. Their general, seeing defeat inevitable, retired to his house, and causing his servants to set it on fire, he perished in the flames. The losses of the English were serious, being one hundred and sixty-nine killed and wounded.

On the 3rd of August the fleet again got under weigh and proceeded towards Nanking, which it reached on the 9th, when the debarkation of the troops began.   In two days everything was ready for an assault, when the Chinese commissioners, who saw that submission was the only practicable thing, now caused the white flag to be hung out, thus signifying their desire to negotiate.   Several friendly conferences having taken place, a treaty of peace was signed on the 29th on board H. M. S. *Cornwallis* by Sir H. Pottinger on the one side, and on the other by Ki-ying, Ili-pu and Niu-kien, and thus ended this first war with China, which was destined to effect such

---

* Circular issued by Sir H. Pottinger, June 24, 1842.

mighty changes in the attitude which this conservative and exclusive country was henceforth to hold in relation to foreign countries.*

Although the war was unquestionably the result of the refusal of the Chinese officials to recognize the English as anything but tributary to their Emperors, there is no doubt that the mandarins who were present at the signing of the treaty all believed that the real cause of it was the opium traffic. Even Sir H. Pottinger, if we may believe the evidence of Capt. Loch, seems to have held the same opinion on this point that the Chinese did, for after the treaty had been signed he proposed to say a few words to the assembled company upon "the great cause that produced the disturbances that led to the war, viz., the trade in opium." Upon hearing this they unanimously declined entering upon the subject, until they were assured that he had introduced it merely as a topic for private conversation. "They then evinced much interest, and eagerly requested to know why we would not act fairly toward them by prohibiting the growth of the poppy in our dominions, and thus effectually stop a traffic so pernicious to the human race." "This," he replied, "in consistency with our constitutional law, could not be done; and," he added, "that even if England chose to exercise so arbitrary a power over the tillers of her soil it would not check the evil, but it would merely throw the market into other hands." He then went on to show that if the Chinese stopped smoking, the production of the article would cease, but if they would not do this they would procure the drug in spite of every enactment. "Would it not, therefore, be better," he said, "to legalize its importation, and by thus securing the co-operation of the rich and of your authorities, thereby greatly limit the facilities which now exist for smuggling." They owned the plausibility of the argument, but expressed themselves persuaded that their imperial master would never listen to a word on the subject.†

---

* The provisions of this famous treaty were: (1.) Lasting peace between England and China. (2.) The opening of the ports of Canton, Amoy, Fuchow, Ningpo and Shanghai to Englishmen for trade and residence, all of whom were to be under the jurisdiction of British consular officers. (3.) The cession of Hongkong. (4.) Payment of an opium indemnity of six million dollars. (5.) Three million dollars to be paid for debts due English merchants. (6.) Twelve million dollars for the expenses of the war. (7.) The entire amount to be paid before December, 1845. (8.) All prisoners of war to be released by the Chinese. (9.) An amnesty for all Chinese who had assisted the English in the war. (10.) A regular tariff to be drawn up. (11.) Official correspondence to be conducted on terms of equality. (12.) Conditions for restoring the places held by the English to be according to the payments of the indemnity. (13.) Time for exchanging ratifications of treaty, etc. A supplementary treaty was signed at the Bogue (October 8, 1843). which provided for the carrying on of trade at the new ports, etc., the stipulations of which were as binding as the various articles of the treaty of Nanking.

† Capt. Loch's "Closing Events of the Campaign in China," pp. 168-175, quoted in *Chinese Repository*, Vol. xiii., p. 69. The connection of the English with this wretched opium business was a most unfortunate one, for though the war was undoubtedly caused by the arrogance of the Chinese and the studied determination of the officials to treat the English as an inferior race and tributary to China, and would have, some time or other, taken place, although opium had never existed, still there is no question but that it was one of the important factors in

In accordance with the stipulations of the treaty consulates were opened in Amoy and Shanghai in November, 1843, and foreign trade was peaceably commenced with the natives. In the following year (July 3) the American treaty was signed, and on October 23 the French one. In connection with the latter a very important event happened, viz., the issuing of a decree by the Emperor that Christianity should be tolerated throughout the empire, and no person professing it should be molested in the exercise of his religion. The honour of bringing about this change was due to the French commissioner, Lagrené, and to their excellencies, Ki-ying and Hwang.* The Chinese government seemed, for the present at least, to have accepted the defeat they had suffered and to be prepared to carry out the articles of the treaty. The twenty-one millions of dollars were paid within the required time, and Chusan was accordingly evacuated by the English troops. The one place that refused to abide by the arrangements that had been made was Canton. The people of that city were determined that no foreigner should have free access to it, and Ki-ying, the viceroy, seemed to have no power to control them. It was not simply that they showed a passive resistance to the carrying out of the stipulations of the treaty; they were also most aggressive in their treatment of the foreigners. At length, after repeated insults, and the attempt of the people of Fatshan to murder a party of Englishmen that visited that city, Sir J. Davis, the Governor of Hongkong, determined to make a military demonstration against Canton.

On the 1st of April, 1847, the expedition, consisting of three steamers, conveying two regiments, started from Hongkong. The guns of the Bogue forts were silenced and spiked, and almost without opposition the force reached the city walls, and the town was commanded by the guns of the men-of-war. The populace, instead of being dismayed, only demanded to be led against the audacious barbarians, whom they declared they would exterminate. Pacific counsels, however, prevailed, and Ki-ying granted the demands of Sir J. Davis, viz., that Canton should be opened to foreigners in two years, that larger space should be given the merchants on

hurrying on the collision. The connection of the English government with the production and sale of opium in India is not one that a great country can ever be proud of. No poet will ever sing its praises and no statues will ever be erected to the memory of the men that have planned and carried out this questionable way of raising a revenue.

* Dr. Morrison, the first Protestant missionary, was sent out by the London Missionary Society, and reached Canton in 1807. He found it impossible to carry on his work there, so bitter was the feeling against Christianity. He consequently entered the service of the East India Co , by which means he was able to reside at Canton and still do Christian work. At the conclusion of the war Protestants of all denominations, from Java, Singapore, Siam, etc., who had been waiting for a favourable opportunity of entering China, now flocked to Hongkong and Macao to make preparations for occupying the treaty ports. The issuing of the edict of toleration, therefore, was a matter of the greatest importance to them, as it gave them the right to preach Christianity, and the natives the privilege of believing in it, without any fear of molestation from the officials.

which to build residences and warehouses, and that Englishmen should have the liberty of going beyond their present bounds for pleasure or exercise, but only to such a distance as would permit of their return home within twenty-four hours. The first and last of these points were certainly not carried out, for in December of this same year six gentlemen were seized and barbarously murdered by the people of a village in the neighbourhood of Canton, and when the two years expired Tau Kwang refused to compel the authorities of this city to admit the English within its walls.

Whilst these events were transpiring there were many signs throughout the country to show that the central government was losing the power to control the empire which it ruled. In A. D. 1845-6 an insurrection of the sons of Jehangir occurred in Turkestan, who, incited by some turbulent chiefs in Kokand, appeared in arms to claim their father's inheritance and to avenge his death. Fortunately, this was soon put down, mainly in consequence of their failing to gain the support of their co-religionists, the Mohammedans. The southern coast of China, too, became infested with powerful fleets of pirates, that defied all the efforts of the authorities to destroy them. Having had the audacity to attack English ships, a crusade against them was ordered by the admiral on the station, and ere long they were suppressed. On land powerful secret societies existed, the chief of which was the Triad, which, though peaceful at present, awaited but some crisis in the nation to exercise their vast machinery for the sorrow of the people at large. Insurrections in the centre of China, and also in the neighbourhood of the Yellow River, where the people were driven to plunder and murder through the poverty they had been reduced to, in consequence of its inundations, all showed that there were widespread causes of discontent, and that it wanted but some great leader to take the initiative, and the country would be ablaze with rebellion. In this perilous condition of affairs Tau Kwang died, A. D. 1850, in the sixty-ninth year of his life, leaving the throne to his fourth son, unconscious at the time that the forces were already gathering that would desolate China for many years, and but for the intervention of the despised foreigner would wrench the empire from the possession of the Manchus.

CHAPTER XXXIV.

THE TS'ING DYNASTY (Continued).

Hien Fung—A. D. 1851-1862.

THIS prince was only nineteen years old when he ascended the throne. He had neither the intellectual vigour nor determination of purpose that his father had, and consequently he was ill-fitted to cope with the great questions that thrust themselves upon the nation during his reign. Ki-ying, who had figured so largely during the time of Tau Kwang, was removed from his office, and many thought that this indicated an anti-foreign feeling in the mind of the young Emperor, especially as Su was appointed viceroy of Canton, a man who had made himself conspicuous by his defending the citizens of that place in their determination not to allow the foreigners to enter their city. This action was hailed by a large and influential party in the state with delight, for such was the gross ignorance of the educated and leading men of China in regard to foreign nations that it was believed that they were utterly beneath the contempt of this country, and that consequently no official relationship with them should be for a moment entertained. The war had taught the Chinese no lesson. They were as arrogant and overbearing as ever, and evidently Hien Fung had come to the throne with those narrow views of statesmanship that were destined to make his reign a troubled one.

In the summer of A. D. 1850 the first act of the great Taiping rebellion was committed by the seizure and fortifying of the market town of Lien-chu, in Kwang-si.* Finding this place an inconvenient

---

* Hung Siu-tsuen, the leader of this movement, was the son of a farmer, and born in A. D. 1813. In the year 1833 he went to the literary examinations at Canton, but failed to get his degree. Whilst there he was given a number of Christian tracts entitled "Good Words to Exhort the Age," but at the time he laid them aside, not caring to study anything that was Christian. The vexation he felt at not passing affected his health, so that he became seriously ill. Whilst he was expecting death, he fell on one occasion into a trance, in which he saw visions of the most wonderful character. Among the people that appeared to him was an old man, who declared that all men were created by him, but that many of them had deserted him for the worship of devils, and handing him a sword gave him a command to destroy all such. This dream was destined to have a most powerful influence over his future life.

About the year A. D. 1843 he again tried to get his degree, but once more failed. He was now persuaded to read the tracts that for ten years had lain covered with dust on his shelves. The effect was marvellous. He was deeply impressed with their correspondence to what he had seen and heard in his visions, and he believed that he was destined to be the future ruler of China. He now adopted such form of Christianity as he could gather from the tracts, and discarded idolatry. He began to preach his new faith, and gained a convert of great value, named Yun-shan. These two shortly after went to visit a relative of Hung's, in Kwangsi, who lived amongst the mountains, near the Miautze. There their preaching and their good moral life seemed to make a great impression upon the simple country folk. Years went by without any very great results, till Yun-shan, who had gone to

one from a military point of view, it was abandoned, and Taitsun was occupied instead. The order and discipline that were maintained amongst the Taipings drew large numbers to them, amongst whom were the chiefs of the Triad Society, but as the objects of the two movements were entirely different from each other these soon withdrew and joined the imperialists. It was whilst encamped at Taitsun that Hung became more convinced than ever that he had received a divine commission to conquer China for himself, and to impress the multitudes that had gathered to his standard he continually issued decrees which he averred had been received by him direct from the Heavenly Father. The Taipings next captured the city of Yungan, where they remained for some time, but feeling their power grow, and driven, too, by the necessity of having to feed such large numbers as had flocked to their camp, they advanced against Kwei-ling, but the imperialists being in force here they failed in their attempts to take it. Nothing daunted by this, they crossed over into Hunan and took Tou, which thus gave them the command of the river Siang. Passing rapidly through the beautiful valley through which it flowed they were everywhere successful till they reached Changsha, the chief city of the province. Here they were stopped by the high walls and massive gates of this formidable city, and after eighty days spent before them in vain, they crossed the Tung-ting Lake, and passing down the Yangtze, carried the great cities of Hanyang and Wuchang by storm. With irresistible force they still pressed on, taking the towns of Nganking and Kiukiang, till on the 8th of March, A. D. 1853, they stood within the walls of Nanking, which from this time became the capital of the rebellion.

The success of the Taipings had been extraordinary. The troops of the empire seemed to have been paralyzed with fear, as they never dared to appear in force against them in the open field. They had started from Yungan numbering ten thousand, but when they appeared before Nanking they counted no fewer than eighty thousand. Hung Siu-tsuen now proclaimed himself Emperor, and five of his leading chiefs were made princes. After a breathing space of two months a large force was despatched to Peking. The reckless daring and bravery of these men may be imagined when the nature of the task they had undertaken is understood. To

---

another part of Kwangsi, preached with such success that he had gathered two thousand adherents. Hung visited him, and the sight of such large numbers undoubtedly made him believe that there was a possibility that his dreams of power might be realized. Slowly he began to prepare for the struggle, which in time was precipitated by the action of the authorities, who became uneasy at the assembling of such multitudes under the guidance of one or two men. The iconoclastic tendencies of the new disciples had also irritated the people, and the destruction of temples had caused conflicts which had compelled the mandarins to interfere. The governor-general of Canton had been duly informed of the state of things, but he felt inadequate to grapple with the difficulty, so Saishangah, the prime minister, and Tahungah, a man who nine years ago had executed one hundred and eight British prisoners in Formosa, were appointed imperial com; missioners to put down the insurrection.

plunge into an unconquered country with no commissariat and no
elaborate system by which they could be supported ; to travel more
than a thousand miles, with the possibility of meeting large armies ;
and to pass great rivers and high mountains, were some of the difficulties they must have been prepared to face. On the 28th of October
they had baffled every obstacle and were encamped at Tsinghai,
near Tientsin. " In six months this insurgent force had traversed
four provinces, taken twenty-six cities, subsisted themselves on the
enemy and defeated every body of imperialists sent against them."*

Not daring to advance, they sent for reinforcements, but
when these joined them there seemed to be no disposition to march
on to the capital. Instead of that they occupied themselves in
conquering and occupying the places that fell in their way as they
wandered about in an aimless manner, till in March, A. D. 1855,
they returned to Ngan-hwui to operate for the future wherever they
were ordered. From this time the character of the movement seems
to have entirely changed. The high incentive which they had
previously had before them of capturing the capital and of founding
a new dynasty being lost, they now degenerated into a vast horde of
robbers, whose hearts were steeled against every human sympathy,
and whose deeds of murder and cruelty rivalled those of Attila
or Tamarlane.

Theological divisions now took place amongst the leaders, and
Hung Siu-tsuen arrogated to himself titles and powers which showed
that he never had any true conception of what Christianity was.
The inherent defect of the whole movement was an utter want of
organization. The rebels could fight and conquer, but they had no
system ready to take the place of the one they were endeavoring to
overthrow. Mere brute force, however it may succeed for a time,
must in the end prove a failure. A year after their return from the
north the Taipings held no more than the two cities of Nanking and
Nganking, with the river banks that connected them, and both of
these towns were blockaded by the imperialists. For three years
they were hemmed in by the imperialists and reduced to the direst
extremity, when on May 6th, A. D. 1860, a spirited sally from
Nanking scattered the besiegers, and a rebel force was once more
let loose to work destruction on society.

Two months after this they were in possession of Kiangnan and
Chehkiang and the famous town of Soochow became theirs. This
beautiful city, noted throughout China, was treated with the utmost
barbarity, and its vast population either murdered or scattered.†

---

* See Williams' " Middle Kingdom," Vol. II., p. 598.
† The writer of this visited this place after it fell into the hands of the rebels.
A sadder scene it would be impossible to imagine. The moat around the city was
literally thick with dead bodies far gone in decomposition, so that the boat had to
be poled, through them. The town was a heap of ruins, and forty thousand Taipings, dressed in silks and satins, the plunder of this famous silk mart, looked
without any compassion upon the scene of desolation that had been caused by
their wickedness.

Ningpo fell into their hands, and Shanghai would have shared the same fate had it not been defended by the English, who repelled their advance by force.

It was at this crisis that the Manchus turned for aid to the foreigner to accomplish what was beyond their own power to perform. An American named Ward was engaged, who became commander of a force of about one hundred foreigners, who captured the city of Sung-kiang from the rebels. The high pay drew considerable numbers to his standard, and soon he had a heterogeneous body at his command that from their success was called the "Ever-victorious Army." Ward having been slain in battle, was succeeded by Burgevine, but he had not the mettle of his predecessor, and after a time Li Hung-chang applied to General Stavely for an able man to take charge of the force. Col. Gordon was recommended by him, and a more suitable man in all the English army could not have been found than he. His success was so great that by June, A. D. 1864, his work was done, and the "Ever-victorious Army" was disbanded. In July of this same year Nanking was captured by the imperialists, and though a small body of rebels escaped, and, travelling south, captured the large city of Changchow, near Amoy, and held it for nearly a year, they were ultimately defeated and scattered, and the great Taiping rebellion was practically at an end. Nine provinces had been desolated by it; flourishing towns and cities had been made heaps of ruins, and wild beasts made their dens within them; and misery and. sorrow, incalculable, had been caused, whilst fully twenty millions of people had been put to death by these ruthless robbers.

Whilst these tragedies were being enacted, the position of China in regard to foreign powers became more and more unfriendly. It was evidently the aim of the imperial government to have as little to do with foreigners as possible, and certainly not to permit them the honor of being on an equal footing with their officers in any official communications they might have to make with them. Naturally, as the result of this policy, complications arose, which were rendered all the more acute by the appointment of Yeh Ming-chin to be Governor-General of Canton. This man was a beau ideal Chinaman of an intensely conservative stamp, who despised the foreigner, and who was determined to uphold the supremacy of his country over every other. When difficult questions arose that might have been settled by a conference he refused to meet any foreign minister. It was impossible, therefore, but that before long a collision would take place that would land England and China in war. That this actually did happen is a matter of history.*

---

* After the capture of Canton, and the seizure of Yeh, it was discovered by the evidence of official documents in his yamên that the insolent policy of Yeh had not only been sanctioned but also suggested by the government at Peking. See Life of Sir H. Parkes.

On the 8th of October, A. D. 1856, twelve of the crew of the lorcha *Arrow* were seized by the orders of Yeh.* In addition to this the English flag, which was flying at the time, was hauled down in anything but a respectful manner, which thus added to the difficulties of the case. It is true, indeed, that at the time this action was performed the registration of the lorcha had expired some ten days before, and therefore, in a strictly legal sense, she was not under English protection. Yeh was not aware of this, however, and therefore it cannot be brought forward in extenuation of his conduct. No difficulty would have been experienced in this case had he appealed to the English Consul, according to Article 9th of the Supplementary Treaty, which demanded that all Chinese wrong-doers in the service of the English should be claimed through the British authorities. It may seem at the present day that the action of Yeh, in thus boarding a vessel flying the English flag to carry off Chinese subjects, was not of sufficient importance to involve two countries in war. In those early days, however, when foreigners had not gained the position they possess unquestioned to-day, it was of vital importance that the rights they had acquired by the sword should not be wrested from them at the caprice of any mandarin, however high in authority. The inviolability of national flags, and the safety of all beneath them, were of vast moment in the intercourse of foreigners with the Chinese, and any attempt to infringe upon these rights had to be at once and vigorously resisted.

Mr. Parkes remonstrated with Yeh, who defended his conduct by saying that he had seized the men, because one of them had been recognized as a pirate, and he demanded the return of the men and an apology. He consented to send back nine, but refused to acknowledge he was in the wrong, when they were promptly returned to him. Further correspondence ensued, and on October 22nd the twelve were sent into the English Consulate, but without an apology, when they were once more sent back to Yeh.

Had another man been governor-general at the time it is almost certain that this affair would have ended in a peaceable manner. His whole policy, however, had been so thoroughly anti-foreign and so high-handed that men never knew what extreme step he might not take at any moment. The inviolability of a nation's flag was a matter of the most supreme importance, for without that no person's safety was secure that came within the jurisdiction of this haughty Chinaman. After in vain endeavoring to get Yeh to acknowledge his wrong, Admiral Seymour advanced with his fleet up the Canton river, and capturing all the forts upon it an English force escaladed the wall of the city at a point nearest to Yeh's official residence, and in a short time Mr. Parkes and the admiral, at the head of a strong

---

* In order to develop the trade of Hongkong the authorities encouraged all kinds of vessels to come to the new port, and they granted licenses, under certain restrictions, to Chinese junks, by which they were allowed to fly the English flag, and thus come under British protection.

guard, entered this place to demand an interview, which had hitherto been refused with so little courtesy.

Finding it impossible to hold so large a place with so small a force, Admiral Seymour wrote home for five thousand men. The English government, determined on war, despatched a body of troops to China, which reached Singapore June 3rd, 1857, and the French having desired to unite with England, Lord Elgin and Baron Gros were appointed plenipotentiaries. A letter from Lord Canning diverted the force to India to assist in the suppression of the mutiny, but by the month of December five thousand English and one thousand French troops were all ready for the campaign.

Yeh having refused to listen to the terms proposed by Lord Elgin, the army advanced against Canton, and on the 27th December landed on the east bank of the river, a short distance from the walls of the town. By three o'clock on the 29th the city was in the hands of the allies, and Yeh, having been captured, was placed on board a man-of-war and despatched to India, where, after a time, he died. The city was now put under the control of a joint commission of Chinese, English and French, who performed their duties with such success that by the end of January, A. D. 1858, the blockade was raised, trade was resumed and the people opened their shops as though they were in the midst of profound peace.

Though the campaign had ended with perfect success so far as Canton was concerned, it was felt that the objects of the war were far from being obtained so long as direct communication with the court at Peking had not been effected. The plenipotentiaries therefore addressed a letter to Yu, the first member of the Privy Council, requesting that a commissioner, with special powers from the Emperor, should meet them in Shanghai to discuss the conditions of peace. The American and Russian ministers at the same time forwarded letters containing the same idea. The reply, as might have been expected, was a most unsatisfactory one, and refused this most reasonable request of the ministers.

Lord Elgin then announced that he would proceed to Taku, and requested a commissioner to meet him there, with whom he could discuss the demands of the allies. Early in May the whole of the fleet lay off the Peiho, ready to back the plenipotentiaries in their demands upon the Chinese. Three officials had been appointed, but upon the discovery that they had not full power they were dismissed and an advance was made upon the Taku forts. These, having been summoned to surrender without any result, were attacked and captured after a rather mild resistance on the part of the garrisons. The gunboats then proceeded to Tientsin, where Lord Elgin took up his residence. The government, terrified by the success of the foreigners, sent Kweiliang and Hwashana, with large powers, to enter into negotiations, with the result that on the 26th June a treaty with England was signed, and on the 4th July Lord Elgin received it, ratified by an imperial edict of Hien Fung. The three other powers also at the same time succeeded in having theirs signed.* It is impossible to overestimate the value and importance of this treaty, both to China and the world. This vast empire, that had been so long isolated from the rest of mankind, and had looked with haughty contempt upon all the peoples outside of it, now undertook, unwillingly it is true, to enter into the comity of nations. An ambassador in Peking meant one in each of the capitals of the powers with which she had entered into treaty. The men of the East would look in the face of the men of the West, not from behind frowning walls and loaded cannon, but in friendly intercourse and in growing mutual knowledge of each other's virtues. The day that the Tientsin treaty was signed was the first in the new life of this nation. The stagnation of ages was now to have an end, and the century would not close before China took her place amongst the kingdoms of the world as one of the great factors in it, whose voice should be heard in some of the great questions that affect our eastern empire. Whilst these negotiations were proceeding in the north, Canton was still held by the allies. In the city itself the utmost order prevailed, but in the outlying country the people, urged and incited by Hwang, the new governor-general, formed themselves into associations for the annoyance and destruction of foreigners. Prices were put on the heads of such, and any stray Englishman that could be seized was put to death. Vigorous measures were adopted, which soon put an end to these disturbances, and Hwang, at the request of Lord Elgin, was disgraced, whilst an order was received from England that Canton should still be held by the English troops. Coming events quickly proved the wisdom of this action, for it soon became apparent that the Chinese government had no intention of carrying out the treaty they had so recently signed. Taken by surprise, and unprepared for the sudden appearance of a foreign force, they yielded for the time being, simply to get rid of the danger and to be able leisurely to prepare to meet a foe whom they were convinced they could easily conquer. This action of the Chinese showed their utter ignorance of Western nations and their methods. In their past history they had faced simply barbarous nations, of which they were the superior both in numbers and civilization. The powers that had appeared at Tientsin were classed amongst these, and were to be treated rather as inferior, than as men on equality with China. Lord Macartney,

---

* This treaty contained fifty-six articles, the most important among which was the right to have an ambassador in Peking ; though in consequence of the stern opposition made to it by the Chinese, Lord Elgin agreed not to insist upon its being carried out immediately. The other was the legalization of opium, with a duty of £10 on each chest. Dr. Wells Williams, who rendered such good service in the arrangement of the details of the tariff, says with regard to this, "While particular provision was made for preventing the importation of salt and the implements and munitions of war, the trade in opium was legalized at a lower rate than was paid on tea and silk entering England. The evils of smuggling it were insufferable, but a heavy duty was desirable as a check and stigma on the traffic." Middle Kingdom, Vol. II., page 657.

they argued, had paid tribute for England, and Lord Amherst had attempted to do the same, and Englishmen for more than a century had patiently borne the greatest insults and indignities from the imperial officers in Canton. It was therefore a thing not to be considered that a treaty that had been wrung from the Emperor in the time of danger should be observed. This was the reasoning, no doubt, of the authorities at Peking.

As the time for the ratification of the treaty drew near, the Chinese commissioners endeavoured to induce the English and French to have this done in Shanghai instead of in Peking. This Messrs. Bruce and Bourboulon refused to consent to, and finding that the Chinese were determined to evade the treaty stipulation, the English and French forces assembled off the mouth of the Peiho on the 20th June, 1859. They found that the Chinese had made every preparation to give them a warm reception. Taku forts had been strongly fortified, whilst across the entrance of the river had been thrown massive booms, backed a little further in by iron stakes and huge rafts of timber. During the night of the 23rd one of the booms was blown up, and next day an advance in force was made. Thirteen gunboats passed through the opening that had been made, whilst six hundred marines and engineers landed to help in the attack on the forts. In the course of a few hours two of the gunboats were sunk, and the rest badly handled, and twenty-five men had been killed and ninety wounded, whilst the land force had been repulsed with a loss of sixty-four killed and fifty-four wounded.*

This repulse confirmed the Chinese, not only in their determination to repudiate the treaty, but also to fight the allies in case they should venture to attack them again. Mr. Ward, the American minister, communicated with Hang-fuh, the governor-general of Chihli, who invited him to Peh-tang, promising to send him on in safety to Peking. Having complied with his request, he and his suite were escorted by an armed guard to the capital, the people all along the route gathering in great crowds to see the foreigners, but everywhere exceedingly polite.† As far as any good purpose was served by this journey he might never have made it at all, for after having been amused by the Commissioner Kwei-liang with the idea that his treaty was going to be ratified at Peking, he was politely escorted back to Peh-tang, where the necessary exchange of ratification was made, August 15th, 1859.

---

* Whilst this engagement was going on, Commodore Tatnal, of the American navy, gave a signal proof of his sympathy with the English in their difficulties by towing boat loads of marines into action, giving as a reason for his conduct that "blood was thicker than water," a sentence that England will never forget, nor the man that uttered it.

† A ridiculous rumour, illustrated by appropriate pictures, respecting this journey, was circulated in Paris, stating that Mr. Ward and his party were conducted from the coast in an immense box, or travelling chamber, drawn overland by oxen, and there put on a raft to be towed up the river and imperial canal, as far as the gate of the capital. Middle Kingdom, Vol. II., page 669.

The English and French being unanimous in their determination to carry on the war, Lord Elgin and Baron Gros were again appointed plenipotentiaries, and a force of about thirteen thousand English, seven thousand French and two thousand five hundred Cantonese coolies, the last to be baggage bearers, etc., assembled off Peh-tang by the 1st August, 1860. By the 12th everything had been landed, and the allied army was on its march to the attack of the Taku forts, an attack which the Chinese had confidently expected would be made from the river.

The journey overland was rendered exceedingly difficult in consequence of the country being flooded. The Chinese, under their general Sangkolinsin, endeavoured to prevent their advance, but in the battle of Sin-ho they were completely routed by the allies, when they retreated upon the forts and entrenched camp at Tang-ku. These, in spite of the bravery of the Tartars, who stubbornly resisted the advance of the English, were captured and occupied, and on the 21st the army was in front of the great northern fort of Taku, which Sir H. Grant had decided to attack first, though General Montauban, the French commander-in-chief, would have preferred to have begun with the southern ones. The fighting commenced early in the morning, when twenty-three pieces of artillery began to play upon the great fortress. The Chinese stood to their guns most manfully, and showed the greatest courage, amidst the showers of missiles that rained about them. Unfortunately for them, during the hottest of the fight a shell exploded their chief magazine, dealing death and destruction amongst the brave men that were defending the walls. After a brief cessation the men were seen at their guns once more, but the discipline of the allies, together with their powerful artillery, ensured the victory, and by noon the place was in their hands. An advance was then made upon the other northern fort, but before their guns could be opened on it a white flag, hoisted by its defenders, showed that they had determined to surrender. Their example was followed by those on the southern bank of the Peiho, and before sunset the whole of the Taku forts were in the possession of the allies.

Without any unnecessary delay, the French and English moved on to Tientsin, where Kwei-liang and two other officials approached the envoys, professedly with the desire of negotiating peace, but really with the purpose of staying their progress towards Peking. Not finding their powers satisfactory, an order was given for the forces (Sept. 8th) to advance to Tungchow. The commissioners had represented that the Emperor was determined on peace, but there were signs of preparation for war along the route that hardly coincided with their express statements, and when Mr. Parkes rode forward with an escort to arrange about the encampment of the troops at Chang-kia-wan he suddenly came upon bodies of men lying in ambush and a battery of twelve guns recently made, all ready for action. Sending back Mr. Loch to inform Sir H. Grant of the state of things, he hurried to the quarters of Prince Tsai to ask an explanation. Getting no satisfaction here, and seeing that the Chinese troops were being moved into position to be ready to meet the advancing enemy, he endeavoured with all his party to return to the English lines. This was a matter of extreme difficulty, for the intervening country was filled with moving bodies of Tartar cavalry, and having to proceed cautiously, longer time was expended on the way, so that before they could reach their countrymen the battle had commenced.

Attempting now to make a detour, they were seized by the Chinese, and had it not been for the interposition of the officer into whose charge they came, they would all have been murdered on the spot. Mr. Parkes, accompanied by Mr. Loch, who had returned to him, were hurried into the presence of Sangkolinsin, who treated them with the greatest insult, compelling them both to knock their heads on the ground before him, at the same time reviling them with the most abusive language, and laughing at the idea that a flag of truce was to be regarded by him as any protection to them. The result was that the whole of the prisoners, divided into two parties, after having been bound most cruelly and barbarously, were forwarded to Peking, where they were confined in the common prisons of the Board of Punishment.

Meanwhile, the battle had been proceeding, but the resistance on the part of the Chinese was not so vigorous as might have been expected from the haughty attitude assumed by their commander-in-chief. In spite of the strong position held by them, and their great strength in cavalry, they were in the course of a few hours compelled to retreat and leave the field to the victors. The moral effect of a charge of Probyn's Horse on their picked Tartar cavalry, in which the latter were broken and scattered in sight of the two armies, had a great deal to do with their defeat. Three days after the battle of Chang-kia-wan (Sep. 21st) Sangkolinsin made a stand at Palikiau (Eight-mile Bridge), determined at all hazards to stay the advance of the allies on Peking, and thus in some measure fulfil the promise he had made the Emperor that no harm should befall his capital. An impetous charge of the French drove the Chinese from the position they had selected, and when the English came up, their defeat was so decided that from this time they never again dared to stand in open field against their victorious enemy.

Sir H. Grant now decided to encamp here until almost his entire force had joined him, together with the siege guns and commissariat stores. He felt that to attack Peking, which now lay at his mercy, he must be provided with all the means at his disposal, in order not to run any risk of disaster. The greatest anxiety now prevailed in the capital. The Emperor had fled to Jehol, the army that had promised to drive the barbarians into the sea had been defeated and driven back, and the allied forces were encamped within a few miles of it. Prince Kung, the brother of the Emperor, after the battle sent commissioners to negotiate, but Lord Elgin would listen to no terms until the prisoners had been released. As there were no signs that he would consent to this, even after the lapse of more than a week, during which time the remainder of the troops, etc., were being brought from Tientsin, Lord Elgin gave the order to advance on Peking, and by the 6th of October the English were encamped near the N. W. gate of the city, and not far from the Emperor's palace, Yuen-ming-yuen (Round Brilliant Garden).

The occupation of this latter building now convinced Prince Kung that if he would prevent the greater calamity of having Peking stormed and captured he must consent to the release of the captives. Accordingly, Messrs. Parkes and Loch and d'Escayrac de Lauture were sent into the English camp, and a few days after, eleven others, in a most wretched and miserable condition, the sole survivors of over thirty persons that had been seized near Tungchow. *

The remainder had died in their prisons, overcome by the terrible tortures they had undergone through being bound too tight by their cruel jailers. The utmost indignation was felt throughout the army when the awful story of their sufferings became known, and in order to mark his indignation against such inhumanity on the part of the officials, Lord Elgin decided that in addition to one hundred thousand pounds to be paid as compensation to the families of the murdered men, the Summer Palace should be destroyed by fire. This was accordingly done, and one cannot but acquiesce in the justice of an act which was intended to teach Hien Fung and the nation a lesson that they would not easily forget.

Prince Kung, having yielded to the demands of the allies, the ratification of the Tientsin treaty and the signing of the Convention took place October 24th, 1860, whilst the same kind of ceremonies were performed by the French on the following day.† These important acts having been performed, the allied troops returned to Tientsin, and by the end of November all had left China, excepting the garrisons at Tientsin and Taku, which two places were to be held until the indemnity had been fully paid up. Hien Fung never returned to Peking, for he died August 17th, 1861, in Jehol, and the supreme conduct of affairs fell into the hands of Prince Kung, a man much more enlightened than he, and one who so thoroughly appreciated the position of affairs that he had determined, in the interests of the empire, to faithfully carry out the treaties that had been made with foreign powers. Hien Fung's only son, a child of six years old, succeeded him on the throne and assumed the title of T'ung Chih.

---

* The party consisted of Messrs. Parkes, Loch, De Morgan, Bowlby, Capt. Brabazon, Lieut. Anderson and six English and twenty Sikh troopers.
† The chief points in the English Convention were the payment of eight million taels for the expenses of the war and the cession of Kowlung to the English.

T'ung Chih—A. D. 1862-1875.

Before Hien Fung's death the whole administrative power had been vested by him in the hands of a council of eight, whilst he himself spent his time in ways that were by no means consistent with those that ought to have characterized the ruler of a great and powerful nation. These men were all intensely conservative and anti-foreign, and looked with aversion upon the concessions that had been made by the treaties that had lately been ratified. Even before the Emperor's decease they had plotted the death of his three brothers, the queen and the young prince's mother, and the appointment of themselves as regents during the minority of his son. Prince Kung, who had certain information of what was going on, determined to be beforehand with the conspirators, and having gained possession of the person of the young Emperor, he apprehended them and caused the leader of the movement to be executed, whilst two others—Princes Chai and Tsin—were allowed to commit suicide. With the degradation and banishment of the rest all danger passed away, and Prince Kung, with the two Empress-Dowagers, formed a Council of Regency that from this time governed China in the name 'of the young ruler.* They were greatly assisted by that wise and liberal statesman, Wen-siang, and also by Kwei-liang, who were members of the Privy Council.

The Chinese government, having seen the utility of Western armaments in their conflict with the Taipings, desired, now that all complications with England were at an end, to have a larger number of such, that they might more effectually crush the rebellion, which by its success at Nanking (May, 1860) had taken a fresh start, and threatened to defy all the resources of the empire to overcome it. Mr. H. N. Lay, the Commissioner of Customs, was given authority to proceed to England to arrange for the construction of a number of steamships and to engage naval officers who could drill the Chinese for a term of three years.† Early in A. D. 1863 the fleet of eight gunboats arrived in China, under the command of Capt. Osborn, R. N., but complications at once arose through a difference of views between Prince Kung and Mr. Lay with regard to the disposition of these ships. The former held that they should form part of the effective fleet of China ; that a Chinese admiral should have joint command with Mr. Lay, and that they should be subject to the control of the provincial authorities. The latter refused to conform

---

* These two Empresses were the widow of Hien Fung and the mother of T'ung Chih, who had been a member of the harem, but had never reached the dignity of being queen.

† In the year 1853, in consequence of a party of Cantonese rebels having forcibly taken possession of Shanghai, the Chinese were unable to collect the foreign Customs there. By the request of the official in charge, the English, French and American ministers assumed the responsibility, and by them a set of Custom House rules were drawn up, which transferred the collection of duties into the hands of the foreigners. Mr. T. Wade was made commissioner, but after a year's service he resigned, and was succeeded by Mr. Lay.

to these ideas. According to his own statement he was "ambitious of obtaining the position of middleman between China and the foreign powers, because I thought I saw a way of solving the problem of placing pacific relations with China upon a sure footing. . . . . My position was that of a foreigner engaged by the Chinese government to perform certain work for them, and not under them. I need scarcely observe, in passing, that the notion of a gentleman acting under an Asiatic barbarian is preposterous."* These words sound strangely to-day after an experience of over thirty years, during which many gentlemen of high intelligence and culture have found it quite consistent with their character to take service under the Chinese government. The dismissal of Mr. Lay under these circumstances is not to be wondered at, especially as his powerful flotilla remained inactive, as far as the Taipings were concerned, at that critical time, when every nerve was being strained to drive them from Soochow, etc. Mr. Lay was succeeded by Mr., now Sir Robert Hart, a man eminently qualified by his superior abilities and high administrative qualities for such a responsible position. Under his guidance the Customs' service has developed into a system, in which a large body of foreigners are lucratively and honourably employed, and from which a very considerable revenue is annually secured to the Chinese government.

In the year A. D. 1867 the regents, seeing that official relationships with the West were inevitable, determined that the various countries there should have an opportunity of learning more fully the character of the Chinese and the nature of their laws and institutions. China had been so thoroughly isolated in the past that the most grotesque and absurd ideas were current regarding it. If there were to be complete harmony between it and foreign powers the first essential was that they should mutually understand and sympathize with each other. China had more to learn than they,' and so in order to bring about a better understanding with each other the Hon. A. Burlinghame, recently U. S. minister in Peking, was appointed, with two mandarins of high rank, envoys to eleven governments in the West. This was a step that astonished and delighted those that were concerned for the advance of China in civilization. Not thirty years had gone by since the Chinese were fighting to keep the foreigners out of their country, and now ambassadors were being sent to foreign nations to invite their friendship and good feeling. Mr. Burlinghame was in many respects well suited to represent the Chinese. He was enthusiastic in the performance of his mission, and though his profound sympathy for China, and his belief in her, that every careful student of her history inevitably gets, led him sometimes to speak in the language of exaggeration, he still did good service by bringing her before the eyes of the people of the West in a way that had never been done in

---

* Blue Book, China, A. D. 1864, quoted in Williams' Middle Kingdom, Vol. II., p. 693.

any previous time. Before his mission had been accomplished he died at St. Petersburg, in February, A. D. 1870.

Unfortunately, as if to counteract whatever favourable impression he might have created, the terrible massacre of Tientsin occurred this year. The government, however, had nothing to do with this, as the awful tragedy happened simply through the indiscretion of the Roman Catholic authorities in the city and the want of wisdom on the part of the French Consul. The people had been highly excited by rumours of what had been going on in the foundling hospital and orphan asylum under the charge of certain Sisters of Mercy. Large numbers of the children had died in consequence of an epidemic and other causes, and the belief had become common that they were put to death for the sake of their eyes, which the Chinese curiously suppose can be made into opium. Permission was asked by the district magistrate to inspect these establishments, but this the French Consul most unwisely refused. This roused the passions of the mob, and on the 21st of June the French consulate, the cathedral and the orphanage were attacked and destroyed, whilst eighteen French and two Russians were murdered in the most cruel and atrocious manner. After a public investigation of the whole matter, an imperial edict was issued, ordering the banishment of the prefect and district magistrate and the execution of twenty of the chief rioters. In addition it was decreed that four hundred thousand taels should be paid as compensation to the French, and that Chung How, the Superintendent of Trade at the time of the riot, should proceed to Paris and there make a formal apology to the government for the affair.

On the 16th of October, A. D. 1872, T'ung Chih was married to Aluteh, the daughter of a distinguished Manchu, and on February 23, A. D. 1873, he attained his majority, and nominally took the reins of power into his own hands, though in point of fact the regents were still the supreme rulers of China. The ministers of England, Germany, France, Russia and the United States thought this a good opportunity for bringing up the question of a personal audience with the new sovereign, without the ceremony of prostration before him, which all previous rulers had demanded. After a considerable amount of discussion, which was carried on with great fairness by Prince Kung and his colleagues, the privilege was granted, and on the 29th of June the Emperor first received the ambassador from Japan, and then those of the great powers just mentioned, thus giving up the claim to superiority over other nations, which China had always claimed, and which had been the fruitful source of trouble and friction between her and foreign powers.*

---

* Although this personal interview with the Emperor was a great advance upon the previous state of things, its graciousness was considerably diminished by the fact that the interview took place in a building where the envoys from tributary states were usually received. It was not till the autumn of 1894, when the Japanese had inflicted such crushing defeats upon the Chinese armies, that the Emperor condescended to see the foreign ambassadors within the precincts of the palace.

This same year became memorable for the suppression of the Mahommedan rebellion in Kansuh by Tso Tsung-tang, a general of great ability, and one whose name was destined ere long to be a well known one throughout the eighteen provinces. He captured the city of Suchau, the last stronghold of the rebels, and treated with such merciless severity those that fell into his hands that the Mahommedans were fain from this time to submit quietly to the rule of the Emperor. Another important event was the suppression of the coolie traffic. Begun in A. D. 1848 to supply labourers to Peru and Cuba, it in time degenerated into a vast system of kidnapping. Voluntary emigrants not coming forward in sufficient numbers, designing and unprincipled men, moved by the hope of gain, inveigled all classes of men into their barracoons, and then shipped them off as free workmen who had willingly contracted to go abroad. As may be imagined, under this system, the greatest atrocities were committed, both by land and sea, and from the time these unhappy men got within the clutches of those that had seized them they lost their liberty and became veritable slaves, with no redress against those that had deprived them of their freedom. The state of things at last became so intolerable that a commission, consisting of three foreigners and two Chinese, was appointed to investigate the whole matter. It was found that fully half a million of coolies had been carried away from China during the twenty-five years during which this traffic had been carried on, and the majority of them against their will. Through the exertions of Mr. Harry Parkes, the English Consul, this abominable system was entirely done away with, and a new one was established in its stead, by which it was secured that every coolie that engaged to go abroad did so willingly, and moreover was protected and secured in his rights by regulations that were drawn up for his protection.

This year was also distinguished by the suppression of the Panthay rebellion. The Panthays were a Mahommedan tribe that, taking advantage of the Taiping troubles, had gained complete possession of the western part of Yunnan, and in A. D. 1867 made Tali their capital, under the rule of Tu Wun-siu, or, as he was better known to the outside world, Sultan Suleiman. Besieged by Gen. Li, and seeing no hope of escape, the insurgents agreed to surrender the city, on condition that if Tu gave himself up the rest of the rebels should be spared. This being agreed to by the Chinese, Tu, dressed in his royal robes, was carried into the Chinese camp, but he died almost immediately after from the large dose of opium he had taken, and the Chinese, in violation of their convention, gave the city to be ravaged by the soldiers, when a large number of the people were ruthlessly massacred.

In the following year complications arose with the Japanese. Three years before, fifty-four Loochooan sailors had been murdered by the savages on the east coast of Formosa. Repeated applications to the Chinese government for redress were made, but in vain, no doubt for the very sufficient reason that it was impossible for them to punish a people who had hitherto defied them with success. The Japanese, determined to take the matter into their own hands, landed a force under Gen. Saigo near the scene of the murders, and commenced operations against the aborigines. War would certainly have resulted with China had not Sir T. Wade mediated with such good effect that the invaders returned to Japan with the understanding that half a million of taels should be paid them for the expenses they had been at in making roads, forts, etc. Thus happily ended an affair that might have led to the most serious and far-reaching consequences. Not long after this troublesome affair had been settled, the Chinese government became involved in a dispute with England with regard to a disaster which had happened to an expedition that had been sent by the Indian government to examine into the capabilities of Yunnan, as a region where trade might be carried on profitably or not. The idea of trading with this province was not a new one, for in A. D. 1868 Major Sladen had been sent at the head of a large party to visit the Panthays in Tali, to see whether trade that had been paralyzed by their cruelty and mismanagement could not be revived. The Chinese merchants in Burmah, who saw danger to themselves in this mission, determined to frustrate it, and it accordingly never got beyond Momein, when it had to return to Bhamo. After a time the Panthays were crushed, trade revived, and an English agent had been appointed to reside at Bhamo. Another mission was organized in A. D. 1874, under Col. Browne, to proceed from the latter place to Hankow, with the special object of reporting on the trade facilities of the country beyond Momein. The party was provided with Chinese passports, and it was arranged that Mr. Margary should be sent through China to meet Col. Browne at Bhamo and act as his guide and interpreter on his journey east. The first part of the programme was carried out with perfect success, and Mr. Margary arrived in Bhamo on the 17th of January, A. D. 1875. On the return journey signs of hostile feeling that had not existed before began to manifest themselves. The fact was, the border tribes, who were in a semi-independent state, looked upon this expedition with suspicion, and there is no doubt but that this feeling was fostered by the Chinese traders.

Col. Browne now sent Margary forward to Manwyne to arrange with Brigadier Li for the reception of the mission.* From Momein, he reported that all was right, and that he was about to start for Manwyne. This was the last that was ever heard from him, for next day (February 20th) he was murdered by the officials at the latter place. Col. Browne, satisfied with Margary's information, proceeded on his journey, but he was soon stopped by the news

---

* This Li was a man of very doubtful reputation. He had been a robber and a rebel, but he had turned loyal, and so, because of his large influence, he had been put in command of the troops that had the care of the frontier.

of his murder and the appearance of a large Chinese force that appeared on the neighbouring heights, and that rapidly advanced to attack his party. Though they numbered several thousand they were repulsed by the small body of Sikh soldiers that formed the escort, who behaved with remarkable steadiness and bravery. Finding it impossible to force his way in the face of such a powerful opposition, he returned to Bhamo, there to await instructions from his superiors.

Shortly before this, viz., on the 12th of January, A. D. 1875, T'ung Chih died of small-pox, and was succeeded by the son of Prince Chun, a younger brother of Prince Kung. By right, Tsai Ching, the son of the latter, had the best claim to the throne, and would no doubt have been elected had not his father occupied the prominent place in the government that he did. The elevation of the son would have meant the retirement of the father into private life, which at that time would not have been for the benefit of the empire. It is a very singular and unexplained circumstance that, although the queen was pregnant at time of T'ung Chih's death, there was no delay to see whether she would have a son, who would have been the legal heir. The election of the new Emperor was made without delay, and very opportunely for the two Empress-Dowagers, Aluteh died before her child could be born. Whether her death was a natural one, or caused by foul means, only the future historian will be able to tell, when the archives of the Hanlin Academy tell their story, after the present dynasty has passed away. The youthful sovereign, who was scarcely four years old, was given the title of Kwang Su, or Brilliant Succession.

Kwang Su—A. D. 1875.

When the news of the murder of Margary reached London the utmost indignation was felt, and stringent orders were sent to Sir T. Wade that the fullest investigation of the whole circumstances of the case should be made, and that the Chinese government should be informed that they were held responsible for the disasters that had occurred. After considerable delay and persistent urging on the part of the English minister, a commission consisting of Hon. T. Grosvenor, Messrs. Davenport and Baber, together with Li Han-chang, was sent to Yunnan to investigate the affair. The only real value of this expedition was to demonstrate to the Chinese that even solitary Englishmen were not to be murdered with impunity, for it was never expected, even by the most sanguine, that the Chinese that were in the secret would ever divulge the names of those who were the guilty parties. The blame was thrown upon the border tribes, but there is no doubt but that the Governor-General of Yunnan and Brigadier Li were the men that were responsible for the attack on the mission, whilst the militia of Manwyne were the murderers of Margary.

Further correspondence and further delays followed the report of the commission, and the Chinese government seemed determined to avoid an honest settlement of the case, but Sir T. Wade's instructions were definite and peremptory, and so, rather than abide the warlike issue that loomed in the near future, terms were agreed upon at Chefoo on the 13th September, 1876. Here the English minister and Li Hung-chang drew up a convention, in which it was decided that two hundred thousand taels should be paid as compensation for the murder; that the Emperor should issue proclamations throughout his empire, directing the high officials everywhere to protect the persons of Englishmen ; and that an embassy should be despatched to London to express the regret of the Chinese government for what had occurred. In addition to the above, regulations were made with regard to opium, transit passes and likin taxes, and four new ports were opened for trade, as well as six on the Yang-tze for the landing of goods.

The same year that witnessed the signing of the Chefoo Convention saw the commencement of Tso Tsung-tang's famous campaign against the Mahommedan rebels in Eastern Turkestan. Yakub Beg, in A. D. 1866, had risen against the son of Jehangir, who ruled in Western Kashgaria, and taking possession of the country, and extending his conquests over neighbouring tribes, he found himself the chief of a large territory, that he held by his own right, without any reference to the Emperor of China, who claimed it as forming part of his own empire. So successful was he that he was styled the "Champion Father," because he seemed to be the avenger that had arisen to redress the wrongs that the Mahommedans had suffered at the hands of the Chinese. The Russians, anxious for their trade routes, and foreseeing that Ili would fall before his arms, seized Kuldja and held it and the region it controlled by force of arms.

The Taiping rebellion and the complications with England prevented the Chinese from dealing at once with this rebel, and so the years passed by without any active interference with him, and it really seemed as though the kingdom he had founded would be a permanent one. Meanwhile the Dunganis had risen, and had been joined by other tribes, and had gained control over large areas in the eastern part of Eastern Turkestan, and over the Tien Shan mountains into Ili, and had penetrated with their victorious forces through Kansuh and into Shensi. The Chinese government now felt that it was not simply the quelling of a rebellion in one of their remote dependencies that demanded their attention, but the very preservation of the empire itself; so Gen. Tso was ordered to advance with all his forces and conquer and suppress the rebels. He began by driving the Dunganis out of China, and he then established his head-quarters at Barkul and Hami. Gradually his troops recaptured city after city, and by consummate generalship he defeated the undisciplined hosts that were opposed to him, so that by the end of the year the Dungani insurrection was at an end, and Chinese law once more reigned over the reconquered territories. Yakub Beg, who now saw that he must fight for his dominions, advanced with all the men he could collect as far east as Turfan, nearly a thousand miles away from Kashgar, his capital. The "Champion Father" proved no match for the Chinese legions. A serious defeat compelled him to retreat, and a second battle, in which he was worsted, drove him out of Kansuh to Korla. Here he died, May A. D. 1877, whether naturally or by poison it is impossible to say.

With his death the campaign was virtually at an end, for he was the one man alone that could hold together the heterogeneous forces that had gathered round his banner. Karashar, Korla, Kashgar, Yarkand and Khoten were all successively captured by the Chinese troops, so that by the beginning of A. D. 1878 the whole of Eastern Turkestan was recovered to the empire. If Ili had been in the possession of the Mahommedans its recovery at this time would have been easy, but unfortunately for the Chinese they had to deal with the Russians, who held Kuldja. Diplomacy, therefore, had now to take the place of arms. Chunghow was accordingly despatched by the regents to negotiate with the Russian government for the restoration of the territory occupied by them. He proved, however, no match for the astute diplomatists that met him in St. Petersburg, and so he concluded a treaty that gave the Russians a most important part of Ili, with all the strong passes in the Tien Shan mountains, the city of Yarkand and an indemnity of five million rubles. On his return to China, January, A. D. 1880, his whole action was repudiated by his government, he was deprived of all his offices, and finally ordered to be executed. Through the intercession of the foreign ambassadors in Peking he was reprieved and set free, and Marquis Tseng was sent to treat with Russia. The happiest results followed from the negotiations that now ensued, for a treaty was ratified August, A. D. 1881, by which the whole of Ili was returned to the Chinese, with the exception of a strip of territory on its extreme western boundary, whilst nine millions of rubles were to be paid to Russia as an indemnity for all claims that she had to make against China.

In the meanwhile, in A. D. 1878, a terrible famine raged through the provinces of Shansi and Shensi, which at the very lowest computation caused the death of eight millions of people. The soil of these two regions is mainly composed of a porous earth named loess, through which the rain rapidly drains, leaving the upper surface dry, and necessitating a constant and copious supply of water, if cultivation is to be carried on with any degree of success. For several years previously the annual rains were deficient, until in this year the earth became so parched that no crops could be planted. The greatest sympathy was shown towards the sufferers. The Chinese government and the rich and poor in different parts of the empire helped considerably, and even far away London sent contributions, and a large number of missionaries went into the famine districts to distribute food to the starving, four of whom died of famine fever.

The year A. D. 1881 was distinguished by the death of the Eastern Empress-Dowager and the permission given to Corea to contract treaties with foreign powers for the purposes of trade, etc.*

In the following year the action of the French in Cochin China led to very serious complications, and ultimately to hostilities with China. For many years they had exercised in a loose and indefinite kind of way a semi-control over that country, but in the year A. D. 1882, moved by reports that the most direct trade route to the south western provinces of China would be by the Red River, they determined to invade Tonquin, the northern part of Annam. In pursuance of this policy the town of Hanoi was captured, and though in defiance of the sovereign rights of China, which she had for many centuries claimed over Cochin China, no resistance was offered by the Chinese government at first to this action of the French. There were, however, others in the country who were determined that the invader should not take possession of their country without at least a stern resistance, and these were the Black Flags. Fighting in consequence was carried on between them and the French, and though the latter captured Sontay they were defeated in an engagement near Hanoi, and were compelled to send to France for more troops. When this arrived they advanced under the command of Admiral Courbet to the attack of Sontay, which had been reoccupied by the Black Flags. After a desperate struggle, in which the French suffered severely, the town was carried. In the beginning of March, A. D. 1884, General Millot, who had superseded Courbet, took Bacninh and caused the Black Flags to retreat. The Chinese government now intervened, and a treaty was signed (11th May), which amongst other things gave over Langson and other places to the French. The Black Flags, however, had their own views with regard to this settlement, and as they had borne the brunt of the fighting they concluded they had a right to have a voice in the disposal of their country. They did not believe that the men with whom they had measured swords, and sometimes defeated, should have so much given them by the Chinese, and accordingly, when the French force was marching to

---

* This permission was granted because of an uneasiness in the mind of the Chinese government in regard to the intentions of Russia respecting Corea, and with the hope that such new relationships would secure her from foreign aggression. She had previously made treaties with Japan, the last of which was contracted in A. D. 1876. In consequence of this consent America in A. D. 1882, and England in A D 1883, entered into treaty relationships with Corea. In A. D. 1885, in consequence of a serious outbreak at Seoul, in which the Japanese were largely concerned, an agreement was entered into between China and Japan, that neither of them was to send troops to Corea without first informing the other. This, as will be seen in the future, was destined to lead to the most serious consequence by and by.

occupy Langson, they attacked it and dispersed it with considerable loss. An apology was demanded from the Chinese government and an indemnity of ten millions sterling. The former they willingly agreed to, but the latter they refused utterly to give. The French had made as great a mistake in their estimate of the Chinese as they had about the Black Flags. Without any formal declaration of war they commenced hostile demonstrations, and a considerable fleet under Admiral Courbet threatened the southern ports of China. Under the idea that hostilities had not yet commenced, part of this was allowed to ascend the Min and anchor close by the Chinese fleet then lying at Pagoda Anchorage. Admiral Courbet in a very ungenerous way took advantage of this, and one day opened fire upon it and destroyed it. Nothing practical resulted from this act, excepting that it increased the ill-will that had previously existed and caused the Chinese to concentrate large forces at Foochow, under the command of the central Asian hero, Tso Tsung-tang, who, though so old, volunteered his services against the enemy of his country. To show that he was in earnest, and that no difficulties were going to stay him, he brought his coffin with him, which ere long he actually needed, for he died near Foochow before the campaign was ended.

The French did not seem to fight with their usual intrepidity. They attacked Tamsuy, which was badly fortified and contained but comparatively a small force of undisciplined Chinese, but to the astonishment of the latter they were repulsed, and though a powerful fleet patrolled the northern end of Formosa they never had the daring to venture upon a second attack. Finally negotiations ensued, a treaty of peace was signed, June 9th, A. D. 1885, by which the French gained very little more than what had been previously given them by the former treaty.

In the year A. D. 1889 Kwang Su was married to a Manchu princess, and great were the rejoicings at this happy event. The expenses attendant upon it were enormous, for it seemed as though the aim of those who were directing the affair was to make it the most magnificent of the kind that had ever happened. Two years after, the young sovereign, who was not yet twenty years of age, received the foreign ambassadors in a public audience. There was considerable dissatisfaction expressed, because this ceremony took place in the "Hall of Tributary Nations," and the question has been brought before the Tsung-li Yamên, or Board for Foreign Affairs, and forcible suggestions have been made that in the future a more appropriate building should be selected in which the representatives of foreign nations should be received by the Emperor. It is inconceivable to all students of Chinese history why England should have allowed herself to be insulted by the Chinese in their demanding that her representative should appear in a building which had been specially reserved for the reception of men that were bringing tribute to the Chinese Emperor as their over-lord. This could not have arisen through the incapacity of the men that appeared on behalf of England at Peking, for some of them have been distinguished for their intelligence and learning. Was it a fear that the demand to be received with the honour due to the country they represented would bring it in collision with China ? Then the fear was groundless, and arose from a want of knowledge of the Chinese character. Firmness in a question that commends itself to the moral sense of the Chinese is a quality that is highly appreciated by them, and no ruler would have the support of the nation in going to war to resist a demand that was based upon right.*

On the 17th March, A. D. 1890, an important treaty was signed at Calcutta, by which it was arranged that trade might be carried on between India and Thibet. Many efforts had been made in former years to get permission for an English mission to travel in the latter country, and passports had been actually issued to Mr. C. Macaulay in A. D. 1884 for this purpose, but in consequence of the inherent dislike of both Chinese and Thibetans to intercourse with the outer world, every plan to get officially into Thibet had signally failed. This treaty provides for trade, communication and pasturage. The frontier between Sikkim and Thibet is defined, and the protectorate of England over the former is recognized by the Chinese government. The town of Ya-tung is appointed as the place where trade is to be carried on, and here a Commissioner of Customs will be appointed by the Inspector-General at Peking, with the sanction of the Tsung-li Yamên, and also an agent of the India government, to see that the provisions of the treaty are properly carried out. On the 1st of May, A. D. 1894, a new station is to be opened inside the Thibetan frontier, to which the Indian authorities will be permitted to send an officer. For the first five years all articles, excepting munitions of war and narcotic drugs, are to be allowed to pass free of duty, after which a tariff will be drawn up defining what articles shall be dutiable and what not. The two officers at Ya-tung will for the present be the means of communication between the two governments. As to pasturage it has been agreed that the Thibetans may cross over into Sikhim, as they have hitherto been wont to do with their flocks, but they must be prepared to come under such rules and regulations as the Indian government may see fit to establish. These rules, however, will be subject to revision every five years. Thus happily has been settled a question that has for a long time puzzled the brains of statesmen. There is no doubt but that with a fuller knowledge of foreigners the reserve of the Thibetans will break down, and a wider and more unrestricted communication will be the result in the future.

The year A. D. 1894 proved to be a most unhappy one in the history of China, bringing not only disaster and disgrace to the

---

* The question has been happily settled, as before mentioned, by the reception of the ambassadors within the precincts of the palace.

Chinese arms, but also grave peril to the dynasty that ruled over it. In the spring of this year a local rebellion broke out in Corea against the government. The cause of this was the utter corruption of the officials who fleeced and misruled the people to an extent hardly parallelled in any other country in the world. These had reduced their system to an art, by which they levied black mail upon every industry in which the people engaged. Through it commerce was restricted, because a part of the gains of almost every sale was demanded by these men, who had spies everywhere abroad to bring information to their masters. Farmers could not look forward to a plenteous harvest with any pleasure, for they knew that any excess that they gathered beyond what was required for the wants of the familÁ would be appropriated by the officials. The consequence was that the aim of every one was to produce simply enough for the immediate wants of his home, so that it might not be invaded by these spoilers in search of plunder.*

The result of this iniquitous system was widespread poverty and discontent. The people, seeing no hope of any redress from their rulers, or from the Chinese, who from their conservative instincts would certainly take the side of the government in any appeal to them, some two or three years ago founded a secret society called the Tong-hak, or National Party, whose aim was the redress of these crushing grievances and the adoption of reforms, such as were imperatively needed throughout the country. After long consultation amongst its leaders it was decided in the spring of this year that the time had arrived when the society should take arms and demand from their rulers a mitigation of the oppressive laws that were rendering life intolerable to the working classes. Thirty thousand men were soon in arms, and so successful were they that they defeated the royal troops, and capturing the chief city of Chung-chong, they prepared to march on Seoul, the capital, to demand, with arms in their hands, the necessary reforms.

In this extremity the king of Corea applied to China for troops to help him in his struggle with his rebellious subjects, and fifteen hundred men, in reply to this appeal, were despatched to the south of Corea to a district on the west coast, lying about a hundred miles from Chemulpo.†

With their arrival the rebellion collapsed, and the Chinese troops returned to their own country, with the exception of five hundred that were marched to Seoul to act as a guard to the king in the case of any further disturbance. This action of the Chinese government was evidently one that had been well considered, nor had the complications likely to arise out of it been sufficiently anticipated. According to the treaty of May, A. D. 1885, it was agreed

---

* The evil was felt particularly in the provinces of Chulla and Chung-chong, where the farmers were so systematically robbed of the fruits of their labours that hope seemed to have fled entirely from their hearts.

† Chemulpo is the port of Seoul, and distant from it about twenty-five miles.

between China and Japan that the soldiers of both countries should be withdrawn from Corea, and neither one should send its troops to it under any circumstances without giving the other due notice of its intentions. The Chinese did indeed notify Japan on the 4th of June of its purpose, but the latter power declares that the communication was not made as promptly as it might have been, and that therefore the spirit of the treaty had not been observed by China. It therefore declared that, as Chinese troops were now encamped in Seoul, it was necessary that Japanese soldiers should also be allowed to be marched there in order to protect the subjects of Japan in this crisis that had been created by the action of China. This being conceded, to the consternation of China, she despached five thousand men under the command of General Oshima, fifteen hundred of whom marched into the capital, whilst the rest encamped at Chemulpo. That this force meant war was evident from the fact that two hundred and fifty horses accompanied it, a considerable number of cannon and all the necessary provisions and equipments for a three months' campaign. When the Japanese were asked the meaning of this large force they declared that it was simply for the protection of their people, an answer that deceived no one, for any danger that might have threatened them had passed away with the collapse of the rebellion.*

* It will be necessary here for the information of the general reader to state briefly the reasons why Japan decided at this time to try issues with the Chinese and determine for ever whether they had the right to be dictators in Corean matters or not. These, concisely stated, are four. (1.) The sense of injustice that rankled in the minds of the whole nation since A. D. 1884. In that year, a riot having taken place in Seoul, the king applied to the Japanese Legation for troops to help him. The request was granted, when the Chinese soldiers marched on the palace, and a bloody encounter ensued, in which the Japanese were defeated. The Chinese, with their haughty contempt of the latter, treated them most barbarously, looted their Legation and plundered the property of the Japanese subjects in the capital. When the people of Japan heard of this they were incensed beyond measure, and loudly cried for war. The Mikado, however, decided for peace, a policy that led to the "Satsuma Rebellion." The nation had never forgotten the matter, and vengeance for the wrongs that had been inflicted was the supreme desire of every loyal man in the country. (2.) The assassination of Kim Ok-kuin, a Corean statesman, who had been involved in the disturbance of A. D 1884, and who had been compelled to fly from his country. This gentleman had resided during the ten years of his exile in Japan, and therefore was a well known personage. He was decoyed to Shanghai (1894), where he was murdered by Corean emissaries, and as the Chinese authorities took no steps to punish them it was believed by Japan that this crime was committed with their sanction. The popular feeling in the latter was intensely excited when the news reached it, and vows were made that it should speedily be avenged. (3.) The Japanese felt they had been the means of opening Corea, and therefore had some right in the control of national matters. To stand aside and let China have full sway would be to undo the work she had already accomplished and hand over the Coreans to despotism and misrule. There were at this time two parties in Corea—the Conservatives and the Progressists. The larger portion of the people belonged to the former, and were out and out opposed to Western ideas and reforms. Amongst the latter were the advanced in thought, who desired the opening up of their country to outside influences, and who could reckon the king amongst their number. (4.) A very important reason for the action of the Japanese at this time was the political condition of their own country. The rapid transition of the latter from despotic to constitutional rule had excited the minds of the military classes against the government, and these were

The result of this action of Japan was to precipitate hostilities. Troops from both countries were hurried into Corea, and though war was not formally declared, it was manifest that in the minds of the Japanese, at least, a state of war existed. Their conduct in the case of the English steamer *Kow-shing* plainly showed this. This vessel had been chartered by Li Hung-chang to convey eleven hundred troops to Corea. On the 25th of July, as she was nearing her destination, she was met by the Japanese man-of-war *Naniwa* and ordered to stop. An officer that came on board told the captain that he must consider himself and all on board as prisoners of war. The Chinese general and soldiers threatened the captain and officers with instant death if they attempted to obey the Japanese, and loaded guns and menacing words showed their determination to carry out their murderous purpose. After a time the *Naniwa* signalled the English to leave the ship, an order that could not possibly be obeyed, and after a short delay a torpedo was fired at her and a broadside of five guns, which sent her to the bottom, only two hundred of the soldiers being eventually saved and two or three of the English crew. Four days after this the Chinese and Japanese troops met each other in hostile array near Yashan, and after three days severe skirmishing the Chinese were compelled to retreat.

The aspect of affairs now became still more serious, for both sides being confident of success, anything like an accommodation of their differences by mutual consultation was entirely out of the question. Accordingly, on the 1st of August war was formally declared between China and Japan, the former power exasperating the latter by calling its people " The Dwarfs " in the royal proclamation, a term that more than anything else aroused the determination of the Japanese not to stop the war until they had avenged themselves on their haughty and comtemptuous enemy.

The first great battle of the war was fought at Ping-yang on the 15th of September, when the Chinese were defeated with the loss of over six thousand men, large quantities of arms and a great supply of provisions. The remnant of the Chinese army was so demoralized that it fled in isolated bands to the north, spreading terror and desolation wherever they went. The Chinese soldiers, when on the march and under the control of their officers, are

---

waiting but for a fitting opportunity to rise in rebellion against it. The crown saw its way out of a very serious crisis by transferring all this restless military energy from Japan to Corea, where it could expend itself upon China.

One thing is certain, viz., that of the two evils the control of Japan over Corea is very much to be preferred to that of China. The latter would simply perpetuate the intolerable misgovernment that has goaded the people into rebellion. The lamentable failure of China in her conflict with Japan, which has arisen solely from her own wretched system of government, plainly declares that she has no moral right to the control of any country outside her own boundaries. The right that she has hitherto claimed over Corea is one founded on force, and not on good government or any concern for the welfare of the people. The swords of her soldiers have given Japan as good a claim as China ever had over that country, and the vast strides that she has taken in civilization give one the hope that Corea will benefit by any control that she may be allowed to exercise over it.

usually a curse to the region through which they pass, but much more so when disorganized and without any commissariat, and under no military discipline. Two days after this decisive victory a naval battle was fought off the mouth of the river Yalu. The Chinese fleet consisted of eleven men-of-war and six torpedo boats, whilst the Japanese had the same number of ships, but no torpedoes. The battle began about ten in the morning and lasted for six hours. The Japanese, who had the fastest ships and better guns, displayed more science and good generalship than the Chinese, though the latter showed considerable pluck. in allowing themselves to be knocked about for so long a time. Four of the Chinese were sunk, whilst another was destroyed by fire. The Japanese ships suffered severely from the fire of their enemy, but they were all subsequently repaired and found capable of joining their squadrons after a time. The victory on this occasion was with the Japanese, and it would have been still more decisive had they had as many torpedoes as the Chinese.

The result of these two engagements was to give the Japanese a decided advantage in their plans for the invasion of China, and the arrival of a second army corps of thirty thousand men under the command of Count Oyama at Kinchow (October 24), thirty-five miles to the north of Port Arthur, gave them such a strong force that they were enabled to advance confidently against the Chinese. Aware of the value of time, the victorious troops hastened from Ping-yang to the Ya-lu, the boundary line between Corea and Manchuria, and crossing that without any serious opposition they took possession (October 25) of Chiu-lien-cheng. A dread of the Japanese arms seemed from this time to have seized upon the hearts of the Chinese troops, and although armies were brought up again and again to fight them, they were never able to stand their ground in any general engagement, but fled before there was any real necessity for their doing so. One can give no other valid excuse, excepting this, for the cowardly way in which they allowed the Japanese to enter Manchuria, the ancestral home of the reigning dynasty, almost without resistance. No sooner did the Japanese make preparations for the passage of the river than a panic seized upon the Chinese on the other side, and they fled in the wildest dismay, thus leaving the roads to Moukden and Peking absolutely open to them, and if they had advanced at once on either place they would have captured it without difficulty.

In all their movements the Japanese showed not only military skill, but also profound commonsense. Wherever they advanced they got the goodwill of the common people, who brought a plentiful supply of fresh provisions into their camp. Everything was paid for with the utmost regularity, and the provost marshals saw to it that no violence or injustice was exercised whilst the troops were on the march or in the camp. How different was the conduct of the Chinese soldiers. Murder, rapine, theft and cruel treatment were the order of the day wherever they went, till at length the people longed for the appearance of the invaders to save them from the barbarity of their own defenders.

Whilst these disasters were occurring to the arms of China, the insufferable pride and contempt for all foreigners had been shown in the murder (August 10) of Rev. Mr. Wylie in Liau-yang by troops on their way to the seat of war and by the insulting attitude that had been assumed in many districts, but especially in Peking, towards them. The government, anxious not to embroil itself with any foreign power, issued a proclamation, commanding the people to refrain from all violence towards foreigners, reminding them that China was at war only with the Dwarfs, and warning them that any insult to them would be severely punished. This action of the executive had a most salutary effect, in the capital at least, and the condign punishment of the murderers of Mr. Wylie must have had a restraining influence upon officers who were conducting troops in the neighbourhood of where foreigners were residing.

On the 60th birthday (November 7) of the Empress-Dowager, a woman whose wise statesmanship had been of such service to China in the various crises through which it had passed during her tenure of power, a very interesting event took place. This was the presentation to her by the Christian women belonging to the Protestant churches in different parts of the empire, of a beautifully printed and bound New Testament, enclosed in a silver casket. It was conveyed to her by the English and American ambassadors in Peking, and was most graciously received by her. That the Emperor was pleased with this gift is evident from the fact that next day two eunuchs in immediate attendance upon himself were sent to the Bible store in the city to purchase copies of both the Old and New Testaments, thus proving that he had intelligently examined the present to the Empress. As far as we know this is the first instance in the history of China when the Bible penetrated into the palace and was looked upon by the eyes of any of its sovereigns, and it is an interesting coincidence that this book, whose teachings could have prevented the calamities that had fallen on the nation through its own corruption, should have appeared at the very time when this proud country was trembling before its despised invaders.

The Japanese, who had shown the greatest energy in their military movements, and who had been steadily making adequate preparations for the investment of Port Arthur, appeared before it on the morning of November 21st, and by two o'clock in the afternoon, with the loss only of about four hundred men, they captured this famous fortress, the forts on the coast being stormed the next day. The news was everywhere received with the most unbounded astonishment. Nature and art had done their very best to make it impregnable, and at least a dozen forts, high up on lofty eminences, with great guns of the newest construction, and narrow defiles heavily mined, by which alone they could be approached, and thirteen thousand men, with abundance of everything they required, rendered it impossible to be taken by assault. A thousand brave men could have held this fortress against the world for a long time, and yet in the course of a few hours the Japanese, who had obtained a plan of the mines, had marched over the road, where they ought to have been sent flying in the air, straight on towards the forts, up the steep banks, till they stood under the very muzzles of the cannon, then over the ramparts, to find that every man had fled, leaving some of the guns unfired in their mad haste to get away. The Japanese sullied their splendid victory by the massacre of the innocent inhabitants, after they had captured the place. Having discovered the mutilated remains of some of their comrades that had been captured by the Chinese soldiers, they became so infuriated that a desperate madness for vengeance seized upon them, and contrary to their usual custom they wreaked it upon the unoffending populace, hundreds of whom were despatched in the most horrible and revolting manner.*

Whilst these successes were being accomplished in the Liau-tung peninsula, the army that had been operating in Manchuria obtained a victory at the battle of Mo-tien-ling, and finding after this that the Chinese never could summon up courage to meet them in any considerable numbers in the field, returned to their head-quarters at An-tung and waited for the development of events. The Chinese government, finding that their soldiers could not be induced to fight, and seeing that peace was their only hope, despatched Mr. Detring to Japan (November 27) to sound the Japanese authorities as to their willingness to come to terms or not. As he was a foreigner, and a man of no special distinction, and moreover had no full powers to treat, he was not received, nor was the question of peace for a moment discussed with him ; and he had to return to China without having accomplished anything.

The Japanese, with that keen military instinct that saw the importance of constant exertion, determined, notwithstanding the severity of the winter, to move the Manchurian army corps to the Liau-tung peninsula and captured the important city of Hai-cheng. This they did with the greatest ease, and shortly after (January 9) the Port Arthur division moving up, took possession, after four hours' fighting, of Kai-ping, the Japanese thus becoming complete masters of the peninsula. Still undeterred by the terrors of king frost, upon whom the Chinese had reckoned so fully, preparations were made for the attack of Wei-hai-wei, where the Chinese fleet had taken refuge, and which next to Port Arthur was the most strongly fortified position the Chinese possessed.

---

* It is the universal conviction amongst the foreigners in China that the speedy capture of Port Arthur was due to treachery amongst the Chinese officers, who were bribed by the Japanese to give them the plan of the mined defile and to cause their men not to stand to their guns when the attack was made

In pursuance of this plan a force of twenty-five thousand men landed (January 23) in Yung-ching bay, on the Shantung promontory, whilst another force three days later occupied Ning-hai without opposition. Whilst these forces were gathering for the conflict, two envoys—Chang Yu-huan and Shau Yu-lien—started (January 26) for Japan to open peace negotiations, but their credentials having been found defective, they were politely bowed out of the country, and the war was continued.

All the necessary plans having been completed, the Japanese advanced upon Wei-hai-wei.* The soldiers occupying the forts around the bay, true to the reputation they had acquired during the war, disgracefully fled without any real fighting and left the ships, that were now commanded by the deserted forts, to their fate. Admiral Ting for several days offered a most heroic defence, and by his sturdy resistance redeemed somewhat the character of the Chinese that had lately sunk so low. All attempts, however, to save Wei-hai-wei were in vain. The forces against it were too strong. The guns from the forts and from the batteries newly erected poured their shot and shell upon the devoted ships, till four of the best of them were sunk. There was no escape from the very jaws of death within which they lay, for the Japanese fleet was cruising outside, and rendered that impossible. A panic began to seize his men, and it was only by personal appeals to them that he could get them to stand to their guns under the rain of fire that poured upon them. Twelve torpedo boats left the harbour under the pretext that they were going to back the enemy outside, but in real'ty to endeavour to save themselves, for they immediately steamed away in different directions as soon as they got out of the bay. At length, on the 12th February, the Admiral, seeing the hopelessness of successfully continuing the defence, hoisted a flag of truce and signified his intention to surrender. The Japanese granted himself and his men the honours of war, but when they came to take possession they found the gallant Admiral lying dead in his cabin, for he had committed suicide to avoid the sterner sentence of the Board of Punishment that would have been meted out to him for his failure to beat the Japanese. This decided success was of immense importance to the victors, for they got possession of the entire remainder of the northern fleet, and thus obtained the undisputed control of the sea, for the southern squadron remained hidden up the Yang-tze and refused to come to the aid of the northern, on the truly Chinese plea that they were not called upon to hazard their safety by going into a station that did not belong to them.

---

* Wei-hai-wei consisted of a larger bay, capable of receiving a considerable fleet. Across its mouth lay the island of Liu-kung-tau, with an entrance into the harbour on each side of it, which was garrisoned with a large body of troops, and was strongly fortified. On the land side of the bay a number of forts had been erected for its defence, and when the Japanese arrived these were occupied by troops that had been sent there to repel any attack on the place.

After the strength of the winter had been broken, and as the Chinese had been gathering larger forces in the neighbourhood of the native city of Newchwang the Japanese determined to advance from Hai-cheng, where they had wintered, and try issues with the foe. After several minor engagements by the way they found themselves face to face with two armies, one under General Sung with forty thousand men, and another under General Wu with thirty thousand. Fortunately for them these two generals were at variance with each other, so that whilst Sung was being attacked and defeated, and his army being scattered in utter confusion, Wu stood sullenly by declaring that the rout of Sung did not concern him. A nemesis, however, was soon to descend upon him, for the victorious Japanese marched against him, and though his men took refuge in the town and fought under cover of the houses, they were defeated with great slaughter and compelled to fly. This was all the more remarkable, as his army consisted of Hunan men, who have the reputation of being the fighting men of China, and who have such a supreme contempt and hatred of foreigners that they have declared they will never allow any of them to defile their province. After the dispersion of these two armies the Japanese marched on to Yin-kow (Newchwang settlement), some thirty miles distant, and took possession of it without any opposition, and so this remarkable campaign, that had not been marred by a single defeat in any general engagement, ended thus gloriously, and, though not expected at the time, with its conclusion came the end of the war.*

The Chinese government, conscious of its danger at this time, despatched Li Hung-chang (March 15) to Japan to sue for peace with full powers to conclude a treaty with that country. Negotia-

---

* The utter and complete collapse of China as a military power, as demonstrated during this contest with Japan, is attributable to the following causes : (1.) The rottenness and corruption of official life throughout the country. Money is the supreme thing in the eyes of a mandarin, and everything, including country, honour, etc., must fall before that. All grades of officials are alike in this Some of the highest names in the land to-day, whose reputation for statesmanship has travelled into Western countries, have been traitors to their country in the late war, for they have been more mindful of their own interests than of the honour of China. The saddest feature about this is that in this demoralizing vice they do not merely represent a privileged class, but the people of China. They all spring from the people, and are a product of a state of things that has existed in society for countless generations. Corruption can only cease to exist when a purer morality shall have permeated and elevated all classes, from the highest to the lowest. (2.) The absence of patriotism. A Chinaman has an intense love for his home but none for his country. Other parts may be invaded and desolated, but the news will cause no thrill of emotion in the hearts of men far removed from the scene. Few would willingly die to save their country. (3.) The impassable gulf that separates the people from the mandarins. The utmost antagonism exists between the two The latter are the spoilers and the former the spoiled. In any war between China and a foreign country the people look upon it as a thing that does not concern them, but is the special business of their rulers, and so long as it does not come near them they look on with supreme indifference. (4.) The inadequacy of the Chinese military system to cope with the one in use in the West. It belongs to a barbarous time, and has been of service when dealing with barbarous tribes and peoples. China must succumb in any war waged by a people that have adopted Western tactics.

tions were begun, but they were interrupted for a time by his being shot in the face by a man whose brothers had suffered severely at the hands of the Chinese. The Japanese authorities were so distressed at this untoward circumstance that to show their abhorrence of the deed they granted an armistice for twenty days, which was subsequently extended to May 8th. Formosa, however, was not included in this, for the Japanese, who had captured the Pescadores (March 24th), were determined not to lose the advantage which these islands gave them in their plan of operation against the former, nor to cease their warfare until they had added it to their own country.

The negotiations for peace ended in the conclusion of a treaty which was signed by the Emperors of China and Japan, and ratifications were exchanged at Chefoo on the 8th of May, and thus the two great powers that had been at deadly variance with each other, were now prepared to lay down their arms and for the future regard each other as friends.*

The army in Formosa, on hearing that the island was to be ceded to the Japanese, was exceedingly indignant, as well as a considerable number of its most prominent inhabitants. Having appealed to the Emperor in vain to withdraw his consent to this part of the treaty, a formal offer of the island was made to the English Consul in Tamsuy. Finding that this was not accepted, they determined to resist the occupation of the Japanese and to hold the island for China till such times as the latter country could send a sufficient force to defy the armies of Japan. In the meanwhile they would take the government into their own hands. Accordingly, on the 25th of May, amidst a salvo of twenty-one guns, the old flag was hauled down and a new one hoisted in its place, and Formosa was declared to be a republic, and its first president was Tang, the late governor, who, to save his life, consented to take this perilous honour. This new form of government was not destined to be of long duration, for the island, having been formally handed over to the Japanese, a force was despatched by them to take possession of it. On the 3rd of June they landed four thousand men to attack Kelung, and so vigorous and enthusiastic was the onslaught that in less than three hours they had captured Palm Island Fort and East Fort, and were driving before them an army of twelve thousand men that had been encamped outside of the town, with the loss to themselves of only eleven killed and twice that number wounded.

---

* The main features of this important treaty were : 1. The independence of Corea. 2. The cession of the Liau-tung peninsula, as well as of Formosa and the Pescadores to the Japanese. 3. An indemnity of Taels 200,000,000, payable in seven years. 4. The opening of Ching-chow and Sha-shih, in Hupeh ; of Chungking, in Szechwan ; of Soochow, in Kiangsu ; and of Hangchow in Chehkiang. In consequence of the protests of Russia, Germany and France, Japan agreed to waive her right to the Liau-tung peninsula and accept a money payment of thirty millions of taels instead. A treaty to this effect was signed at Peking, November 7th, 1895.

The panic that followed this success of the Japanese may be more easily imagined than described. The president, who had been constantly watched and guarded by the suspicious soldiers, lest he should escape, managed by a bribe of $15,000 to his bodyguard to steal out from his yamên at two o'clock in the morning (June 5) and get on board a steamer in the harbour of Tamsuy. When daylight came and it was known amongst the soldiery that he had fled, the wildest disorder at once ensued, and all law and order from this time ceased. Pandemonium seemed to be set loose, and robbery and murder and pillage became the business of every lawless ruffian and vagabond that had been waiting, like vultures for their prey, for this very opportunity. All the official residences were looted and set on fire, whilst thousands of soldiers, mad and excited, struggled fiercely with each other for the money in the treasury. Crowds of roughs, who had appeared like magic when the strong arm of law was paralyzed, attacked the arsenal and stripped it of everything movable and wrecked and carried off property to the value of $1,000,000. One of the worst consequences of the spoliation of this place was the arming of the rabble with the rifles that they found there. Murder now became more common, for every one wanted to practise his hand with his new weapon, and the passion for killing became a mania. In the midst of all this frenzy and madness the powder magazine was exploded, and large numbers of those engaged in the looting were blown to atoms.

Finding that these wild and maddened crowds were preparing to attack the foreigners three of these went out to the Japanese camp, some ten miles off, to invite them to come to their rescue. A polite reception awaited them, and five hundred men accompanied them on their return. With their arrival the danger at once disappeared, for every soldier had fled in dismay. Peaceable possession was taken of Taipeh and Tamsuy, and the Japanese rule was at once established in these two places, much to the comfort of the law-abiding citizens.

Although the northern part of the island came under the immediate rule of the Japanese it was not till the end of October that the whole of it was subjugated. Liu Yung-fu, the general of the Black Flags, in command of the southern portion of Formosa, refused to submit and declared himself president of the republic, which he held was still in existence in spite of the victories of the Japanese in the north. He was a man of great vigor of character, and during his term of power ruled well. He kept his wild troops in order, established a foreign customs, issued bank notes, organized a post office with a new set of stamps and made the power of his new government to be felt amongst all classess.

Unfortunately for the stability of his rule neither he nor his men had the courage to meet the Japanese in the field of battle. On the approach of the latter Liu fled secretly in a junk to the mainland, and his troops surrendered almost without a shot. Had the soldiers fought as desperately as the common people did the Japanese would have found considerable difficulty in conquering Formosa. In many a conflict in the interior of the country with the Hakkas they found in them assailants worthy of their steel. There was more real fighting in this island than there was in the previous campaigns in China, and it was only the superior discipline of the Japanese that enabled them to overcome the brave but undisciplined numbers that dared to contest with them the possession of their country.

The utter collapse of China in her war with Japan led to very serious political results, such as were ultimately to affect and determine the whole Eastern question. Foreign nations that had been wont to treat China with a certain degree of respect, and to tolerate the haughty way in which she was accustomed to consider grievances that were brought to her notice, now proceeded to take action in various matters such as they would never have dreamed of doing before the war. That she should have been so thoroughly beaten and disgraced by such an insignificant foe, as they considered the Japanese to be, produced in their minds a certain amount of contempt that made them determined to take things into their own hands, and to refuse to submit to the calm insolence and vexatious delays with which the Chinese government had been used to treat the representatives of foreign powers. The first to assert the new spirit of quiet contempt for the Chinese were the Germans. On the 1st of November, 1897, two German missionaries resident in the province of Shantung were murdered by a band of robbers. Reparation was sternly demanded from the Chinese government, and not content with the usual slow diplomatic action with which they had invariably endeavoured to wear out the patience of the Western powers, men-of-war were despatched and a body of troops were landed in Shantung, the result being that the Chinese authorities had to concede all the demands of the German government.

An indemnity was paid for the murder of the men, special mining and railway rights were granted, and most serious of all Kiau-chao was leased to it for ninety-nine years. Thus, as a result of the disgrace of China, a footing was gained in the empire, which really meant the supremacy of the German flag in the course of time over a larger area than that represented by the port that had been leased for so long a period. This transaction was to have more serious consequences than were ever dreamt of by those who were the actors in it.

The Chinese were not the only aggrieved parties in this spoliation of their country. The Russians looked upon the aggressive movement of the Germans with the greatest suspicion and dislike, as it seemed to interfere with their settled policy that Manchuria and Northern China were the sphere of influence that belonged to them, and that any movement that had the appearance of interfering with that was to be deprecated and opposed to the very utmost.

As it would have been impossible for Russia to take any open action to oppose the Germans, without revealing her designs on China to the world, she demanded from the former that Port Arthur and Talien-wan should be leased to her on the same terms that Kiau-chao had been ceded to the Germans. China was too conscious of her weakness to dare to refuse, and so the port that was to become so famous throughout the world, and where such terrific sacrifice of life was to be made within a very few years, came into the possession of a power that was planning to dominate one of the richest possessions of the Manchu dynasty.

The English, taking advantage of the general weakness of the empire, and jealous because of the advantages that had been gained by Germany and Russia, made a claim for Wei-hai-wei, and out of gratitude for the assistance that Great Britain had given her to enable her to pay the indemnity for the expenses of the war, China not only gave her a lease of that port for twenty-five years, but also later on, in A. D. 1899, granted her an extension of territory on the hinterland of Hongkong.

The concession that the Chinese had been compelled to make to the Russians was highly resented by the Japanese. The former, in conjunction with France and Germany, had intervened to prevent the latter from reaping the full benefit of their victorious war with China, and now they were being compelled to stand by whilst Russia, without any sacrifice, was taking possession of what rightfully, as the spoils of war, belonged to them. The Liau-tung peninsula, moreover, was legally theirs, for by the treaty of Shemoneseki (April 17th, A. D. 1895) China had ceded the whole of it to them, and that they had no present control over it was simply because the three above-mentioned powers, in contempt of Japan and in defiance of her rights, had stepped in and prevented China from carrying out her engagements with her.

Little did Russia dream of the Nemesis that was awaiting her in the near future, or of the fierce indignation that she had aroused in the hearts of the Japanese people by the ungenerous treatment of them, and by her utter want of conscience in depriving them of the territory that China had consented to hand over to them.

The statesmen of Japan now recognized that they had a powerful and inveterate foe in Russia, and if they were to retain their national existence in the future, the question would have finally to be settled on the battlefield. It was a matter of life and death, and the sooner they made preparations for the contest that was inevitable, the better would it be for them in the struggle that was to decide the fate of their country.

From that time, with steady persistence and with a determination that knew no faltering, the nation set itself the mighty task of preparing its armies and its navy to meet the forces of the great Russian power and to save itself from being annihilated by it. The Japanese are born administrators. They never leave anything to chance, and so in the drilling of their soldiers and in the training of their ships, every detail that could render them more effective was thought out and attended to. The latest invention in guns, the best strategic methods that the nations of the West had learned, the highest scientific results that the greatest thinkers of other countries had discovered, were all adopted by the Japanese authorities in order to make their soldiers and their sailors more efficient in the carrying out of the one master purpose that had taken possession of every class in the nation.

All this was done so quietly and with so little ostentation that the outside world never dreamed of the tremendous revolution that was taking place in the life of Japan, or that silently but surely a new empire was being built up that ere long would astonish the whole world with the powers that were being developed.

The utter defeat of the Chinese in their contest with the Japanese was destined to have far-reaching results. A contempt of the Western nations and the threatened break up of the empire by the process of spoliation was one of these. The most important immediate effect, however, was the influence that the disastrous campaign had upon the Chinese themselves. It certainly broke up the stolid apathy and indifference that had hitherto been a marked feature in their national life, and the spirit of patriotism was aroused that from this time was destined to weld the various parts of the empire more closely than had ever been experienced in any period of its past history.

A wave of horror and indignation swept throughout the country as the story of the reverses that had been endured at the hands of the Japanese spread from town to town, and village to village, till the whole of its four hundred millions of people had heard with the fiercest indignation of the humiliation of the empire. Never before had the remotest parts of this great country been so welded together by a common sympathy as when the tale of the disasters that had fallen upon its armies was told with bated breath and quivering hearts by countless crowds that at first refused to believe that such an insignificant power as Japan could have defeated the enormous forces that China could put into the field.

Hitherto the idea of patriotism had been scarcely grasped by the Chinese, as is abundantly proved by the fact that the language contains no word that will express this sentiment. The Chinaman's heart had in the past been centered in his clan and in the old ancestral home where his fathers had lived and died, and whilst these were safe he cared little what became of the rest of the world outside of these.

With the news, however, of the disgrace that had befallen the imperial arms, a new instinct seemed to have been born within the heart of the nation, and China, with its immense plains and mighty rivers and lofty mountains, and its peoples so numerous that they appeared to defy calculation, became a potent factor in the thoughts and aspirations of men whose conceptions of their country had been narrowed down to the local surroundings amidst which they had been bred and born. It was indeed worth all the pain and the humiliation that had come upon the nation to have got an inspiration that would bind the hearts of the four hundred millions of "the black-haired race" by the common tie of a love for their country.

There was one man in the empire that felt profoundly concerned, because of the sorrows and the disasters that had been brought upon his country, and that was the Emperor Kuang Hsü. This man's character has suffered severely from adverse criticism. He has been represented as weak and unstable in purpose, and too impetuous in carrying out the great reforms that he deemed essential for the welfare of his country.

"I have been accused," he said to one of the reformers who had assisted him with valuable advice, "of being rash and precipitate and of attempting great political changes without due consideration. This is an entire mistake. I have thought over the condition of my country with great seriousness for several years. Plan after plan has come before my mind, but each one I was afraid to put into action, lest I should make some blunder that would bring sorrow upon my empire. In the meanwhile China is being dismembered. Shantung has been occupied by the Germans. The Liau-tung peninsula practically belongs to the Russians, and Formosa has been given over to the Japanese. Whilst I am waiting and considering my country is falling to pieces, and now, when I attempt heroic measures, I am accused of rashness. Shall I wait till China has slipped from my hands and I am left a crownless king?"

One day a chief of the eunuchs came into his library, in which he spent many hours every day in study. It contained a most valuable collection of historical books which the Emperor was continually consulting in order that he might get hints from the statesmen and master minds of the past in the art of governing an empire. He hoped in some mysterious way to catch some special inspiration from those great men that influenced the destinies of China in the remote past, and from a study of their methods be enabled to avert the calamities that were falling so fast upon China.

When the eunuch entered the room, he saw that the face of his royal master was clouded with sadness. "Call in the attendants," he said to him, "and have all these books at once burned." The man was horror struck, and falling on his knees, he besought the Emperor to delay the carrying out of his purpose. "The books are valuable," he said. "They have been handed down from the past as a precious legacy to the successive rulers that have sat on the dragon throne. No such a collection exists anywhere else, and their destruction would be an irreparable loss that never could be made good." Kuang Hsü replied, "What good have I ever received from these ancient books? I have studied them with care, I have pondered over the thoughts of the statesmen of the past, but I have received no lesson as to how I should meet the difficulties in which my empire is plunged at the present moment. The times have changed and the old-fashioned thoughts of men that lived in the far-off ages will not serve for the changed conditions in which we are living to-day. Foreign powers are at my very gates and the empire is crumbling away at their touch ; let the books be burned."

Of all the Emperors, whose stories have been told in the preceding pages, not one has ever shown the tender concern and love for the people that Kuang Hsü has done. Many of them have far excelled him in strength of character and in regal powers of mind, but in the long array of names that we find that stand conspicuous in the history of the Chinese empire, no man has surpassed him in his absolute love and devotion for his people. One incident alone in his life will show that this statement is not an extravagant one. When the forces of the foreign powers that were hastening to the relief of the men and women who were besieged in Peking drew near to the city, preparations were made by the Court for a flight to Si-ngan, the provincial capital of Shensi. As the mournful procession reached the gate through which the members of the royal family, and the great officers of State that accompanied them were to pass into the country beyond, Kuang Hsü protested against his being compelled to abandon his capital. With tears in his eyes, and with a faltering voice, he begged to be allowed to stay behind and die with his people who, he feared, might be called upon to pass through great sufferings 'after the foreign soldiers had captured the town. His appeal was made in vain, and he was forced to follow in the train of the Empress-Dowager, who had been the main cause of the calamities that were making her a refugee from her own Court.

So convinced was the Emperor that the only way to save his country was by deep and radical changes that in A. D. 1898 he began to institute a number of reforms, that from a Chinese point of view were of a most startling and revolutionary character. He proposed, for example, that the system of examination for literary degrees that had been in vogue for centuries should be radically changed, and such subjects, and that a knowledge of ancient and modern history, the government and institutions of foreign countries, modern arts and sciences, should be demanded by the imperial examiners as a *sine qua non* from all those that came up for their degrees. It was hoped by this new system that the intense conservatism of the scholars of China, who had always been the opponents of reform, would gradually receive its death-blow, and the possibility of a new life for the empire be secured without a revolution.

Another great reform aimed at by the Emperor was the establishment of colleges and technical schools for the study of scientific knowledge, whilst the common schools of the country, where the Confucian classics were the only text-books, should be gradually supplanted by others, where subjects of a more general and useful character should be taught. In order to carry out this last idea an edict was actually issued ordering that all the heathen temples, with certain specified exceptions, should have the idols removed from them, and that the local mandarins should see that they were turned into school-houses and made ready for the reception of the children that resided in their neigbourhood.

The most remarkable thing about this royal command was the absolute submission with which it was received. No outcry was raised and no opposition of any kind was offered, and thus the remarkable spectacle was witnessed of a nation being deprived of its gods, and in some sense of its religion, without any protest being made or any tumult being raised in any direction by those who, by a stroke of the pen, were deprived of the visible forms of their religious belief.

The Emperor's mind at this time was deeply impressed with the idea that the needs of the empire were so urgent and so imperative that the best thoughts of the most profound thinkers in the country were needed for a crisis like this. He accordingly issued an edict giving the right to anyone to memorialize the throne who considered that he had any thoughts or suggestions that might be of service to aid in the deliverance of his country. Such a liberal and progressive policy had never been heard of in the past, and the men that were dreaming of a new future for China saw in this action of Kuang Hsü an indication that a new *régime* had indeed been instituted that portended far-reaching reforms in the future.

The reforms of Kuang Hsü, whilst looked upon favourably by the nation in general, were viewed with the utmost dislike by the Empress-Dowager and by the more conservative ministers and nobles at Peking. Plans accordingly were secretly formed to frustrate the benign intention of the Emperor for the salvation of his empire. Troops were silently collected in the capital, and on the 22nd of September, 1898, Kuang Hsü was suddenly seized by the order of the Empress-Dowager and compelled to abdicate his throne, whilst she appointed herself regent to govern the country in his stead.

Her first act (September 24th) was to annul all the reforms that had been inaugurated by the unhappy Emperor, and her next was to plan for the punishment and murder of the band of young reformers that had assisted him in devising the new schemes and movements that were to regenerate China. Many of these were seized and banished, others were imprisoned, whilst others again were executed, glorying in their death and declaring that reforms might be staged, but the nation ere long would insist upon them being carried out.

On the 1st day of the Chinese New Year (January 31st, 1900) Kuang Hsü was compelled to announce to the whole empire that he had abdicated the throne and that Pu Chiu, the son of Prince Tuan, was to succeed to the Dragon Throne. Much to the disappointment of the Empress-Dowager this action of hers called forth the most vigorous opposition from all who were interested in the reform movement, and telegrams were received from various quarters by the Emperor imploring him not to abdicate, as the Chinese everywhere looked to him as the only man in the empire who could carry out the great changes that were needed for the salvation of the country. The ambassadors of the foreign powers joined in the protest, so the scheme of the Empress-Dowager to get rid of the Emperor was frustrated. Pu Chiu was appointed heir-apparent, whilst Kuang Hsü was kept a State prisoner.

In the meanwhile a very serious insurrectionary movement was being organized in the province of Shantung by the members of a secret society who are now widely known as the " Boxers." The origin of this treasonable association was the disasters that had come upon China in the late war with Japan, which were all put down, not to the superior fighting powers of that country, but to the mismanagement of the government. A feeling of bitter hostility had consequently been engendered against the Manchu dynasty. There seems to be very little reason for doubting that in the early period of the movement the expulsion of the Tartars and the establishment of a native dynasty were the main objects that were in the mind of every member of the society.

By a stroke of genius the Empress-Dowager managed to enlist the services of the Boxers on her side in the determined purpose which she had formed of expelling all foreigners, of whatever nationality they might be, from China.

The Boxers, confident in the knowledge that there would be no opposition to them from the government, commenced their destructive campaign by burning and plundering the houses of the native Christians in Shantung. They were assisted in their operations by the general apathy of the mandarins and by the reputation they had obtained of being in the possession of magical powers. It was universally believed the bullets had no power of wounding them, and that cannon balls would recoil upon those that fired them, but would never injure any Boxer.

The movement spread from Shantung into the province of Chih-li, the Boxers distinguishing themselves by the savage cruelty with which they tortured and murdered the Christians wherever they encountered them. Pao-ting-fu was captured and burned, Tientsin was in a most perilous condition, and even the capital (Peking) was threatened by the insurgents. As these kept advancing towards the city, a force of soldiers of various nationalities was despatched to the assistance of the foreigners there, and not very long after their arrival all communication with the outer world was cut off and the famous siege of the legations by the Boxers and the Chinese regular forces was commenced.

The state of things became so serious, and the position of the foreign ambassadors in the capital so critical, that the representatives of the Western powers felt that there was no course left to them but to take up arms and appeal to force. The Boxers had gradually increased in numbers and in their reputation for invincibility, and they were confident that they could drive the Barbarians back again into the ocean, from whence they had come, and deliver China for ever from their hated presence.

The government, which was rarely the Empress-Dowager, profoundly sympathizing with these views, and only waiting for a favourable opportunity to put them into action, naturally refrained from taking any efficient measures for the suppression of these turbulent and fanatical disturbers of the peace, and whatever military action was taken was half-hearted and only adopted for the sake of appearance.

It was determined therefore to assume the offensive, even though no declaration of war had been proclaimed either by China or any of the foreign powers. The allied fleets that were lying off Taku on the 16th of June sent in an ultimatum to the General in command of the forts, demanding either their surrender or the withdrawal of the forces occupying them.

As these terms were promptly rejected by the Chinese, the ships weighed anchor and proceeded to the various stations that had been appointed them and made preparations for bombardment. To the credit of the enemy it may be said that he did not wait to be attacked, but gallantly opened fire upon the advancing vessels. A furious engagement was the result, which ended in the capture of the famous forts and the rout and dispersion of the garrisons. The Chinese government was so exasperated at this proceeding of the allies that they at once declared war practically against the whole of the Western powers, and an ultimatum was sent by the Chinese Foreign Office in Peking to the whole of the legations ordering every one of those connected with them to quit the city within twenty-four hours.

The government whose hand had been forced by the capture of the Taku forts, now openly allied themselves with the Boxers and proceeded to a rigorous siege of the men and women that were cooped up in the British Legation, and who defended themselves with a heroism and a dogged perseverance that finally saved them from utter destruction. In addition to the soldiers that were the chief fighters there was a large number of women and children, also a considerable body of native Christians who had taken refuge with the foreigners when they were compelled to leave their homes to escape the fury of the Boxers and of the regular soldiers of the government.

During the time they were surrounded by the thousands of trained men that thirsted for their blood, viz., from the 20th of June (the day on which Baron von Kettler, the German ambassador, was ruthlessly killed by some of the imperial soldiers) until August the 14th, when General Gaselee entered Peking with the relief force, all classes of those who were besieged worked together most heartily, and each one did his share in helping to keep the enemy from succeeding in his murderous designs.

Whilst this famous siege was being carried on, exciting events were being enacted in the great plains that stretched between Peking and Tientsin. The Boxers, elated by their successes and really believing that they were invulnerable to any fire that the foreigners could bring upon them, made several attacks on the latter city. These, after great loss of life, were repulsed, and the allies, feeling the danger and indignity of being subject to such ferocious assaults, finally decided to capture Tientsin. This was done after severe fighting, and the Boxers and the forces of the regular army that had shown extraordinary courage in their fighting with the allied forces retired into the interior.

A determined effort was now made to relieve the foreigners in Peking. A previous attempt (June 10th) that had been made by Admiral Seymour signally failed, and the British force of one thousand men came perilously near to being annihilated.

The expedition that was now formed consisted of about fifteen thousand men, and was composed for the most part of British, American, Japanese, Russian, and German troops. In the course of ten days or so they had reached Peking and taken it by assault. The Empress-Dowager, the Emperor, and the chief nobles of the Court fled in hot haste from the city, and after suffering severe hardships arrived at Si-ngan-fu, an ancient capital of China.

This ignominious flight of the Empress-Dowager from her capital to avoid being captured by the victorious foreigners whom she had planned to drive out of the country or to have them barbarously murdered, was a first Nemesis upon her for her savage and unwomanly conduct. Nothing less than the utter extermination of the foreigners in her dominions would seem to satisfy her, or assuage the hatred that rankled deeply in her heart against them. She accordingly issued a secret edict to the viceroys throughout the empire, giving them stringent orders that they should take immediate measures to have them ruthlessly destroyed without mercy and without pity.

Some of these high officials, who were filled with an anti-foreign hatred, and who wished at the same time to curry favour with the Empress-Dowager, proceeded with alacrity to carry out the murderous orders she had issued, and massacres of missionaries and of native Christians filled the minds of all those who heard the tragic stories with the utmost horror. In Pao-ting-fu the missionaries were almost all exterminated, as well as those of the converts that fell into the hands of the Boxers, who seemed in their savage fury to have lost every particle of human kindness and compassion that had ever existed in their hearts.

A most tragic scene was enacted in Tai-yuan-fu, the chief city in the province of Shansi. The governor was Yu Hsien, who was a devoted creature of the Empress-Dowager, and who was at the same time a most rancorous and bitter hater of all foreigners. On July 9th he had all the missionaries with their wives and children, to the number of forty-five, seized and brought to his official residence, where in his own presence he had them slaughtered by his soldiers. It is stated that he was so dissatisfied with the slowness with which they did their cruel work that he called for a sword, and with his own hands put several of the martyrs to death. It is satisfactory to know that this wretch paid the penalty of his misdeeds with his life before many months had passed by.

In Manchuria the persecution of missionaries and their converts was carried on systematically and relentlessly. Many of them managed to escape from the country, but it is estimated that fully two hundred Protestant and Roman Catholic missionaries were murdered, whilst several thousand native Christians shared the same fate as their pastors.

It is pleasing to know that whilst war and bloodshed were rampant in the North, the rest of China was comparatively tranquil. The viceroys of the eastern and southern provinces refused to obey the secret edict of the Empress-Dowager. They were perfectly aware that China had not the power to contend successfully with all the great powers of the West. They accordingly came to an agreement with the consuls of the foreign nations that if their troops would not extend their operations beyond the North, where the actual fighting was being carried on, they would guarantee that peace would be preserved over those vast regions over which their authority extended. This compact was faithfully kept by both sides, and so China was preserved from disasters that might have overwhelmed her. With the capture and occupation of Peking by the allied troops, and the flight of the royal family and the members of the Court, the war was virtually at an end. It was a wild but heroic attempt to shake off the grip of the foreign powers that was being laid more tightly every year upon China. The whole nation was undoubtedly at one with the Empress-Dowager in her desire to give back to the empire the proud position that not many decades ago it possessed of being able to dictate her own terms to any of the Western powers that came humbly knocking at her gates, and praying to be allowed to be admitted, even on the humblest terms. The very madness of her methods, in that she was prepared to fight all the countries of Europe and America, showed how desperately in earnest she was. Up to this time she had ever had the reputation of being a wise and able stateswoman, and her long reign as regent, when the reins of power were held by her, testified to her great administrative ability and the wisdom with which she had guided the car of State through many a difficult and perplexing negotiation with foreign powers. It was felt by her, and indeed by the whole nation, with very few exceptions, that the foreigners were a danger to the empire. Their presence in China, it was universally believed, was not simply for trade, but that they might rend the eighteen provinces between them and become possessors of them. The uprising of the Boxers with their heroism, and their supernatural powers that they firmly believed rendered them absolutely immune from shot and shell, seemed to show that the supreme moment had arrived when the deliverance of the empire could be accomplished with certainty and success.

That the movement should be a lamentable failure was a foregone conclusion. China was in no condition to fight with even one of the Western powers, but when she stood up to meet in battle the forces of them all combined, then defeat and disaster were inevitable. One cannot, however, but admire the pluck and the patriotism of the Empress-Dowager that led her into so perilous a condition in order that her country might be saved from the grasp of the Barbarians. Her methods were savage and relentless, and her scheme for the wholesale destruction of them filled the West with horror and indignation. It must be remembered that they were eminently Oriental, and were less brutal and ferocious than some similar designs that are not unknown in the history of foreign nations. The massacre of St. Bartholomew far exceeded in deliberate cruelty, and in utter savagery of execution, any of the terrible scenes that were enacted during the reign of terror, when the Boxers and the imperial soldiers were let loose upon the missionaries and their converts. No attempt ought to be made to defend the murder of so many men and women who had come to China on purpose to elevate and raise the nation, and yet still one must recognize that it was no mere thirst for blood that led to the terrible massacres, but a mistaken belief that the only way to accomplish deliverance was by the utter extermination of all foreigners no matter to what country they might belong.

The allied forces not only took possession of the capital, but they also became masters of all the surrounding country for a considerable distance. One would like to be able to chronicle that the troops used their victory with moderation, and that life and property were held sacred after the Chinese army had fled in disorder and had ceased to fight. The truth is the very reverse was the case. Looting and pillage became the order of the day, especially amongst certain nationalities, whom it would be invidious to particularize, and the lives of many of the common people were sacrificed during the search for plunder that was unblushingly made by even those that wore the uniform of soldiers, but whom success had often turned into the veriest robbers and murderers.

As the Court had fled, and the high mandarins had followed in their train, it was difficult at first to find anyone with whom the allies could discuss the terms of peace. After a time, however, Li Hung-chang and Prince Ching appeared upon the scene, having been appointed plenipotentaries by the Empress-Dowager, and after prolonged conferences, the following are some of the terms that were agreed to:—

1. A monument was to be erected on the spot where Baron von Kettler was murdered, and a prince of the blood was to proceed to Germany and make an ample apology to the Emperor for the wrong that had been done to his ambassador.

2. Eleven princes and high mandarins were to be put to death for their share in the tragedies that had aroused the indignation of the West.

3. An indemnity of four hundred and fifty million taels was to be paid by instalments extending over a period of forty years. To help the government to raise this large sum the duties on imports were increased by five per cent.

4. The Taku and other forts on the coast of Chihli were to be demolished and permanent guards of foreign soldiers were to be stationed in Peking so as to safeguard the various embassies that were established there, and save them from any future possible catastrophes.

The allies, with the exception of Russia, kept steadily to the determination of not allowing the dismemberment of the empire. This latter power, though ostensibly agreeing with the terms of peace that had been made with China, never for one moment abandoned the purpose that her statesmen had formed of finally annexing Manchuria to the dominions of the Czar.

This design was carefully concealed and she promised that by a certain date her troops should retire from that province, and that it should be handed back to the Chinese government. She professed that the unsettled condition of the country would render that impossible for the present; but it was patent to all the world that this was a mere shallow excuse, and that her real purpose was the permanent possession of the country that had been the home of the fathers of the Manchu dynasty. Unfortunately the concession that the Chinese had granted the Russians of building a railway through Northern Manchuria afforded a most substantial reason why the latter could not withdraw all their forces from the country. The line ran through an immense extent of territory, and really required an army to be constantly in occupation to protect it from marauders and to secure the safety of the thousands of employees that were scattered along such an extended line of country. If there had been any ordinary prevision in the statesmen that granted the Russians the concession to construct the line, they would have seen that when they give them this right to do so they really made them a present of the strip of country through which the line would have to pass. If they had formally handed over to them the whole of the territory along which the railway ran, they could hardly have more thoroughly secured it to them than they did when they signed the convention that gave them practically the right to remain for ever, and protect what had been built at such an enormous cost of public money. That the Russians felt that they held military possession of the country, and that to all intents and purposes it was part and parcel of Russia, is evident from the fact that because of an attack by the Chinese on some Cossack soldiers it was determined that the town of Blagovestchensk, on the river Amur, should be seized and its inhabitants utterly destroyed.

This was done in the most ruthless and savage manner, and thousands of men, women, and children were driven at the point of the bayonet into the river that flowed near by, and where they miserably perished. If this was not done by orders from the high authorities at St. Petersburg, it was a great crime that was quietly condoned by them, for no punishment visited the perpetrators of these dastardly and inhuman atrocities. But a Nemesis was soon to come upon the Russian nation for its absolute disregard for human life, and for its apparent loss of political honour. Promises had been made and specified dates had been given when Manchuria was to be evacuated and the Russian troops were to return to their own country. With the near approach of each period when it had been promised that the country should revert to China, fresh excuses for delay were manufactured until finally, when pressed to name a date when the withdrawal would actually take place, Russia declared that she was not to be coerced into making any pledges of any kind on the subject, and that she would not even undertake to say that she would ever leave Manchuria at all.

There was something more serious, however, than even this attitude of the Russian authorities with regard to the evacuation of the great province that they had practically seized. Russia evidently was not going to be content with that, for her diplomatic action showed that she was casting longing eyes upon Corea as well, and that she would never rest satisfied until she had become Lord Paramount of it, and had secured a port by which she could find an exit to the sea. The Japanese, who claimed the Hermit Land as their special sphere of influence, became alarmed when they realized that the object of the Russians was to drive them out of the country, and to occupy the position that they claimed belonged to them. Nine years had nearly gone by since Russia had treated her with the utmost contempt and had actually gained possession of territory that they had won at the point of the sword. Their wrongs had rankled within their breasts. Silently but determinedly, and with faces set as stern as fate, they had trained their navy on the newest and most scientific principles to meet the Russian ships at sea, and they had drilled their soldiers to a state of perfection such as no armies in the world perhaps had ever before attained. With untiring perseverance they had manœuvered with their men in the heats of summer and in the storms of winter, so as to make them fit under any circumstances to meet their foe with the certainty of success.

And now the time had come to put all these years of training, and the severe discipline that had made the Japanese soldier as perfect a fighter as any human being could be, to the test. It was evident that Russia was going to threaten the very national existence of Japan. She was to be ousted out of Corea, the one breathing space to which the nation could look in the future for the outflow of its congested population, and when they had been driven back to their own islands it would be easy for the enemy to cross the narrow strait that divided the Corean and Japanese coasts from each other, and carry the war into the very heart of their country.

With absolute unanimity the entire people girded themselves for the gigantic struggle, and it would seem as though every man that was called to the ranks was prepared to die, and every home that sent him forth had counted the cost, and was willing to surrender him as a sacrifice to perish, if necessary, for the welfare of the State.

The Japanese ambassador at St. Petersburg practically began the bloody campaigns that were to deluge the hills and plains of Manchuria with blood by demanding that Russia should fulfil her pledges that she had repeatedly given to China, and withdraw their soldiers from that province.

The Russian authorities, for statesmen they did not possess, looked upon this request with the utmost contempt. That Japan, of all the countries in the world, should dare to formulate any demand from her was something that was to be highly resented, and consequently but scant courtesy was shown in dealing with the great questions that the Japanese ambassador pressed upon the attention of the Russian Foreign Office. If the Minister in St. Petersburg had not been so blinded by the scorn that they felt for such an insignificant power as Japan, they would have been struck by the insistence and by the dignity with which the demands of Japan were formulated. There evidently was a purpose behind them that would never be satisfied until at least some of them had been finally conceded. They were satisfied that Japan never could fight, and never intended to take up the sword to back up her diplomatic action, and so she could be quietly ignored and treated with the scantiest of courtesy. In all the correspondence that was carried on during the latter part of 1903, and the month of January, 1904, the Japanese won the admiration of all thinking and impartial men, by the calm dignity with which they presented their case and the good temper with which they bore what to every one seemed to be the unreasonable delays of the Russian Foreign Office in replying to the Japanese despatches. That the latter did not wish for war was manifest from the large concessions that they were prepared to make in order to avert that. In the first instance they had categorically stated that there were two things that Japan insisted upon being conceded, viz., the evacuation of Manchuria by Russia, and her recognition of Japan's suzerainty over Corea. Russia would grant neither of these points.

After some time Japan withdrew the first stipulation and proposed that a line should be drawn from East to West through the northern part of Corea, and that all the territory lying to the north of that should be under the control of Russia, whilst all south of it should be recognized as belonging to Japan. This most reasonable concession was not accepted, and the Japanese, being convinced that Russia meant in time to drive them entirely out of the Hermit Kingdom, broke off diplomatic relations and prepared for war. This momentous decision took place on February 8th, 1904, and now a drama was to be enacted which for heroism and for sacrifice of human life the world had rarely seen in all the long centuries of the past.

The Japanese had everything ready, even to the minutest detail, both on sea and land, for the mighty conflict, and with a promptness and despatch that have characterised all their movements in the war, on the very next day they made an attack with torpedoes on the Russian fleet in Port Arthur, disabling two battleships and a cruiser, whilst on the 10th day they landed 19,000 troops in Corea and occupied Seoul, and on the very same day a battle was fought with the *Variag* and *Koreitz*, two Russian men-of-war, off the harbour of Chemulpo. After an engagement of about two hours both ships fled before the terrible fire of the Japanese men-of-war, and were sunk not very far from where they had been moored before they responded to the call of the enemy to come out and fight them.

The news of these successful attacks spread with wonderful rapidity all over the world, and created the most profound impressions of surprise. None were more astonished, however, than the Russians who had been so accustomed to look upon Japan as a power that was to be utterly neglected, that they could not understand how such promptitude and such military ability could have been developed in so short a space of time. If their Intelligence Department had been only moderately alive to its duties, years ago it would have discovered the steady, unceasing preparations that were being made day and night, and with a purpose that never faltered, for the campaign that had opened so successfully for Japan.

And now that the war had commenced in earnest, Russia began to organize her forces to meet a foe that was still looked upon with contempt, and as one that would easily be crushed when their armies met on the battlefield. So certain did this seem that the Russian commander-in-chief declared, when he was starting to take command of the forces in Manchuria, that he would never make peace with Japan who had dared to measure herself with Russia, until he stood with his victorious army in Tokio and dictated terms to the conquered nation in its own capital.

The Japanese were perfectly alive to the very serious nature of the enterprise upon which they had embarked, as was shown by the immense exertions they had made and by the large forces they had without any delay put on the field. By the middle of March they had landed 100,000 men in Corea. This in itself was a gigantic operation, but in addition they had kept up the struggle with Port Arthur, and amidst the most inclement weather five of their battleships and two of their cruisers had bombarded Vladivostock (March 6th, 1904).

The Russians by this time seemed to begin to realize that the war on which they had entered so lightly was a much more serious matter than they had anticipated, for by the close of April they had massed 50,000 troops on the Yalu, whilst General Kuropatkin had under his own immediate command fully 300,000 more.

Fortune, however, seemed to be against them from the very outset, and a want of enterprise characterised the whole of the forces, both naval and military. They were tremendously lacking in the initiative, and perhaps they dreamed that Japan, being an Oriental power, would take things in such a leisurely fashion that they could well forestall any attempts that might be made by her. They were soon to have a rough awakening in their estimate of the foe they were to meet.

The early disasters in Port Arthur had cast a gloom over the spirits of the men there, which, however, was lifted by the arrival of Admiral Makaroff to take command of that fortress.

His ability and enterprise would most certainly have given a new turn to affairs, when unfortunately (April 13th) his battleship *Petropavolovsk*, was blown up by a Japanese mine, and he and nearly all on board perished in the waters in which she sank. His loss was a great misfortune to the Russian cause, for there was no one with anything like the genius that he possessed to take his place.

But events were hurrying on, and the Japanese soldiers, with firm and persistent tread, were marching steadily on in the direction of their foes. These showed their want of strategy in allowing them so easily to cross the Yalu, and to fight the first pitched battle of the war near Kiu-lien-cheng, where the Russians suffered a most decided defeat (May 1st), being compelled to retire before their victorious enemy, and to abandon twenty-eight of their guns, two companies of artillery being taken prisoners, whilst over 2,000 men were killed and wounded in the battle.

The Russians, instead of sending large reinforcements to stay the onward march of the Japanese, retired to Kinchow and Namshan, which they heavily fortified, so as to make them almost impregnable. The Japanese, however, were to give the Russians and the world at large a lesson in fighting, and to teach them that the word impregnable, in the ordinary military sense of the term, was forever to have a new signification. After sixteen hours of incessant fighting, and after crossing a series of wire netting, where they were mowed down by the fire of the Russians, they carried fort after fort at the point of the bayonet, and the Russians were compelled to retreat on Port Arthur (May 26th). Four days after Dalny was occupied by General Oku, and that famous fortress was thus isolated, and the siege proper may be said to have commenced from that date.

With the possession of Dalny, with its docks and piers and railway station uninjured, the Japanese were enabled to land the forces and stores that were needed for the army that was advancing into Manchuria, and also to complete the investment of Port Arthur, within whose series of fortifications there were more than 30,000 soldiers, whilst anchored in its harbour there was a very formidable fleet that could render effective service in the defence of the whole.

The Japanese fleet, under the now famous Admiral Togo, cruised about outside, just beyond the range of the heavy guns of the many strongly armed forts that stood in rings around Port Arthur, and did everything that human foresight and courage could suggest to render the blockade as effective as possible. He was not content simply to lie off and wait the coming of the enemy's ships to attack him. His torpedo boats, in the wildest and stormiest weather, often boldly ventured close to the entrance of the harbour, and occasionally inflicted damage upon the Russians and also themselves, suffering the loss of the brave men who with heroic daring risked their lives in carrying out the orders of the admiral.

The Japanese land forces, in the meanwhile, were advancing steadily along the line of the railway, which the Russians had contructed for the purpose of connecting Port Arthur with the various places held by them in Manchuria. Although the Russian soldiers fought with great bravery, they found it impossible to stay the victorious march of their indomitable foes, and they were compelled to slowly retreat before them. Two places—Siu-yen and Samake—were occupied by them (June 1st), whilst at the same time an army under General Nogi was advancing to lay siege to Port Arthur.

The Russians seemed doomed to defeat, for a great victory at Telissu, after three days of most severe fighting, was gained by the Japanese, at an expense to the Russians of 10,000 men, whilst they were compelled to retreat before an enemy that seemed to have lost all consciousness that they could be beaten.

But it was not simply on land that the arms of the Japanese were successful. Admiral Togo encountered the Russian fleet outside of Port Arthur (June 22rd), when a battleship was sunk, and some of their other men-of-war were disabled, and they were compelled to beat a hasty retreat and gain the protection of the heavy guns on shore.

The Japanese land forces that continued to advance after the battle of Telissu, having captured all the main roads that led to Liau-yang, came up with the Russian army that lay in and around that city. After prolonged and most terrible fighting the place was captured, the Russians losing two hundred guns and immense quantities of military stores. General Kuropatkin retreated and was closely followed by Generals Oku and Kuroki with the forces that had gained so splendid a victory.

Before this great disaster to the Russian arms had taken place, the fleet in Port Arthur had suffered a terrible defeat at the hands of that most indefatigable and brilliant fighter, Admiral Togo. On the 10th of August it steamed out in battle array from the harbour, and was promptly met by the Japanese, when an engagement took place that soon ended in the utter defeat and dispersion of the Russian ships. Some regained the shelter of the harbour, whilst others fled to Tsingtau, some to Shanghai, whilst one at least, the *Diana*, travelled as far as Saigon, where she still remains dismantled and interned by the French authorities.

Four days after this decisive engagement, the three men-of-war from Vladivostock, that had evidently come south to unite with the Port Arthur fleet, were encountered by Admiral Kamimura, and after a fight of five hours retreated in great haste ; but one of them, the *Rurik*, being a slow sailer was sunk by the Japanese, six hundred of her crew being picked up whilst in a drowning condition by their generous-hearted foes. The other two reached Vladivostock, but in a most terribly damaged condition.

After the great and exhausting battle of Liau-yang, and the retreat of the Russian forces to the river Taitse, which they strongly fortified and entrenched with all the military skill that the Russian engineers possessed, a lull in the fighting took place. Not that the Japanese were inactive, for the very reverse was the case. Before they could hope for any success against the powerful army in front of them, a very important flanking movement would have to be carried out. This was most brilliantly effected and the Tai-ling Pass, which might be called the key to Moukden, was occupied by the Japanese forces.

The possession of this highly strategical position was of the utmost importance to the Japanese, for they could now bring up supplies by the river Liau, which, previous to this time, had all to be transported by railway. It would seem, indeed, as though sorrow and disaster were to dog the steps of the Russians during the unlucky month of September, not only on the field but also in the fighting around Port Arthur. In the latter place fort after fort was captured, and during three days' severe fighting no fewer than six were torn from the enemy's grasp (September 25th), the situation in that beleagured fortress becoming every day more distressing and perilous.

The position of General Kuropatkin became most serious, for place after place was captured by the Japanese, till finally he was driven behind the formidable entrenchments that he had bestowed great labour on, on the right bank of the river Sha-ho. Here, after five days of the most fierce and incessant fighting, the Russians were once more defeated with great slaughter, leaving 13,333 dead on the field as counted by the Japanese, whilst the latter in killed and wounded suffered the loss of 15,879 men.

This great battle that was fought with such terrible persistency, and with the most reckless bravery, seemed to exhaust both armies, for no active movements took place for some time after the Russians had retreated upon Moukden. It had been the severest of all the great engagements that had yet been fought ; indeed, one of the peculiarities of the campaign so far had been that each battle had been more sanguinary and more destructive of life and property than the one that preceded it. That the Japanese should dare to advance and attack their formidable foe, and that the Russians should await the onset of men that had been consistently victorious, are splendid proofs of the indomitable courage and absolute disregard for life that were manifested by both the combatants.

During this time of apparent inactivity the siege of Port Arthur was being vigorously pressed, and fort after fort was being captured. The 30th of November proved a most disastrous one for the Russians, for on that day the celebrated 203 metre fort was captured after the most terrific loss of life by the Japanese. As this completely dominated the town and harbour of Port Arthur, it meant that before long the Russians would have to surrender. That they were conscious of this is proved by the heroic but vain attempt that was made (December 2nd) to recapture it.

The Japanese lost no time in utilizing their success, for in the course of a few days the fleet that lay anchored in the harbour were so damaged by the incessant hail of fire that was rained upon them that they were put completely out of action and could take no part in the defence of the place.

General Stoessel, considering that the fortress was untenable, surrendered it (January 1st, 1905) to General Nogi, and on the 5th of January marched out with 48,000 troops, including 16,000 sick and wounded, and the investing force took possession on the same day. To the astonishment of the whole world it was discovered that the stories of the terrible suffering and privations that the garrison had endured from want of provisions were entirely mythical and had no foundation in fact. Food was found to be most abundant, whilst the ammunition was so plentiful that the siege could have been maintained for several months longer.

The most astounding thing, however, was the fact that when the garrison marched out, instead of the 5,000 men that it had been represented to the world were the sole effective numbers that had survived the slaughter of the rest of the defenders of the fortress, it was found that there were actually over 30,000 unwounded soldiers that were quite capable, both from numbers and bravery of holding the fortress for some considerable time against the attacks of the Japanese.

The surrender was a most disgraceful one, and reflected the greatest descredit upon General Stoessel, whom the world had been holding up for months as one of the great heroes in the military world. It was also a most unfortunate one for General Kuropatkin, for it let loose Nogi and his victorious troops to swell the ranks of the forces that were to drive him from Moukden and to send the Russian armies in rout and disaster from the plains of Manchuria.

During the months of January and February desultory fighting was carried on with almost invariable success to the Japanese, whose ultimate aim in all these numerous engagements was the driving the Russians out of Moukden, and the capture of the strong pass of Tieh-ling, which constituted the gateway into the rich and fertile plains of Manchuria that lay to the south of it.

By the end of February the Japanese had carried everything before them, and they stood in the presence of 450,000 valiant Russians who were prepared to sacrifice their lives rather than yield the positions they held to the foe. As the Japanese meant business, there was but slight delay, when once they had come in touch with the enemy, in beginning the attack. The fighting qualities on both sides were pretty nearly equal, but the brilliant strategy of the Japanese give them a decided predominance.

After the severest fighting, in which the most heroic deeds were performed and the most terrible loss of life on both sides, the Russians were compelled to retreat (March 13), and so closely were they pressed by the victorious Japanese that they soon became disordered, and the flight ended in a most distressing and disgraceful rout, during which 40,000 prisoners were captured, whilst immense military stores were seized by the Japanese. Never in the world's history had there been such a battle as this. For thirteen successive days incessant attacks and counter attacks had been made. The sound of firing, and the screaming and bursting of shells, and the horrible carnival of death had gone on with pitiless monotony. If ever there was a hell upon earth, it was during those terrible days of battle, when human lives were being slaughtered, and men seemed to lose every noble human instinct, in the one mad passion to slay and destroy life.

In killed, wounded, and prisoners, the Russians lost 175,000 men, whilst the Japanese losses fully amounted to the half of that number. The Russians had hoped to be able to make a stand at Tieh-ling, where their military stores were accumulated, and where the natural strength of the position would give them a breathing space, before the enemy appeared before it, to try and wrest it from them. In this, however, they were doomed to disappointment, for the Japanese pressed their pursuit with such vigor that four days after the great battle of Moukden, the Japanese captured this strongly fortified pass (March 16th), and the Russians had once more to flee before the victorious foe, leaving all their stores and artillery in their hands.

The victory of Moukden and the capture of Tieh-ling proved most decisive in their results; and the Russian armies, no longer able to face the Japanese, were compelled to retreat in the direction of Harbin, to await reinforcements and to reorganize their shattered forces that had suffered so heavily both in men and materials in the recent battles in which they had been engaged.

The Japanese, too, whilst they remained masters on the field, had suffered too grievously to permit them to advance very far from their base, until the gaps that had been made in their regiments by the shot and shell of the Russians had been refilled by new troops from home. It is true that the latter were not entirely inactive, and that various places on the route of the retreating Russians had fallen into their hands; still no great movements were made by either side, but preparations were made by both for a greater battle in the near future, when the question to whom Manchuria should finally belong would be settled by the arbitrament of arms.

In the meanwhile the Russians had determined to assist their land forces by sending out an immense fleet, under the command of Admiral Rozhdiestvensky, which should endeavour to destroy the navy of the Japanese, and not only cut off the supplies of their armies in Manchuria, but also be able to bring the war into Japan itself, and thus retrieve their fortunes that had sunk to the lowest ebb through the successive misfortunes that had fallen on their arms.

For several months then ships of the great Russian Armada, accompanied by a whole fleet of colliers and transports, slowly made their way to the East, until they finally rendezvoused off the coast of Cochin China, in Kamranh Bay.

After a considerable delay the admiral at length set sail for Vladivostock with over thirty battleships, cruisers and torpedo boats, whilst men looked on with the greatest auxiety to see how the Japanese, who had managed to conceal their ships and their plans from the world, would fare in the presence of such a mighty and imposing force.

On the 27th of May, 1905, the Russian fleet was sighted at early dawn by the Japanese scouts, and the whole of their fleet that lay behind the island of Tsushima weighed anchor and proceeded at half speed in the direction of the advancing foe. By two o'clock in the afternoon, when the battle really commenced, the Russians were completely enveloped by the Japanese who had stationed a squadron at each end of the straits of Tsushima, so that there was no escape for them, and they had either to fight or to surrender.

The battle from the very first was entirely in favour of the Japanese. A gale of wind was blowing at the time from the east, which caused the Russian ships to roll heavily and thus to expose their hulls to the terrific storm of shot and shell that were hurled against them. The heavy rolling sea at the same time prevented the gunners on board the ships from firing with accuracy against the Japanese.

As night came on and darkness fell upon the Straits, the Japanese destroyer flotilla took up the work of destruction, and through the livelong night made incessant attacks upon the unfortunate Russian ships. Next day the battle was resumed by the whole of the ships under Admiral Togo, with the result that the great Baltic fleet was practically annihilated, for at the close of the fight eighteen ships had been sent to the bottom of the sea, whilst two battleships and two coast defence armoured cruisers had hauled down their flags and had surrendered to the Japanese. The rest of the imposing Armada had vanished, and Japan, as far as her enemy was considered, became mistress of the sea. Her losses had been comparatively trifling, consisting simply of three destroyers and eight hundred men killed and wounded, whilst the Russians had to deplore the loss of their whole fleet, with 14,000 men killed or drowned.

The news of this astounding victory produced the greatest amazement wherever it was published. That the Japanese would give the Russians a good deal of trouble was anticipated by the most of those who cared to give an opinion on the subject, but that they should come out of the fight practically unscathed, whilst the Russian Armada should virtually be destroyed, was something that was never dreamed of by the greatest believers in the prowess of the Japanese.

When the news reached St. Petersburg there was general dismay, but one good effect of the disaster was the willingness of the Czar to consider the question of peace, which up to this point he would never consent to discuss. President Roosevelt, who had been most earnest in his efforts to put an end to this most sanguinary war, made an appeal to the Russian Emperor, through his Ambassador to the United States, with the happy result that both Russia and Japan consented to send plenipotentiaries to Washington to agree, if possible, upon terms that would restore harmony between the two nations.

The moral effect of the great victory of the Japanese over the Russians in the Straits of Tsushima was very pronounced and far-reaching. It was soon discovered that the destruction of the Russian fleet had been the result of a variety of causes. The main factor undoubtedly was the bravery and heroism with which the Japanese sailors engaged the great Armada that had come out to the East to give a death-blow to their country. Their enthusiasm was aroused to the highest pitch by the famous signal that Admiral Togo flung out when the moment for attack had come: "The destiny of our empire depends upon this action. You are all expected to do your very utmost."

These words, no doubt more telling and effective in the language of the men who were called upon to fight than they appear in an English garb, stirred the whole fleet with the determination to conquer or die. There was to be no retreat and no talk of surrender.

They were to die to the very last man if necessary in order to save their country.

Another very important item in the great contest was the splendid strategy of Admiral Togo. After weeks of manœuvering he had succeeded in getting his enemy into the very place that he had selected in which to fight him. He had lured him into the fatal Straits, and then had so closed both ends that there was no possibility of advance or retreat without meeting a force that was superior in every way to him.

The splendid aim of the Japanese gunners made victory a certainty. Although the Russians in many instances showed the most reckless bravery and preferred to go down with their ships rather than surrender, the fact that at the close of the engagement only three of their torpedo boats had been sunk, whilst none of the larger ships had been put out of action, showed how infinitely superior the Japanese firing had been to that of their unfortunate enemy.

Another very potent cause for the disaster to the Muscovite arms was the incapacity, if not the positive cowardice, of some of the higher officers that fought under the orders of Admiral Rozhdiestvensky. One admiral fled during the evening of the 27th, whilst the fleet was being hotly engaged, with three of his cruisers, and never stayed to see what would be the fate of his unhappy comrades-in-arms.

In addition to the above there was the undoubted fact that some of the ships were in a state of mutiny, as is attested by the report of Rozhdiestvensky to the Czar, in which he specifically mentioned that the crews of the *Seniavin* and *Apraxine* had refused to fight when they were attacked by the Japanese. When these facts are taken into consideration, it can hardly be wondered at that the conflict in the Straits of Tsushima should have been as disastrous and as tragic as it was.

The great reverse seemed to the outside world to be so terrible that the question of peace between the two belligerents might well be now considered. Up to this time the Russians had refused to entertain the subject at all, as they had the greatest faith that the Armada would restore the prestige of their arms, and inflict such a crushing defeat on the Japanese navy that they would be able to dictate terms to their hitherto victorious enemy.

These hopes having been dashed by the practical annihilation of their navy, President Roosevelt offered to act as mediator between the two parties, and after strenuous efforts and considerable correspondence both the Russians and the Japanese consented to appoint plenipotentiaries to meet in Washington to discuss the terms upon which they could agree to cease hostilities.

The Russians, whilst consenting to these arrangements, showed no serious earnestness in the matter, so that the impression went abroad that it was not peace that they desired so much as an opportunity of reinforcing their armies in Manchuria, to gain, if possible, a crowning victory that would restore to them their lost prestige. This but proves the utter incapacity of the rulers of Russia to understand the situation. They seem by their incompetency to be hurrying on their country to destruction. They have neither the brain power to direct their armies in their contest with Japan, neither have they the sense to know how to make peace with a foe that is their superior both in the field and in the cabinet.

After the great battle of Moukden a lull took place in the active movements of both armies, though both sides, and especially the Japanese, began to make strenuous preparations for the next great battle which the latter hoped would end in such a decisive victory that the Russians would be driven out of Manchuria, and they be left masters of the field.

So well did the Japanese conceal their movements that only occasional rumours reached the outside world, and telegrams, that could not altogether be relied upon, vaguely informed an anxious world that forces amounting to 450,000 men were being slowly but surely concentrating for the one great aim of enveloping the Russian armies and making them prisoners.

At last, in the beginning of July, telegrams announced that a Japanese force had landed on the island of Saghalien and had captured Notoro, with the light-house on it. This was rapidly followed by the reduction of other places, so that before the end of the month the whole of the island was in the hands of the Japanese.

Whilst the subjugation of the island was going on Olga Bay was occupied by the Japanese, and at the same time 50,000 troops were landed to the north of Vladivostock, preparatory to an attack on that famous fortress.

In the meanwhile China had been affected in no slight degree by the stirring events that had been taking place in the territories, which through the folly and treachery of her officials had been handed over to the Russians. The need of reforms which had been so wisely seen by the Emperor Kwang Su, but which had been barbarously and ruthlessly put a stop to by the Empress-Dowager, has now been felt in an acute measure, and edicts have been issued ordering that, in order to be able to deal with foreign affairs in a more intelligent manner and more for the interest of China, Prince Chu Chak, Tai Hung, Vice-President of Board of Revenue, Chu Sai, Cabinet Minister, and Tuan Fang, Governor of Hupeh, should proceed to the countries, both East and West, and study the legislation and administration of those countries, so as to see wherein China may be able to benefit by the experience of those countries.

An imperial edict also has been issued abolishing torture in the examination or punishment of prisoners, a mighty step in this great land of China, which from times immemorial has always held that the ends of justice never could be secured without it. That a system that for many ages has been considered by the rulers of China as the only possible way by which crime and lawlessness could be successfully met, should disappear by a stroke of the vermillion pen is a marvellous evidence of how the influence of the West is beginning to tell upon this ancient empire.

That the humane act of the Emperor will not be carried out in its entirety by the mandarins is only what may be expected ; still the fact remains that torture is illegal, and that any official that has the temerity to employ it does so at his own peril.   The nation may well breathe a sigh of relief at this most momentous action of Kwang Su, for it is not simply the criminal classes that will be relieved of the terror and sufferings that they might have been subjected to whenever they came within the grip of the law.   The theory of the Chinese that every accused man is guilty, whether he be so or not, has led to the gravest injustice and the most cruel wrongs being perpetrated on innocent persons.   Where a person has refused to acknowledge an offence that he never committed, torture has been applied of so severe and intolerable a character that many an innocent person, unable to endure the agony, has owned up to crimes that were perpetrated by others, and for which he has finally suffered the penalty of death.

All that barbarous system has now come to an end, and the public will never again be horrified by witnessing such scenes, as "the slicing process," by which some unfortunate individual was slowly done to death, by the gradual excision of parts of the body, until the spirit, unable to endure the awful agony, left the maimed and mutilated body in the midst of fiercest sufferings that the ingenuity of man could devise.

A remarkable result of the war is seen in the growing solidarity of the Chinese people.   The sight of Japan standing up alone in front of the great Russian empire, and through her unity of purpose and her heroism defeating a power that the nations of the West have rarely dared to encounter, has made the thinkers of this land pause and question how it is that a country that twenty years ago was an unrecognized factor in the politics of the East, has all at once, and as if by magic, developed into a first-rate power.

The secret of it all is the fact that the Japanese are dominated by a patriotism that makes them willing to sacrifice everything they possess for their country.

This thought is one that is entirely new to the Chinese.   Up to the present patriotism, such as we understand by that word in the West, has never really been felt by the masses of the Chinese empire.   To them the clan has been the supreme thought in their lives, and so there has never been any common bond to bind the various peoples of the eighteen provinces into one compact whole, and cause them to throb with a common purpose.

The marvellous successes of the Japanese, the construction of telegraphs and railroads, and above all the remarkable growth and freedom of the press in the outports under foreign rule, have produced a growing feeling of unity, which may be considered as the first signs of a patriotism that shall weld the far-off peoples of this extensive empire into one homogeneous whole.

A striking proof of this is seen in the united action which the leading men in Shanghai, Tientsin, Amoy and Canton have taken in regard to the wrongs which the Chinese consider they have had to suffer from the illiberal and harsh way in which the Chinese "Exclusion Treaty" has been carried out in the United States. In order to express their indignation, the men of the North are combining with those of Mid-China and with those in the extreme South, and they have decreed that all trade with America shall be boycotted, until some amendment be made in the forthcoming treaty between the United States and China. Unfortunately the leaders of the popular movement are demanding more than the American Government can possibly concede, and that is free entry of all classes of Chinese into their country. The labour question will first of all have to be satisfactorily settled before any concession can be granted to such large and wide-reaching demands. What is needed at the present moment is that statesmen, by exceptional ability, should appear on the scene who shall be able to grapple with an international question that is bristling with difficulties. That the Chinese government have never yet been ready to concede what the popular leaders demand, is evident from the fact that foreigners, of whatever nationality, cannot freely travel throughout China, nor can they carry on business, excepting at the places opened to them by treaty. China is not an open country in the sense that England is, where no restrictions are placed upon the coming and going of any foreign subject. To demand free access to the United States for any and every Chinaman shows that the present movement to boycott the Americans is largely influenced by the wrongs and insults that the Chinese declare they have suffered from them in the carrying out of the Exclusion Treaty, rather than by any large and liberal ideas on the question of international comity.

The disastrous battle of Tsushima was so terrible in its effects that the Western world felt that the time had come when the war should be put an end to. After considerable negotiations both Russia and Japan consented to appoint plenipotentiaries to meet together in America, and try and settle the terms upon which hostilities could be suspended and peace be agreed upon between the two belligerents.

On the 8th of August, 1905, the high officials assembled in Portsmouth, N. H., and began discussions, which lasted for nearly a month, whilst the whole world looked on with painful interest and with intense anxiety as to how they would end.

The Czar had made two stipulations, viz., that there was to be no cession of Russian territory, and no war indemnity to be paid to the Japanese. As the latter demanded both it was felt that the prospects of peace were anything but bright.

At length, when it seemed that the conference would break up without any result being attained, Japan, to the amazement of the whole world, agreed to withdraw her demand for an indemnity, also that she would be content with the half of Saghalien, instead of the whole island, which she actually had in her possession. She also consented not to insist upon the handing over to her of the interned Russian warships, or upon the limitation of Russian naval strength in the Pacific.

These difficulties having been removed out of the way, a treaty of peace was agreed to by both Russia and Japan, and signed on September 6th, to the great joy of all lovers of peace. It consisted of the following articles:—

1.   Russia agreed to recognize the paramount position of Japan in Korea.

2.   Russia and Japan shall simultaneously evacuate Manchuria, which with certain limitations is to be handed over to China.

3.   Russia agrees to transfer to Japan the lease of the Liao-tung Peninsula.

4.   That the half of the island of Saghalien, south of fifty degrees north latitude shall belong to Japan.

5.   That the Chinese Eastern Railway, ten miles south of Harbin, shall belong to Japan.

6.   Russia agrees not to use for military purposes that portion of the Siberian Railway that runs through Manchuria and terminates at Vladivostock.

7.   It is agreed that Japan shall enjoy with Russia equal fishing rights on the Siberian littoral.

8.   The open door in Manchuria.

9.   Both Russia and Japan agree not to construct any military works or fortifications on Saghalien.

10.   That Russia shall pay to Japan the sum say of 150,000,000 yen for the support of the prisoners captured by the latter during the war.

And now the great war is over, the greatest in some respects that has ever been fought in the history of the world. The Russians have been thoroughly humiliated and defeated. They have shown ability neither for war nor for the finer arts of statesmanship.

The Japanese, on the other hand, have amazed the world, not simply by the heroism of their soldiers, but by the completeness of their military preparations, that enabled them to win victory after victory, without sustaining a single defeat during the whole of their campaigns with Russia.

They have also signally manifested their humanity by the way in which they have treated the wounded and captured Russians, and finally they have shown their magnanimity by their generosity in not insisting upon an indemnity, lest by doing so they should prolong a war that has been conspicuous for the great destruction of human life.

There is no doubt but that the brilliant successes of the Japanese have powerfully influenced the people and rulers of China. The recent deliberations in the palace for the abolishing of the present system of literary examinations, and the proposal in high quarters for a parliament for China, are but symptoms of the great change that has taken place in public opinion in this land, and they are at the same time omens of what may be expected to happen in the near future, when Japan begins to assert her influence over the country that she has delivered from the grasp of the Russians.

A great future is already dawning for China.

APPENDIX A.

A Chapter on the Population of China.

THE question of the population of China has always been a perplexing one, and from the absence of sufficient data, one impossible to be settled satisfactorily. It has therefore been deemed advisable to refrain from any special mention of it in the body of the history and to discuss it in a separate chapter by itself, though even by this method the results obtained will be far from absolutely correct. The taking of the census in the present is done in such a loose and slovenly way, and is entrusted to men who are so illiterate and of such low social position, that there is no wonder that the statistics compiled by them should be looked upon with anything but satisfaction. There is no evidence that the censuses of former days are any more reliable than those taken in more modern times.

Up to the 13th century of the Christian era we have to depend upon Ma Toan-liu for any information that we possess of the early statistics of population. He gives 13,704,923 as the result of a census taken in the 9th century B.C. As these numbers included only persons between the ages of 15 and 65, and excluded all officials and slaves, and all that had to give personal service to the state, and, more-over, only referred to those that lived to the north of the Yangtze, it is evident that the census was taken simply to ascertain the actual number of taxable people. Supposing that the above numbers represented 75 per cent of the whole, the population would thus be 18,273,230.

From A. D. 2–155 Mr. Ma gives ten censuses which show an average of sixty-three millions, the highest being eighty-three and the lowest forty-seven millions. The disastrous wars that took place during the period of the " Warring States," and the terrible loss of life caused by those struggles, will account for the com-paratively small increase in the population in eight hundred years. The civil broils that occurred towards the end of the Former Han, and the desolating strifes that were the result of them, will also account for the still further reduced numbers that the censuses had to show.

After the collapse of the Later Han Dynasty the population was once more vastly reduced by the constant and savage wars that were the result of the division of the country into three kingdoms, and it was not till the time of the Western Tsin, when the empire came under the sway of one sovereign, and the people were protected in their homes, that their numbers began once more to show an increase. Ma declares that the population in A. D. 280 was 14,163,863, or reckoning as we did before, actually 18,885,150.

During the time of the Eastern Tsin serious troubles broke out in the state, that ended in the division of the empire into north and south, and which involved the people in disastrous wars, when invading hosts plundered and murdered to their hearts' content and turned many a fruitful populous region into a veritable wilderness. With the return of settled rule the population again increased, and so we find that in the year A.D. 606 it was 46,019,956. What percentage this was of the whole, and what classes were included and what excluded by the census takers, we have no means of ascertaining.

Though the Sui dynasty exercised complete control over the whole country the people were greatly oppressed, and many reduced to the direst poverty and distress by the expensive and luxurious habits of Yang Ti, all of which had a depressing influence on population.

During the T'ang dynasty (A.D. 618-907) up to the year A.D. 841 Ma gives fifteen censuses, but these are all so unsatisfactory and so difficult to be reconciled the one with the other that they cannot be relied upon for the purpose of precise information. It would seem from one of them (A.D. 754) that the population was about seventy millions, but what percentage these were of the whole we have no means of determining.

With the disappearance of the T'ang, troubles came upon the country during the ...nsettled period of the Five Dynasties, which again retarded the increase of population, but with the establishment of the Sung dynasty and the steady increase of wealth and prosperity the numbers began to rise, till in A.D. 1021 the census showed over forty-three millions of people. Eighty years pass by, during which no great calamities seemed to have disturbed the citizens of the empire,.and coming to A.D. 1102 we find the population has mounted up to about one hundred millions. The repeated invasions of the Kins, and the disasters that followed their almost invariable successes, that culminated in the withdrawal of the Court to Nanking, and the virtual abandonment of the northern provinces to the savage and ruthless invaders, had such a disastrous effect on the population that in A.D. 1223 it had dwindled down to about sixty-three millions. Considering that these returns did not include the provinces that were lost in consequence of their seizure by the Kins the decrease will seem a reasonable one.

The invasion of the Mongols, and the awful slaughter that took place wherever these conquering hordes marched, again diminished the numbers of this unfortunate empire, so that in A.D. 1290 the census shows only 58,834,711.

During the Ming dynasty, between A.D. 1381-1580, sixteen censuses have been reported, which give an average for the two centuries of about 56½ millions, the highest being 66½ millions, A.D. 1412, and the lowest about 46¾, A. D. 1506. Although we have these very definite statements given us by the censuses we must not accept them as indicating the actual population of the empire. We have no means of testing these statistics by knowing what classes were included or excluded, and what districts in consequence of local rebellions did not come within the duties of the census taker. At the present day the census is taken every year, but where any particular region is in a state of disaffection, that cannot be done, for the very sufficent reason that the control of the mandarins is too weak to carry out the imperial commands. In former days, when law at various crises in the history of the empire was inoperative, this must have been continually happening, and so, apparently without sufficient reason, we find an unaccountable decrease in the numbers of the people. A thorough acquaintance with Chinese methods will help us to understand many things that would otherwise be perplexing.

During the present dynasty a large number of censuses have been taken, the most prominent of which are :—

A.D. 1711, which gives 28,605,716. (See *Chinese Repository*). This did not give all the population, was made possibly for the purposes of taxation and for ascertaining how many were fit to be enrolled in the army for fighting purposes.

A.D. 1753, population 103,050,060. (See " General Statistics " and *Chinese Repository*). This gives an average annual increase of 1,772,484 for forty-two years, which is by no means excessive, when we consider the facilities that this country affords for meeting the wants, etc., of its people.

A.D. 1792, population 307,467,200. (See " General Statistics " and Dr. Morrison's Anglo-Chinese College Report). This gives an annual average growth of population of 5,241,464, which is reasonable. It is true, indeed, that the Chinese Commissioner Chau stated to Lord Macartney in this same year that the population of the empire was three hundred and thirty-three millions. As there is no means of verifying this statement we prefer to accept the former number as more reliable.

A.D. 1812, population 361,693,879. (See *Chinese Repository*.) This estimate has been considered by various writers to be a very satisfactory one and approximately correct.

A.D. 1881, population 380 millions. (See Chinese Customs' Report.) This last ought to be the most reliable of any census that has hitherto been made public. The gentlemen who have the duty of making up the report are highly intelligent, painstaking and scrupulous in ascertaining the truth. They have, besides, facilities for getting at the statistics of the empire such as no other foreigners have. We may rest assured therefore that these numbers are nearer the truth than any that have been yet given the public. They, of course, apply only to China proper, Thibet, Eastern Turkestan and Manchuria, not being included. The population of these latter is unknown, and therefore it would be folly to put down the guesses of men who are by no means unanimous in their estimates. In dealing with the figures given in the early censuses, especially where great diminution of population occurs, one must bear in mind that famines, flooding of the Yellow River, droughts and annual mortality from fevers, dysentery, cholera and such like, which latter are awfully destructive from the absence of truly medical knowledge, are quite sufficient to account in a very large degree for the serious decrease in the numbers of the people. [For a fuller treatment of the subject see *Chinese Repository* and Williams' *Middle Kingdom.*]

APPENDIX B.

Genealogical Tables of Chinese and Tartar Dynasties.

THE LEGENDARY PERIOD.

The Ages of the five Rulers.

Dynastic Titles.								Personal Appellation.
T'ai Hau	...	...	...	...	B. C.	2852	... ...	Fuh-hi.
Yen Ti	...	...	...	...	,,	2737	... ...	Shin-nung.
Hwang Ti	...	...	...	...	,,	2697	... ...	Yew-nai.
Shau Hau	...	...	...	...	,,	2597	... ...	Kin-t'ien.
Chwan Hu	...	...	...	...	,,	2513	... ...	Kau-yang.
Ti Kuh	...	...	...	...	,,	2435	... ...	Kau-sin.
Ti Chih	...	...	...	...	,,	2365	...	
T'ang Ti Yau	...	...	...	...	,,	2356	...	
Yu Ti Shun	...	...	...	...	,,	2255	...	

The Hia Dynasty—B. C. 2205-1766.

Dynastic Title.					According to Common Reckoning.			According to Bamboo Records.*	
The Great Yu	...	...	...	...	B. C.	2205	... ...	B. C.	1989
K'i	...	...	...	...	,,	2197	... ...	,,	1978
T'ai K'ang	...	...	...	...	,,	2188	... ...	,,	1957
Chung K'ang	...	...	...	...	,,	2159	... ...	,,	1951
Siang	...	...	...	...	,,	2146	... ...	,,	1942
Interregnum of Forty Years, beginning	,,	2118	... ...	,,	1914
Shau K'ang	...	...	...	...	,,	2079	... ...	,,	1874
Ch'u	...	...	...	...	,,	2057	... ...	,,	1851
Hwai	...	...	...	...	,,	2040	... ...	,,	1832
Mang	...	...	...	...	,,	2014	... ...	,,	1788
Sieh	...	...	...	...	,,	1996	... ...	,,	1729
Pu Kiang	...	...	...	...	,,	1980	... ...	,,	1701
Kiung	...	...	...	...	,,	1921	... ...	,,	1642
Kin	...	...	...	...	,,	1900	... ...	,,	1621
K'ung Kia	...	...	...	...	,,	1879	... ...	,,	1611
Kau	...	...	...	...	,,	1848	... ...	,,	1600
Fa	...	...	...	...	,,	1837	... ...	,,	1595
Kieh Kwei	...	...	...	...	,,	1818	... ...	,,	1588

* These Bamboo Records were tablets that were said to have been discovered in the tomb of King Siang, of Wei, which had been ruthlessly opened by some plunderers in the year A.D. 279. They contained about one hundred thousand characters, and were deposited in the imperial library by Wu Ti, the founder of the Western Tsin dynasty. These bamboo tablets contained nearly twenty different works of between seventy and eighty chapters or books.—Dr. Legge's Shoo King, Prolegomena, page 105, etc.

LEGENDARY PERIOD.—(CONTINUED.)
The Shang Dynasty—B. C. 1766-1121.

Dynastic Title.					According to Common Reckoning.			According to Bamboo Records.	
T'ang	...	...	...	...	B. C.	1766	... ...	B. C.	1557
T'ai Kia	...	...	...	...	,,	1753	... ...	,,	1539
Yu Ting	...	...	...	...	,,	1720	... ...	,,	1527
T'ai Kung	...	...	...	...	,,	1691	... ...	,,	1508
Siau Kia	...	.	...	...	,,	1666	... ...	,,	1503
Yung Ki	...	...	...	...	,,	1649	... ...	,,	1486
T'ai Mow	...	...	...	...	,,	1637	... ...	,,	1474
Chung Ting	...	...	...	...	,,	1562	... ...	,,	1399
Wai Jen	...	...	...	...	,,	1549	... ...	,,	1390
Ho Tan Kia	...	...	...	...	,,	1534	... ...	,,	1380
Tsu Yih	...	...	...	...	,,	1525	... ...	,,	1371
Tsu Sin	...	...	...	...	,,	1506	... ...	,,	1352
Yu Kia	...	...	...	...	,,	1490	... ...	,,	1338
Tsu Ting	...	...	...	...	,,	1465	... ...	,,	1333
Nan Kung	...	...	...	...	,,	1433	... ...	,,	1324
Yang Kia	...,	...	...	...	,,	1408	... ...	,,	1318
P'an Kung	...	...	...	...	,,	1401	... ...	,,	1314
Siau Sin	...	...	...	...	,,	1373	... ...	,,	1286
Siau Yih	...	...	...	...	,,	1352	... ...	,,	1283
Wu Ting	...	...	...	...	,,	1324	... ...	,,	1273
Tsu Kung	...	...	...	...	,,	1265	... ...	,,	1214
Tsu Kia	...	...	...	...	,,	1258	... ...	,,	1203
Lin Sin	...	...	...	...	,,	1225	... ...	,,	1170
Kung Ting	...	...	...	...	,,	1219	... ...	,,	1166
Wu Yih	...	...	...	...	,,	1198	... ...	,,	1158
T'ai Ting	...	...	...	...	,,	1194	... ...	,,	1123
Ti Yih	...	...	...	...	,,	1191	... ...	,,	1110
Chow Sin	...	...	...	...	,,	1154	... ...	,,	1101

SEMI-HISTORICAL AND HISTORICAL PERIOD.
The Chow Dynasty—B. C. 1122-255.

Dynastic Title.					According to Common Reckoning.			According to Bamboo Records.	
Wu	...	...	...	...	B. C.	1122	... ...	B. C.	1049
Ch'ung	...	...	...	...	,,	1115	... ...	,,	1043
K'ang	...	...	...	...	,,	1078	... ...	,,	1006
Chau	...	...	...	...	,,	1052	... ...	,,	980
Muh	...	...	...	...	,,	1001	... ...	,,	961
Kung	...	...	...	...	,,	946	... ...	,,	906
I	...	...	...	...	,,	934	... ...	,,	860
Hiau	...	...	...	...	,,	909	... ...	,,	869
I	...	...	...	...	,,	894	... ...	,,	854
Li	...	...	...	...	,,	878	... ...	,,	852
Suan	...	...	...	...	,,	827	... ...	,,	861
Yew	...	...	...	...	,,	781	... ...	,,	780
P'ing	...	...	...	...	,,	770	... ...	,,	770
Hwan	...	...	...	...	,,	719	... ...	,,	718

Dynastic Title.				According to Common Reckoning.			According to Bamboo Records.	

Historical Period begins about B. C. 781-719.

Chwang	...	...	...	...	B. C. 696	...	...	B. C. 695
Hi	...	...	...	...	,, 681	...	...	,, 680
Hwei	...	...	...	...	,, 676	...	...	,, 676
Siang	...	...	...	...	,, 651	...	...	,, 651
K'ing	...	...	...	...	,, 618	...	...	,, 617
K'wang	...	...	...	...	,, 612	...	...	,, 611
Ting	...	...	...	...	,, 606	...	...	,, 605
Kien	...	...	...	...	,, 585	...	...	,, 584
Ling	...	...	...	...	,, 571	...	...	,, 570
King	...	...	...	...	,, 544	...	...	,, 543
King	...	...	...	...	,, 519	...	...	,, 518
Yuan	...	...	...	...	,, 475	...	...	,, 474
Ching Ting	...	...	...	...	,, 468	...	...	,, 467
K'au	...	...	...	...	,, 440	...	...	,, 439
Wei Lieh	...	...	...	...	,, 425	...	...	,, 424
Ngan	...	...	...	...	,, 401	...	...	,, 400
Lieh	...	...	...	...	,, 375	...	...	,, 374
Hien	...	...	...	...	,, 368	...	...	,, 367
Shen Tsing	...	...	...	...	,, 320	...	...	,, 319
Nan	...	...	...	...	,, 314	...	...	,, 313
Tung Chow Kun	...	...	...	...	,, 255	...	...	,, —

The Ts'in Dynasty—B. C. 255-206.

Dynastic Title.

Chau Siang Wang	...	...	...	B. C. 255	...	...	The 52nd year of his reign as ruler of state of Ts'in.
Hian Wun Wang	...	...	...	,, 250	...	...	Reigned only three days
Chwan Siang Wang	...	...	...	,, 249			
Prince Chung	...	...	...	,, 246			
Shih Hwang Ti	...	...	...	,, 221	...	...	Title taken by Cheng when declared Emperor.
Urh Shih Hwang Ti	...	...	...	,, 209			

The Han Dynasty; also called the Former Han and Western Han, because of its capital being in Ch'ang-ngan—B. C. 206-A. D. 25.

Dynastic Title.							Title of Reign.
Kau Ti or Kau Tsu	...	...	...	B. C. 206	...	...	Actually ascended the throne B.C. 202.
Hwei Ti	...	...	...	,, 194			
Kau How or Lu Shih	...	...	...	,, 187			
Wun Ti	..	...	...	,, 179			
King Ti	...	...	...	,, 156	...	...	Chung Yuan.
Wu Ti	...	...	...	,, 140	...	...	Kien Yuan, etc.
Chau Ti	...	...	...	,, 86	...	...	Shih Yuan, etc.
Suan Ti	...	...	...	,, 73	...	...	Pen Shih, etc.
Yuan Ti	...	...	...	,, 48	...	...	Ch'u Yuan, etc.

Dynastic Title.								Title of Reign.
Ch'eng Ti	...	...	...	...	B. C.	32	... ...	Kieu Shih, etc.
Ngai Ti	...	...	...	...	,,	6	... ...	Kien P'ing, etc.
P'ing Ti	...	...	...	...	A. D.	1	... ...	Yuan Sbih.
Ju Tze Ying	...	...	...	...	,,	6	... ...	Ku Sheh.
Wang Mang (the usurper)	...	...	...	,,	9	... ...	Shih Kien Kwoh.
Hway Yang Wang	...	...	...	,,	23	... ...	Keng Shih.

*The After Han Dynasty, also called the Eastern Han, because its
Capital was at Loh-yang—A. D. 25-221.*

Dynastic Title.								Title of Reign.
Kwang Wu Ti	...	...	...	...	A. D.	25	... ...	Kien Wu, etc.
Ming Ti	...	...	...	...	,,	58	... ...	Yung P'ing.
Chang Ti	...	...	...	,,	76	... ...	Kien Ch'u, etc.
Ho Ti	...	...	...	...	,,	89	... ...	Yung Yuan, etc.
Shang Ti	...	...	...	...	,,	106	... ...	Yen P'ing.
Ngan Ti	...	...	...	...	,,	107	.. ...	Yung Ch'u, etc.
Shun Ti	...	...	...	...	,,	126	... ...	Yung Kien, etc.
Ch'ung Ti	...	...	...	...	,,	145	... ...	Yung Kai.
Chih Ti	...	...	...	...	,,	146	... ...	Pen Ch'u.
Hwan Ti	...	...	...	...	,,	147	... ...	Kieu Ho, etc.
Ling Ti	...	...	...	...	,,	168	... ...	Kien Ning, etc.
Hien Ti	...	...	...	...	,,	190	... ...	Ch'u P'ing, etc.

THE EPOCH OF THE THREE KINGDOMS—A. D. 221-265.

The Minor Han.

Dynastic Title.								Title of Reign.
Chau Lieh Ti	...	...	...	...	A. D.	221	... ...	Chang Wu.
How Tsu	...	...	...	..	,,	223	... ...	Kien Hing, etc.

The Wei Dynasty.

Dynastic Title.								Title of Reign.
Wen Ti	...	...	...	...	A. D.	220	... ...	Hwang Ch'u.
Ming Ti	...	...	...	...	,,	227	... ...	T'ai Ho, etc.
Fei Ti	...	...	...	...	,,	240	... ...	Cheng Shih.
Shau Ti	...	...	...	...	,,	254	... ...	Cheng Yuan.
Yuan Ti	...	...	...	...	,,	260	... ...	King Yuan.

The Wu Dynasty.

Dynastic Title.								Title of Reign.
Ta Ti (really sovereign in A. D. 229)			A. D.	222	... ...	Hwang Wu.
Fei Ti	...	...	...	...	,,	252	... ...	Kien Hing.
King Ti	...	...	...	...	,,	258	... ...	Yung Ngan.
Mo Ti (deposed A. D. 280)	...	...	,,	264	... ...	Yuan Hing.

The Western Ts'in Dynasty—A. D. 265-317.

Dynastic Title.								Title of Reign.
Wu Ti	...	...	...	...	A. D.	265	...	...	T'ai Shih, etc.
Hwei Ti	...	...	...	...	,,	290	...	...	Yung Hi, etc.
Hwai Ti	...	...	...	...	,,	307	...	...	Yung Kia.
Min Ti	...	...	...	...	,,	313	..	...	Kien Hing.

The Eastern Ts'in Dynasty—A. D. 317-420.

Dynastic Title.								Title of Reign.
Yuan Ti	...	...	...	...	A. D.	317	...	...	Kien Wu, etc.
Ming Ti	...	...	...	...	,,	323	...	...	T'ai Ning.
Ch'eng Ti	...	...	...	...	,,	326	...	...	Hien Ho, etc.
K'ang Ti	...	...	...	...	,,	343	...	...	Kien Yuan.
Muh Ti	...	...	...	...	,,	345	...	...	Yung Ho, etc.
Ngai Ti	...	...	...	...	,,	362	...	...	Lung Ho, etc.
Ti Yih	...	...	...	...	,,	366	...	...	T'ai Ho.
Kien Wen Ti	...	...	...	...	,,	371	...	...	Hien Ngan.
Hiau Wu Ti	...	...	...	...	,,	373	...	...	Ning K'ang, etc.
Ngan Ti	...	...	...	...	,,	397	...	...	Lung Ngan, etc.
Kung Ti	...	...	...	...	,,	419	...	...	Yuan Hi.

EPOCH OF DIVISION BETWEEN NORTH AND SOUTH.

The Sung Dynasty—A. D. 420-479.

Dynastic Title.								Title of Reign.
Wu Ti	...	...	...	...	A. D.	420	...	...	Yung Ch'u.
Shau Ti	...	...	...	...	,,	423	...	...	King P'ing.
Ying Yang Wang								—
Wen Ti	...	...	...	...	,,	424	...	...	Yuan Kia.
Hiau Wu Ti	...	...	...	...	,,	454	...	...	Hiau Kien, etc.
Fei Ti	...	...	...	...	,,	465	...	...	King Ho.
Ming Ti	...	...	...	...	,,	465	...	...	T'ai Shih, etc.
Ts'ang Wu Wang	...	...	...	...	,,	473	...	...	Yuan Hwei.
Tsu Li								—
Shun Ti	...	...	...	...	,,	477	...	...	Shang-ming.

The T'si Dynasty—A. D. 479-502.

Dynastic Title.								Title of Reign.
Kau Ti	...	...	...	...	A. D.	479	...	...	Kien Yuan.
Wu Ti	...	...	...	...	,,	483	...	...	Yung Ming.
Yu Lin Wang	...	...	...	...	,,	494	...	...	Lung Ch'ang.
Hai Ling Wang	...	...	...	...	,,	494	..	...	Yen Hing.
Ming Ti	...	...	...	...	,,	494	...	...	Kien Wu, etc.
Tung Hwun How	...	...	...	...	,,	499	...	...	Yung Yuan.
Ho Ti	...	...	...	...	,,	501	...	...	Chung Hing.

The Liang Dynasty—A. D. 502-557.

Dynastic Title.					A.D.			Title of Reign.
Wu Ti	...	...	...	...	A. D.	502 ...	...	T'ien Kien, etc.
Kien Wen Ti	...	...	...	...	,,	550 ...	...	Ta Pau.
Yu Chang Wang	...				,,	551 ...	...	T'ien Cheng.
Yuan Ti	...	...	...	...	,,	552 ...	...	Ch'eng Sheng.
Cheng Yang How	...	...	...		,,	555 ...	...	T'ien Ch'eng.
King Ti	...	...	...	...	,,	555 ...	...	Shau T'ai, etc.

The Ch'en Dynasty—A. D. 557-589.

Dynastic Title.					A.D.			Title of Reign.
Wu Ti	...	...	...	, ...	A. D.	557 ...	...	Yung Ting.
Wen Ti	...	...	...	...	,,	560 ...	...	T'ien Kia, etc.
Lin Hai Wang	...	...	...	...	,,	567 ...	...	Kwang Ta.
Suan Ti	...	...	...	...	,,	569 ...	...	Ta Kien.
How Tsu	...	...	..	...	,,	583 ...	...	Chih Tuh, etc.

The Northern Western and Eastern Wei Dynasties (House of Toba), as well as the Northern Ts'i and Northern Chow Dynasties, ruled over the northern portion of China whilst the Sung, Ts'i, Liang and Ch'en held supremacy over the south.

The Sui Dynasty—A. D. 589-618.

Dynastic Title.					A.D.			Title of Reign.
Kau Tsu	...	...	...	...	A. D.	589 ...	...	K'ai Hwang.
Yang Ti	...	...	...	...	,,	605 ...	...	Ta Yeh.
Kung Ti Yew	...	...	...	...	,,	617 ...	...	I Ning.
Kung Ti T'ung	...	...	...	...	,,	618 ...	...	Hwang T'ai.

The T'ang Dynasty—A. D. 618-907.

Dynastic Title.					A.D.			Title of Reign.
Kau Tsu	...	...	...	...	A. D.	618 ...	...	Wu Tuh.
T'ai Tsung	...	...	...	...	,,	627 ...	...	Cheng Kwan.
Kau Tsung	...	...	...	...	,,	650 ...	...	Yung Hwei, etc.
Chung Tsung	...	...	...	...	,,	684 ...	...	Sz Chung.
Jui Tsung	...	...	...	...	,,	684 ...	...	Wen Ming.
Wu How (usurped the throne twenty years)	...	...	...	...	,,	684 ...	...	Kwang Tsuh, etc.
Chung Tsung (again became Emperor).								
Jui Tsung	...	...	...	...	,,	710 ...	...	King Yun, etc.
Huan Tsung	...	...	...	...	,,	713 ...	...	K'ai Yuan, etc.
Su Tsung	...	...	...	...	,,	756 ...	...	Chih Tuh, etc.
Tai Tsung	...	..	...	...	,,	763 ...	...	Kwang Tuh, etc.
Teh Tsung	...	...	...	...	,,	780 ...	...	Kien Chung, etc.
Shun Tsung	...	...	...	...	,,	805 ...	...	Yung Cheng.
Hien Tsung	...	...	...	...	,,	806 ...	...	Yuan Ho.
Mu Tsung	...	...	...	...	,,	821 ...	...	Ch'ang K'ing.
King Tsung	...	...	...	...	,,	825 ...	...	Pau Li.
Wen Tsung	...	...	...	...	,,	827 ...	...	T'ai Ho, etc.
Wu Tsung	...	...	...	...	,,	841 ...	...	Hwei Ch'ang.
Suan Tsung	...	...	...	...	,,	847 ...	...	T'ai Chung.
I Tsung	...	...	...	...	,,	860 ...	...	Hien T'ung.
Hi Tsung	...	...	...	...	,,	874 ...	...	K'ien Fu, etc.
Chau Tsung	...	...	...	...	,,	889 ...	...	Lung Ki, etc.
Chau Suan Ti	...	...	...	...	,,	905 ...	...	T'ien Yew.

EPOCH OF THE FIVE DYNASTIES.

The After Liang Dynasty.

Dynastic Title.							Title of Reign.
T'ai Tsu	...	...	...	...	A.D.	907	K'ai P'ing.
Mo Ti	...	...	...	...	,,	913	Kien Hwa.

The After T'ang Dynasty.

Dynastic Title.							Title of Reign.
Chwang Tsung	...	...	...	...	A.D.	923	T'ung Kwang.
Ming Tsung	...	...	...	...	,,	926	T'ien Ch'ung, etc.
Min Ti	...	...	...	...	,,	934	Ying Shun.
Fei Ti	...	...	...	...	,,	934	Ts'ing T'ai.

The After Tsin Dynasty.

Dynastic Title.							Title of Reign.
Kau Tsu	...	...	...	...	A.D.	936	T'ien Fuh.
Ch'uh Ti	...	...	...	...	,,	943	K'ai Yun.

The After Han Dynasty.

Dynastic Title.							Title of Reign.
Kau Tsu	...	...	...	...	A.D.	947	T'ien Fuh.
Yin Ti	...	...	...	...	,,	948	K'ien Yew.

The After Chow Dynasty.

Dynastic Title.							Title of Reign.
T'ai Tsu	...	...	...	...	A.D.	951	Kwang Shun.
Shih Tsung	...	...	...	...	,,	954	Hien Tuh.
Kung Ti	...	...	...	...	,,	960	Hien Tuh.

The Sung Dynasty.

Dynastic Title.							Title of Reign.
T'ai Tsu	...	...	...	...	A.D.	960	Kien Lung, etc.
T'ai Tsung	...	...	...	...	,,	976	T'ai P'ing, etc.
Chen Tsung	...	...	...	...	,,	998	Hien P'ing, etc.
Jin Tsung	...	...	...	...	,,	1023	T'ien Shung, etc.
Ying Tsung	...	...	...	...	,,	1064	Che P'ing, etc.
Shen Tsung	...	...	...	...	,,	1068	Hi Ning, etc.
Cheh Tsung	...	...	...	...	,,	1086	Yuan Yew, etc.
Hwei Tsung	...	...	...	...	,,	1101	Kien Chung, etc.
K'in Tsung	...	...	...	...	,,	1126	Tsing K'ang.

The Southern Sung Dynasty.

Dynastic Title.							Title of Reign.
Kau Tsung	...	...	...	...	A.D.	1127	Kien Yen, etc.
Hiau Tsung	...	...	...	...	,,	1163	Lung Hing, etc.
Kwang Tsung	...	...	...	...	,,	1190	Shau Hi.
Ning Tsung	...	...	...	...	,,	1195	K'ing Yuan, etc.
Li Tsung	...	...	...	...	,,	1225	Pau K'ing, etc.
Tu Tsung	...	...	...	...	,,	1265	Hien Shun.
Kung Ti	...	...	...	...	,,	1275	Tuh Yew.
Twan Tsung	...	...	...	...	,,	1276	King Yen.
Ti Ping	...	...	...	...	,,	1278	Siang Hing.

The Yuan Dynasty.

Dynastic Title.								Title of Reign.
T'ai Tsu	...	...	...	...	A. D.	1206	...	... Temuchin or Ghengis.
T'ai Tsung	...	...	...	...	,,	1229	...	... Ogdai.
Ting Tsung	...	...	...	...	,,	1246	.	... Gayuk.
Hien Tsung	...	...	...	...	,,	1251	...	... Mangu.
She Tsu, or Kublai	.	...	...	,,	1260	...	... Chung T'ung.
Kublai's reign over China began 1280							...	... Che Yuan.
Ch'eng Tsung	...	...	...	...	,,	1295	...	... Yuan Chung, etc.
Wu Tsung	...	...	...	...	,,	1308	...	... Che Ta.
Ien Tsung	...	...	...	...	,,	1313	...	... Hwang K'ing, etc.
Ying Tsung	...	...	...	...	,,	1321	...	... Che Che.
Tai Ting Ti	...	...	...	...	,,	1324	...	... Tai Ting, etc.
Ming Tsung	...	...	...	...	,,	1329	...	... T'ien Li.
Wen Ti	...	...	...	...	,,	1330	...	... T'ien Li.
Shun Ti	...	...	...	...	,,	1333	...	... Yuan T'ung, etc.

The Ming Dynasty.

Dynastic Title.								Title of Reign.
T'ai Tsu	...	...	..	...	A. D.	1368	...	... Hung Wu.
Hwei Ti	...	...	...	...	,,	1399	...	... Kien Wen.
Ch'eng Tsu	...	...	...	...	,,	1403	...	... Yung Loh.
Ien Tsung	...	...	...	...	,,	1425	...	... Hung Hi.
Suan Tsung	...	...	...	...	,,	1426	...	... Suan Tuh.
Ying Tsung	...	...	...	...	,,	1436	...	... Chung T'ung.
Tai Tsung, King Ti	...	...	...	,,	1450	...	... King T'ai.
Ying Tsung, again Emperor	...	...	,,	1457	...	... T'ien Shun.
Hien Tsung	...	...	...	...	,,	1465	...	... Ch'eng Hwa.
Hiau Tsung	...	...	...	...	,,	1488	...	... Hung Che.
Wu Tsung	...	...	...	...	,,	1506	...	... Chung Tuh.
Shih Tsung	...	...	...	...	,,	1522	...	... Kia Tsing.
Muh Tsung	...	...	...	...	,,	1567	...	... Lung K'ing.
Shen Tsung	...	...	...	...	,,	1573	...	... Wan Li.
Kwang Tsung	...	...	...	...	,,	1620	...	... Tai Ch'ang.
Hi Tsung	...	...	...	...	,,	1621	...	.. T'ien K'i.
Chwang Lieh Ti	...	...	...	...	,,	1628	...	... Ts'ung Chung.

The Ts'ing Dynasty.

Dynastic Title.								Title of Reign
Hiau Tsu Suan	...	...	...	...	A. D.	1583		
T'ai Tsu Kau	...	...	...	...	,,	1616	...	... T'ien Ming.
T'ai Tsung Wen	...	...	...	...	,,	1627	...	... T'ien Tsung, etc.
She Tsu Chang	...	...	...	...	,,	1644	...	... Shun Chih.
Sheng Tsu Jen	...	...	...	...	,,	1662	...	... K'ang Hi.
She Tsung Hien	...	...	...	...	,,	1723	...	... Yung Ching.
Kau Tsung Shun	...	...	...	...	,,	1736	...	... K'ien Lung.
Jen Tsung Jui	...	...	...	...	,,	1796	...	... Kia K'ing.
Suan Tsung Ch'eng	...	...	...		1821	...	... Tau Kwang.
Wen Tsung Hien	...	...	...	,,	1851	...	... Hien Fung.
The present Emperor came to his majority 1873	...	...	...	,,	1862	...	... { T'ung Chih. ' Kwang Su.

The Tartar Dynasty.

The Liau Dynasty (*Khitan Tartars*).

Dynastic Title.								Title of Reign.
T'ai Tsu	...	...	...	...	A. D.	907	... ...	Shen Ts'eh.
T'ai Tsung. Title Liau, taken A.D. 937				,,		927	... ...	T'ien Hien.
She Tsung	...	...	...	...	,,	947	... ...	T'ien Luh.
Muh Tsung	...	...	...	...	,,	951	... ...	Ying Li.
King Tsung	...	...	...	...	,,	968	... ...	Pau Ming, etc.
Sheng Tsung	...	...	...	...	,,	183	... ...	T'ung Ho, etc.
Hing Tsung	...	...	...	...	,,	1031	... ...	King Fuh, etc.
Tau Tsung	...	...	...	...	,,	1055	... ...	Ts'ing Ming, etc.
T'ien Cha	...	...	...	...	,,	1101	... ...	K'ien K'ing, etc.

The Western Liau Dynasty.

Dynastic Title.								Title of Reign.
Tuh Tsung	...	...	...	...	A. D.	1125	... ...	Yen K'ing, etc.
Kan T'ien How	...	...	...	...	,,	1136	... ...	Hien Ts'ing.
Jen Tsung	...	...	...	...	,,	1142	... ...	Shau Hing.
Ch'eng T'ien	...	...	...	...	,,	1154	... ...	Ts'ung Fuh, etc.
Mo Tsu	...	...	...	...	,,	1168	... ...	T'ien Hi.

The Kin Dynasty (*Nuchen Tartars*).

Dynastic Title.								Title of Reign.
T'ai Tsu	...	...	...	...	A. D.	1115	... ...	Show Kwoh, etc.
T'ai Tsung	...	...	...	...	,,	1123	... ...	T'ien Hwei.
Hi Tsung	..	...	...	...	,,	1135	... ...	T'ien Hwei, etc.
This man reckoned rule from first year of his predecessor.								
Hai Ling Wang	...	...	...	...	,,	1149	... ...	T'ien Tuh.
She Tsung	...	...	...	...	,,	1161	... ...,	Ta Ting.
Chang Tsung	...	...	...	...	,,	1190	... ...	Ming Ch'ang, etc.
Wei Shau Wang	...	...	...	...	,,	1209	... ...	Ta Ngan, etc.
Suan Tsung	...	...	...	...	,,	1213	... ...	Chung Yew, etc.
Ngai Tsung	...	...	...	...	,,	1224	... ...	Chung Ta, etc.
Mo Ti	...	...	..	...	,,	1234	... ...	Shung Ch'ang.

APPENDIX C.

The Eighteen Provinces of China and its Colonies.

Chihli, Shantung, Shansi, Honan, Kiangsu, Nganhwui, Kiangsi, Chehkiang, Fuhkien, Hupeh, Hunan, Kwangtung, Kwangsi, Yunnan, Kweichow, Szchwan, Shensi, Kansuh.

The area of these is 1,297,999 square miles. They are divided into 267 departments and 537 countries, and have 8 Governor Generals and 16 Governors as supreme rulers under the Emperor.

Divisions of Manchuria.

Shingking, Kirin and Heh-lung-kiang.

Divisions of Mongolia.

Inner Mongolia, Outer Mongolia, Tsing-hai, and Uliasutai.

Divisions of Ili or Chinese Turkestan.

Songaria, Eastern Turkestan.

Thibet has been considered by the Chinese to be under their jurisdiction, but latterly the Thibetans have been gradually taking the rule more into their own hands, and whatever authority the former claim to have is more nominal than real.

INDEX.

72528